always up to date

The law changes, but Nolo is on top of it! We offer several ways to make sure you and your Nolo products are up to date:

1 **Nolo's Legal Updater**
We'll send you an email whenever a new edition of this book is published! Sign up at **www.nolo.com/legalupdater**.

2 **Updates @ Nolo.com**
Check **www.nolo.com/update** to find recent changes in the law that affect the current edition of your book.

3 **Nolo Customer Service**
To make sure that this edition of the book is the most recent one, call us at **800-728-3555** and ask one of our friendly customer service representatives. Or find out at **www.nolo.com**.

please note

We believe accurate, plain-English legal information should help you solve many of your own legal problems. But this text is not a substitute for personalized advice from a knowledgeable lawyer. If you want the help of a trained professional—and we'll always point out situations in which we think that's a good idea—consult an attorney licensed to practice in your state.

13th edition

How to File for
Chapter 7
Bankruptcy

by Attorneys Stephen Elias,
Albin Renauer & Robin Leonard

NOLO

THIRTEENTH EDITION	MAY 2006
Editor	LISA GUERIN
Book Design	TERRI HEARSH
Proofreading	SUSAN CARLSON GREENE
Index	SONGBIRD INDEXING SERVICES
Printing	CONSOLIDATED PRINTERS, INC.

Elias, Stephen.
   How to file for Chapter 7 bankruptcy / by Stephen Elias, Albin Renauer & Robin
Leonard.--13th ed.
     p. cm.
   Includes index.
   ISBN 1-4133-0451-6
    1. Bankruptcy--United States--Popular works. I. Title: Chapter 7 bankruptcy. II.
Renauer, Albin. III. Leonard, Robin. IV. Title.

KF1524.6.E4 2006
346.7307'8--dc22

2005058985

Quantity sales: For information on bulk purchases or corporate premium sales, please contact the
Special Sales Department. For academic sales or textbook adoptions, ask for Academic Sales.
800-955-4775, Nolo, 950 Parker Street, Berkeley, CA 94710.

3 1984 00243 6176

About Our Cover

Astrid plays an integral role at Guide Dogs for the Blind
(www.guidedogs.com)—her pups become loyal helpers and
confidence-boosters to visually impaired people. In much the
same way, Nolo books and software will guide you step by
step through the unfamiliar legal tangles of life's big events.

Dedications

To Mom and Dad, who gave me what money can't buy, and to whom I'm forever indebted.

—A.R.

To everyone who uses this and other Nolo books, for their courage and for having the good sense to take the law into their own hands.

—S.R.E., R.L., and A.R.

Acknowledgments

For their support and creative contributions to the early editions of this book, the authors gratefully acknowledge the following people:

Jake Warner, Mary Randolph, Terri Hearsh, Toni Ihara, Lisa Goldoftas, Marguerite Kirk, Susan Levinkind, Mike Mansel, Kim Wislee, Jess Glidewell, Les Peat, Lee Ryan, Marian Shostrom, Bobbe Powers, Virginia Simons, Jim Snyder, and the late A. Richard Anton.

The current edition would not have been possible without the assistance of:

Deanne Loonin, who updated several chapters of this edition and acted as a valuable sounding board throughout

Leslie Kane, who graciously reviewed many sections of this edition, bringing her knowledge and experience as a bankruptcy attorney to those pages, and

Ella Hirst, who tackled several large and difficult research projects with proficiency and good cheer.

Table of Contents

4 Your House

5 Secured Debts

6 Complete and File Your Bankruptcy Paperwork

7 Handling Your Case in Court

Glossary

Appendixes

1   State and Federal Exemption Tables

2   Worksheets and Charts

3   Tear-Out Forms

Index

Introduction

This book shows you how to file for Chapter 7 bankruptcy, a legal remedy that provides a fresh financial start to consumers and businesses by canceling all or many of their debts. The typical Chapter 7 bankruptcy is a routine process that requires no special courtroom or analytical skills. Under the new bankruptcy law that went into effect on October 17, 2005, most filers will have to:

- get credit counseling from an agency approved by the United States Trustee's office (filers must complete this counseling before filing for bankruptcy)
- file a packet of official forms and evidence of their recent wages (if they've been working)
- attend a five-minute, out-of-court meeting with a bankruptcy court official (called a "trustee")
- give the trustee a copy of their most recent tax return at least seven days before this meeting
- take a two-hour budget management course, and
- wait for three to six months for their bankruptcy to become final and their debts to be discharged.

Higher-income filers face an additional hurdle. Some Chapter 7 filers—about 15%, according to a recent study—will also have to do some calculations to find out whether they could afford to pay back a portion of their debt over a five-year period. This additional requirement is called the "means test," and filers who could afford to repay some of their debts according to its calculations may not be allowed to file for Chapter 7. The means test won't affect most filers, however, because it applies only if your average income in the six months before you file is more than the state median income for a family of your size—a category into which most Chapter 7 filers don't fall. Ch.1, Section C, explains how to calculate your income and compare it to the state median; Ch. 6, Section J, explains the means test in detail.

You may be thinking, "If this process is so straightforward for most people, why is this book so big?" The answer is that few people will need the whole book—most will use only a few chapters. However, the more property, income, and debts you have, the more information you'll need to fully understand your options. This book is designed both for the routine cases and for cases that have one or more complicating twists.

A. How to Use This Book

This book provides detailed information on Chapter 7 bankruptcy, including who is eligible to file; what happens to your property when you file; which debts are wiped out by your bankruptcy discharge; how to complete the required paperwork; how to handle routine court appearances; what kinds of help are available from lawyers, bankruptcy petition preparers, and legal reference books; and what to expect after your bankruptcy case is over.

Not every reader will need all of this information, however. If you have already decided to file for Chapter 7 and you understand what will happen to your property and debts, you can proceed straight to Ch. 6 for step-by-step instructions on completing the official bankruptcy forms. If you don't own a home or any other valuable property, you might want to skip Chs. 3 and 4, which explain how your property is handled in bankruptcy. And if none of your debts are "secured" (that is, you haven't pledged collateral or otherwise given the creditor the right to take your property if you don't pay the debt) you can certainly skip past Ch. 5.

Use this chart to figure out where to find the information you need.

Question	Where to Find the Answer
How does Chapter 7 bankruptcy work?	Ch. 1, Section B
Am I eligible to file for Chapter 7?	Ch. 1, Section C
Is my income low enough to qualify for Chapter 7?	Ch. 1, Section C, and Ch. 6, Section J
Does it make sense for me to use Chapter 7?	Ch. 1, Section D
Do I have options other than filing for bankruptcy?	Ch. 1, Section E
Can I avoid being evicted by filing for bankruptcy?	Ch. 2, Section C
Does bankruptcy stop my creditors from trying to collect what I owe them?	Ch. 2, Sections A and B
What will happen to my car if I file?	Ch. 3 and Ch. 5
What will happen to my house if I file?	Ch. 4
What personal property might I lose if I file?	Ch. 3
Can I keep property that I've pledged as collateral for a debt?	Ch. 5
Should I sign a reaffirmation agreement promising to repay a debt even after I file for bankruptcy?	Ch. 5
Will I lose my retirement account or pension?	Ch. 3, Section B
Where can I get the credit counseling required by the new bankruptcy law?	Chapter 1, Section B
Can I get my student loans cancelled or reduced in bankruptcy?	Ch. 9, Section B
Is there any way I can keep valuable property when I file for Chapter 7?	Ch. 3, Section C
Which debts will be wiped out after my bankruptcy?	Ch. 9, Section A
Which debts will I still have to pay after my bankruptcy?	Ch. 9, Section B
Can I get my tax debts wiped out in bankruptcy?	Ch. 9, Section B
How will my bankruptcy affect someone who cosigned for one of my debts?	Ch. 1, Section D
What will happen if I forget to list a debt on my bankruptcy papers?	Ch. 8, Section B
Can I give property away to friends or relatives to avoid losing it in bankruptcy?	Ch. 1, Section C
How will bankruptcy affect my child support obligations?	Ch. 2, Section B, and Ch. 9, Section B
How do I fill out the bankruptcy forms?	Ch. 6
How do I file my bankruptcy forms?	Ch. 6, Section L
What happens at the meeting of the creditors?	Ch. 1, Section B, and Ch. 7, Section A
Can I change my bankruptcy papers once I file them?	Ch. 7, Section B
Will I need an attorney to handle my bankruptcy?	Section C, below
How can I find a lawyer?	Ch. 10, Section C
If I can't afford a lawyer, what other types of help are available to me?	Ch. 10, Sections A, B, and D
Can I be fired because I filed for bankruptcy?	Ch. 8, Section F
How can I rebuild my credit after bankruptcy?	Ch. 8, Section G

B. What This Book Doesn't Cover

This book explains routine Chapter 7 bankruptcy procedures. You must be an individual, married couple, or small business owner with personal liability for your business debts to use this book. If your situation proves to be complicated, you might need more help than we can provide here. Throughout the book, we alert you to potential problems that might merit seeking some assistance. (See Ch. 10 for more on help beyond this book.)

This book doesn't cover the following situations:

- **Chapter 13 bankruptcies (repayment plans).** Chapter 13 allows people to repay a portion of their debts, with court supervision. Whether you are eligible to file for Chapter 13 bankruptcy depends on the type of debt you have and how much income you can devote to repaying the debt over a three- to five-year period. This book doesn't tell you how to file a Chapter 13 bankruptcy. (For that, you'll need a copy of *Chapter 13 Bankruptcy: Repay Your Debts*, by Stephen Elias and Robin Leonard (Nolo). However, it does help you figure out whether you might qualify to file for Chapter 13 and how to choose between that and Chapter 7, if both are available to you. Most of the forms you must complete for a Chapter 7 bankruptcy are also used in Chapter 13, so any work you do to prepare for a Chapter 7 bankruptcy won't be wasted if you later decide to file for Chapter 13 bankruptcy instead.

- **Bankruptcies for people in business partnerships.** If you're a partner in a business (other than a husband-wife partnership), filing for a personal bankruptcy will affect your business; we don't address that situation in this book. However, if you are partners with your spouse and are filing jointly, then this book will work just fine.

- **Bankruptcies for people who are major stockholders in privately held corporations.** If you are a major owner of a privately held corporation, filing for bankruptcy could affect the corporation's legal and tax status. This book doesn't cover your situation.

- **Business reorganizations.** This book doesn't cover procedures under Chapter 11 of the bankruptcy laws, which allow a business to continue operating while paying off all or a portion of its debts under court supervision.

- **Farm reorganizations.** A special set of bankruptcy statutes, called Chapter 12, lets family farmers continue farming while paying off their debts over time. This book doesn't cover Chapter 12 bankruptcies or the potentially complex question of whether a farmer is better off filing for Chapter 7, Chapter 12, Chapter 11, or Chapter 13 bankruptcy. If you're a farmer, check with a bankruptcy lawyer. If you decide to file for Chapter 7 bankruptcy, this book should give you the information you need.

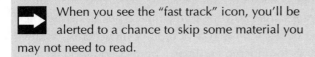

Icons Used in This Book

 When you see the "fast track" icon, you'll be alerted to a chance to skip some material you may not need to read.

 Information following this icon is for married couples only.

 This icon cautions you about potential problems.

 This icon highlights good advice or suggests time-saving tips.

 This icon refers you to related information in the book.

 Suggested references for additional information follow this icon.

 This icon tells you that it would be a good idea consult a bankruptcy lawyer.

 This icon reminds you of something you need to do.

C. If You Need More Help

If you need help with your bankruptcy, you have a number of options. Getting help may be as simple as using a bankruptcy petition preparation service to provide you with clerical and filing assistance. Or, it may involve consulting a bankruptcy attorney for advice or representation, or hitting the law library and figuring things out for yourself. In Ch. 10, we explain how to find the kind of help you need. Throughout the book, we do our best to point out where you may need assistance, although only you can judge whether you're in over your head.

 When you're looking for a bankruptcy lawyer, act locally. Bankruptcy law comes primarily from Congress and is meant to be uniform across the country. But when disputes arise about those laws, bankruptcy

courts must decide what the laws mean—and they don't all decide the issues in the same way. Also, the property you can keep in a Chapter 7 bankruptcy is determined primarily by state—not federal—laws. As a result, bankruptcy law and practice vary significantly from court to court and from region to region. This book can't possibly address every variation. When you need a bankruptcy lawyer, find someone who's familiar with your local bankruptcy court and the state exemption laws available to you.

Here are some common situations in which you may require the assistance of a bankruptcy lawyer:

- Your average income during the six months before you file is more than your state's median income, and it looks like you won't be able to pass the means test. (See Ch. 1, Section C, and Ch. 6, Section J, for more information on these calculations.)
- You want to hold onto a house or motor vehicle and the information we provide on these subjects doesn't adequately address your situation or answer all of your questions.
- You want to get rid of a student loan or income tax debt that won't be wiped out in bankruptcy unless you convince a court that it should be discharged.
- A creditor files a lawsuit in the bankruptcy court claiming that a specific debt should survive your bankruptcy because you incurred it through fraud or other misconduct.
- The bankruptcy trustee (the court official in charge of your case) seeks to have your whole bankruptcy dismissed because you didn't give honest and complete answers to questions about your assets, liabilities, and economic transactions.
- The U.S. Trustee asks the court to dismiss your case—or force you into Chapter 13—because your income is high enough to fund a Chapter 13 repayment plan, or because the trustee believes that your filing is an abuse of the Chapter 7 bankruptcy process for other reasons.
- You have recently given away or sold valuable property for less than it is worth.
- You went on a recent buying spree with your credit card (especially if you charged more than $500 on luxury goods within the past 90 days).

- You want help negotiating with a creditor or the bankruptcy court, and the amount involved justifies hiring a bankruptcy lawyer to assist you.
- You have a large lien on your property because of a court judgment against you, and you want to remove the lien in your bankruptcy case.
- A creditor is asking the court to allow it to proceed with its collection action despite your bankruptcy filing (for instance, a creditor wants to foreclose on your house because you are behind on your mortgage payments).
- You are being evicted by your landlord because you have fallen behind on your rent.

D. The New Bankruptcy Law: A Work in Progress

On April 17, 2005, President Bush signed a bill that made fundamental changes to the American consumer bankruptcy system. These changes, most of which took effect on October 17, 2005, are expected to have a major impact on many who file for bankruptcy to wipe out their debt.

Written primarily by the banking and credit card industries, the new bankruptcy law places a number of new hurdles in the way of those who seek the "fresh start" bankruptcy has traditionally offered. Among the changes enacted by the new law are provisions that make it harder to wipe out certain types of debts; force more debtors to repay a portion of their debts; require debtors to undergo credit and budget counseling; impose more obligations on bankruptcy attorneys (which will drive some attorneys out of the field and cause those who remain to raise their fees); and subject bankruptcy filers to increased scrutiny from the court and the United States Attorney General.

This book incorporates all of the provisions and requirements of the new bankruptcy law, and provides blank and sample copies of the very latest bankruptcy forms. Because the new law makes such profound changes to the bankruptcy system, however, no one can know exactly how courts will interpret its provisions in the months and years to come. As bankruptcy cases are filed under the new rules, we will learn how these legal changes play out in actual practice—including how courts will define the new terms included in the law. This book includes the best available information on the effect of the new rules, but, of course, we can't predict the future. To make sure you have the latest information, check for updates on Nolo's website at www.nolo.com. ∎

CHAPTER

1

Should You File for Chapter 7 Bankruptcy?

In the chapters that follow, we explain how to complete the required bankruptcy paperwork, what happens to your debts and property when you file for bankruptcy, how to get help with your bankruptcy, and how to pick up the financial pieces once your bankruptcy is final, among other things. But before you get to these important topics, you need to figure out whether you can—and should—file for Chapter 7 bankruptcy in the first place. This chapter will give you an overview of the bankruptcy process and help you decide whether Chapter 7 bankruptcy is right for you.

A. Bankruptcy in America: The Big Picture

Although you may not care much about the larger bankruptcy picture, understanding it will help you keep your situation in perspective. Knowing that you're not alone should also reassure you if you are feeling isolated or even like a failure.

1. Why People File for Bankruptcy

Over 1.5 million individuals and couples file for bankruptcy each year. Studies show that the most common reasons for these bankruptcies are:

- job loss, followed by an inability to find work that pays nearly as well
- medical expenses that aren't reimbursed by insurance or government programs
- divorce or legal separation, and
- small business failures.

Of course, none of these events would necessarily require bankruptcy if the people who experience them had adequate savings to weather the storm. But, for a number of reasons, most of us lack such savings. In fact, many of us are up to our eyeballs in debt, making ends meet from paycheck to paycheck. And when a recession hits, or jobs leave the country *en masse* and the pink slips start flowing, many otherwise stalwart citizens find themselves turning to bankruptcy for relief. Let's take a closer look at how we got so financially overextended.

2. Why You Shouldn't Feel Guilty About Filing for Bankruptcy

The American economy is based on consumer spending. Roughly two-thirds of the gross national product comes from consumers like us spending our hard-earned dollars on goods and services we deem essential to our lives. If you ever had any doubt about how important consumer spending is to our economy, remember that President George W. Bush wasted no time after the events of September 11, 2001, in urging Americans to spend more. And many other government leaders told us that spending was our patriotic duty. As Americans, we learn almost from birth that it's a good thing to buy all sorts of goods and services. A highly paid army of persuaders surrounds us with thousands of seductive messages each day that all say, "buy, buy, buy."

These sophisticated advertising techniques (which often cross the line into manipulation) convince us to buy. And for those of us who can't afford to pay as we go, credit card companies are relentless in offering credit to even the most deeply indebted of us. In fact, over 3 billion credit card solicitations are mailed to U.S residents each year—that's ten solicitations for every man, woman, and child. And, perhaps surprisingly, the largest growth sectors for credit cards are college students and people with bad credit ratings. The college students are targeted because they are customers of the future—and because their parents can be expected to bail them out if they get carried away with their new purchasing power. And people with bad credit are solicited in large numbers because creditors have discovered that they will pay huge interest rates for debts run up on their cards, which leads to equally huge profits.

Readily available credit makes it easy to live beyond our means and difficult to resist the siren songs of the advertisers. If, because of illness, loss of work, or just plain bad planning, we can't pay for the goods or services we need, feelings of fear and guilt are often our first responses. But, as we've also seen, the American economy depends on our spending—the more, the better. In short, much of American economic life is built on a contradiction.

Credit Card Companies Have Loaded the Dice

As anyone who has ever tried to rent a car—or even a movie—knows, it's tough to get by without a credit card. And once you get that card, most credit card companies will make it very easy for you to take on more debt than you can handle. By charging high interest rates and penalties, credit card companies can cause your original debt to soar beyond any reasonable expectation. In many cases, the interest rates are so high that the companies involved would have been prosecuted for loan sharking in the not-too-distant past—before the credit card industry systematically lobbied to do away with usury laws or to create exceptions to those laws for credit card interest rates. Credit card companies keep this system working by encouraging us to make the minimum payment, which stimulates us to make more credit purchases and eases us into debt loads far beyond our ability to ever pay them off. We now all owe our souls to the company store.

In this age of $50 billion bailouts for poorly managed financial institutions, should you really feel guilt ridden about the debts you've run up? That's something only you can decide, but remember that large creditors expect defaults and bankruptcies and treat them as a cost of doing business. The reason banks issue so many credit cards is that it is a very profitable business, even though some credit card debt is wiped out in bankruptcies and never repaid.

Bankruptcy is a truly worthy part of our legal system, based as it is on forgiveness rather than retribution. Certainly, it helps keep families together, frees up income and resources for children, reduces suicide rates, and keeps the ranks of the homeless from growing even larger. And, perhaps paradoxically, every successful bankruptcy returns a newly empowered person to the ranks of the "patriotic" consumer. If you suddenly find yourself without a job; socked with huge, unexpected medical bills you can't pay; or simply snowed under by an impossible debt burden, bankruptcy provides a chance for a fresh start and a renewed, positive outlook on life.

3. What About the Downside?

Bankruptcy can also have its disadvantages—economically, emotionally, and in terms of your future credit rating. The bankruptcy process can get intrusive. As part of your filing, you are required to disclose your financial activities during the previous year or two, as well as your debts and current property holdings.

Bankruptcy also carries a certain stigma. (Otherwise, why would we spend so much time talking you out of feeling bad about it?) Some people would rather struggle under a mountain of debt than accept the label of "bankrupt."

If you have a bankruptcy on your record, you will need to convince those who have business dealings with you that you made every effort to meet your financial obligations before turning to bankruptcy. Whether you are renting or buying a home, buying or leasing a car, or seeking financing for a business, your bankruptcy will be counted against you, at least for several years. And while you will be able to get credit cards after bankruptcy, you will have to pay the highest interest rate, at least for a while.

While these facts may seem like downsides, they collectively have an upside. For several years, you will find it very easy to be debt-free—you will have to pay as you go because it will be tough to get credit. Filing for bankruptcy can be a harsh wakeup call, one that will give you a new perspective on the credit system. A bankruptcy temporarily removes you from the credit hamster wheel and gives you some time and space to learn to live credit free (or, at least, to fashion a saner relationship to the credit industry).

B. An Overview of Chapter 7 Bankruptcy

This book explains how to file for Chapter 7 bankruptcy. Its name comes from the chapter of the federal statutes that contains the bankruptcy law (Chapter 7 of Title 11 of the United States Code). Chapter 7 bankruptcy is sometimes called "liquidation" bankruptcy—it cancels most of your debts, but you have to let the bankruptcy trustee liquidate (sell) your nonexempt property for the benefit of your creditors.

(People who file for bankruptcy are allowed to keep certain necessities of life, known as "exempt" property, as explained further in "What Is Exempt Property?" below.) By comparison, Chapter 13 bankruptcy is called a "reorganization" bankruptcy because it allows you to keep all of your property if you are willing to restructure your debt and pay some of it off over time.

Here is a brief overview of the Chapter 7 bankruptcy process, from start to finish.

1. What Bankruptcy Costs

The whole Chapter 7 bankruptcy process takes about three to six months, costs $299 in filing fees, and usually requires only one brief meeting, out of court, with the bankruptcy trustee—the official appointed by the bankruptcy judge to process your bankruptcy on behalf of the court. If you use a lawyer, you can expect to pay an additional $1,000 or more in legal fees. Of course, you can save most of this money by representing yourself with the help of this book (and, perhaps, a bankruptcy petition preparer). See Ch. 10 for information on finding lawyers and petition preparers.

2. Mandatory Credit Counseling

Before you can file for bankruptcy, you must consult a nonprofit credit counseling agency. The purpose of this consultation is to see whether there is a feasible way to handle your debt load outside of bankruptcy, without adding to what you owe.

To qualify for bankruptcy relief, you must show that you received credit counseling from an agency approved by the U.S Trustee's office for your region within the 180-day period before you filed. Once you complete the counseling, the agency will give you a certificate showing that you participated. It will also give you a copy of any repayment plan you worked out with the agency. This requirement doesn't apply if no credit counseling agency is available to you in your region.

The purpose of credit counseling is to give you an idea of whether you really need to file for bankruptcy or whether an informal repayment plan would get you back on your economic feet. Counseling is required even if it's pretty obvious that a repayment plan isn't feasible (that is, your debts are too high and your income is too low) or you are facing debts that you find unfair and don't want to pay. (Credit card balances inflated by high interest rates and penalties are particularly unpopular with many filers, as are emergency room bills and deficiency judgments based on auctions of repossessed cars.)

The law requires only that you participate—not that you go along with whatever the agency proposes. Even if a repayment plan is feasible, you aren't required to agree to it. However, if the agency does come up with a plan, you must file it along with the other required bankruptcy paperwork. See Ch. 6, Section A, for more information on the credit counseling requirement, including how to get the certificate of completion that you'll have to file with your other bankruptcy papers.

Rules Counseling Agencies Must Follow

In addition to providing services without regard to your ability to pay, counseling agencies have to meet a number of other requirements. They must:

- disclose to you their funding sources, their counselor qualifications, the possible impact of their proposed plan on your credit report, the costs of the program, if any, and how much of the costs will be born by you

- provide counseling that includes an analysis of your current financial condition, factors that caused the condition, and how you can develop a plan to respond to the problems without adding to your debt

- use trained counselors who don't receive any commissions or bonuses based on the outcome of the counseling services (that is, the counselors themselves may not receive kickbacks, although kickbacks to the agency may be legal), and

- maintain adequate financial resources to provide continuing support services over the life of any repayment plan (that is, if they propose a three-year payment plan, they must have adequate reserves to service your case for three years).

3. Filing Your Papers

To begin a Chapter 7 bankruptcy case, you must complete a packet of forms and file them with the bankruptcy court in your area. Many filers are shocked to see the long list of documents that might be required in a Chapter 7 case, particularly after Congress added even more paperwork requirements in the new bankruptcy law. But don't be alarmed: Many of these forms require very little time and effort to fill in, and most filers won't have to complete them all. Just take things one step at a time, following the detailed instructions in Ch. 6, and you'll do just fine.

Once you file the papers described below, the court will send a notice of your bankruptcy to all of the creditors listed in your bankruptcy documents. You will get a copy as well. This notice (called a "341 notice" because it is required by Section 341 of the bankruptcy code) sets a date for the meeting of creditors (see Section 7, below) and gives creditors the deadlines for filing objections to your bankruptcy or to the discharge of particular debts.

a. The Voluntary Petition

You begin a Chapter 7 case by filing a "Voluntary Petition": the official court form that requests a bankruptcy discharge of your debts. This form asks for some basic information, including your name, address, and the last four digits of your Social Security number; information about your creditors, debts, and property; and whether you have lived, maintained a residence or business, or had assets in the district where you are filing for most of the 180-day period before you file (this gives you the right to file in that district). You'll find line-by-line instructions for completing the Voluntary Petition in Ch. 6, Section E.

b. Additional Documents

You will have to submit quite a few more documents, either when you file the petition or within 15 days after you file (there are a few exceptions to the 15-day limit). These documents include lists of your creditors, assets, debts, income, and financial transactions prior to filing; copies of your most recent federal tax return and wage stubs; a list of property you are claiming as exempt (that is, property that you are entitled to keep even though you are filing for bankruptcy); information on what you plan to do with property that serves as collateral for a loan (such as a car or home); and proof that you have completed credit counseling.

Perhaps the most important form—made necessary by the new bankruptcy law—requires you to compute your average income during the six months prior to your bankruptcy filing date and compare that to the median income for your state. If your income is more than the median, the same form takes you through a series of questions (called the "means test") designed to determine whether you could file a Chapter 13 bankruptcy and pay some of your unsecured debts over time. The outcome of this test will determine whether you can file for Chapter 7 bankruptcy. (See Section C1, below, and Ch. 6, Section J, for detailed information about these calculations.)

After you file, you may want to amend some or all of your forms to correct mistakes you discover or to reflect agreements you reach with the trustee. Amending these forms is fairly simple—we explain how to do it in Ch. 7.

Emergency Filing

If you need to stop creditors quickly, you can do so without filing all of the bankruptcy forms we describe in Ch. 6 (although you'll eventually have to complete the full set). In some situations, speed is essential. For example, if you face foreclosure and your house is going to be sold in a few days, or your car is about to be repossessed, filing an emergency petition will stop the repossession or foreclosure cold.

To put an end to collection efforts, you can simply file the three-page Voluntary Petition together with a form called a Creditors Matrix, which lists the name, address, and zip code of each of your creditors. The automatic stay, which stops collection efforts and lawsuits against you, will then go into effect. (See Section 4, below, and Ch. 2 for more information on the automatic stay.) You'll have 15 days to file the rest of the forms. (Bankruptcy Rule 1007(c).) See Ch. 6 for line-by-line instructions on completing the paperwork.

You should file on an emergency basis only if you absolutely must. Many emergency filers fail to meet the 15-day deadline and have their petitions dismissed as a result. Because you are rushing, you tend to make mistakes that have to be corrected later, which just adds work and potential errors to the process. But if filing an emergency petition is the only way to stop a potentially disastrous creditor action, go for it. Just remember to hit your deadline for filing the rest of the forms.

What Is Exempt Property?

Each state has laws that determine which items of property are exempt in bankruptcy, and in what amounts. These items cannot be seized by creditors or by the bankruptcy trustee. Instead, you are allowed to hang on to them, even though you have filed for bankruptcy.

Each state's exemptions are different, and the exemptions you can use depend on how long you have lived in the state where you currently reside. (See Section D4, below, and Ch. 3 for more on these new residency requirements.) Many states exempt "personal effects" (things such as electric shavers, hair dryers, and toothbrushes), ordinary household furniture, clothing, and health aids without regard to their value.

Other kinds of property are exempt only up to a limit. For example, in many states, furniture or a car is exempt to several thousands of dollars. This exemption limit means that any equity in the property above the limit isn't exempt. (Equity is the market value minus what you still owe.)

Typically, the following items are exempt:

- part of the equity in motor vehicles (the amount varies from state to state)
- reasonably necessary clothing (no fur coats)
- reasonably necessary household goods and furnishings
- household appliances
- jewelry, to a few hundred dollars
- personal effects
- life insurance (cash or loan value or proceeds), (the amount varies from state to state)
- part of the equity in a residence (the amount varies from state to state)
- pensions
- public benefits
- tools of a trade or profession, to a certain value, and
- unpaid but earned wages.

For detailed information on exemptions for personal property, see Ch. 3. You'll find information on exemptions for your home in Ch. 4.

4. Bankruptcy's Magic Wand: The Automatic Stay

Often, people filing for bankruptcy have faced weeks, months, or even years of harassment by creditors demanding payment and threatening lawsuits and collection actions. Bankruptcy puts a stop to all this. By filing your bankruptcy petition, you instantly create a federal court order (called an "Order for Relief" and colloquially known as the "automatic stay") that requires your creditors to stop all collection efforts. So, at least temporarily, most creditors cannot call you, write dunning letters, legally grab (garnish) your wages, empty your bank account, go after your car, house, or other property, or cut off your utility service or welfare benefits. As explained in Ch. 2, the automatic stay is not absolute: Some creditors are not affected by the automatic stay, and others can get the stay lifted to collect their particular debt, as long as they get the judge's permission first.

Renters beware. The automatic stay's magic does not extend to certain eviction actions. And even if the automatic stay does kick in to temporarily halt your eviction when you file for bankruptcy, the bankruptcy court will almost always lift the stay and let the eviction proceed, upon the landlord's request. See Ch. 2, Section C, for more information on the automatic stay and eviction proceedings.

5. Court Control Over Your Financial Affairs

By filing for bankruptcy, you are technically placing the property you own and the debts you owe in the hands of the bankruptcy trustee (see Section 6, below). You can't sell or give away any of the property that you own when you file, or pay any of your prefiling debts, without the trustee's consent. However, with a few exceptions, you can do what you wish with property you acquire and income you earn after you file for bankruptcy. You are also allowed to borrow money after you file.

6. The Trustee

The bankruptcy court exercises control over your property and debts by appointing an official called a "trustee" to manage your case. Your trustee's name and contact information will be in the official notice of filing you receive in the mail several days after you file your petition. The trustee (or the trustee's staff) will examine your papers to make sure they are complete and to look for property to sell for the benefit of your creditors. The trustee's primary duty is to see that your creditors are paid as much as possible. The trustee is mostly interested in what you own and what property you claim as exempt, but will also look at your financial transactions during the previous year (in some cases these can be undone to free up assets that can be distributed to your creditors). The more assets the trustee recovers for creditors, the more the trustee is paid.

How Trustees Get Paid

In Chapter 7 cases, trustees receive a flat fee of $60 per case. In addition, trustees are entitled to pocket a percentage of the funds the trustee disburses to the debtor's creditors: 25% of the first $5,000 disbursed, 10% of the next $45,000, and so on. Most Chapter 7 cases involve no disbursements (because typically there are no nonexempt assets), so the trustee usually has to settle for the $60 fee. But these financial incentives make trustees ever vigilant to situations where they can actually grab some property and earn a statutory "commission."

Some courts appoint full-time trustees (called "standing" trustees) to handle all cases filed in that courthouse. Other courts appoint trustees on a rotating basis from a panel of bankruptcy lawyers (called "panel" trustees). Either way, the trustees have the same responsibilities. However, full-time trustees usually do a better job of scrutinizing bankruptcy papers for possible mistakes, whether intentional or accidental.

The U.S. Trustee

The U.S. Trustee Program is a division of the U.S. Department of Justice. Each U.S. trustee oversees several bankruptcy courts. Individual cases within those courts are assigned to assistant U.S. trustees, who also employ attorneys, auditors, and investigators. U.S. trustees work closely with their Department of Justice colleagues from the FBI and other federal agencies to ferret out fraud and abuse in the bankruptcy system. The U.S. trustees (and the assistant U.S. trustees) also supervise the work of the panel or standing trustees, who are appointed by the courts.

You will most likely encounter the U.S. trustee if:

- your bankruptcy papers suggest that you may be engaging in fraudulent behavior
- your case is selected for a random audit (one out of every 250 bankruptcy cases is supposed to be audited under the new bankruptcy law)
- your bankruptcy schedules show that you don't pass the means test (see Section C1, below), or
- you use a bankruptcy petition preparer (BPP) to help you with your paperwork (see Ch. 10, Section B, for more on BPPs), and the trustee believes that the BPP has done something illegal—typically, that the BPP has not just helped you complete your papers, but has given you legal advice, something that only lawyers are allowed to do. In this situation, your bankruptcy won't be affected, but the U.S. trustee may want you to act as a witness against the BPP.

7. The Meeting of Creditors

As explained in Section 3, above, you will receive a notice of the date of the creditors' meeting shortly after you file your bankruptcy papers. This meeting is typically held somewhere in the courthouse or federal building (but almost never in a courtroom). The trustee runs the meeting and, after swearing you in, may ask you questions about your bankruptcy and the documents you filed. For instance, the trustee might ask how you arrived at the value you assigned to an item of property listed in your papers, whether you have given anything away in the last year, and whether the information you put in your papers is 100% accurate. All together, this questioning rarely takes more than a few minutes. Creditors rarely attend this meeting—but if they do, they will also have a chance to question you under oath, usually about where collateral is located or about information you gave them to obtain a loan. In most bankruptcy cases, this will be the only personal appearance you have to make. We discuss the creditors' meeting in more detail, and provide information on other situations when you might have to appear in court, in Ch. 7.

8. What Happens to Your Property in a Chapter 7 Bankruptcy

In your bankruptcy papers, you'll be asked which items of your property you claim as exempt. Each state allows debtors to keep certain types of property, or a certain amount of equity in that property. The exemptions available to you depend on where you have lived prior to filing for bankruptcy. (For more information, see "What Is Exempt Property?" above, and Ch. 3.)

If, after the creditors' meeting, the trustee determines that you have some nonexempt property, you may be required to either surrender that property or provide the trustee with its equivalent value in cash. The trustee is highly unlikely to search your home or seize your property, but will order you to turn over property listed in your schedules or identified during your creditors' meeting or in other proceedings. If you don't turn over the property, the bankruptcy judge can order you to do it (and hold you in contempt if you don't). Plus, the court can dismiss your bankruptcy petition if you fail to cooperate with the trustee.

If the property isn't worth very much or would be cumbersome for the trustee to sell, the trustee may "abandon" it—which means that you get to keep it, even though it's nonexempt. As it turns out, all of the property that most Chapter 7 debtors own is either exempt or essentially worthless for purposes of raising money for the creditors. As a result, few debtors end up having to surrender any of their property—unless the property is collateral for a secured debt. (See Section 9, below, and Ch. 5 for a detailed discussion of secured debts.)

9. How Your Secured Debts Are Treated

If you've pledged property as collateral for a loan, the loan is called a secured debt. The most common examples of collateral are houses and motor vehicles. If you are behind on your payments, the creditor can ask to have the automatic stay lifted so it can repossess the property or foreclose on the mortgage. However, if you are current on your payments, you can keep the property and continue making payments as before—unless you have enough equity in the property to justify its sale by the trustee for the benefit of your unsecured creditors. (See Ch. 5 for more information on secured debts.)

If a creditor has recorded a lien against your property without your consent (for example, because the creditor obtained a money judgment against you in court), that debt is also secured. However, in some cases and with certain types of property, you may be able to wipe out the debt and keep the property free of the lien. This is called "lien avoidance," and it is also covered in Ch. 5.

10. How Contracts and Leases Are Treated in Bankruptcy

If you're a party to a contract or lease that's still in effect, the trustee may take your place as a party to the contract—known as "assuming" the contract—and enforce it for the benefit of your unsecured creditors. Alternatively, the trustee can decide not to step in as a party to the contract—called "rejecting" the contract—in which case, your obligations under the contract are discharged as an unsecured debt. For example, suppose you have a five-year lease on some commercial property when you file for bankruptcy. If you've got a good lease (perhaps at a below-market rate, with a few years left on it, for property in an up-and-coming part of town), the trustee may decide to assign the lease to a third party in exchange for money to pay your unsecured creditors. In this situation, the trustee will assume the lease and assign it to the highest bidder, even if the lease forbids assignments: The trustee's rights trump any transfer restrictions in the lease.

However, if the trustee doesn't think selling the lease is worth the trouble (as is almost always the case), the trustee will take no action, which is the same thing as rejecting the lease. Of course, you and the landlord can renew the lease at any time.

Under the new bankruptcy law, you can assume the lease on personal property (such as a car or business equipment) rather than having the trustee assume it. However, you will be allowed to do this only if you are able to cure any defaults on the lease, as required by the creditor. (Ch. 6 provides instructions for completing Schedule G, a required bankruptcy form in which you list all current contracts and leases, and the Statement of Intention, another required form in which you tell your creditors and the trustee whether you would like to assume any leases.)

What If You Change Your Mind About Chapter 7 Bankruptcy After Filing?

If you don't want to go through with your Chapter 7 bankruptcy after you file, you can ask the court to dismiss your case. A court will generally agree, as long as the dismissal won't harm the creditors. For example, if you have substantial nonexempt equity in your house, the court will probably deny your request so the trustee can sell the house to make some money for your unsecured creditors. (See Ch. 4 for more on what happens to your home in bankruptcy.) Even if your case is dismissed, you can usually file again if you want to, although you may have to wait 180 days if you requested dismissal after a creditor filed a motion to lift the automatic stay. (See Ch. 2 for more information on the automatic stay.)

As an alternative to having your case dismissed, you may exercise your one-time "right to convert" the case to a Chapter 13 bankruptcy, as long as you really intend to propose and follow a repayment plan. This will keep your property out of the trustee's hands, because in Chapter 13 you don't have to surrender property if you complete your repayment plan. (See Section E4, below.)

11. Personal Financial Management Counseling

The new bankruptcy law requires all debtors to attend a two-hour course on managing finances in order to receive a bankruptcy discharge. You must take this course from an agency approved by the U.S. Trustee Program. (For a list of approved agencies, go to the U.S. Trustee's website, www.usdoj.gov/ust, and click "Credit Counseling & Debtor Education.") If no course is available in your area, you will be excused from this requirement. You will be charged fees on a sliding scale, but you can't be denied services because of your inability to pay.

12. The Bankruptcy Discharge

At the end of the bankruptcy process, all of your debts are discharged except:

- debts that automatically survive bankruptcy, unless the bankruptcy court rules otherwise (child support, most tax debts, and student loans are examples), and
- debts that the court has declared nondischarge-able as a result of an action brought by the creditor, as might be the case with debts incurred by fraudulent or willful and malicious acts on your part.

Ch. 9 explains which debts are—and are not—discharged at the end of your bankruptcy case.

13. After Bankruptcy

Once you receive your bankruptcy discharge, you are free to resume your economic life without reporting your activities to the bankruptcy court—unless you receive (or become eligible to receive) an inheritance, insurance proceeds, or proceeds from a divorce settlement within 180 days after your filing date. In that case, you have a duty to report those assets to the trustee. If you don't, and they are discovered, the trustee (and the court, if necessary) can order you to turn over the assets and your discharge can be revoked.

After bankruptcy, you cannot be discriminated against by public or private employers solely because of the bankruptcy, although this ban on discrimination has exceptions (discussed in Ch. 8). You can start rebuilding your credit almost immediately, but it will

take several years to get decent interest rates on a credit card, mortgage, or car note. You can't file for a subsequent Chapter 7 bankruptcy until eight years have passed since your last filing date. You can file for Chapter 13 bankruptcy any time, but you can't get a Chapter 13 discharge until four years have passed since you filed for Chapter 7. (See Section E4, below.)

C. Who Can File for Chapter 7?

Filing for Chapter 7 bankruptcy is one way to solve debt problems—but it isn't available to everyone. Here are some situations in which you may not be able to use Chapter 7.

1. You Can Afford a Chapter 13 Repayment Plan

Under the old bankruptcy rules, most filers were free to choose the type of bankruptcy that seemed best for them—and most chose Chapter 7 rather than Chapter 13. The new bankruptcy law takes this choice away from some filers with higher incomes. One goal of the new law is to force people who have the economic ability to pay back some of their debts over time to file under Chapter 13, rather than allowing them to liquidate their debts outright in Chapter 7. If the U.S. Trustee decides, based on the information about your income, debts, and expenses you provide in your required paperwork, that you could afford a Chapter 13 plan under the new rules, it will file a motion to have your case dismissed—and that motion will probably be granted by the court.

To figure out whether you will be allowed to use Chapter 7, you must:

- determine your "current monthly income" (see Subsection a, below), and
- compare your current monthly income to the median family income in your state (see Subsection b, below).

If your current monthly income is no more than the state median income, you are free to file for Chapter 7. If your income exceeds the state median income, you will have to do some calculations (called the means test) to determine whether you can afford to pay off at least some of your unsecured debts in a Chapter 13 plan. (If you have to take the means test, you can find step-by-step instructions in Ch. 6, Section J.)

Certain Disabled Veterans Can Skip the Math

If you are a disabled veteran, and the debts you wish to discharge were incurred while you were on active duty or engaged in homeland defense activities, the court is legally required to treat you as if your income is less than the state median—even if it is actually higher. This means that you'll be able to file for Chapter 7 regardless of your income or expenses.

The new law doesn't clearly indicate what will happen if some of your debts were incurred while you were on active duty, and others were incurred before or afterwards. We'll have to wait and see how courts interpret this provision.

a. Determine Your Current Monthly Income

The new bankruptcy law defines current monthly income as your average monthly income over the six-month period before you filed for bankruptcy. You must include almost all types of income, whether or not they are taxable—this means, for example, that if you are including wages in your income, you must use your gross earnings, not the net income you actually take home after taxes are withheld and other deductions are made. For filers who lost a job or other income during the six months before filing for bankruptcy, this current income figure may be significantly more than what they are actually earning each month by the time they file for bankruptcy.

EXAMPLE: John and Marcia are married and have two young children. They fell quickly into debt after John was forced out of his job because of a work-related injury on April 1, 2006. Three months later, on July 1, 2006, John and Marcia decide to file for bankruptcy.

To compute their current monthly income, Marcia adds up the family's income for the period from January 1, 2006, through June 30, 2006 (the six-month period before their filing date). This includes John's gross salary for the first three months (he made $8,000 a month as a software engineer), plus $1,800 in workers' compensation benefits for each of the last three months. Marcia made $1,000 during each of the first three months, and had no income for the last three months. The total family income for the six-month period is $32,400. The family's current monthly income is $32,400 divided by six, or $5,400, even though the amount they actually took in during each of the three months before filing was only $1,800.

Use the Current Monthly Income Worksheet, below (and in Appendix 2), to calculate your current monthly income by:

- adding up all of the income you received during the six months before filing for bankruptcy, and
- dividing by six to come up with a monthly average.

You should include all of the following types of income on the form:

- wages, salary, tips, bonuses, overtime, and commissions
- gross income from operating a business, profession, or farm
- interest, dividends, and royalties
- rents and other income from real property
- pension and retirement income
- regular contributions someone else makes to you or your dependents' household expenses, including child or spousal support
- regular contributions of your spouse, if he or she isn't filing for bankruptcy with you
- unemployment compensation
- workers' compensation insurance
- state disability insurance, and
- annuity payments.

Current Monthly Income Worksheet

Use this worksheet to calculate your current monthly income; use figures for you and your spouse if you plan to file jointly.

Line 1. Calculate your total income over the last six months from wages, salary, tips, bonuses, overtime, and so on.

   A. Month 1 $ _____

   B. Month 2   _____

   C. Month 3   _____

   D. Month 4   _____

   E. Month 5   _____

   F. Month 6   _____

   G. TOTAL WAGES (add Lines A–F) $ _____

Line 2. Add up all other income for the last six months.

   A. Business, profession, or farm income   _____

   B. Interest, dividends, and royalties   _____

   C. Rents and real property income   _____

   D. Pension and retirement income   _____

   E. Alimony or family support   _____

   F. Spousal contributions (if not filing jointly)   _____

   G. Unemployment compensation   _____

   H. Workers' compensation   _____

   I. State disability insurance   _____

   J. Annuity payments   _____

   K. Other   _____

   L. TOTAL OTHER INCOME $ _____

Line 3. Calculate total income over the six months prior to filing.

   A. Enter total wages (Line 1G).   _____

   B. Enter total other income (Line 2L).   _____

   C. TOTAL INCOME OVER THE SIX MONTHS PRIOR TO FILING. Add Lines A and B together. $ _____

Line 4. Average monthly income over the six months prior to filing. This is called your current monthly income.

   A. Enter total six-month income (Line 3C).   _____

   B. CURRENT MONTHLY INCOME. Divide Line A by six. $ _____

Income You Don't Have to Include

Your current monthly income includes income from all sources, **except:**

- payments you receive under the Social Security Act (including Social Security retirement, Social Security Disability Insurance, Supplemental Security Income, Temporary Assistance for Needy Families, and possibly state unemployment insurance)
- payments to you as a victim of war crimes or crimes against humanity, based on your status as a victim of such crimes, and
- payments to victims of international or domestic terrorism.

---

b. Compare Your Income to Your State's Family Median Income

The census bureau publishes *annual* family median income figures for all 50 states. To compare your current *monthly* income to the family median income for your state, you'll need to multiply your current monthly income by 12 (or divide the annual family median income figure by 12). Let's do it the first way. In John and Marcia's case, the family's current monthly income ($5,400) multiplied by 12 would be $64,800.

Once you've got your current monthly income and your family median income for the same time period (one month or one year), compare them to see whether your current monthly income is more or less than the median. You can find the most recent family median income figures in the Median Family Income chart in Appendix 2. You can also find up-to-date figures at the website of the U.S. Trustee at www.usdoj.gov/ust/ bapcpa/meanstesting.htm or the United States Census Bureau, www.census.gov (click "State Family Income" from the homepage).

You can see from the chart in Appendix 2 that John and Marcia's current monthly income would be more than the family median income in most states.

For Larger Families

Although the U.S. Census Bureau generates median figures for families that have up to seven members, Congress does not want you to use these figures if you have a larger family. The Census figures are to be used for families that have up to four members (these are the numbers you will find in Appendix 2). If there are more than four members of your family, you must add a set amount per additional person to the four-member family median income figure for your state (currently, this amount is $6,300).

---

c. What to Do Next

If, like most bankruptcy filers, your current monthly income is equal to or below the state's median, then you will be allowed to file for Chapter 7 bankruptcy. Keep reading this chapter to make sure that Chapter 7 is the best way to handle your debt problems.

If, on the other hand, your income exceeds the state median income, you'll need to take the means test to figure out whether you'll be allowed to file for Chapter 7 or you'll be limited to Chapter 13. You can find the means test form, and step-by-step instructions for completing it, in Ch. 6, Section J. If you pass the means test, you'll be able to file for Chapter 7, and you should return here and continue reading. If you don't pass the means test, you might consider filing for Chapter 13 bankruptcy with the help of Nolo's *Chapter 13 Bankruptcy*, by Stephen Elias and Robin Leonard. You should also take a look at the alternatives to bankruptcy discussed in Section E.

2. You Previously Received a Bankruptcy Discharge

You cannot file for Chapter 7 bankruptcy if you obtained a discharge of your debts under Chapter 7 in a case begun within the past eight years, or under Chapter 13 in a case begun within the previous six years. (11 U.S.C. § 727.) However, if you obtained a Chapter 13 discharge in good faith after paying at least 70% of your unsecured debts, the six-year bar does not apply.

The eight- and six-year periods run from the date you filed for the earlier bankruptcy, not the date you received your discharge.

EXAMPLE: Brenda files a Chapter 7 bankruptcy case on January 31, 2006. She receives a discharge on April 20, 2006. Brenda files another Chapter 7 bankruptcy on February 1, 2014. The second bankruptcy is allowed because eight years have passed since the date the earlier bankruptcy was filed (even though fewer than eight years have passed since Brenda received a discharge in the earlier case).

3. A Previous Bankruptcy Was Dismissed Within the Previous 180 Days

You cannot file for Chapter 7 bankruptcy if your previous Chapter 7 or Chapter 13 case was dismissed within the past 180 days because:
- you violated a court order, or
- you requested the dismissal after a creditor asked for relief from the automatic stay. (11 U.S.C. §109(g).)

4. You Defrauded Your Creditors

Bankruptcy is geared towards the honest debtor who got in too deep and needs a fresh start. A bankruptcy court will not help someone who has played fast and loose with creditors.

Certain activities are red flags to the courts and trustees. If you have engaged in any of them within the past several years, do not file for bankruptcy until you consult with a bankruptcy lawyer. These no-nos are:
- unloading assets to your friends or relatives
- incurring debts for luxury items when you were clearly broke, and
- concealing property or money from your spouse during a divorce proceeding.

EXAMPLE: Joan wants to file for bankruptcy but is worried that she'll lose her house. Before filing, Joan puts the house in her mother's name on the understanding that her mother will deed it back to her after the bankruptcy is completed. Before filing, Joan learns that this is a definite no-no and can land her in serious trouble. She retransfers the house back into her own name and files a Chapter 7 bankruptcy. The trustee learns of the transactions and successfully opposes Joan's discharge on the ground that she acted fraudulently. The fact that she undid the fraud before filing won't necessarily help her.

5. You Are Attempting to Defraud the Bankruptcy Court

Misleading the court is a terrible idea. If you lie, cheat, or attempt to hide assets, your current debt crisis may no longer be your biggest legal problem. You must sign your bankruptcy papers under "penalty of perjury," swearing that everything in them is true. If you get caught deliberately failing to disclose property, omitting material information you are asked to provide about your financial affairs during previous years, or using a false Social Security number (to hide your identity as a prior filer), you will not get any bankruptcy relief, and you may be prosecuted for perjury or fraud on the court. People go to prison for that.

The U.S. Trustee Program Actively Roots Out Fraud

The U.S. Trustee Program, a branch of the U.S. Department of Justice, is actively engaged in fighting bankruptcy-related fraud. Copies of all bankruptcy petitions filed in your district are passed on to the U.S. Trustee for that district, where they are scrutinized. The U.S. Trustee also performs random audits of roughly one out of every 250 cases filed. While the trustee in charge of your case is also supposed to be on the lookout for fraudulent behavior, the U.S. Trustee is a law enforcement agency and is likely to be much more thorough. This is nothing you need worry about as long as you are scrupulously honest in your paperwork and disclosures.

The "Open Letter to Debtors and Their Counsel," set out below, reflects a view held by more and more bankruptcy courts. Just remember, you're signing papers under penalty of perjury, and the courts expect you to be careful and accurate. The more accurate you are with the information in your papers, the less likely you are to run into any trouble.

Open Letter to Debtors and Their Counsel

I have noticed a disturbing trend among debtors and their counsel to treat the schedules and statement of affairs as "working papers" which can be freely amended as circumstances warrant and need not contain the exact, whole truth.

Notwithstanding execution under penalty of perjury, debtors and their counsel seem to think that they are free to argue facts and values not contained in the schedules or even directly contrary to the schedules. Some debtors have felt justified signing a statement that they have only a few, or even a single creditor, in order to file an emergency petition, knowing full well that the statement is false.

Whatever your attitude is toward the schedules, you should know that as far as I am concerned they are the sacred text of any bankruptcy filing. There is no excuse for them not being 100% accurate and complete. Disclosure must be made to a fault. The filing of false schedules is a federal felony, and I do not hesitate to recommend prosecution of anyone who knowingly files a false schedule.

I have no idea where anyone got the idea that amendments can cure false schedules. The debtor has an obligation to correct schedules he or she knows are false, but amendment in no way cures a false filing. Any court may properly disregard [a] subsequent sworn statement at odds with previous sworn statements. I give no weight at all to amendments filed after an issue has been raised.

As a practical matter, where false statements or omissions have come to light due to investigation by a creditor or trustee, it is virtually impossible for the debtor to demonstrate good faith in a Chapter 13 case or entitlement to a discharge in a Chapter 7 case. I strongly recommend that any of you harboring a cavalier attitude toward the schedules replace it with a good healthy dose of paranoia.

Dated: September 10, 1997

Alan Jaroslovsky

Alan Jaroslovsky
U.S. Bankruptcy Judge, N.D. Cal., Santa Rosa

D. Does Chapter 7 Bankruptcy Make Economic Sense?

If you are inclined to file for Chapter 7 bankruptcy, take a moment to decide whether it makes economic sense. If filing for Chapter 7 won't help you out of your current debt problems, will force you to give up property you want to keep, or is unnecessary because of your financial situation, for example, then Chapter 7 might not be the best option.

 If you are married, consider the debts and property of both spouses as you read this section. In Ch. 6, Section C, you will have an opportunity to decide whether you are better off filing jointly or filing alone.

1.   Are You Judgment Proof?

Most unsecured creditors are required to obtain a court judgment before they can start collection procedures such as a wage garnishment or seizure and sale of personal property. Taxes, child support, and student loans are exceptions to this general rule. If your debts are mainly of the type that require a judgment, the next question is whether you have any income or property that is subject to seizure by your creditors if they obtain a judgment. For instance, if all of your income comes from Social Security (which can't be taken by creditors), and all of your property is exempt (see Ch. 3), there is nothing your creditors can do with their judgment. That makes you judgment proof. While you may still wish to file for bankruptcy to get a fresh start, nothing bad will happen to you if you don't file, no matter how much you owe. For more on what it means to be judgment proof, see Section E1, below.

Even though you may be judgment proof, you may want to file for bankruptcy to stop harassment by your creditors. In most cases, you can stop creditors from making telephone calls to your home or work by simply telling them to stop. You can also send them a letter like the one shown below, which almost always does the trick.

Sample Letter Telling Collection Agency to Stop Contacting You

Sasnak Collection Service
49 Pirate Place
Topeka, Kansas 69000

November 11, 2004

Attn: Marc Mist
Re: Lee Anne Ito
Account No. 88-90-92

Dear Mr. Mist:

For the past three months, I have received several phone calls and letters from you concerning an overdue Rich's Department Store account.

This is my formal notice to you under 15 U.S.C. § 1692c(c) to cease all further communications with me except for the reasons specifically set forth in the federal law.

This letter is not meant in any way to be an acknowledgment that I owe this money.

Very truly yours,

Lee Anne Ito

Lee Anne Ito

2. Will Bankruptcy Discharge Enough of Your Debts?

Certain categories of debts may survive Chapter 7 bankruptcy, depending on the circumstances. These are commonly referred to as nondischargeable debts—and it may not make much sense to file for Chapter 7 bankruptcy if your primary goal is to get rid of them.

There are three categories of nondischargeable debts:
- debts that always survive bankruptcy
- debts that survive bankruptcy unless the bankruptcy court rules that a particular exception applies, and
- debts that survive bankruptcy only if the bankruptcy court says that they should.

If most of your debts are the kind that automatically survive bankruptcy or that survive unless a particular exception applies, hold off on filing your Chapter 7 bankruptcy until you have at least read Ch. 9 and learned what is likely to happen to these debts in your case. In particular, you should be concerned about:
- back child support and alimony
- debts other than support that arise from a marital settlement agreement or divorce decree
- student loans
- government fines, penalties, or court-ordered restitution
- tax arrearages (including debts incurred to pay a tax arrearage—for example, if you used a credit card to pay back taxes), and
- court judgments for injuries or death resulting from your drunk-driving convictions.

The following types of debts can survive bankruptcy, but only if the creditor mounts a successful challenge to them in the bankruptcy court:
- debt incurred on the basis of fraud, such as lying on a credit application or writing a bad check
- debt for luxury items that you recently bought on credit with no intention of paying for them
- debt from willful and malicious injury to another person or another's property, including assault, battery, false imprisonment, libel, and slander, and
- debt from larceny (theft), breach of trust, or embezzlement.

<table>
<tr><td>

Sorting It All Out

If your debt load consists primarily of debts that will be discharged unless a creditor convinces the court that they shouldn't be, it may make sense to file for bankruptcy and hope that the creditor doesn't challenge the discharge. Many creditors don't—mounting a challenge to the discharge of a debt usually requires a lawyer, and lawyers don't come cheap. Also, many lawyers advise their clients to write off the debt rather than throw good money after bad in a bankruptcy court challenge.

If your debt load consists primarily of debts that will survive your bankruptcy unless you convince the court otherwise, you must decide whether the debts are large enough to warrant paying an attorney to argue your position in court that the debts should be discharged. For example, if you owe $50,000 in student loans and have a good argument that they should be discharged, it will be worth your while to file for bankruptcy and pay an attorney $1,000 to push the issue. (You could also do this yourself, although this sort of procedure is difficult to navigate without competent expert help.) If, on the other hand, the amount in question is small and your chances of victory slim, you may choose to forgo bankruptcy altogether.

</td></tr>
</table>

Chapter 13 might be a better choice. In some situations, Chapter 13 offers relief that is not available in Chapter 7. For example, if you are facing foreclosure on your home because of mortgage defaults, or if you have debts that you can discharge in Chapter 13 but not in Chapter 7, you might want to consider using Chapter 13. See Section E4, below, for more on Chapter 13 bankruptcy.

3. Will a Cosigner Be Stuck With Your Debts?

If someone else cosigned a loan or otherwise took on a joint obligation with you, that person can be held wholly responsible for the debt if you don't pay it. If you receive a Chapter 7 bankruptcy discharge, you may no longer be liable for the debt—but your cosigner will still be on the hook. Especially if your cosigner is

a friend or relative, you might not want to stick him or her with your debt burden.

If you have a cosigner whom you want to protect, you'll need to use one of the alternatives to Chapter 7 bankruptcy that are outlined in Section E, below. By arranging to pay the debt over time, you can keep creditors from going after your cosigner for payment. And, if you decide to file for Chapter 13, you can include the debt in your repayment plan to keep creditors off your cosigner's back.

4. How Much Property Will You Have to Give Up?

Chapter 7 bankruptcy essentially offers this deal: If you are willing to give up your nonexempt property (or exempt property of equivalent value) to be sold for the benefit of your creditors, the court will erase some or all of your debt. If you can keep most of the things you care about, Chapter 7 bankruptcy can be a very effective remedy for your debt problems. But if Chapter 7 bankruptcy would force you to part with treasured property, you may need to look for another solution.

The laws that control what property you can keep in a Chapter 7 bankruptcy are called exemptions. Each state's legislature produces a set of exemptions for use by people who are sued in that state. These same exemptions are available to people who file for bankruptcy in that state and meet the residency requirements described below. In 15 states (and the District of Columbia), debtors who meet the residency requirements can choose between their state's exemptions or another set of exemptions created by Congress (known as federal bankruptcy exemptions). States that currently allow debtors this choice are Arkansas, Connecticut, Hawaii, Massachusetts, Michigan, Minnesota, New Hampshire, New Jersey, New Mexico, Pennsylvania, Rhode Island, Texas, Vermont, Washington, and Wisconsin.

As it does in so many things, California has adopted its own unique exemption system. Rather than using the federal exemptions, California offers two sets of state exemptions for those who meet the residency requirements described below. As in the 15 states that have the federal bankruptcy exemptions, people filing for bankruptcy in California (who meet the residency requirements) must choose one or the other set of California's state exemptions.

Property that is not exempt can be taken from you and sold by the trustee to pay your unsecured creditors. You can avoid this result by finding some cash to pay the trustee what the property is worth, or convincing the trustee to accept some exempt property of roughly equal value as a substitute. Also, if nonexempt property lacks sufficient value to produce money at a public sale, the trustee may decide to let you keep it. For instance, few trustees bother to take well-used furniture or second-hand electronic gadgets or appliances. These items generally aren't worth what it would cost to sell them.

As you've no doubt figured out, the key to getting the most out of the bankruptcy process is to use exemptions to keep as much of your property as possible, while erasing as many debts as you can. To make full and proper use of your exemptions, you'll want to:

- learn which exemptions are available to you
- become familiar with the exemptions you can use, and
- use the available exemptions in the way that lets you keep more of your treasured property.

Ch. 3 gives step-by-step instructions for figuring out whether your personal property is exempt under the state laws available for use in your bankruptcy, and Ch. 4 covers exemptions for your home. Here, we provide a brief overview of exemptions.

a. Residency Requirements for Using Exemptions

When it passed the new bankruptcy law, Congress wanted to discourage people from moving to a new state to take advantage of its more generous exemptions for homes and other valuable property. To achieve this goal, the new bankruptcy law imposes:

- a two-year residency requirement to claim a state's exemptions for personal and real property, and
- a $125,000 limit on the homestead exemption you can claim if you didn't acquire your home at least 40 months before filing for bankruptcy (if your state's homestead exemption is less than $125,000—as many are—then this rule won't affect you).

If you have not lived (or been domiciled) in your current state for at least two years before filing, you must use the exemptions of the state where you were living for the better part of the 180-day period ending two years before your filing date. In other words, if you file for bankruptcy on January 1, 2008, and you have not lived in your current state for two years, you will have to use the exemptions available in the state where you lived for most of the period between July 5, 2005 and December 31, 2005. These somewhat bewildering rules are explained in detail in Ch. 3; the 40-month rule for claiming the homestead exemption is covered in Ch. 4.

b. Property That Is Typically Exempt

Certain kinds of property are exempt in almost every state, including:

- equity in your home, to a certain value (commonly called the homestead exemption)
- equity in motor vehicles, to a certain value (usually between $1,000 and $5,000)
- reasonably necessary clothing (no mink coats)
- reasonably needed household furnishings and goods (the second TV may have to go if it has any value)
- household appliances
- jewelry, to a certain value
- personal effects
- life insurance (cash or loan value, or proceeds), to a certain value
- retirement funds necessary for current support
- tools of your trade or profession, to a certain value
- a portion of unpaid but earned wages, and
- public benefits (welfare, Social Security, unemployment compensation) accumulated in a bank account.

Many states also provide a "wildcard" exemption—an exemption for a set dollar amount that you can apply to any property that would otherwise not be exempt. (See Ch. 3 for more on wildcard exemptions.) Also, if you are using the federal exemptions or the California "System 2" exemptions and you don't need to protect equity in a home, you can use some or all of the homestead exemption as a wildcard.

How Property Is Valued for Exemption Purposes

Under the old rules, you could value your property at roughly what you could get for it at your own garage sale. The new bankruptcy law uses a new standard: You must value property at what it would cost to buy it from a retail vendor, taking the property's age and condition into account. (11 U.S.C. §§ 506 and 527(b).) For cars, this "replacement value" will be the retail amount listed in the Kelly Blue Book or similar price guides. For other property, you will have to use the amount for which similar property is sold on eBay, or at used clothing or furniture stores, flea markets, and the like.

c. Property That Is Typically Nonexempt

In most states, you will have to give up or pay the trustee for the following types of property (in legal terms, these items are "nonexempt"):

- expensive musical instruments (unless you're a professional musician)
- cameras, camcorders, and personal digital assistants
- stamp, coin, and other collections
- valuable family heirlooms
- cash, bank accounts, stocks, stock options, bonds, royalties, and other investments
- business assets
- real estate you're not living in
- boats, planes, and off-road vehicles
- a second car or truck, and
- a second or vacation home.

If it appears that you have a lot of nonexempt property, read Ch. 3 before deciding whether to file for bankruptcy. That chapter helps you determine exactly how much of your property is not exempt and suggests ways to:

- buy it from the trustee (if you really want to hold on to it)
- use exempt property to barter with the trustee, or
- retain the value of your nonexempt property by selling some of it and buying exempt property with the proceeds before you file.

If Chapter 7 Bankruptcy Won't Let You Keep Treasured Property

If it looks like Chapter 7 bankruptcy is destined to come between you and property that you really want to keep, consider filing for Chapter 13 bankruptcy (or using one of the other alternatives discussed in Section E, below). Chapter 13 bankruptcy lets you keep your property regardless of its exempt status, as long as you will have sufficient income over the next three to five years to pay off all or a portion of your unsecured debts and to pay any priority debts you have (such as back child support, alimony, and taxes) in full. However, even in Chapter 13, you will be required to propose a plan that pays your unsecured creditors a total amount that is at least equal to the value of your nonexempt property.

EXAMPLE 1: Several years ago, John and Louise inherited a genuine Chinese jade vase, their most prized possession. It's worth $10,000. They don't want to give it up but are in desperate financial shape, with debts of more than $60,000.

If they file for Chapter 7 bankruptcy, their debts will be discharged, but they will probably lose the vase, assuming it's not exempt in their state and there's no wildcard exemption available that will cover its value. In Chapter 13 bankruptcy, however, they could keep the vase and pay their debts out of their income over the next three to five years, provided their payments to their unsecured creditors over the life of the plan total at least $10,000. After several anguished days, John and Louise decide to file for Chapter 7 bankruptcy and give up the vase.

John and Louise might be tempted to hide the vase and hope the trustee doesn't discover it. That would be a crime (perjury), for which they could be fined or jailed. It's also an abuse of the bankruptcy process that could get their petition dismissed and prevent them from filing again for six months and discharging the debts they listed in their schedules. A much safer alternative (but still risky in some states) would be to sell the vase before they file and use the proceeds to buy exempt property. (See Ch. 3 for information on how to do this.) Or, John and Louise might offer the trustee exempt property in place of the vase.

EXAMPLE 2: Over the years, Mari has carefully constructed an expensive computer system that she uses primarily for hobbies but also as a work tool for her marginal desktop publishing business. The computer system does not qualify for a specific exemption in her state. Over a substantial period of time, Mari has also amassed a debt of $100,000, consisting primarily of ten bank credit cards, medical bills, and department store charge accounts.

If Mari files for Chapter 7 bankruptcy, she can discharge all of her debts, because they are unsecured and she did not incur them fraudulently. However, unless a wildcard exemption protects the computer system's value, Mari must either surrender most of the computer equipment so it can be sold for the benefit of her creditors (though she may be able to keep the pieces essential to her desktop publishing business) or find a way to replace them with exempt property of equivalent value. Mari decides that canceling her debts is far more important to her than hanging on to the entire system, and proceeds to file for Chapter 7 bankruptcy.

E. Alternatives to Chapter 7 Bankruptcy

In many situations, filing for Chapter 7 bankruptcy is the best remedy for debt problems. In others, however, another course of action makes more sense. This section outlines your main alternatives.

1. Do Nothing

Surprisingly, the best approach for some people who are deeply in debt is to take no action at all. If you're living simply (that is, with little income and property) and look forward to a similar life in the future, you may be what is known as "judgment proof." This means that anyone who sues you and obtains a court judgment won't be able to collect—simply because you don't have anything they can legally take. (As a famous song of the 1970s said, "Freedom's just another

word for nothing left to lose.") Except in highly unusual situations (for example, if you are a tax protester or willfully refuse to pay child support), you can't be thrown in jail for failing to pay your debts.

Normally, creditors cannot take your property or income without first suing you and obtaining a court judgment (except for taxing authorities and student loan collectors). However, even if the creditor is armed with a court judgment, the law prevents creditors (except the IRS, of course) from taking property that is exempt under your state's general exemption laws, including food, clothing, personal effects, and furnishings. (See Section D4, above.) And creditors won't go after your nonexempt property unless it is worth enough to cover the creditor's costs of seizure and sale.

Before taking property, creditors usually try to go after your wages and other income. But a creditor can take only 25% of your net wages to satisfy a court judgment, unless it is for child support or alimony. Often, you can keep more than 75% of your wages if you can demonstrate that you need the extra amount to support yourself and your family. Income from a pension or other retirement benefit is usually treated like wages. Creditors cannot touch public benefits such as welfare, unemployment insurance, disability insurance, SSI, or Social Security.

To sum up, if you don't have a steady job or other source of income that a creditor can snatch, or you can live on 75% of your wages (or perhaps a little more), you needn't fear a lawsuit. Similarly, if most of your property is exempt, there is little the creditor can seize to repay the debt. In these situations, most creditors don't bother trying to collect the debt at all.

Now that you have the good news, here's some bad: Judgments usually last for five to ten years, and they can be renewed for longer periods. In this age of computers, credit reporting bureaus, and massive databases that track our every activity, you may have to live with your decision to do nothing for a long, long time. And, in many cases, interest on your debt will continue to accrue, which means the $10,000 you owe today could become a $100,000 debt in the future.

Even if you are judgment proof, you may be better off dealing with your debt situation now, either through bankruptcy or through one of the other alternatives discussed below. For example, if you don't file for bankruptcy and later receive a windfall—lottery winnings or an unexpected inheritance—you may lose the windfall to your creditors. Windfalls you receive after you file bankruptcy, on the other hand, are yours to keep.

Doing Nothing May Add to Your Tax Obligations

Deciding to simply live with your debts could increase your tax burdens. The IRS treats certain forgiven debts (debts for which a creditor agrees to take less than is owed, or nothing) and debts written off (debts that the creditor has stopped trying to collect, declared uncollectible, and reported as a tax loss to the IRS) as taxable income to you. (26 U.S.C. § 108.) Any bank, credit union, savings and loan, or other financial institution that forgives or writes off all or part of a debt for $600 or more must send you and the IRS a Form 1099-C at the end of the tax year. When you file your tax return, you must report the write-off as income and pay taxes on it.

There are three exceptions to this rule that apply to consumers. Even if the financial institution issues a Form 1099-C, you do not have to report the income if:

- The forgiveness or write-off is intended as a gift. (This would be unusual.)
- You discharge the debt in bankruptcy.
- You were insolvent before the creditor agreed to waive the debt or wrote off the debt.

The Internal Revenue Code does not define "insolvent." Generally, it means that your debts exceed the value of your assets. To figure out whether you are insolvent, total up your assets and your debts, including the debt that was forgiven or written off. If you conclude that you were insolvent when the debt was written off, you will need to attach an explanatory letter to your tax return listing your assets and debts.

2. Negotiate With Your Creditors

If you have some income, or you have assets you're willing to sell, you may be a lot better off negotiating with your creditors than filing for bankruptcy. Through negotiation, you may be able to come up with a new payment plan that allows you to get back on your feet.

Or you may be able to settle your debt for less than you owe.

 Negotiating with creditors. How to negotiate with your creditors is covered in detail in *Solve Your Money Troubles*, by Robin Leonard (Nolo). That book explains how to deal with creditors when you owe money on a variety of debts, including credit cards, mortgage loans, car loans, child support, and alimony.

3. Get Outside Help to Design a Repayment Plan

Many people have trouble negotiating with creditors, either because they don't have the skills and negotiating experience to do a good job or because they find the whole process exceedingly unpleasant. Indeed, because the ability to negotiate is an art, many people benefit from outside help.

If you don't want to negotiate with your creditors, you can turn to a lawyer or to a credit counseling agency. These agencies come in two basic varieties: nonprofit and for profit. They all work on the same basic principle: A repayment plan is negotiated with all of your unsecured creditors. You make one monthly payment to the agency, which distributes the payment to your creditors as provided in the plan. As long as you make the payments, the creditors will not take any action against you. And if you succeed in completing the plan, one or more of your creditors may be willing to extend you new credit on reasonable terms.

The nonprofit agencies tend to be funded primarily by the major creditors (in the form of a commission for each repayment plan they negotiate) and by moderate fees charged the user (roughly $20–$25 per plan negotiated). The for-profit agencies are funded by the same sources but tend to charge much higher fees than the nonprofit agencies.

The big downside to entering into one of the repayment plans is that if you fail to make a payment, the creditors may pull the plug on the deal and come after you, regardless of how faithful you've been in the past. When that happens, you may find that you would have been better off filing for bankruptcy in the first place. For more on the pros and cons of repayment plans, see *Solve Your Money Troubles*, by Robin Leonard (Nolo).

Credit Counseling Agencies Under the New Bankruptcy Law

With a few exceptions, all bankruptcy filers are now required to get credit counseling (see Section B2, above). You must get this counseling from a nonprofit agency that meets a number of requirements and has been approved by the U.S. trustee. If you decide to get help with a repayment plan, you would do well to choose one of these agencies—the U.S. Trustee's office oversees their operation, which gives you some protection against fraudulent practices. You can find a list of approved agencies at the U.S. Trustee's website, at www. usdoj.gov/ust.

4. Pay Over Time With Chapter 13 Bankruptcy

Chapter 13 bankruptcy lets you enter into a court-approved plan to deal with your debts over three to five years. Some debts must be paid in full (back taxes and child support are the most common examples), while others may be paid only in part. The basic idea is that you must devote all of your disposable income to whatever plan is approved by the bankruptcy court. With a few exceptions, Chapter 13 doesn't require you to give up any property—for that reason, it's the bankruptcy of choice for folks who have significant amounts of nonexempt property or property that has a sentimental value.

If you do file for a Chapter 13 bankruptcy, the minimum amount you will have to pay to your unsecured creditors is roughly equal to the value of your nonexempt property. But you may have to pay more: The new bankruptcy law provides guidelines for calculating exactly how much you must pay into your plan, based on the size of your income:

- If your current monthly income (as defined by the bankruptcy law—see Section C1, above) is more than the median family income for your state, you must pay all of your "disposable income" into your plan for five years. To calculate your disposable income, you must use expenses dictated by the IRS, which could be significantly less than your actual expenses. This means that you may be obligated to pay more money

into your plan than you actually have left over each month, after paying your bills and living expenses.
- If your current monthly income is less than the state median, you can propose a three-year repayment plan. You can also calculate your disposable income using your actual expenses, rather than the IRS standards.

To file for Chapter 13 bankruptcy, you fill out the same forms as in a Chapter 7 bankruptcy and file them with the bankruptcy court along with a filing fee of $274. In addition, you must file copies of your federal tax returns for the past four years (which means you must be current with your taxes) and a plan to repay your debts under the new bankruptcy law's guidelines. With the possible exception of current payments on your mortgage and car note, you make payments under the plan directly to the bankruptcy trustee, who in turn distributes the money to your creditors. When you complete your plan, any remaining unpaid balances on unsecured, dischargeable debts are wiped out.

Chapter 13 requires you to pay off your debts over time, but few filers pay back 100% of what they owe. The typical Chapter 13 plan pays 100% of child support (unless the support has been assigned to a government agency, in which case the plan might pay a lesser percentage), back taxes, and other debts classified as "priority" debts, and some lesser percentage of other unsecured debts, depending on the debtor's income and the value of the debtor's nonexempt property.

Like Chapter 7 bankruptcy, Chapter 13 bankruptcy doesn't wipe out all types of debts. Domestic support obligations, criminal penalties, certain tax debts, debts arising from injuries caused by your intoxicated driving, certain debts or creditors you don't list on your bankruptcy papers, and debts arising from your fraudulent conduct all will survive your bankruptcy filing, whether you file under Chapter 7 or Chapter 13. And, as in Chapter 7, student loan debts will be discharged only if you can show that repaying the loan would cause a substantial hardship. (For more on each of these types of debts, see Ch. 9.) Debts arising from a civil judgment against you for maliciously or willfully injuring or killing someone will also survive a Chapter 13 bankruptcy.

In addition to these debts, there are certain debts that are discharged only in Chapter 13—that is, these debts will survive Chapter 7 bankruptcy, but will be wiped out at the end of your repayment plan if you file under Chapter 13. These debts include:

- marital debts created in a divorce or settlement agreement
- debts incurred to pay a nondischargeable tax debt
- court fees
- condominium, cooperative, and homeowners' association fees
- debts for loans from a retirement plan, and
- debts that couldn't be discharged in a previous bankruptcy.

You can file for Chapter 13 bankruptcy at any time, even if you got a Chapter 7 bankruptcy discharge the day before. However, you can't get your Chapter 13 discharge until four years have passed since you filed the Chapter 7 case.

If you start, but are not able to finish, a Chapter 13 repayment plan—for example, you lose your job six months into the plan and can't make the payments—the trustee may modify your plan. The trustee may give you a grace period (if the problem seems temporary), reduce your total monthly payments, or extend the repayment period. As long as it looks like you're acting in good faith, the trustee will try to accommodate and help you across rocky periods. If it's clear you won't be able to complete the plan because of circumstances beyond your control, the court might let you discharge your debts on the basis of hardship. Examples of hardship would be a sudden plant closing in a one-factory town, or a debilitating illness.

If the bankruptcy court won't let you modify your plan or give you a hardship discharge, you still have two options:

- You can convert your case to a Chapter 7 bankruptcy (unless you received a Chapter 7 discharge in a case filed within the previous eight years).
- You can ask the bankruptcy court to dismiss your Chapter 13 petition, which would leave you in the same position you were in before you filed, except you'll owe less because of the payments you made on your debts. If your Chapter 13 bankruptcy is dismissed, your creditors may add any interest that was abated during your Chapter 13 case to the total amount you owe.

Do You Qualify for Chapter 13 Bankruptcy?

Like Chapter 7, there are several requirements you must meet in order to qualify for Chapter 13 bankruptcy:

- **You must file as an individual.** Only individuals, not business entities (such as partnerships or corporations), can file for Chapter 13.
- **Your debt must not be too high.** Your total secured debt (debt which is secured by collateral or otherwise gives the creditor the right to seize property if you don't pay) may not exceed $922,975, and your total unsecured debt may not exceed $307,675.
- **You must be able to propose a legally feasible repayment plan.** If you have sufficient income to pay all of your priority debts (for instance child support and tax debts), make required monthly payments —and pay back any arrearages—on your secured debts (such as a mortgage or car note), and pay at least some money towards your unsecured debts over the next five years, you can probably propose a Chapter 13 plan that will pass legal muster. One way to figure out whether you can propose a feasible plan is to take the means test—an eligibility requirement for Chapter 7 that asks higher income filers to show that they cannot propose a feasible Chapter 13 repayment plan. If the means test shows that you will have at least some money left over each month to pay towards your unsecured debts, you should be able to come up with a feasible Chapter 13 plan. The means test is covered in detail in Ch. 6, Section J.

You may qualify for Chapter 13 even if you don't have sufficient disposable income to complete your plan. The new bankruptcy law assumes that your monthly income during your plan will be the same as your average income during the six months before you filed for bankruptcy. If you lost a job or otherwise experienced a drop in income during those six months, your actual income could be quite a bit less than the law assumes it will be. In addition, certain higher-income filers will have to calculate their expenses using IRS standards, which are often less than their actual living expenses. All this means that you may not be able, as a practical matter, to make the payments required by a Chapter 13 plan, even if you qualify to file under the figures used in the new law.

Chapter 13 May Reduce Secured Debts That Are Heavy With Interest

Chapter 13 bankruptcy allows you to break a secured debt into two parts: the part that is secured by the fair market value of the collateral, and any part of the debt that is unsecured because it exceeds the value of the collateral. You must pay the replacement value of the collateral (the secured part) in your Chapter 13 plan, but you can discharge the unsecured portion along with your other unsecured debts. This procedure is popularly referred to as a "cramdown."

For example, people often owe more on a car than the car is worth. This is because the car note includes a lot of interest, and most cars depreciate in value fairly rapidly. Chapter 13 allows you to cram down the debt on the car to the car's replacement value (what it would cost to purchase the car from a retail vendor, considering its age and condition) and get rid of the rest of the debt over the life of your plan. You can also cram down debts for other types of property, including real estate in some situations. However, there are a couple of exceptions to the cramdown rule:

- You can cram down a car contract only if you bought the car more than 30 months before filing for bankruptcy.
- You can cram down contracts on other types of property only if you bought the property more than a year before filing for bankruptcy.

 Resources for Chapter 13 bankruptcy. For more general information on Chapter 13 bankruptcy, get a copy of *The New Bankruptcy: Is It Right for You?*, by Stephen Elias (Nolo). If you are interested in filing for Chapter 13 bankruptcy, see *Chapter 13 Bankruptcy: Repay Your Debts,* by Stephen Elias and Robin Leonard (Nolo). That book provides all the forms and instructions necessary to complete your own Chapter 13 bankruptcy.

5. Family Farmers Should Consider Chapter 12 Bankruptcy

Chapter 12 bankruptcy, which is very similar to Chapter 13, is specially designed for family farmers and provides a way to keep the farm while paying off debts over time. If you are a farmer, we recommend you speak with a bankruptcy attorney about Chapter 12 bankruptcy before choosing to file a Chapter 7 bankruptcy.

6. Corporations and Partnerships Should Consider Chapter 11 Bankruptcy

Chapter 11 bankruptcy is usually reserved for corporations and partnerships. Individuals occasionally file for Chapter 11 bankruptcy, however, if their debts exceed either of Chapter 13 bankruptcy's debt limits of $922,975 (secured debts) or $307,675 (unsecured debts), and they think they'll have enough steady income to pay off a portion of their debts over a several year period. This book doesn't cover Chapter 11 bankruptcies—few bankruptcy attorneys recommend them for individuals. ■

The Automatic Stay

One of the most powerful features of bankruptcy is the automatic stay: a court order that goes into effect as soon as you file, protecting you from certain actions by your creditors. The automatic stay stops most debt collectors dead in their tracks and keeps them at bay for the rest of your case. Once you file, all collection activity (with a few exceptions, explained below) must go through the bankruptcy court—and most creditors cannot take any further action against you directly while the bankruptcy is pending.

The purpose of the automatic stay is, in the words of Congress, to give debtors a "breathing spell" from their creditors, and a break from the financial pressures that drove them to file for bankruptcy. In a Chapter 7 bankruptcy, it serves another purpose as well: to preserve the status quo at the time you file. The automatic stay ensures that the trustee—not your creditors—will be responsible for ultimately deciding which property you will be able to keep, which property you will have to give up, and how the proceeds will be divided if the trustee takes and sells any of your belongings.

This chapter explains how the automatic stay applies to typical debt collection efforts, including a couple of situations in which you might not get the protection of the automatic stay. It also covers how the automatic stay works in eviction proceedings, vital information for any renter who files for bankruptcy.

You don't need bankruptcy to stop your creditors from harassing you. Many people begin thinking about bankruptcy when their creditors start phoning them at home and on the job. Federal law prohibits this activity by debt collectors once you tell the creditor, in writing, that you don't want to be called. And if you orally tell debt collectors that you refuse to pay, they cannot, by law, contact you except to send one last letter making a final demand for payment before filing a lawsuit. While just telling the creditor to stop usually works, you may have to send a written follow-up letter. (You can find a sample letter in Ch. 1, Section D.)

A. Actions Prohibited by the Stay

When you file for any kind of bankruptcy, the automatic stay goes into effect. It's "automatic" because you don't have to ask the court to issue the stay, and the court doesn't have to take any special action to make it effective—once you file, the stay is in place, automatically. The stay prohibits creditors and collection agencies from taking any action to collect most kinds of debts you owe them—unless the law or the bankruptcy court says they can.

Under the new bankruptcy law, however, the stay is not as automatic as it once was. In some circumstances, the creditor can file an action in court to have the stay lifted (called a Motion to Lift Stay). In others, the creditor can simply begin collection proceedings without seeking advance permission from the court.

The good news is that the most common type of creditor collection actions are still stopped dead by the stay—harassing calls by debt collectors, threatening letters by attorneys, and lawsuits to collect payment for credit card and health care bills. This section explains which collection actions are stopped by the automatic stay.

1. Credit Card Debts, Medical Debts, and Attorney Fees

Anyone trying to collect credit card debts, medical debts, attorney fees, debts arising from breach of contract, or legal judgments against you (other than child support and alimony) must cease all collection activities after you file your bankruptcy case. They cannot:

- file a lawsuit or proceed with a pending lawsuit against you
- record liens against your property
- report the debt to a credit reporting bureau, or
- seize your property or income, such as money in a bank account or your paycheck.

2. Public Benefits

Government entities that are seeking to collect overpayments of public benefits such as SSI, Medicaid, or Temporary Assistance to Needy Families (welfare) benefits cannot reduce or terminate your benefits to get that money back while your bankruptcy is pending. If, however, you become ineligible for benefits, including Medicare benefits, bankruptcy doesn't prevent denial or termination of the benefits on that ground.

3. Criminal Proceedings

If a case against you can be broken down into criminal and debt components, only the criminal component will be allowed to continue—the debt component will be put on hold while your bankruptcy is pending. For example, if you were convicted of writing a bad check and have been sentenced to community service and ordered to pay a fine, your obligation to do community service will not be stopped by the automatic stay (but your obligation to pay the fine will).

4. IRS Liens and Levies

Certain tax proceedings are not affected by the automatic stay (see Section B1, below, for more information). The automatic stay does, however, stop the IRS from issuing a lien or seizing (levying against) any of your property or income.

5. Foreclosures

Foreclosures are initially stayed by your bankruptcy filing. However, the stay won't apply if you filed another bankruptcy case within the previous two years and the court, in that proceeding, lifted the stay and allowed the lender to proceed with the foreclosure. In other words, the law doesn't allow you to prevent a foreclosure by filing serial bankruptcies. For detailed information on what happens to your home in bankruptcy, see Ch. 4.

6. Utilities

Companies providing you with utilities (such as gas, heating oil, electricity, telephone, and water) may not discontinue service because you file for bankruptcy. However, they can shut off your service 20 days after you file if you don't provide them with a deposit or other means to assure future payment.

B. When the Stay Doesn't Apply

The stay doesn't put a stop to every type of collection action, nor does it apply in every situation. Congress has determined that certain debts or proceedings are sufficiently important to "trump" the automatic stay. In these situations (described in Section 1, below), collection actions can continue just as if you had never filed for bankruptcy.

In addition to the specific types of collection actions that can continue despite the stay (such as child support enforcement—see Section A, above), there are circumstances in which you can lose the protection of the stay through your own actions. These are described in Section 2, below.

1. Actions Not Stopped by the Stay

The automatic stay does not prohibit the following types of actions from proceeding.

a. Divorce and Child Support

Almost all proceedings related to divorce or parenting continue as before—they are not affected by the automatic stay. These include actions to:
- set and collect current child support and alimony
- collect back child support and alimony from property that is not in the bankruptcy estate (see Ch. 3, Sections A and B, for more information on what's in the bankruptcy estate
- determine child custody and visitation
- establish paternity in a lawsuit
- modify child support and alimony
- protect a spouse or child from domestic violence
- withhold income to collect child support
- report overdue support to credit bureaus
- intercept tax refunds to pay back child support, and
- withhold, suspend, or restrict drivers' and professional licenses as leverage to collect child support.

b. Tax Proceedings

The IRS can continue certain actions, such as conducting a tax audit, issuing a tax deficiency notice, demanding a tax return, issuing a tax assessment, or demanding payment of an assessment.

c. Pension Loans

The stay doesn't prevent withholding from a debtor's income to repay a loan from an ERISA-qualified pension (this includes most job-related pensions and individual retirement plans). See Ch. 3, Section B, for more on how pensions are treated in bankruptcy.

2. How You Can Lose the Protection of the Stay

Even in circumstances where the stay would otherwise apply, you can lose its protection through your own actions. The stay won't protect you from collection efforts if:

- you had a previous bankruptcy case pending within a year of your current bankruptcy filing, or
- you don't meet the deadlines for dealing with property that serves as collateral for a secured debt.

a. Prior Dismissals

Under the new bankruptcy law, the automatic stay will last only 30 days if you had a prior bankruptcy case pending within the year before you file (unless you can get the court to extend it). (11 U.S.C. §§ 362(c)(3) and (4).) And if you had two cases pending in the last year, the automatic stay will never kick in at all (unless the court orders it). There are two lessons here for debtors:

- don't let your case be dismissed (a dismissed case counts as a pending case), and
- if your case is dismissed and you want to file again within the year, you should talk to an attorney.

One Dismissal in the Past Year

With a couple of exceptions, if you had a bankruptcy case dismissed during the previous year for any reason, voluntarily or involuntarily, the court will presume that your new filing is in bad faith, and the stay will terminate after 30 days in your new case. You, the trustee, the U.S. Trustee, or the creditor can ask the court to continue the stay beyond the 30-day period, but the court will do this only if you (or whoever else makes the request) can show that your current case was not filed in bad faith.

The motion to continue the stay must be scheduled for hearing within the 30-day period after you file for bankruptcy, and must give creditors adequate notice of why the stay should be extended. This means the motion must:

- be filed within several days after you file for bankruptcy, (unless you obtain an "Order Shortening Time" from the judge, a simple procedure)
- be served on all creditors on whom you want the stay to apply, and
- provide specific reasons that your filing was not in bad faith and the stay should be extended.

When deciding whether to extend the stay beyond 30 days, the court will look at a number of factors to decide whether your current filing is in good faith. Here are some of the factors that will work against you:

- More than one prior bankruptcy case was filed by (or against) you in the past year.
- Your prior case was dismissed because you failed to file any required documents on time (for instance, you didn't give the trustee your most recent tax return at least seven days before the first meeting of creditors) or amend the petition on a timely basis when required to do so. If you failed to file these documents inadvertently or because of a careless error, that won't help you with the judge—unless you used an attorney in the prior case. Judges are more willing to give debtors the benefit of the doubt here if their attorney was responsible for the mistake.
- The prior case was dismissed while a creditor's request for relief from the stay was pending.
- Your circumstances haven't changed since your previous case was dismissed.

Two Dismissals in the Past Year

If you had more than two cases dismissed during the previous year, no stay will apply in your current case unless you convince the court, within 30 days of your filing, that your current case was not filed in bad faith and that a stay should therefore be granted. The court will look at the factors outlined above, to decide whether you have overcome the presumption of bad faith.

b. Missing Deadlines for Handling Secured Debts

If you have property that secures a debt—that is, property that the creditor has a right to take if you don't pay the debt—you will have to file a Statement of Intention with court and serve it on (send or hand it to) your creditors. The Statement of Intention explains what you want to do with the collateral. You have several choices:

- give the property back to the creditor and get rid of the debt (this is called "surrendering" the property)
- keep the property and pay the creditor what it would cost to replace it, given its age and condition; this is often less than what you still owe on the debt, or
- keep the property and reaffirm the contract, which means that you will continue to owe some or all of the debt after your bankruptcy.

The bankruptcy rules require you to serve this Statement of Intention within 30 days after filing your bankruptcy case, and to actually carry out your stated intention—by giving back the property, paying its replacement value to the creditor, or signing a reaffirmation agreement—within 30-45 days after your first creditors' meeting (because the law is contradictory on this time limit, you should take action within 30 days, to be on the safe side). If you don't meet these deadlines, the stay will no longer apply to that property (although it will continue to protect you otherwise). For example, assume you want to continue paying on your car note, but you don't serve your Statement of Intention on time. The stay will no longer protect your car or prevent the creditor from repossessing it. The Statement of Intention is discussed in more detail in Ch. 6, Section H; you can find lots more information on secured debts, including tips that will help you decide which of these options makes the most sense in your case, in Ch. 5.

C. Evictions

In the past, many people filed for Chapter 7 bankruptcy to stop the sheriff from enforcing a judgment for possession (an eviction order). While landlords could come into court and ask the judge to lift the automatic stay and let the eviction proceed, many landlords didn't know they had this right—and many others didn't have the wherewithal to hire an attorney (or the confidence to handle their own case). In other words, filing for Chapter 7 bankruptcy often stopped court-ordered evictions dead in their tracks for the duration of the bankruptcy (typically, four to six months).

Today, things are a bit different. The new bankruptcy law gives landlords the right to evict a tenant, despite the automatic stay, if:

- the landlord got a judgment for possession before the tenant filed for bankruptcy (if the judgment was for nonpayment of rent, there is a possible exception to this rule—see Section C1, below), or
- the landlord is evicting the tenant for endangering the property or the illegal use of controlled substances on the property.

If the landlord does not already have a judgment at the time you file, and he or she wants to evict you for reasons other than endangering the property or using controlled substances (for example, the eviction is based on your failure to pay rent or violation of another lease provision), the automatic stay will prevent the landlord from beginning or continuing with eviction proceedings. However, the landlord can always ask the judge to lift the stay—and courts tend to grant these requests.

1. If the Landlord Already Has a Judgment

If your landlord has already obtained a judgment of possession against you at the time you file for bankruptcy, the automatic stay won't help you (with the possible exception described below). The landlord may proceed with the eviction just as if you never filed for bankruptcy.

If the eviction order is based on your failure to pay rent, you may be able to have the automatic stay reinstated. However, this exception applies only if your state's law allows you to stay in your rental unit and "cure" (pay back) the rent delinquency after the landlord has a judgment for possession. Here's what you'll have to do to take advantage of this exception:

Step 1: As part of your bankruptcy petition, you must file a certification (a statement under oath) stating that your state's laws allow you to cure the rent delinquency after the judgment is obtained, and to continue living in your rental unit. Very few states allow this. To find out whether yours is one of them, ask the sheriff or someone at legal aid (if you have legal aid in your area). In addition, when you file your bankruptcy petition, you must deposit with the court clerk the amount of rent that will become due during the 30-day period after you file.

Once you have filed your petition containing the certification and deposited the rent, you are protected from eviction for 30 days unless the landlord successfully objects to your initial certification before the 30-day period ends. If the landlord objects to your certification, the court must hold a hearing on the objection within ten days, so theoretically you could have less than 30 days of protection if the landlord files and serves the objection immediately.

Step 2: To keep the stay in effect longer, you must, before the 30-day period runs out, file and serve a second certification showing that you have fully cured the default in the manner provided by your state's law. However, if the landlord successfully objects to this second certification, the stay will no longer be in effect and the landlord may proceed with the eviction. As in Step 1, the court must hold a hearing within ten days if the landlord objects.

If you really want to keep your apartment, talk to a lawyer. As you can see, these new rules are somewhat complicated. If you don't interpret your state's law properly, file the necessary paperwork on time, and successfully argue your side if the landlord objects, you could find yourself put out of your home. A good lawyer can tell you whether it's worth fighting an eviction—and, if so, how to go about it.

2. Endangering the Property or Illegal Use of Controlled Substances

Under the new bankruptcy law, an eviction action will not be stayed by your bankruptcy filing if your landlord wants you out because you endangered the property or engaged in the "illegal use of controlled substances" on the property. And your landlord doesn't have to have a judgment in hand when you file for bankruptcy: The landlord may start an eviction action against you or continue with a pending eviction action even after

your filing date if the eviction is based on property endangerment or drug use.

To evict you on these grounds after you have filed for bankruptcy, your landlord must file and serve on you a certification showing that:

- the landlord has filed an eviction action against you based on property endangerment or illegal drug use on the property, or
- you have endangered the property or engaged in illegal drug use on the property during the 30-day period prior to the landlord's certification.

If your landlord files this certification, he or she can proceed with the eviction 15 days later unless, within that time, you file and serve on the landlord an objection to the truth of the statements in the landlord's certification. If you do that, the court must hold a hearing on your objection within ten days. If you prove that the statements in the certification aren't true or have been remedied, you will be protected from the eviction while your bankruptcy is pending. If the court denies your objection, the eviction may proceed immediately.

As a practical matter, you will have a very difficult time proving a negative—that is, that you weren't endangering the property or using drugs. Similarly, once allegations of property endangerment or drug use are made, it's hard to see how they would be "remedied."

Landlords can always ask the court to lift the automatic stay to begin or continue an eviction on any grounds. Although the automatic stay will kick in unless one of these exceptions apply, the judge can lift the stay upon the landlord's request. And many courts are willing to do so, because most evictions will have no effect on the bankruptcy estate—that is, your tenancy isn't something that the trustee can turn into money to pay your creditors. As a general rule, bankruptcy courts are inclined to let landlords exercise their property rights regardless of the tenant's debt problems.

Need help with your landlord? For more information on dealing with landlords—including landlords that are trying to evict you—see *Every Tenant's Legal Guide,* by Janet Portman and Marcia Stewart (Nolo).

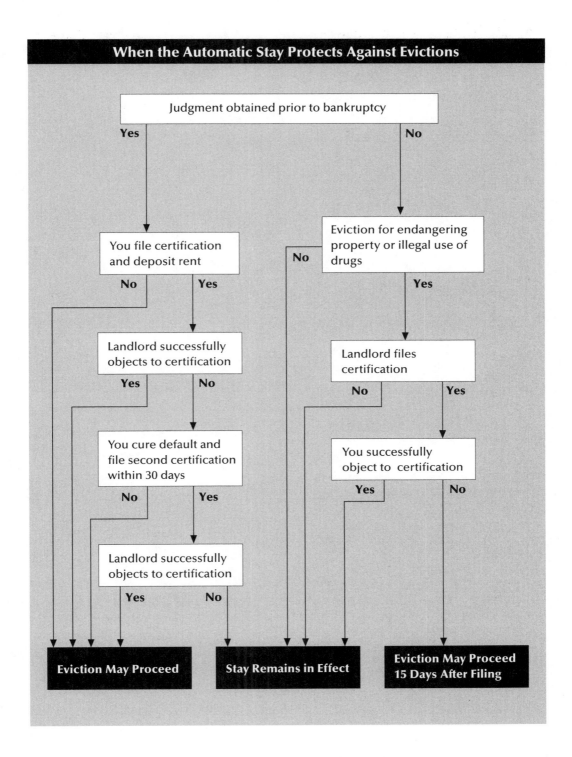

Your Property and Bankruptcy

This chapter explains what happens to your personal property when you file for Chapter 7 bankruptcy. Sections A and B explain what property is subject to the reach of the bankruptcy court. Section C covers exemptions: state and federal laws that determine what property you can keep when you file for bankruptcy. Happily, most people find that they can keep virtually all their personal property through the bankruptcy process.

Once you have figured out what property you can keep through bankruptcy, you may be able to exchange some of your nonexempt property for exempt items before you file. Section D offers suggestions—and important cautions—if you want to try this.

More information on homes and collateral. This chapter covers personal property only, not real estate. If you own your home, Ch. 4 explains how to figure out whether you'll be able to keep it. And, if you own personal property that serves as collateral for a debt, that property is handled a bit differently. The special rules for these debts (called "secured" debts) are explained in Ch. 5.

A. Property in Your Bankruptcy Estate

When you file for Chapter 7 bankruptcy, almost everything you own when you file becomes subject to the bankruptcy court's authority. (The exceptions, listed in Section B, below, include pensions, tuition and individual education accounts, and, if you are filing alone, property you own with a spouse as tenants by the entirety.)

All property subject to the court's jurisdiction is collectively called your "bankruptcy estate." With a few exceptions (discussed below), property you acquire after you file isn't included in your bankruptcy estate. If you originally filed for Chapter 13 bankruptcy and now want to convert your case to a Chapter 7 bankruptcy, everything you owned on the date you filed your Chapter 13 petition and still possess is the property of your Chapter 7 bankruptcy estate. (11 U.S.C. § 348(f)(1)(A).)

Using the Information in This Chapter

This chapter will help you:

- **Decide whether bankruptcy is appropriate.** Knowing what you own and how much you can get for it will help you decide whether or not to file for Chapter 7 bankruptcy. It may be easier simply to sell off some property (especially property that you would have to give up anyway if you filed for bankruptcy) and pay creditors directly rather than to go through bankruptcy.

- **Determine what property you can keep.** You'll be able to keep some property no matter how much it is worth. However, your right to keep property in bankruptcy often depends on its value. For instance, many states allow you to keep a car, but only if your equity is less than a certain amount ($1,500 is a common limit). If you own considerably more equity, you will have to turn the car over to the trustee to be sold (or find a way to pay the trustee the equivalent value in cash or other exempt property). After the sale, you'll get $1,500 from the proceeds (in this example), and your creditors will get the rest.

- **Summarize information about your property before you file.** If you decide to file for bankruptcy, you'll need to fill out forms listing what property you own, how much it's worth, and what you claim as exempt. The work you do in this chapter can be transferred to those forms.

1. Property You Own and Possess

Property that you own and possess—for example, clothing, books, computers, cameras, TV, stereo system, furniture, tools, car, real estate, boat, artworks, and stock certificates—is included in your bankruptcy estate.

Property that belongs to someone else is not part of your bankruptcy estate—even if you control the property—because you don't have the right to sell it or give it away. Here are some examples.

EXAMPLE 1: A parent establishes a trust for her child and names you as trustee to manage the money in the trust until the child's 18th birthday. You possess and control the money, but it's solely for the child's benefit under the terms of the trust; you cannot use it for your own purposes. It isn't part of your bankruptcy estate.

EXAMPLE 2: Your sister has gone to Zimbabwe for an indefinite period and has loaned you her computer system while she's gone. Although you might have use of the equipment for years to come, you don't own it. It isn't part of your bankruptcy estate.

EXAMPLE 3: You are making monthly payments on a leased car. You are entitled to possess the car as long as you make the monthly payments, but you don't own it. It is not part of your bankruptcy estate (but the lease itself is).

2. Property You Own but Don't Possess

Any property you own is part of your bankruptcy estate, even if you don't have physical possession of it. For instance, you may own a share of a vacation cabin in the mountains but never go there yourself. Or you may own furniture or a car that someone else is using. Other examples include a deposit held by a stockbroker, stock options, contractual rights to a royalty or commission, or a security deposit held by your landlord or the utility company.

3. Property You Have Recently Given Away

People contemplating bankruptcy are often tempted to unload their property on friends and relatives or pay favorite creditors before they file. Don't bother. Property given away or paid out shortly before you file for bankruptcy is still part of your bankruptcy estate—and the trustee has the legal authority to take it back. Be sure to include this property on the Personal Property Checklist in Section C, below.

a. Giving Away Property

You might be thinking about signing over the title certificate to an item of property to a relative or the person you live with, then not listing it in your bankruptcy papers. This is both dishonest and foolhardy. On your bankruptcy forms, which you must sign under penalty of perjury, you must list all property transactions made within the previous year. Knowingly failing to report a transaction is perjury—a felony. And, if the unreported transfer is discovered, the trustee can seize the item from whoever has it and sell it to pay your creditors if you didn't receive a reasonable amount for the item—selling an item for less than it's worth is the same as giving a gift for bankruptcy purposes—or if the transfer either left you insolvent or gave you a big push in that direction.

A prosecution for perjury isn't the only calamity that may befall you if you transfer property with the intent to defraud your creditors. The court may refuse to discharge *any* of your debts. (11 U.S.C. § 727(a)(2).)

b. Paying Off a Favorite Creditor

You can't pay a favorite creditor, such as a relative or friend, before you file for bankruptcy, then leave your other creditors with less than they would have otherwise received. Bankruptcy law calls payments and repossessions made shortly before filing for bankruptcy "preferences." The trustee can sue the creditor for the amount of the preference and make it a part of the bankruptcy estate, so that it can be distributed among all of your creditors. In general, a preference exists when you pay or transfer property worth more than $600 to a creditor:

- within 90 days before filing for bankruptcy, or
- within one year before filing if the creditor was close to you—for example, a friend, relative, or business partner, or a corporation owned by you. (11 U.S.C. § 547.)

Even though you can't pay a favorite creditor before you file, there is nothing to prevent payment after you file, as long as you do it with postfiling income or property that isn't in your bankruptcy estate.

4. Property You Are Entitled to Receive but Don't Yet Possess When You File

Property to which you are legally entitled at the time you file for bankruptcy is included in your bankruptcy estate, even if you haven't actually received it yet. The most common examples are wages you have earned but have not yet been paid and tax refunds that are legally owed to you. Here are some other examples:

- vacation or severance pay earned before you filed for bankruptcy.
- property you've inherited, but not yet received, from someone who has died. If you're a beneficiary in the will or revocable living trust of someone who is alive, you don't have to list that on your bankruptcy papers—the benefactor could change the will or trust before he or she dies. If the benefactor has already died, however, you have a legal right to receive the property and you must list it.
- property you will receive from a trust. If you receive periodic payments from a trust but aren't entitled to the full amount of the trust yet, the full amount of the trust is considered property of your bankruptcy estate and should be listed on Worksheet B and your bankruptcy papers. Although the bankruptcy trustee may not be able to get the money (depending on the type of trust), you don't want to be accused of hiding it.
- proceeds of an insurance policy, if the death, injury, or other event that triggers payment has oc-curred. For example, if you were the beneficiary of your father's life insurance policy, and your father has died but you haven't received your money yet, that amount is part of your bankruptcy estate.
- a legal claim to monetary compensation (sometimes called a legal "cause of action"), even if the value of the claim hasn't yet been determined. For example, if you have a claim against someone for injuring you in a car accident, you must include this potential source of money in your bankruptcy papers, even if the amount you will receive (if any) has not yet been determined in a lawsuit, settlement agreement, or insurance claim.

- accounts receivable (money you are owed for goods or services you've provided). Even if you don't think you'll be paid, that money is considered part of your bankruptcy estate. It's the trustee's job to go after the money; leaving it off the bankruptcy forms can get you into trouble.
- money earned (but not yet received) from property in your bankruptcy estate. This includes, for example, rent from commercial or residential real estate, royalties from copyrights or patents, and dividends earned on stocks.

5. Proceeds From Property of the Bankruptcy Estate

If property in your bankruptcy estate earns income or otherwise produces money after you file for bankruptcy, this money is also part of your bankruptcy estate. For example, suppose a contract to receive royalties for a book you have written is part of your bankruptcy estate. Any royalties you earn under this contract after you file for bankruptcy are also property of the estate. The one exception to this rule is money you earn from providing personal services after filing for bankruptcy, which isn't part of your bankruptcy estate. Continuing our example, work on a new edition of the book after you file for bankruptcy would be considered personal services. The royalties you earn for that new work would not be part of your bankruptcy estate.

Another example of money that ends up in your bankruptcy estate (and thus is not yours to keep) are proceeds from what's called a "contingent future interest." This bit of legalese refers to money that you will receive if certain things happen in the future. The mere possibility that you will receive property after filing for bankruptcy is enough to put that property in your bankruptcy estate once you do file. For example, in one case an employee had the right to participate in a profit-sharing plan, but only if he was still employed by the company at the end of the year. He filed for bankruptcy before the end of the year, but remained employed and received a hefty check, which the trustee claimed belonged to the bankruptcy estate, at least in part. The court ruled that the debtor's interest in the profit sharing plan was a "contingent future interest" (contingent on whether the debtor remained employed), and that the check based on that interest belonged in the bankruptcy estate even though it wasn't received until after the filing date. (*In re Edwards*, 273 B.R. 527 (Bankr. E.D. Mich. 2000).)

6. Certain Property Acquired Within 180 Days After You File for Bankruptcy

Most property you acquire—or become entitled to acquire—after you file for bankruptcy isn't included in your bankruptcy estate. But there are exceptions. If you acquire (or become entitled to acquire) certain items within 180 days after you file, you must report them to the bankruptcy court—and the bankruptcy trustee may take them. (11 U.S.C. § 541(a)(5).)

The 180-day rule applies to:

- property you inherit during the 180-day period
- property (not including alimony) from a property settlement agreement or divorce decree that goes into effect during the 180-day period, and
- death benefits or life insurance policy proceeds that become owed to you during the 180-day period.

You must report these items on a supplemental form, even if your bankruptcy case is over. You can find instructions for filing the supplemental form in Ch. 7, Section B.

If you convert from Chapter 7 to Chapter 13, the 180-day period runs from the date you originally filed for Chapter 7, not from the date you converted to Chapter 13. (*In Re Carter*, 260 B.R. 130 (Bankr. W.D Tenn. 2001).)

Are Stock Options Part of Your Bankruptcy Estate?

If you own stock options, you have the right to purchase stock at the price that was assigned when the stock options were granted. Most of the time, you have to wait for a while after you get the options before being able to buy the stock (stock options "vest" when that waiting period is up). Making such a purchase is called "exercising your stock options." Whether stock options are part of your bankruptcy estate depends on when you received them and when they vest.

As a general rule, stock options that you own when you file for bankruptcy are part of your bankruptcy estate. In addition, any stock you purchase by exercising your stock options is also part of the estate, even if you exercise those options after you file for bankruptcy. Courts treat these stock purchases as proceeds earned on property of the estate.

Sometimes, your stock options do not vest (that is, you cannot exercise them) until you have been with your company for a certain period of time. In that case, your bankruptcy estate will include only those stock options that have already vested on the date you file for bankruptcy .

To calculate the value of your stock options, multiply the number of vested stock options you own by the difference between your option price and the fair market value of the stock. (Value of options = [number of vested stock options] x [fair market value – option price].) Even if the potential value of your options is very uncertain, they are still part of your bankruptcy estate and the trustee will take them if they are marketable.

7. Your Share of Marital Property

How much of your marital property—the property you and your spouse own together—is included in your bankruptcy estate depends on two factors: (1) whether you file jointly or alone, and (2) the laws of your state regarding marital property.

If you file jointly, all marital property that fits into one of the categories listed in Subsections 1 through 5 above belongs to your bankruptcy estate.

However, if you are married and you file for bankruptcy alone, some marital property may not be part of your bankruptcy estate. Whether property is part of the estate depends on whether you live in a community property, tenancy by the entirety, or common law property state.

a. Community Property States

These are the community property states: Alaska (if the spouses sign a written agreement to treat the property as community property), Arizona, California, Idaho, Louisiana, Nevada, New Mexico, Texas, Washington, and Wisconsin.

In these states, the general rule is that all property either spouse earns or receives during the marriage is community property and is owned jointly by both spouses. Exceptions are gifts and inheritances received specifically by one spouse, and property owned by one spouse before the marriage or acquired after permanent separation—these are the separate property of the spouse who acquired or received them.

If you are married, live in a community property state, and file for bankruptcy, all the community property you and your spouse own is considered part of your bankruptcy estate, even if your spouse doesn't file. This is true even if the community property might not be divided 50-50 if you were to divorce.

EXAMPLE: Paul and Sonya live in California, a community property state. Sonya contributed $20,000 of her separate property toward the purchase of their house. All the rest of the money used to pay for the house is from community funds, and the house is considered community property. If Paul and Sonya were to divorce and split the house proceeds, Sonya would be entitled to $20,000 more than Paul as reimbursement for her down payment. But they aren't divorced, and Paul files for bankruptcy without Sonya. Their house is worth $250,000. Paul must list that entire value on his bankruptcy papers—that is, he can't subtract the $20,000 Sonya would be entitled to if they divorced.

The separate property of the spouse filing for bankruptcy is also part of the bankruptcy estate. But the separate property of the spouse *not* filing for bankruptcy is not part of the bankruptcy estate.

EXAMPLE: Paul owns a twin-engine Cessna as his separate property (he owned it before he married Sonya). Sonya came to the marriage owning a grand piano. Because only Paul is filing for bankruptcy, Paul's aircraft will be part of his bankruptcy estate, but Sonya's piano won't be.

You may need to do some research into your state's property laws to make sure you understand which of your property is separate and which is community. See Ch. 10 for tips on research.

b. Tenancy by the Entirety States

States that recognize some form of tenancy by the entirety are Delaware, District of Columbia, Florida, Hawaii, Illinois, Indiana, Maryland, Massachusetts, Michigan, Missouri, North Carolina, Ohio, Pennsylvania, Rhode Island, Tennessee, Vermont, Virginia, and Wyoming.

Real estate (and personal property in some states) a couple owns as tenants by the entirety belongs to the marriage, rather than to one spouse or another. If both spouses file for bankruptcy, the trustee can use property held in tenancy by the entirety to pay creditors. If only one spouse files for bankruptcy, this property is generally exempt from claims for which only one spouse is liable. Because the property belongs to the marriage, one spouse cannot give it away or encumber it with debts on his or her own. The property is not exempt from claims owed jointly by the couple, however.

In sum, if none of the filing spouse's debts are owed jointly with the nonfiling spouse, property held in tenancy by the entirety will probably be abandoned by the trustee, because it cannot be taken and sold for the benefit of any creditor. We discuss this further in Ch. 4.

c. Common Law Property States

If your state is not listed above as a community property or tenancy by the entirety state, it is a "common law" property state. When only one spouse files for bankruptcy in a common law property state, all of that spouse's separate property plus half of the couple's jointly owned property go into the filing spouse's bankruptcy estate.

The general rules of property ownership in common law states are:

- Property that has only one spouse's name on a title certificate (such as a car, a house, or stocks), is that spouse's separate property, even if it was bought with joint funds.
- Property that was purchased or received as a gift or inheritance by both for the use of both spouses is jointly owned, unless title is held in only one spouse's name (which means it belongs to that spouse separately, even if both spouses use it).
- Property that one spouse buys with separate funds or receives as a gift or inheritance for that spouse's separate use is that spouse's separate property (unless, again, a title certificate shows differently).

d. Same-Sex Couples

If you are in a relationship with someone of the same sex, you may be wondering whether you can file for bankruptcy together with your partner—and what effect bankruptcy will have on property you own together. Many issues involving same-sex marriage and domestic partnerships are still up in the air, and, because same-sex marriage has only recently become a possibility, it isn't clear how things will shake out.

If you and your partner have married (Massachusetts is the only state that currently allows same-sex couples to marry) or registered as domestic partners in a state that offers registered partners some of the benefits of marriage (such as California, Connecticut, Hawaii, Maine, New Jersey, and Vermont), you might be considering a joint bankruptcy filing. Thus far, however, such efforts have not been successful, primarily because federal law does not recognize same-sex marriage and allows states to disregard such marriages performed in other states. This law, known as the Defense of Marriage Act (DOMA), also defines marriage, for purposes of federal law, as a union between a man and a woman. The DOMA has led at least one court to deny a lesbian couple who had married in Canada the right to file jointly for bankruptcy.

There is even less certainty as to how state exemptions and property ownership laws will be applied to same-sex couples who are married or registered in one of these states. For example, a New Jersey Tax Court recently allowed a disabled veteran's claim that the home he owned with his male partner was exempt from taxes, because the men had registered as domestic partners in New Jersey and owned the home in tenancy by the entirety—a form of property ownership previously reserved to married couples.

This uncertainty extends only to couples that have married or registered, however. If you and your partner are neither married nor registered in a state that gives partners marriage-like benefits, any property you own together will be treated like property owned with any other person: The share that you own will be part of the bankruptcy estate, and will be subject to the court's jurisdiction. Your partner will be treated as a codebtor on any debts you owe jointly. But your partner will not be part of your bankruptcy case.

If you and your partner or spouse are considering filing jointly or have concerns about the treatment of your debts and property in bankruptcy, you should consult with a bankruptcy attorney who is familiar with legal issues facing same-sex couples.

B. Property That Isn't in Your Bankruptcy Estate

Property that is not in your bankruptcy estate is not subject to the bankruptcy court's jurisdiction, which means that the bankruptcy trustee can't take it to pay your creditors under any circumstances.

The most common examples of property that doesn't fall within your bankruptcy estate are:

- property you buy or receive after your filing date (with the few exceptions described in Section A, above)
- pensions subject to the federal law known as ERISA (commonly, defined-benefit pensions)
- property pledged as collateral for a loan, if a licensed lender (pawnbroker) retains possession of the collateral

- property in your possession that belongs to someone else (for instance, property you are storing for someone), and
- wages that are withheld, and employer contributions that are made for employee benefit and health insurance plans.

Retirement accounts are exempt, no matter which exemptions you use. When it passed the new bankruptcy law, Congress created a broad exemption for all types of tax-exempt retirement accounts, including 401(k)s, 403(b)s, profit-sharing and money purchase plans, IRAs (including Roth, SEP, and SIMPLE IRAs), and defined-benefit plans. These exemptions are unlimited—that is, the entire account is exempt, regardless of how much money is in it—except in the case of traditional and Roth IRAs. For these types of IRAs only, the exemption is limited to a total value of $1 million per person (this figure will be adjusted every three years for inflation). These accounts are exempt regardless of whether you use the federal or a state exemption system.

Under the new bankruptcy law, funds placed in a qualified tuition program or Coverdell education savings account are also not part of your bankruptcy estate, as long as:

- you deposit the funds into the account at least one year before filing for bankruptcy, and
- the beneficiary of the account is your child, stepchild, grandchild, step-grandchild, or in some cases, foster child.

Funds placed in the account more than two years before you file are excluded from the bankruptcy estate without limit. However, you can exclude only $5,000 of the contributions you make between one and two years before filing. And contributions made within the year before filing are not excluded at all.

Experts disagree over how to interpret this provision. Some believe that, although the statute appears to exclude all contributions made more than two years before filing, the total exclusion for educational accounts and tuition program will be capped at $5,000, regardless of when the funds were deposited. Talk to a bankruptcy lawyer if you need more information on this issue.

C. Property You Can Keep

Your property is everything you own. If you own your own home (or you have any ownership interest in land or buildings of any kind), you are the proud owner of what is called "real property." If you don't own any real estate, everything you own is considered personal property.

When filing for Chapter 7 bankruptcy, you may be able to keep your home. (See Ch. 4 for more information.) However, you will probably have to give up any other real estate you own, which will be sold for the benefit of your creditors. You will also be able to keep some or all of your personal property. How much you get to keep will depend on whether the property is considered exempt under the state exemption system available to you (or under the federal exemption statute, if the state where you file allows you to choose between the federal and state exemptions).

This section describes how exemptions work and how to figure out which exemptions you can use. Once you know which exemptions are available to you, you can start applying those exemptions to your personal property to figure out which items you'll be able to keep. To help you keep track, we've included a Personal Property Checklist, which you can use to take an inventory of your property. Then, using the Property Exemption Worksheet, you'll be able to figure out, item by item, whether you'll be able to hang on to your property.

1. How Exemptions Work

Figuring out exactly what property you're legally entitled to keep if you file for bankruptcy takes some work, but it's very important. It's your responsibility—and to your benefit—to claim all exemptions to which you're entitled. If you don't claim property as exempt, you could lose it unnecessarily to your creditors.

Exempt property is the property you can keep during and after bankruptcy. Nonexempt property is the property that the bankruptcy trustee is entitled to take and sell to pay your creditors. Therefore, the more you can claim as exempt, the better off you are.

In Ch. 1, we explained that each state's legislature produces a set of exemptions for use by people who are residents of that state. Fifteen states (and the District of Columbia) allow debtors to choose between their state's exemptions or another set of exemptions created by Congress (called federal bankruptcy exemptions). States that currently allow debtors this choice are Arkansas, Connecticut, Hawaii, Massachusetts, Michigan, Minnesota, New Hampshire, New Jersey, New Mexico, Pennsylvania, Rhode Island, Texas, Vermont, Washington, and Wisconsin. You have to choose one system or the other—you can't mix and match some exemptions from one and some from the other. However, if you use one system when you first file your petition and later on decide that the other system would work better for you, you can amend Schedule C—the form where you list your exemption claims—to change systems.

California has adopted its own unique exemption system. Although California doesn't allow debtors to use the federal exemptions, California offers two sets of state exemptions. With a few important exceptions, the alternative California exemptions are the same as the federal exemptions. As in the 15 states that have the federal bankruptcy exemptions, people filing for bankruptcy in California must choose one or the other set of California's state exemptions.

You might be able to keep your nonexempt property. You won't have to surrender a specific item of nonexempt property to the trustee if you pay the property's value in cash, or if the trustee is willing to accept exempt property of roughly equal value instead. Also, the trustee might reject or abandon the item if it would be too costly or cumbersome to sell. In that case, you also get to keep it. So when we say that you have to give up property, remember that you still might be able to barter with the trustee to keep it.

a. Types of Exemptions

Both state and federal exemptions come in several basic flavors.

1. Exemptions to a Limited Amount

Some exemptions protect the value of your ownership in a particular item only up to a set dollar limit. For instance, the New Mexico state exemptions allow you to keep $4,000 of equity in a motor vehicle. If you were filing for Chapter 7 bankruptcy in that state and using the state exemption list, you could keep your car if it was worth $4,000 or less. You could also keep the

car if selling it would not raise enough money to pay what you still owe on it and give you the full value of your $4,000 exemption. For example, if you own a car worth $20,000 but still owe $16,000 on it, selling it would raise $16,000 for the lender and $4,000 for you (thanks to the exemption). The trustee wouldn't take the car because there would be nothing left over to pay your other creditors. Instead, you would be allowed to keep it as long as you are—and remain—current on your payments.

However, if your equity in the car exceeded the $4,000 exemption, the trustee might sell the car to raise money for your other creditors. To continue our example, let's say you owe only $10,000 on that car. Selling the car for $20,000 would pay off the lender in full, pay your $4,000 exemption, and leave a portion of the remaining $6,000 (after the costs of sale are deducted) to be distributed to your other creditors. In this scenario, you are entitled to the full value of your exemption—$4,000—but not to the car itself.

2. Exemptions Without Regard to Value

Another type of exemption allows you to keep specified property items regardless of their value. For instance, the Utah state exemptions allow you to keep a refrigerator, freezer, microwave, stove, sewing machine, and carpets with no limit on their value. For comparison purposes, another Utah state exemption places a $500 limit on "heirlooms, sofas, chairs, and related furnishings." Go figure.

3. Wildcard Exemptions

Some states (and the federal exemption list) also provide a general-purpose exemption, called a wildcard exemption. This exemption gives you a dollar amount that you can apply to any type of property. If you play poker, you undoubtedly have played a game where a particular card is designated a wildcard, which means you can use it as a queen of diamonds, a two of spades, or any other card you want to make the most of the other cards in your hand. The same principle applies here. For example, suppose you own a $3,000 boat in a state that doesn't exempt boats but does have a wildcard of $5,000. You can take $3,000 of the wildcard and apply it to the boat, which means the boat will now be considered exempt. And if you have other nonexempt property, you can apply the remaining $2,000 to that property.

You can also use a wildcard exemption to increase an existing exemption. For example, if you have $5,000 worth of equity in your car but your state only allows you to exempt $1,500 of its value, you will likely lose the car. However, if your state has a $5,000 wildcard exemption, you could use the $1,500 motor vehicle exemption and $3,500 of the wildcard exemption to exempt your car entirely. And you'd still have $1,500 of the wildcard exemption to use on other nonexempt property.

b. Why State Exemptions Vary So Much

Each state's exemptions are unique. The property you can keep, therefore, varies considerably from state to state. Why the differences? State exemptions are used not only for bankruptcy purposes but also to shelter property that otherwise could be taken by creditors who have obtained court judgments. The exemptions reflect the attitudes of state legislators about how much property, and which property, a debtor should be forced to part with when a victorious creditor collects on a judgment. These attitudes are rooted in local values and concerns. But in many cases there is another, more pressing, reason why state exemptions differ. Some state legislatures have raised exemption levels in recent times, while other states last looked at their exemptions many decades ago. In states that don't reconsider their exemptions very often, you can expect to find lower dollar amounts.

c. New Residency Requirements for Using State Exemptions

Prior to the new bankruptcy law, filers used the exemptions of the state where they lived when they filed for bankruptcy. Under the new rules, however, some filers will have to use the exemptions of the state where they *used* to live. Congress was concerned about people gaming the system by moving to states with liberal exemptions just to file for bankruptcy. As a result, it passed residency requirements filers have to meet before they can use a state's exemption system.

Here are the new rules that apply to exemptions for everything but a home:

- If you have lived or made your residence in your current state for at least two years, you can use that state's exemptions.

- If you have lived or made your residence in your current state for more than 91 days but less than two years, you must use the exemptions of the state where you lived for the better part of the 180-day period immediately prior to the two-year period preceding your filing.

- If you have lived or made your residence in your current state for fewer than 91 days, you can either file in the state where you lived immediately before (as long as you lived there for at least 91 days) or wait until you have logged 91 days in your new home and file in your current state. Once you figure out where you can file, you'll need to use whatever exemptions are available to you according to the rules set out above.

- If the state you are filing in offers a choice between the state and federal bankruptcy exemptions, you can use the federal exemption list regardless of how long you've been living in the state.

- If these rules deprive you of the right to use *any* state's exemptions, you can use the federal exemption list. For example, some states allow their exemptions to be used only by current state residents, which might leave former residents who haven't lived in their new home state for at least two years without any available state exemptions.

A longer residency requirement applies to homestead exemptions: If you acquired a home in your current state within the 40 months before you file for bankruptcy (and you didn't purchase it with the proceeds from selling another home in that state), your homestead exemption will be subject to a cap of $125,000, even if the state homestead exemption available to you is larger. For detailed information on homestead exemptions, see Ch. 4.

EXAMPLE 1: Sammie Jo lives in South Carolina from July 2005 until January 2007, when she gets lucky at a casino, moves to Texas, and buys a car for $15,000. In March 2008, Sammie Jo files for bankruptcy in Texas. Her car is now worth $14,000. Because Sammie Jo has been living in Texas for only 14 months—not two years—she can't use the Texas exemption for cars, which can be up to $30,000, depending on the value of other personal property a filer claims as exempt. Because Sammie Jo filed in March 2008, she must use the exemptions of the state where she lived for most of the nine-month period ending two years before she filed, or March 2006. Sammie Jo lived in South Carolina for the six months prior to March 2006, so she must use the South Carolina exemptions. As it turns out, the South Carolina exemption for cars is only $1,200, which means that Sammie Jo will probably lose her car if she uses the South Carolina exemptions.

As it turns out, however, Texas gives filers the option of using either its state exemptions or the federal bankruptcy exemptions. Under the new law, the rules of the state where a person files determine whether the federal exemptions are available, even if that person has not lived in the state long enough to use its *state* exemptions. This means that Sammie Jo can use the federal exemptions instead of the South Carolina state exemptions. Under the federal exemptions, Sammie Jo is entitled to exempt a motor vehicle worth up to $2,950—still not enough to cover her car. But wait. The federal exemptions also provide a wildcard of $975, plus $9,250 of unused homestead exemption. Sammie Jo doesn't own her home, so she can add the entire wildcard of $10,225 to her $2,950 vehicle exemption, for a total exemption of $13,175 she can apply to her car. While Sammie Jo still has $825 of nonexempt equity in her car ($14,000 minus $13,175), the trustee will probably let her keep it. The cost of storing the car and selling it at auction would likely eat up that nonexempt equity, leaving little or nothing for Sammie Jo's creditors (or the trustee's commission).

EXAMPLE 2: Julia lived in North Dakota for many years, until she moved to Florida on January 15, 2007. She files for bankruptcy in Florida on November 30, 2008. Because she has live in Florida for slightly less than two years when she files, she must use the exemptions from the state where she lived for the better part of the 180-day period that ended two years before she filed—which is North Dakota. As it turns out, Julia's most valuable possession is a prepaid medical savings account with $20,000 in it. While the account would be exempt under Florida law, North Dakota has no exemption for this type of property. Nor are the federal

exemptions available in Florida. So the trustee will probably seize the medical savings account and use the money in it to pay Julia's creditors. Had Julia waited another month and a half to file, she would have been able to use Florida's exemptions and keep her medical savings account.

⚠ These residency requirements may be declared unconstitutional. Some bankruptcy experts believe that using residency requirements to discourage bankruptcy filers from moving may be unconstitutional, because it burdens filers' fundamental right to travel. Because this issue is sure to be raised early on by any attorney whose client would suffer financial harm due to these residency requirements, you should check for updates at www.nolo.com before relying on the information in this section. If you are interested in reading the leading case on this "right to travel" issue, see *Shapiro v. Thompson*, 394 U.S. 618 (1969), available at www.oyez.org/oyez/resource/case/351.

d. If You Are Married and Filing Jointly

If the federal bankruptcy exemptions are available in the state where you file and you decide to use them, you may double all of the exemptions if you are married and filing jointly. (See Ch. 6 for more on whether to file jointly.) This means that you and your spouse can each claim the full amount of each exemption. If you decide to use your state's exemptions, you may be able to double some exemptions but not others. For instance, in the California exemption System 1 list, the $2,300 limit for motor vehicles may not be doubled, but the $6,075 limit on tools of the trade may be doubled in some circumstances. In order for you to double an exemption for a single piece of property, title to the property must be in both of your names. In Appendix 1, we've noted whether a court or state legislature has expressly allowed or prohibited doubling. If the chart doesn't say one way or the other, it is probably safe to double. However, keep in mind that this area of the law changes rapidly—legislation or court decisions issued after the publication date of this book will not be reflected in the chart. (See Ch. 10 for information on doing your own legal research.)

Think Creatively About Exemptions

"Tools of the trade" is a common exemption category. The term used to mean hand tools, but now it refers more broadly to the things you need in order to do the job you rely on for support. Here are some examples of property that could be considered tools of the trade in various fields:

- Art camera, scanner (artist)
- Car, truck, or van that is used for more than just commuting (sales manager, insurance adjuster, physician, firewood salesperson, traveling salesperson, real estate salesperson, mechanic)
- Cream separator, dairy cows, animal feed (farmer)
- Drills, saws (carpenter)
- Electric motor, lathe (mechanic)
- Guitar, acoustic amplifier, coronet, violin and bow, organ, speaker cabinet (musician)
- Hair dye, shampoo, cash register, furniture, dryer, fan, curler, magazine rack (barber, beauty parlor operator)
- Oven, mixer (baker)
- Personal computer, printer (insurance salesperson, lawyer, accountant)
- Photographic lens (photographer)
- Power chain saw (firewood salesperson)
- Sewing machine (tailor)
- Truck (logger, tire retreader, truck driver, farmer, electrician)

The ideas listed above are examples of tools of the trade. Be sure to review the tools of the trade exemption rules available to you.

2. Applying Exemptions to Your Property

The Personal Property Checklist and Property Exemption Worksheet will help you figure out what personal property you own and whether you will get to keep it if you file for bankruptcy. You also can use this information to complete the official forms that accompany your bankruptcy petition, if you later decide to file.

a. Inventory Your Property

If you decide to file for bankruptcy, you will be required to list all property that belongs in your bankruptcy estate. Whether or not you can hold on to that property, or at least some of the property's value in dollar terms, depends on what the property is worth and which exemptions are available to you. The best way to start figuring out what you'll be able to keep—and get a jump on your filing paperwork—is to create an inventory (list) of your property.

Use the Personal Property Checklist shown below—you can find a blank, tear-out copy in Appendix 2—to create an inventory of your possessions. Place a checkmark in the box next to each item you own. If you are married and filing jointly, list all property owned by you and your spouse.

Personal Property Checklist

Cash on hand (include sources)
- ☐ In your home
- ☐ In your wallet
- ☐ Under your mattress

Deposits of money (include sources)
- ☐ Bank account
- ☐ Brokerage account (with stockbroker)
- ☐ Certificates of deposit (CDs)
- ☐ Credit union deposit
- ☐ Escrow account
- ☐ Money market account
- ☐ Money in a safe deposit box
- ☐ Savings and loan deposit

Security deposits
- ☐ Electric
- ☐ Gas
- ☐ Heating oil
- ☐ Security deposit on a rental unit
- ☐ Prepaid rent
- ☐ Rented furniture or equipment
- ☐ Telephone
- ☐ Water

Household goods, supplies, and furnishings
- ☐ Antiques
- ☐ Appliances
- ☐ Carpentry tools
- ☐ China and crystal
- ☐ Clocks
- ☐ Dishes
- ☐ Food (total value)
- ☐ Furniture (list every item; go from room to room so you don't miss anything)
- ☐ Gardening tools
- ☐ Home computer (for personal use)
- ☐ Iron and ironing board
- ☐ Lamps
- ☐ Lawn mower or tractor

- ☐ Microwave oven
- ☐ Patio or outdoor furniture
- ☐ Radios
- ☐ Rugs
- ☐ Sewing machine
- ☐ Silverware and utensils
- ☐ Small appliances
- ☐ Snow blower
- ☐ Stereo system
- ☐ Telephone and answering machines
- ☐ Televisions
- ☐ Vacuum cleaner
- ☐ Video equipment (VCR, camcorder)

Books, pictures, and other art objects; stamp, coin, and other collections
- ☐ Art prints
- ☐ Bibles
- ☐ Books
- ☐ Coins
- ☐ Collectibles (such as political buttons, baseball cards)
- ☐ Family portraits
- ☐ Figurines
- ☐ Original artworks
- ☐ Photographs
- ☐ Records, CDs, audiotapes
- ☐ Stamps
- ☐ Videotapes

Apparel
- ☐ Clothing
- ☐ Furs

Jewelry
- ☐ Engagement and wedding rings
- ☐ Gems
- ☐ Precious metals
- ☐ Watches

Firearms, sports equipment, and other hobby equipment

☐ Board games

☐ Bicycle

☐ Camera equipment

☐ Electronic musical equipment

☐ Exercise machine

☐ Fishing gear

☐ Guns (rifles, pistols, shotguns, muskets)

☐ Model or remote-controlled cars or planes

☐ Musical instruments

☐ Scuba diving equipment

☐ Ski equipment

☐ Other sports equipment

☐ Other weapons (swords and knives)

Interests in insurance policies

☐ Credit insurance

☐ Disability insurance

☐ Health insurance

☐ Homeowners' or renters' insurance

☐ Term life insurance

☐ Whole life insurance

Annuities

Pension or profit-sharing plans

☐ IRA

☐ Keogh

☐ Pension or retirement plan

☐ 401(k) plan

Stock and interests in incorporated and unincorporated companies

Interests in partnerships

☐ Limited partnership interest

☐ General partnership interest

Government and corporate bonds and other investment instruments

☐ Corporate bonds

☐ Municipal bonds

☐ Promissory notes

☐ U.S. savings bonds

Accounts receivable

☐ Accounts receivable from business

☐ Commissions already earned

Family support

☐ Alimony (spousal support, maintenance) due under court order

☐ Child support payments due under court order

☐ Payments due under divorce property settlement

Other debts for which the amount owed you is known and definite

☐ Disability benefits due

☐ Disability insurance due

☐ Judgments obtained against third parties you haven't yet collected

☐ Sick pay earned

☐ Social Security benefits due

☐ Tax refund due under returns already filed

☐ Vacation pay earned

☐ Wages due

☐ Workers' compensation due

Any special powers that you or another person can exercise for your benefit, other than those listed under "real estate"

☐ A right to receive, at some future time, cash, stock, or other personal property placed in an irrevocable trust

☐ Current payments of interest or principal from a trust

☐ General power of appointment over personal property

An interest in property due to another person's death

☐ Any interest as the beneficiary of a living trust, if the trustor has died

☐ Expected proceeds from a life insurance policy where the insured has died

☐ Inheritance from an existing estate in probate (the owner has died and the court is overseeing the distribution of the property), even if the final amount is not yet known

☐ Inheritance under a will that is contingent on one or more events occurring, but only if the owner has died

All other contingent claims and claims where the amount owed you is not known, including tax refunds, counterclaims, and rights to setoff claims (claims you think you have against a person, government, or corporation, but you haven't yet sued on)

☐ Claims against a corporation, government entity, or individual

☐ Potential tax refund on a return that is not yet filed

Patents, copyrights, and other intellectual property

☐ Copyrights

☐ Patents

☐ Trade secrets

☐ Trademarks

☐ Trade names

Licenses, franchises, and other general intangibles

☐ Building permits

☐ Cooperative association holdings

☐ Exclusive licenses

☐ Liquor licenses

☐ Nonexclusive licenses

☐ Patent licenses

☐ Professional licenses

Automobiles and other vehicles

☐ Car

☐ Minibike or motor scooter

☐ Mobile or motor home if on wheels

☐ Motorcycle

☐ Recreational vehicle (RV)

☐ Trailer

☐ Truck

☐ Van

Boats, motors, and accessories

☐ Boat (canoe, kayak, rowboat, shell, sailboat, pontoon, yacht)

☐ Boat radar, radio, or telephone

☐ Outboard motor

Aircraft and accessories

☐ Aircraft

☐ Aircraft radar, radio, and other accessories

Office equipment, furnishings, and supplies

☐ Artwork in your office

☐ Computers, software, modems, printers

☐ Copier

☐ Fax machine

☐ Furniture

☐ Rugs

☐ Supplies

☐ Telephones

☐ Typewriters

Machinery, fixtures, equipment, and supplies used in business

☐ Military uniforms and accoutrements

☐ Tools of your trade

Business inventory

Livestock, poultry, and other animals

☐ Birds

☐ Cats

☐ Dogs

☐ Fish and aquarium equipment

☐ Horses

☐ Other pets

☐ Livestock and poultry

Crops—growing or harvested

Farming equipment and implements

Farm supplies, chemicals, and feed

Other personal property of any kind not already listed

☐ Church pew

☐ Health aids (such as a wheelchair or crutches)

☐ Hot tub or portable spa

☐ Season tickets

b. Using the Property Exemption Worksheet

Now that you have a comprehensive list of your property, you can decide how to use the exemptions available to you to your best advantage. This will require you to come up with a value for each item, decide which exemption system to use (if you have a choice), then figure out how to apply those exemptions to your property.

To do this, use the Property Exemption Worksheet in Appendix 2. A portion of the worksheet is set out below. As you can see, it includes four columns:

1. a description of the property
2. the property's replacement value
3. the exemption (if any) that applies to the property, and
4. the number of the statute where that exemption appears (you'll need this information when you complete your bankruptcy forms).

Complete each of these columns following the instructions below.

Column 1: Using your completed checklist as a guide, describe each item of property and its location.

For personal property, identify the item (for example, 1994 Ford Mustang) and its location (for example, residence). For cash on hand and deposits of money, indicate the source of each, such as wages or salary, insurance policy proceeds, or the proceeds from selling an item of property. Although cash on hand is usually not exempt, you may be able to exempt all or some of it if you can show that it came from an exempt source, such as unemployment insurance.

Column 2: Enter the replacement value of each item of property in Column 1. (Under the former rules, filers used the market value—what they could get for the property if they sold it at their own garage sale. The new bankruptcy law requires filers to use the replacement value, which is typically a higher figure.)

It's easy to enter a dollar amount for cash, bank deposits, bonds, and most investment instruments. For items that are tougher to value, such as insurance, annuities, pensions, and business interests, you may need to get an appraisal from someone who has some financial expertise.

For your other property, estimate its replacement value—that is, what you could buy it for from a retail vendor, considering its age and condition. As long as you have a reasonable basis for your estimates, the lower the value you place on property, the more of it you will probably be allowed to keep through the bankruptcy process. But be honest when assigning values. Trustees have years of experience and a pretty good sense of what property is worth. It's okay to be wrong as long as you have an arguable basis for the value you list and briefly explain any uncertainties. If you can't come up with a replacement value, leave this column blank. If you file for bankruptcy, you can simply indicate that the value is unknown. If the trustee is concerned about the value, you will be asked at your creditors' meeting to provide more detail.

Property Exemption Worksheet

1 Property	2 Replacement Value	3 Exemption	4 Statute No.
1. Cash on hand			
_____	_____	_____	_____
_____	_____	_____	_____
_____	_____	_____	_____
_____	_____	_____	_____

Here are some tips for valuing specific items:

- **Cars.** Unfortunately, the new replacement value requirement doesn't exactly square with the way car values are determined by the Kelley Blue Book, the most common source for car prices. To be absolutely safe in your estimate, use the average retail price for your car (based on its mileage) listed at the website of the National Automobile Dealers Association, www.nada.com. If your car is inoperable or in poor condition (with obvious and significant body damage or serious mechanical problems), you can reasonably list the replacement value as zero. Because such cars are not sold by car dealers, there's no way to figure out what a retail merchant would charge for such a car.
- **Older goods.** If the items are sold in used goods stores (for example, used furniture stores, Goodwill stores, or hospice outlets), check their prices. If not, you can check the want ads in a local flea market or penny-saver newspaper. EBay is also a good source for values: You can find retail merchants selling a wide variety of used goods at www.ebay.com.
- **Life insurance.** List the current cash surrender value of your policy, (call your insurance agent to find out what it is). Term life insurance has a cash surrender value of zero. Don't list the amount of benefits the policy will pay, unless you're the beneficiary of an insurance policy and the insured person has died.
- **Stocks and bonds.** Check the listing in a newspaper business section. If you can't find the listing, or the stock isn't traded publicly, call your broker and ask what it's worth. If you have a brokerage account, use the value from your last statement. For information on how to calculate the value of any stock options you own, see "Are Stock Options Part of Your Bankruptcy Estate?", above.
- **Jewelry, antiques, and other collectibles.** Any valuable jewelry or collections should be appraised.

Add up the amounts in Column 4 and enter the total in the space provided on the last page.

Ignore liens against your personal property when computing the property's value. If you owe money to a major consumer lender such as Beneficial Finance, the lender may have a lien on some or all of your personal property. You can usually remove this lien in the course of your bankruptcy. Similarly, you may have a lien against your personal property if a creditor has obtained a court judgment against you. These liens, too, can frequently be removed. See Ch. 5 to find out more about personal property liens and your options for dealing with them.

Columns 3 and 4. Identify exemptions for your personal property.

You can find every state's exemptions in Appendix 1. If the state exemption system you're using allows you to choose the federal exemptions instead of your state's exemptions, you can find these listed directly after Wyoming.

Focus on the property you really want to keep. If you have a lot of property and get bogged down in exemption jargon and dollar signs, start with the property you would feel really bad about losing. After that, if you are so inclined, you can search for exemptions that would let you keep property that is less important to you.

If You Can Only Use Your State's Exemptions

Unless you are using the exemptions for Arkansas, Connecticut, Hawaii, Massachusetts, Michigan, Minnesota, New Hampshire, New Jersey, New Mexico, Pennsylvania, Rhode Island, Texas, Vermont, Washington, or Wisconsin, you must use that state's exemptions.

Step 1: In Column 3, list the amount of the exemption or write "no limit" if the exemption is unlimited. In Column 4, list the number of the statute identified in Appendix 1 for the exemption that may reasonably be applied to the particular property item. If you need more information or an explanation of terms, use the notes at the beginning of Appendix 1 and the glossary. In evaluating whether your cash on hand and deposits are exempt, look to the source of the money, such as welfare benefits, insurance proceeds, or wages.

Err on the side of exemption. If you can think of a reason why a particular property item might be exempt, list it even if you aren't sure that the exemption applies. If you later decide to file for Chapter 7 bankruptcy, you will only be expected to do your best to fit the exemptions to your property. Of course, if you do misapply an exemption and the bankruptcy trustee or a creditor files a formal objection within the required time, you may have to scramble to keep the property that you mistakenly thought was exempt.

Step 2: If a particular exemption has no dollar limit, then apply that exemption to all property items that seem to fall into that category. If there is a limit (for instance, $1,000 worth of electronic products), total the value of all property items you wish to claim under that exemption. Then compare the total with the exemption limit. If the total is less than the limit, then there is no problem. However, if the total is more than the limit, you may have to either give the trustee enough of the property to bring your total back under the limit or apply a wildcard exemption to the extra property, if the state system you are using has one.

If You Live in California or a State That Allows You to Choose the Federal Exemptions

If the state system you're using allows you to use the federal bankruptcy exemptions or you qualify to use the California exemptions where you have a choice between two state systems, you'll need to decide which exemption system to use. You can't use some exemptions from one system and some from the other. If you own a home in which you have equity, your choice will often be dictated by which system gives you the most protection for that equity. In California, for example, the homestead exemption in System 1 protects up to $150,000 in equity, while the System 2 list only protects $18,675. Most homeowners in California end up choosing System 1, for obvious reasons.

Unless your choice of exemption lists is dictated by your home equity, you'll be best served by going through the Property Exemption Worksheet twice. The first time through, use the state exemptions (or System 1 in California). The second time, use the federal bankruptcy exemptions (or System 2 in California).

After you apply both exemption lists to your property, compare the results and decide which exemption list will do you the most good. You may find federal exemptions that don't exist in the state's exemption list, or that are more generous than the state's exemptions. Or vice versa. You may be sorely tempted to pluck some exemptions out of one list and add them to the other list. Again, this can't be done. You'll either have to use your state's exemption list or the federal bankruptcy exemptions—you can't mix and match them.

EXAMPLE: Paula Willmore has lived in Albuquerque, New Mexico, for several years. Other than clothing, household furniture, and personal effects, the only property Paula owns is a vintage 1967 Chevy Camaro Rally Sport. Paula often checks out local car magazines and knows that the model she owns typically sells for about $10,000, although this price varies by several thousand dollars based on the car's condition. Paula wants to know what will happen to her car if she files for Chapter 7 bankruptcy.

Because Paula has lived in New Mexico for more than two years, she will use that state's exemption rules. Her first step is to locate the exemptions for New Mexico in Appendix 1. At the bottom of the New Mexico exemption listings for personal property, Paula finds an entry for motor vehicles and sees that the exemption is $4,000. Paula begins to worry that she may lose her car, which is worth more than double the exemption limit.

Paula's next step is to search the New Mexico state exemptions for a wildcard exemption. (See Section 1, above, for an explanation of wildcard exemptions.) Paula discovers (at the bottom of the list) that she has a $2,500 wildcard exemption that she can apply to any property, including the Camaro. Add that to the $4,000 regular motor vehicle exemption, and Paula can now exempt $6,500. This amount still doesn't cover the Camaro's replacement value, which means the trustee would probably sell it, give Paula her $6,500 exemption, and distribute the rest of the sales proceeds to Paula's unsecured creditors.

Paula next checks to see whether New Mexico allows debtors to use the federal bankruptcy exemptions. She looks at the top of the exemption page and sees a note that the federal bankruptcy exemptions are available in her state. Hoping that the federal bankruptcy exemptions will give her a higher exemption limit for her Camaro, she turns to the end of Appendix 1 (right after Wyoming) and finds the federal bankruptcy exemption list. Under personal property she sees a listing for motor vehicles in the amount of $2,950—not high enough.

Paula examines the federal bankruptcy exemptions to see whether they provide a wildcard exemption. She discovers that the federal bankruptcy exemptions let you use up to $9,250 of the homestead exemption as a wildcard. Because Paula has no home equity to protect, she can apply most of the wildcard to the Camaro, in addition to the federal exemption for motor vehicles of $2,950. Further, Paula sees that she can get an additional wildcard exemption of $975 under the federal exemption system, just in case she has other non-exempt property.

Because Paula is most concerned about keeping her car, and because the federal bankruptcy exemptions let her keep her car while the state exemptions don't, Paula decides to use the federal bankruptcy exemption list.

Five Steps to Applying Exemptions to Your Personal Property

1. Check the exemptions you are using for specific property items that you want to keep.
2. If the state exemptions don't cover the property you want to keep (either because they don't exempt that property at all or because they exempt less than your property is worth), look for a wildcard exemption in the state exemption list.
3. If the state also lets you use the federal bankruptcy exemptions (or you live in California), see whether a federal exemption (or a System 2 exemption in California) covers your property.
4. If the federal bankruptcy exemptions are available to you but don't seem to cover your property, see whether the federal bankruptcy wildcard exemption will work.
5. If you have the choice of two exemption systems, decide which exemption list you want to use. Don't mix and match. (In California, if you own your home and have more than $20,000 in equity, you'll probably want to use System 1. If you don't own a home, System 2 will often be a better choice.)

Tip #1: Double your exemptions if you're married and filing jointly, unless the state exemption list prohibits it. If you're using the federal bankruptcy exemptions, you may double all exemptions.

Tip #2: While you're figuring out which of your property is exempt, write down in Column 4 the numbers of the statutes that authorize each exemption. (You can find these in Appendix 1.) You will need this information when you fill out Schedule C of your bankruptcy papers.

Using Federal Nonbankruptcy Exemptions

If you are using state exemptions, you are also entitled to use a handful of exemptions called "federal nonbankruptcy exemptions." As the name suggests, these exemptions are generally used in cases other than bankruptcies, but you can also use them in a bankruptcy case. (In California, they apply only if you're using System 1.)

Skim the list at the end of Appendix 1 to see if any of these exemptions would help you. If they would, you can use them in addition to the state exemptions. If they duplicate each other, though, you cannot add them together for any one category. For example, if both your state and the federal nonbankruptcy exemptions let you exempt 75% of disposable weekly earnings, you cannot combine the exemptions to keep all of your wages—75% is all you get.

D. Selling Nonexempt Property Before You File

If you want to reduce the amount of nonexempt property you own before you file for bankruptcy, you might consider selling the nonexempt property and using the proceeds to buy exempt property. Or you might want to use the proceeds to pay certain types of debts. But be careful: If the court learns that you sold the property and believes that you did so in order to defraud, hinder, or shortchange your creditors, your efforts to shelter the property will fail. The court will treat any exempt property you purchase as nonexempt property. And, if the court believes you acted fraudulently, your bankruptcy discharge may be at risk.

Talk to a lawyer first. Before you sell nonexempt property, consult a bankruptcy attorney. Your local bankruptcy court may automatically consider these kinds of transfers attempts to defraud your creditors. (See Section 2, below.) The only sure way to find out what is and isn't permissible in your area is to ask an attorney familiar with local bankruptcy court practices. A consultation on this sort of issue should not run more than $100 and is well worth the cost if it will help you hold on to the value of your nonexempt property by converting it to exempt property.

1. How to Proceed

There are several ways to turn your nonexempt property into exempt property:

a. Replace Nonexempt Property With Exempt Property

You may:
- Sell a nonexempt asset and use the proceeds to buy an asset that is completely exempt. For example, you can sell a nonexempt coin collection and purchase clothing, which in most states is exempt without regard to value.
- Sell a nonexempt asset and use the proceeds to buy an asset that is exempt up to the amount received in the sale. For example, you can sell a nonexempt coin collection worth $1,200 and purchase a car that is exempt up to $1,200 in value.
- Sell an asset that is only partially exempt and use the proceeds to replace it with a similar asset of lesser value. For example, if a television is exempt up to a value of $200, you could sell your $500 television and buy a workable second-hand one for $200, putting the remaining cash into other exempt assets such as clothing or appliances.
- Use cash (which isn't exempt in most states) to buy an exempt item, such as furniture or work tools.

b. Pay Debts

If you choose to reduce your nonexempt property by selling it and using the proceeds to pay debts, keep the following points in mind:
- **It's usually unwise to pay off a debt that could be discharged in bankruptcy.** Many debts (such as credit card bills) can be completely discharged in bankruptcy. The only reason you should consider paying a dischargeable debt is to pay a debt for which a relative or friend is a cosigner, so that the friend or relative is not stuck paying the whole debt after your liability is discharged. Also, you might want to pay off a small credit card balance in order to keep the card out of your bankruptcy (you don't have to list it if you don't owe anything on it).
- **If you pay a creditor more than $600, you may want to wait to file for bankruptcy.** You should wait at least 90 days before you file for bankruptcy

if the total payments to any one regular "arm's length" creditor during that period exceed $600. Otherwise, the payment may be considered a preference, and the trustee may be able to get the money back and add it to your bankruptcy estate. (11 U.S.C. §§ 547(b), (c)(7), and (f).) If the creditor you pay is a relative, close friend, or company in which you are an officer, you should wait at least one year before filing. (See Section A3, above, for further explanation.) The $600 limit applies only if you owe primarily consumer debts; if you owe primarily business debts or taxes, you can pay a creditor up to $5,000 without it being considered a preference.

- **You can pay regular bills.** You can pay regular monthly bills right up until you file for bankruptcy. So keep paying your phone bills, rent, and mortgage.
- **Think twice before paying secured debts.** If you want to use the proceeds from nonexempt property to pay off a debt secured by collateral, read Ch. 5 of this book first. If the collateral for the debt isn't exempt, paying off the debt won't do you much good, because the trustee will take the collateral anyway when you file for bankruptcy. If the collateral is exempt, you may be able to keep it even if you don't pay off the debt before you file for bankruptcy.

EXAMPLE: John owes $5,000 on his 2002 Toyota truck, which is worth $4000. John sells his non-exempt musical equipment, pays off the $5,000 note, and files bankruptcy. It turns out that John can exempt only $1,000 in the motor vehicle. The trustee orders John to turn over the truck, which John does. The trustee sells the truck and gives John his $1,000 exemption. Not only did John lose his truck, but he also no longer has his musical equipment.

A better alternative: Because John owes more on the truck than it's worth, he could hold on to it through bankruptcy, making regular payments on the loan. The trustee would not take the truck away to sell it, because there would be no money left for unsecured creditors if the truck were sold with $5,000 in debt still hanging over it. And John might be able to hold on to the musical equipment for a small price paid to the trustee.

You Can Pay Favored Creditors After You File

You may be tempted to leave certain creditors off your bankruptcy papers, perhaps because the creditor is a relative, a local provider of important services (doctor, lawyer, veterinarian, department store), or your employer. Unfortunately, bankruptcy requires that all creditors be identified on the appropriate schedules. However, just because you got rid of a debt doesn't mean you can't pay it—as long as you wait until after you file and don't use property of the estate. For instance, if you file for bankruptcy on March 12, 2007, you can use your income earned after that date to pay the creditor, since that income is not part of your bankruptcy estate. One last point: While you are free to pay off a discharged debt, the creditor is not permitted to hound you for it.

2. Fraudulent Transactions

There's one major limitation on selling nonexempt property and using it to purchase exempt property: You can't do it to defraud, cheat, hinder, or delay your creditors. The new bankruptcy law allows the court to look into any conversion of exempt property to nonexempt property that occurs during the *ten years* before you file. In addition, if you transfer property to a friend, family member, or other close associate for less than the property is worth, this transfer will automatically be viewed as fraudulent if it occurred during the two years before you filed.

If a creditor or the trustee complains about a prebankruptcy transaction, and the court concludes that you were motivated by greed rather than the desire to get a fresh start, the court may let the trustee take the new property and sell it to pay for your creditors—even if that type of property is exempt under the exemptions you are using. In extreme cases, the court may even deny you a bankruptcy discharge.

There are two main factors a judge looks at:

- **Your motive.** The bankruptcy court will probably go along with your sale and purchase if the exempt property you end up with is a necessity or will clearly help you make a fresh start. For example, it's probably fine to sell a second (and usually nonexempt) car and buy some tools needed for your cabinetmaking business, or school clothing or books for your children. But if you sell your second car and buy a $3,000 diamond ring with the proceeds, a court might consider it a greedy attempt to cheat your creditors, even if the ring is exempt under your state's laws. Put a little differently, if the court thinks that you're trying to preserve the value of your nonexempt property for use after bankruptcy rather than acquiring property you really need, your conversion attempt will probably fail.

- **The amount of property involved.** If the amount of nonexempt property you get rid of before you file is enough to pay most of your debts, the court may dismiss your case.

3. Five Guidelines for Prebankruptcy Planning

Here are five important guidelines for staying out of trouble when you're making these kinds of prebankruptcy transactions.

a. **Accurately report all your transactions** on Form 7, the Statement of Financial Affairs. (See Ch. 6 for more on completing the official bankruptcy forms.) If the subject comes up with the trustee, creditors, or the court, freely admit that you tried to arrange your property holdings before filing for bankruptcy so that you could better get a fresh start. Courts see frankness about your prebankruptcy activities as a sign of honorable intentions. If you lie or attempt to conceal what you did or why you did it, the bankruptcy trustee or court may conclude that you had fraudulent intentions and either not allow the transaction or—even worse—deny you a bankruptcy discharge.

b. **Sell and buy for equivalent value.** If you sell a $500 nonexempt item and purchase an exempt item obviously worth $500, you shouldn't have a problem. If, however, you sell a $500 nonexempt item and purchase a $100 exempt item, be prepared to account for the $400 difference. Otherwise, the court will probably assume that

you're trying to cheat your creditors and either force you to cough up the $400 (if you still have it) or, possibly, dismiss your bankruptcy case.

c. **Sell and buy property at reasonable prices.** When you sell nonexempt property in order to purchase exempt property, make the price as close to the item's market value as possible. This is especially true if you sell to a friend or relative. If you sell your brother a $900 stereo system for $100, a creditor or the trustee may cry foul, and the judge may agree.

At the other end of the transaction, if you pay a friend or relative significantly more for exempt property than it is apparently worth, the court may suspect that you're just trying to transfer your assets to relatives to avoid creditors.

d. **Don't make last-minute transfers or purchases.** The longer you can wait to file for bankruptcy after making these kinds of property transfers, the less likely the judge is to disapprove. For example, judges frequently rule that a hasty transaction on the eve of filing shows an intent to cheat creditors. The open, deliberate, and advance planning of property sales and purchases, however, is usually considered evidence that you didn't intend to defraud. But even this isn't foolproof. One court ruled that the debtor's deliberate planning over a year before filing was evidence of an intent to cheat creditors. This conflict reinforces our earlier warning: You must find out your bankruptcy court's approach before you sell nonexempt property.

e. **Don't just change the form of property ownership.** Simply changing the way property is held from a nonexempt form to an exempt form is usually considered fraudulent.

EXAMPLE: Although he's married, Jeff owns a house as his separate property. Also, Jeff incurred virtually all of his debts alone, so he plans to file for bankruptcy alone. In Jeff's state, the homestead exemption is only $7,500. Jeff's equity in his home is nearly $30,000. Jeff's state also exempts property held as tenancy by the entirety, so Jeff transfers ownership of the house to himself and his wife as tenants by the entirety. That would normally exempt the house from all debts Jeff incurred separately. But because Jeff merely changed the form of property ownership, rather than buying exempt property or paying off debts to give himself a fresh start, the bankruptcy court would probably find the transfer fraudulent and take Jeff's house. (Jeff would get $7,500 from the sale as his homestead exemption.)

⚠ **Community property warning.** As mentioned earlier, if you're married and live in a community property state (Alaska, Arizona, California, Idaho, Louisiana, Nevada, New Mexico, Texas, Washington, or Wisconsin), the trustee can usually take both your share of community property and your spouse's, even if your spouse doesn't file for bankruptcy. So you might be tempted to change all or a portion of the community property into your spouse's separate property. Beware: Creditors or the trustee are apt to cry fraud, and the trustee is likely to take the property anyway.

To give you an idea of what judges consider improper behavior shortly before filing for bankruptcy, here are some transactions that courts have found to be fraudulent:

- A debtor bought goods on credit but never paid for them. He then sold those goods and bought property that he tried to exempt.
- A debtor with nonexempt property was forced into involuntary bankruptcy by a creditor. The debtor convinced the creditor to drop the forced bankruptcy. Then the debtor sold the nonexempt property, purchased exempt property, and filed for Chapter 7 bankruptcy.
- A debtor sold nonexempt property that was worth enough to pay off all her debts (but didn't pay them off).

- A debtor sold nonexempt items for amounts well below what they were worth.
- A debtor sold valuable property to a nonfiling spouse for one dollar.
- A debtor transferred nonexempt property the day after a creditor won a lawsuit against him, then filed for bankruptcy.
- A debtor in a state with an "unlimited" homestead exemption sold all her nonexempt property and used the proceeds to pay off a large portion of her mortgage.
- A debtor bought a piano and harpsichord and a whole life insurance policy, all exempt in his state. He didn't play either instrument, and he had no dependents who needed insurance protection.

Taking Out Loans to Pay Nondischargeable Debts

Some people are tempted to borrow money to discharge debts that aren't dischargeable—for instance, a student loan—and then list the new loan as a dischargeable unsecured debt. Be careful if you do this. A court could consider your actions fraudulent and dismiss your bankruptcy. If the court doesn't dismiss your case, the creditor may ask the court to declare the debt nondischargeable. If you take out the loan while you're broke and file for bankruptcy soon after, you probably will be penalized. And, if you borrow money or use your credit card to pay off a nondischargeable tax debt, you will not be able to discharge the loan or credit card charge. (11 U.S.C. § 523(a)(14).)

CHAPTER

4

Your House

If you own a home, Chapter 7 bankruptcy may not be the best strategy to deal with your debts. Before you decide to file, you must be aware of two important points:

- Chapter 7 bankruptcy won't ultimately prevent a foreclosure on a mortgage or deed of trust, although the automatic stay (see Ch. 2) will put it on hold while your bankruptcy case is pending (unless the creditor gets the judge to authorize the foreclosure). If you want to keep your home, you must keep making your mortgage payments before, during, and after bankruptcy. If you've already missed mortgage payments, you'll have to make them up to prevent foreclosure. (See Section B, below.)
- If you have nonexempt equity in your home (that is, equity that isn't protected by a homestead or other exemption), you risk losing your home if you file for Chapter 7 bankruptcy—assuming the amount of equity will cover the costs of sale and then some. (Real estate exemptions are discussed in Section C, below.)

Chapter 13 bankruptcy provides many opportunities for saving a home that are unavailable to a Chapter 7 filer. We explain the broad outlines of a Chapter 13 bankruptcy in Ch. 1. Also see *The New Bankruptcy: Will It Work for You?*, by Stephen Elias (Nolo).

This chapter explains how filing for Chapter 7 bankruptcy—or pursuing alternative strategies—affects your ability to hold on to your home. Of course, your home isn't your only consideration in deciding whether or not to file for bankruptcy, so make sure to read Ch. 1 of this book before making the decision. If you're still uncertain about what to do after reading these chapters, see a bankruptcy lawyer. If your home is important to you, it's worth spending some extra money to save it.

Be aware of the following:
- The procedures and strategies discussed in this chapter are complex. We recommend that you talk to a lawyer before filing. A mistake in estimating your equity or applying a homestead exemption could cost you your home.
- We offer this information to make you aware of several options that may be available to you. Your state's laws may give you additional rights that are not listed here.
- If you own two homes, or you want to protect equity in a home that is not your residence, a consultation with a bankruptcy lawyer is a must.
- The rules for how community property and "tenancy by the entirety" ownership is treated in bankruptcy can get complex when only one spouse files. If you are married, own your home, and plan on filing alone, see a bankruptcy lawyer first.

A. How Bankruptcy Affects a Typical Homeowner

Here's an overview of how bankruptcy affects you as a homeowner.

1. Mortgage Payments

You must keep making your mortgage payments. As you probably know all too well, you don't really "own" much of your home—a bank or other lender that has a mortgage or deed of trust on the home probably owns most of it. (Throughout this chapter, we use the term "mortgage" to include deeds of trust.)

Until the mortgage is paid off, the lender has the right to foreclose if you miss mortgage payments. Chapter 7 bankruptcy doesn't change this. (See Section B, below.)

2. Liens on Your House

Bankruptcy won't eliminate liens on your home that were created with your consent or certain non-consensual liens (such as tax liens or mechanics' liens). If you've pledged your home as security for loans other than your mortgage—for example, you took out a home equity loan or second mortgage—or a creditor such as the IRS has recorded a lien, those creditors, too, have claims against your home.

Who Gets What From the Sale of a Home in Bankruptcy?

Mortgage lenders and priority lienholders get paid first…

…then you get the amount of your homestead exemption…

…then other lienholders (if any proceeds are left over)…

…then unsecured creditors (if any proceeds are left over)

If there is a judgment lien on your home—that is, if a creditor sued you, obtained a court judgment, and recorded a lien at the land records office—you may be able to get rid of the lien entirely without paying a cent

to the lienholder. And, in some states, if your home is sold in bankruptcy, you will get your homestead amount ahead of secured creditors holding judicial liens.

You can get rid of the lien created by a judgment by filing a "motion to avoid a judicial lien." You may also be able to get rid of some liens by filing a separate lawsuit in bankruptcy court. We explain these procedures in Ch. 5.

3. Keeping Your House

Even if you keep up with your mortgage payments, you may still lose your house unless a homestead exemption protects your equity (the difference between what your house is worth and what you owe the mortgage lender and all lienholders). If you were to sell your home today, without filing for bankruptcy, the money raised by the sale would go first to the mortgage lender to pay off the mortgage, then to lienholders to pay off the liens, and finally to pay off the costs of sale and any taxes due. If anything were left over, you'd get it.

How a Homestead Exemption Works: An Example

This chart applies only to those states that use dollar-amount homestead exemptions. If your state bases the homestead exemption on acreage, your lot size will determine whether or not you keep your home. (See Section C, below.)

This example is based on a $100,000 home with a $35,000 homestead exemption.

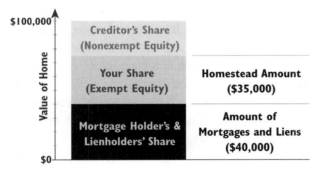

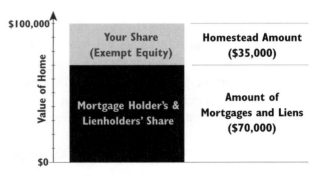

If you have nonexempt equity in your home, the trustee will sell your home. Here, the homeowner's total equity is $60,000 ($100,000 [value of home] – $40,000 [mortgages and liens against home]). The homeowner's nonexempt equity is $25,000 ($60,000 [total equity] – $35,000 [homestead exemption]). Because the homeowner has $25,000 in nonexempt equity, the trustee will sell the house and use the nonexempt equity to pay unsecured creditors.

If you don't have any nonexempt equity, the trustee won't sell your home. Here, the homeowner's total equity is $30,000 ($100,000 [value of home] – $70,000 [mortgages and liens against home]). The homeowner doesn't have any nonexempt equity ($30,000 [total equity] – $35,000 [homestead exemption] = less than zero).

If you file for bankruptcy and the trustee has your house sold, the creditors will get paid in pretty much the same order, with one big difference. In a bankruptcy sale, whatever is left after the mortgages, liens, costs of sale, and taxes have been paid goes not to you, but to your unsecured creditors—unless a homestead exemption entitles you to some or all of it.

As a practical matter, the trustee won't bother to sell your house if there will be nothing left over for your unsecured creditors. Thus, the amount of your homestead exemption often determines whether or not you'll lose your home in bankruptcy.

If the bankruptcy trustee calculates that there would be leftover proceeds from a sale of your home to give to your unsecured creditors, the trustee will, almost always, take your home and sell it at auction to get that money, unless you can pay the trustee the amount that your unsecured creditors would get from the sale.

Section C of this chapter, below, explains how to figure out whether a homestead exemption will prevent the trustee from selling your home.

B. If You're Behind on Your Mortgage Payments

If you're behind on your mortgage payments but want to keep your house, your first strategy should be to negotiate with the lender and try other nonbankruptcy alternatives discussed in this section. (This section deals only with secured debts created by agreements. For a discussion of eliminating judicial liens on your home, see Ch. 5.)

Chapter 7 bankruptcy's automatic stay won't prevent foreclosure if you fall behind on your mortgage payments. At most, it will postpone foreclosure for a month or so.

About the only way Chapter 7 bankruptcy can help you hang on to your home is by discharging your other debts, which will allow you to devote more money to getting current on your mortgage to prevent foreclosure.

⚠ **If foreclosure is looming.** If you think foreclosure is a real possibility, immediately see a lawyer who is experienced in debt problems. Don't wait until the last minute. The lawyer may need several months to negotiate

with the lender or plan for an eventual bankruptcy so that you get the most out of it. The lawyer can also look for other ways to challenge the foreclosure—for example, because the lender didn't give you proper notice of the foreclosure or because of problems with the original mortgage.

1. Negotiating With the Lender

If you've missed a few mortgage payments, most lenders will be willing to negotiate. What the lender agrees to will depend on your credit history, the reason for your missed payments, and your financial prospects.

> **EXAMPLE:** Doug misses a few house payments because he had a car accident and couldn't work for two months. It looks like he'll be back to work soon. The bank will probably work out a deal with Doug rather than immediately move to foreclose.

2. Mortgage Workouts

Not all lenders are receptive to informal negotiations. Many will require you to proceed through a more formal process called a "mortgage workout." A workout is an agreement you make with the lender that changes how you pay the delinquency on your mortgage or otherwise keeps you out of foreclosure.

Over the years, lenders have learned that high foreclosure rates can cost them lots of money. As a result, they are often willing to renegotiate payment terms with borrowers in default in order to avoid foreclosure. If you think you have the resources to keep your home by renegotiating the payments, you should consider talking to the lender about a workout.

Here are some workout options your lender might agree to:

- Pay back missed payments over a few months. For example, if your monthly payment is $1,000 and you missed two payments ($2,000), the lender might let you pay $1,500 for four months.
- Reduce or suspend your regular payments for a specified time, then add a portion of your overdue amount to your regular payments later on.
- Extend the length of your loan and add the missed payments at the end.

- For a period of time, suspend the amount of your monthly payment that goes towards the principal, and require payment of interest, taxes, and insurance only.
- Refinance your loan to reduce future monthly payments.
- Let you sell the property for less than you owe the lender and waive the rest of the loan. This is called a "short sale."

Before you contact the lender about a workout, you should prepare information about your situation, including:

- an assessment of your current financial situation and a reasonable budget for the future
- a plan to deal with other essential debts, such as utility bills and car payments
- a hardship letter explaining why you fell behind on your mortgage (emphasize the most sympathetic aspects of your situation)
- information about the property and its value, and
- information about your loan and the amount of the default.

You should also find out whether your mortgage is insured by the Federal Housing Administration (FHA) or the U.S. Department of Housing and Urban Development (HUD). Borrowers with these types of mortgages have some special rights that those with "conventional" mortgages don't have.

It's a good idea to look for a nonprofit debt counselor or lawyer who has experience with mortgage workouts to help you. For information on HUD-approved counseling agencies in your area, call 800-569-4287 (TDD 800-877-8339). It's best to start the workout negotiations as early as possible

Be advised that workouts are not for everyone—nor will lenders always agree to a workout. Be realistic about your situation before you approach the lender. If it is likely that you will lose your house anyway because of your dire financial situation or because you have other pressing financial problems, it doesn't make sense to keep paying your mortgage through a workout.

3. If the Lender Starts to Foreclose

If your debt problems look severe or long-lasting, the lender may take steps toward foreclosure. Again, if you're faced with foreclosure and want to keep your house, consult a lawyer who specializes in debt

problems to work out a strategy to save your home.

In most cases, the lender will "accelerate" the debt or "call the loan" before foreclosure actually occurs. This means you must pay the entire balance immediately. If you don't, the lender will foreclose.

EXAMPLE: Don and Louise bought a $100,000 home by putting $20,000 down and getting an $80,000 mortgage. Their monthly house payments are $900. After paying on the mortgage for several years, they've recently missed three consecutive payments. The bank accelerated the loan and is now demanding the entire $76,284 balance. Because they can't pay it, the bank begins foreclosure proceedings.

Foreclosure can take anywhere from three to 18 months, depending on where you live and what type of loan you have. During this time, you have several options:

- Sell your house. If you don't get any offers that will cover what you owe your lender, a short sale may be possible.
- Get another lender to give you a loan that pays off all or part of the first loan and puts you on a new schedule of monthly payments. If the original lender has accelerated the loan, you'll need to refinance the entire balance of the loan to prevent foreclosure. If the lender hasn't accelerated the loan, however, you can prevent foreclosure simply by paying the missed payments, taxes, and insurance, plus interest. But be careful when deciding whether to refinance. In many cases, refinancing hurts more than it helps. Many lenders have figured out clever ways to hide high costs and fees in refinancing deals.
- If you are at least 62 years old and have significant equity in your home, consider getting a reverse mortgage. You can use this type of loan to pay off the lender and receive some money each month, based on your equity. (For more on reverse mortgages, see Section D1, below.)
- File for Chapter 13 bankruptcy if you can't come up with the needed money in a lump sum right away and you can propose a feasible repayment plan. Chapter 13 bankruptcy allows you to "cure the default"—make up missed payments over time and make the regular payments as they come due. (See Section D2, below.)

4. Defenses to Foreclosure

You may be able to delay or stop the foreclosure if you have defenses to paying the mortgage or if the lender has not properly followed state foreclosure procedures. If you think you might have a defense to foreclosure, contact a lawyer immediately. Some possible defenses are:

- **Interest rate that violates state or federal law.** Some states limit how much interest can be charged on a loan. Federal law prohibits lenders from making deceptive or false representations about the loan and from charging high closing costs and fees. If your interest is very high or your lender didn't tell you the truth about the terms of your loan, consult a lawyer.
- **Violations of the federal Truth in Lending law.** The federal Truth in Lending law requires the lender to give you certain information about your loan before you sign the papers. If the lender failed to provide this information, you may be able to cancel the mortgage. But this applies only to loans not used to purchase your home.
- **Home improvement fraud.** If you got ripped off by a home improvement contractor, you may be able to cancel a loan for that work.
- **Failure to follow foreclosure procedures.** Each state requires lenders to follow specific procedures when foreclosing on a home. If the lender doesn't follow these rules (for example, by not giving proper notice of the foreclosure or failing to inform you of certain rights), you may be able to delay the foreclosure.

Finding defenses to foreclosure is not easy, nor is raising these defenses in court. If you think you might have a defense to foreclosure, consult an attorney. (See Ch. 10 for information on how to find a good lawyer.)

5. If Foreclosure Is Unavoidable

If you've exhausted the suggestions described above and it looks like foreclosure is inevitable, be aware that losing your home in a bankruptcy sale will often be a better deal than losing it in a foreclosure sale, for two reasons.

First, a forced sale of your home in bankruptcy is supervised by the bankruptcy trustee, who will want to sell the house for as much as possible. In a foreclosure sale, the foreclosing creditor will try to get only a high enough price to cover the amount due on the mortgage. If you have a homestead exemption on the house, the more the house is sold for, the more you get for your homestead exemption. (See Section C, below.)

Second, debtors are rarely entitled to the homestead exemption if the house is sold through foreclosure. In a bankruptcy sale, however, you are entitled to your homestead amount in cash, if there are proceeds left over after the secured creditors have been paid off.

In the end, what happens to your home will be up to the bankruptcy trustee. If there is enough equity in your home to produce some money for your unsecured creditors, the trustee will sell it, pay off the mortgage and other lienholders, give you your exemption, and distribute the rest. If there is not enough equity to generate money for your unsecured creditors, the trustee will release his or her authority over the home (called abandonment) and let the mortgage holder pursue any remedies available to it, which will most likely result in foreclosure if you owe an arrearage.

Getting Your Equity Out of Your Home

Many people who fall behind on their mortgage payments discover that the longer they can stall the foreclosure, the longer they can live rent free in the home. In essence, this is a backdoor way to get a sizable chunk of equity out of your home without selling it or taking it into bankruptcy. For example, if your mortgage payment is $1,500 a month and you manage to live in the house for a year without making your payments, you've pulled the equivalent of $18,000 equity out of your home. And, if you have no equity in your home to begin with, that $18,000 is gravy.

There are, of course, downsides to this behavior, such as having a foreclosure on your credit record and possibly incurring tax liabilities. Still, people in economic crisis mode can find at least some comfort in not having all of their equity swallowed up in a foreclosure or losing it in a bankruptcy because of a low or nonexistent homestead exemption.

C. Will the Trustee Sell Your Home?

If you file for Chapter 7 bankruptcy, the fact that you've kept up on your house payments may not protect you from losing it. The trustee will still have your house sold if the sale will produce some cash to pay your unsecured creditors (and you aren't able to pay the trustee an equivalent amount). If the sale won't produce cash, the trustee will not take the house.

Whether the sale will produce cash depends on two factors:

- whether you have any equity in your home, and
- if so, whether that equity is exempt.

Use the Homeowners' Worksheet that follows to figure out the answers to these questions. (You'll find a tear-out copy of the worksheet in Appendix 2.)

Part I: Do You Have any Equity in Your Home?

Line 1: Estimated market value of your home

Estimate how much money your home could produce in a quick as-is sale. The trustee will often use this value in deciding whether to sell the home. However, the trustee may instead use the full market value of your property. So, if there is significant difference between the quick sale value and full value of the home, use the latter to be on the safe side. To get a rough idea of what your home is worth in either type of sale, ask a realtor what comparable homes in your neighborhood have sold for. Or look in newspaper real estate sections. You can also generate rough home valuation estimates from websites such as www.domania.com, www.homegain.com, or www.realtor.com.

Line 2: Costs of sale

Costs of sale vary, but they tend to be about 5% of the sales price. The trustee does not technically have to subtract the costs of sale in determining whether to take your home, but most do. (If you want to err on the side of caution, put "0" in this blank.) On Schedule A, you can note that you are deducting the costs of sale from the property's fair market value.

Line 3: Amount owed on mortgages and other loans

Enter the amount needed to pay off your mortgage and any other loans that are secured by the home as collateral. If you can't come up with a reasonably reliable estimate, contact each lender and ask how much is necessary to cancel the debt.

Line 4: Amount of liens

Enter the amount of all liens recorded against your home (other than liens created by mortgages and home equity loans). Liens are claims against your home that have been recorded with the land records office. The three most common types of liens are tax liens, mechanics' liens, and judgment liens. Tax liens can be recorded against your home by the county, state, or federal government for failure to pay property, income, or other taxes. People who do work on your home and claim that you didn't pay them what you owe can record mechanics' or materialmen's liens against your home. And judgment liens can be recorded by anyone who has sued you and won.

If you think there might be liens on your home, visit the county land records office. Tell the clerk you'd like to check your title for liens. The clerk should direct you to an index (often on microfiche) that lists all property in the county by the owner's last name. Next to your home should be a list of any liens recorded against it.

Line 5 = Line 2 + Line 3 + Line 4

Add up the total costs that would have to be paid if you were to sell your home.

Line 6 (Your Equity) = Line 1 – Line 5

If Line 1 is more than Line 5, subtract Line 5 from Line 1, and put the result on Line 6. For bankruptcy purposes, this is your equity in the property—that is, the amount the house will sell for, less the amount that will have to be paid to others from the proceeds.

If the amount on Line 5 is more than the amount on Line 1, you have no equity; you can stop here. There will be no reason for the trustee to take your home in bankruptcy—once all of the liens and mortgage(s) are paid off, there would be nothing left to distribute to your unsecured creditors.

If you do have equity, go on to Part II to determine how much of it is protected by an applicable exemption.

The Trustee's Power to Eliminate Liens—And How It May Cost You Your House

When property has liens on it for more than the property is worth, it is "oversecured." If a trustee sells oversecured property, there won't be enough money to pay off all liens, which means that one or more lienholders will be left with nothing. And there certainly won't be any money to pay unsecured creditors, who get paid only after all lienholders have been paid off.

The trustee's job is to find money to pay unsecured creditors, so the trustee usually won't bother selling an oversecured home. The picture changes, however, if the trustee can knock out enough lienholders to free up some equity. Once that happens, it might make sense to sell the home.

All states have laws that specify how to record, or "perfect," a lien. The rules are complex, and lienholders often make mistakes. Trustees may challenge liens they believe were recorded improperly. By successfully knocking out liens, the trustee can turn an oversecured property into one that, when sold, will yield some cash after the remaining lienholders get their share. When the trustee eliminates enough liens to make equity available (above the amount of your homestead exemption), it may be worth the trustee's time and effort to sell your home.

Legal research note. If you do legal research about equity and homestead exemptions, note that the word "equity" has multiple meanings. "Unencumbered" equity is the value of your home, minus the mortgage and the liens you can't get rid of. (That's what we mean when we say equity.) Then there's "encumbered" equity, which is the value of your home minus only the mortgage. Sometimes courts refer to encumbered equity simply as "equity."

Part II: If You Have Equity, Is It Protected by an Exemption?

This part assumes that, in Part I, you found that you have some amount of home equity. Here in Part II,

we'll determine how much of that equity you can claim as exempt—that is, how much of it you're entitled to keep.

Before you can figure out how much of your equity is protected by an exemption, you must determine which set of exemptions to use. The new bankruptcy law imposes strict residency requirements on filers seeking to use a homestead exemption. Filers who don't meet these requirements may have to use the exemptions of the state where they used to live—and will be subject to a $125,000 limit on the amount of equity they can exempt. (Because most states protect less than $125,000 in home equity, this cap won't affect the majority of filers.) The purpose of these rules is to prevent filers from moving to another state to take advantage of its better homestead protection.

Here are the rules:

- If you bought your home at least 40 months ago, you can use the homestead exemption of the state where your home is.
- If you bought your home at least two years ago, you can use the homestead exemption of the state where your home is. However, if you bought your home within the last 40 months, your homestead exemption is capped at $125,000, unless you bought the home with the proceeds from the sale of another home in the same state.
- If you bought your home within the last two years, then you must use the homestead exemption of the state where you were living for the better part of the 180-day period that ended two years before your filing date. And you are still subject to the $125,000 limit.

EXAMPLE 1: Four years ago, John and Susie retired and moved from Massachusetts to Maine, where they bought a home. If they file for bankruptcy in Maine, they can use Maine's exemptions, because they have lived there for more than 40 months. If they had moved to Maine three years ago, they would still be able to use Maine's exemptions, but their homestead exemption would be capped at $125,000. Maine's homestead allowance for joint filers who are at least 61 years old is $140,000, so John and Susie would lose $15,000 worth of homestead exemption ($140,000 exemption minus the $125,000 cap).

EXAMPLE 2: After moving from Vermont to Boston in 2006, Julius and his family buy a fine old Boston home for $700,000. After borrowing heavily against the home because of financial reversals, Julius files for bankruptcy in early 2008, when he owns $250,000 in equity. Although the Massachusetts homestead exemption of $500,000 would cover Julius's equity, he can claim only $125,000 of that exemption because he moved to Massachusetts from another state within the last 40 months.

EXAMPLE 3: Eighteen months ago, Fred moved from Florida to Nevada, where he purchased his current home with $400,000 he received from an inheritance. Fred files for bankruptcy in his current home state of Nevada. Because Fred lived in Florida for two years prior to moving to Nevada, he must use Florida's homestead exemption—and because Fred hasn't lived in Nevada for 40 months, his exemption is subject to the $125,000 cap. The cap imposes an extreme penalty on Fred. Florida offers an unlimited homestead exemption, while Nevada's homestead exemption is $350,000. Because of the cap, however, Fred can protect only $125,000 of his equity, which means that the trustee will undoubtedly sell his home, give Fred his $125,000, and use the rest to pay off his unsecured creditors.

EXAMPLE 4: Joan moves from Maryland to Vermont, where she buys a home. Less than two years after moving, Joan files for bankruptcy. Because Joan was living in Maryland for years before moving to Vermont, she must use either Maryland's state homestead allowance or the federal homestead allowance (Maryland gives filers a choice of exemptions). Maryland provides no homestead exemption at all, but the federal homestead exemption is approximately $20,000. It isn't hard for Joan to figure out that she should use the federal exemption system.

If you are filing in a state that allows you to choose between the state and federal exemption lists, you are always entitled to use the federal exemptions, regardless of how long you have lived in the state. The federal homestead exemption allows you to protect about $20,000 in equity, and married couples can double that amount. Homeowners filing in states that allow a choice will probably be better off using the federal exemptions, unless the state homestead exemption exceeds $20,000.

The cap also applies to filers who commit certain types of misconduct. No matter how long you have lived in the state where you are filing, your homestead exemption will be capped at $125,000 if you have been convicted of a felony which demonstrates that your bankruptcy filing is abusive, you owe a debt arising from a securities act violation, or you have committed a crime or an intentional, willful, or reckless act that killed or caused serious personal injury to someone in the last five years. The court may decide to lift the cap if it finds that the homestead exemption is reasonably necessary for you to support yourself and your dependents.

Line 7: Does the available homestead exemption protect your kind of dwelling?

Only three states do not have a homestead exemption. If you are using the exemptions in one of these three states, enter $0 on Line 11.

States With No Homestead Exemption		
Maryland	New Jersey	Pennsylvania

For all other states, check the table in Appendix 1 to see if your type of dwelling is protected. Some types of dwellings may not be covered, including:

- **Mobile homes.** Most states specifically include mobile homes in their homestead exemptions. Other states include any "real or personal property used as a residence." This would include a trailer, mobile home, or houseboat, as long as you live in it. Some states don't detail the types of property that qualify as a homestead. If your mobile home does not qualify for a homestead exemption, it would be protected only by the exemption for a "motor vehicle."
- **Co-ops or condominiums.** Some homestead laws specifically cover co-ops or use language that says the exemption protects "any property used as a dwelling."
- **Apartments.** Most homestead statutes *do not* protect apartments, though a few do.

Homeowners' Worksheet

Part I. Do you have any equity in your home?

1. Market value of your home ....$_____
2. Costs of sale (if unsure, put 5% of market value)...........$_____
3. Amount owed on all mortgages....................................$_____
4. Amount of all liens on the property ....$_____
5. Total of Lines 2, 3, and 4 ....$_____
6. Your equity (Line 1 minus Line 5).. $_____

If Line 6 is less than zero, skip the rest of the worksheet. The trustee will have no interest in selling your home.

Part II. Is your property protected by an exemption?

7. Does the available homestead exemption protect your kind of dwelling?
   - ☐ Yes. Go on to Line 8.
   - ☐ No. Enter $0 on Line 11, then continue on to Line 12.
8. Do you have to file a "declaration of homestead" to claim the homestead exemption?
   - ☐ Yes, but I have not filed it yet. (You should. See instructions.)
   - ☐ Yes, and I have already filed it.
   - ☐ No
9. Is the homestead exemption based on lot size?
   - ☐ No, it is based on equity alone. Go to Line 10.
   - ☐ No, it is unlimited (true only of the exemptions for Washington, DC).

If you are using the D.C. exemptions, you can stop here. Your home is protected.

   - ☐ Yes. The exemption is limited to property of _____ acres.

If your property is smaller than this limit, you can stop here. Your home is protected. If your property exceeds this limit, see the instructions.

   - ☐ Yes, but there is an equity limit as well. The exemption is limited to property of ___ acres.

If your property is smaller than this limit, go on to Line 10. If your property exceeds this limit, see the instructions.

10. Do you own the property with your spouse in "tenancy by the entirety"?
    - ☐ Yes. *See the instructions and talk to a bankruptcy attorney to find out whether your house is fully protected.*
    - ☐ No. Go on to Line 11.
11. Is the dollar amount of the homestead exemption limited?
    - ☐ Yes. Enter the dollar limit here: $_____
    - ☐ No dollar limit. *You can stop here. Your home is protected.*
12. Can you protect more equity with a wildcard exemption?
    - ☐ Yes. Enter the dollar amount here: $_____
    - ☐ No.
13. How much of your equity is protected?
    Total of Lines 11 and 12: $_____

If the total exceeds $125,000 and you are subject to the $125,000 cap on homestead exemptions, write "$125,000" on this line. See the instructions for more information.

14. Is your home fully protected?
    Subtract Line 13 from Line 6: $_____

If this total is a negative number, your home is protected. If this total is a positive number, you have unprotected equity in your home, and the trustee might choose to sell it (or allow you to keep it in exchange for cash or exempt property roughly equal in value to your unprotected equity).

If your type of dwelling is not covered, enter $0 on Line 11.

If it is unclear whether your type of dwelling is covered by the available homestead exemption, you may need to do some legal research. (See Ch. 9 for help getting started.)

Line 8: Do you have to file a "declaration of homestead" to claim the exemption?

States That May Require a Declaration of Homestead		
Alabama	Montana	Utah
Idaho	Nevada	Virginia
Massachusetts	Texas	Washington

To claim a homestead exemption in Virginia, you must have a declaration of homestead on file with the land records office for the county where the property is located when you file for bankruptcy. The other states on this list vary in what they require and when. If you are using exemptions for one of these states, the safest approach is to file a declaration of homestead.

Requiring you to record a declaration before you can get the benefit of a homestead exemption may violate the bankruptcy laws. (*In re Leicht*, 222 B.R. 670 (1st Cir. BAP 1998).) Regardless of the legalities, however, you will be best served by filing your declaration of homestead before you file for bankruptcy.

Other states allow (but do not require) you to file a homestead declaration in certain circumstances. In Texas, for example, you may file a homestead declaration to claim protection for property you own but are not currently living in.

EXAMPLE: John and Doris live in Texas. They have retired and have decided to rent out their spacious country home and live in an apartment closer to town. They can still claim their country home as their homestead by recording a declaration of homestead with the land records office in the county where their country home is.

In some states, a "declared" homestead offers additional protection in situations other than bankruptcy. Also, if you own more than one piece of real estate, some states allow a creditor to require you to file a declaration of homestead to clarify which property you are claiming as your homestead.

Line 9: Lot Size: Does the homestead exemption limit the size of the lot you can protect?

Most states place a limit on the value of property you can claim as your homestead exemption, but a few states have no such limits. Find out what kind of homestead exemption system your state uses by looking at the lists below.

Unlimited Homestead Exemption
District of Columbia

If you are lucky enough to be using the District of Columbia exemptions, congratulations: You can skip the rest of this chapter. Your home is not at risk in a Chapter 7 bankruptcy.

Homestead Exemption Based on Lot Size Only		
Arkansas	Kansas	Texas
Florida	Oklahoma	
Iowa	South Dakota	

In these states, you can easily determine whether your home is exempt. The homestead exemption is based simply on acreage. Look in Appendix 1 for the acreage limitation for the state. (In Oklahoma, if you use more than 25% of the property as a business, the one-acre urban homestead exemption cannot exceed $5,000.)

If your property is less than the maximum allowable acreage, your home is fully protected. You can skip the rest of this chapter

If your property exceeds the maximum allowable acreage, the trustee will sell the excess acreage if you have any equity in it (unless you are able to buy it back from the trustee for a negotiated amount). Enter $0 in Line 11 of the worksheet.

Homestead Exemption Based on Lot Size and Equity		
Alabama	Michigan	Nebraska
Hawaii	Minnesota	Oregon
Louisiana	Mississippi	

These states use the size of your lot and the amount of your equity to determine whether your home is exempt. First look in Appendix 1 for the state acreage limitation; enter it on Line 9.

If your property exceeds the maximum allowable acreage, the trustee will want to sell the excess acreage (or get the equivalent in value from you) if you have enough equity in it.

If your lot size is within the allowed acreage, your exemption is determined by the equity amount limit. Proceed to Line 10.

Homestead Exemption Based on Equity Alone

Federal exemptions, and Alaska, Arizona, California, Colorado, Connecticut, Georgia, Idaho, Illinois, Indiana, Kentucky, Maine, Massachusetts, Missouri, Montana, Nevada, New Hampshire, New Mexico, New York, North Carolina, North Dakota, Ohio, Rhode Island, South Carolina, Tennessee, Utah, Vermont, Virginia, Washington, West Virginia, Wisconsin, Wyoming

---

If the state homestead exemption is based on equity alone, or if you are using the federal exemptions, go to Line 10.

Line 10: Do you own the property with your spouse in "tenancy by the entirety"?

If you are married and live in the right state, you may be able to exclude your home from your bankruptcy estate—which means you can keep it, no matter how much equity you own or how large your state's homestead exemption is—if you own it with your spouse in tenancy by the entirety.

Tenancy by the entirety (TBE) is a form of property ownership available to married couples in about half of the states, some of which have laws that prohibit TBE property from being sold to pay debts that are owed by only one spouse. This rule has no dollar limit—if this type of law applies, you can keep TBE property, regardless of its value. Some state laws also protect personal property owned in tenancy by the entirety, such as checking accounts.

To qualify for this type of property protection, all of the following must be true:

- You are married.
- You are filing for bankruptcy alone, without your spouse. If you file jointly, your TBE property is not protected.
- All of the debts you are trying to discharge are yours alone; none are debts that you owe jointly with your spouse.
- You and your spouse own property in one of these states:

Delaware, District of Columbia, Florida, Hawaii, Illinois, Indiana, Maryland, Massachusetts, Michigan, Missouri, North Carolina, Ohio, Pennsylvania, Rhode Island, Tennessee, Vermont, Virginia, Wyoming

---

Unlike exemptions, tenancy by the entirety protection depends on the law of the state where your property is, not where you live. For example, if you and your spouse live in Minnesota but own a condo in Florida as tenants by the entirety, Florida law protects your condo from being seized to pay debts owed by only one spouse, even though Minnesota law offers no such protection.

- You and your spouse own the home as tenants by the entirety. In some of these states, the law presumes that married people own their property as tenants by the entirety, unless they specify that they wish to own it in some other way (as joint tenants, for example).

If you meet these five criteria, this protection could be extremely valuable to you. You may want to see a bankruptcy attorney to figure out the best way to take full advantage of it.

Line 11: Is the dollar amount of the homestead exemption limited?

Most states place a dollar limit on the homestead exemption—for example, New York allows you to exempt up to $50,000 in equity, while Massachusetts allows you to exempt up to $500,000. If the state homestead exemption you're using works this way, write down the amount of equity the exemption protects on Line 11. If your state allows you to use the federal exemptions and you plan to do so, write down the federal exemption instead. (See Appendix 1 for these figures.)

In some states, if you own your home with your spouse and you file jointly for bankruptcy, you can each claim the full homestead exemption amount (this is called "doubling"). Other states limit both spouses to the one exemption. When you look at Appendix 1, check carefully to see whether doubling is prohibited. If the chart doesn't mention doubling one way or the other, assume that you and your spouse can double.

Line 12: Can you protect more equity with a wildcard exemption?

Some states allow you to add a wildcard exemption to the amount of your homestead exemption. Although these wildcard amounts are usually small, they might be enough to tip the balance in favor of keeping your home.

Wildcard Exemptions That Can Be Applied to Real Estate	
California, System 2	$1,000
Connecticut	1,000
Georgia	600
Indiana	4,000
Kentucky	1,000
Maine	400
Maryland (This is the only exemption you can use on your home; there is no homestead exemption.)	5,500
Missouri	1,250
New Hampshire	8,000
Ohio	400
Pennsylvania	300
Vermont	400
Virginia (if you're a disabled veteran)	2,000
West Virginia	800
Federal	975

Other states have wildcard exemptions, but they apply only to personal property.

If the state where you're filing appears on this list, write the wildcard exemption amount on Line 12. If your state doesn't have a wildcard exemption that you can use for real estate, leave this line blank.

Line 13: How much of your equity is protected?

Add Lines 11 (the state homestead exemption available to you) and 12 (any wildcard exemption you can add to your homestead exemption). This is the amount of home equity you can protect in bankruptcy. If you aren't subject to the $125,000 cap (which generally applies if you have moved from one state to another in the 40 months before filing for bankruptcy—see the instructions for Part II, above), write this amount on Line 13.

If you are subject to the $125,000 cap, it might limit the amount of equity you can protect. If the total of Lines 11 and 12 doesn't exceed $125,000, it doesn't matter—the cap won't affect you, and you can write the total amount on Line 13. However, if the total is more than $125,000 and the cap applies, you can protect only $125,000 in equity. Even if your state law would otherwise allow you to take a larger exemption, you'll be limited to $125,000, and this is what you should write on Line 13.

Line 14: Is your home fully protected?

Subtract Line 13 from Line 6, and enter the total on Line 14. If you generate a negative number, all of your home equity should be protected by the applicable exemptions, if your estimates are correct. The trustee probably won't have your home sold, because there would be no proceeds left over (after your mortgage holder was paid off and you received your exempt amount of equity) to pay your unsecured creditors.

If, however, you generate a positive number, your equity exceeds the applicable exemption—in other words, you have unprotected equity in your home. If your estimates are right, the trustee can force the sale of your home to pay off your creditors, unless you can pay the trustee the value of your unprotected equity (perhaps by selling property that would otherwise be exempt). From the proceeds of the sale, your secured creditors will be paid the amounts of their mortgages, liens, and so forth; you will receive the amount of your exemption; and your unsecured creditors will get the rest.

If you have unprotected equity, you shouldn't file for Chapter 7 bankruptcy if you want to keep your house. The trustee will almost certainly sell your home, unless you can come up with the cash to keep it. You'll probably fare better—and hold on to your home longer—by using your equity to help pay off your debts, either directly or through a reverse mortgage, or to fund a Chapter 13 reorganization plan. Some of these strategies are discussed in Section D, below.

This worksheet is for estimate purposes only. If this worksheet shows that your equity is equal to or near the maximum amount of your state's homestead exemption, take note: The trustee can challenge the value you claim for your home—and may determine that it's worth more than you think. If this happens, and the trustee concludes that your equity exceeds the amount you can claim as exempt, the trustee may seek to have your home sold. If your estimates show that you might be close to the exemption limit, get some advice from an experienced bankruptcy lawyer.

D. Ways to Prevent the Loss of Your House in Bankruptcy

If you have nonexempt equity in your home and would lose it if you filed for bankruptcy, you probably want to explore other options. We outline some of them here, but you should ask an experienced bankruptcy lawyer for help.

1. Reduce Your Equity Before Filing for Bankruptcy

If you can reduce your nonexempt equity before you file, you may be able to pay off your other debts and avoid bankruptcy. And, if you later file for bankruptcy, you may be able to save your home.

There are two ways to reduce your equity:
- borrow against the equity, or
- sell part ownership of your house.

You can use the proceeds to buy exempt property or to pay off other debts.

Consult a local bankruptcy lawyer before reducing your equity. If you do file for bankruptcy after reducing your equity, the bankruptcy court in your area might view your actions as an abuse of the bankruptcy process and dismiss your bankruptcy petition. This is more likely if you reduced your equity within two years of filing. How to stay out of trouble is discussed in Ch. 3, Section D.

a. Borrow Against Your Equity

If you borrow against your equity, you won't reduce your overall debt burden. You may be able to lower your overall monthly bills, however, if you can get a lower interest rate or a longer-term equity loan to pay off short-term, high-interest debts. You can also fully deduct the interest you pay on home equity loans from your income taxes.

Be careful when you shop for a loan. Many lenders offer loans with very high rates to people in financial trouble. Although you may be desperate to save your home, taking out another loan with high interest rates or high costs and fees will only get you into deeper financial trouble. Also, be extra cautious about taking out a loan with a balloon payment (a large lump sum of money due at the end of the loan term). If you can't make the balloon payment when it comes due, you will lose your home. Most people can't come up with $25,000, $50,000, or $100,000 all at once. You might be able to refinance your home to pay off the balloon, but don't count on it.

b. Sell Some of Your Equity

Another way to protect your equity is to sell some of your house. By owning your home jointly with someone else, your equity is reduced.

Selling a portion of your equity may appeal to you—after all, what you need now is more cash, not another monthly bill. Perhaps a friend or relative would be willing to buy a half share in your home. If you pursue this strategy, you may need to wait a year after the sale before filing for bankruptcy. Otherwise, the bankruptcy trustee might void the sale, especially if it appears that you gave your friend or relative a bargain on the price.

Even a year may not be sufficient in some courts if the judge views your actions as defrauding your creditors. (See Ch. 3, Section D.) Be sure to consult a local bankruptcy attorney who is aware of local practice before you try this.

Also, think long and hard about whether you want to share ownership of your home. A co-owner can sell his or her interest, force a sale of the property, die and leave it to someone else, and so on. Again, consult a bankruptcy lawyer before you sell. This strategy can be fraught with complications and traps for the uninformed.

c. Consider a Reverse Mortgage

If you are at least 62 years old and you own substantial equity in your home, a reverse mortgage may be just the ticket. When you get a reverse mortgage, you borrow against your home equity and receive monthly payments that you can use to fix your home, pay down your debts, or pay them off altogether. This allows you to use your equity without getting deeper into the type of debt trouble that might cause you to lose your home.

You don't have to pay a reverse mortgage loan back during your lifetime—instead, the loan is collected after your death, from your home equity. Of course, this also means that your heirs are less likely to inherit your home (it may have to be sold to pay off the reverse mortgage). For more information about reverse mortgages, visit the website of the Federal Trade Commission, at www.ftc.gov/bcp/conline/pubs/homes/rms.pdf.

2. If You File for Bankruptcy

If you do file for Chapter 7 bankruptcy, you may be able to keep the trustee from selling your house through one of the following methods:

- **Offer to substitute cash for the amount of non-exempt equity.** You may be able to convince the trustee not to sell your house if you can come up with as much cash as would be available from the proceeds to pay unsecured creditors. You may be able to raise the cash by selling exempt property or using income you earn after you file.

  EXAMPLE: The Robertsons have approximately $5,000 of nonexempt equity in their home. All of their home furnishings are exempt. After discussing the matter with the trustee, they sell three pieces of furniture and a camera for a total of $1,800 and scrape together $2,700 extra cash from income earned since they filed for bankruptcy. They offer the cash to the trustee as a substitute for the nonexempt equity. The trustee accepts the money, because the creditors will end up with almost as much as they would have gotten if the home were sold—and the trustee will be spared the hassle of selling the Robertsons' home.

- **File for (or convert to) Chapter 13 bankruptcy.** Chapter 13 bankruptcy lets you pay your debts out of your income rather than by selling your property. If you file for Chapter 13 bankruptcy, you won't have to give up your home, even if you have nonexempt equity. (However, you will have to pay your unsecured creditors at least the value of your nonexempt property over the life of your plan.) Chapter 13 bankruptcy also permits you to spread out repayments of missed installments, taxes, and late charges on a mortgage. And, if your lender has begun foreclosure proceedings, Chapter 13 bankruptcy can halt them as long as your house hasn't yet been sold. (See Ch. 1, Section E, of this book for more on Chapter 13.)

  You can convert to Chapter 13 bankruptcy any time during a Chapter 7 bankruptcy proceeding. If you miss mortgage payments after you file for Chapter 7 bankruptcy, however, some courts won't let you include them in your Chapter 13 repayment plan. So try to make all payments due after you file for Chapter 7. If the lender won't accept them (because it wants to proceed with foreclosure), save the money so you can make up the payments later. ∎

Secured Debts

This chapter explains how bankruptcy law handles secured debts. In Section A, you'll learn how to tell whether a debt is secured. Section B explains what happens to secured debts in bankruptcy. In Section C, you'll learn about ways to turn secured debts into unsecured ones—and why that's important. Section D explains the choices bankruptcy gives you for dealing with secured debts that can't be turned into unsecured ones. Finally, Section E has step-by-step, do-it-yourself instructions for some simple procedures for handling secured debts. (If you opt for one of the complex procedures, Section E explains the basics, but you'll need the help of a lawyer.)

Along the way, you'll need to learn a bit of peculiar terminology and a few detailed rules, but it's worth it: You might be able to save a lot of money and keep property you'd otherwise lose.

Before we get into the details and the paperwork, here's a brief summary of what's likely to happen to your secured debts and the property that secures them. First, the bad news:

- If you have a mortgage on your home or a home equity loan, bankruptcy won't get rid of it.
- If the government has a lien on your home for unpaid taxes, you can't remove it.

Now, the good news:

- If you have a car loan and you want to keep your car, you may be able to keep it by just paying the car's current replacement value (what you could buy it for, considering its age and condition), rather than the amount due on the loan. (You'll need to come up with this amount in a lump sum. If you can't raise the cash, you'll have to work out a new agreement with the lender or surrender the car and buy a cheaper one. If the car is unreliable or in poor condition, that's probably a good choice. On the other hand, the replacement value may be low enough to warrant paying for the car, despite its condition.)
- If you have a car loan and you decide to give up your car, bankruptcy will eliminate any remaining balance due on the loan.
- If you lost a lawsuit or small claims case, and your opponent recorded a judgment lien on your property for the amount you owe, you can probably get rid of this lien, depending on what you were sued for, whether the property is

exempt, and how much equity you have in the property.

That's the big picture for the most common kinds of secured debts. Now it's time to learn the details about:

- which of your debts are secured
- which secured debts you can turn into unsecured ones (via lien avoidance), and
- how to deal with the debts that remain secured.

➡ **You may be able to skip this chapter.** If you have no secured debts, you won't need the information in this chapter.

A. Secured Debts

A secured debt is linked to a specific item of property, called collateral, that guarantees payment of the debt. If you don't pay, the creditor is entitled to take the collateral. For example, mortgages and car loans are secured debts.

When you fill out your bankruptcy forms, you list all of your secured debts on Schedule D. Keep in mind that there are two kinds of secured debts: those you agree to, such as a mortgage, and those created without your consent, such as a lien against your property recorded by the IRS because you haven't paid your taxes.

1. Liens You Agree To: Security Interests

If you agree to pledge property as collateral—that is, as a guarantee that you will pay a debt—the lien on your property is called a security interest. If you signed a security agreement, it may well have given the creditor the right to take the property (the collateral) if you miss a payment.

Here are some common examples of security interests:

- **Mortgages** (called deeds of trust in some states), which are loans to buy or refinance a house or other real estate. The real estate is collateral for the loan. If you fail to pay, the lender can foreclose.
- **Home equity loans** (second mortgages) from banks or finance companies, such as loans to do work on your house. The house is collateral for the loan. If you fail to pay, the lender can foreclose.

Important Definitions: Liens Created by Secured Debts

Various types of liens are created by secured debts. The type of lien on your property often determines which lien reduction or lien-eliminating procedures you can use.

You may want to skip this list of definitions for now and refer to it when we describe specific kinds of liens.

Security Interests—Liens You Agree To

If you voluntarily pledge property as collateral—that is, as a guarantee that you will pay a debt—the lien on your property is called a security interest. Many written security agreements give the creditor the right to take the property if you miss a payment. The most common types of security interests are the following:

Purchase-money security interests. If you purchase an item on credit and pledge it as collateral for the debt, the lien on the collateral is called a purchase-money security interest. Typical purchase-money secured debts are automobile loans and debts for large furniture purchases.

These kinds of liens cannot be eliminated in bankruptcy. If you want to keep the property, you will either have to honor the original contract and continue making payments, or pay the value of the property up-front to keep the property. (See Section B2, below.)

Nonpurchase-money security interests: If you pledge property you already own as collateral for a loan, the lien is called a nonpurchase-money security interest. If you keep the property—for example, you borrow from a lending company or credit union and pledge your car or stereo equipment as security for the loan—the loan is called *nonpossessory*.

These kinds of liens can be eliminated in bankruptcy if the collateral is exempt and meets the criteria described in Section C2, below.

If you don't retain possession of the property (for instance, if you turn property over to a pawnshop), the loan is called *possessory*. These liens cannot be eliminated in bankruptcy as described in Section C2, below.

Liens Created Without Your Consent

If a creditor gets a lien on your property without your consent, it is called a nonconsensual lien. There are three major types of nonconsensual liens.

Judicial liens. A judicial lien is created against your property by somebody who wins a money judgment in a lawsuit against you, then takes the additional steps necessary to record a lien against your property. If a judicial lien is on exempt property, you can probably eliminate it in bankruptcy, unless it arose out of a mortgage foreclosure. (See Section C2, below.)

Statutory liens. Nonconsensual liens can also be created automatically by law. For example, in most states, when you hire someone to work on your house, the worker or supplier of materials automatically gets a mechanics' lien or materialmen's lien on the house if you don't pay. Liens like these are called statutory liens.

> **EXAMPLE:** Sam's home suffered severe water damage after a pipe burst in the upstairs bathroom. He had the damage repaired at a cost of $4,000. Now, because of unexpected medical bills, he can't pay the plumber and carpenter the last $2,000 he owes them for the work done on the house. The carpenter and plumber have a statutory lien on his house for $2,000.

Tax liens. Federal, state, and local governments have the authority to impose liens on your property if you owe delinquent taxes. Tax liens are usually impossible to eliminate in bankruptcy.

- **Loans for cars, boats, tractors, motorcycles, or RVs.** Here, the vehicle is the collateral. If you fail to pay, the lender can repossess it.
- **Store charges with a security agreement.** Almost all store purchases on credit cards are unsecured. Some stores, however (notably Sears) print on the credit card slip or other receipt that the store "retains a security interest in all hard goods (durable goods) purchased" or make customers sign security agreements when they use their store charge card. For example, if you buy a major appliance on credit, the store may require you to sign a security agreement in which you agree that the item purchased is collateral for your repayment. If you don't pay back the loan, the seller can take the property. (In Vermont, a bankruptcy court has ruled that store charges are unsecured, not secured, under Vermont state law. *In re Oszajca*, 199 B.R. 103 (D. Vt. 1996).)
- **Personal loans from banks, credit unions, or finance companies.** Often you must pledge valuable personal property, such as a paid-off motor vehicle, as collateral.

2. Liens Created Without Your Consent: Nonconsensual Liens

A creditor can, in some circumstances, get a lien on your property without your consent. These are called nonconsensual liens. In theory, a nonconsensual lien gives the creditor the right to force the sale of the property in order to get paid. In practice, however, few creditors force a sale of property, because so much time and expense are involved. Instead, they wait until you sell or refinance the property—when the lien must be paid off to give the new owner clear title to the property.

a. Types of Nonconsensual Liens

There are three major types of nonconsensual liens:
- **Judicial liens.** A judicial lien can be imposed on your property only after somebody sues you and wins a money judgment against you. In most states, the judgment creditor then must record (file) the judgment with the county or state; the recorded judgment creates the lien on your real estate in that county or state. In a few states, a judgment

entered against you by a court automatically creates a lien on the real estate you own in that county—that is, the judgment creditor doesn't have to record the judgment to get the lien.
- **Statutory liens.** Some liens are created automatically by law. For example, in most states, when you hire someone to work on your house, the worker or supplier of materials automatically gets a mechanics' lien (also called a materialmen's lien) on the house if you don't pay. So does a homeowners' association, in some states, if you don't pay your dues or special assessments.
- **Tax liens.** Federal, state, and local governments have the authority to impose liens on your property if you owe delinquent taxes. If you owe money to the IRS or other taxing authority, the debt is secured *only* if the taxing authority has recorded a lien against your property (and you still own the property) or has issued a notice of tax lien and the equity in your home or retirement plan is sufficient to cover the amount of the debt.

b. Property Affected by Such Liens

Identify the property affected by each lien. If you are like most people, the property most likely to be affected by such liens are your house and your car—but not always. Let's look at this by type of lien.
- **Judicial liens.** In every state, a judicial lien affects real estate you own in the county where the lien is recorded or the judgment is entered. In most states, a judicial lien does not cover your personal property.

    However, in some states, a judicial lien also affects your personal property in the county. And that's not the end of it. A judgment creditor can also file the judgment with the state motor vehicles department, imposing a lien on any car, truck, motorcycle, or other motor vehicle you own. You may not know about this lien until the creditor files a claim with the bankruptcy court describing its interest as secured, or until you check with the motor vehicles department.
- **Statutory liens.** Statutory liens affect your real estate.
- **Tax liens.** A lien recorded by a local government for unpaid property tax affects your real estate. Similarly, if your state taxing authority sends you

a bill and you don't contest it or pay it, the state can record a tax lien against your real estate in that state. And, if you don't pay an IRS bill, the IRS can record a Notice of Federal Tax Lien at your county land records office or your Secretary of State's office. While the lien attaches to all of your property, for practical purposes a lien will be valid only if your real estate, retirement account, or bank account contains enough equity to cover the debt.

Secured Debts and Bankruptcy

Bankruptcy eliminates your personal liability for secured debts, but the creditor's lien remains. Sometimes you can take further steps in bankruptcy to eliminate or reduce a lien.

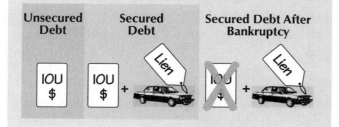

B. What Chapter 7 Bankruptcy Does to Secured Debts

Bankruptcy has a different effect on secured debts than on other kinds of debts, because a secured debt consists of two parts:

- The first part is no different from an unsecured debt: It is personal liability for the debt, which is what obligates you to pay the debt to the creditor. Bankruptcy wipes out your personal liability if the debt is dischargeable. (See Ch. 9.) Once your personal liability is eliminated, the creditor cannot sue you to collect the debt.

- The second part of a secured debt is the creditor's legal claim (lien or security interest) on the property that is collateral for the debt. A lien gives the creditor the right to repossess the property or force its sale if you do not pay the debt. The claim sticks with the property even if you give the property to someone else. Bankruptcy, by itself,

does not eliminate liens. But, during bankruptcy, you may be able to take additional steps to eliminate, or at least reduce, liens on secured property.

EXAMPLE: Mary buys a couch on credit from a furniture store. She signs a contract that states she must pay for the couch over the next year. The contract also states that the creditor (the store) has a security interest in the couch and can repossess it if any payment is more than 15 days late. In this type of secured debt, Mary's obligation to pay the debt is her personal liability, and the store's right to repossess the couch is the lien. Bankruptcy eliminates her obligation to pay for the couch, but the creditor retains its lien and can repossess the couch if she doesn't pay.

You may lose property if you have nonexempt equity. Remember, if your equity in collateral securing a debt is higher than the exemption you can claim in it, the trustee can take the collateral, sell it, pay off the secured creditor, pay you your exemption amount, and distribute the balance to your unsecured creditors. Fortunately, most filers find that they owe more on collateral than it is worth, primarily because of the interest figured into their payments and, in the case of personal property, the depreciation of the property's value over time. In these situations, the trustee has no interest in taking the property—because the proceeds would all go to the secured creditor and nothing would be left to distribute to unsecured creditors—and the filer could use one of the options discussed in this section.

1. Eliminating Liens in Bankruptcy

As mentioned above, there are several steps you can take during bankruptcy to eliminate or reduce liens. But these procedures are neither automatic nor required —you have to request them.

The most powerful of these procedures lets you eliminate (avoid) some types of liens on certain kinds of exempt property without paying anything to the creditor. (See Ch. 3 for a definition of exempt property.) With the lien eliminated, you get to keep the property free and clear without paying anything more to the creditor.

Other procedures let you eliminate a creditor's lien (and keep the property) by paying the creditor either the amount of the lien or the current replacement value of the property, whichever is less.

Finally, you can rid yourself of a lien simply by surrendering the property to the creditor.

The choice of which procedure to use on each item of secured property is up to you.

2. If You Don't Eliminate Liens

If you take no steps to eliminate a lien as a part of your bankruptcy case, the lien will survive your bankruptcy intact, and the creditor will be free to take the property or force its sale. Fortunately, the courts are very liberal about reopening a case to allow a debtor to file a motion to avoid a lien. So if, after your bankruptcy case is over, you discover a lien that you missed while your bankruptcy case was open, don't worry. Reopening a bankruptcy is a routine procedure.

> **EXAMPLE:** After Mary's bankruptcy case is over, she reads this book and realizes that she can avoid a particular lien. She quickly contacts a bankruptcy attorney, who helps her file a motion to reopen her case so she can file her motion to avoid the lien.

If the property is valuable and could be easily resold (an automobile, for example), the creditor will surely repossess the item at the first opportunity unless you agree to keep making payments. (See Section C4, below.) If, however, the property is of little value and not worth the cost of repossessing (such as Mary's couch), the creditor may do nothing; this is called abandoning the property.

If the property is of the type with a "title" or ownership document, such as a house or car, and the creditor does nothing, the lien simply remains on the property until you sell it. At that time, the lien must be paid out of the proceeds of the sale if the buyer wants to have clear title to the property. On the other hand, if the property has no ownership title document, as would be the case with Mary's couch, a computer, or a washer and dryer set, the creditor has no practical way to enforce the lien. In some cases, if the property is declining in value and it is clear that you aren't going to take steps to keep it, the creditor might request the bankruptcy

court's permission to take the property even before the bankruptcy case is over. For example, if you own a new photocopier subject to a security interest and the copier depreciates in value at a fairly steep rate (say 30% a year), the creditor would want it back as soon as possible to maximize the proceeds from its resale.

C. Ways to Deal With Secured Debts in Bankruptcy

There are several ways to deal with secured debts in bankruptcy. Some options are included on the Statement of Intention form; others are not. All but the first option allow you to keep property. These options are explained below, beginning with a description of each option, then going into advantages, disadvantages, restrictions, when it makes sense to use that option, and how it works.

You may want to skim through these options for now, and then refer back to them as you read Section D, below. That section discusses which option is best for specific kinds of property, including houses and cars.

1. Surrender Property

Description. Surrendering secured property simply means allowing the creditor to repossess or take the item or foreclose on the lien. It completely frees you from the debt—your surrender of the property satisfies the lien, and the bankruptcy discharges your personal liability.

Advantage. A quick and easy way to completely rid yourself of a secured debt.

Disadvantage. You lose the property.

Restrictions. None. You can surrender any kind of property to get rid of any kind of lien.

When to use it. For property that you don't need or want or that would cost too much to keep.

How it works. You simply list the property as surrendered on your Statement of Intention and send a copy of the form to the creditor within 45 days after you file for bankruptcy. It's then up to the creditor to contact you to arrange a time to pick up the property. You must make the property available to the creditor within 30 days after the first creditors' meeting. If the creditor never takes the property, it's yours to keep. (This might happen if, for example, the lien is on your household furniture and the furniture is a couple of years old and not worth the cost of picking it up, storing it, and selling it at auction.) Section E1, below, contains step-by-step instructions for surrendering property.

2. Avoid (Eliminate) Liens

Description. Lien avoidance is a procedure by which you ask the bankruptcy court to "avoid" (eliminate or reduce) liens on your exempt property.

How much of a lien can be avoided depends on the value of the property and the amount of the exemption. If the property is entirely exempt or is worth less than the legal exemption limit, the court will eliminate the entire lien and you'll get to keep the property without paying anything. If the property is worth more than the exemption limit, the lien will be reduced to the difference between the exemption limit and either the property's value or the amount of the debt, whichever is less. (11 U.S.C. § 522(f)(2).)

EXAMPLE: A creditor has a $500 lien on Harold's guitar, which is worth $300. In Harold's state, the guitar is exempt only to $200. He could get the lien reduced to $100. The other $400 of the lien is eliminated (avoided).

$500 lien		
	$300	= value of item
	− 200	= exemption amount
	$100	= amount of lien remaining after lien avoidance

Advantages. Lien avoidance costs nothing, involves only a moderate amount of paperwork, and allows you to keep property without paying anything. It is the best and most powerful tool for getting rid of liens.

Disadvantages. Some paperwork is involved. Also, by trying to avoid a lien on exempt property, you may reopen the issue of whether the property is exempt in the first place. This may happen if the property was deemed exempt by default (that is, the property is exempt because the trustee and creditors failed to

timely challenge the debtor's claim of exemption). Some courts have allowed creditors to raise the issue of the property's exempt status at a hearing on a motion to avoid a lien. Other courts have ruled that creditors cannot raise this issue—the property is deemed exempt and the only issue to discuss at the hearing is whether the lien may be avoided.

As a practical matter, motions to avoid a lien are rarely contested.

Restrictions. Lien avoidance has several important restrictions, as follows.

a. Security Interests

A security interest (a secured debt you agree to) can be avoided only if it meets the criteria listed below.

- The lien must be the result of a loan which you obtained by pledging property you already own as collateral. This is called a "nonpossessory, nonpurchase-money security interest."

  That sounds complicated, but it makes sense when you break it down:
  - Nonpossessory means the creditor does not physically keep the collateral you've pledged as collateral. You keep it in your possession; the creditor only retains a lien on it. (In contrast, if you leave your property at a pawn shop to get a loan, that is a possessory security interest—for which this lien avoidance procedure is not available.)
  - Nonpurchase-money means that the money loaned was not the money used to purchase the collateral.
  - Security interest means the lien was created by a voluntary agreement between you and the creditor.

  The most common examples of nonpossessory, nonpurchase-money security interests are home equity loans and personal loans for which a car is pledged as collateral. Unfortunately, as explained below, these two most common types of collateral are not included in the list of eligible property. Consequently, the situations in which you can use this procedure, as a practical matter, are quite limited.

- The property you pledged must be exempt under the exemption you are using. (Remember that residency requirements may limit the exemptions available to you—see Ch. 3, Section C for more information.)
- The collateral you pledged must be any of the following property:
  - household furnishings, household goods, clothing, appliances, books, and musical instruments or jewelry that are primarily for your personal, family, or household use
  - health aids professionally prescribed for you or a dependent
  - animals or crops held primarily for your personal, family or household use—but only the first $5,000 of the lien can be avoided, or
  - implements, professional books, or tools used in a trade (yours or a dependent's)—but only the first $5,000 of the lien can be avoided.

A security interest cannot be removed from real estate or from a motor vehicle unless the vehicle is a tool of your trade. Generally, a motor vehicle is not considered a tool of trade unless you use it as an integral part of your business—for example, if you do door-to-door sales or delivery work. It is not considered a tool of trade if you simply use it to get to and from your workplace, even if you have no other means of commuting.

What Are Household Goods?

Under the new bankruptcy law, household goods are limited to:
- clothing
- furniture
- appliances
- one radio
- one television
- one VCR
- linens
- china
- crockery
- kitchenware
- educational equipment and materials primarily for the use of your minor dependent children
- medical equipment and supplies
- furniture exclusively for the use of your minor children, or your elderly or disabled dependents
- your personal effects (including your wedding rings and the toys and hobby equipment of your minor dependent children) and those of your dependents, and
- one personal computer and related equipment.

Items in the following categories are not considered to be household goods and you cannot avoid liens on them:
- works of art (unless they are by you or a relative)
- electronic entertainment equipment with a fair market value of more than $500 total (not including the one television, one radio, and one VCR listed above)
- items acquired as antiques that have a fair market value of more than $500 total
- jewelry (other than wedding rings) that has a fair market value of more than $500 total, and
- a computer (excluding the personal computer and related equipment listed above), motor vehicle (including a tractor or lawn tractor), boat, or a motorized recreational device, conveyance vehicle, watercraft, or aircraft.

b. Nonconsensual Liens

A nonconsensual lien (a secured debt you didn't agree to) can be avoided only if it meets two criteria:

- The lien must be a judicial lien, which can be removed from *any* exempt property, including real estate and cars. (See Ch.3, Section C.)
- You must be able to claim the property as exempt.

When to use it: Use lien avoidance whenever possible, especially if a lien can be completely wiped out. Even if you don't need the property, you can avoid the lien, sell the property, and use the money for things you do need.

To keep things simple, you may want to avoid liens only on property that is completely exempt. Then the lien will be eliminated entirely and you'll own the property free and clear, without paying anything to the creditor.

Even partial lien avoidance can be beneficial, but sooner or later you'll have to pay the remaining amount of the lien to the creditor if the property has a title document or is being subjected to repossession or foreclosure on what's left of the lien. Most often, you'll have to pay off the lien in a lump sum, but some creditors may be willing to accept installments, especially if you compromise on the value of the lien.

How it works: You request lien avoidance by checking the column "Property is claimed as exempt" on the Statement of Intention and typing and filing a motion. (Complete instructions for preparing and filing a motion to avoid a lien are in Section E2, below.) Although it may sound complicated, lien avoidance is usually a routine procedure that involves just a little time.

Eliminating Judicial Liens on Oversecured Property

To determine whether you can eliminate a judicial lien, apply this simple formula. Add the following items:

- all consensual liens on the property (for example, a mortgage and home equity loan)
- all tax liens, and
- your exemption amount.

If the total of all these items is greater than the value of the property, then you can completely eliminate judicial liens on the property. The Judicial Lien Worksheet, below, will help you do the math. Here are a few sample calculations:

EXAMPLE A

Value of property.......... $200,000
Mortgage..... 100,000
Second mortgage....... 20,000
Exemption....... 10,000
TOTAL....................... 130,000
Amount available for judicial liens.................. 70,000
Amount of judicial lien...... 30,000

RESULT: Lien cannot be eliminated

EXAMPLE B

Value of property.......... $200,000
Mortgage..... 150,000
Second mortgage....... 20,000
Exemption....... 10,000
TOTAL....................... 180,000
Amount available for judicial liens.................. 20,000
Amount of judicial lien...... 30,000

RESULT: $10,000 of lien can be eliminated $20,000 of lien cannot be eliminated

EXAMPLE C

Value of property.......... $200,000
Mortgage.... 160,000
Second mortgage...... 40,000
Exemption...... 10,000
TOTAL....................... 210,000
Amount available for judicial liens............................0
Amount of judicial lien..... 30,000

RESULT: Judicial lien can be completely eliminated

One more point to remember: For the purposes of bankruptcy's lien avoidance provisions, judicial liens get the lowest priority, behind consensual liens and tax liens, regardless of when the liens were perfected and regardless of what state law says. So, in Example C above, it would not matter if the $30,000 judgment lien was created before or after the $40,000 second mortgage: The judicial lien can be eliminated either way.

Judicial Lien Worksheet

1. Value of your home..._____

2. Amount of first mortgage ...._____

3. Amount of other mortgages and home equity loans ....._____

4. Amount of tax liens ...._____

5. Amount of mechanics' liens ...._____

6. Total of Lines 2 through 5 ...._____
   (Total of all liens that are not judicial liens)

   *If Line 6 is greater than Line 1, you can stop here—you can
   eliminate all judicial liens. Otherwise, go on to Line 7.*

7. Line 1 minus Line 6. ...._____
   This is the amount of equity you can protect with an exemption.

8. **Exemption Amount** ...._____

   *If Line 8 is greater than Line 7 you can stop here —you can
   eliminate all judicial liens. Otherwise, go on to Line 9.*

9. Line 7 minus Line 8..._____
   This is the amount of the judicial liens that you can't eliminate.

10. **Amount of judicial liens**.. _____

    *If Line 9 is greater than Line 10, you can stop here — you cannot
    eliminate judicial liens from this property.
    Otherwise, go on to Line 11.*

11. Line 10 minus Line 9. ...._____
    This is the portion of the judicial lien that you can eliminate.
    (Line 9 is the portion of judicial lien you cannot eliminate.)

3. Redeem Property

Description. In bankruptcy, you have the right to "redeem" property, which involves buying it back from the creditor rather than having the creditor take it and sell it to someone else. You pay the creditor the property's current replacement value (what you would have to pay a retail vendor for that type of property, considering its age and condition), usually in a lump sum.

In return, the creditor delivers title to you in the same manner as if you had completely performed on the original agreement. You then own the property free and clear.

> **EXAMPLE:** Susan and Gary owe $500 on some household furniture with a replacement value of $200. They can keep the furniture and eliminate the $500 lien by paying the creditor the $200 within 30 days after the first creditors' meeting.

Advantage. Redemption is a great option if you owe more than the property is worth. The creditor must accept the current replacement value of the item as payment in full. If you and the creditor are unable to agree on the replacement value of the property, the court will decide the issue in a proceeding called a "valuation" hearing. (Ch. 3, Section C, explains how to figure out the replacement value of various types of property.)

Disadvantage. For most debtors, redemption will require an immediate lump sum payment of the value of the item. It may be difficult for you to come up with that much cash on short notice. You can try to get the creditor to voluntarily accept your redemption payments in installments, but courts cannot require a creditor to accept installment payments.

Restrictions. You have the right to redeem property only if all of the following are true:

- The debt is a consumer debt. This means it was incurred "primarily for a personal, family, or household purpose." This includes just about everything except business debts.
- The property is tangible personal property. Tangible property is anything you can touch. A car, furniture, a boat, a computer, and jewelry are all examples of tangible property. Stocks are intangible. The property must also be personal property, which simply means it can't be real estate.
- The property is either:
  - claimed as exempt (exempt property is explained in Ch. 3, Section C), or
  - abandoned by the trustee. A trustee will abandon property that has little or no nonexempt value beyond the amount of the liens. The trustee may notify you of the abandonment or may simply wait for your discharge to be granted, at which time the property is deemed to have been abandoned. Either way, once the property is abandoned, you can redeem it by paying the secured creditor its replacement value. When you fill out your bankruptcy papers, if you know you'll want to redeem an item of property if the trustee abandons it, check the redeem column on Form 8, Statement of Intention. If you haven't done this and the trustee abandons the property, you may have to amend your Statement of Intention. Call the trustee and find out. (Ch. 7 explains how to amend a form.)

When to use it. Use redemption only if you owe more than it would cost to purchase the property and lien avoidance is not available. Redemption usually makes sense for keeping small items of household property, because raising money for the lump sum payment probably will not be that difficult.

Redemption can also be used for automobiles, which are not eligible for lien avoidance and are likely to be repossessed if a lien remains after bankruptcy and you don't agree to keep making payments. If the creditor won't agree to installment payments, however, raising the cash necessary to redeem an automobile may be difficult.

How it works. You and the creditor must agree on the value of the property, then draft and sign a redemption agreement. Agreeing on the replacement value may take a little negotiation, although retail values are readily available for most cars that are in decent condition. Also, sometimes you can get the creditor to agree to accept payments in installments by agreeing to a higher value. Whatever you agree to, put it in the redemption agreement. See Section E3, below, for sample agreements and full instructions.

How to Value Your Car

The best website to check for a used car's retail value (which is its replacement value) is the National Auto Dealers Association, www.nadaguides.com. The site posts an average resale value for particular cars, which will usually be sufficient proof of the vehicle's value. You can also check the Kelley Blue Book (www.kbb.com) for the value of cars in various conditions. You'll notice that older cars in poor condition are not valued by these sites. For instance, if your car has serious body damage or an expensive, looming mechanical failure (such as a transmission that needs to be replaced), you can reasonably place a value of $0 on the vehicle and negotiate from there.

4. Reaffirm a Debt

Description. When you reaffirm a debt, both the creditor's lien on the collateral and your personal liability under the Reaffirmation Agreement survive bankruptcy intact—often, just as if you never filed for bankruptcy. You and the creditor draw up an agreement that sets out the amount you owe and the terms of the repayment. In return, you get to keep the property as long as you stay current on your payments.

If you default on your payments, the creditor can repossess the collateral. You can also be held liable for the difference between what the property is resold for and the unpaid amount of the agreement. This is called a "deficiency balance." Nearly all states permit deficiency balances for most types of property. About half of the states, however, don't allow them on repossessed personal property if the original purchase price was less than a few thousand dollars.

You can cancel a Reaffirmation Agreement by notifying the creditor before either of the following, whichever occurs later:

- the date of your discharge, or
- 60 days after you filed the Reaffirmation Agreement with the bankruptcy court (this often happens at the discharge hearing). (11 U.S.C. § 524(c)(2).)

If your case is already closed, however, you will not be able to switch to the other options listed in this chapter.

Advantages. Reaffirmation can be used when lien avoidance and/or redemption are unavailable or impractical. It provides a sure way to keep property, as long as you abide by the terms of the Reaffirmation Agreement.

Disadvantages. Because reaffirmation leaves you personally liable, there is no way to "walk away" from the debt, even if the property becomes worthless or you simply decide you no longer want it. You'll still be legally bound to pay the agreed-upon amount even if the property is damaged or destroyed. And because you can't file for Chapter 7 bankruptcy again until eight years have passed since your earlier bankruptcy discharge, you'll be stuck with the debt.

> **EXAMPLE:** Tasha owns a computer worth $900. She owes $1,500 on it. She reaffirms the debt for the full $1,500. Two months after bankruptcy, she spills a soft drink into the disk drive and the computer is a total loss. Now, she has not only lost the computer, but, because she reaffirmed the debt, she still has to pay the creditor $1,500.

Restrictions. Reaffirmation can be used on any kind of property and any kind of lien, but the creditor must agree to the terms of the reaffirmation. If you are not represented by an attorney, the court must approve the agreement as well.

The court can disapprove the agreement if it appears that the agreement would be an undue hardship on you. The court will presume that an undue hardship exists if you won't have enough income left over, after deducting your expenses, to make the required payments. In this situation, you will have to overcome the presumption of undue hardship—by showing that you can afford to pay for the property—at the discharge hearing scheduled by the court. Even if you are represented by an attorney, the court will have to review and approve your agreement if your income and expenses demonstrate that you won't be able to make the payments.

When to use it. Because of the disadvantages of reaffirmation, you should use it only if redemption and lien avoidance are unavailable or impractical.

Use reaffirmation primarily for property you can't live without—and only if you have good reason to believe you'll be able to pay off the balance.

For some types of property, such as automobiles or your home, reaffirmation may be the only practical way to keep the item. Also, reaffirmation can be a sensible way to keep property that is worth significantly more than what you owe on it.

If you do decide to reaffirm, try to get the creditor to accept less than the full amount you owe as full payment of the debt. (This doesn't apply when you reaffirm your mortgage.) As a general rule, you should never reaffirm a debt for more than what it would cost you to replace the property.

How it works. You and the creditor agree to the terms of the reaffirmation in a written Reaffirmation Agreement, which is filed with the court. If you are representing yourself, you must appear at a hearing—before you receive your discharge—where the judge will review the agreement and decide whether it is in your best interests or it would impose an undue hardship. If you want to reaffirm a debt in order to keep the collateral, make sure you keep current on your payments so you can stay on the creditor's good side. If you fall behind, the creditor has the right to demand that you get current before agreeing to a reaffirmation contract, but you usually have some room to negotiate.

A sample Reaffirmation Agreement appears at the end of the chapter. The agreement includes a number of disclosures and warnings that are required by the new bankruptcy law. These provisions are intended to put you on notice of how much you'll be paying overall, the interest rate, and your liability to pay the debt in full, even if something happens to the collateral. In Part D of the agreement, you must explain why you are reaffirming the debt and provide information on your income and expenses, so the court can determine whether the agreement creates an undue hardship for you.

You Can No Longer Retain Property Unless You Reaffirm or Redeem

Under the old bankruptcy law, many courts allowed debtors to both discharge a secured debt and keep the collateral, as long as they stayed current on their payments. However, the new bankruptcy law makes clear that you must redeem or reaffirm the debt if you want the bankruptcy court to protect your right to keep the collateral. If you fail to redeem or reaffirm the debt by the deadline—30 days after the creditors' meeting—the creditor is entitled to take back the collateral.

EXAMPLE: Joanie signed a five-year car note on her 2003 Mercedes S Class. After making payments for three years, she files for Chapter 7 bankruptcy. She still owes $18,000 on the note. If she signs a Reaffirmation Agreement within 45 days after her creditors' meeting, she can keep the car as long as she continues making her $750 monthly payments. If she surrenders the car as part of her bankruptcy case, she will discharge her $18,000 liability on the car note. If, however, she tries to keep the car without reaffirming or redeeming, the creditor has a right to repossess the car.

Although the creditor has a legal right to repossess collateral for a secured debt, it might not choose to exercise that right. If the collateral isn't worth much on the open market, the creditor may prefer to continue receiving your payments than to take and resell the property. The more the collateral is worth, however, the more likely the creditor is to repossess and sell it at auction. You can always approach the creditor to see whether it will agree in advance to let you keep the property without reaffirming or redeeming the debt. If you don't reach an agreement, however, you risk repossession, even if you faithfully make your payments each month.

Some state laws add another twist: In some states, a creditor is prohibited from taking collateral if you are current on the payments, even though bankruptcy law would allow it to do so. If you want more information, consult a bankruptcy lawyer. (See Ch. 10 for tips on finding and working with an attorney.)

5. Pay Off the Lien Later in a Follow-Up Chapter 13 Bankruptcy

Description. You can file what some bankruptcy practitioners call a "Chapter 20" bankruptcy—that is, filing for Chapter 13 bankruptcy immediately after completing a Chapter 7 bankruptcy. You use the Chapter 13 bankruptcy to deal with any liens remaining after your Chapter 7 case has wiped out your personal liability. And, if the lien exceeds the value of the property, you can often get the lien fully discharged by simply paying the current replacement value of the item, rather than the full amount of the lien.

You can do this only if the Chapter 13 plan lasts at least four years past the date when you filed for Chapter 7 bankruptcy. The new bankruptcy law prohibits you from receiving a Chapter 13 discharge within four years of filing a Chapter 7 case in which a discharge was granted.

> **EXAMPLE:** Fred has a $20,000 lien on his car, which has a replacement value of $10,000. He files for Chapter 7 bankruptcy on April 1, 2007, and decides not to reaffirm or redeem the debt. The $20,000 debt is discharged in his Chapter 7 case, but the lien remains—which means the creditor still has the right to repossess his car. Before the repossession takes place, Fred files for Chapter 13 bankruptcy, proposes a four-year repayment plan to deal with the lien, and gets the lien reduced to the car's replacement value ($10,000). If the judge approves his plan, Fred will be able to keep the car and pay a lot less for it, over a longer period of time, than he would have had to pay if he'd reaffirmed the loan in his Chapter 7 bankruptcy.

Because this book covers Chapter 7 bankruptcies only, space does not permit us to give a full explanation of how to do a successful follow-up Chapter 13 case. For more information, see *Chapter 13 Bankruptcy: Repay Your Debts*, by Stephen Elias and Robin Leonard (Nolo).

Advantage. Filing a follow-up Chapter 13 case allows you to pay off remaining liens over time, even if the creditor is demanding immediate payment.

Disadvantage. This strategy requires you to file for Chapter 13 bankruptcy, which means you must fill out another set of bankruptcy forms and pay another filing fee. This strategy also requires you to give up all of your disposable income over at least the next four years to the bankruptcy trustee. Staying involved in the bankruptcy system for four more years means that it may take that much longer before you can begin to rebuild your credit.

Restrictions. There are no restrictions on the use of the Chapter 20 technique, except that you'll have to wait four years for your discharge. To file for Chapter 13 bankruptcy, however, your unsecured debts cannot exceed $307,675 and your secured debts cannot exceed $922,975.

When to use it. This remedy makes sense only if lien avoidance is not available or redemption is not practical. It can be particularly useful for dealing with liens on property you need to keep, if you cannot raise the lump sum necessary to redeem the property.

How it works. You file your Chapter 13 petition as soon as you get your Chapter 7 discharge—or even earlier, if necessary, to prevent the creditor from taking the property. Then you work with the bankruptcy court trustee to set up an appropriate Chapter 13 payment plan.

6. Lien Elimination Techniques Beyond the Scope of This Book

Deep in the recesses of the Bankruptcy Code are other procedures for eliminating certain kinds of nonconsensual liens. 11 U.S.C. § 522(h) gives a debtor the power to use a wide range of lien avoidance techniques available to the bankruptcy trustee. The techniques are found in Sections 545, 547, 548, 549, 553, and 724(a) of the Bankruptcy Code. These liens include:

- nonjudicial liens securing the payment of penalties, fines, or punitive damages, and
- nonconsensual liens that were recorded or perfected while you were already insolvent or within the 90 days before you filed for bankruptcy.

To use these procedures, you'll need the help of a bankruptcy attorney.

D. Choosing the Best Options

Now it's time pick the best option for each of your secured debts. If an item has more than one lien on it, you might use different procedures to deal with each lien. For example, you might eliminate a judicial lien on exempt property through lien avoidance and redeem the property to satisfy a purchase-money security interest.

Schedule D and the Statement of Intention Form

When you file for Chapter 7 bankruptcy, you must list on Schedule D all creditors who hold secured claims. (See Ch. 6.) And, you must inform the bankruptcy trustee and your affected creditors what you plan to do about the property that secures those debts. You do this by filing a form called the Chapter 7 Individual Debtor's Statement of Intention and mailing a copy of the form to each creditor listed on it.

There are line-by-line instructions on how to fill out these forms in Ch. 6. To make the decisions requested on the Statement of Intention, though, you'll need the information from this section. Here are some timing tips:

- Try to decide what to do with each item of secured property before you file for bankruptcy.
- The Statement of Intention is due within 45 days after you file for bankruptcy but is often filed right after you file your other papers.
- The law requires you to carry out your stated intentions within 30 days after the creditors' meeting—if you miss the deadline, your collateral will no longer be protected by the automatic stay, which leaves the creditor free to take it.

If you change your mind after you file your Statement of Intention, you can amend the form using the instructions in Ch. 7, Section B.

Don't pay too much. If the option you're considering would require you to pay more than the current market value of the property you want to keep, it's a bad deal. There are usually ways you or a lawyer can keep any item of secured property by paying no more than its current replacement value.

1. What Property Should You Keep?

Be realistic about how much property you will be able to afford to keep after bankruptcy. Face the fact that you may not be able to keep everything, and decide which items you can do without. These questions will help you decide whether an item is worth keeping:

- How important is the property to you?
- Will you need the property to help you make a fresh start after bankruptcy?
- How much would it cost to keep the property? (This will depend on the procedure you use.)
- Would it be more expensive to redeem the property or to replace it?
- If you're considering reaffirming the debt, will you realistically be able to make the payments after bankruptcy?
- If you're considering surrendering your property and buying a replacement item, will you need a loan to purchase it? If so, will you be able to get such a loan after bankruptcy?

EXAMPLE 1: Fran bought a sports car two years ago for $16,000. Now Fran is unemployed but is about to start a new job. She still owes $13,000 on the car, and it is currently worth $10,000. Although she likes the car, she can't come up with the $10,000 in cash to redeem it, and she doesn't want to remain personally liable for the $13,000 debt. If Fran is willing to lower her standards a little, she can buy a reliable used car to get her to work and back for about $3,000. She decides to surrender the car. Now she will have to buy the lower-priced car, but she may have difficulty getting a loan for it.

EXAMPLE 2: Joe owns a six-year-old Toyota with a replacement value of $2,000. It is security for a debt of $2,500. If Joe files for bankruptcy, he will probably be able to keep the car by paying the secured creditor only $2,000 (the value of the car). Joe decides it's worth paying that amount. He knows the car is reliable and will probably last another six years. He also believes it would be a hassle to find a car of comparable quality at that price, and it's his only means of getting to work. And, after some realistic budgeting, Joe concludes that making the payments after bankruptcy will not wreck his budget. He has probably made the right decision.

EXAMPLE 3: Now assume that Joe makes a different decision: Instead of redeeming the debt for $2,000, he decides to discharge the $2,500 debt and continue making payments to the creditor. Joe figures that the creditor would rather receive the payments than go through the expense and hassle of repossessing a car that would sell for only $2,000. If Joe is wrong, however, he will have no recourse against the possession.

2. Real Estate or Motor Vehicles

Liens on real estate or cars involve special considerations.

a. Your Home

Filing for bankruptcy when you own your home is discussed in Ch. 4, but here's a reminder: If you own your home and are behind on the payments, Chapter 13 bankruptcy will allow you to keep your house if your proposed repayment plan is feasible. Chapter 7 bankruptcy, on the other hand, does not offer a procedure for catching up on unpaid mortgage payments ("curing an arrearage"). Unless you can become current on your payments—using property or income you acquire after your filing date—Chapter 7 will not stop foreclosure.

If you are current on your mortgage, however, Chapter 7 bankruptcy might help you eliminate other liens on your house. To determine whether any liens can be eliminated, total up the amount of your mortgage(s), applicable homestead exemption, and other liens on your home. If the total exceeds the value of your home, you can probably eliminate some of the liens.

You can use lien avoidance to get rid of judicial liens if they conflict with your homestead exemption. And you can do this without a lawyer's help. (Lien avoidance is explained in Section C2, above; the necessary forms are in Section E2, below.)

With the help of a lawyer, you might be able to eliminate other types of liens, including "unrecorded" tax liens and liens for penalties, fines, or punitive damages from a lawsuit. (See Section C6, above.)

b. Your Car

Because repossessed motor vehicles can easily be resold, if a lien remains on your car, the creditor will probably act quickly to either repossess it or force its sale (unless you stay current on your payments and the creditor wouldn't gain much by taking and selling the car). Still, if you intend to keep your car, you should deal with liens on it during bankruptcy.

If your automobile is exempt, any judicial liens on it can be eliminated through lien avoidance. (See Section C2, above.)

The purchase-money security interest held by the seller can be dealt with only through redemption or reaffirmation. Raising the lump sum amount necessary for a redemption is your best option. (See Section C3, above.) If that is not possible, your only realistic option is to reaffirm the debt (see Section C4, above), unless you are willing to gamble that the creditor will let you keep the car as long as you make your payments.

If your automobile falls within the tool of trade exemption, you can use lien avoidance for any non-purchase money liens on the vehicle. (See Section C2, above.)

3. Exempt Property

Property that is exempt under the laws available to you (remember, you can use your current state's exemptions only if you have lived there for at least two years before filing—see Ch. 3, Section C) might also be subject to a lien. Under the new bankruptcy law, there are four ways to deal with liens on exempt property:
- give the property back (if there's no property, there's no lien)
- get rid of the lien in a lien avoidance action
- redeem the property, or
- reaffirm the debt.

If you are keeping the property, you should use lien avoidance whenever possible to eliminate judicial liens and nonpurchase-money security interests. Use redemption whenever the lien exceeds the replacement value of the property and you can raise the cash necessary to buy the property back.

If you can't raise the lump sum necessary for redemption, you'll have to either reaffirm the debt or attempt to pay off the lien outside of bankruptcy. The option you choose will depend on how anxious the creditor is to repossess the item. If the property is of little value, you can probably get away with informally paying off the lien. Property of greater value, however, may require reaffirmation. Remember never to agree to pay more than it would cost to replace the property.

Also, remember that even if you can get liens wiped out, you still may not get to keep the property if your equity in the property is worth more than your exemption amount. The trustee will want to sell the property, pay you your exemption amount, and distribute the remaining portion among your unsecured creditors. (See Section 4, below, for what happens to nonexempt property, including equity that exceeds the available exemption.)

In this situation, the only way to hold on to the property is to buy it back from the trustee. How much you will have to pay depends on several factors, but keep in mind this basic rule: The amount you offer to the trustee has to leave your unsecured creditors no worse off than they would have been had the trustee sold the property to somebody else.

EXAMPLE: Mindy has a $1,000 asset on which she can claim a $500 exemption. There is a $200 judicial lien on the asset. Mindy cannot avoid the lien, because it does not "impair" her exemption. If the trustee sold the property, Mindy would get her $500 exemption, the lienholder would get $200, and the remaining $300 would go to Mindy's unsecured creditors. If Mindy wanted to buy the property from the trustee, she'd have to offer $500: $200 for the lienholder and $300 for her unsecured creditors.

As you can see, the amount you have to offer the trustee will vary from case to case, depending on the amount of the liens, the amount of your exemption, and whether you or the trustee can eliminate the liens on the asset. You can consult with the trustee to work out the particulars.

4. Nonexempt Property

If you want to keep nonexempt property, your options are limited. You can:

- redeem the property if the trustee abandons it (abandoning property means that the trustee releases it from the bankruptcy estate; a trustee will abandon property when there is not enough value in it to justify selling it to raise money for the unsecured creditors)
- reaffirm the debt, or
- risk trying to pay off the lien informally, outside of bankruptcy.

a. Property Worth More Than the Debt

If your nonexempt property is worth significantly more than the liens on it, you probably won't have a chance to keep it. The trustee is likely to sell the property, pay off the liens, and distribute the rest of the proceeds to your unsecured creditors.

EXAMPLE: Elena pledges her $4,000 car as security for a $900 loan. The $900 lien is the only lien on her car, and only $1,200 of the $4,000 is exempt. If Elena files for bankruptcy, the trustee will take the car, sell it, pay off the $900 lien, give Elena her $1,200 exemption, and distribute the rest of the proceeds to Elena's creditors.

If the trustee does not take the property and you want to keep it, your best bet is probably to reaffirm the debt. This will prevent the creditor from taking the property. (See Sections C4, above and E4, below, for complete instructions.)

b. Property Worth Less Than the Debt

If the property is worth less than the liens on it, the trustee will probably abandon the property.

EXAMPLE: When Stan bought his $500 sofa on credit from the Reliable Furniture Co., he pledged the sofa as security. Since then, the sofa has declined in value to only $100, but he still owes $250 on it. The trustee will abandon the property, because selling it would yield no proceeds for the unsecured creditors.

The trustee might also abandon property if the collateral has more than one lien on it and the combined total of all the liens exceeds the value of the collateral. In this case, the creditors with the lowest-priority liens are called undersecured creditors. (State and federal law determine the priority of the liens. Most of the time, the most recent lien is the lowest-priority lien, but certain types of liens always have priority over others.)

EXAMPLE: Aaron's car is currently worth $3,000. He pledged his car as collateral for the loan he used to buy it. That loan has a remaining balance of $2,200. He later pledged his car for two personal loans on which he owes $500 each. In addition, there is a judgment lien against his car for $1,000. The total balance of all liens is $4,200.

In this situation, the original $2,200 purchase-money loan is fully secured, and so is the first personal loan for $500. The other $500 loan is secured only by the remaining $300 in equity, so it is an undersecured claim. And there is nothing securing the $1,000 judgment.

When the trustee abandons the property, you have the right to redeem it at its current replacement value. This is your best option, if you can come up with the necessary lump sum payment. Redemption eliminates all liens on the property. (See Section C3, above.)

If you can't come up with the lump sum necessary to redeem the property, reaffirmation is the only sure way to keep it. If you are willing to gamble that the creditor won't take the property as long as you keep up your payments, you always have the option of simply continuing to pay off the lien outside of bankruptcy. Whatever option you choose, just remember not to pay more than the property is worth.

Planning reminder. Once you've filed for bankruptcy, a creditor cannot legally take your property unless the court lifts the automatic stay or you miss the deadlines for dealing with your secured debts (see Ch. 2). It's much easier to hold on to property in the first place than it is to get it back after the creditor repossesses it. So, if you have some exempt property that a creditor is about to take and you haven't filed for bankruptcy yet, you may want to file right away to prevent the seizure.

Getting Back Exempt Property Repossessed Just Before Bankruptcy

If, during the 90 days before you filed for bankruptcy, a secured creditor took exempt property that would qualify for either lien avoidance or redemption, you may be able to get the property back. But you must act quickly, before the creditor resells the property. If the creditor has already resold the property, you probably can't get it back. Repossessed cars are usually resold very quickly, but used furniture may sit in a warehouse for months.

Legally, the creditor must give back such property because the repossession is an illegal preference, which means that the property is still part of the bankruptcy estate. (11 U.S.C. §§ 542, 543, 547; see Ch. 2, Section A.) In practice, however, the creditor won't give the property back unless the court orders it (which usually means you'll need the help of a lawyer) or unless you make a reasonable offer of cash for the item.

Assuming you don't want to hire a lawyer, you probably won't be able to get an item back unless you talk the creditor into allowing you to redeem it or reaffirm the debt. The creditor might prefer to have cash in hand rather than used property sitting in a warehouse. If you plan to avoid the lien on the exempt item and not pay anything, however, the creditor probably won't turn over the property unless forced to by court order.

Whether hiring a lawyer is worth the expense to get back an exempt item so you can avoid the lien depends on how badly you need the property and what you'll save through lien avoidance. Compare what it would cost to redeem the property or buy replacement property. If those options are cheaper, or you decide you can get along without the property, don't bother with the court order.

E. Step-by-Step Instructions

Once you decide what to do with each item of secured property, you must list your intentions on your Statement of Intention, file that form, and then carry out the procedures within 30 days after the creditors' meeting. (See Ch. 6 for instructions.)

1. How to Surrender Property

If you plan to surrender any secured property, here's how to proceed.

Step 1: When you fill out your Statement of Intention, state that you are surrendering the property that secures the debt. (Instructions for completing the form are in Ch. 6.)

Step 2: The creditor, who will receive a copy of the Statement of Intention form, must make arrangements to pick up the property. It's not your responsibility to deliver. But you can call your creditors, explain the situation, and ask if they want the property back. If they don't, great—you don't have to worry about it anymore. If they do pick it up, get a receipt. (See sample receipt below.)

Receipt for Surrender of Property

1. This receipt certifies that ___[name of repossessor (print)]___ took the following item(s): _(List items)___

   _____

   _____

   _____

   on ___[date]___, 20__, because of debt owed to [name of creditor (print)].

2. [Name of repossessor (print)] is an authorized agent of [name of creditor (print)].

   Signed: __[Your signature]_____

   Dated: _____

   Signed: __[Repossessor's signature]____

   Dated: _____

---

2. How to Avoid Liens on Exempt Property

To avoid a lien, you claim the property as exempt on Schedule C, file a separate request (motion) with the bankruptcy court, and formally serve the motion on the creditor by mail.

You request lien avoidance by typing and filing a motion. It is simple and can be done without a lawyer. In most courts, you must file your motion with the court within 30 days after you file for bankruptcy. But some courts require it to be filed before the creditors' meeting. Check your local rules.

What goes in your motion papers depends on the kind of lien you're trying to get eliminated. Refer to Section C2, above, to determine whether or not lien avoidance is possible and, if so, what kind of lien you want the court to avoid. Read Subsection a, below, if you're dealing with a nonpossessory nonpurchase money security interest, and Subsection b, below, if you want to avoid a judicial lien. Subsection c, below, discusses tax liens, but that isn't a do-it-yourself procedure.

a. Nonpossessory, Nonpurchase-Money Security Interests

You will need to fill out one complete set of forms for each affected creditor—generally, each creditor holding a lien on that property. Sample forms are shown below. Some courts have their own forms; If yours does, use them and adapt these instructions to fit.

Checklist of Forms for Motion to Avoid Nonpossessory, Nonpurchase-Money Security Interest

☐ Motion to Avoid Nonpossessory, Nonpurchase-Money Security Interest

☐ Notice of Motion to Avoid Nonpossessory, Nonpurchase-Money Security Interest

☐ Order to Avoid Nonpossessory, Nonpurchase-Money Security Interest

☐ Proof of Service by Mail

Step 1: If your court publishes local rules, refer to them for time limits, format of papers, and other details of a motion proceeding.

Step 2: Type the top half of the pleading form (where you list your name, the court, the case number, and so on, following the examples shown below. This part of the form is known as the "caption." It is the same for all pleadings.

Step 3: If you're using a computer to prepare the forms, save the caption portion and reuse it for other pleadings. If you're using a typewriter to prepare the forms, stop when you've typed the caption and photocopy the page you've made so far, so you can reuse it for other pleadings.

Step 4: Using one of the copies that you just made, start typing again just below the caption and prepare a Motion to Avoid Nonpossessory, Nonpurchase-Money Security Interest, as shown in the example.

Step 5: Most courts require you only to file the motion with the court and serve the creditor with a notice explaining that the lien will be avoided by default if the creditor doesn't respond and request a hearing. (These are colorfully called "scream or die" motions—see the sample Motion to Avoid Judicial Lien, below, for language you can use instead of a formal notice if your district follows this procedure.) Because motions to avoid liens are usually pretty straightforward and are usually granted, many creditors don't bother to respond. If they do, however, either you or the creditor will have to schedule a hearing.

Step 6: If a hearing is required, call the court clerk and give your name and case number. Say you'd like to file a motion to avoid a lien and need to find out when and where the judge will hear arguments on your motion. Under some local rules the clerk will give you a hearing date; ask for one at least 31 days in the future, because you must mail notice of your motion to the creditor at least 30 days before the hearing (unless local rules state differently).

Write down the information. If the clerk won't give you the information over the phone, go to the bankruptcy court with a copy of your motion filled out. File that form and schedule the hearing. Write down the information about when and where your motion will be heard by the judge.

If there will be a hearing, prepare a Notice of Motion that lists the date, time, and place of the hearing. (See the sample Notice of Motion to Avoid Nonpossessory, Nonpurchase-Money Security Interest.) If you are filing in a district that requires a hearing only if the creditor requests one, use the language in the sample Notice of Motion and Motion to Avoid Judicial Lien, below, to give the creditor proper notice of this procedure.

Step 7: Prepare a proposed Order to Avoid Nonpossessory, Nonpurchase-Money Security Interest. This is the document the judge signs to grant your request. Specify exactly what property the creditor has secured in the space indicated in the sample. You can get this information from the security agreement you signed. Make two extra copies, and take them with you to the hearing if there is one. The court's local rules may require you to file the proposed order with the rest of your motion papers.

Step 8: Prepare at least two Proofs of Service by Mail, one for each affected creditor and one for the trustee. These forms state that a friend or relative of yours, who is at least 18 years old and not a party to the bankruptcy, mailed your papers to the creditor(s) or the trustee. Fill in the blanks as indicated. Have your friend sign and date the form at the end as shown on the sample. See "How to Serve the Creditor," below, for more information.

Step 9: Make at least three extra copies of all forms.

Step 10: Keep the Proofs of Service. Have your friend mail one copy of the Motion, Notice of Motion, and proposed Order to each affected creditor and the trustee.

Motion to Avoid Nonpossessory, Nonpurchase-Money Security Interest

UNITED STATES BANKRUPTCY COURT

_____ DISTRICT OF _____

In re)
) [Set forth here all names including
) married, maiden, and trade names used
) by debtor within last 8 years]
)   Debtor(s)   )   Case No. _____
)
)   Chapter 7
Address _____)
)
Employer's Tax Identification (EIN) No(s). [if any]: _____
)
Last four digits of Social Security No(s): _____)

MOTION TO AVOID NONPOSSESSORY, NONPURCHASE-MONEY SECURITY INTEREST

1. Debtors _____[your name(s)]_____, filed a voluntary petition for relief under Chapter 7 of Title 11 of the United States Code on _____[date you filed for bankruptcy]_____.

2. This court has jurisdiction over this motion, filed pursuant to 11 U.S.C. § 522(f), to avoid a nonpossessory nonpurchase-money security interest held by _____[name of lienholder]_____ on property held by the debtor.

3. On or about _[date you incurred the debt]_, debtors borrowed $ _[amount of loan]_ from _[name of creditor]_. As security for loan, _[name of creditor]_ insisted upon, and the debtors executed, a note and security agreement granting to _[name of creditor]_ a security interest in and on the debtor's personal property, which consisted of _[items held as security as they are listed in your loan agreement]_ which are held primarily for the family and household use of the debtors and their dependents.

4. All such possessions of debtors have been claimed as fully exempt in their bankruptcy case.

5. The money borrowed from _[name of creditor]_ does not represent any part of the purchase money of any of the articles covered in the security agreement executed by the debtors, and all of the articles so covered remain in the possession of the debtors.

6. The existence of _[name of creditor]_'s lien on debtor's household and personal goods impairs exemptions to which the debtors would be entitled under 11 U.S.C. § 522(b).

WHEREFORE, pursuant to 11 U.S.C. § 522(f), debtors pray for an order avoiding the security interest in their personal and household goods, and for such additional or alternative relief as may be just and proper.

Dated: _____

Dated: _____   _____ Debtor in Propria Persona

_____ Debtor in Propria Persona

_____ Address

Notice of Motion to Avoid Nonpossessory, Nonpurchase-Money Security Interest

UNITED STATES BANKRUPTCY COURT

_____ DISTRICT OF _____

In re)
) [Set forth here all names including
) married, maiden, and trade names used
) by debtor within last 8 years]
)   Debtor(s)   )   Case No. _____
)
)   Chapter 7
Address _____)
)
Employer's Tax Identification (EIN) No(s). [if any]: _____
)
Last four digits of Social Security No(s): _____)

NOTICE OF MOTION TO AVOID NONPOSSESSORY, NONPURCHASE-MONEY SECURITY INTEREST

Please take notice of motion set for a hearing on: _____[leave blank]_____, 20___

at _____ o'clock _____ .m. at _____[leave blank]_____, in

courtroom _____[leave blank]_____.

Order to Avoid Nonpossessory, Nonpurchase-Money Security Interest

UNITED STATES BANKRUPTCY COURT

DISTRICT OF _____

In re

    [Set forth here all names including
    married, maiden, and trade names used
    by debtor within last 8 years]

                 Debtor(s)   Case No. _____

                           Chapter 7

Address _____

Employer's Tax Identification (EIN) No(s). [if any]: _____

Last four digits of Social Security No(s): _____

ORDER TO AVOID NONPOSSESSORY, NONPURCHASE-MONEY SECURITY INTEREST

The motion of the above-named debtor(s) _[your name(s)]_____ , to avoid the lien
of the respondent, _[Name of creditor]_____ , is sustained.

The lien is a nonpossessory, nonpurchase-money lien that impairs the debtor's exemptions in the following property:

    [list all items held as security as listed in your loan agreement]

Unless debtor's bankruptcy case is dismissed, the lien of the respondent is hereby extinguished and the lien shall not survive bankruptcy or affix to or remain enforceable against the aforementioned property of the debtor.

_[Name of creditor]_____ shall take all necessary steps to remove any record of the lien from the aforementioned property of the debtor.

Dated: _[leave blank for judge to sign]_____

      [leave blank for judge to sign]
      U.S. Bankruptcy Judge

Proof of Service by Mail

UNITED STATES BANKRUPTCY COURT

DISTRICT OF _____

In re

    [Set forth here all names including
    married, maiden, and trade names used
    by debtor within last 8 years]

                 Debtor(s)   Case No. _____

                           Chapter 7

Address _____

Employer's Tax Identification (EIN) No(s). [if any]: _____

Last four digits of Social Security No(s): _____

PROOF OF SERVICE BY MAIL

I, _____ _[friend's name]_____ , declare that: I am a resident or employed in the County of _[county where friend lives or works]_, State of _[state where friend lives or works]_. My residence/business address is _____ _[friend's address]_____ . I am over the age of eighteen years and not a party to this case.

On _____ _[leave blank]_____ , 20___, I served the:

    [list papers served]

on _____ _[lender or lienholder's name]_____ , by placing true and correct copies thereof enclosed in a sealed envelope with postage thereon fully prepaid in the United States Mail at _[city of post office where papers will be mailed]_, address as follows:

    [address of affected lender or lienholder and trustee]

I declare under penalty of perjury that the foregoing is true and correct, and that this declaration was executed on

Date: _____ , 20___ at _____
                     City and State

                 _____
                 Signature

Step 11: File (in person or by mail) the original (signed) Notice of Motion, Motion (and proposed Order, if required in your area), and Proof of Service with the bankruptcy court.

Step 12: The trustee or creditors affected by your motion may submit a written response. However, most courts will grant your motion if the trustee or creditor doesn't file a response to the motion and you ask the court to enter a default judgment in your favor (see Step 14, below).

Step 13: If there is a hearing, attend it. The hearing is usually very short, ten minutes or less. Because you filed the motion, you argue your side first. Explain briefly how your property falls within the acceptable categories of exempt property, that the lien is a nonpossessory nonpurchase-money security interest, and that the lien impairs your exemption. (11 U.S.C. § 522(f)(2).) "Impairs your exemption" means that because of the lien, your ownership interest in this item of exempt property has been reduced.

The trustee or creditor (or an attorney) responds. The judge either decides the matter and signs your proposed order or takes it "under advisement" and mails you the order in a few days.

Step 14: If the creditor doesn't show up at the hearing, or if the creditor doesn't file a response to your motion when it is required to do so (see Step 12, above), file and serve a Request for Entry of Order by Default. (See the sample request with the papers for avoiding a judicial lien, below, to get an idea of what this should look like. Of course, you'll have to change the language so it refers to a nonpossessory, nonpurchase-money security interest rather than a judicial lien.) This document tells the court that you followed all of the proper procedures and gave the creditor notice of your motion, but the creditor didn't respond as it was required to do. The Request asks the court to grant your motion by default. You must prepare another Proof of Service and serve this request on the creditor.

Get an attorney, if you need one. If you are having trouble figuring out how to draft the necessary paperwork to avoid a lien, think about asking a lawyer for help—especially if the lien is substantial.

How to Serve the Creditor

Under the new bankruptcy law, you must provide notice to the creditor by following these rules:

- If the creditor provided you with a contact address and a current account number within the 90 days before you filed for bankruptcy, you must use that address and include the account number and the last four digits of your Social Security or taxpayer identification number with your papers.
- If the creditor was prohibited from communicating with you during this 90-day period, you must use the address and account number contained in the two written communications you received most recently from the creditor.
- If the creditor has filed a preferred contact address with the court, you must use that address.

If your creditor is a business, you must serve a live human being who represents the creditor—you can't just send your motion to "Visa" or "First Bank," for example. Here's how to find that warm body:

- Call the creditor and ask for the name and address of the person who accepts service of process for the business.
- If you don't know how to reach the creditor, contact your state's Secretary of State office and ask for the name and address of the person who is listed as the registered agent for service of process for the company. Many states make this information available online, too.

Request for Entry of Order by Default

1　[Your Name]
2　[Your Address]
3　[Your Address]
　　[Your Phone #]
　　[Last four digits of taxpayer ID #]
4　Debtor is Self-Represented

7　IN THE UNITED STATES BANKRUPTCY COURT
8　[The district where your court is located]

10　In the Matter of　　　) Case No:　[Enter your Case #]
11　[Your Name],　　　　　) Chapter 7
12　Debtor　　　　　　　　)

15　REQUEST FOR ENTRY OF ORDER BY DEFAULT
16　Now comes debtor [your name], who declares and says under
17　penalty of perjury this [day, month, year] at [your city and
18　state] that the following statements are true and correct:
19　1. On [date], Debtor [your name] caused a Notice of
20　Motion and Motion to Avoid Judicial Lien on Real Estate to be
21　served on [name of person motion was served on].
22　2. A copy of the Notice of Motion and Motion and a pro-
23　posed order are attached to this request. Also attached is a
24　Proof of Service of this request on [name of person motion was
25　served on], the trustee, and the U.S. Trustee.
26　3. The trustee and the U.S. trustee were also served with
27　the Notice of Motion and Motion to Avoid Lien on [date trustee
28　and U.S. Trustee were served]

1　4. A proof of service duly executed by [name of person
2　who served your notice of motion and motion] as to service of
3　the Notice of Motion and Motion is on file with the court.
4　5. The Notice of Motion and Motion complies in all
5　respects with Bankruptcy Local Rule [number of rule you used
6　to provide Notice of Motion] of the United States Bankruptcy
7　Court for the [name of court's district]
8　6. The debtor has received no response from any of the
9　served parties as of [current date], 21 days after the service
10　of the Notice of Motion and Motion.
11　WHEREFORE, Debtor respectfully requests that the Court enter
12　by default the attached Order to Avoid Judicial Lien on Real
13　Estate.

15　　　　　　　　　Date: [current date]

16　　　　　Signed: [your name]

19　　　　PROOF OF SERVICE BY MAIL (Bankruptcy Rule 7004)
20　　　I, [name of process server], declare that I am a
21　resident of or employed in the [county and state]. My address
22　is [process server's address]. I am over the age of eighteen
23　years of age and am not a party to this case.
24　On [date of service by mail], I served the Notice
25　of Motion and Motion to Avoid Judicial Lien on Real Estate
26　on the following parties by placing true and correct copies
27　thereof enclosed in a sealed envelope with postage thereon
28　fully prepaid, in the United States Mail at [city and state]
　　addressed as follows:

Request for Entry of Order by Default, continued

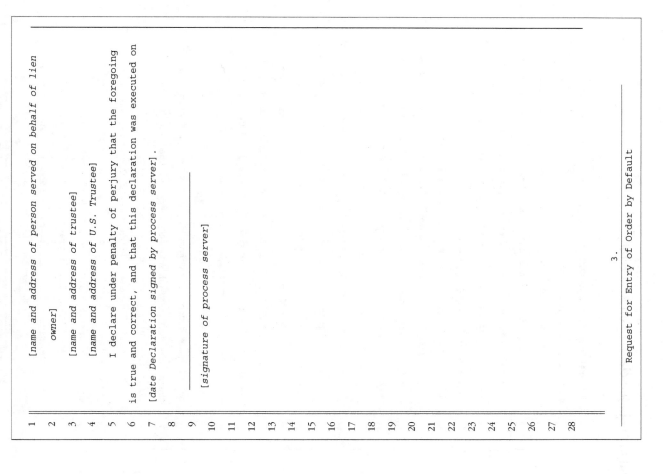

1
2
3
4
5
6
7
8
9
10
11
12
13
14
15
16
17
18
19
20
21
22
23
24
25
26
27
28

[name and address of person served on behalf of lien
    owner]

[name and address of trustee]

[name and address of U.S. Trustee]

    I declare under penalty of perjury that the foregoing
is true and correct, and that this declaration was executed on
[date Declaration signed by process server].

_____
[signature of process server]

3.

Request for Entry of Order by Default

Notice of Motion and Motion to Avoid Judicial Lien on Real Estate

```
1   [Your Name]
2   [Your Address]
3   [Your Address]
    [Last four digits of taxpayer ID #]
4   Debtor is Self-Represented
5
6
7            IN THE UNITED STATES BANKRUPTCY COURT
8            [The district where your court is located]
9
10  In the Matter of        ) Case No:  [Enter your Case #]
11  [Your Name]             ) Chapter 7
12  Debtor                  )
13  _____)
14               NOTICE OF MOTION AND
15       MOTION TO AVOID JUDICIAL LIEN ON REAL ESTATE
16       PLEASE TAKE NOTICE that Debtor [your name] is moving the
17  Court to avoid a judicial lien held by [name of lien owner]
18  on certain real property owned by the Debtor.
19       This motion is being brought under procedures prescribed
20  by Bankruptcy Local Rule [number of applicable local rule]
21  of the United States Bankruptcy Court for the [Name of your
22  court's district].
23       If you wish to object to the motion, or request a hearing
24  on the motion, your objection and/or request must be filed and
25  served upon debtor within 20 days of the date this notice was
26  mailed.
27       You must accompany any request you make for a hearing,
28  or any objection to the relief sought by Debtor, with any
```

Notice and Motion to Avoid Judicial Lien on Real Estate

1.

```
1   declarations or memoranda of law you wish to present in
2   support of your position.
3        If you do not make a timely objection to the requested
4   relief, or a timely request for hearing, the Court may enter
5   an order granting the relief by default and either 1) set a
6   tentative hearing date or 2) require that Debtor provides you
7   at least 10 day's written notice of hearing (in the event an
8   objection or request for hearing is timely made).
9        1.  Debtor [your name] commenced this case on [date of your
10  bankruptcy filing] by filing a voluntary petition for relief under
11  Chapter 7 of Title 11 of the United States Bankruptcy Code.
12       2.  This court has jurisdiction over this motion, filed
13  pursuant to 11 U.S.C. Sec. 522(f) to avoid and cancel a judicial
14  lien held by [name of lien owner] on real property used as the
15  debtor's residence, under 28 U.S.C. Sec. 1334.
16       3.  On [date lien recorded against property], creditors
17  recorded a judicial lien against the following debtor's
18  residence at [address of property]. The said judicial lien is
19  entered of record as follows: [lien recording information as
20  shown in the Recorder's Office]
21       4.  The debtor's interest in the property referred to in
22  the preceding paragraph and encumbered by the lien has been
23  claimed as fully exempt in [his/her] bankruptcy case.
24       5.  The existence of [lien owner's] lien on debtor's real
25  property impairs an exemption to which the debtor would be
26  entitled under 11 U.S.C. [Sec. 522(b)/522(c)].
27       WHEREFORE, debtor prays for an order against [lien
28  owner] avoiding and canceling the judicial lien in the above-
```

Notice and Motion to Avoid Judicial Lien on Real Estate

2.

Notice of Motion and Motion to Avoid Judicial Lien on Real Estate

```
 1   mentioned property, and for such additional or alternative
 2   relief as may be just and proper.
 3
 4                    Date: [current date]
 5
 6                          [your name]
 7
 8        PROOF OF SERVICE BY MAIL (Bankruptcy Rule 7004)
 9        I, [name of process server], declare that I am a
10   resident of or employed in the [county and state]. My address
11   is [process server's address]. I am over the age of eighteen
12   years of age and am not a party to this case.
13        On [date of service by mail], I served the Notice
14   of Motion and Motion to Avoid Judicial Lien on Real Estate
15   on the following parties by placing true and correct copies
16   thereof enclosed in a sealed envelope with postage thereon
17   fully prepaid, in the United States Mail at [city and state]
18   addressed as follows:
19        [name and address of person served on behalf of lien
         owner]
20   [name and address of trustee]
21   [name and address of trustee]
22   [name and address of U.S. Trustee]
23        I declare under penalty of perjury that the foregoing
24   is true and correct, and that this declaration was executed on
25   [Date Declaration signed by process server].
26
27   [Signature of process server]
28
                              3.
         Notice and Motion to Avoid Judicial Lien on Real Estate
```

Order to Avoid Judicial Lien on Real Estate

```
 1   [Your Name]
 2   [Your Address]
 3   [Your Address]
     [Your Phone #]
     [Last four digits of taxpayer ID #]
 4   Debtor is Self-Represented
 5
 6
 7           IN THE UNITED STATES BANKRUPTCY COURT
 8           [The district where your court is located]
 9
10   In the Matter of        )  Case No:  [Enter your Case #]
11   [Your Name],            )  Chapter 7
12   Debtor                  )
13                           )
14      ORDER TO AVOID JUDICIAL LIEN ON REAL ESTATE
15       Upon request of Debtor for relief by default under Bankruptcy
16   Local Rule [number of local rule], and good cause appearing
17   therefore, the motion of the above-named debtor [your name] to
18   avoid the lien of respondent [name of lien owner] is sustained.
19       It is hereby ORDERED AND DECREED that the judicial lien held
20   by [name of lien owner] in and on Debtor's residential real
21   estate at [address of real estate] entered of record at [where
22   lien entered in official records] for [amount of lien] and any
23   other amounts due thereunder be hereby canceled.
24       It is further ORDERED that unless debtor's bankruptcy case
25   is dismissed, [name of lien owner] and its successors shall
26   take all steps necessary and appropriate to release the judi-
27   cial lien and remove it from the local judgment index.
28
     Dated: _____
                                          U.S. BANKRUPTCY JUDGE
                              1.
                       Order Avoiding Lien
```

b. Judicial Lien

To eliminate a judicial lien, follow the steps in Subsection a, above, but use the Sample Notice of Motion and Motion to Avoid Judicial Lien and Order to Avoid Judicial Lien forms as examples.

The sample forms are for eliminating a judicial lien on your home. To eliminate a lien on personal property, you will need to change the language accordingly.

Checklist of Forms for Motion to Avoid Judicial Lien

☐ Motion to Avoid Judicial Lien or Motion to Avoid Judicial Lien (on Real Estate)
☐ Notice of Motion to Avoid Judicial Lien
☐ Order to Avoid Judicial Lien
☐ Proof of Service (use form from Section K1, above)
☐ Request for Entry of Order by Default and Proof of Service by Mail (if the creditor doesn't respond)

You may have to prove the value of the property in question. Typically, when you file for bankruptcy and assign a value to your property, the only person who may check your figures is the trustee—and that doesn't happen very often. However, if a creditor opposes your motion to avoid a judicial lien, the creditor can make you prove the property's value, because the more the property is worth, the less the lien impairs the exemption. For instance, if you listed property as worth $50,000 and the exemption is $45,000, a lien exceeding $5,000 would impair the exemption and entitle you to have the lien removed. But if the evidence you provide at the hearing shows that the property is worth $60,000, a lien of less than $15,000 wouldn't impair the exemption, because you would be able to take your $45,000 exemption and still pay the full lien. So, be prepared to show how you determined the value of your property.

Use an attorney, if necessary. If you are having trouble figuring out how to draft the necessary paperwork to avoid a lien, think about asking a lawyer for help—especially if the lien is substantial.

c. Tax Liens

If your federal tax debt is secured, you may have a basis for challenging the lien. Quite often, the IRS makes mistakes when it records a notice of federal tax lien.

Help from a lawyer. You will need the help of a tax or bankruptcy attorney—preferably one who has experience in both areas—to challenge a tax lien.

Here are some possible grounds for asking the court to remove the lien:

- The notice of federal tax lien was never recorded, though the IRS claims it was.
- The notice of federal tax lien was recorded after the automatic stay took effect.
- The notice of federal tax lien was recorded in the wrong county—it must be recorded where you own real estate for it to attach to the real estate in that county.
- The notice of federal tax lien was recorded against the wrong assets, such as your child's house, not yours.

Even if the notice of federal tax lien was recorded correctly, you still may have a basis to fight it if either of the following is true:

- The lien expired—liens last only ten years.
- The lien is based on an invalid tax assessment by the IRS.

3. How to Redeem Property

If you want to redeem exempt or abandoned property, list the property on your Statement of Intention as property to be retained and check the column that says property will be redeemed. (More instructions are in Ch. 6.) You must pay the creditor the current replacement value of the property within 45 days after the creditors' meeting.

Explore lien avoidance first. If lien avoidance (Section C2, above) is available, you may be able to get rid of a lien on exempt property without paying anything.

a. Agreeing on the Value of the Property

Before you can redeem property, you and the creditor must agree on what the property is worth. If you believe the creditor is setting too high a price for the property, tell the creditor why you think the property is worth less—it needs repair, it's falling apart, it's damaged or stained, or whatever. If you can't come to an agreement, you can ask the bankruptcy court to rule on the matter. But you will probably need an attorney to help you make this request, so it is not worth your while unless the property is worth more than the lawyer will cost, and you and the creditor are very far apart in your estimates of the property's value.

You and the creditor should sign a redemption agreement that sets forth the terms of your arrangement and the amount you are going to pay, in case there is a dispute later. (See the sample forms in Subsection d, below.)

b. If the Creditor Won't Cooperate

The creditor may refuse to let you redeem property, because the creditor claims that it isn't one of the types of property described in Section C3, above, or because you can't agree on the value. If so, you will need to file a formal complaint in the bankruptcy court to have a judge resolve the issue. You will need an attorney to help you, so think twice about whether you really want to redeem the property. It may be better just to let the creditor have it.

c. Paying in Installments

If you can't raise enough cash to pay the creditor within 45 days after the creditors' meeting, try to get the creditor to let you pay in installments. Some creditors will agree if the installments are substantial and you agree to pay interest on them. But a creditor is not required to accept installments; it can demand the entire amount in cash.

If the creditor refuses to accept installments, you can ask the bankruptcy court to delay your deadline for making the payment for a month or two. But, to do so, you will need to file a formal complaint in the bankruptcy court. Again, you will need an attorney to help you, so it may not be worth it.

d. Paperwork

Below are two sample redemption agreements you can use to type up your agreement with the creditor. Form 1 is for installments and Form 2 is for a lump sum payment. Type the form on legal paper (the blank paper in Appendix 3 with numbers down the left side) and put your bankruptcy case number on it in case you need to file it later. You should fill out a separate form for every item of property you want to redeem. Have the creditor sign it.

There is no need to file these agreements with the trustee. Keep them with your other bankruptcy papers, in case the trustee or the judge wants to see them.

Agreement for Installment Redemption of Property

UNITED STATES BANKRUPTCY COURT

_____ DISTRICT OF _____

In re _____)

       [Set forth here all names including   )

       married, maiden, and trade names used   )

       by debtor within last 8 years]   )

                       Debtor(s)   )   Case No. _____

Address _____)

)

_____)   Chapter 7

)

Employer's Tax Identification (EIN) No(s). *[if any]:*   )

_____)

Last four digits of Social Security No(s): _____   )

AGREEMENT FOR INSTALLMENT REDEMPTION OF PROPERTY

_____ (Debtor) and

_____(Creditor) agree that:

   1. Creditor owns a security interest in _____ (Collateral).

   2. The replacement value of Collateral is $_____.

   3. Creditor's security interest is valid and enforceable despite the Debtor's bankruptcy case.

   4. If Debtor continues to make payments of $_____ a month on Creditor's security

interest, Creditor will take no action to repossess or foreclose its security.

   5. Debtor's payments will continue until the amount of $_____, plus interest (to be

computed at the same annual percentage rate as in the original contract between the parties), is paid.

   6. Upon being fully paid as specified in Paragraph 5, Creditor will take all steps necessary to terminate

its security interest in Collateral.

   7. If Debtor defaults, Creditor will have its rights under the original contract.

Dated: _____   _____

                                     Debtor in Propria Persona

Dated: _____   _____

                                     Creditor

Agreement for Lump Sum Redemption of Property

UNITED STATES BANKRUPTCY COURT

_____ DISTRICT OF _____

In re _____   )

           [Set forth here all names including   )

           married, maiden, and trade names used   )

           by debtor within last 8 years]   )

                      Debtor(s)   )   Case No. _____

Address _____   )

)

_____   )   Chapter 7

)

Employer's Tax Identification (EIN) No(s). *[if any]*:   )

_____   )

Last four digits of Social Security No(s): _____   )

AGREEMENT FOR REDEMPTION OF PROPERTY

_____ (Debtor) and

_____(Creditor) agree that:

    1. Creditor owns a security interest in _____ (Collateral).

    2. The replacement value of Collateral is $_____.

    3. Creditor's security interest is valid and enforceable despite the Debtor's bankruptcy case.

    4. Debtor agrees to pay the full value of the collateral no later than _____.

    5. Upon receiving the payment specified in Paragraph 4, Creditor will take all steps necessary to

terminate its security interest in Collateral.

Dated: _____   _____

                                        Debtor in Propria Persona

Dated: _____   _____

                                        Creditor

4. How to Reaffirm a Debt

Bankruptcy courts frown on Reaffirmation Agreements, because they obligate debtors to make payments after bankruptcy, which contradicts bankruptcy's purpose. Nevertheless, if you do decide to reaffirm a debt, you must list it as such on your Statement of Intention. Within 30 days after the creditors' meeting, you must be willing to sign a reaffirmation agreement. The law provides that either you or the creditor must file the Reaffirmation Agreement and, if you aren't represented by an attorney, file a motion asking the court to approve it. If you are dealing with a major creditor, you can count on the creditor to provide the agreement, get your signature, and file it with the court. After all, these creditors are familiar with Reaffirmation Agreements, and they want you to be legally obligated to repay the loan after your bankruptcy discharge is granted. But if the creditor doesn't take care of the details and you want to make sure you can hold on to the collateral, you will have to prepare, sign, and file the agreement yourself. You can find a Reaffirmation Agreement that complies with the new law below (and in Appendix 3).

The Reaffirmation Agreement includes a request for a discharge hearing. After you file the agreement, you will receive notice of the scheduled hearing in the mail. At the hearing, the court will make sure that you understand the consequences of signing the agreement. The court must approve the agreement unless it appears, based on your income and expense schedules, that you won't be able to make the required payments. In that case, the judge will disapprove the agreement and send you and the creditor back to the drawing board. At that point, the creditor may decide to repossess the property or agree to a new plan that will bring your payments down to an acceptable level.

Don't agree to pay too much. If the creditor requires you to reaffirm for the full amount owed on the collateral (an amount that is greater than the current replacement value of the collateral), select another option unless you really, really want the property and won't be able to get similar property after bankruptcy. In general, you should try to avoid staying on the hook for a debt for more than it would cost you to replace the property.

Your right to cancel a Reaffirmation Agreement. The Bankruptcy Code gives you the right to cancel any Reaffirmation Agreement by notifying the creditor at any time:

- before you receive your discharge, or
- within 60 days after the Reaffirmation Agreement is filed with the bankruptcy court,

whichever is later. (11 U.S.C. § 524(c)(2).)

Notice to the creditor should be by certified mail, return receipt requested. This precludes the creditor from later claiming it didn't receive notice.

Canceling your reaffirmation will leave your debt in the same condition as if you had never filed the Reaffirmation Agreement. That is, your personal liability for the debt will be discharged (assuming the debt is dischargeable), and the creditor will be able to enforce its lien on your property by either repossessing it or foreclosing on it. If your bankruptcy case is still open, you can still try other options discussed in this chapter.

As mentioned, the new bankruptcy law requires you to surrender the collateral, redeem it, or reaffirm the debt. Filers can no longer discharge the debt while keeping the collateral simply by staying current on their payments. However, there is nothing to prevent a creditor from letting you continue to make the payments and choosing not to repossess the collateral. Also, the laws of some states prohibit creditors from repossessing property as long as the debtor is current on his or her payments.

This approach clearly risks losing the collateral—the creditor can decide to end the informal arrangement and repossess at any time. However, your debt will be discharged. If you choose this approach, indicate on the Statement of Intention that you are surrendering the property. The creditor will have the right to repossess, even if you continue making payments.

Because this approach isn't officially sanctioned by law, you will face another potential problem: Even after you have paid off the lien with interest, it will remain on the public record unless the creditor takes steps to have it removed. This won't be an issue if you never sell the property. But if you need clear title to the property in order to sell it later, you'll need to go to court and prove that you paid off the lien. To keep track of how much you have paid, keep copies of every check or money order you send the creditor.

Reaffirmation Agreement

B 240 - Reaffirmation Agreement
(10/05)

P. 2

United States Bankruptcy Court
District of _____

In re _____,
    Debtor

Case No. _____
Chapter _____

REAFFIRMATION AGREEMENT

[Indicate all documents included in this filing by checking each applicable box.]

☐ Part A: Disclosures, Instructions, and Notice to Debtor (Pages 1 - 5)
☐ Part B: Reaffirmation Agreement
☐ Part C: Certification by Debtor's Attorney
☐ Part D: Debtor's Statement in Support of Reaffirmation Agreement
☐ Part E: Motion for Court Approval
☐ Proposed Order Approving Reaffirmation Agreement

☐ *[Check this box if]* Creditor is a Credit Union as defined in §19(b)(1)(a)(iv) of the Federal Reserve Act

PART A: DISCLOSURE STATEMENT, INSTRUCTIONS AND NOTICE TO DEBTOR

1. DISCLOSURE STATEMENT

Before Agreeing to Reaffirm a Debt, Review These Important Disclosures:

SUMMARY OF REAFFIRMATION AGREEMENT

This Summary is made pursuant to the requirements of the Bankruptcy Code.

AMOUNT REAFFIRMED

a. The amount of debt you have agreed to reaffirm: $ _____

b. All fees and costs accrued as of the date of this disclosure statement, related to the amount of debt shown in a, above: $ _____

c. The total amount you have agreed to reaffirm (Add lines a. and b.):

Your credit agreement may obligate you to pay additional amounts which may come due after the date of this disclosure. Consult your credit agreement.

ANNUAL PERCENTAGE RATE

[The annual percentage rate can be disclosed in different ways, depending on the type of debt.]

a. If the debt is an extension of "credit" under an "open end credit plan," as those terms are defined in § 103 of the Truth in Lending Act, such as a credit card, the creditor may disclose the annual percentage rate shown in (I) below or, to the extent this rate is not readily available or not applicable, the simple interest rate shown in (ii) below, or both.

(I) The Annual Percentage Rate disclosed, or that would have been disclosed, to the debtor in the most recent periodic statement prior to entering into the reaffirmation agreement described in Part B below or, if no such periodic statement was given to the debtor during the prior six months, the annual percentage rate as it would have been so disclosed at the time of the disclosure statement: _____%.

— *And/Or* —

(ii) The simple interest rate applicable to the amount reaffirmed as of the date this disclosure statement is given to the debtor: _____%. If different simple interest rates apply to different balances included in the amount reaffirmed, the amount of each balance and the rate applicable to it are:

$ _____ @ _____%;
$ _____ @ _____%;
$ _____ @ _____%.

b. If the debt is an extension of credit other than under an open end credit plan, the creditor may disclose the annual percentage rate shown in (I) below, or, to the extent this rate is not readily available or not applicable, the simple interest rate shown in (ii) below, or both.

(I) The Annual Percentage Rate under §128(a)(4) of the Truth in Lending Act, as disclosed to the debtor in the most recent disclosure statement given to the debtor prior to entering into the reaffirmation agreement with respect to the debt or, if no such disclosure statement was given to the debtor, the annual percentage rate as it would have been so disclosed: _____%.

— *And/Or* —

(ii) The simple interest rate applicable to the amount reaffirmed as of the date this disclosure statement is given to the debtor: _____%. If different simple interest rates apply to different balances included in the amount reaffirmed,

Reaffirmation Agreement

P. 3

the amount of each balance and the rate applicable to it are:

$ _____ @ _____ %;
$ _____ @ _____ %;
$ _____ @ _____ %.

c. If the underlying debt transaction was disclosed as a variable rate transaction on the most recent disclosure given under the Truth in Lending Act:

The interest rate on your loan may be a variable interest rate which changes from time to time, so that the annual percentage rate disclosed here may be higher or lower.

d. If the reaffirmed debt is secured by a security interest or lien, which has not been waived or determined to be void by a final order of the court, the following items or types of items of the debtor's goods or property remain subject to such security interest or lien in connection with the debt or debts being reaffirmed in the reaffirmation agreement described in Part B.

Item or Type of Item   Original Purchase Price or Original Amount of Loan

Optional—At the election of the creditor, a repayment schedule using one or a combination of the following may be provided:

Repayment Schedule:

Your first payment in the amount of $ _____ is due on _____ (date), but the future payment amount may be different. Consult your reaffirmation agreement or credit agreement, as applicable.

---Or---

Your payment schedule will be: _____ (number) payments in the amount of $ _____ each, payable (monthly, annually, weekly, etc.) on the _____ (day) of each (week, month, etc.), unless altered later by mutual agreement in writing.

---Or---

A reasonably specific description of the debtor's repayment obligations to the extent known by the creditor or creditor's representative.

P. 4

2. INSTRUCTIONS AND NOTICE TO DEBTOR

Reaffirming a debt is a serious financial decision. The law requires you to take certain steps to make sure the decision is in your best interest. If these steps are not completed, the reaffirmation agreement is not effective, even though you have signed it.

1. Read the disclosures in this Part A carefully. Consider the decision to reaffirm carefully. Then, if you want to reaffirm, sign the reaffirmation agreement in Part B (or you may use a separate agreement you and your creditor agree on).

2. Complete and sign Part D and be sure you can afford to make the payments you are agreeing to make and have received a copy of the disclosure statement and a completed and signed reaffirmation agreement.

3. If you were represented by an attorney during the negotiation of your reaffirmation agreement, the attorney must have signed the certification in Part C.

4. If you were not represented by an attorney during the negotiation of your reaffirmation agreement, you must have completed and signed Part E.

5. The original of this disclosure must be filed with the court by you or your creditor. If a separate reaffirmation agreement (other than the one in Part B) has been signed, it must be attached.

6. If the creditor is not a Credit Union and you were represented by an attorney during the negotiation of your reaffirmation agreement, your reaffirmation agreement becomes effective upon filing with the court unless the reaffirmation is presumed to be an undue hardship as explained in Part D. If the creditor is a Credit Union and you were represented by an attorney during the negotiation of your reaffirmation agreement, your reaffirmation agreement becomes effective upon filing with the court.

7. If you were not represented by an attorney during the negotiation of your reaffirmation agreement, it will not be effective unless the court approves it. The court will notify you and the creditor of the hearing on your reaffirmation agreement. You must attend this hearing in bankruptcy court where the judge will review your reaffirmation agreement. The bankruptcy court must approve your reaffirmation agreement as consistent with your best interests, except that no court approval is required if your reaffirmation agreement is for a consumer debt secured by a mortgage, deed of trust, security deed, or other lien on your real property, like your home.

Reaffirmation Agreement, continued

P. 5

YOUR RIGHT TO RESCIND (CANCEL) YOUR REAFFIRMATION AGREEMENT

You may rescind (cancel) your reaffirmation agreement at any time before the bankruptcy court enters a discharge order, or before the expiration of the 60-day period that begins on the date your reaffirmation agreement is filed with the court, whichever occurs later. To rescind (cancel) your reaffirmation agreement, you must notify the creditor that your reaffirmation agreement is rescinded (or canceled).

Frequently Asked Questions:

What are your obligations if you reaffirm the debt? A reaffirmed debt remains your personal legal obligation. It is not discharged in your bankruptcy case. That means that if you default on your reaffirmed debt after your bankruptcy case is over, your creditor may be able to take your property or your wages. Otherwise, your obligations will be determined by the reaffirmation agreement which may have changed the terms of the original agreement. For example, if you are reaffirming an open end credit agreement, the creditor may be permitted by that agreement or applicable law to change the terms of that agreement in the future under certain conditions.

Are you required to enter into a reaffirmation agreement by any law? No, you are not required to reaffirm a debt by any law. Only agree to reaffirm a debt if it is in your best interest. Be sure you can afford the payments you agree to make.

What if your creditor has a security interest or lien? Your bankruptcy discharge does not eliminate any lien on your property. A "lien" is often referred to as a security interest, deed of trust, mortgage or security deed. Even if you do not reaffirm and your personal liability on the debt is discharged, because of the lien your creditor may still have the right to take the security property if you do not pay the debt or default on it. If the lien is on an item of personal property that is exempt under your State's law or that the trustee has abandoned, you may be able to redeem the item rather than reaffirm the debt. To redeem, you make a single payment to the creditor equal to the current value of the security property, as agreed by the parties or determined by the court.

NOTE: When this disclosure refers to what a creditor "may" do, it does not use the word "may" to give the creditor specific permission. The word "may" is used to tell you what might occur if the law permits the creditor to take the action. If you have questions about your reaffirming a debt or what the law requires, consult with the attorney who helped you negotiate this agreement reaffirming a debt. If you don't have an attorney helping you, the judge will explain the effect of your reaffirming a debt when the hearing on the reaffirmation agreement is held.

P. 6

PART B: REAFFIRMATION AGREEMENT.

I (we) agree to reaffirm the debts arising under the credit agreement described below.

1. Brief description of credit agreement:

2. Description of any changes to the credit agreement made as part of this reaffirmation agreement:

SIGNATURE(S):

Borrower: _____   Co-borrower, if also reaffirming these debts:

_____   _____
(Print Name)   (Print Name)

(Signature)   (Signature)
Date: _____   Date: _____

Accepted by creditor:

_____
(Print Name)

(Signature)
Date of creditor acceptance: _____

Reaffirmation Agreement, continued

P. 7

PART C: CERTIFICATION BY DEBTOR'S ATTORNEY (IF ANY).

[Check each applicable box.]

☐ I hereby certify that (1) this agreement represents a fully informed and voluntary agreement by the debtor; (2) this agreement does not impose an undue hardship on the debtor or any dependent of the debtor; and (3) I have fully advised the debtor of the legal effect and consequences of this agreement and any default under this agreement.

☐ *[If applicable and the creditor is not a Credit Union.]* A presumption of undue hardship has been established with respect to this agreement. In my opinion, however, the debtor is able to make the required payment.

Printed Name of Debtor's Attorney: _____

Signature of Debtor's Attorney: _____

Date: _____

P. 8

PART D: DEBTOR'S STATEMENT IN SUPPORT OF REAFFIRMATION AGREEMENT

[Read and complete numbered paragraphs 1 and 2, OR, if the creditor is a Credit Union and the debtor is represented by an attorney, read the un-numbered paragraph below. Sign the appropriate signature line(s) and date your signature.]

1. I believe this reaffirmation agreement will not impose an undue hardship on my dependents or me. I can afford to make the payments on the reaffirmed debt because my monthly income (take home pay plus any other income received) is $ _____, and my actual current monthly expenses including monthly payments on post-bankruptcy debt and other reaffirmation agreements total $ _____, leaving $ _____ to make the required payments on this reaffirmed debt. I understand that if my income less my monthly expenses does not leave enough to make the payments, this reaffirmation agreement is presumed to be an undue hardship on me and must be reviewed by the court. However, this presumption may be overcome if I explain to the satisfaction of the court how I can afford to make the payments here: _____

2. I received a copy of the Reaffirmation Disclosure Statement in Part A and a completed and signed reaffirmation agreement.

Signed: _____

     _____
     (Debtor)

     _____
     (Joint Debtor, if any)

Date: _____

— Or —

[If the creditor is a Credit Union and the debtor is represented by an attorney]

I believe this reaffirmation agreement is in my financial interest. I can afford to make the payments on the reaffirmed debt. I received a copy of the Reaffirmation Disclosure Statement in Part A and a completed and signed reaffirmation agreement.

Signed: _____

     _____
     (Debtor)

     _____
     (Joint Debtor, if any)

Date: _____

Reaffirmation Agreement, continued

P. 9

United States Bankruptcy Court
_____ District of _____

In re _____ , Case No. _____
           (Debtor)   Chapter _____

ORDER APPROVING REAFFIRMATION AGREEMENT

The debtor(s) _____ have filed a motion for approval of the
                (Name(s) of debtor(s))

reaffirmation agreement dated _____ made between the debtor(s) and
                               (Date of agreement)

_____ . The court held the hearing required by 11 U.S.C. § 524(d)
(Name of creditor)

on notice to the debtor(s) and the creditor on _____ .
                                                 (Date)

COURT ORDER: The court grants the debtor's motion and approves the reaffirmation
                 agreement described above.

                                    BY THE COURT

Date: _____

                                    _____
                                    United States Bankruptcy Judge

PART E: MOTION FOR COURT APPROVAL
(To be completed only if the debtor is not represented by an attorney.)

MOTION FOR COURT APPROVAL OF REAFFIRMATION AGREEMENT

I (we), the debtor(s), affirm the following to be true and correct:

I am not represented by an attorney in connection with this reaffirmation agreement.

I believe this reaffirmation agreement is in my best interest based on the income and
expenses I have disclosed in my Statement in Support of this reaffirmation agreement, and
because (provide any additional relevant reasons the court should consider):

Therefore, I ask the court for an order approving this reaffirmation agreement.

Signed: _____
        (Debtor)

        _____
        (Joint Debtor, if any)

Date: _____

CHAPTER

6

Complete and File Your Bankruptcy Paperwork

This chapter shows you how to take all of the necessary steps to prepare your case for filing under Chapter 7. For the most part, the process is very simple, as long as you follow all of the instructions we provide.

⚠️ **Chapter 7 bankruptcy can be a very straightforward process, but only if you follow the rules.** If you don't—even if your error is accidental—your bankruptcy case might be dismissed. And the consequences of dismissal can be dire: Not only will you continue to owe your debts and face creditor collection actions, but you might also lose the protection of the automatic stay in any future bankruptcy case you file (See Ch. 2, Section B, for more information).

A. Gather the Necessary Documents

The new bankruptcy law places some new paperwork burdens on filers. In addition to completing a sizable stack of official bankruptcy forms, you must also submit a number of other papers. Along with your bankruptcy forms, you will have to file:

- a certificate showing that you completed a credit counseling workshop (see Section 1, below)
- your most recent tax return or a transcript of the return (see Section 2, below), and
- your wage stubs for the last 60 days, if you were working (see Section 3, below).

1. The Credit Counseling Certificate

As explained in Ch. 1, every person who files a consumer bankruptcy has to first attend credit counseling. This credit counseling must be provided by an agency approved by the United States Trustee's Office within the 180-day period before you file for bankruptcy. The counseling can be done by phone, on the Internet, or in person.

You can obtain a list of approved counselors by visiting the U.S Trustee's Office website at www.usdoj .gov/ust (click "Credit Counseling & Debtor Education"). The agencies are listed by state, but you can use any agency in any state or region.

Follow These Rules to Stay Out of Trouble

If you keep these golden rules in mind, you'll save yourself a lot of time and trouble:

- Don't file for Chapter 7 bankruptcy unless you are sure it is the right choice (Ch. 1 explains how to decide whether bankruptcy makes sense and, if so, which type of bankruptcy will best suit your situation).
- Don't file until you have completed all of your documents as directed in this chapter.
- Don't file until you have a certificate showing that you have completed your credit counseling workshop (see Section A, above).
- If you can, pay your filing fee in full rather than in installments, so you don't have to worry about your case being dismissed if you miss a payment.
- Be absolutely complete and honest in filling out your paperwork.
- File all of your documents at the same time (unless you have to file an emergency petition to stop an impending foreclosure, wage garnishment, or repossession).
- Don't file your case until you have your most recent federal tax return (or a transcript) in your hands.
- Serve your tax return (or transcript) on the trustee and any creditors who request it) as soon after you file as possible. If you don't serve it seven days before the creditors' meeting, your case could be dismissed.
- Immediately amend your paperwork if the trustee asks you to.
- Don't forget your personal financial management counseling. You won't receive a discharge until you get a certificate showing that you have completed this course, which you must file within 45 days after your creditors' meeting.

We will repeat these rules throughout this chapter, as we discuss the required forms and procedures.

a. Repayment Plans

The purpose of this counseling is to get you to sign up for a debt repayment plan instead of filing for bankruptcy. Indeed, if the plan makes sense and you believe you can faithfully make the payments required to complete it, you might reasonably consider signing up for it. However, keep in mind that even if you make the required payments on the plan month after month, the creditors can pull out of the plan if you later fall behind—and they can go after you for the remaining debt. If you then decide to file for bankruptcy protection, you will have paid back all that money for no good reason. This is why most bankruptcy professionals—including the authors of this book—discourage their clients from signing up for a debt repayment plan.

Even if you have no intention of signing up for a plan, you are still required to cooperate with the debt counseling agency in fashioning a plan if they think one is possible. You then have to file this plan along with your certificate of completion and your other bankruptcy papers. If the U.S. Trustee suspects that you might be able to complete a Chapter 13 repayment plan (see Section J, below), it will review the agency's plan as part of its decision-making process.

b. Counseling Fees

Most of these credit counseling agencies charge a modest sum ($25–$50 is common) for the counseling, the issuance of a repayment plan (if it gets that far), and the certificate of completion that you'll need to file with your other bankruptcy papers. Some credit counseling agencies don't charge anything for the counseling, but require a fee of $50 or more for the certificate.

Agencies are legally required to offer their services without regard to your ability to pay. (11 U.S.C. § 111(c)(2)(B).) If an agency wants to charge more than you can afford, inform the agency of this legal requirement. If the agency doesn't back down, make notes of your conversations (including who you talked to, what they said, and the date when you talked), and then inform the agency that you are going to report it to the U.S. Trustee's Office for failing to take your poverty into account. If that doesn't bring down the price, go ahead and report the agency. You'll be doing

others in your same situation a great favor. You can contact the U.S. Trustee's Office by sending an email to ustrustee.program@usdoj.gov.

c. Exceptions to the Counseling Requirement

You don't have to get counseling if the U.S. Trustee certifies that there is no appropriate agency available to you in the district where you will be filing. However, counseling can be provided by telephone or online if the U.S. Trustee approves, so it is unlikely that approved debt counseling will ever be unavailable.

You can also avoid the requirement if you move the court to grant an exception and prove that "exigent circumstances" prevented you from getting counseling. This means that:

- you had to file for bankruptcy immediately (perhaps to stop a foreclosure), and
- you were unable to obtain counseling within five days after requesting it.

A foreclosure may not be "exigent" enough. One court has found that a debtor who waits until the last minute to seek credit counseling might not qualify for an exception to the counseling requirement. In *Dixon v. La Barge, Jr.,* No. 05-6059 (BAP 8th Circuit, Feb. 17, 2006), the court found that no exigent circumstances existed when a debtor filed for bankruptcy on the day of a scheduled foreclosure sale. In that case, the debtor claimed to have learned that he could file for Chapter 7 bankruptcy—and that he would have to complete credit counseling—on the night before he filed.

If the court grants an exception, you must complete the counseling within 30 days after you file (you can ask the court to extend this deadline by 15 days).

You may also escape the credit counseling requirement if, after notice and hearing, the bankruptcy court determines that you couldn't participate because of:

- a physical disability that prevents you from attending counseling (this exception probably won't apply if the counseling is available on the Internet or over the phone)
- mental incapacity (you are unable to understand and benefit from the counseling), or
- your active duty in a military combat zone.

2. Your Tax Return or Transcript

Under the new bankruptcy law, you are supposed to give the trustee and the U.S. Trustee your most recent IRS tax return no later than seven days before your creditors' meeting. (11 U.S.C. § 521(e)(2).) You also have to provide the return to any creditor who asks for it. To protect your privacy, you can redact (black out) your birthdate and Social Security number. If you don't provide your tax return on time, your case could be dismissed.

If you can't find a copy of your most recent tax return, you can ask the IRS to give you a transcript of the basic information in your return—and you can use the transcript as a substitute for your return. Because it can take some time to receive the transcript, you should make your request as soon as you can.

⚠ **If you haven't filed tax returns.** Some bankruptcy commentators believe that the new bankruptcy law requires you to be current on your taxes—that is, you must have filed all previous tax returns—in order to file for Chapter 7. It's isn't clear yet whether courts will agree with this interpretation. As a practical matter, you should find out how your bankruptcy trustee sees the issue and do what he or she requires. If you are required to get current on your filing, find a good tax preparer or enrolled agent to help you catch up.

3. Wage Stubs

If you are employed, you receive stubs or "advisements" with your paycheck. You are required to produce these stubs for the 60-day period prior to filing. If you have already tossed your stubs, you have two options: Wait 60 days (and keep your stubs) before filing, or go ahead and file, hand over the stubs you have, and explain why you don't have 60 days' worth.

If you are not employed, don't worry about this requirement.

B. Get Some Information From the Court

Every bankruptcy court has its own requirements for filing bankruptcy papers. If your papers don't meet these local requirements, the court clerk may reject them. So, before you begin preparing your papers, find out your court rules.

Finding the Right Bankruptcy Court

Because bankruptcy is a creature of federal, not state, law, you must file for bankruptcy in a special federal court. There are federal bankruptcy courts all over the country.

The federal court system divides the country into judicial districts. Every state has at least one judicial district; most have more. You can file in any of the following districts:

- the district where you have been living for the greater part of the 180-day period before you file
- the district where you are domiciled—that is, where you maintain your home, even if you have been living elsewhere (such as on a military base) temporarily
- the district where your principal place of business is located (if you are a business debtor), or
- the district where the majority of your business assets are located.

Most readers will be using the first option—and many will probably file in the large city closest to their home. To find a bankruptcy court in your state, check the government listings in your white pages (under "United States, Courts"), call directory assistance, ask your local librarian, or visit the court directory link at www.bankruptcydata.com. If you live in a state with more than one district, call the court in the closest city and ask whether that district includes your county or zip code.

EXAMPLE: For the past two months, you've lived in San Luis Obispo, which is in California's Central judicial district. Before that you lived in Santa Rosa, in California's Northern judicial district. Because you spent more of the past six months in the Northern District than in the Central, you should file in the bankruptcy court in the Northern District. If it's too inconvenient to file there, you could wait another month, when you would qualify to file in the Central district court.

In urban areas especially, you may get no response to a letter or phone call. You may need to visit the court and get the information in person. Or, the information may be available on the Internet. Almost all bankruptcy courts have websites with this sort of information. To find your court's website, visit www. uscourts.gov/courtlinks.

1. Fees

The total fee to file for Chapter 7 bankruptcy is $299. Fees change, however, so make sure you verify them with the court. This fee is due upon filing, unless the court waives the fee or gives you permission to pay in installments. (To make these requests, you must complete Form 3A or 3B, as explained below.)

2. Local Forms

In addition to the official forms that every bankruptcy court uses (they are listed in Section D, below), your local bankruptcy court may require you to file one or two additional forms that it has developed. For example, different courts have different forms that you must file along with your wage stubs (see Section A, above). You can get all local forms from your local bankruptcy court or a local stationery store, or you can download them from your court's website. (Go to www.uscourts.gov/courtlinks for a list of links to local courts.) Of course, we can't include all local forms in this book or tell you how to fill them out. Most, however, are self-explanatory. If you need help in obtaining or understanding them, see a local bankruptcy lawyer or visit a bankruptcy petition preparer (See Ch. 10 for information on petition preparers.)

3. Local Court Rules

Most bankruptcy courts publish local rules that govern the court's procedures. These rules mainly govern hearings conducted by the bankruptcy judge and aren't relevant in routine bankruptcy cases, which usually involve only filing papers and appearing at a creditors' meeting. Still, on occasion, a rule does affect a routine Chapter 7 bankruptcy. You can get your local rules from the bankruptcy court—in person or on its website—but be prepared to comb through reams of material to find the one or two rules that might apply in your case.

4. Number of Copies

Before filing your papers, find out how many copies your court requires. Most ask for an original and one copy. The original will be scanned into the court's database, and your copy will be "conformed" for your records. (A conformed copy is either stamped or receives a computer-generated label, with information showing that you filed, the date of your filing, your case number, and the tentative date of your creditors' meeting.) A few courts still require you to provide an original and four copies.

5. Order of Papers and Other Details

Every court has a preferred order in which it wants to receive the forms in the package you submit for filing. Most courts also have rules indicating whether the forms should be hole-punched or stapled, and other details. If you mess up, most clerks will put your forms in the correct order or punch and staple your papers in the right way. Some, however, will make you do it yourself. This can be a major pain if you are filing by mail. Every court has an exhibit of the standard Chapter 7 filing with the forms arranged correctly. If you want to get it right the first time, visit the court and carefully examine the court's sample filing, taking notes of which forms fall in which order.

Below is a sample letter you can adapt to your situation and send to the court, requesting the information discussed above. Include a large, self-addressed envelope. Call and ask the court if you need to affix return postage. Again, if you live in an urban area, you'll probably have to visit the court to get this information.

Sample Letter to Bankruptcy Court

Sandra Smith
432 Oak Street
Cincinnati, OH 45219
123-456-7890

July 2, 20XX

United States Bankruptcy Court
Atrium Two, Room 800
221 East Fourth Street
Cincinnati, OH 45202

Attn: COURT CLERK

TO THE COURT CLERK:

Please send me the following information:

1. Copies of all local forms required by this court for an individual (not corporation) filing a Chapter 7 bankruptcy and for making amendments.
2. The number of copies or sets required for filing.
3. The order in which forms should be submitted.
4. Complete instructions on this court's emergency filing procedures and deadlines.

I would also appreciate answers to four other questions:

1. Do you require a separate creditor mailing list (matrix)? If so, do you have specific requirements for its format?
2. Is the filing fee still $299? If not, please advise.
3. Should I two-hole punch my papers or is that done by the court?
4. Should I staple the papers or use paper clips?

I've enclosed a self-addressed envelope for your reply. Thank you.

Sincerely,

Sandra Smith

Sandra Smith

C. For Married Filers

If you are married, you and your spouse will have to decide whether one of you should file alone or whether you should file jointly. To make this decision, you'll first have to make sure that you're married in the eyes of the federal law (a trickier issue than you might think), then consider how filing together or separately will affect your debts and property.

1. Are You Married?

If you are married to a partner of the opposite sex, and you were married with a valid state license, you are married for purposes of filing a joint petition—and you can skip down to Section 2, below. However, if you were not married with a license and ceremony, or if you are married to a same-sex partner, read on.

a. Common Law Marriage

Some states allow heterosexual couples to establish "common law" marriages, which the states will recognize as valid marriages even though the couples do not have a state marriage license or certificate. Contrary to popular belief, a common law marriage is not created when two people simply live together for a certain number of years. In order to have a valid common law marriage, the couple must do all of the following:

- live together for a significant period of time (not defined in any state)
- hold themselves out as a married couple—typically this means using the same last name, referring to the other as "my husband" or "my wife," and filing a joint tax return, and
- intend to be married.

Alabama, Colorado, the District of Columbia, Georgia, Idaho, Iowa, Kansas, Montana, New Hampshire (but only for inheritance purposes), Ohio, Oklahoma, Pennsylvania, Rhode Island, South Carolina, Texas, and Utah recognize some form of common law marriage, but the rules for what constitutes a marriage differ from state to state. And, several of these states will only recognize common law marriages that were created before a certain date.

If you live in one of these states and you meet your state's requirements for a common law marriage, you have the option to file jointly, if you wish.

b. Same-Sex Marriage

If you married your same-sex partner in a country or province that recognizes same-sex marriage, or in Massachusetts after that state began allowing same-sex marriage, it's not clear whether you can file jointly. At least one court has refused to allow a lesbian couple who had married in Canada to file a joint bankruptcy petition, based on a provision of federal law that defines marriage as a union between a man and a woman. (See Ch. 3, Section A, for more information.) If you choose to file jointly with your same-sex spouse, you may well face opposition on these grounds from the trustee or the U.S. Trustee. Consider consulting with a bankruptcy attorney who has some experience with issues facing same-sex couples before you decide how to proceed.

2. Should You File Jointly?

Unfortunately, there is no simple formula that will tell you whether it's better to file alone or with your spouse. In the end, it will depend on which option allows you to discharge more of your debts and keep more of your property. Here are some of the factors you should consider:

- If you are living in a community property state and most of your debts were incurred, and your property acquired, during marriage, you should probably file jointly. Even if only one spouse files, all community property is considered part of the bankruptcy estate. The same is true for debts—that is, all community debts are listed and discharged even though only one spouse files. (See Ch. 3, Section A, for more on community property.)
- If you have recently married, you haven't acquired any valuable assets as a married couple, and one of you has all the debts, it may make sense for that spouse to file for bankruptcy alone (especially if the nonfiling spouse has good credit to protect).
- You may want to file alone if you and your spouse own property as tenants by the entirety (see Ch. 3, Section A), you owe most of the debts in your own name, and you live in a state that excludes such property from the bankruptcy estate when one spouse files. This is a particularly important consideration if you own your home as tenants by the entirety—filing jointly could cause you to lose your home. (See Ch. 4 for more information.)
- If the exemption system you are using allows married spouses to double their exemptions,

filing jointly may help you hang on to more of your property. (See Ch. 3 for more information on exemptions, and Appendix 1 for state-by-state information on doubling.)
- If you are still married but separated, you may have to file alone if your spouse won't cooperate. Still, if your debts and property are joint rather than separate, a joint filing would probably be to your best advantage.

If you are uncertain about how to file, see a lawyer. Deciding whether to file jointly or alone can have significant consequences. Because the best choice will depend on your unique situation, we advise you to talk to a bankruptcy lawyer if you have any questions about which option makes more sense.

D. Required Forms and Documents

Bankruptcy uses official forms prescribed by the federal office of the courts. In addition, the new law requires you to file certain documents, as described in Section A. Here we provide complete lists of (1) the official forms you will be completing in this chapter, and (2) the documents that you will have to file along with the official forms. We also explain how to get these forms and documents.

1. Checklist of Required Bankruptcy Forms

These are the standard forms that must be filed in every Chapter 7 bankruptcy:

- ❏ Form 1—Voluntary Petition
- ❏ Form 3A—(if you want to pay your filing fee in installments)
- ❏ Form 3B—(if you apply for a fee waiver)
- ❏ Form 6, which consists of:
    - ❏ Schedule A—Real Property
    - ❏ Schedule B—Personal Property
    - ❏ Schedule C—Property Claimed as Exempt
    - ❏ Schedule D—Creditors Holding Secured Claims
    - ❏ Schedule E—Creditors Holding Unsecured Priority Claims
    - ❏ Schedule F—Creditors Holding Unsecured Nonpriority Claims

❏ Schedule G—Executory Contracts and
   Unexpired Leases
❏ Schedule H—Codebtors
❏ Schedule I—Current Income
❏ Schedule J—Current Expenditures
❏ Summary of Schedules A through J
❏ Declaration Concerning Debtor's Schedules
❏ Form 7—Statement of Financial Affairs
❏ Form 8—Chapter 7 Individual Debtor's Statement
   of Intention
❏ Form 21—Full Social Security Number Disclosure
❏ Form B22A—Statement of Current Monthly
   Income and Means Test Calculation
❏ Form B201—Notice to Individual Consumer
   Debtor Under § 342 of the Bankruptcy Code
❏ Mailing Matrix
❏ Required local forms, if any.

With the exception of Form B22A, which might
require you to do a fair bit of math, the forms are very
straightforward and easy to complete, as long as you
take them one at a time. Also, you probably won't have
to spend time on each of them, even though they will
be part of your filing package. For instance, if you don't
own real estate, you can simply check the None box on
Schedule A and proceed to Schedule B.

All together, these forms usually are referred to as
your "bankruptcy petition," although technically your
petition is only Form 1. (In case you're wondering,
Forms 2, 4, and 5 aren't used in voluntary Chapter 7
bankruptcy filings.)

Fee Waiver

You may ask the court to waive the fees by filing
Form 3B. To qualify, you must be unable to pay in
installments and your income must be below 150%
of the poverty line. You can find a blank copy of
the form in Appendix 3; as you'll see, it is fairly
complicated and asks you to repeat much of the
information from your other papers. There is some
doubt as to whether courts will grant requests for
fee waivers, but there's no harm in trying.

---

2. Checklist of Required Documents

As explained in Section A, above, the new bankruptcy
law requires filers to submit some documents along
with their forms. The documents you must file are:

❏ your most recent federal tax return (or a transcript
   of the return obtained from the IRS)
❏ a certificate showing that you have completed the
   required credit counseling
❏ any repayment plan that was developed during
   your credit counseling, and
❏ your pay stubs for the previous 60 days (along
   with an accompanying form, if your local court
   requires one).

3. Where to Get the Official Forms

Appendix 3 of this book includes tear-out copies of all
of the required bankruptcy forms. You can type the
necessary information in the blanks, or complete the
forms by hand. Other options include:

• Get free, fill-in-the-blanks PDF forms from the
  website of the U.S. Trustee, www.usdoj.gov/ust
  (click "Data Enabled Form Standard" from the
  home page). You can enter your information on
  the computer, but you can't save your entries.
  And, because this site doesn't have every required
  form, you'll have to use a few forms from the
  federal judiciary site (see below) or Appendix 3 of
  this book.

• Get nonfillable PDF forms from the website of the
  federal judiciary, www.uscourts.gov (click "U.S.
  Bankruptcy Courts," then "Bankruptcy Forms").
  This site includes a complete set of forms, but
  you can't fill them in on the computer—you'll
  have to type or print your information.

• Purchase a software package that includes
  the forms. (Our favorite is Blankrupter 4.0, a
  software program available for $49.95 from
  BlumbergExcelsior, www.blumberg.com.
  Although you'll have to lay out some cash, you
  can fill out the forms on your computer and save
  your entries. What's more, the program uses the
  basic information you enter to complete every
  form to which it applies, which can be a real
  time saver.) If you have to take the means test
  (because your income is higher than your state's
  median income), you can use the program's
  means test calculator, which incorporates the

IRS and Census Bureau figures. If you edit your entries, the program automatically revises the means test presumption and fills out the appropriate forms; you won't have to re-enter data or do side calculations.

4. Tips for Completing the Forms

Here are some tips that will make filling in your forms easier and the whole bankruptcy process smoother. A sample completed form accompanies each form's instructions. Refer to it while you fill in your bankruptcy papers.

Use your worksheets and credit counseling plan (if you have one). If you've completed the worksheets in Chs. 1, 3, 4, and 5, you've already done a lot of the work. These worksheets will save you lots of time when you prepare your bankruptcy forms, so keep them handy. If you skipped any of those chapters, refer to the worksheets and accompanying instructions for help in figuring out what to put in your bankruptcy forms.

Make several copies of each form. That way, you can make a draft, changing things as you go until the form is complete and correct. Prepare final forms to file with the court only after you've double checked your drafts. If you use the pdf, fill-in-the-blanks forms available from the U.S. Trustee's website (see Section 3, above), remember that you can't save the information in the forms. It's easiest to do a draft by hand, then complete the form and print it all at once.

Type your final forms. If you are using the Nolo forms or the nonfillable PDF forms available from the federal judiciary website (see Section 3, above), you could write in your information by hand. However, the trustee handling your case will likely be friendlier if forms are typewritten. If you don't have access to a typewriter, many libraries have typewriters available to the public (for a small rental fee), or you can hire a bankruptcy form preparation service to prepare your forms using the information you provide. (See Ch. 10 for more on these services.)

Be ridiculously thorough. Always err on the side of giving too much information rather than too little. If you leave information out, the bankruptcy trustee may become suspicious of your motives. If you leave creditors off the forms, the debts you owe these creditors might not be discharged—hardly the result you would want. If you intentionally or carelessly fail to list all your property and debts, or fail to accurately describe your recent property transactions, the court, upon a request by the trustee, may rule that you acted with fraudulent intent. It may deny your bankruptcy discharge altogether, and you may lose some property that you could otherwise have kept.

Respond to every question. Most of the forms have a box to check when your answer is "none." If a question doesn't have a "none" box and the question doesn't apply to you, type in "N/A" for "not applicable." This will let the trustee know that you didn't overlook the question. Occasionally, a question that doesn't apply to you will have a number of blanks. Put "N/A" in only the first blank if it is obvious that this applies to the other blanks as well. If it's not clear, put "N/A" in every blank.

Explain uncertainties. If you can't figure out which category on a form to use for a debt or an item of property, list the debt or item in what you think is the appropriate place and briefly note next to your entry that you're uncertain. The important thing is to disclose the information somewhere. The bankruptcy trustee will sort it out, if necessary.

Be scrupulously honest. As part of your official bankruptcy paperwork, you must complete declarations, under penalty of perjury, swearing that you've been truthful. It's important to realize that you could be prosecuted for perjury if it's evident that you deliberately lied.

Use continuation pages if you run out of room. The space for entering information is sometimes skimpy, especially if you're filing jointly. Most of the forms come with preformatted continuation pages that you can use if you need more room. But if there is no continuation form in Appendix 3, prepare one yourself, using a piece of regular, white 8 ½ by 11" paper. Put "see continuation page" next to the question you're working on and enter the additional information on the continuation page. Label the continuation pages with your name and the form name, and indicate "Continuation Page 1," "Continuation Page 2," and so on. Be sure to attach all continuation pages to their appropriate forms when you file your bankruptcy papers.

Get help, if necessary. If your situation is complicated, you're unsure about how to complete a form, or you run into trouble when you go to file your papers, consult a bankruptcy attorney or do some legal research before proceeding. (See Ch. 10.)

Refer to—but don't copy—the sample forms.
Throughout this chapter, we have included the completed sample forms of Carrie Anne Edwards, who lives in California. These forms are intended to be used as examples, so you can see what a completed form should look like. However, everyone's bankruptcy situation is different—and obviously, you will owe different debts, own different property, have different bank accounts and Social Security numbers, and otherwise be utterly dissimilar from this fictional gal. DO NOT COPY THESE EXAMPLES, even if you live in California, because they won't fit your precise situation.

E. Form 1—Voluntary Petition

A completed sample Voluntary Petition and line-by-line instructions follow.

Emergency Filing

Although people usually file all of their bankruptcy forms at once, you don't absolutely have to. If you really need to stop creditors quickly—because of a foreclosure or threatened repossession, you can simply file the three-page Voluntary Petition together with your credit counseling certificate, the statement of your Social Security number (Form B21,) and a form called a Matrix, which lists the name, address, and zip code of each of your creditors. The automatic stay, which stops most collection efforts against you, will then go into effect. You have 15 days to file the rest of the forms. (Bankruptcy Rule 1007(c).) See Section M, below, for instructions.

Although it's an option if you're really in a jam, we urge you to not do an emergency filing unless it's absolutely necessary. That 15-day extension goes by fast; many people blow the deadline, then have their cases dismissed. So, if at all possible, file all your paperwork at the same time.

First Page

Court Name. At the top of the first page, fill in the first two blanks with the name of the judicial district you're filing in, such as the "Central District of California." If your state has only one district, enter "XXXXXX" in the first blank and your state in the second blank. If your state divides its districts into divisions, enter the division after the state name, such as "Northern District of California, Santa Rosa Division."

Name of Debtor. Enter your full name (last name first), as used on your checks, driver's license, and other formal documents. If you are married and filing jointly (see Section C, above), put one of your names as the debtor (on the left) and the other formal name as the "joint debtor (spouse)," on the right. If you are married but filing separately, enter "N/A" in the second blank.

All Other Names. The purpose of this box is to make sure that your creditors will know who you are when they receive notice of your bankruptcy filing. If you have been known by any other name in the last six years, list it here. If you've operated a business as a sole proprietor during the previous six years, include your trade name (fictitious or assumed business name) preceded by "dba" for "doing business as." But don't include minor variations in spelling or form. For instance, if your name is John Lewis Odegard, you don't have to put down that you're sometimes known as J.L. But if you've used the pseudonym J.L. Smith, you should list it. If you're uncertain, list any name that you think you may have used with a creditor. Do the same for your spouse (in the box to the right) if you are filing jointly. If you're filing alone, type "N/A" anywhere in the box to the right.

Soc. Sec./Tax I.D. No. Enter only the last four digits of your Social Security number. If you have a taxpayer's I.D. number, enter the complete number. Do the same for your spouse (in the box to the right) if you are filing jointly. If you're filing alone, type "N/A" anywhere in the box to the right.

Street Address of Debtor. Enter your current street address. Even if you get all of your mail at a post office box, list the address of your personal residence.

Street Address of Joint Debtor. Enter your spouse's current street address (even if it's the same as yours) if you are filing jointly—again, no post office boxes. If you're filing alone, type "N/A" anywhere in the box.

County of Residence. Enter the county in which you live. Do the same for your spouse if you're filing jointly. Otherwise, type "N/A" in the box. If you are doing business, enter the county where your (or your

(Official Form 1) (10/05)

United States Bankruptcy Court **Northern District of California**	**Voluntary Petition**

Name of Debtor (if individual, enter Last, First, Middle): Edwards, Carrie Anne	Name of Joint Debtor (Spouse) (Last, First, Middle):
All Other Names used by the Debtor in the last 8 years (include married, maiden, and trade names):	All Other Names used by the Joint Debtor in the last 8 years (include married, maiden, and trade names):
Last four digits of Soc. Sec./Complete EIN or other Tax ID No. (if more than one, state all) xxx-xx-6287	Last four digits of Soc. Sec./Complete EIN or other Tax ID No. (if more than one, state all)
Street Address of Debtor (No. & Street, City, and State): 3045 Berwick St Lakeport, CA <div align="right">ZIP Code 95453</div>	Street Address of Joint Debtor (No. & Street, City, and State): <div align="right">ZIP Code</div>
County of Residence or of the Principal Place of Business: Lake	County of Residence or of the Principal Place of Business:
Mailing Address of Debtor (if different from street address): PO Box 1437 Lakeport, CA <div align="right">ZIP Code 95453</div>	Mailing Address of Joint Debtor (if different from street address): <div align="right">ZIP Code</div>
Location of Principal Assets of Business Debtor (if different from street address above):	

Type of Debtor (Form of Organization) (Check one box)	Nature of Business (Check all applicable boxes.)	Chapter of Bankruptcy Code Under Which the Petition is Filed (Check one box)
■ Individual (includes Joint Debtors) ☐ Corporation (includes LLC and LLP) ☐ Partnership ☐ Other (If debtor is not one of the above entities, check this box and provide the information requested below.) State type of entity:	☐ Health Care Business ☐ Single Asset Real Estate as defined in 11 U.S.C. § 101 (51B) ☐ Railroad ☐ Stockbroker ☐ Commodity Broker ☐ Clearing Bank ☐ Nonprofit Organization qualified under 15 U.S.C. § 501(c)(3)	■ Chapter 7 ☐ Chapter 11 ☐ Chapter 15 Petition for Recognition of a Foreign Main Proceeding ☐ Chapter 9 ☐ Chapter 12 ☐ Chapter 15 Petition for Recognition of a Foreign Nonmain Proceeding ☐ Chapter 13
		Nature of Debts (Check one box) ■ Consumer/Non-Business ☐ Business

Filing Fee (Check one box)	Chapter 11 Debtors
■ Full Filing Fee attached ☐ Filing Fee to be paid in installments (Applicable to individuals only) Must attach signed application for the court's consideration certifying that the debtor is unable to pay fee except in installments. Rule 1006(b). See Official Form 3A. ☐ Filing Fee waiver requested (Applicable to chapter 7 individuals only). Must attach signed application for the court's consideration. See Official Form 3B.	Check one box: ☐ Debtor is a small business debtor as defined in 11 U.S.C. § 101(51D). ☐ Debtor is not a small business debtor as defined in 11 U.S.C. § 101(51D). ——————— Check if: ☐ Debtor's aggregate noncontingent liquidated debts owed to non-insiders or affiliates are less than $2 million.

Statistical/Administrative Information	THIS SPACE IS FOR COURT USE ONLY
☐ Debtor estimates that funds will be available for distribution to unsecured creditors. ■ Debtor estimates that, after any exempt property is excluded and administrative expenses paid, there will be no funds available for distribution to unsecured creditors.	

Estimated Number of Creditors

1- 49	50- 99	100- 199	200- 999	1000- 5,000	5001- 10,000	10,001- 25,000	25,001- 50,000	50,001- 100,000	OVER 100,000
■	☐	☐	☐	☐	☐	☐	☐	☐	☐

Estimated Assets

$0 to $50,000	$50,001 to $100,000	$100,001 to $500,000	$500,001 to $1 million	$1,000,001 to $10 million	$10,000,001 to $50 million	$50,000,001 to $100 million	More than $100 million
☐	☐	■	☐	☐	☐	☐	☐

Estimated Debts

$0 to $50,000	$50,001 to $100,000	$100,001 to $500,000	$500,001 to $1 million	$1,000,001 to $10 million	$10,000,001 to $50 million	$50,000,001 to $100 million	More than $100 million
☐	☐	■	☐	☐	☐	☐	☐

spouse's) business assets are located, if it's different than your mailing address.

Mailing Address of Debtor. Enter your mailing address if it is different from your street address. If it isn't, put "N/A." Do the same for your spouse (in the box to the right) if you are filing jointly.

Location of Principal Assets of Business Debtor. If you—or your spouse, if you are filing jointly—have been self-employed or operated a business as a sole proprietor within the last two years, you may be considered a "business debtor." This means you will have to provide additional information on Form 7. (See the instructions for that form, below.) If your business owns any assets—such as machines or inventory—list their primary location. If they are all located at your home or mailing address, enter that address.

Type of Debtor. Check the first box—"Individual(s)"—even if you have been self-employed or operated a sole proprietorship during the previous two years. If you are filing bankruptcy for a corporation, partnership, or other type of business entity, you shouldn't be using this book.

Nature of Business. See a bankruptcy lawyer if any of these business descriptions apply to you or your spouse. For instance, if you or your spouse own an assisted living facility (11 U.S.C. Section 101 (27A)), you would need a lawyer's services, because the law has gotten quite complicated regarding how health care businesses are treated in bankruptcy.

Chapter of Bankruptcy Code Under Which the Petition is Filed. Check "Chapter 7."

Nature of Debts. Check "Consumer/Non-Business" if you aren't in business and haven't been for the previous two years. If you're self-employed or in business as a sole proprietor, check "Consumer/Non-Business" if most of your debts are owed personally— not by your business. If, however, the bulk of your debts are due to the operation of your business, check "Business." If you are in doubt, check "Business." Later on this category will be very important. For instance, even if your income is above the state median, you won't have to take the means test if you are a business debtor. (See the instructions for Form B22A, in Section J, below, for more on the means test.)

Filing Fee. If you will attach the entire fee, check the first box. If you plan to ask the court for permission to pay in installments, check the second box. (Instructions for applying to the court are in Section M, below.) If you wish to apply for a full waiver of the filing fee, check the third box and see Section M, below.

⚠️ **Federal agencies disagree over whether fee waivers are available.** As you'll see, there is an ongoing dispute in the federal government regarding fee waivers. The agency responsible for creating the forms has provided a form for fee waivers, which refers to a rule that provides for the waivers. However, the agency responsible for making the rules has refused to issue a rule permitting the waivers.

Chapter 11 Debtors. Leave this section blank.

Statistical/Administrative Information. Here there are a number of boxes. The first set of boxes tells the trustee whether you think there will be assets available to be sold for the benefit of your unsecured creditors. If you did your homework in Ch. 3 and Ch. 4, you will have a good idea of whether all of your assets can be claimed as exempt, or whether some will have to be surrendered to the trustee. Check the top or bottom box accordingly. If you check the bottom box, your creditors will be told that there is no point in filing a Proof of Claim unless they hear differently from the trustee. If you check the top box, your creditors will be told to file Proof of Claims. If you haven't a clue yet about your property and exemptions, come back to this question after you've completed Schedules A, B, and C.

Similarly, if you can provide pretty good estimates of the other information requested (estimated number of creditors, assets, and debts), fill in the appropriate box on the form. If not, come back to these questions when you've completed more of your paperwork.

Second Page

Name of Debtor(s). Enter your name and your spouse's, if you are filing jointly.

Prior Bankruptcy Case Filed Within Last 8 Years. If you haven't filed a bankruptcy case within the previous eight years, type "N/A" in the first box. If you—or your spouse, if you're filing jointly—have, enter the requested information. A previous Chapter 7 bankruptcy bars you from filing another one until eight years have passed since you filed the previous case. And, if you filed a Chapter 7 bankruptcy case that was dismissed for cause within the previous 180 days, you

(Official Form 1) (10/05)	FORM B1, Page 2

Voluntary Petition

(This page must be completed and filed in every case)

Name of Debtor(s):
Edwards, Carrie Anne

Prior Bankruptcy Case Filed Within Last 8 Years (If more than one, attach additional sheet)		
Location Where Filed: - None -	Case Number:	Date Filed:

Pending Bankruptcy Case Filed by any Spouse, Partner, or Affiliate of this Debtor (If more than one, attach additional sheet)		
Name of Debtor: - None -	Case Number:	Date Filed:
District:	Relationship:	Judge:

Exhibit A	**Exhibit B**
(To be completed if debtor is required to file periodic reports (e.g., forms 10K and 10Q) with the Securities and Exchange Commission pursuant to Section 13 or 15(d) of the Securities Exchange Act of 1934 and is requesting relief under chapter 11.) ☐ Exhibit A is attached and made a part of this petition.	(To be completed if debtor is an individual whose debts are primarily consumer debts.) I, the attorney for the petitioner named in the foregoing petition, declare that I have informed the petitioner that [he or she] may proceed under chapter 7, 11, 12, or 13 of title 11, United States Code, and have explained the relief available under each such chapter. I further certify that I delivered to the debtor the notice required by §342(b) of the Bankruptcy Code. X _____ Signature of Attorney for Debtor(s) Date

Exhibit C	**Certification Concerning Debt Counseling by Individual/Joint Debtor(s)**
Does the debtor own or have possession of any property that poses or is alleged to pose a threat of imminent and identifiable harm to public health or safety? ☐ Yes, and Exhibit C is attached and made a part of this petition. ■ No	■ I/we have received approved budget and credit counseling during the 180-day period preceding the filing of this petition. ☐ I/we request a waiver of the requirement to obtain budget and credit counseling prior to filing based on exigent circumstances. (Must attach certification describing.)

Information Regarding the Debtor (Check the Applicable Boxes)

Venue (Check any applicable box)

■   Debtor has been domiciled or has had a residence, principal place of business, or principal assets in this District for 180 days immediately preceding the date of this petition or for a longer part of such 180 days than in any other District.

☐   There is a bankruptcy case concerning debtor's affiliate, general partner, or partnership pending in this District.

☐   Debtor is a debtor in a foreign proceeding and has its principal place of business or principal assets in the United States in this District, or has no principal place of business or assets in the United States but is a defendant in an action or proceeding [in a federal or state court] in this District, or the interests of the parties will be served in regard to the relief sought in this District.

Statement by a Debtor Who Resides as a Tenant of Residential Property
Check all applicable boxes.

☐   Landlord has a judgment against the debtor for possession of debtor's residence. (If box checked, complete the following.)

_____
(Name of landlord that obtained judgment)

_____
(Address of landlord)

☐   Debtor claims that under applicable nonbankruptcy law, there are circumstances under which the debtor would be permitted to cure the entire monetary default that gave rise to the judgment for possession, after the judgment for possession was entered, and

☐   Debtor has included in this petition the deposit with the court of any rent that would become due during the 30-day period after the filing of the petition.

may have to wait to file again, or you may not be able to discharge all your debts. (See Ch. 2, Section B, for more information.) If either situation applies to you, see a bankruptcy lawyer before filing.

Pending Bankruptcy Case Filed by any Spouse, Partner, or Affiliate of this Debtor. "Affiliate" refers to a related business under a corporate structure. "Partner" refers to a business partnership. Again, you shouldn't use this book if you're filing as a corporation, partnership, or other type of business entity. If your spouse has a bankruptcy case pending anywhere in the country, enter the requested information. Otherwise, type "N/A" in the first box.

Exhibit A. This is solely for people who are filing for Chapter 11 bankruptcy. Leave it blank.

Exhibit B. This is solely for people who are represented by an attorney. If you are representing yourself or using a bankruptcy petition preparer, leave this section blank.

Exhibit C. If you own or have in your possession any property that might cause "imminent and identifiable" harm to public health or safety (for example, real estate that is polluted with toxic substances, or explosive devices such as hand grenades or dynamite), check the "yes" box, fill in Exhibit C (see Appendix 3), and attach Exhibit C to this Petition. If you are unsure about whether a particular piece of property fits the bill, err on the side of inclusion.

Certification Concerning Debt Counseling by Individual/Joint Debtor(s). With rare exceptions, individuals filing for Chapter 7 bankruptcy are required to participate in debt counseling sessions within 180 days of their bankruptcy filing (see Section A, above, for more details). Most of you will check the top box. If you must file now and haven't had an opportunity to get credit counseling, check the bottom box and attach a certification (statement under penalty of perjury) explaining why you didn't have time to get your credit counseling done. Although the petition asks you to certify that you have received both budget and credit counseling, the question refers only to credit counseling. You are also required to undergo budget counseling, but that happens later (within 45 days after your meeting of creditors—see Ch. 7).

Information Regarding the Debtor. Most filers will check the top box. (See Section B, above.) Check the middle box if it is appropriate (it won't be for most users of this book, which is intended for individuals and sole proprietors). Leave the bottom box blank. If it applies to you, see a lawyer.

Statement by a Debtor Who Resides as a Tenant of Residential Property. As explained in Ch. 2, certain evictions are allowed to proceed after you file for bankruptcy, despite the automatic stay. The questions in this section are intended to figure out whether your landlord has already gotten a judgment for possession (eviction order), and whether you might be able to postpone the eviction. See Ch. 2, Section C, for the information you need to complete these boxes, if they apply.

Third Page

Signature(s) of Debtor(s) (Individual/Joint). You—and your spouse, if you are filing jointly—must sign where indicated. If you are filing alone, type "N/A" on the joint debtor signature line. Include your telephone number and the date. You—and your spouse, if you are filing jointly—declare that you are aware that you may file under other sections of the bankruptcy code, and that you still choose to file for Chapter 7 bankruptcy. (These provisions are described in Ch. 1, Section E.) If you think you want to pursue one of those options, put your Chapter 7 petition aside and either consult a lawyer or find a book that explains your proposed alternative in more detail. For example, check out *Chapter 13 Bankruptcy: Repay Your Debts,* by Stephen Elias and Robin Leonard (Nolo).

Signature of Attorney. If you are representing yourself, type "debtor not represented by attorney" in the space for the attorney's signature. If you are represented by a lawyer, fill in the blanks accordingly.

Signature of Non-Attorney Petition Preparer. If a bankruptcy petition preparer typed your forms, have that person complete this section. Otherwise, type "N/A" on the first line.

(Official Form 1) (10/05)   FORM B1, Page 3

Voluntary Petition	Name of Debtor(s):
(This page must be completed and filed in every case)	Edwards, Carrie Anne

Signatures

Signature(s) of Debtor(s) (Individual/Joint)	**Signature of a Foreign Representative**

Signature(s) of Debtor(s) (Individual/Joint)

I declare under penalty of perjury that the information provided in this petition is true and correct.
[If petitioner is an individual whose debts are primarily consumer debts and has chosen to file under chapter 7] I am aware that I may proceed under chapter 7, 11, 12, or 13 of title 11, United States Code, understand the relief available under each such chapter, and choose to proceed under chapter 7.
[If no attorney represents me and no bankruptcy petition preparer signs the petition] I have obtained and read the notice required by §342(b) of the Bankruptcy Code.

I request relief in accordance with the chapter of title 11, United States Code, specified in this petition.

X _____
Signature of Debtor

X _____
Signature of Joint Debtor

_____
Telephone Number (If not represented by attorney)

_____
Date

Signature of a Foreign Representative

I declare under penalty of perjury that the information provided in this petition is true and correct, that I am the foreign representative of a debtor in a foreign proceeding, and that I am authorized to file this petition.

(Check only one box.)

☐ I request relief in accordance with chapter 15 of title 11. United States Code. Certified copies of the documents required by §1515 of title 11 are attached.

☐ Pursuant to §1511 of title 11, United States Code, I request relief in accordance with the chapter of title 11 specified in this petition. A certified copy of the order granting recognition of the foreign main proceeding is attached.

X _____
Signature of Foreign Representative

_____
Printed Name of Foreign Representative

_____
Date

Signature of Attorney

X Debtor not represented by attorney
Signature of Attorney for Debtor(s)

_____
Printed Name of Attorney for Debtor(s)

_____
Firm Name

_____
Address

_____
Telephone Number

_____
Date

Signature of Non-Attorney Bankruptcy Petition Preparer

I declare under penalty of perjury that: (1) I am a bankruptcy petition preparer as defined in 11 U.S.C. § 110; (2) I prepared this document for compensation and have provided the debtor with a copy of this document and the notices and information required under 11 U.S.C. §§ 110(b), 110(h), and 342(b); and, (3) if rules or guidelines have been promulgated pursuant to 11 U.S.C. § 110(h) setting a maximum fee for services chargeable by bankruptcy petition preparers, I have given the debtor notice of the maximum amount before preparing any document for filing for a debtor or accepting any fee from the debtor, as required in that section. Official Form 19B is attached.

_____
Printed Name and title, if any, of Bankruptcy Petition Preparer

_____
Social Security number (If the bankrutpcy petition preparer is not an individual, state the Social Security number of the officer, principal, responsible person or partner of the bankruptcy petition preparer.)(Required by 11 U.S.C. § 110.)

_____
Address

X _____

_____
Date

Signature of Debtor (Corporation/Partnership)

I declare under penalty of perjury that the information provided in this petition is true and correct, and that I have been authorized to file this petition on behalf of the debtor.

The debtor requests relief in accordance with the chapter of title 11, United States Code, specified in this petition.

X _____
Signature of Authorized Individual

_____
Printed Name of Authorized Individual

_____
Title of Authorized Individual

_____
Date

Signature of Bankruptcy Petition Preparer or officer, principal, responsible person, or partner whose social security number is provided above.

Names and Social Security numbers of all other individuals who prepared or assisted in preparing this document unless the bankruptcy petition preparer is not an individual:

If more than one person prepared this document, attach additional sheets conforming to the appropriate official form for each person.

A bankruptcy petition preparer's failure to comply with the provisions of title 11 and the Federal Rules of Bankruptcy Procedure may result in fines or imprisonment or both 11 U.S.C. §110; 18 U.S.C. §156.

F. Form 6—Schedules

Form 6 refers to a series of schedules that provides the trustee and court with a picture of your current financial situation. Most of the information needed for these schedules is included in the Personal Property Checklist, Property Exemption Worksheet, and Homeowners' Worksheet that you (hopefully) completed in Chs. 3 and 4.

Use the correct address for your creditors. Many of these schedules ask you to provide addresses for the creditors you list. For creditors who have dunned you with written requests or demands for payment, you should provide the address that the creditor listed as a contact address on at least two written communications you received from the creditor within the 90-day period prior to your anticipated filing date. If the creditor has not contacted you within that 90-day period, provide the contact address that the creditor gave in the last two communications it sent to you. If you no longer have the address of your original creditor, use the contact address of the most recent creditors. If a creditor is a minor child, simply put "minor child" and the appropriate address. Don't list the child's name.

1. Schedule A—Real Property

Here you list all the real property you own as of the date you'll file the petition. Don't worry about whether a particular piece of property is exempt; you don't have to claim your exemptions until you get to Schedule C. If you completed the Personal Property Checklist, Property Exemption Worksheet, and Homeowner's Worksheet in Ch. 3 and Ch. 4, get them out. Much of that information goes on Schedule A.

A completed sample of Schedule A and line-by-line instructions follow. Even if you don't own any real estate, you still must complete the top of this form.

Tab this page. You might want to put a sticky note alongside the instructions for Schedule A, because we'll keep referring back to the instructions on these pages.

In re. (This means "In the matter of.") Type your name and the name of your spouse, if you're filing jointly. "In re [your name(s)]" will be the name of your bankruptcy case.

Case No. If you made an emergency filing, fill in the case number assigned by the court. Otherwise, leave this blank.

If you don't own real estate, type "N/A" anywhere in the first column, type "0" in the total box at the bottom of the page, and move on to Schedule B.

Real Property Defined

Real property—land and things permanently attached to land—includes more than just a house. It can also include unimproved land, vacation cabins, condominiums, duplexes, rental property, business property, mobile home park spaces, agricultural land, airplane hangars, and any other buildings permanently attached to land.

You may own real estate even if you can't walk on it, live on it, or get income from it. This might be true, for example, if:

- you own real estate solely because you are married to a spouse who owns real estate and you live in a community property state, or
- someone else lives on property that you are entitled to receive in the future under a trust agreement.

There's a separate schedule for leases and timeshares. If you hold a timeshare lease in a vacation cabin or property, lease a boat dock, lease underground portions of real estate for mineral or oil exploration, or otherwise lease or rent real estate of any description, don't list it on Schedule A. All leases and timeshares should be listed on Schedule G. (See the instructions for that schedule in Section 7, below.).

Description and Location of Property. For each piece of real property you own, list the type of property—for example, house, farm, or undeveloped lot—and street address. You don't need to include the legal description of the property (the description on the deed).

Nature of Debtor's Interest in Property. In this column, you need to provide the legal definition for the interest you (or you and your spouse) have in the real estate. The most common type of interest—outright ownership—is called "fee simple." Even if you still

Form B6A
(10/05)

In re   Carrie Anne Edwards _____,   Case No. _____
                                                    Debtor

SCHEDULE A. REAL PROPERTY

Except as directed below, list all real property in which the debtor has any legal, equitable, or future interest, including all property owned as a cotenant, community property, or in which the debtor has a life estate. Include any property in which the debtor holds rights and powers exercisable for the debtor's own benefit. If the debtor is married, state whether husband, wife, or both own the property by placing an "H," "W," "J," or "C" in the column labeled "Husband, Wife, Joint, or Community." If the debtor holds no interest in real property, write "None" under "Description and Location of Property."

Do not include interests in executory contracts and unexpired leases on this schedule. List them in Schedule G - Executory Contracts and Unexpired Leases.

If an entity claims to have a lien or hold a secured interest in any property, state the amount of the secured claim. See Schedule D. If no entity claims to hold a secured interest in the property, write "None" in the column labeled "Amount of Secured Claim."

If the debtor is an individual or if a joint petition is filed, state the amount of any exemption claimed in the property only in Schedule C - Property Claimed as Exempt.

Description and Location of Property	Nature of Debtor's Interest in Property	Husband, Wife, Joint, or Community	Current Value of Debtor's Interest in Property, without Deducting any Secured Claim or Exemption	Amount of Secured Claim
Residence Location: 3045 Berwick St, Lakeport CA	Fee Simple	–	140,000.00	140,000.00

	Sub-Total >	140,000.00	(Total of this page)
	Total >	140,000.00	

_0_ continuation sheets attached to the Schedule of Real Property

(Report also on Summary of Schedules)

owe money on your mortgage, as long as you have the right to sell the house, leave it to your heirs, and make alterations, your ownership is fee simple. A fee simple interest may be owned by one person or by several people jointly. Normally, when people are listed on a deed as the owners—even if they own the property as joint tenants, tenants in common, or tenants by the entirety—the ownership interest is in fee simple. Other types of real property interests include:

- **Life estate.** This is the right to possess and use property only during your lifetime. You can't sell the property, give it away, or leave it to someone when you die. Instead, when you die, the property passes to whomever was named in the instrument (trust, deed, or will) that created your life estate. This type of ownership is usually created when the sole owner of a piece of real estate wants his surviving spouse to live on the property for the rest of her life, but then have the property pass to his children. In this situation, the surviving spouse has a life estate. Surviving spouses who are beneficiaries of A-B, spousal, or marital by-pass trusts have life estates.

- **Future interest.** This is your right to own property sometime in the future. A common future interest is owned by a person who—under the terms of a deed or irrevocable trust—will inherit the property when its current possessor dies. Note that the fact that you are named in a will or living trust doesn't create a future interest, because the person who signed the deed or trust can easily amend the document to cut you out.

- **Contingent interest.** This ownership interest doesn't come into existence unless one or more conditions are fulfilled. Wills sometimes leave property to people under certain conditions. If the conditions aren't met, the property passes to someone else. For instance, Emma's will leaves her house to John provided that he takes care of her until her death. If John doesn't care for Emma, the house passes to Emma's daughter Jane. Both John and Jane have contingent interests in Emma's home.

- **Lienholder.** If you are the holder of a mortgage, deed of trust, judgment lien, or mechanic's lien on real estate, you have an ownership interest in the real estate.

- **Easement holder.** If you are the holder of a right to travel on or otherwise use property owned by someone else, you have an easement.

- **Power of appointment.** If you have a legal right, given to you in a will or transfer of property, to sell a specified piece of someone's property, that's called a power of appointment and should be listed.

- **Beneficial ownership under a real estate contract.** This is the right to own property by virtue of having signed a binding real estate contract. Even though the buyer doesn't yet own the property, the buyer does have a "beneficial interest"—that is, the right to own the property once the formalities are completed. For example, property buyers have a beneficial ownership interest in property while the escrow is pending.

If you have trouble figuring out which of these definitions best fits your type of ownership interest, leave the column blank and let the trustee help you sort it out.

Husband, Wife, Joint, or Community. If you're not married, put "N/A." If you are married, indicate whether the real estate is owned:

- by the husband (H)
- by the wife (W)
- jointly by husband and wife as joint tenants, tenants in common, or tenants by the entirety (J), or
- jointly by husband and wife as community property (C).

For more information on ownership of property by married couples, see Ch. 3, Section A.

Current Value of Debtor's Interest in Property, without Deducting any Secured Claim or Exemption. Enter the current fair market value of your real estate ownership interest. If you filled in the Homeowners' Worksheet in Ch. 4, use the value you came up with there.

Don't figure in homestead exemptions or any mortgages or other liens on the property. Just put the actual current market value as best you can calculate it. However, you can deduct the costs of sale from the market value and enter the difference, as long as you explain what you did on the schedule. (See Ch. 4 for information on valuing real estate.)

If you own the property with someone else who is not joining you in your bankruptcy, list only your ownership share in this column. For example, if you and your brother own a home as joint tenants (each owns 50%), split the property's current market value in half and list that amount here.

If your interest is intangible—for example, you are a beneficiary of real estate held in trust that won't be distributed for many years—enter an estimate provided by a real estate appraiser or put "don't know" and explain why you can't be more precise.

Total. Add the amounts in the fourth column and enter the total in the box at the bottom of the page. The form reminds you that you should also enter this total on the Summary of Schedules (see the instructions for completing the summary, below).

Amount of Secured Claim. List mortgages and other debts secured by the property. If there is no secured claim of any type on the real estate, enter "None." If there is, enter separately the amount of each outstanding mortgage, deed of trust, home equity loan, or lien (judgment lien, mechanic's lien, materialmen's lien, tax lien, or the like) that is claimed against the property. If you don't know the balance on your mortgage, deed of trust, or home equity loan, call the lender. To find out the existence and values of liens, visit the land records office in your county and look up the parcel in the records; the clerk can show you how. Or, you can order a title search through a real estate attorney or title insurance company. If you own several pieces of real estate and there is one lien on file against all the real estate, list the full amount of the lien for each separate property item. Don't worry if, taken together, the value of the liens is higher than the value of the property; it's quite common.

How you itemize liens in this schedule won't affect how your property or the liens will be treated in bankruptcy. The idea here is to notify the trustee of all possible liens that may affect your equity in your real estate.

If you are simply unable to obtain this information, and you can't afford the help of a lawyer or title insurance company, put "unknown." This will be okay for the purpose of filing your papers, but you may need to get the information later. For example, a question might come up as to whether the equity in your home is protected by your exemption. Suppose your exemption is $10,000 and your equity is $30,000. You would probably lose the house and get $10,000,

and your creditors would get $20,000, less the costs of sale. But if there were an unknown lien on the property for $20,000, then you wouldn't have to lose the house, because there would be nothing left over for the unsecured creditors. So it's to your benefit to get this information any way you can.

2. Schedule B—Personal Property

Here you must list and evaluate *all* of your personal property, including property that is security for a debt and property that is exempt. If you didn't fill in the Personal Property Checklist and Property Exemption Worksheet in Ch. 3, turn to that chapter for explanations and suggestions about what property you should list in each of the schedule's categories.

Be honest and thorough. When listing all of your stuff on a public document like Schedule B, you might feel tempted to cheat a little. Don't give in to the temptation to "forget" any of your assets. Bankruptcy law doesn't give you the right to decide that an asset isn't worth mentioning. Even if, for example, you've decided that your CD collection is worthless given the advent of the IPod, you still have to list it. You can explain on the form why you think it's worthless. If you omit something and get caught, your case can be dismissed—or your discharge revoked—leaving you with no bankruptcy relief for your current debts. Remember, you can use exemptions to keep much of your property; if no exemption is available, you may be able to buy the property back from the trustee.

A completed sample of Schedule B and line-by-line instructions follow. If you need more room, use an attached continuation page, or create a continuation page yourself. (See Section D, above.)

In re and **Case No.** Follow the instructions for Schedule A.

Type of Property. The form lists general categories of personal property. You leave this column as is.

None. If you own no property that fits in a category listed in the first column, enter an "X" in the "None" column. But make sure that you really don't own anything in this category.

Description and Location of Property. List specific items that fall in each general category. If you filled out the Personal Property Checklist and Property Exemption Worksheet in Ch. 3, you already have this

Form B6B
(10/05)

In re   Carrie Anne Edwards   Case No. _____
_____ ,
                        Debtor

SCHEDULE B. PERSONAL PROPERTY

Except as directed below, list all personal property of the debtor of whatever kind. If the debtor has no property in one or more of the categories, place an "x" in the appropriate position in the column labeled "None." If additional space is needed in any category, attach a separate sheet properly identified with the case name, case number, and the number of the category. If the debtor is married, state whether husband, wife, or both own the property by placing an "H," "W," "J," or "C" in the column labeled "Husband, Wife, Joint, or Community." If the debtor is an individual or a joint petition is filed, state the amount of any exemptions claimed only in Schedule C - Property Claimed as Exempt.

Do not list interests in executory contracts and unexpired leases on this schedule. List them in Schedule G - Executory Contracts and Unexpired Leases.

If the property is being held for the debtor by someone else, state that person's name and address under "Description and Location of Property."
In providing the information requested in this schedule, do not include the name or address of a minor child. Simply state "a minor child."

Type of Property	N O N E	Description and Location of Property	Husband, Wife, Joint, or Community	Current Value of Debtor's Interest in Property, without Deducting any Secured Claim or Exemption
1. Cash on hand		Cash in wallet	-	50.00
2. Checking, savings or other financial accounts, certificates of deposit, or shares in banks, savings and loan, thrift, building and loan, and homestead associations, or credit unions, brokerage houses, or cooperatives.		Bank of America Checking Account #12345 Lakeport California from wages WestAmerica Bank, Lakeport CA Savings Account	- -	150.00 300.00
3. Security deposits with public utilities, telephone companies, landlords, and others.	X			
4. Household goods and furnishings, including audio, video, and computer equipment.		All items at replacement value Stereo system ($300), washer dryer set (200), refrigerator (400), electric stove (250), misc furniture (couch, 2 chairs, 2 end tables) (500), minor appliances (blender, toaster, mixer) (125), roll top desk (700), vacuum (50), bed and bedding (650), 20 inch tv (75), lawnmower (200), swing set, childrens toys (240), snowblower (160), oriental rug (2500) Location: 3045 Berwick St, Lakeport CA	-	6,350.00
5. Books, pictures and other art objects, antiques, stamp, coin, record, tape, compact disc, and other collections or collectibles.		250 books at used book store prices Location: 3045 Berwick St, Lakeport CA stamp collection at stamp dealer price Location: 3045 Berwick St, Lakeport CA	- -	1,250.00 2,500.00

Sub-Total >   10,600.00
(Total of this page)

__3__   continuation sheets attached to the Schedule of Personal Property

Form B6B
(10/05)

In re   Carrie Anne Edwards   ,   Case No. _____
                                    Debtor

SCHEDULE B. PERSONAL PROPERTY
(Continuation Sheet)

Type of Property	N O N E	Description and Location of Property	Husband, Wife, Joint, or Community	Current Value of Debtor's Interest in Property, without Deducting any Secured Claim or Exemption
6. Wearing apparel.		normal clothing at used clothing store prices Location: 3045 Berwick St, Lakeport CA	-	800.00
7. Furs and jewelry.		diamond necklace at used jewelry store price (800), watch at flea market price (75) Location: 3045 Berwick St, Lakeport CA	-	875.00
8. Firearms and sports, photographic, and other hobby equipment.		Mountain bike at used bicycle store price (250), Digital camera priced at ebay (200), sword collection priced at antique store Location: 3045 Berwick St, Lakeport CA	-	1,250.00
9. Interests in insurance policies. Name insurance company of each policy and itemize surrender or refund value of each.	X			
10. Annuities. Itemize and name each issuer.	X			
11. Interests in an education IRA as defined in 26 U.S.C. § 530(b)(1) or under a qualified State tuition plan as defined in 26 U.S.C. § 529(b)(1). Give particulars. (File separately the record(s) of any such interest(s). 11 U.S.C. § 521(c); Rule 1007(b)).	X			
12. Interests in IRA, ERISA, Keogh, or other pension or profit sharing plans. Give particulars.		TIAA/CREF (ERISA Qualified Pension), not in bankruptcy estate	-	0.00
		IRA, Bank of America, Lakeport CA (25,000), not in bankruptcy estate	-	0.00
13. Stock and interests in incorporated and unincorporated businesses. Itemize.		5,000 shares in BLP Bankruptcy Services, Inc, a close corporation Location of certificates: 3045 Berwick St, Lakeport CA (valued at $.10 a share	-	500.00
14. Interests in partnerships or joint ventures. Itemize.	X			

Sub-Total >   3,425.00
(Total of this page)

Sheet 1 of 3 continuation sheets attached
to the Schedule of Personal Property

Form B6B
(10/05)

In re   Carrie Anne Edwards   Case No. _____
                                                    ,
                                          Debtor

SCHEDULE B. PERSONAL PROPERTY
(Continuation Sheet)

Type of Property	N O N E	Description and Location of Property	Husband, Wife, Joint, or Community	Current Value of Debtor's Interest in Property, without Deducting any Secured Claim or Exemption
15. Government and corporate bonds and other negotiable and nonnegotiable instruments.		U.S. Savings Bonds, all certificates at Ameritrust, 10 Financial Way, Cleaveland Heights OH 41118	-	1,000.00
		Negotiable promissory note from Jonathan Edwards, Carrie's brother, dated 11/3/XX Location: 3045 Berwick St, Lakeport CA	-	500.00
16. Accounts receivable.	X			
17. Alimony, maintenance, support, and property settlements to which the debtor is or may be entitled. Give particulars.	X			
18. Other liquidated debts owing debtor including tax refunds. Give particulars.		Wages for 6/1/XX to 8/1/XX from ABC Typing Services	-	500.00
19. Equitable or future interests, life estates, and rights or powers exercisable for the benefit of the debtor other than those listed in Schedule A - Real Property.	X			
20. Contingent and noncontingent interests in estate of a decedent, death benefit plan, life insurance policy, or trust.	X			
21. Other contingent and unliquidated claims of every nature, including tax refunds, counterclaims of the debtor, and rights to setoff claims. Give estimated value of each.	X			
22. Patents, copyrights, and other intellectual property. Give particulars.		Copyright in book published by Nolo Press (Independent Paralegal's Handbook)	-	Unknown
23. Licenses, franchises, and other general intangibles. Give particulars.	X			

Sub-Total >   2,000.00
(Total of this page)

Sheet __2__ of __3__ continuation sheets attached
to the Schedule of Personal Property

Form B6B
(10/05)

In re   Carrie Anne Edwards   ,   Case No._____
                                    Debtor

SCHEDULE B. PERSONAL PROPERTY
(Continuation Sheet)

Type of Property	N O N E	Description and Location of Property	Husband, Wife, Joint, or Community	Current Value of Debtor's Interest in Property, without Deducting any Secured Claim or Exemption
24. Customer lists or other compilations containing personally identifiable information (as defined in 11 U.S.C. § 101(41A)) provided to the debtor by individuals in connection with obtaining a product or service from the debtor primarily for personal, family, or household purposes.	X			
25. Automobiles, trucks, trailers, and other vehicles and accessories.		2002 Buick LeSabre fully loaded in good condition (replacement value from nada.com)	-	8,500.00
26. Boats, motors, and accessories.	X			
27. Aircraft and accessories.	X			
28. Office equipment, furnishings, and supplies.		Used computer valued at Ebay price, used in business	-	800.00
		Copier (used Xerox) no known market for replacement value	-	Unknown
29. Machinery, fixtures, equipment, and supplies used in business.	X			
30. Inventory.	X			
31. Animals.	X			
32. Crops - growing or harvested. Give particulars.	X			
33. Farming equipment and implements.	X			
34. Farm supplies, chemicals, and feed.	X			
35. Other personal property of any kind not already listed. Itemize.	X			

Sheet __3__ of __3__ continuation sheets attached
to the Schedule of Personal Property

Sub-Total >   9,300.00
(Total of this page)
Total >   25,325.00

(Report also on Summary of Schedules)

information. If not, be sure to go over the Personal Property Checklist, which lists types of property to include in each category. Although the categories in the checklist correspond to the categories in Schedule B, the checklist describes some of them differently (where we felt the Schedule B descriptions weren't clear).

⚠ **Use the property's replacement value.** As explained in Ch. 3, the new bankruptcy law requires you to use the property's replacement value—what it would cost to purchase the property from a retail vendor, given its age and condition—when estimating what it's worth. See Ch. 3 for tips on finding replacement values for various types of property.

Separately list all items worth $50 or more. Combine small items into larger categories whenever reasonable. For example, you don't need to list every spatula, colander, garlic press, and ice cream scoop; instead, put "kitchen cookware" (unless one of these items exceeds $50). If you list numerous items in one category (as is likely for household goods and furnishings), you may need to attach a continuation sheet.

For each category of property listed, you must describe where it is located. If your personal property is at your residence, just enter "Residence" or your home address in the box. If someone else holds property for you (for example, you loaned your aunt your color TV), put that person's name and address in this column. The idea is to tell the trustee where all your property is located.

Here are further instructions for filling in some of the blanks.

Item 1: Include all cash you have on the date you file the petition.

Items 1 and 2: Explain the source of any cash on hand or money in financial accounts—for example, from wages, Social Security payments, or child support. This will help you (and the trustee) decide later whether any of this money qualifies as exempt property.

Item 11: Although an education IRA and a qualified state tuition plan may technically not be part of the bankruptcy estate, list them here anyway. Also, you are required to file any records you have of these interests as an attachment to Schedule B.

Item 12: Although ERISA-qualified pension plans, IRAs, and Keoghs may not be part of your bankruptcy estate, list them here anyway and describe each plan in detail. In the Current Value column, enter the value of the pension, if known.

Item 13: Include stock options.

Item 16: If you are a sole proprietor or independent contractor, you likely will be owed money by one or more of your customers. Specify each such debt by customer name, the reason for the debt, and the date the debt was incurred. These debts belong to your bankruptcy estate and may be collected by the trustee unless you are able to claim them as exempt.

Item 17: List all child support or alimony arrears— that is, money that should have been paid to you but hasn't been. Specify the dates the payments were due and missed, such as "$250 monthly child support payments for June, July, August, and September 20XX." Also list any debts owed you from a property settlement incurred in a divorce or dissolution.

Item 18: List all money owed to you and not yet paid, other than child support, alimony, and property settlements. If you've obtained a judgment against someone, but haven't been paid, list it here. State the defendant's name, the date of the judgment, the court that issued the judgment, the amount of the judgment, and the kind of case (such as car accident).

Item 19: An "equitable or future interest" means that sooner or later you will get property that is currently owned by someone else. Your expectation is legally recognized and valuable. For instance, if your parents' trust gives them the right to live in the family home, that's a "life estate." If the trust gives you the home when they die, you have an "equitable interest" in the home while they're alive. "Powers exercisable for the benefit of the debtor" means that a person has been given the power to route property your way, but it hasn't happened by the time you file your bankruptcy petition. In sum, if it looks like property is coming your way eventually, and that property hasn't been listed in Schedule A, list it here.

Item 20: You have a contingent interest in property if, for example, you are named the remainder beneficiary of an irrevocable trust (a trust that can't be undone by the person who created it). It's contingent because you may or may not get anything from the trust—it all depends on whether there's anything left by the time it gets to you. A noncontingent interest means you will get the property sooner or later, for example, under the terms of an insurance policy. Also list here any wills or revocable living trusts where you are named as a beneficiary. Even though you don't have any right to inherit under these documents (they can be changed at any time prior to the person's death), the trustee wants to know this information because the inheritance becomes part of your bankruptcy estate if the person dies within the six-month period following your bankruptcy filing date.

Item 21: List all claims that you have against others that might end up in a lawsuit. For instance, if you were recently rear-ended in an automobile accident and are struggling with whiplash, you may have a cause of action against the other driver (and that driver's insurer). Failure to list this type of claim here can result in your inability to pursue it after bankruptcy.

Item 22: This question asks about assets commonly known as intellectual property. State what the patent, copyright, trademark, or the like is for. Give the number assigned by the issuing agency and length of time the patent, copyright, trademark, or other right will last. Keep in mind that both copyright and trademark rights may exist without going through a government agency. If you claim trademark rights through usage, or copyright through the fact that you created the item and reduced it to tangible form, describe them here.

Item 23: List all licenses and franchises, what they cover, the length of time remaining, who they are with, and whether you can transfer them to someone else.

Item 24: Describe customer lists or other compilations containing personally identifiable information that you obtained from people as part of providing them with consumer goods or services.

Items 25-27: Include the make, model, and year of each item.

Item 32: For your crops, list whether they've been harvested, whether they've been sold (and, if so, to whom and for how much), whether you've taken out any loan against them, and whether they are insured.

Husband, Wife, Joint, or Community. If you're not married, put "N/A" at the top of the column.

If you are married and live in a community property state, then property acquired during the marriage is community property and you should put "C" in this column. Gifts and inheritances received by one spouse are separate property, as is property a spouse owned prior to marriage or after separation. Identify this property with an "H" (for husband) or "W" (for wife), as appropriate.

If you live in any state that is not a community property state, write "J" if you own the property jointly with a spouse, and "H" or "W" if a spouse owns that property as an individual.

Current Value of Debtor's Interest in Property, Without Deducting any Secured Claim or Exemption. You can take the information requested here from the Property Exemption Worksheet in Ch. 3. List the replacement value of the property, without regard to any secured interests or exemptions. For example, if you own a car with a replacement value of $6,000, you still owe $4,000 on the car note, and your state's motor vehicle exemption is $1,200, put down $6,000 for the market value of the car.

Total. Add the amounts in this column and put the total in the box at the bottom of the last page. If you used any continuation pages in addition to the preprinted form, remember to attach those pages and include the amounts from those pages in this total.

3. Schedule C—Property Claimed as Exempt

On this form, you claim all property you think is legally exempt from being sold to pay your unsecured creditors. In the overwhelming majority of Chapter 7 bankruptcies filed by individuals, all—or virtually all—of the debtor's property is exempt.

 If you own a home. Be sure to read Ch. 4 before completing Schedule C.

When you work on this form, you'll need to refer frequently to several other documents. Have in front of you:

- the worksheets from Ch. 3 and Ch. 4
- your drafts of Schedules A and B
- the list of state or federal bankruptcy exemptions you'll be using, provided in Appendix 1, and
- if you're using a state's exemptions, the additional nonbankruptcy federal exemptions, provided in Appendix 1.

Set out below is a sample completed Schedule C and line-by-line instructions.

Form B6C
(10/05)

In re   Carrie Anne Edwards _____,   Case No. _____

                                    Debtor

SCHEDULE C. PROPERTY CLAIMED AS EXEMPT

Debtor elects the exemptions to which debtor is entitled under: ☐ Check if debtor claims a homestead exemption that exceeds
(Check one box) $125,000.
☐ 11 U.S.C. §522(b)(2)
■ 11 U.S.C. §522(b)(3)

Description of Property	Specify Law Providing Each Exemption	Value of Claimed Exemption	Current Value of Property Without Deducting Exemption
Real Property Residence Location: 3045 Berwick St, Lakeport CA	C.C.P. § 703.140(b)(1)	0.00	140,000.00
Cash on Hand Cash in wallet	C.C.P. § 703.140(b)(5)	50.00	50.00
Checking, Savings, or Other Financial Accounts, Certificates of Deposit Bank of America Checking Account #12345 Lakeport California	C.C.P. § 703.140(b)(5)	150.00	150.00
from wages			
WestAmerica Bank, Lakeport CA Savings Account	C.C.P. § 703.140(b)(5)	300.00	300.00
Household Goods and Furnishings All items at replacement value	C.C.P. § 703.140(b)(3)	6,350.00	6,350.00
Stereo system ($300), washer dryer set (200), refrigerator (400), electric stove (250), misc furniture (couch, 2 chairs, 2 end tables) (500), minor appliances (blender, toaster, mixer) (125), roll top desk (700), vacuum (50), bed and bedding (650), 20 inch tv (75), lawnmower (200), swing set, childrens toys (240), snowblower (160), oriental rug (2500) Location: 3045 Berwick St, Lakeport CA			
Books, Pictures and Other Art Objects; Collectibles 250 books at used book store prices Location: 3045 Berwick St, Lakeport CA	C.C.P. § 703.140(b)(5)	1,250.00	1,250.00
stamp collection at stamp dealer price Location: 3045 Berwick St, Lakeport CA	C.C.P. § 703.140(b)(5)	2,500.00	2,500.00
Wearing Apparel normal clothing at used clothing store prices Location: 3045 Berwick St, Lakeport CA	C.C.P. § 703.140(b)(3)	800.00	800.00

___1___ continuation sheets attached to **Schedule of Property Claimed as Exempt**

Form B6C
(10/05)

In re Carrie Anne Edwards   ,   Case No._____
                              Debtor

SCHEDULE C. PROPERTY CLAIMED AS EXEMPT
(Continuation Sheet)

Description of Property	Specify Law Providing Each Exemption	Value of Claimed Exemption	Current Value of Property Without Deducting Exemption
Furs and Jewelry diamond necklace at used jewelry store price (800), watch at flea market price (75) Location: 3045 Berwick St, Lakeport CA	C.C.P. § 703.140(b)(4)	875.00	875.00
Firearms and Sports, Photographic and Other Hobby Equipment Mountain bike at used bicycle store price (250), Digital camera priced at ebay (200), sword collection priced at antique store Location: 3045 Berwick St, Lakeport CA	C.C.P. § 703.140(b)(5)	1,250.00	1,250.00
Stock and Interests in Businesses 5,000 shares in BLP Bankruptcy Services, Inc, a close corporation Location of certificates: 3045 Berwick St, Lakeport CA (valued at $.10 a share	C.C.P. § 703.140(b)(5)	500.00	500.00
Government & Corporate Bonds, Other Negotiable & Non-negotiable Inst. U.S. Savings Bonds, all certificates at Ameritrust, 10 Financial Way, Cleaveland Heights OH 41118	C.C.P. § 703.140(b)(5)	1,000.00	1,000.00
Negotiable promissory note from Jonathan Edwards, Carrie's brother, dated 11/3/XX Location: 3045 Berwick St, Lakeport CA	C.C.P. § 703.140(b)(5)	500.00	500.00
Other Liquidated Debts Owing Debtor Including Tax Refund Wages for 6/1/XX to 8/1/XX from ABC Typing Services	C.C.P. § 703.140(b)(5)	500.00	500.00
Automobiles, Trucks, Trailers, and Other Vehicles 2002 Buick LeSabre fully loaded in good condition (replacement value from nada.com)	C.C.P. § 703.140(b)(2) C.C.P. § 703.140(b)(5)	2,975.00 5,525.00	8,500.00
Office Equipment, Furnishings and Supplies Used computer valued at Ebay price, used in business	C.C.P. § 703.140(b)(6)	800.00	800.00

Sheet __1__ of __1__ continuation sheets attached to the Schedule of Property Claimed as Exempt

Looking at the sample Schedule C exemptions, you might notice that a particular exemption can apply to more than one category of personal property from Schedule B. That's because the exemption categories are set up by each state, but the property categories are determined by the feds, who also wrote Schedule B. As a result, the property and exemption categories don't necessarily have any relation to each other. For example, the California "tools of the trade" exemption (see Appendix 1) could apply to a number of the property categories, including Category 28 (Office equipment, furnishings, and supplies), Category 33 (Farming equipment and implements), Category 25 (Automobiles, trucks, trailers and other vehicles, and accessories), and Category 5 (Books, etc).

Give Yourself the Benefit of the Doubt

When you claim exemptions, give yourself the benefit of the doubt—if an exemption seems to cover an item of property, claim it. You may find that you're legally entitled to keep much of the property you're deeply attached to, such as your home, car, and family heirlooms.

Your exemption claims will be examined by the trustee and, possibly, a creditor or two, although historically few creditors monitor bankruptcy proceedings. In close cases, bankruptcy laws require the trustee to honor rather than dishonor your exemption claims. In other words, you're entitled to the benefit of the doubt.

If the trustee or a creditor successfully objects to an exemption claim, you've lost nothing by trying. See Ch. 7 for more on objections to claimed exemptions.

In re and **Case No.** Follow the instructions for Schedule A.

Debtor elects the exemptions to which the debtor is entitled under: If you're using the federal exemptions, check the top box. Everybody else, check the second box. See Ch. 3 for information on the new residency requirements for using a state's exemptions and tips on how to choose between the federal and state exemption systems. As we point out in Ch. 3, if you are living in a state that offers the federal exemption system, but

you haven't been there long enough to meet the two-year residency requirement, you can choose the federal system (and check the top box on Schedule C).

Property out of state. You'll generally choose the exemptions of the state you live in when you file as long as you've lived there for at least two years. If you want to protect your equity in a home in a state other than the one you file in, see a lawyer.

Check if debtor claims a homestead exemption that exceeds $125,000. Check this box if:
- the exemptions of the state you are using allow a homestead of more than $125,000
- you have more than $125,000 equity in your home, and
- you acquired your home at least 40 months prior to your bankruptcy filing date.

If you didn't acquire your home at least 40 months before filing, and you didn't purchase it from the proceeds of selling a home in the same state, your homestead exemption may be capped at $125,000, regardless of the exemption available in the state where your home is located. See Ch. 4 for detailed information on the homestead exemption cap.

The following instructions cover one column at a time. But rather than listing all your exempt property in the first column and then completing the second column before moving on to the third column, you might find it easier to list one exempt item and complete all columns for that item before moving on to the next exempt item.

Description of Property. To describe the property you claim as exempt, take these steps:

Step 1: Turn to Ch. 3, Section C, to find out which exemptions are available to you and which property to claim as exempt (if you have already used the Property Exemption Worksheet to identify your exempt property, skip this step).

Step 2: Decide which of the real estate you listed on Schedule A, if any, you want to claim as exempt. Remember that state homestead allowances usually apply only to property you are living in when you file, but that you can use a wildcard exemption for any type of property. Use the same description you used in the Description and Location of Property column of Schedule A.

Step 3: Decide which of the personal property you listed on Schedule B you want to claim as exempt. For each item identified, list both the category of property (preprinted in the Types of Property column) and the specific item, from the Description and Location of Property column. Do not include the location of the property. If the exemptions you are using apply to an entire category, such as clothing, simply list "clothing" as the item you are exempting.

Specify Law Providing Each Exemption. You'll find citations to the specific laws that create exemptions in the state and federal exemption lists in Appendix 1. Remember to use the rules for choosing your exemptions explained in detail in Ch. 3.

You can simplify this process by entering, anywhere on the form, the name of the statutes you are using. The name is noted at the top of the exemption list you use. For example, you might type "All law references are to the Florida Statutes Annotated unless otherwise noted."

For each item of property you are claiming as exempt, enter the citation (number) of the specific law that creates the exemption, as set out on the exemption list. If you are combining part or all of a wildcard exemption with a regular exemption, list both citations. If the wildcard and the regular exemption have the same citation, list the citation twice and put "wildcard" next to one of the citations. If you use any reference other than one found in the state statutes you are using, such as a federal nonbankruptcy exemption or a court case, list the entire reference for the exempt item.

Value of Claimed Exemption. Claim the full exemption amount allowed, up to the value of the item. The amount allowed is listed in Appendix 1.

Bankruptcy law allows married couples to double all exemptions unless the state expressly prohibits it. That means that each of you can claim the entire amount of each exemption, if you are both filing. If your state's chart in Appendix 1 doesn't say your state forbids doubling, go ahead and double.

If you are using part or all of a wildcard exemption, in addition to a regular exemption, list both amounts. For example, if the regular exemption for an item of furniture is $200, and you plan to exempt it to $500 using $300 from your state's wildcard exemption, list $200 across from the citation you listed for the regular exemption and $300 across from the citation you listed for the wildcard exemption (or across from the term "wildcard").

⚠️ **Don't claim more than you need for any particular item.** For instance, if you're allowed household furniture up to a total amount of $2,000, don't inflate the value of each item of furniture simply to get to $2,000. Use the values as you stated them on Schedule B.

Current Value of Property Without Deducting Exemption. Enter the current (replacement) value of the item you are claiming as exempt. For most items, this information is listed on Schedules A and B. However, if you listed the item as part of a group in Schedule B, list it separately here and assign it a separate replacement value.

4. Schedule D—Creditors Holding Secured Claims

In this schedule, you list all creditors who hold claims secured by your property. This includes:

- holders of a mortgage or deed of trust on your real estate
- creditors who have won lawsuits against you and recorded judgment liens against your property
- doctors or lawyers to whom you have granted a security interest in the outcome of a lawsuit, so that the collection of their fees would be postponed (the expected court judgment is the collateral)
- contractors who have filed mechanics' or materialmen's liens on your real estate
- taxing authorities, such as the IRS, that have obtained tax liens against your property
- creditors with either a purchase-money or nonpurchase-money security agreement (for explanation of this jargon, see "Nature of Lien" below), and
- all parties who are trying to collect a secured debt, such as collection agencies and attorneys.

Credit Card Debts

Most credit card debts, including cards issued by a bank, gasoline company, or department store, are unsecured and should be listed on Schedule F. Some department stores, however, claim to retain a security interest in all durable goods, such as furniture, appliances, electronics equipment, and jewelry, bought using the store credit card. Also, if you were issued a bank or store credit card as part of a plan to restore your credit, you may have had to post property or cash as collateral for debts incurred on the card. If either of these exceptions apply to you, list the credit card debt on Schedule D.

Line-by-line instructions and a completed sample of Schedule D follow.

In re and **Case No.** Follow instructions for Schedule A.

Check this box if debtor has no creditors holding secured claims to report on this Schedule D. Check the box at the bottom of the Schedule's instructions if you have no secured creditors, then skip ahead to Schedule E. Everyone else, keep reading.

Creditor's Name and Mailing Address, Including Zip Code and Account Number. List all secured creditors, preferably in alphabetical order. For each, fill in the last four digits of the account number, if you know it; the creditor's name; and the complete mailing address, including zip code. As mentioned earlier, the mailing address should be the contact address shown on at least two written communications you received from the creditor during the previous 90 days. Call the creditor to get this information if you don't have it.

If you have more than one secured creditor for a given debt, list the original creditor first, followed by the other creditors. For example, if you've been sued or hounded by a collection agency, list the information for the collection agency after the original creditor.

If, after typing up your final papers, you discover that you've missed a few creditors, don't retype your papers to preserve perfect alphabetical order. Simply add the creditors at the end. If your creditors don't all fit on the first page of Schedule D, make as many copies of the preprinted continuation page as you need to list them all.

Codebtor. Someone who owes money with you probably isn't the first person you think of as your creditor. But if someone else agreed to cosign your loan, lease, or purchase, then creditors can go after your codebtor, who will then look to you to cough up the money. So, if someone else (other than a spouse with whom you are filing jointly) can be legally forced to pay your debt to a listed secured creditor, enter an "X" in this column and list the codebtor in the creditor column of this Schedule. You'll also need to list the codebtor as a creditor in Schedules E, F, and H (explained below).

The most common codebtors are:

- cosigners
- guarantors (people who guarantee payment of a loan)
- ex-spouses with whom you jointly incurred debts before divorcing
- joint owners of real estate or other property
- coparties in a lawsuit
- nonfiling spouses in a community property state (most debts incurred by a nonfiling spouse during marriage are considered community debts, making that spouse equally liable with the filing spouse for the debts), and
- nonfiling spouses in states other than community property states, for debts incurred by the filing spouse for basic living necessities such as food, shelter, clothing, and utilities.

Husband, Wife, Joint, or Community. Follow the instructions for Schedule A.

Date Claim Was Incurred, Nature of Lien, and Description and Value of Property Subject to Lien. This column calls for a lot of information for each secured debt. If you list two or more creditors on the same secured claim (such as the lender and a collection agency), simply put ditto marks (") in this column for the second creditor. Let's take these one at a time.

Date Claim Was Incurred. For most claims, the date the claim was incurred is the date you signed the security agreement. If you didn't sign a security agreement with the creditor, the date is most likely the date a contractor or judgment creditor recorded a lien against your property or the date a taxing authority notified you of a tax liability or assessment of taxes due.

Form B6D
(10/05)

In re   Carrie Anne Edwards   ,   Case No._____
                                                    Debtor

SCHEDULE D. CREDITORS HOLDING SECURED CLAIMS

State the name, mailing address, including zip code, and last four digits of any account number of all entities holding claims secured by property of the debtor as of the date of filing of the petition. The complete account number of any account the debtor has with the creditor is useful to the trustee and the creditor and may be provided if the debtor chooses to do so. List creditors holding all types of secured interests such as judgment liens, garnishments, statutory liens, mortgages, deeds of trust, and other security interests.

List creditors in alphabetical order to the extent practicable. If a minor child is a creditor, indicate that by stating "a minor child" and do not disclose the child's name. See 11 U.S.C§112; Fed.R.Bankr.P. 1007(m). If all secured creditors will not fit on this page, use the continuation sheet provided.

If any entity other than a spouse in a joint case may be jointly liable on a claim, place an "X" in the column labeled "Codebtor", include the entity on the appropriate schedule of creditors, and complete Schedule H-Codebtors. If a joint petition is filed, state whether husband, wife, both of them, or the marital community may be liable on each claim by placing an "H", "W", "J", or "C" in the column labeled "Husband, Wife, Joint, or Community." If the claim is contingent, place an "X" in the column labeled "Contingent". If the claim is unliquidated, place an "X" in the column labeled "Unliquidated". If the claim is disputed, place an "X" in the column labeled "Disputed". (You may need to place an "X" in more than one of these three columns.)

Report the total of all claims listed on this schedule in the box labeled "Total" on the last sheet of the completed schedule. Report this total also on the Summary of Schedules.

☐   Check this box if debtor has no creditors holding secured claims to report on this Schedule D.

CREDITOR'S NAME AND MAILING ADDRESS INCLUDING ZIP CODE, AND ACCOUNT NUMBER (See instructions above.)	C O D E B T O R	Husband, Wife, Joint, or Community	DATE CLAIM WAS INCURRED, NATURE OF LIEN, AND DESCRIPTION AND VALUE OF PROPERTY SUBJECT TO LIEN	C O N T I N G E N T	U N L I Q U I D A T E D	D I S P U T E D	AMOUNT OF CLAIM WITHOUT DEDUCTING VALUE OF COLLATERAL	UNSECURED PORTION, IF ANY
		H W J C						
Account No. 444555666777 GMAC PO Box 23567 Duchesne, UT 84021			November, 2002 Purchase Money Security 2002 Buick LeSabre fully loaded in good condition (replacement value from nada.com)					
			Value $ 8,500.00				1,000.00	0.00
Account No. 64-112-1861 Grand Junction Mortgage 3456 Eight St. Clearlake, CA 95422			5/2005 First Mortgage Residence Location: 3045 Berwick St, Lakeport CA					
			Value $ 140,000.00				135,000.00	0.00
Account No. 55555555555 Lending Tree PO Box 3333 Palo Alto, CA 94310			12/xx Second Mortgage Residence Location: 3045 Berwick St, Lakeport CA					
			Value $ 140,000.00				5,000.00	0.00
Account No. 								
			Value $					

    0   continuation sheets attached

	Subtotal (Total of this page)	141,000.00
	Total (Report on Summary of Schedules)	141,000.00

Nature of Lien. What kind of property interest does your secured creditor have? Here are the possible answers:

- **First mortgage.** You took out a loan to buy your house. (This kind of lien is a specific kind of purchase-money security interest.)

- **Purchase-money security interest.** You took out a loan to purchase the property that secures the loan—for example, a car note. The creditor must have perfected the security interest by filing or recording it with the appropriate agency within 20 days. (*Fidelity Financial Services, Inc. v. Fink*, 522 U.S. 211 (1998).) Otherwise, the creditor has no lien and you should list the debt on Schedule F (unsecured debt) instead.

- **Nonpossessory, nonpurchase-money security interest.** You borrowed money for a purpose other than buying the collateral. This includes refinanced home loans, home equity loans, or loans from finance companies.

- **Possessory, nonpurchase-money security interest.** This is what a pawnshop owner has when you pawn your stuff.

- **Judgment lien.** This means someone sued you, won a court judgment, and recorded a lien against your property.

- **Tax lien.** This means a federal, state, or local government agency recorded a lien against your property for unpaid taxes.

- **Child support lien.** This means that another parent or government agency has recorded a lien against your property for unpaid child support.

- **Mechanics' or materialmen's lien.** This means someone performed work on your real property or personal property (for example, a car) but didn't get paid, and recorded a lien on that property. Such liens can be an unpleasant surprise if you paid for the work, but your contractor didn't pay a subcontractor who got a lien against your property.

- **Unknown.** If you don't know what kind of lien you are dealing with, put "Don't know nature of lien" after the date. The bankruptcy trustee can help you figure it out later.

Description of Property. Describe each item of real estate and personal property that is collateral for the secured debt listed in the first column. Use the same description you used on Schedule A for real property, or Schedule B for personal property. If a creditor's lien covers several items of property, list all items affected by the lien.

Value of Property. The amount you put here must be consistent with what you put on Schedule A or B. If you put only the total value of a group of items on Schedule B, you must now get more specific. For instance, if a department store has a secured claim against your washing machine, and you listed your "washer/dryer set" on Schedule B, now you must provide the washer's specific market value. You may have already done this on the Property Exemption Worksheet. If not, see the instructions for "Current Value" on Schedule B.

Contingent, Unliquidated, Disputed. Indicate whether the creditor's secured claim is contingent, unliquidated, or disputed. Check all categories that apply. If you're uncertain of which to choose, check the one that seems closest. If none apply, leave them blank. Briefly, these terms mean:

- **Contingent.** The claim depends on some event that hasn't yet occurred and may never occur. For example, if you cosigned a secured loan, you won't be liable unless the principal debtor defaults. Your liability as cosigner is contingent upon the default.

- **Unliquidated.** This means that a debt may exist, but the exact amount hasn't been determined. For example, say you've sued someone for injuries you suffered in an auto accident, but the case isn't over. Your lawyer has taken the case under a contingency fee agreement—he'll get a third of the recovery if you win, and nothing if you lose—and has a security interest in the final recovery amount. The debt to the lawyer is unliquidated because you don't know how much, if anything, you'll win.

- **Disputed.** A claim is disputed if you and the creditor do not agree about the existence or amount of the debt. For instance, suppose the IRS says you owe $10,000 and has put a lien on your property, and you say you owe $500. List the full amount of the lien, not the amount you think you owe.

You're not admitting you owe the debt. You may think you don't really owe a contingent, unliquidated, or disputed debt, or you may not want to "admit" that you owe the debt. By listing a debt here, however, you aren't admitting anything. Instead, you are making sure that, if you owe the debt after all, it will be discharged in your bankruptcy (if it is dischargeable; see Ch. 9).

Amount of Claim Without Deducting Value of Collateral. For each secured creditor, list the amount it would take to pay off the secured claim, regardless of what the property is worth. The lender can give you this figure. In some cases, the amount of the secured claim may be more than the property's value.

> **EXAMPLE:** Your original loan was for $13,000, plus $7,000 in interest (for $20,000 total). You've made enough payments so that $15,000 will cancel the debt. You would put $15,000 in this column.

If you have more than one creditor for a given secured claim (for example, the lender and a collection agency), list the debt only for the lender and put ditto marks (") for each subsequent creditor.

Subtotal/Total. Total the amounts in the Amount of Claim column for each page. Do not include the amounts represented by the ditto marks if you listed multiple creditors for a single debt. On the final page of Schedule D, which may be the first page or a preprinted continuation page, enter the total of all secured claims.

Unsecured Portion, If Any. If the replacement value of the collateral is equal to or greater than the amount of the claim, enter "0," meaning that the creditor's claim is fully secured. If the replacement value of the collateral is less than the amount of the claim(s) listed, enter the difference here.

> **EXAMPLE:** If the current value of your car is $5,000 but you still owe $6,000 on your car loan, enter $1,000 in this column ($6,000 − $5,000). This is the amount of the loan that is unsecured by the collateral (your car).

If you list an amount in this column for a creditor, do not list this amount again on Schedule F (where you will list all other creditors with unsecured claims). Otherwise, this unsecured amount will be listed twice.

5. Schedule E—Creditors Holding Unsecured Priority Claims

Schedule E identifies certain creditors who may be entitled to be paid first—by the trustee—out of your nonexempt assets. Even if you don't have any nonexempt assets to be distributed, you still need to fill this form out if you have any unsecured priority debts.

Set out below are a sample completed Schedule E and line-by-line instructions.

In re and **Case No.** Follow the instructions for Schedule A.

Check this box if debtor has no creditors holding unsecured priority claims to report on this Schedule E. Priority claims are claims that must be paid first in your bankruptcy case. The most common examples are unsecured income tax debts and past due alimony or child support. There are several other categories of priority debts, however. Read further to figure out whether or not you can check this box.

Types of priority claims. These are the categories of priority debts, as listed on Schedule E. Check the appropriate box on the form if you owe a debt in that category.

Domestic support obligations. Check this box for claims for domestic support that you owe to, or that are recoverable by, a spouse, former spouse, or child; the parent, legal guardian, or responsible relative of such a child; or a governmental unit to whom such a domestic support claim has been assigned to the extent provide.

Extensions of credit in an involuntary case. Don't check this box. You are filing a voluntary, not an involuntary, case.

Wages, salaries, and commissions. If you own a business and owe a current or former employee wages, vacation pay, or sick leave that was earned within 90 days before you file your petition or within 90 days of the date you ceased your business, check this box. If you owe money to an independent contractor who did work for you, and the money was earned within 90 days before you file your petition or within 90 days of the date you ceased your business, check this box only if, in the 12 months before you file for bankruptcy, this independent contractor earned at least 75% of his or her total independent contractor receipts from you. Only the first $10,000 owed per employee or independent contractor is a priority debt.

Form B6E
(10/05)

In re   Carrie Anne Edwards   Case No._____

                                      Debtor

SCHEDULE E. CREDITORS HOLDING UNSECURED PRIORITY CLAIMS

A complete list of claims entitled to priority, listed separately by type of priority, is to be set forth on the sheets provided. Only holders of unsecured claims entitled to priority should be listed in this schedule. In the boxes provided on the attached sheets, state the name, mailing address, including zip code, and last four digits of the account number, if any, of all entities holding priority claims against the debtor or the property of the debtor, as of the date of the filing of the petition. Use a separate continuation sheet for each type of priority and label each with the type of priority.

The complete account number of any account the debtor has with the creditor is useful to the trustee and the creditor and may be provided if the debtor chooses to do so. If a minor child is a creditor, indicate that by stating "a minor child" and do not disclose the child's name. See 11 U.S.C.§112; Fed.R.Bankr.P. 1007(m).

If any entity other than a spouse in a joint case may be jointly liable on a claim, place an "X" in the column labeled "Codebtor", include the entity on the appropriate schedule of creditors, and complete Schedule H-Codebtors. If a joint petition is filed, state whether husband, wife, both of them or the marital community may be liable on each claim by placing an "H", "W", "J", or "C" in the column labeled "Husband, Wife, Joint, or Community". If the claim is contingent, place an "X" in the column labeled "Contingent". If the claim is unliquidated, place an "X" in the column labeled "Unliquidated". If the claim is disputed, place an "X" in the column labeled "Disputed". (You may need to place an "X" in more than one of these three columns.)

Report the total of claims listed on each sheet in the box labeled "Subtotal" on each sheet. Report the total of all claims listed on this Schedule E in the box labeled "Total" on the last sheet of the completed schedule. Report this total also on the Summary of Schedules.

Report the total of amounts entitled to priority listed on each sheet in the box labeled "Subtotal" on each sheet. Report the total of all amounts entitled to priority listed on this Schedule E in the box labeled "Total" on the last sheet of the completed schedule. If applicable, also report this total on the Means Test form.

☐ Check this box if debtor has no creditors holding unsecured priority claims to report on this Schedule E.

TYPES OF PRIORITY CLAIMS (Check the appropriate box(es) below if claims in that category are listed on the attached sheets.)

■ **Domestic support obligations**

Claims for domestic support that are owed to or recoverable by a spouse, former spouse, or child of the debtor, or the parent, legal guardian, or responsible relative of such a child, or a governmental unit to whom such a domestic support claim has been assigned to the extent provided in 11 U.S.C. § 507(a)(1).

☐ **Extensions of credit in an involuntary case**

Claims arising in the ordinary course of the debtor's business or financial affairs after the commencement of the case but before the earlier of the appointment of a trustee or the order for relief. 11 U.S.C. § 507(a)(3).

☐ **Wages, salaries, and commissions**

Wages, salaries, and commissions, including vacation, severance, and sick leave pay owing to employees and commissions owing to qualifying independent sales representatives up to $10,000* per person earned within 180 days immediately preceding the filing of the original petition, or the cessation of business, which ever occurred first, to the extent provided in 11 U.S.C. § 507 (a)(4).

☐ **Contributions to employee benefit plans**

Money owed to employee benefit plans for services rendered within 180 days immediately preceding the filing of the original petition, or the cessation of business, whichever occurred first, to the extent provided in 11 U.S.C. § 507(a)(5).

☐ **Certain farmers and fishermen**

Claims of certain farmers and fishermen, up to $4,925* per farmer or fisherman, against the debtor, as provided in 11 U.S.C. § 507(a)(6).

☐ **Deposits by individuals**

Claims of individuals up to $2,225* for deposits for the purchase, lease, or rental of property or services for personal, family, or household use, that were not delivered or provided. 11 U.S.C. § 507(a)(7).

■ **Taxes and certain other debts owed to governmental units**

Taxes, customs duties, and penalties owing to federal, state, and local governmental units as set forth in 11 U.S.C § 507(a)(8).

☐ **Commitments to maintain the capital of an insured depository institution**

Claims based on commitments to the FDIC, RTC, Director of the Office of Thrift Supervision, Comptroller of the Currency, or Board of Governors of the Federal Reserve System, or their predecessors or successors, to maintain the capital of an insured depository institution. 11 U.S.C. § 507(a)(9).

☐ **Claims for death or personal injury while debtor was intoxicated**

Claims for death or personal injury resulting from the operation of a motor vehicle or vessel while the debtor was intoxicated from using alcohol, a drug, or another substance. 11 U.S.C. § 507(a)(10).

*Amounts are subject to adjustment on April 1, 2007, and every three years thereafter with respect to cases commenced on or after the date of adjustment.

_____2_____ continuation sheets attached

Form B6E - Cont.
(10/05)

In re   Carrie Anne Edwards   ,   Case No. _____
                                                    Debtor

SCHEDULE E. CREDITORS HOLDING UNSECURED PRIORITY CLAIMS
(Continuation Sheet)

Domestic Support Obligations

TYPE OF PRIORITY

CREDITOR'S NAME, AND MAILING ADDRESS INCLUDING ZIP CODE, AND ACCOUNT NUMBER (See instructions.)	CODEBTOR	H W J C	DATE CLAIM WAS INCURRED AND CONSIDERATION FOR CLAIM	CONTINGENT	UNLIQUIDATED	DISPUTED	AMOUNT OF CLAIM	AMOUNT ENTITLED TO PRIORITY
Account No.			2005					
Jon Edwards 900 Grand View Jackson, WY 83001		-	Child support				2,500.00	2,500.00
Account No.								
Account No.								
Account No.								
Account No.								

Sheet 1 of 2 continuation sheets attached to
Schedule of Creditors Holding Unsecured Priority Claims

Subtotal
(Total of this page)   2,500.00   2,500.00

Form B6E - Cont.
(10/05)

In re   Carrie Anne Edwards   ,   Case No. _____
                                          Debtor

SCHEDULE E. CREDITORS HOLDING UNSECURED PRIORITY CLAIMS
(Continuation Sheet)

Taxes and Certain Other Debts
Owed to Governmental Units

TYPE OF PRIORITY

CREDITOR'S NAME, AND MAILING ADDRESS INCLUDING ZIP CODE, AND ACCOUNT NUMBER (See instructions.)	C O D E B T O R	H W J C	DATE CLAIM WAS INCURRED AND CONSIDERATION FOR CLAIM	C O N T I N G E N T	U N L I Q U I D A T E D	D I S P U T E D	AMOUNT OF CLAIM	AMOUNT ENTITLED TO PRIORITY
Account No. IRS Columbus, OH 43266			April 15, 20XX tax liability and interest				3,000.00	3,000.00
Account No.								
Account No.								
Account No.								
Account No.								

Sheet _2_ of _2_ continuation sheets attached to
Schedule of Creditors Holding Unsecured Priority Claims

Subtotal (Total of this page)	3,000.00	3,000.00
Total (Report on Summary of Schedules)	5,500.00	5,500.00

Contributions to employee benefit plans. Check this box if you own a business and you owe contributions to an employee benefit fund for services rendered by an employee within 180 days before you file your petition, or within 180 days of the date you ceased your business.

Certain farmers and fishermen. Check this box only if you operate or operated a grain storage facility and owe a grain producer, or you operate or operated a fish produce or storage facility and owe a U.S. fisherman for fish or fish products. Only the first $4,925 owed per person is a priority debt.

Deposits by individuals. If you took money from people who planned to purchase, lease, or rent goods or services from you that you never delivered, you may owe a priority debt. For the debt to qualify as a priority, the goods or services had to have been planned for personal, family, or household use. Only the first $2,225 owed (per person) is a priority debt.

Taxes and certain other debts owed to governmental units. Check this box if you owe unsecured back taxes or if you owe any other debts to the government, such as fines imposed for driving under the influence of drugs or alcohol. Not all tax debts are unsecured priority claims. For example, if the IRS has recorded a lien against your real property, and the equity in your property fully covers the amount of your tax debt, your debt is a secured debt. It should be on Schedule D, not on this schedule.

Commitments to maintain the capital of an insured depository institution. Don't check this box. It is for business bankruptcies.

Claims for death or personal injury while debtor was intoxicated. Check this box if there are claims against you for death or personal injury resulting from your operation of a motor vehicle or vessel while intoxicated from using alcohol, a drug, or another substance. This priority doesn't apply to property damage—only to personal injury or death.

If you didn't check any of the priority debt boxes, go back and check the first box, showing you have no unsecured priority claims to report. Then go on to Schedule F.

If you checked any of the priority debt boxes, make as many photocopies of the continuation page as the number of priority debt boxes you checked. You will

need to complete a separate sheet for each type of priority debt, as follows:

In re and **Case No.** Follow the instructions for Schedule A.

Type of Priority. Insert the category for one of the boxes you checked (for example, "Domestic support obligations").

Creditor's Name and Mailing Address, Including Zip Code and Account Number. List the name and complete mailing address (including zip code) of each priority creditor, as well as the account number, if you know it. The address should be the one provided by the creditor in two written communications you have received from the creditor within the past 90 days, if possible. You may have more than one priority creditor for a given debt. For example, if you've been sued or hounded by a collection agency, list the collection agency in addition to the original creditor.

Codebtor. If someone else can be legally forced to pay your debt to a priority creditor, enter an "X" in this column and list the codebtor in the creditor column of this schedule. You'll also need to list the codebtor as a creditor in Schedule F and Schedule H. Common codebtors are listed in the instructions for Schedule D.

Husband, Wife, Joint, or Community. Follow the instructions for Schedule A.

Date Claim Was Incurred and Consideration for Claim. State the date you incurred the debt—this may be a specific date or a period of time. Also briefly state what the debt is for. For example, "goods purchased," "hours worked for me," or "deposit for my services."

Contingent, Unliquidated, Disputed. Follow the instructions for Schedule D.

Amount of Claim. For each priority debt other than taxes, put the amount it would take to pay off the debt in full, even if it's more than the priority limit. For taxes, list only the amount that is unsecured (and therefore a priority). You should list the secured amount on Schedule D. If the amount isn't determined, write "not yet determined" in this column.

Subtotal/Total. Total the amounts in the Amount of Claim column on each page. If you use continuation pages for additional priority debts, enter the total of all priority debts on the final page.

Amount Entitled to Priority. If the priority claim is larger than the maximum indicated on the first page of Schedule E (for example, $10,000 of wages owed to

. each employee), put the maximum here. If the claim is less than the maximum, put the amount you entered in the Total Amount of Claim column here.

6. Schedule F—Creditors Holding Unsecured Nonpriority Claims

In this schedule, list all creditors you haven't listed in Schedules D or E. You should include even debts that are or may be nondischargeable, such as a student loan. Even if you believe that you don't owe the debt or you owe only a small amount and intend to pay it off, you must include it here. It's essential that you list every creditor to whom you owe, or possibly owe, money. The only way you can legitimately leave off a creditor is if your balance owed is $0.

Even if you plan (and want) to repay a particular creditor, list the debt and get it discharged, anyway. The creditor will be legally barred from trying to collect the debt, but you can always pay the debt voluntarily out of property or income you receive after you file for bankruptcy.

> **EXAMPLE:** Peter owes his favorite aunt $8,000. Peter files for bankruptcy and lists the debt, which is discharged when Peter's bankruptcy is over. Peter can voluntarily repay the $8,000 out of wages he earns any time after he files, because the wages he earns after filing are not part of his bankruptcy estate. He cannot use property that belongs to the bankruptcy estate, however, until he receives a discharge. The important thing is, repayment is completely voluntary on Peter's part. Peter's aunt can't sue him in court to enforce payment of the debt.

Inadvertent errors or omissions on this schedule can come back to haunt you. If you don't list a debt you owe to a creditor, it might not be discharged in bankruptcy if your estate has assets that are distributed to your other creditors by the trustee, or if the creditor is otherwise prejudiced by being left out (although it is sometimes possible in these circumstances to reopen the bankruptcy and include the creditor). Also, leaving a creditor off the schedule might raise suspicions that you deliberately concealed information, perhaps to give that creditor preferential treatment in violation of bankruptcy rules.

Below are a sample completed Schedule F and line-by-line instructions. Use as many preprinted continuation pages as you need.

In re and **Case No.** Follow the instructions for Schedule A.

Check this box if debtor has no creditors holding unsecured claims to report on this Schedule F. Check this box if you have no unsecured nonpriority debts. This would be very rare.

Creditor's Name and Mailing Address, Including Zip Code and Account Number. List, preferably in alphabetical order, the name and complete mailing address of each unsecured creditor, as well as the account number (if you know it). If you have more than one unsecured creditor for a given debt, list the original creditor first, followed by the other creditors. For example, for a particular debt, you might have the name, address, and account number for the original creditor, a collection agency run by the original creditor, an independent collection agency, an attorney debt collector, and an attorney who has sued you.

It's best to list all the creditors, because it never hurts to be thorough. But you could omit the intermediate collectors and just list the original creditor and the latest collector or attorney. Or, if you no longer have contact information for the original creditor, listing the latest collector will do

When you are typing your final papers, if you get to the end and discover that you left a creditor off, don't start all over again in search of perfect alphabetical order. Just add the creditor to the end of the list.

Form B6F
(10/05)

In re   Carrie Anne Edwards   ,   Case No. _____
                                                    Debtor

SCHEDULE F. CREDITORS HOLDING UNSECURED NONPRIORITY CLAIMS

State the name, mailing address, including zip code, and last four digits of any account number, of all entities holding unsecured claims without priority against the debtor or the property of the debtor, as of the date of filing of the petition. The complete account number of any account the debtor has with the creditor is useful to the trustee and the creditor and may be provided if the debtor chooses to do so. If a minor child is a creditor, indicate that by stating "a minor child" and do not disclose the child's name. See 11 U.S.C.§112; Fed.R.Bankr.P. 1007(m). Do not include claims listed in Schedules D and E. If all creditors will not fit on this page, use the continuation sheet provided.

If any entity other than a spouse in a joint case may be jointly liable on a claim, place an "X" in the column labeled "Codebtor", include the entity on the appropriate schedule of creditors, and complete Schedule H - Codebtors. If a joint petition is filed, state whether husband, wife, both of them, or the marital community maybe liable on each claim by placing an "H", "W", "J", or "C" in the column labeled "Husband, Wife, Joint, or Community".

If the claim is contingent, place an "X" in the column labeled "Contingent". If the claim is unliquidated, place an "X" in the column labeled "Unliquidated". If the claim is disputed, place an "X" in the column labeled "Disputed". (You may need to place an "X" in more than one of these three columns.)

Report the total of all claims listed on this schedule in the box labeled "Total" on the last sheet of the completed schedule. Report this total also on the Summary of Schedules.

☐   Check this box if debtor has no creditors holding unsecured claims to report on this Schedule F.

CREDITOR'S NAME, AND MAILING ADDRESS INCLUDING ZIP CODE, AND ACCOUNT NUMBER (See instructions above.)	CODEBTOR	Husband, Wife, Joint, or Community			DATE CLAIM WAS INCURRED AND CONSIDERATION FOR CLAIM. IF CLAIM IS SUBJECT TO SETOFF, SO STATE.	CONTINGENT	UNLIQUIDATED	DISPUTED	AMOUNT OF CLAIM
		H	W	J C					
Account No. Alan Accountant 5 Green St. Cleveland, OH 44118		-			4 /XX Tax preparation				500.00
Account No. 41 89-0000-2613-5556 American Allowance PO Box 1 New York, NY 10001		-			1/xx to 4/xx credit card charges				5,600.00
Account No. Angel of Mercy Hospital 4444 Elevisior St. Belmont, CA 94003		-			12/xx uninsured surgery and medical treatment				34,000.00
Account No. Bob Jones III 4566 Fifth Ave. New York, NY 10020		-			5/xx Auto accident--negligence claim				75,000.00

  2   continuation sheets attached

Subtotal (Total of this page)   115,100.00

Form B6F - Cont.
(10/05)

In re   Carrie Anne Edwards   Case No. _____

                                     Debtor

SCHEDULE F. CREDITORS HOLDING UNSECURED NONPRIORITY CLAIMS
(Continuation Sheet)

CREDITOR'S NAME, AND MAILING ADDRESS INCLUDING ZIP CODE, AND ACCOUNT NUMBER (See instructions.)	CODEBTOR	H W J C	DATE CLAIM WAS INCURRED AND CONSIDERATION FOR CLAIM. IF CLAIM IS SUBJECT TO SETOFF, SO STATE.	CONTINGENT	UNLIQUIDATED	DISPUTED	AMOUNT OF CLAIM
Account No. Bonnie Johnson 3335 Irving St Clearlake, CA 95422		-	8/xx Personal loan				5,500.00
Account No. 845061-86-3 Citibank 200 East North St Columbus, OH 43266		-	20xx Student loan				10,000.00
Account No. 4401 Dr. Dennis Dentist 45 Superior Way Cleveland, OH 44118		-	12/xx to 6/xx dental work				1,050.00
Account No. 555671 Dr. Helen Jones 443 First St. Soledad, CA 94750		-	4/xx to 8/xx Pediatric Care				5,000.00
Account No. Fannie's Furniture 55544 Grove St. Berkeley, CA 94710	X	-	12/xx used bedroom set				1,300.00

Sheet no. __1__ of __2__ sheets attached to Schedule of
Creditors Holding Unsecured Nonpriority Claims

                                       Subtotal
 (Total of this page)   22,850.00

Form B6F - Cont.
(10/05)

In re   Carrie Anne Edwards   ,   Case No. _____

Debtor

SCHEDULE F. CREDITORS HOLDING UNSECURED NONPRIORITY CLAIMS
(Continuation Sheet)

CREDITOR'S NAME, AND MAILING ADDRESS INCLUDING ZIP CODE, AND ACCOUNT NUMBER (See instructions.)	CODEBTOR	H W J C	DATE CLAIM WAS INCURRED AND CONSIDERATION FOR CLAIM. IF CLAIM IS SUBJECT TO SETOFF, SO STATE.	CONTINGENT	UNLIQUIDATED	DISPUTED	AMOUNT OF CLAIM
Account No. 222387941 Illuminating Co. 20245 Old Hwy 53 Clearlake, CA 95422	-		3/xx to 7/xx electrical work on house				750.00
Account No. John White Esq. PO Box 401 Finley, CA 95435	-		2/xx to 8/xx Legal representation in lawsuit against neighbor for incursion on property				3,450.00
Account No. 11210550 PG&E 315 North Forbes St. Lakeport, CA 95453	-		12/xx to 6/xx gas and electric service				1,200.00
Account No. 487310097 Sears PO Box 11 Chicago, IL 60619	-		20xx to 200xx Dept store and catalog charges				3,800.00
Account No.							

Sheet no. __2__ of __2__ sheets attached to Schedule of Creditors Holding Unsecured Nonpriority Claims

Subtotal (Total of this page)	9,200.00
Total (Report on Summary of Schedules)	147,150.00

Creditors That Are Often Overlooked

One debt may involve several different creditors. Remember to include:

- your ex-spouse, if you are still obligated under a divorce decree or settlement agreement to pay joint debts, turn any property over to your ex, or make payments as part of your property division
- anyone who has cosigned a promissory note or loan application you signed
- any holder of a loan or promissory note that you cosigned for someone else
- the original creditor, anybody to whom the debt has been assigned or sold, and any other person (such as a bill collector or attorney) trying to collect the debt, and
- anyone who may sue you because of a car accident, business dispute, or the like.

Codebtor. If someone else can be legally forced to pay your debt to a listed unsecured creditor, enter an "X" in this column and list the codebtor as a creditor in this schedule. Also, list the codebtor in Schedule H. The instructions for Schedule D list common codebtors.

Husband, Wife, Joint, or Community. Follow the instructions for Schedule A.

Date Claim Was Incurred and Consideration for Claim. If Claim Is Subject to Setoff, So State. State when the debt was incurred. It may be one date or a period of time. With credit card debts, put the approximate time over which you ran up the charges, unless the unpaid charges were made on one or two specific dates. Then state what the debt was for. You can be general ("clothes" or "household furnishings") or specific ("refrigerator" or "teeth capping").

If you are entitled to a setoff against the debt—that is, the creditor owes you some money, too—list the amount and why you think you are entitled to the setoff. If there is more than one creditor for a single debt, put ditto marks (") in this column for the subsequent creditors.

Contingent, Unliquidated, Disputed. Follow the instructions for Schedule D.

Amount of Claim. List the amount of the debt claimed by the creditor, even if you dispute the amount. That way, it will all be wiped out if it's dischargeable. If

there's more than one creditor for a single debt, put the debt amount across from the original creditor and put ditto marks (") across from each subsequent creditor you have listed. Be as precise as possible when stating the amount. If you must approximate, write "approx." after the amount.

Subtotal/Total. Total the amounts in the last column for this page. Do not include the amounts represented by the ditto marks if you listed multiple creditors for a single debt. On the final page (which may be the first page or a preprinted continuation page), enter the total of all unsecured, nonpriority claims. On the first page in the bottom left-hand corner, note the number of continuation pages you are attaching.

7. Schedule G—Executory Contracts and Unexpired Leases

In this form, you list every executory contract or unexpired lease to which you're a party. "Executory" means the contract is still in force—that is, both parties are still obligated to perform important acts under it. Similarly, "unexpired" means that the contract or lease period hasn't run out—that is, it is still in effect. Common examples of executory contracts and unexpired leases are:

- car leases
- residential leases or rental agreements
- business leases or rental agreements
- service contracts
- business contracts
- timeshare contracts or leases
- contracts of sale for real estate
- personal property leases, such as equipment used in a beauty salon
- copyright and patent license agreements
- leases of real estate (surface and underground) for the purpose of harvesting timber, minerals, or oil
- future homeowners' association fee requirements
- agreements for boat docking privileges, and
- insurance contracts.

If you're behind in your payments. If you are not current on payments that were due under a lease or executory contract, the delinquency should also be listed as a debt on Schedule D, E, or F. The sole purpose of this schedule is to identify existing contractual obligations that you still owe or that someone owes you. Later, you will be given the opportunity to state whether you want the lease or contract to continue in effect.

Below are a sample completed Schedule G and line-by-line instructions.

In re and **Case No.** Follow the instructions for Schedule A.

Check this box if debtor has no executory contracts or unexpired leases. Check this box if it applies; otherwise, complete the form.

Name and Mailing Address, Including Zip Code, of Other Parties to Lease or Contract. Provide the name and full address (including zip code) of each party—other than yourself—to each lease or contract. These parties are either people who signed agreements or the companies for whom these people work. If you're unsure about whom to list, include the person who signed an agreement, any company whose name appears on the agreement, and anybody who might have an interest in having the contract or lease enforced. If you still aren't sure, put "don't know."

Description of Contract or Lease and Nature of Debtor's Interest. For each lease or contract, give:

- a description of the basic type (for instance, residential lease, commercial lease, car lease, business obligation, or copyright license)
- the date the contract or lease was signed
- the date the contract is to expire (if any)
- a summary of each party's rights and obligations under the lease or contract, and
- the contract number, if the contract is with any government body.

What Happens to Executory Contracts and Unexpired Leases in Bankruptcy

The trustee has 60 days after you file for bankruptcy to decide whether an executory contract or unexpired lease should be assumed (continued in force) as property of the estate or terminated (rejected). If the lease or contract would generate funds for your unsecured creditors, then it will be assumed; otherwise it will be rejected. As a general matter, most leases and contracts are liabilities and are rejected by the trustee. However, you have the right to assume a lease on personal property (for instance, a car lease) on your own, as long as you give the creditor written notice and the creditor agrees. (11 U.S.C. Section 365 (p).) You provide this written notice in the Statement of Intention (see the instructions for the Statement in Section H, below).

As a general rule, people filing Chapter 7 bankruptcies are not parties to leases or contracts that would likely add value to their bankruptcy estates. This isn't an absolute rule, however. If the trustee could sell a lease to someone else for a profit (because you're paying less than market rent, for example), the trustee might assume the lease and assign it for a lump sum that could be distributed to your creditors. But this would be highly unusual. Trustees aren't looking for ways to put you on the street or penalize you for getting a great rent deal.

It's also possible that you'll want to get out of a contract or lease, such as a residential or auto lease or a timeshare you can't afford. Be sure to state at the bankruptcy meeting or even on your papers that you would like the trustee to terminate the agreement. But remember this is up to the trustee to decide.

If the lease is assigned or terminated or the contract is terminated, you and the other parties to the agreement are cut loose from any obligations, and any money you owe the creditor will be discharged in your bankruptcy, even if the debt arose after your filing date. For example, say you are leasing a car when you file for bankruptcy. You want out of the lease. The car dealer cannot repossess the car until the trustee terminates the lease, which normally must occur within 60 days of when you file. During that 60-day period, you can use the car without paying for it. The payments you don't make during this period will be discharged as if they were incurred prior to your bankruptcy.

Bankruptcy law has special rules for executory contracts related to intellectual property (copyright, patent, trademark, or trade secret), real estate, and timeshare leases. If you are involved in one of these situations, see a lawyer.

Form B6G
(10/05)

In re   Carrie Anne Edwards   Case No. _____
_____ ,
                          Debtor

SCHEDULE G. EXECUTORY CONTRACTS AND UNEXPIRED LEASES

Describe all executory contracts of any nature and all unexpired leases of real or personal property. Include any timeshare interests. State nature of debtor's interest in contract, i.e., "Purchaser", "Agent", etc. State whether debtor is the lessor or lessee of a lease. Provide the names and complete mailing addresses of all other parties to each lease or contract described. If a minor child is a party to one of the leases or contracts, indicate that by stating "a minor child" and do not disclose the child's name. See 11 U.S.C. § 112; Fed.R. Bankr. P. 1007(m).

☐ Check this box if debtor has no executory contracts or unexpired leases.

Name and Mailing Address, Including Zip Code, of Other Parties to Lease or Contract	Description of Contract or Lease and Nature of Debtor's Interest. State whether lease is for nonresidential real property. State contract number of any government contract.
Beauty Products Leasing Co. 44332 Grove St. Geismar, LA 70734	Laser skin treatment machine. Lease for 5 year period that expires in 2010
Herman Jones 45543 Woodleigh Court Smith River, CA 95567	Sales contract for debtor's home entered into between debtor and Herman Jones on 2 /1/XX

___0___ continuation sheets attached to Schedule of Executory Contracts and Unexpired Leases

8. Schedule H—Codebtors

In Schedules D, E, and F, you identified those debts for which you have codebtors—usually, a cosigner, guarantor, ex-spouse, nonfiling spouse in a community property state, nonfiling spouse for a debt for necessities, nonmarital partner, or joint contractor. You must also list those codebtors here. In addition, you must list the name and address of any spouse or former spouse who lived with you in Puerto Rico or in a community property state during the eight-year period immediately preceding your bankruptcy filing. (To remind you, the community property states are Alaska, Arizona, California, Idaho, Louisiana, Nevada, New Mexico, Texas, Washington, and Wisconsin.) If you are married but filing separately, include all names used by your spouse during the eight-year period.

In Chapter 7 bankruptcy, your codebtors will be wholly responsible for your debts, unless they, too, declare bankruptcy.

Below are a sample completed Schedule H and line-by-line instructions.

In re and **Case No.** Follow instructions for Schedule A.

Check this box if debtor has no codebtors. Check this box if it applies; otherwise, complete the form.

Name and Address of Codebtor. List the name and complete address (including zip code) of each codebtor. If the codebtor is a nonfiling, current spouse, put all names by which that person was known during the previous eight years.

Name and Address of Creditor. List the name and address of each creditor (as listed on Schedule D, E, or F) to which each codebtor is indebted.

EXAMPLE: Tom Martin cosigned three different loans—with three different banks—for debtor Mabel Green, who is filing for bankruptcy. In the first column, Mabel lists Tom Martin as a codebtor. In the second, Mabel lists each of the three banks.

If you are married and filing alone. If you live in a community property state, your spouse may be a codebtor for most of the debts you listed in Schedules D, E, and F. This is because, in these states, most debts incurred by one spouse are owed by both spouses. In this event, don't relist all the creditors in the second column. Simply write "all creditors listed in Schedules D, E, and F, except:" and then list any creditors who you owe alone.

If you lived with a former spouse in a community property state or Puerto Rico in the eight-year period prior to filing, list his or her name and address.

Form B6H
(10/05)

In re   Carrie Anne Edwards   Case No. _____
_____,
Debtor

SCHEDULE H. CODEBTORS

Provide the information requested concerning any person or entity, other than a spouse in a joint case, that is also liable on any debts listed by debtor in the schedules of creditors. Include all guarantors and co-signers. If the debtor resides or resided in a community property state, commonwealth, or territory (including Alaska, Arizona, California, Idaho, Louisiana, Nevada, New Mexico, Puerto Rico, Texas, Washington, or Wisconsin) within the eight year period immediately preceding the commencement of the case, identify the name of the debtor's spouse and of any former spouse who resides or resided with the debtor in the community property state, commonwealth, or territory. Include all names used by the nondebtor spouse during the eight years immediately preceding the commencement of this case. If a minor child is a codebtor or a creditor, indicate that by stating "a minor child" and do not disclose the child's name. See 11 U.S.C. § 112; Fed. Bankr. P. 1007(m).

☐ Check this box if debtor has no codebtors.

NAME AND ADDRESS OF CODEBTOR	NAME AND ADDRESS OF CREDITOR
Bonnie Johnson 3335 Irving St. Clearlake, CA 95422	Fannie's Furniture 55544 Grove St. Berkeley, CA 94710

   0   continuation sheets attached to Schedule of Codebtors

9. Schedule I—Current Income of Individual Debtor(s)

In this Schedule, you calculate your actual current income (not your average monthly income in the six months before you file, which you'll have to calculate in Form B22A, below).

Directly below are a sample completed Schedule I and line-by-line instructions. If you're married and filing jointly, you must fill in information for both spouses. If you are married but filing alone, fill in the information only for yourself.

In re and **Case No.** Follow the instructions for Schedule A.

Debtor's Marital Status. Enter your marital status. Your choices are single, married, separated (you aren't living with your spouse and plan never to again), widowed, or divorced. You are divorced only if you have received a final judgment of divorce from a court.

Dependents of Debtor and Spouse. List all people, according to their relationship with you (son, daughter, and so on), for whom you and your spouse provide at least 50% of support. There is no need to list their names. This list may include your children, your spouse's children, your parents, other relatives, and domestic partners. It does not include your spouse.

Employment. Provide the requested employment information. If you have more than one employer, enter "See continuation sheet" just below the box containing the employment information, then complete a continuation sheet. If you are retired, unemployed, or disabled, enter that in the blank for "occupation."

Income. Enter your estimated monthly gross income from regular employment, before any payroll deductions are taken. In the second blank, put your estimated monthly overtime pay. Add them together and enter the subtotal in Item 3.

⚠ **Make sure the numbers add up.** As you juggle these income and deduction numbers, remember that you need to use a monthly amount. This means you may need to convert the numbers on your pay stub or other documents if you're paid weekly, every two weeks, or twice a month.

Item 4: Less Payroll Deductions. In the four blanks, enter the deductions taken from your gross salary. The deductions listed are the most common ones, but you may have others to report. Other possible deductions are state disability taxes, wages withheld or garnished for child support, credit union payments, or perhaps payments on a student loan or a car.

Item 5: Subtotal of Payroll Deductions. Add your payroll deductions and enter the subtotal.

Item 6: Total Net Monthly Take Home Pay. Subtract your payroll deductions subtotal from your income subtotal.

Item 7: Regular income from operation of business or profession or farm. If you are self-employed or operate a sole proprietorship, enter your monthly income from that source here. If it's been fairly steady for at least one calendar year, divide the amount you entered on your most recent tax return (IRS Schedule C: Profit or Loss From Business) by 12 for a monthly amount. If your income hasn't been steady for at least one calendar year, enter the average monthly net income from your business or profession over the past three months. In either case, you must attach a detailed statement of your income (you can use your Schedule C).

Item 8: Income from real property. Enter the monthly income from real estate rentals, leases, or licenses (such as mineral exploration, oil, and the like).

Item 9: Interest and dividends. Enter the average estimated monthly interest you receive from bank or security deposits and other investments, such as stocks.

Item 10: Alimony, maintenance or support payments payable to the debtor for the debtor's use or that of dependents listed above. Enter the average monthly amount you receive for your support (alimony, spousal support, or maintenance) or for your children (child support).

Item 11: Social Security or other government assistance. Enter the total monthly amount you receive in Social Security, SSI, public assistance, disability payments, veterans' benefits, unemployment compensation, workers' compensation, or any other government benefit. If you receive food stamps, include their monthly value. Specify the source of the benefits.

Item 12: Pension or retirement income. Enter the total monthly amount of all pension, annuity, IRA, Keogh, or other retirement benefits you currently receive.

Item 13: Other monthly income. Specify any other income (such as royalty payments or payments from a trust) you receive on a regular basis, and enter the

Form B6I
(10/05)

In re   Carrie Anne Edwards _____   Case No. _____
                                    Debtor(s)

SCHEDULE I. CURRENT INCOME OF INDIVIDUAL DEBTOR(S)

The column labeled "Spouse" must be completed in all cases filed by joint debtors and by a married debtor in a chapter 7, 11, 12, or 13 case whether or not a joint petition is filed, unless the spouses are separated and a joint petition is not filed. Do not state the name of any minor child.

Debtor's Marital Status:	DEPENDENTS OF DEBTOR AND SPOUSE	
Divorced	RELATIONSHIP: Daughter Son	AGE: 12 14

Employment:	DEBTOR	SPOUSE
Occupation	Retail	
Name of Employer	Macy's	
How long employed	2 months	
Address of Employer	2356 Cleveland Ave. Santa Rosa, CA 95402	

INCOME: (Estimate of average monthly income)	DEBTOR	SPOUSE
1. Current monthly gross wages, salary, and commissions (Prorate if not paid monthly.)	$ 3,900.00	$ N/A
2. Estimate monthly overtime	$ 0.00	$ N/A
3. SUBTOTAL	$ 3,900.00	$ N/A
4. LESS PAYROLL DEDUCTIONS		
a. Payroll taxes and social security	$ 500.00	$ N/A
b. Insurance	$ 0.00	$ N/A
c. Union dues	$ 0.00	$ N/A
d. Other (Specify): _____	$ 0.00	$ N/A
_____	$ 0.00	$ N/A
5. SUBTOTAL OF PAYROLL DEDUCTIONS	$ 500.00	$ N/A
6. TOTAL NET MONTHLY TAKE HOME PAY	$ 3,400.00	$ N/A
7. Regular income from operation of business or profession or farm. (Attach detailed statement)	$ 0.00	$ N/A
8. Income from real property	$ 0.00	$ N/A
9. Interest and dividends	$ 0.00	$ N/A
10. Alimony, maintenance or support payments payable to the debtor for the debtor's use or that of dependents listed above.	$ 500.00	$ N/A
11. Social security or other government assistance (Specify): _____	$ 0.00	$ N/A
_____	$ 0.00	$ N/A
12. Pension or retirement income	$ 0.00	$ N/A
13. Other monthly income (Specify): royalties from book on bankruptcy	$ 1,000.00	$ N/A
_____	$ 0.00	$ N/A
14. SUBTOTAL OF LINES 7 THROUGH 13	$ 1,500.00	$ N/A
15. TOTAL MONTHLY INCOME (Add amounts shown on lines 6 and 14)	$ 4,900.00	$ N/A

16. TOTAL COMBINED MONTHLY INCOME: $ _____ 4,900.00 _____   (Report also on Summary of Schedules)

17. Describe any increase or decrease in income reasonably anticipated to occur within the year following the filing of this document:

monthly amount here. You may have to divide by three, six, or 12 if you receive the payments quarterly, semiannually, or annually.

Item 14: Subtotal of Lines 7 through 13. Add up your additional income (Items 7 through 13).

Item 15: Total Monthly Income. Combine Items 6 and 14.

Item 16: Total Combined Monthly Income. If you are filing jointly, add your total income to your spouse's total income and enter the result here.

Item 17: Describe any increase or decrease in income reasonably anticipated to occur within the year following the filing of this document. If you indicate that you will soon be enjoying a significantly higher income, you might face a motion from the U.S. Trustee seeking to force you into Chapter 13. But you must be accurate and complete, so you need to disclose that fact here. Of course, if your income is due to decrease any time soon, you should use this part of the form to indicate that as well.

10. Schedule J—Current Expenditures of Individual Debtor(s)

In this form, you must list your family's total monthly expenditures, even if you're married and filing alone. Be complete and accurate. Expenditures for items the trustee considers luxuries won't be considered reasonable and will be disregarded for the purpose of figuring your net income on this form. For instance, payments on expensive cars or investment property may be disregarded by the trustee. Reasonable expenditures for housing, utilities, food, medical care, clothing, education, and transportation will be counted. Be ready to support high amounts with bills, receipts, and canceled checks.

EXAMPLE 1: Joe owes $100,000 (excluding his mortgage and car), earns $4,000 a month, and spends $3,600 a month for the other items listed on Schedule J, including payments on a midpriced car and a moderately priced family home. Joe would probably be allowed to proceed with a Chapter 7 bankruptcy because his monthly disposable income ($400) wouldn't put much of a dent in his $100,000 debt load, even over a five-year period.

EXAMPLE 2: Same facts, except that Joe's Schedule J expenditures total only $2,200 a month. In this case, the court might rule that because Joe has $1,800 a month in disposable income, he could pay off most of his $100,000 debt load over a three- to five-year period, either informally or under a Chapter 13 repayment plan. The court could dismiss Joe's Chapter 7 bankruptcy petition or pressure him to convert it to Chapter 13 bankruptcy.

EXAMPLE 3: Same facts as Example 2, but Joe is incurably ill and will soon quit working. The court will more than likely allow him to proceed with a Chapter 7 bankruptcy.

Most bankruptcy experts believe that the means test set out in Form B22A (see the instructions for the form, below) is the only test for deciding whether a person's Chapter 7 bankruptcy filing could be presumed to be "abusive." However, nothing in the bankruptcy law prevents a trustee from opposing a Chapter 7 filing on the basis that the numbers shown in Schedules I and J indicate that the filing is abusive under all the circumstances. (11 U.S.C. Section 707(b)(1).) So, you should be aware that expenses for luxuries or a large discrepancy between your income and expenses as shown on Schedules I and J may result in a challenge to your Chapter 7 filing by the trustee or U.S. Trustee.

Review the sample completed Schedule J and the guidelines below for filling it out.

Once again, be accurate. Creditors sometimes try to use the information on these forms to prove that you committed fraud when you applied for credit. If a creditor can prove that you lied on a credit application, the debt may survive bankruptcy. (See Ch. 9 for more information.) If being accurate on this form will substantially contradict information you previously gave a creditor, see a bankruptcy attorney before filing.

In re and **Case No.** Follow the instructions for Schedule A.

Check this box if a joint petition is filed and debtor's spouse maintains a separate household. If you and your spouse are jointly filing for bankruptcy but maintain separate households (for example, you've recently separated), check this box and make sure that you each fill out a separate Schedule J.

Form B6J
(10/05)

In re ___Carrie Anne Edwards_____   Case No. _____
                                          Debtor(s)

SCHEDULE J. CURRENT EXPENDITURES OF INDIVIDUAL DEBTOR(S)

Complete this schedule by estimating the average monthly expenses of the debtor and the debtor's family. Pro rate any payments made bi-weekly, quarterly, semi-annually, or annually to show monthly rate.

☐   Check this box if a joint petition is filed and debtor's spouse maintains a separate household. Complete a separate schedule of expenditures labeled "Spouse."

1. Rent or home mortgage payment (include lot rented for mobile home)	$ 1,465.00
a. Are real estate taxes included? Yes __X__ No _____	
b. Is property insurance included? Yes __X__ No _____	
2. Utilities: a. Electricity and heating fuel	$ 150.00
b. Water and sewer	$ 150.00
c. Telephone	$ 175.00
d. Other See Detailed Expense Attachment	$ 130.00
3. Home maintenance (repairs and upkeep)	$ 75.00
4. Food	$ 600.00
5. Clothing	$ 300.00
6. Laundry and dry cleaning	$ 100.00
7. Medical and dental expenses	$ 300.00
8. Transportation (not including car payments)	$ 750.00
9. Recreation, clubs and entertainment, newspapers, magazines, etc.	$ 100.00
10. Charitable contributions	$ 0.00
11. Insurance (not deducted from wages or included in home mortgage payments)	
a. Homeowner's or renter's	$ 0.00
b. Life	$ 0.00
c. Health	$ 0.00
d. Auto	$ 100.00
e. Other _____	$ 0.00
12. Taxes (not deducted from wages or included in home mortgage payments)	
(Specify) _____	$ 0.00
13. Installment payments: (In chapter 11, 12 and 13 cases, do not list payments to be included in the plan.)	
a. Auto	$ 50.00
b. Other Payment on home equity loan	$ 100.00
c. Other _____	$ 0.00
d. Other _____	$ 0.00
14. Alimony, maintenance, and support paid to others	$ 0.00
15. Payments for support of additional dependents not living at your home	$ 0.00
16. Regular expenses from operation of business, profession, or farm (attach detailed statement)	$ 0.00
17. Other Child care	$ 300.00
Other _____	$ 0.00
18. TOTAL MONTHLY EXPENSES (Report also on Summary of Schedules)	$ 4,845.00

19. Describe any increase or decrease in expenditures anticipated to occur within the year following the filing of this document:

_____

20. STATEMENT OF MONTHLY NET INCOME

a.	Total monthly income from Line 16 of Schedule I	$ 4,900.00
b.	Total monthly expenses from Line 18 above	$ 4,845.00
c.	Monthly net income (a. minus b.)	$ 55.00

Form B6J
(10/05)

In re　Carrie Anne Edwards　　　　　　　　　　　　　　　　　Case No. _____
　　　　　　　　　　　　　　　Debtor(s)

SCHEDULE J. CURRENT EXPENDITURES OF INDIVIDUAL DEBTOR(S)
Detailed Expense Attachment

Other Utility Expenditures:

Satellite TV	$　　　90.00
DSL	$　　　40.00
Total Other Utility Expenditures	$　　　130.00

Expenditures Items 1–17. For each listed item, fill in your monthly expenses. If you make some payments biweekly, quarterly, semiannually, or annually, prorate them to show your monthly payment. Here are some pointers:

- Do not list payroll deductions you listed on Schedule I.
- Include payments you make for your dependents' expenses in your figures as long as those expenses are reasonable and necessary for the dependents' support.
- Utilities—Other: This includes garbage, Internet, and cable TV service.
- Installment payments—Other: In this blank, put the amount of any installment payments you are making on a secured debt or a debt you plan on reaffirming (agreeing to owe and pay the secured debt on basically the same terms as preceded the bankruptcy). Do not put payments you have been making on a credit card or other debt that does not involve collateral and that you plan to discharge in your bankruptcy.

Item 18. Total Monthly Expenses. Total up all your expenses.

Item 19. Describe any increase or decrease in expenditures in the next year. For instance if you plan to pay off a car note during the coming year, indicate that fact.

Item 20. Deduct your total expenses on Line 18 from your total income on Line 16 of Schedule I. This will show at a glance whether you have significantly more income than expenses.

⚠ **Don't underestimate your expenses.** As indicated above, a significant net income might lead the trustee to challenge your Chapter 7 filing. Sometimes people give low estimates of their expenses, because they don't want to appear to be living beyond their means. If this describes your situation, go back over your expenses and make sure they are accurate.

11. Summary of Schedules

This form helps the bankruptcy trustee and judge get a quick look at your bankruptcy filing. Below is a completed Summary and line-by-line instructions.

Court Name. Copy this information from Form 1—Voluntary Petition.

In re and **Case No.** Follow the instructions for Schedule A.

Name of Schedule. This lists the schedules. Don't add anything.

Attached (Yes/No). You should have completed all of the schedules, so type "Yes" in this column for each schedule, even if you added no information.

No. of Sheets. Enter the number of pages you completed for each schedule. Remember to count continuation pages. Enter the total at the bottom of the column.

Amounts Scheduled. For each column—Assets, Liabilities, and Other—copy the totals from Schedules A, B, D, E, F, I, and J and enter them where indicated. Add up the amounts in the Assets and Liabilities columns and enter their totals at the bottom. (Once you've completed this form, you can go back and fill in the "Statistical/Administrative Information" section on Form 1—Voluntary Petition (see Section E).)

Statistical Summary of Certain Liabilities. The second page of the summary sheet asks you to list the amounts of particular types of debts, including child support, student loans, and loans from a pension plan. Fill in the requested amounts from Schedules E and F.

Form 6-Summary
(10/05)

United States Bankruptcy Court
Northern District of California

In re   Carrie Anne Edwards   ,   Case No. _____

                                             Debtor

Chapter _____ 7 _____

SUMMARY OF SCHEDULES

Indicate as to each schedule whether that schedule is attached and state the number of pages in each. Report the totals from Schedules A, B, D, E, F, I, and J in the boxes provided. Add the amounts from Schedules A and B to determine the total amount of the debtor's assets. Add the amounts of all claims from Schedules D, E, and F to determine the total amount of the debtor's liabilities. Individual debtors must also complete the "Statistical Summary of Certain Liabilities."

NAME OF SCHEDULE	ATTACHED (YES/NO)	NO. OF SHEETS	AMOUNTS SCHEDULED		
			ASSETS	LIABILITIES	OTHER
A - Real Property	Yes	1	140,000.00		
B - Personal Property	Yes	4	25,325.00		
C - Property Claimed as Exempt	Yes	2			
D - Creditors Holding Secured Claims	Yes	1		141,000.00	
E - Creditors Holding Unsecured Priority Claims	Yes	3		5,500.00	
F - Creditors Holding Unsecured Nonpriority Claims	Yes	3		147,150.00	
G - Executory Contracts and Unexpired Leases	Yes	1			
H - Codebtors	Yes	1			
I - Current Income of Individual Debtor(s)	Yes	1			4,900.00
J - Current Expenditures of Individual Debtor(s)	Yes	2			4,845.00
Total Number of Sheets of ALL Schedules		19			
Total Assets			165,325.00		
Total Liabilities				293,650.00	

Form 6-Summ2
(10/05)

United States Bankruptcy Court
Northern District of California

In re   Carrie Anne Edwards   ,   Case No. _____

                               Debtor

                                             Chapter _____ 7 _____

STATISTICAL SUMMARY OF CERTAIN LIABILITIES (28 U.S.C. § 159)
[Individual Debtors Only]

Summarize the following types of liabilities, as reported in the Schedules, and total them.

Type of Liability	Amount
Domestic Support Obligations (from Schedule E)	2,500.00
Taxes and Certain Other Debts Owed to Governmental Units (from Schedule E)	3,000.00
Claims for Death or Personal Injury While Debtor Was Intoxicated (from Schedule E)	0.00
Student Loan Obligations (from Schedule F)	0.00
Domestic Support, Separation Agreement, and Divorce Decree Obligations Not Reported on Schedule E	0.00
Obligations to Pension or Profit-Sharing, and Other Similar Obligations (from Schedule F)	0.00
TOTAL	5,500.00

The foregoing information is for statistical purposes only under 28 U.S.C § 159.

12. Declaration Concerning Debtor's Schedules

In this form, you are required to swear that everything you have said on your schedules is true and correct. Deliberate lying is a major sin in bankruptcy and could cost you your bankruptcy discharge, a fine of up to $500,000, and up to five years in prison.

Below is a completed Declaration and instructions.

In re and **Case No.** Follow the instructions for Schedule A.

Declaration Under Penalty of Perjury by Individual Debtor. Enter the total number of pages in your schedules (the number on the Summary plus two). Enter the date and sign the form. Be sure that your spouse signs and dates the form if you are filing jointly.

Certification and Signature of Non-Attorney Bankruptcy Petition Preparer. If a BPP typed your forms, have that person complete this section. Otherwise, type "N/A" anywhere in the box.

Declaration Under Penalty of Perjury on Behalf of Corporation or Partnership. Enter "N/A" anywhere in this blank.

Official Form 6-Decl.
(10/05)

United States Bankruptcy Court
Northern District of California

In re   Carrie Anne Edwards   Case No. _____

                     Debtor(s)   Chapter   7 _____

DECLARATION CONCERNING DEBTOR'S SCHEDULES

DECLARATION UNDER PENALTY OF PERJURY BY INDIVIDUAL DEBTOR

I declare under penalty of perjury that I have read the foregoing summary and schedules, consisting of _____21_____ sheets *[total shown on summary page plus 2]*, and that they are true and correct to the best of my knowledge, information, and belief.

Date   October 25, 2005 _____   Signature   /s/ Carrie Anne Edwards _____

                                                Carrie Anne Edwards
                                                Debtor

Penalty for making a false statement or concealing property: Fine of up to $500,000 or imprisonment for up to 5 years or both.
18 U.S.C. §§ 152 and 3571.

G. Form 7—Statement of Financial Affairs

This form gives information about your recent financial transactions, such as payments to creditors, sales, or other transfers of property and gifts. Under certain circumstances, the trustee may be entitled to take back property that you transferred to others prior to filing for bankruptcy, and sell it for the benefit of your unsecured creditors.

The questions on the form are, for the most part, self-explanatory. Spouses filing jointly combine their answers and complete only one form.

If you have no information for a particular item, check the "None" box. If you fail to answer a question and don't check "None," you will have to amend your papers—that is, file a corrected form—after you file. Add continuation sheets if necessary.

⚠️ **Be honest and complete.** Don't give in to the temptation to leave out a transfer or two, assuming that the trustee won't find or go after the property. You must sign this form under penalty of perjury. And, if the trustee or a creditor discovers that you left information out, your bankruptcy will probably be dismissed and you may be prosecuted.

A completed Statement of Financial Affairs and instructions follow.

Court Name. Copy this information from Form 1—Voluntary Petition.

In re and **Case No.** Follow the instructions for Schedule A.

1. Income from employment or operation of business. Enter your gross income for this year and for the previous two years. This means the total income before taxes and other payroll deductions or business expenses are removed.

2. Income other than from employment or operation of business. Include interest, dividends, royalties, workers' compensation, other government benefits, and all other money you have received from sources other than your job or business during the last two years. Provide the source of each amount, the dates received, and the reason you received the money so that the trustee can verify it if he or she desires.

3. Payments to creditors. Here you list payments you've recently made to creditors. There are two kinds of creditors: regular creditors and insiders. An insider—defined on the first page of the Statement of Financial Affairs—is essentially a relative or close business associate. All other creditors are regular creditors.

a. Individual or joint debtor(s) with primarily consumer debts. List payments made to a regular creditor that total more than $600, if the payment was made:

- to repay a loan, installment purchase, or other debt, and
- during the 90 days before you file your bankruptcy petition.

If you have made payments exceeding $600 during that 90-day period to satisfy a domestic support obligation (child support or alimony), identify that payment with an asterisk. Include payments as part of a creditor repayment plan negotiated by an approved budget and credit counseling agency.

b. Debtor whose debts are not primarily consumer debts. If your debts are primarily business debts, list all payments or other transfers made to a creditor within 90 days of filing regarding property that is worth $5,000 or more.

c. All debtors. List all payments or other transfers made to an insider creditor, if the payments or transfers were made within one year before you file your bankruptcy petition. Include alimony and child support payments.

The purpose of these questions is to find out whether you have preferred any creditor over others. If you have paid a regular creditor during the 90 days before you file, or an insider during the year before you file, the trustee can demand that the creditor turn over the amount to the court, so the trustee can use it to pay your other unsecured creditors. (See Ch.3, Section A.) The trustee may ask you to produce written evidence of any payments you list here, such as copies of canceled checks, check stubs, or bank statements.

4. Suits and administrative proceedings, executions, garnishments and attachments.

a. Include all court actions that you are currently involved in or that you were involved in during the year before filing. Court actions include personal injury cases, small claims actions, contract disputes,

Official Form 7
(10/05)

United States Bankruptcy Court
Northern District of California

In re   Carrie Anne Edwards   Case No. _____
                                           Debtor(s)   Chapter   7 _____

STATEMENT OF FINANCIAL AFFAIRS

        This statement is to be completed by every debtor. Spouses filing a joint petition may file a single statement on which the information for both spouses is combined. If the case is filed under chapter 12 or chapter 13, a married debtor must furnish information for both spouses whether or not a joint petition is filed, unless the spouses are separated and a joint petition is not filed. An individual debtor engaged in business as a sole proprietor, partner, family farmer, or self-employed professional, should provide the information requested on this statement concerning all such activities as well as the individual's personal affairs. Do not include the name or address of a minor child in this statement. Indicate payments, transfers and the like to minor children by stating "a minor child." See 11 U.S.C. § 112; Fed. R. Bankr. P. 1007(m).

        Questions 1 - 18 are to be completed by all debtors. Debtors that are or have been in business, as defined below, also must complete Questions 19 - 25. **If the answer to an applicable question is "None," mark the box labeled "None."** If additional space is needed for the answer to any question, use and attach a separate sheet properly identified with the case name, case number (if known), and the number of the question.

DEFINITIONS

        "In business." A debtor is "in business" for the purpose of this form if the debtor is a corporation or partnership. An individual debtor is "in business" for the purpose of this form if the debtor is or has been, within six years immediately preceding the filing of this bankruptcy case, any of the following: an officer, director, managing executive, or owner of 5 percent or more of the voting or equity securities of a corporation; a partner, other than a limited partner, of a partnership; a sole proprietor or self-employed full-time or part-time. An individual debtor also may be "in business" for the purpose of this form if the debtor engages in a trade, business, or other activity, other than as an employee, to supplement income from the debtor's primary employment.

        "Insider." The term "insider" includes but is not limited to: relatives of the debtor; general partners of the debtor and their relatives; corporations of which the debtor is an officer, director, or person in control; officers, directors, and any owner of 5 percent or more of the voting or equity securities of a corporate debtor and their relatives; affiliates of the debtor and insiders of such affiliates; any managing agent of the debtor. 11 U.S.C. § 101.

---

1. Income from employment or operation of business

None
☐

        State the gross amount of income the debtor has received from employment, trade, or profession, or from operation of the debtor's business, including part-time activities either as an employee or in independent trade or business, from the beginning of this calendar year to the date this case was commenced. State also the gross amounts received during the **two years** immediately preceding this calendar year. (A debtor that maintains, or has maintained, financial records on the basis of a fiscal rather than a calendar year may report fiscal year income. Identify the beginning and ending dates of the debtor's fiscal year.) If a joint petition is filed, state income for each spouse separately. (Married debtors filing under chapter 12 or chapter 13 must state income of both spouses whether or not a joint petition is filed, unless the spouses are separated and a joint petition is not filed.)

        AMOUNT   SOURCE
        $144,600.00   2003 ($55,100) (employment at Microsoft as software engineer)
                           2004 ($50,100) (employment at Microsoft)

                           Jan-Oct 2005 (39,400) (employment at Microsoft and Macy's)

2

2. Income other than from employment or operation of business

None
☐

State the amount of income received by the debtor other than from employment, trade, profession, or operation of the debtor's business during the **two years** immediately preceding the commencement of this case. Give particulars. If a joint petition is filed, state income for each spouse separately. (Married debtors filing under chapter 12 or chapter 13 must state income for each spouse whether or not a joint petition is filed, unless the spouses are separated and a joint petition is not filed.)

AMOUNT	SOURCE
$32,000.00	Oct 04-Oct 05 (12,000 royalties, 6000 child support October 03-Oct 04 (8,000 royalities, 6000 child support)

3. Payments to creditors

None
☐

Complete a. or b., as appropriate, and c.

a.   *Individual or joint debtor(s) with primarily consumer debts.* List all payments on loans, installment purchases of goods or services, and other debts to any creditor made within **90 days** immediately preceding the commencement of this case if the aggregate value of all property that constitutes or is affected by such transfer is not less than $600. Indicate with an (*) any payments that were made to a creditor on account of a domestic support obligation or as part of an alternative repayment schedule under a plan by an approved nonprofit budgeting and creditor counseling agency. (Married debtors filing under chapter 12 or chapter 13 must include payments by either or both spouses whether or not a joint petition is filed, unless the spouses are separated and a joint petition is not filed.)

NAME AND ADDRESS OF CREDITOR	DATES OF PAYMENTS	AMOUNT PAID	AMOUNT STILL OWING
Loantree PO Box 305 Lucerne, CA 95458	12/xx	$800.00	$0.00

None
■

b.   *Debtor whose debts are not primarily consumer debts:* List each payment or other transfer to any creditor made within **90 days** immediately preceding the commencement of the case if the aggregate value of all property that constitutes or is affected by such transfer is not less than $5,000. (Married debtors filing under chapter 12 or chapter 13 must include payments by either or both spouses whether or not a joint petition is filed, unless the spouses are separated and a joint petition is not filed.)

NAME AND ADDRESS OF CREDITOR	DATES OF PAYMENTS/ TRANSFERS	AMOUNT PAID OR VALUE OF TRANSFERS	AMOUNT STILL OWING

None
■

c.   *All debtors:* List all payments made within **one year** immediately preceding the commencement of this case to or for the benefit of creditors who are or were insiders. (Married debtors filing under chapter 12 or chapter 13 must include payments by either or both spouses whether or not a joint petition is filed, unless the spouses are separated and a joint petition is not filed.)

NAME AND ADDRESS OF CREDITOR AND RELATIONSHIP TO DEBTOR	DATE OF PAYMENT	AMOUNT PAID	AMOUNT STILL OWING

4. Suits and administrative proceedings, executions, garnishments and attachments

None
☐

a. List all suits and administrative proceedings to which the debtor is or was a party within **one year** immediately preceding the filing of this bankruptcy case. (Married debtors filing under chapter 12 or chapter 13 must include information concerning either or both spouses whether or not a joint petition is filed, unless the spouses are separated and a joint petition is not filed.)

CAPTION OF SUIT AND CASE NUMBER	NATURE OF PROCEEDING	COURT OR AGENCY AND LOCATION	STATUS OR DISPOSITION
Bob Jones III v. Carrie Edwards Case # cv34457	Negligence action for auto accident	Lake County Superior Court 255 N. Forbes St. Lakeport, CA 95453	Trial pending

3

None ☐   b. Describe all property that has been attached, garnished or seized under any legal or equitable process within **one year** immediately preceding the commencement of this case. (Married debtors filing under chapter 12 or chapter 13 must include information concerning property of either or both spouses whether or not a joint petition is filed, unless the spouses are separated and a joint petition is not filed.)

NAME AND ADDRESS OF PERSON FOR WHOSE BENEFIT PROPERTY WAS SEIZED	DATE OF SEIZURE	DESCRIPTION AND VALUE OF PROPERTY
JNR Adjustment Co. PO Box 27070 Minneapolis, MN 55427	4/XX	wage garnishment for two months totaling $510 for judgment on debt owed to DVD club.

5. Repossessions, foreclosures and returns

None ☐   List all property that has been repossessed by a creditor, sold at a foreclosure sale, transferred through a deed in lieu of foreclosure or returned to the seller, within **one year** immediately preceding the commencement of this case. (Married debtors filing under chapter 12 or chapter 13 must include information concerning property of either or both spouses whether or not a joint petition is filed, unless the spouses are separated and a joint petition is not filed.)

NAME AND ADDRESS OF CREDITOR OR SELLER	DATE OF REPOSSESSION, FORECLOSURE SALE, TRANSFER OR RETURN	DESCRIPTION AND VALUE OF PROPERTY
Eskanos & Adler 2325 Clayton Rd. Concord, CA 94520	4/XX	Repossessed furniture worth $800

6. Assignments and receiverships

None ■   a. Describe any assignment of property for the benefit of creditors made within **120 days** immediately preceding the commencement of this case. (Married debtors filing under chapter 12 or chapter 13 must include any assignment by either or both spouses whether or not a joint petition is filed, unless the spouses are separated and a joint petition is not filed.)

NAME AND ADDRESS OF ASSIGNEE	DATE OF ASSIGNMENT	TERMS OF ASSIGNMENT OR SETTLEMENT

None ■   b. List all property which has been in the hands of a custodian, receiver, or court-appointed official within **one year** immediately preceding the commencement of this case. (Married debtors filing under chapter 12 or chapter 13 must include information concerning property of either or both spouses whether or not a joint petition is filed, unless the spouses are separated and a joint petition is not filed.)

NAME AND ADDRESS OF CUSTODIAN	NAME AND LOCATION OF COURT CASE TITLE & NUMBER	DATE OF ORDER	DESCRIPTION AND VALUE OF PROPERTY

7. Gifts

None ■   List all gifts or charitable contributions made within **one year** immediately preceding the commencement of this case except ordinary and usual gifts to family members aggregating less than $200 in value per individual family member and charitable contributions aggregating less than $100 per recipient. (Married debtors filing under chapter 12 or chapter 13 must include gifts or contributions by either or both spouses whether or not a joint petition is filed, unless the spouses are separated and a joint petition is not filed.)

NAME AND ADDRESS OF PERSON OR ORGANIZATION	RELATIONSHIP TO DEBTOR, IF ANY	DATE OF GIFT	DESCRIPTION AND VALUE OF GIFT

8. Losses

None ■   List all losses from fire, theft, other casualty or gambling within **one year** immediately preceding the commencement of this case **or since the commencement of this case.** (Married debtors filing under chapter 12 or chapter 13 must include losses by either or both spouses whether or not a joint petition is filed, unless the spouses are separated and a joint petition is not filed.)

DESCRIPTION AND VALUE OF PROPERTY	DESCRIPTION OF CIRCUMSTANCES AND, IF LOSS WAS COVERED IN WHOLE OR IN PART BY INSURANCE, GIVE PARTICULARS	DATE OF LOSS

4

9. Payments related to debt counseling or bankruptcy

None
☐ List all payments made or property transferred by or on behalf of the debtor to any persons, including attorneys, for consultation concerning debt consolidation, relief under the bankruptcy law or preparation of the petition in bankruptcy within **one year** immediately preceding the commencement of this case.

NAME AND ADDRESS OF PAYEE	DATE OF PAYMENT, NAME OF PAYOR IF OTHER THAN DEBTOR	AMOUNT OF MONEY OR DESCRIPTION AND VALUE OF PROPERTY
Jim McDonald Esq. 444 State St. Ukiah, CA	7/xx	$100 for bankruptcy telephone advice

10. Other transfers

None
■ a. List all other property, other than property transferred in the ordinary course of the business or financial affairs of the debtor, transferred either absolutely or as security within **two years** immediately preceding the commencement of this case. (Married debtors filing under chapter 12 or chapter 13 must include transfers by either or both spouses whether or not a joint petition is filed, unless the spouses are separated and a joint petition is not filed.)

NAME AND ADDRESS OF TRANSFEREE, RELATIONSHIP TO DEBTOR	DATE	DESCRIBE PROPERTY TRANSFERRED AND VALUE RECEIVED

None
■ b. List all property transferred by the debtor within **ten years** immediately preceding the commencement of this case to a self-settled trust or similar device of which the debtor is a beneficiary.

NAME OF TRUST OR OTHER DEVICE	DATE(S) OF TRANSFER(S)	AMOUNT OF MONEY OR DESCRIPTION AND VALUE OF PROPERTY OR DEBTOR'S INTEREST IN PROPERTY

11. Closed financial accounts

None
☐ List all financial accounts and instruments held in the name of the debtor or for the benefit of the debtor which were closed, sold, or otherwise transferred within **one year** immediately preceding the commencement of this case. Include checking, savings, or other financial accounts, certificates of deposit, or other instruments; shares and share accounts held in banks, credit unions, pension funds, cooperatives, associations, brokerage houses and other financial institutions. (Married debtors filing under chapter 12 or chapter 13 must include information concerning accounts or instruments held by or for either or both spouses whether or not a joint petition is filed, unless the spouses are separated and a joint petition is not filed.)

NAME AND ADDRESS OF INSTITUTION	TYPE OF ACCOUNT, LAST FOUR DIGITS OF ACCOUNT NUMBER, AND AMOUNT OF FINAL BALANCE	AMOUNT AND DATE OF SALE OR CLOSING
WestAmerica Bank 444 North Main St. Lakeport, CA 95453	Checking Acct #4444444 Final balance ($50)	

12. Safe deposit boxes

None
■ List each safe deposit or other box or depository in which the debtor has or had securities, cash, or other valuables within **one year** immediately preceding the commencement of this case. (Married debtors filing under chapter 12 or chapter 13 must include boxes or depositories of either or both spouses whether or not a joint petition is filed, unless the spouses are separated and a joint petition is not filed.)

NAME AND ADDRESS OF BANK OR OTHER DEPOSITORY	NAMES AND ADDRESSES OF THOSE WITH ACCESS TO BOX OR DEPOSITORY	DESCRIPTION OF CONTENTS	DATE OF TRANSFER OR SURRENDER, IF ANY

5

13. Setoffs

None
■

List all setoffs made by any creditor, including a bank, against a debt or deposit of the debtor within **90 days** preceding the commencement of this case. (Married debtors filing under chapter 12 or chapter 13 must include information concerning either or both spouses whether or not a joint petition is filed, unless the spouses are separated and a joint petition is not filed.)

NAME AND ADDRESS OF CREDITOR	DATE OF SETOFF	AMOUNT OF SETOFF

14. Property held for another person

None
☐

List all property owned by another person that the debtor holds or controls.

NAME AND ADDRESS OF OWNER	DESCRIPTION AND VALUE OF PROPERTY	LOCATION OF PROPERTY
Bonnie Johnson 3335 Irving St Clearlake, CA 95422	Poodle (Binkie) $300	Edwards residence

15. Prior address of debtor

None
☐

If the debtor has moved within **three years** immediately preceding the commencement of this case, list all premises which the debtor occupied during that period and vacated prior to the commencement of this case. If a joint petition is filed, report also any separate address of either spouse.

ADDRESS	NAME USED	DATES OF OCCUPANCY
21 Scarborough Rd. South Cleveland Heights OH 41118	Carrie Edwards	1/1/XX-- 5/1/XX

16. Spouses and Former Spouses

None
☐

If the debtor resides or resided in a community property state, commonwealth, or territory (including Alaska, Arizona, California, Idaho, Louisiana, Nevada, New Mexico, Puerto Rico, Texas, Washington, or Wisconsin) within **eight years** immediately preceding the commencement of the case, identify the name of the debtor's spouse and of any former spouse who resides or resided with the debtor in the community property state.

NAME
Torrey Edwards

17. Environmental Information.

For the purpose of this question, the following definitions apply:

"Environmental Law" means any federal, state, or local statute or regulation regulating pollution, contamination, releases of hazardous or toxic substances, wastes or material into the air, land, soil, surface water, groundwater, or other medium, including, but not limited to, statutes or regulations regulating the cleanup of these substances, wastes, or material.

"Site" means any location, facility, or property as defined under any Environmental Law, whether or not presently or formerly owned or operated by the debtor, including, but not limited to, disposal sites.

"Hazardous Material" means anything defined as a hazardous waste, hazardous substance, toxic substance, hazardous material, pollutant, or contaminant or similar term under an Environmental Law

None
■

a. List the name and address of every site for which the debtor has received notice in writing by a governmental unit that it may be liable or potentially liable under or in violation of an Environmental Law. Indicate the governmental unit, the date of the notice, and, if known, the Environmental Law:

SITE NAME AND ADDRESS	NAME AND ADDRESS OF GOVERNMENTAL UNIT	DATE OF NOTICE	ENVIRONMENTAL LAW

6

None ■   b. List the name and address of every site for which the debtor provided notice to a governmental unit of a release of Hazardous Material. Indicate the governmental unit to which the notice was sent and the date of the notice.

SITE NAME AND ADDRESS	NAME AND ADDRESS OF GOVERNMENTAL UNIT	DATE OF NOTICE	ENVIRONMENTAL LAW

None ■   c. List all judicial or administrative proceedings, including settlements or orders, under any Environmental Law with respect to which the debtor is or was a party. Indicate the name and address of the governmental unit that is or was a party to the proceeding, and the docket number.

NAME AND ADDRESS OF GOVERNMENTAL UNIT	DOCKET NUMBER	STATUS OR DISPOSITION

18 . Nature, location and name of business

None ■   a. *If the debtor is an individual,* list the names, addresses, taxpayer identification numbers, nature of the businesses, and beginning and ending dates of all businesses in which the debtor was an officer, director, partner, or managing executive of a corporation, partner in a partnership, sole proprietor, or was self-employed in a trade, profession, or other activity either full- or part-time within **six years** immediately preceding the commencement of this case, or in which the debtor owned 5 percent or more of the voting or equity securities within **six years** immediately preceding the commencement of this case.

If the debtor is a partnership, list the names, addresses, taxpayer identification numbers, nature of the businesses, and beginning and ending dates of all businesses in which the debtor was a partner or owned 5 percent or more of the voting or equity securities, within **six years** immediately preceding the commencement of this case.

If the debtor is a corporation, list the names, addresses, taxpayer identification numbers, nature of the businesses, and beginning and ending dates of all businesses in which the debtor was a partner or owned 5 percent or more of the voting or equity securities within **six years** immediately preceding the commencement of this case.

NAME	LAST FOUR DIGITS OF SOC. SEC. NO./ COMPLETE EIN OR OTHER TAXPAYER I.D. NO.	ADDRESS	NATURE OF BUSINESS	BEGINNING AND ENDING DATES

None ■   b. Identify any business listed in response to subdivision a., above, that is "single asset real estate" as defined in 11 U.S.C. § 101.

NAME	ADDRESS

The following questions are to be completed by every debtor that is a corporation or partnership and by any individual debtor who is or has been, within **six years** immediately preceding the commencement of this case, any of the following: an officer, director, managing executive, or owner of more than 5 percent of the voting or equity securities of a corporation; a partner, other than a limited partner, of a partnership, a sole proprietor or self-employed in a trade, profession, or other activity, either full- or part-time.

*(An individual or joint debtor should complete this portion of the statement **only** if the debtor is or has been in business, as defined above, within six years immediately preceding the commencement of this case. A debtor who has not been in business within those six years should go directly to the signature page.)*

19. Books, records and financial statements

None ■   a. List all bookkeepers and accountants who within **two years** immediately preceding the filing of this bankruptcy case kept or supervised the keeping of books of account and records of the debtor.

NAME AND ADDRESS	DATES SERVICES RENDERED

None ■   b. List all firms or individuals who within the **two years** immediately preceding the filing of this bankruptcy case have audited the books of account and records, or prepared a financial statement of the debtor.

NAME	ADDRESS	DATES SERVICES RENDERED

None ■   c. List all firms or individuals who at the time of the commencement of this case were in possession of the books of account and records of the debtor. If any of the books of account and records are not available, explain.

NAME   ADDRESS

None ■   d. List all financial institutions, creditors and other parties, including mercantile and trade agencies, to whom a financial statement was issued by the debtor within **two years** immediately preceding the commencement of this case.

NAME AND ADDRESS   DATE ISSUED

20. Inventories

None ■   a. List the dates of the last two inventories taken of your property, the name of the person who supervised the taking of each inventory, and the dollar amount and basis of each inventory.

DATE OF INVENTORY   INVENTORY SUPERVISOR   DOLLAR AMOUNT OF INVENTORY
                                                           (Specify cost, market or other basis)

None ■   b. List the name and address of the person having possession of the records of each of the two inventories reported in a., above.

DATE OF INVENTORY   NAME AND ADDRESSES OF CUSTODIAN OF INVENTORY
                                                 RECORDS

21 . Current Partners, Officers, Directors and Shareholders

None ■   a. If the debtor is a partnership, list the nature and percentage of partnership interest of each member of the partnership.

NAME AND ADDRESS   NATURE OF INTEREST   PERCENTAGE OF INTEREST

None ■   b. If the debtor is a corporation, list all officers and directors of the corporation, and each stockholder who directly or indirectly owns, controls, or holds 5 percent or more of the voting or equity securities of the corporation.

                                                           NATURE AND PERCENTAGE
NAME AND ADDRESS   TITLE   OF STOCK OWNERSHIP

22 . Former partners, officers, directors and shareholders

None ■   a. If the debtor is a partnership, list each member who withdrew from the partnership within **one year** immediately preceding the commencement of this case.

NAME   ADDRESS   DATE OF WITHDRAWAL

None ■   b. If the debtor is a corporation, list all officers, or directors whose relationship with the corporation terminated within **one year** immediately preceding the commencement of this case.

NAME AND ADDRESS   TITLE   DATE OF TERMINATION

23 . Withdrawals from a partnership or distributions by a corporation

None ■   If the debtor is a partnership or corporation, list all withdrawals or distributions credited or given to an insider, including compensation in any form, bonuses, loans, stock redemptions, options exercised and any other perquisite during **one year** immediately preceding the commencement of this case.

NAME & ADDRESS   AMOUNT OF MONEY
OF RECIPIENT,   DATE AND PURPOSE   OR DESCRIPTION AND
RELATIONSHIP TO DEBTOR   OF WITHDRAWAL   VALUE OF PROPERTY

8

24. Tax Consolidation Group.

None ■ If the debtor is a corporation, list the name and federal taxpayer identification number of the parent corporation of any consolidated group for tax purposes of which the debtor has been a member at any time within **six years** immediately preceding the commencement of the case.

NAME OF PARENT CORPORATION   TAXPAYER IDENTIFICATION NUMBER (EIN)

25. Pension Funds.

None ■ If the debtor is not an individual, list the name and federal taxpayer identification number of any pension fund to which the debtor, as an employer, has been responsible for contributing at any time within **six years** immediately preceding the commencement of the case.

NAME OF PENSION FUND   TAXPAYER IDENTIFICATION NUMBER (EIN)

DECLARATION UNDER PENALTY OF PERJURY BY INDIVIDUAL DEBTOR

I declare under penalty of perjury that I have read the answers contained in the foregoing statement of financial affairs and any attachments thereto and that they are true and correct.

Date October 25, 2005   Signature /s/ Carrie Anne Edwards
                                           Carrie Anne Edwards
                                           Debtor

Penalty for making a false statement: Fine of up to $500,000 or imprisonment for up to 5 years, or both. 18 U.S.C. §§ 152 and 3571

divorces, paternity actions, support or custody modification actions, and the like. Include:

- **Caption of suit and case number.** The caption is the case title (such as Molly Maytag v. Ginny Jones). The case number is assigned by the court clerk and appears on the first page of any court-filed paper.
- **Nature of proceeding.** A phrase, or even a one-word description, is sufficient. For example, "suit by debtor for compensation for damages to debtor's car caused by accident," or "divorce."
- **Court or Agency and location.** This information is on any summons you received or prepared.
- **Status or disposition.** State whether the case is awaiting trial, is pending a decision, is on appeal, or has ended.

b. If, at any time during the year before you file for bankruptcy, your wages, real estate, or personal property was taken from you under the authority of a court order to pay a debt, enter the requested information. If you don't know the exact date, put "on or about" the approximate date.

5. Repossessions, foreclosures and returns. If, at any time during the year before you file for bankruptcy, a creditor repossessed or foreclosed on property you had bought and were making payments on, or had pledged as collateral for a loan, give the requested information. For instance, if your car, boat, or video equipment was repossessed because you defaulted on your payments, describe it here. Also, if you voluntarily returned property to a creditor because you couldn't keep up the payments, enter that here.

6. Assignments and receiverships.

a. If, at any time during the 120 days (four months) before you file for bankruptcy, you assigned (legally transferred) your right to receive benefits or property to a creditor to pay a debt, list it here. Examples include assigning a percentage of your wages to a creditor for several months or assigning a portion of a personal injury award to an attorney. The assignee is the person to whom the assignment was made, such as the creditor or attorney. The terms of the assignment should be given briefly—for example, "wages assigned to Snorkle's Store to satisfy debt of $500."

b. Identify all of your property that has been in the hands of a court-appointed receiver, custodian, or other official during the year before you file for bankruptcy. If you've made child support payments directly to a court, and the court in turn paid your child's other parent, list those payments here.

7. Gifts. Provide the requested information about gifts you've made in the past year. The bankruptcy court and trustee want this information to make sure you haven't improperly unloaded any property before filing for bankruptcy. List all charitable donations of more than $100 and gifts to family members of more than $200.

You don't have to list gifts to family members that are "ordinary and usual," but there is no easy way to identify such gifts. The best test is whether someone outside of the family might think the gift was unusual under the circumstances. If so, list it. Forgiving a loan is also a gift, as is charging interest substantially below the market rate. Other gifts include giving a car or prepaid trip to a business associate.

8. Losses. Provide the requested information. If the loss was for an exempt item, most states let you keep the insurance proceeds up to the limit of the exemption. (See Appendix 1.) If the item was not exempt, the trustee is entitled to the proceeds. In either case, list any proceeds you've received or expect to receive. If you experience a loss after you file, you should promptly amend your papers, as this question applies to losses both before you file and afterwards.

9. Payments related to debt counseling or bankruptcy. If you paid an improperly high fee to an attorney, bankruptcy petition preparer, debt consultant, or debt consolidator, the trustee may try to get some of it back to distribute to your creditors. Be sure to list all payments someone else made on your behalf, as well as payments you made directly.

10. Other transfers.

a. List all real and personal property that you've sold or given to someone else during the year before you file for bankruptcy. Some examples are selling or abandoning (junking) a car, pledging your house as security (collateral) for a loan, granting an easement on real estate, or trading property. Also, describe any transfer within the past year to your ex-spouse as part of a marital settlement agreement. If you are filing alone, describe gifts to your current spouse made during that same period.

Don't include any gifts you listed in Item 7. Also, don't list property you've parted with as a regular part of your business or financial affairs. For example, if you operate a mail order book business, don't list the books you sold during the past year. Similarly, don't put down payments for regular goods and services, such as your phone bill, utilities, or rent. The idea is to disclose transfers of property that might legally belong in your bankruptcy estate.

EXAMPLE 1: Two years before filing for bankruptcy, Jack sold some personal electronic mixing equipment to a friend for a modest sum. This sale wasn't made within the previous year, so Jack needn't list it here.

EXAMPLE 2: John has accumulated a collection of junked classic cars to resell to restoration hobbyists. Within the past year, John has sold three of the cars for a total of $20,000. Because this is part of John's regular business, he needn't report the sales here. However, as a sole proprietor, John will be completing Questions 18 through 20.

EXAMPLE 3: Within the year before filing for bankruptcy, Louise, a nurse, sold a vintage Jaguar E-type for $17,000. Because this isn't part of her business, Louise should list this sale here.

b. List all transfers of your own property you have made in the previous ten years to an irrevocable trust that lists you as a beneficiary. These types of trusts—referred to as self-settled trusts—are commonly used by wealthy people to shield their assets from creditors and by disabled people to preserve their right to receive government benefits. However, in bankruptcy, self-settled trusts don't work, and the assets in the trust can be seized by the trustee to pay your unsecured creditors.

11. Closed financial accounts. Provide information for each account in your name or for your benefit that was closed or transferred to someone else during the past year.

12. Safe deposit boxes. Provide information for each safe deposit box you've had within the past year.

13. Setoffs. A setoff is when a creditor, often a bank, uses money in a customer's account to pay a debt owed to the creditor by that customer. Here, list any setoffs your creditors have made during the last 90 days.

14. Property held for another person. Describe all the property you've borrowed from, are storing for, or hold in trust for someone else. Examples include funds in an irrevocable trust held for someone else as beneficiary but controlled by you, as trustee, and property you're holding as executor or administrator of an estate. This type of property is not part of your bankruptcy estate. However, you must disclose it so the trustee is aware of it and can ask for more details. (Some people dishonestly describe all of their property as being in trust or otherwise belonging to someone else, hoping to avoid having to give it to the trustee. Disclosures in this part of the Statement of Financial Affairs allow the trustee to explore this possibility.)

A trustee who becomes interested in property you describe here may invoke several court procedures designed to get more information. However, it is unlikely that the trustee will invade your house to seize the property. If you can establish that the property truly belongs to someone else—by producing the trust document, for example—you needn't worry about losing it in your bankruptcy case.

EXAMPLE: You are renting an unfurnished apartment owned by a friend. The friend has left a valuable baby grand piano in your care. If and when you decide to move, you have agreed to place the piano in storage for your friend. Because you don't own the piano, but rather are taking care of it for your friend, you would describe it here.

15. Prior address of debtor. If you have moved within the three years before you file for bankruptcy, list all of your residences within those three years.

16. Spouses and Former Spouses. If you lived in a community property state (or Puerto Rico) within eight years prior to filing for bankruptcy, list the name of your spouse and of any former spouses who lived with you in the community property state. To remind you, community property states are Alaska, Arizona, California, Idaho, Louisiana, Nevada, New Mexico, Texas, Washington, and Wisconsin.

17. Environmental Information. Few individuals will have much to say here. It's intended primarily for businesses that do business on polluted premises. Still, read the questions carefully and provide the requested information, if applicable.

18. Nature, location and name of business. Provide all of the information requested on Line a if you are in business or have been in business for the previous six years. Note that the definition of business is very broad: It includes not only sole proprietors, but anyone self-employed in a trade, profession, or other activity either full- or part-time or a business in which the debtor owned five percent or more of the voting or equity securities within the six-year period. It is very important that you answer this question completely so that the trustee will have a good idea of how you earned your money over the past six years and what you did with your business interests (if you are no longer in business).

➡️ **Skip ahead if you don't own a business.** Only business debtors have to provide responses on Lines 19 through 25. If you aren't one, go on to Line 26.

If the majority of your business income for any one business comes from renting, leasing, or otherwise operating a single piece of real property (other than an apartment building with fewer than four units), include your business name and the address of the property on Line b.

19. Books, records and financial statements.

   a. Identify every person other than yourself—usually a bookkeeper or accountant—who was involved in the accounting of your business during the previous two years. If you were the only person involved in your business's accounting, check "None."

   b. If your books weren't audited during the past two years, check "None." Otherwise, fill in the requested information.

   c. Usually, you, your bookkeeper, your accountant, an ex-business associate, or possibly an ex-mate will have business records. If any are missing, explain (you'll be better off if the loss of your records was beyond your control).

   d. You may have prepared a financial statement if you applied to a bank for a loan or line of credit for your business or in your own name. If you're self-employed and applied for a personal loan to purchase a car or house, you probably submitted

a financial statement as evidence of your ability to repay. Such statements include:

- balance sheets (these compare assets with liabilities)
- profit and loss statements (these compare income with expenses), and
- financial statements (these provide an overall financial description of a business).

20. Inventories. If your business doesn't have an inventory because it's a service business, check "None." If your business deals in products, but you were primarily the middle person or original manufacturer, put "no inventory required" or "materials purchased for each order as needed." If you have an inventory, fill in the information requested in Items a and b.

21 through 25. These items are intended for filers who are part of a business entity, such as a partnership, corporation, or limited liability company. Our book is designed for individuals only, so you should be able to check "None" for each of these items. If you are part of a business entity, consult with a bankruptcy lawyer before filing.

Declaration Under Penalty of Perjury by Individual Debtor. Sign and date this section. If you're filing jointly, be sure your spouse dates and signs it as well.

If completed on behalf of a partnership or corporation. Type "N/A."

Certification and Signature of Non-Attorney Bankruptcy Petition Preparer. If a BPP typed your forms, have that person complete this section. Otherwise, type "N/A" anywhere in the box.

Be sure to insert the number of continuation pages, if any, you attached.

H. Form 8—Chapter 7 Individual Debtor's Statement of Intention

This form is very important if you owe any secured debts (Schedule D) or are a party to any unexpired leases (Schedule G). This is where you inform the trustee and your secured creditors what you want to happen to the collateral for each of your secured debts. Briefly, you may:

- reaffirm the debt under a Reaffirmation Agreement that will continue your liability for all or part of the debt despite your bankruptcy

- redeem the debt by buying the collateral at its replacement value, or
- voluntarily surrender the collateral.

These options were discussed in detail in Ch. 5; you should return to that chapter now if you want more guidance on your options here.

If you are a party to a lease (for instance, a car lease), you may indicate on this form that you want to assume the lease (provided your creditor agrees).

 If you are married. If you're filing jointly, complete only one form, even though it says "Individual Debtor's Statement of Intention."

Below is a completed Statement of Intention and instructions.

Court Name. Copy this information from Form 1— Voluntary Petition.

In re and **Case No.** Follow the instructions for Schedule A.

Chapter. Type in "7."

First, check all of the boxes that apply. The first box refers to your Schedules A, B, and D. Don't check that box until you have filed those schedules and included the property that secures the debt (the collateral) and the creditor. Check the second box and attach any leases or contracts that you identified in Schedule G. Check the third box if you have any secured debts, leases, or contracts you have to deal with.

 If you have no secured debts, don't check the third box and skip ahead to the signature section of the form.

If you've decided to give up any (or all) property you've pledged as collateral for a secured debt, or the property has already been taken and you don't want to get it back, describe the property and creditor and check the first column (Property will be Surrendered). (If you need more space, use a continuation page.) If you want to redeem the property, check the appropriate box. If you want to reaffirm the debt, check the last box.

You'll notice that a column allows you to claim secured property as exempt. You'll want to check that box—and none of the others—if you are planning on removing (avoiding) the lien the secured creditor has on the property. If you do that, you can keep

the property free and clear of both the lien and the underlying debt. See Ch. 5 for a detailed discussion of lien avoidance.

If you have any leases or contracts that you wish to assume, provide the requested information and put a check in the column that states you'll assume the obligation.

Another Possible Option for Dealing with Your Secured Property

Under the old bankruptcy law, many bankruptcy courts allowed debtors to keep the property and discharge the debt, as long as they continued to make their payments. This remedy was called "retain and pay," and was the remedy of choice for many debtors. The new bankruptcy law appears to reject this remedy, forcing debtors to either surrender the property, redeem the property, reaffirm the debt, or avoid the lien. Nevertheless, some consumer law experts believe that the laws of some states will permit debtors to retain and pay, despite the new bankruptcy law.

Even if there is no more retain and pay remedy, you may able to achieve the same result by dealing directly with your creditors. If you have a creditor who will work with you in this way, check the "Property will be Surrendered" box but continue making payments as long as the creditor lets you keep the property. This informal arrangement can be risky, though, because the creditor can pull the plug on you at any time, leaving you no recourse. If you really want to hold on to the collateral and you are living in a state that doesn't allow the retain and pay approach, you'll probably be better off reaffirming the debt.

Save up those monthly payments. Often, secured creditors will not accept payments while your bankruptcy case is open, but will expect you to get current after the bankruptcy discharge, when the automatic stay is no longer in place. If a creditor refuses your payments during bankruptcy, be sure to save the money so you'll be able to pay for the property you intend to keep.

Form 8
(10/05)

United States Bankruptcy Court
Northern District of California

In re   Carrie Anne Edwards _____   Case No. _____

                               Debtor(s)   Chapter   7 _____

CHAPTER 7 INDIVIDUAL DEBTOR'S STATEMENT OF INTENTION

■   I have filed a schedule of assets and liabilities which includes debts secured by property of the estate.

■   I have filed a schedule of executory contracts and unexpired leases which includes personal property subject to an unexpired lease.

■   I intend to do the following with respect to property of the estate which secures those debts or is subject to a lease:

Description of Secured Property	Creditor's Name	Property will be Surrendered	Property is claimed as exempt	Property will be redeemed pursuant to 11 U.S.C. § 722	Debt will be reaffirmed pursuant to 11 U.S.C. § 524(c)
2002 Buick LeSabre fully loaded in good condition (replacement value from nada.com)	GMAC				X
Residence Location: 3045 Berwick St, Lakeport CA	Grand Junction Mortgage				X
Residence Location: 3045 Berwick St, Lakeport CA	Lending Tree				X

Description of Leased Property	Lessor's Name	Lease will be assumed pursuant to 11 U.S.C. § 362(h)(1)(A)
Laser skin treatment machine. Lease for 5 year period that expires in 2010	Beauty Products Leasing Co.	X

Date   October 25, 2005 _____   Signature   /s/ Carrie Anne Edwards _____

                                                 Carrie Anne Edwards

                                                 Debtor

Credit Card Debts

If you owe money on a bank or department store credit card and want to keep the card through bankruptcy, contact the bank or store before you file. If you offer to reaffirm the debt, some banks or stores may let you keep the credit card. If you do reaffirm it, list it on the Statement of Intention, even though, technically, it isn't a secured debt. But think twice before you do this. If you don't reaffirm the debt, it will be discharged in bankruptcy—giving you the fresh start that is, after all, the point of the process.

Signature. Date and sign the form. If you're married and filing jointly, your spouse must also date and sign the form.

Certification of Non-Attorney Bankruptcy Petition Preparer. If a BPP typed your forms, have that person complete this section. Otherwise, type "N/A" anywhere in the box.

I. Form 21—Statement of Social Security Number

This schedule requires you to list your full Social Security number. It will be available to your creditors and the trustee but, to protect your privacy, will not be part of your regular bankruptcy case file.

J. Form B22A—Statement of Current Monthly Income and Means Test Calculation

➡ **Business debtors can skip ahead.** This form is only for debtors whose debts are primarily consumer debts. If more than 50% of your debt load is attributable to the operation of a business, you are a business debtor and need not complete this form.

This form helps the U.S. Trustee decide whether your income and expenses qualify you to file for Chapter 7 bankruptcy, or whether you will have to use Chapter 13.

In Ch. 1, Section C, we explained how to calculate your current monthly income and compare it with your state's median income. As discussed there, if your current monthly income is above your state's median income, you will have to take a means test. Parts II and III of this form are where you calculate your current monthly income; if it exceeds the state median, you'll have to fill out the means test beginning with Part IV.

If You Fail the Means Test

If the information you provide on this form shows that you can pay more than 25% of the debts you listed in Schedule F over a five-year period, your Chapter 7 filing will be presumed to be abusive, and the U.S. Trustee will ask the court to either dismiss your Chapter 7 filing or, with your consent, convert your case to a Chapter 13 case. If this happens to you, we highly recommend that you obtain the services of an attorney to help you stay in Chapter 7, unless you are willing to sign up for a five-year repayment plan. If you do, you can use most of the bankruptcy papers filed in your Chapter 7 case in your Chapter 13 case.

Below is a completed Statement of Current Monthly Income and instructions.

In re and **Case No.** Follow the instructions for Schedule A.

Check the box as directed in Parts I, III, and VI of this statement. Don't check any of the boxes for now. You will decide which box to check later, after you figure out whether you have to take the means test and, if so, whether you pass it.

Part I: Exclusion for Disabled Veterans

If all of the facts in the Veteran's Declaration are true of your situation, check the indicated boxes and sign the verification in Part VIII. To qualify for this exclusion, you must have a disability rating of at least 30%, and more than half of your debt must have been incurred while you were either on active duty or performing homeland defense activity.

If you qualify for the veteran's exclusion, you don't have to calculate your current income or take the means test on this form; you can file for Chapter 7. If you don't meet the qualifications of this category,

Form B22A (Chapter 7) (10/05)

In re   Carrie Anne Edwards
_____
                      Debtor(s)

Case Number: _____
                      (If known)

> According to the calculations required by this statement:
>
> ☐ **The presumption arises.**
>
> ■ **The presumption does not arise.**
>
> (Check the box as directed in Parts I, III, and VI of this statement.)

STATEMENT OF CURRENT MONTHLY INCOME AND MEANS TEST CALCULATION
FOR USE IN CHAPTER 7 ONLY

In addition to Schedules I and J, this statement must be completed by every individual Chapter 7 debtor, whether or not filing jointly, whose debts are primarily consumer debts. Joint debtors may complete one statement only.

Part I. EXCLUSION FOR DISABLED VETERANS

1	If you are a disabled veteran described in the Veteran's Declaration in this Part I, (1) check that box at the beginning of the Veteran's Declaration, (2) check the box for "The presumption does not arise" at the top of this statement, and (3) complete the verification in Part VIII. Do not complete any of the remaining parts of this statement. ☐ **Veteran's Declaration.** By checking this box, I declare under penalty of perjury that I am a disabled veteran (as defined in 38 U.S.C. § 3741(1)) whose indebtedness occurred primarily during a period in which I was on active duty (as defined in 10 U.S.C. § 101(d)(1)) or while I was performing a homeland defense activity (as defined in 32 U.S.C. §901(1)).

Part II. CALCULATION OF MONTHLY INCOME FOR § 707(b)(7) EXCLUSION

2	**Marital/filing status.** Check the box that applies and complete the balance of this part of this statement as directed. a. ■ Unmarried. **Complete only Column A ("Debtor's Income") for Lines 3-11.** b. ☐ Married, not filing jointly, with declaration of separate households. By checking this box, debtor declares under penalty of perjury: "My spouse and I are legally separated under applicable non-bankruptcy law or my spouse and I are living apart other than for the purpose of evading the requirements of § 707(b)(2)(A) of the Bankruptcy Code." **Complete only column A ("Debtor's Income") for Lines 3-11.** c. ☐ Married, not filing jointly, without the declaration of separate households set out in Line 2.b above. **Complete both Column A ("Debtor's Income") and Column B ("Spouse's Income") for Lines 3-11.** d. ☐ Married, filing jointly. **Complete both Column A ("Debtor's Income") and Column B ("Spouse's Income") for Lines 3-11.**

	All figures must reflect average monthly income for the six calendar months prior to filing the bankruptcy case, ending on the last day of the month before the filing. If you received different amounts of income during these six months, you must total the amounts received during the six months, divide this total by six, and enter the result on the appropriate line.	**Column A** Debtor's Income	**Column B** Spouse's Income
3	Gross wages, salary, tips, bonuses, overtime, commissions.	$ 3,900.00	$

4	Income from the operation of a business, profession or farm. Subtract Line b from Line a and enter the difference on Line 4. Do not enter a number less than zero. **Do not include any part of the business expenses entered on Line b as a deduction in Part V.**		$ 0.00	$

		Debtor	Spouse
a.	Gross receipts	$ 0.00	$
b.	Ordinary and necessary business expenses	$ 0.00	$
c.	Business income	Subtract Line b from Line a	

5	Rents and other real property income. Subtract Line b from Line a and enter the difference on Line 5. Do not enter a number less than zero. **Do not include any part of the operating expenses entered on Line b as a deduction in Part V.**		$ 0.00	$

		Debtor	Spouse
a.	Gross receipts	$ 0.00	$
b.	Ordinary and necessary operating expenses	$ 0.00	$
c.	Rental income	Subtract Line b from Line a	

6	Interest, dividends, and royalties.	$ 1,000.00	$
7	Pension and retirement income.	$ 0.00	$
8	Regular contributions to the household expenses of the debtor or the debtor's dependents, including child or spousal support. Do not include contributions from the debtor's spouse if Column B is completed.	$ 500.00	$

Form B22A (Chapter 7) (10/05)

9	Unemployment compensation. Enter the amount in column A and, if applicable, Column B. However, if you contend that unemployment compensation received by you or your spouse was a benefit under the Social Security Act, do not list the amount of such compensation in Column A or B, but instead state the amount in the space below: Unemployment compensation claimed to be a benefit under the Social Security Act Debtor $ 0.00 Spouse $	$ 0.00	$
10	Income from all other sources. If necessary, list additional sources on a separate page. **Do not include** any benefits received under the Social Security Act or payments received as a victim of a war crime, crime against humanity, or as a victim of international or domestic terrorism. Specify source and amount. Debtor Spouse a. $ $ b. $ $ Total and enter on Line 10	$ 0.00	$
11	**Subtotal of Current Monthly Income for § 707(b)(7).** Add Lines 3 thru 10 in Column A, and, if Column B is completed, add Lines 3 through 10 in Column B. Enter the total(s).	$ 5,400.00	$
12	**Total Current Monthly Income for § 707(b)(7).** If Column B has been completed, add Line 11, Column A to Line 11, Column B, and enter the total. If Column B has not been completed, enter the amount from Line 11, Column A.	$ 5,400.00	

Part III. APPLICATION OF § 707(b)(7) EXCLUSION

13	**Annualized Current Monthly Income for § 707(b)(7).** Multiply the amount from Line 12 by the number 12 and enter the result.	$ 64,800.00
14	**Applicable median family income.** Enter the median family income for the applicable state and household size. (This information is available by family size at www.usdoj.gov/ust/ or from the clerk of the bankruptcy court.) a. Enter debtor's state of residence: _____ CA _____ b. Enter debtor's household size: _____ 3 _____	$ 61,655.00
15	**Application of Section 707(b)(7).** Check the applicable box and proceed as directed. ☐ **The amount on Line 13 is less than or equal to the amount on Line 14.** Check the box for "The presumption does not arise" at the top of page 1 of this statement, and complete Part VIII; do not complete Parts IV, V, VI or VII. ■ **The amount on Line 13 is more than the amount on Line 14.** Complete the remaining parts of this statement.	

Complete Parts IV, V, VI, and VII of this statement only if required. (See Line 15.)

Part IV. CALCULATION OF CURRENT MONTHLY INCOME FOR § 707(b)(2)

16	**Enter the amount from Line 12.**	$ 5,400.00
17	**Marital adjustment.** If you checked the box at Line 2.c, enter the amount of the income listed in Line 11, Column B that was NOT regularly contributed to the household expenses of the debtor or the debtor's dependents. If you did not check box at Line 2.c, enter zero.	$ 0.00
18	**Current monthly income for § 707(b)(2).** Subtract Line 17 from Line 16 and enter the result.	$ 5,400.00

Part V. CALCULATION OF DEDUCTIONS UNDER § 707(b)(2)

Subpart A: Deductions under Standards of the Internal Revenue Service (IRS)

19	**National Standards: food, clothing, household supplies, personal care, and miscellaneous.** Enter "Total" amount from IRS National Standards for Allowable Living Expenses for the applicable family size and income level. (This information is available at www.usdoj.gov/ust/ or from the clerk of the bankruptcy court.)	$ 1,017.00
20A	**Local Standards: housing and utilities; non-mortgage expenses.** Enter the amount of the IRS Housing and Utilities Standards; non-mortgage expenses for the applicable county and family size. (This information is available at www.usdoj.gov/ust/ or from the clerk of the bankruptcy court).	$ 458.00

Form B22A (Chapter 7) (10/05)

20B	**Local Standards: housing and utilities; mortgage/rent expense.** Enter, in Line a below, the amount of the IRS Housing and Utilities Standards; mortgage/rent expense for your county and family size (this information is available at www.usdoj.gov/ust/ or from the clerk of the bankruptcy court); enter on Line b the total of the Average Monthly Payments for any debts secured by your home, as stated in Line 42; subtract Line b from Line a and enter the result in Line 20B. **Do not enter an amount less than zero.**		
	a.	IRS Housing and Utilities Standards; mortgage/rental expense	$ 781.00
	b.	Average Monthly Payment for any debts secured by your home, if any, as stated in Line 42	$ 1,565.10
	c.	Net mortgage/rental expense	Subtract Line b from Line a.	$ 0.00

21	**Local Standards: housing and utilities; adjustment.** If you contend that the process set out in Lines 20A and 20B does not accurately compute the allowance to which you are entitled under the IRS Housing and Utilities Standards, enter any additional amount to which you contend you are entitled, and state the basis for your contention in the space below: _____	$ 0.00

22	**Local Standards: transportation; vehicle operation/public transportation expense.** You are entitled to an expense allowance in this category regardless of whether you pay the expenses of operating a vehicle and regardless of whether you use public transportation. Check the number of vehicles for which you pay the operating expenses or for which the operating expenses are included as a contribution to your household expenses in Line 8. ☐ 0 ☑ 1 ☐ 2 or more. Enter the amount from IRS Transportation Standards, Operating Costs & Public Transportation Costs for the applicable number of vehicles in the applicable Metropolitan Statistical Area or Census Region. (This information is available at www.usdoj.gov/ust/ or from the clerk of the bankruptcy court.)	$ 338.00

23	**Local Standards: transportation ownership/lease expense; Vehicle 1.** Check the number of vehicles for which you claim an ownership/lease expense. (You may not claim an ownership/lease expense for more than two vehicles.) ☑ 1 ☐ 2 or more. Enter, in Line a below, the amount of the IRS Transportation Standards, Ownership Costs, First Car (available at www.usdoj.gov/ust/ or from the clerk of the bankruptcy court); enter in Line b the total of the Average Monthly Payments for any debts secured by Vehicle 1, as stated in Line 42; subtract Line b from Line a and enter the result in Line 23. **Do not enter an amount less than zero.**		
	a.	IRS Transportation Standards, Ownership Costs, First Car	$ 471.00
	b.	Average Monthly Payment for any debts secured by Vehicle 1, as stated in Line 42	$ 50.00
	c.	Net ownership/lease expense for Vehicle 1	Subtract Line b from Line a.	$ 421.00

24	**Local Standards: transportation ownership/lease expense; Vehicle 2.** Complete this Line only if you checked the "2 or more" Box in Line 23. Enter, in Line a below, the amount of the IRS Transportation Standards, Ownership Costs, Second Car (available at www.usdoj.gov/ust/ or from the clerk of the bankruptcy court); enter in Line b the total of the Average Monthly Payments for any debts secured by Vehicle 2, as stated in Line 42; subtract Line b from Line a and enter the result in Line 24. **Do not enter an amount less than zero.**		
	a.	IRS Transportation Standards, Ownership Costs, Second Car	$ 0.00
	b.	Average Monthly Payment for any debts secured by Vehicle 2, as stated in Line 42	$ 0.00
	c.	Net ownership/lease expense for Vehicle 2	Subtract Line b from Line a.	$ 0.00

25	**Other Necessary Expenses: taxes.** Enter the total average monthly expense that you actually incur for all federal, state and local taxes, other than real estate and sales taxes, such as income taxes, self employment taxes, social security taxes, and Medicare taxes. **Do not include real estate or sales taxes.**	$ 500.00

26	**Other Necessary Expenses: mandatory payroll deductions.** Enter the total average monthly payroll deductions that are required for your employment, such as mandatory retirement contributions, union dues, and uniform costs. **Do not include discretionary amounts, such as non-mandatory 401(k) contributions.**	$ 0.00

27	**Other Necessary Expenses: life insurance.** Enter average monthly premiums that you actually pay for term life insurance for yourself. **Do not include premiums for insurance on your dependents, for whole life or for any other form of insurance.**	$ 0.00

Form B22A (Chapter 7) (10/05)

28	**Other Necessary Expenses: court-ordered payments.** Enter the total monthly amount that you are required to pay pursuant to court order, such as spousal or child support payments. **Do not include payments on past due support obligations included in Line 44.**	$	0.00
29	**Other Necessary Expenses: education for employment or for a physically or mentally challenged child.** Enter the total monthly amount that you actually expend for education that is a condition of employment and for education that is required for a physically or mentally challenged dependent child for whom no public education providing similar services is available.	$	0.00
30	**Other Necessary Expenses: childcare.** Enter the average monthly amount that you actually expend on childcare. **Do not include payments made for children's education.**	$	300.00
31	**Other Necessary Expenses: health care.** Enter the average monthly amount that you actually expend on health care expenses that are not reimbursed by insurance or paid by a health savings account. **Do not include payments for health insurance listed in Line 34.**	$	300.00
32	**Other Necessary Expenses: telecommunication services.** Enter the average monthly expenses that you actually pay for cell phones, pagers, call waiting, caller identification, special long distance or internet services necessary for the health and welfare of you or your dependents. **Do not include any amount previously deducted.**	$	175.00
33	**Total Expenses Allowed under IRS Standards.** Enter the total of Lines 19 through 32.	$	3,509.00

<table>
<tr><td colspan="4" align="center">**Subpart B: Additional Expense Deductions under § 707(b)**</td></tr>
<tr><td colspan="4" align="center">**Note: Do not include any expenses that you have listed in Lines 19-32**</td></tr>
</table>

34	**Health Insurance, Disability Insurance and Health Savings Account Expenses.** List the average monthly amounts that you actually expend in each of the following categories and enter the total.		
	a. Health Insurance $ 0.00		
	b. Disability Insurance $ 0.00		
	c. Health Savings Account $ 0.00		
	Total: Add Lines a, b and c	$	0.00
35	**Continued contributions to the care of household or family members.** Enter the actual monthly expenses that you will continue to pay for the reasonable and necessary care and support of an elderly, chronically ill, or disabled member of your household or member of your immediate family who is unable to pay for such expenses.	$	0.00
36	**Protection against family violence.** Enter any average monthly expenses that you actually incurred to maintain the safety of your family under the Family Violence Prevention and Services Act or other applicable federal law.	$	0.00
37	**Home energy costs in excess of the allowance specified by the IRS Local Standards.** Enter the average monthly amount by which your home energy costs exceed the allowance in the IRS Local Standards for Housing and Utilities. **You must provide your case trustee with documentation demonstrating that the additional amount claimed is reasonable and necessary.**	$	0.00
38	**Education expenses for dependent children less than 18.** Enter the average monthly expenses that you actually incur, not to exceed $125 per child, in providing elementary and secondary education for your dependent children less than 18 years of age. **You must provide your case trustee with documentation demonstrating that the additional amount claimed is reasonable and necessary and not already accounted for in the IRS Standards.**	$	0.00
39	**Additional food and clothing expense.** Enter the average monthly amount by which your food and clothing expenses exceed the combined allowances for food and apparel in the IRS National Standards, not to exceed five percent of those combined allowances. (This information is available at www.usdoj.gov/ust/ or from the clerk of the bankruptcy court.) **You must provide your case trustee with documentation demonstrating that the additional amount claimed is reasonable and necessary.**	$	37.00
40	**Continued charitable contributions.** Enter the amount that you will continue to contribute in the form of cash or financial instruments to a charitable organization as defined in 26 U.S.C. § 170(c)(1)-(2).	$	0.00
41	**Total Additional Expense Deductions under § 707(b).** Enter the total of Lines 34 through 40	$	37.00

Form B22A (Chapter 7) (10/05)

	Subpart C: Deductions for Debt Payment			
42	**Future payments on secured claims.** For each of your debts that is secured by an interest in property that you own, list the name of the creditor, identify the property securing the debt, and state the Average Monthly Payment. The Average Monthly Payment is the total of all amounts contractually due to each Secured Creditor in the 60 months following the filing of the bankruptcy case, divided by 60. Mortgage debts should include payments of taxes and insurance required by the mortgage. If necessary, list additional entries on a separate page.			

	Name of Creditor	Property Securing the Debt	60-month Average Payment
a.	GMAC	2002 Buick LeSabre fully loaded in good condition (replacement value from nada.com)	$ 50.00
b.	Grand Junction Mortgage	Residence Location: 3045 Berwick St, Lakeport CA	$ 1,465.10
c.	Lending Tree	Residence Location: 3045 Berwick St, Lakeport CA	$ 100.00
		Total: Add Lines	$ 1,615.10

43 **Past due payments on secured claims.** If any of the debts listed in Line 42 are in default, and the property securing the debt is necessary for your support or the support of your dependents, you may include in your deductions 1/60th of the amount that you must pay the creditor as a result of the default (the "cure amount") in order to maintain possession of the property. List any such amounts in the following chart and enter the total. If necessary, list additional entries on a separate page.

	Name of Creditor	Property Securing the Debt in Default	1/60th of the Cure Amount
a.	-NONE-		$
		Total: Add Lines	$ 0.00

44 **Payments on priority claims.** Enter the total amount of all priority claims (including priority child support and alimony claims), divided by 60. — $ 91.67

45 **Chapter 13 administrative expenses.** If you are eligible to file a case under Chapter 13, complete the following chart, multiply the amount in line a by the amount in line b, and enter the resulting administrative expense.

a.	Projected average monthly Chapter 13 plan payment.	$ 0.00
b.	Current multiplier for your district as determined under schedules issued by the Executive Office for United States Trustees. (This information is available at www.usdoj.gov/ust/ or from the clerk of the bankruptcy court.)	x 8.90
c.	Average monthly administrative expense of Chapter 13 case	Total: Multiply Lines a and b	$ 0.00

46 **Total Deductions for Debt Payment.** Enter the total of Lines 42 through 45. — $ 1,706.77

	Subpart D: Total Deductions Allowed under § 707(b)(2)	
47	**Total of all deductions allowed under § 707(b)(2).** Enter the total of Lines 33, 41, and 46.	$ 5,252.77

	Part VI. DETERMINATION OF § 707(b)(2) PRESUMPTION	
48	Enter the amount from Line 18 (Current monthly income for § 707(b)(2))	$ 5,400.00
49	Enter the amount from Line 47 (Total of all deductions allowed under § 707(b)(2))	$ 5,252.77
50	**Monthly disposable income under § 707(b)(2).** Subtract Line 49 from Line 48 and enter the result.	$ 147.23
51	**60-month disposable income under § 707(b)(2).** Multiply the amount in Line 50 by the number 60 and enter the result.	$ 8,833.80

Form B22A (Chapter 7) (10/05)

52	**Initial presumption determination.** Check the applicable box and proceed as directed.
	☐ **The amount on Line 51 is less than $6,000.** Check the box for "The presumption does not arise" at the top of page 1 of this statement, and complete the verification in Part VIII. Do not complete the remainder of Part VI.
	☐ **The amount set forth on Line 51 is more than $10,000.** Check the box for "The presumption arises" at the top of page 1 of this statement, and complete the verification in Part VIII. You may also complete Part VII. Do not complete the remainder of Part VI.
	■ **The amount on Line 51 is at least $6,000, but not more than $10,000.** Complete the remainder of Part VI (Lines 53 through 55).

53	**Enter the amount of your total non-priority unsecured debt**	$ 147,150.00
54	**Threshold debt payment amount.** Multiply the amount in Line 53 by the number 0.25 and enter the result.	$ 36,787.50

55	**Secondary presumption determination.** Check the applicable box and proceed as directed.
	■ **The amount on Line 51 is less than the amount on Line 54.** Check the box for "The presumption does not arise" at the top of page 1 of this statement, and complete the verification in Part VIII.
	☐ **The amount on Line 51 is equal to or greater than the amount on Line 54.** Check the box for "The presumption arises" at the top of page 1 of this statement, and complete the verification in Part VIII. You may also complete Part VII.

Part VII. ADDITIONAL EXPENSE CLAIMS

56	**Other Expenses.** List and describe any monthly expenses, not otherwise stated in this form, that are required for the health and welfare of you and your family and that you contend should be an additional deduction from your current monthly income under § 707(b)(2)(A)(ii)(I). If necessary, list additional sources on a separate page. All figures should reflect your average monthly expense for each item. Total the expenses.

	Expense Description	Monthly Amount
a.		$
b.		$
c.		$
d.		$
	Total: Add Lines a, b, c, and d	$

Part VIII. VERIFICATION

57	I declare under penalty of perjury that the information provided in this statement is true and correct. *(If this is a joint case, both debtors must sign.)*
	Date: February 10, 2006 Signature: /s/ Carrie Anne Edwards
	Carrie Anne Edwards
	(Debtor)

continue on to Part II. Your income may still qualify you for Chapter 7 bankruptcy.

Part II. Calculation of Monthly Income for § 707(b)(7) Exclusion

Line 2a. If you are unmarried, check this box and follow the instructions (complete only Lines 3 through 11 in Column A).

Line 2b. If you are married, but filing separately because you have separate households, check this box and complete only Lines 3 through 11 in Column A. To check this box, you are declaring, under penalty of perjury, that you are legally separated under the laws of your state or that you are living separately for reasons other than to qualify for Chapter 7 bankruptcy.

Line 2c. If you are married but filing separately for reasons other than those stated in Section 2c, check this box and complete Lines 3 through 11 in Columns A and B.

Line 2d. If you are married and filing jointly, check this box and complete Lines 3 through 11 in Columns A and B.

⚠️ **Use the right figures.** All figures you enter in Lines 3 through 11 must be averages of the six-month period that ends on the last day of the month before you file. For instance, if you file on September 9, the six-month period ends on August 31. If the amounts are the same for each of those six months (for example, because you've held the same job and worked the same amount of hours during that period), then use those amounts. If the amounts vary, add up everything you've earned in that category for the six-month period, then divide the total by six to get a monthly average.

Line 3. Enter your average monthly earnings over the last six months for gross wages, salary, tips, bonuses, overtime, and commissions. ("Gross" means before any taxes, Social Security, or other amounts are withheld.)

Line 4. If you operate a business, profession, or farm, you'll need to compute your average monthly expenses for the six-month period and subtract them from your income for that period. The lowest figure you can enter is zero.

Line 5. Enter your average monthly rental income for the six-month period (if you have any), and deduct ordinary and necessary operating expenses for that same period.

Line 6. Enter your average monthly income from interest, dividends, and royalties over the last six months.

Line 7. Here's where you include your average monthly pension and retirement income. Don't include Social Security retirement benefits.

Line 8. Enter the monthly average of any amounts regularly contributed by someone else to your household expenses. If you are filing separately but your spouse's income is included in Column B, don't include any contributions that your spouse makes to your household—his or her income is already being taken into account.

Line 9. Your average monthly unemployment compensation goes here. If you want, you can argue that unemployment compensation should be excluded under the general Social Security exclusion (see Line 10) and omit it from Columns A and B. However, you'll need to enter the amount you receive in the boxes supplied for this purpose.

Line 10. Insert the average monthly amount you received from any other source. Do not include money or benefits received under the SSI, SSA, or TANF programs. These are Social Security benefits and are excluded from your current monthly income computation.

Line 11. Compute the subtotals for Column A and B (if used). Remember, these subtotals should reflect an average monthly figure for all of the items you entered in Lines 3 through 10.

Line 12. Add the subtotals for Line A and B together. This is what the new bankruptcy law calls your "current monthly income." Because it's a six-month average, it might not match your actual monthly income at the time you file, especially if you've had a job loss or become unable to work in the last six months.

Part III: Application of § 707(b)(7) Exclusion

This is where the rubber meets the road: In this part, you must compare the current monthly income figure you calculated in Part II with the median family income for your state. If your income is higher than the median, you'll have to fill out the rest of the form—and you may be barred from using Chapter 7. If your income is equal to or less than the median, you can skip the rest of the form and file your Chapter 7 papers.

Line 13. Convert your monthly figure on Line 12 to an annual figure by multiplying it by 12. This is your current annual income.

Line 14. Enter the median income for your state for your household size. Note that your household size might be larger than your actual family size. For instance, you may have a relative or friend who is living with you as part of your household; if so, include the friend as a household member. The most recent state median income figures (2004) as of the date this book is published are in Appendix 2. To make sure that you are using the most current figures, however, you should visit the U.S. Trustee's website, www.usdoj.gov/ust, and click "Means Testing Information." Scroll down a bit for the link to the state median income figures.

Line 15. Do the math. If your income exceeds the state median, check the bottom box on Line 15 and continue to Part IV. If your income does not exceed the median, check the top box on Line 15, then sign and date the form in Part VIII. Finally, return to the first page of the form, where you should check the bottom box ("The presumption does not arise") in the top, right-hand corner.

Consider postponing your filing. If you conclude that you'll have to take the means test, think about whether your income will decrease in the next few months. If you recently lost a high-paying job or had a sudden decrease in commissions or royalties, for example, your average income over the past six months might look pretty substantial. But in a few months, when you average in your lower earnings, it will come down quite a bit—perhaps even to less than the state median. If so, you might want to delay your bankruptcy filing if you can.

Part IV. Calculation of Current Monthly Income For § 707(b)(2)

This is the beginning of the means test. With a couple of exceptions, the values you will be entering in the form are fairly straightforward. The purpose of the means test is to find out whether you have enough income to pay some of your unsecured, nonpriority debts over a five-year (60-month) period. (Your unsecured, nonpriority debts are those you listed in Schedule F, above.)

Line 16. Enter the total from Line 12.

Line 17. If you checked the box on Line 2c (married, not filing jointly, and not making the declaration in Item 2b), you can subtract the amount of your spouse's income (as listed in Line 11, Column B) that was NOT regularly contributed to your household expenses or those of your dependents. For example, if Line 11, Column B shows that your nonfiling spouse has a monthly income of $2,000, but your spouse contributes only $400 a month to your household, you can enter $1,600 here.

Line 18. Subtract the amount on Line 17 from the amount on Line 16. Enter the total here.

Part V. Calculation of Deductions Under § 707(b)(2)

In this part, you will figure out what expenses you can deduct from your current monthly income. After you subtract all allowed expenses, you will be left with your monthly disposable income—the amount you would have left over, in theory, to pay into a Chapter 13 plan.

Subpart A: Deductions under Standards of the Internal Revenue Service (IRS)

If you have to complete this part of the form—that is, if your current monthly income exceeds the state median income—you are not allowed to subtract all of your actual expenses. Instead, you must calculate some of your expenses according to standards set by the IRS. (The IRS uses these standards to decide how much a delinquent taxpayer should have to give the agency each month to repay back taxes on an installment plan.)

Line 19. Enter the total IRS National Standards for Allowable Living Expenses for your family size and income level. This is the amount the IRS believes you should get to spend for food, clothing, household supplies, personal care, and miscellaneous other items. You can get these figures from www.usdoj.gov/ust. Click "Means Testing Information," then scroll down to the National Standards link. (If you are filing in Alaska or Hawaii, you must use a different set of standards, which reflect the higher cost of living in these states. Links to these standards appear just below the National Standards link.) You also can get these figures from your court clerk.

Line 20A. Enter the amount of the IRS Housing and Utilities Standards, non-mortgage expenses for your county and family size. Get these figures from www. usdoj.gov/ust. Click "Means Testing Information," then scroll down to the IRS Housing and Utilities Standards section and enter your state in the drop-down menu. Find the figures for your county and family size, then enter the figure that appears under the heading "Non-Mortgage."

Line 20B. On Line a, enter the amount of the IRS Housing and Utility Standards, mortgage/rental expenses for your county and family size. These figures appear on the U.S. Trustee's website, on the same chart as non-mortgage expenses—follow the instructions for Line 20A, above.

On Line b, enter the average monthly payment for any debts secured by your home, including a mortgage, home equity loan, taxes, and insurance. The average monthly payment is the total of all amounts contractually due to each secured creditor in the 60 months following the filing of the bankruptcy case, divided by 60.

On Line c, subtract Line b from Line a. This may turn out to be a negative figure—if so, enter a zero in the right-hand column. Later in the means test, you'll be able to add your average monthly payment back in as an expense.

Line 21. If your actual rental or mortgage expense is higher than that allowed by the IRS, you can claim an adjustment here. For instance if the IRS mortgage/rental expense for a family of two is $550, you pay an actual rent of $900, and that amount is average for the area in which you live, enter the additional $350 here and explain why you should be able to subtract it (that you couldn't possibly find housing in your area for less, for example).

Line 22. You are entitled to claim an expense here regardless of whether you actually have one. First, indicate the number of cars for which you pay operating expenses or for which somebody else contributes the operating expenses as part of the amount entered on Line 8. Then, enter the appropriate amount from the IRS Transportation Standards, Operating Costs & Public Transportation Costs chart for your number of vehicles. These amounts vary by region; the chart divides the country into Metropolitan Statistical Area or Census Region.

You can get these figures from www.usdoj.gov/ust. Click "Means Testing Information," then scroll down to the Local Transportation Expense Standards drop-down menu and choose your region. You can claim a transportation expense even if you don't have a car. For instance, in San Francisco, people without a car can claim $317, people with one car can claim $376, and people with two or more cars can claim $466.

Line 23. These are your expenses for owning or leasing a car. On Line 23a, enter the IRS Local Transportation Standards for ownership of a first car. This amount is actually a national figure; currently, it is $475. To make sure you are using the most up-to-date numbers, check the website of the U.S. Trustee, www.usdoj.gov/ust. Click "Means Testing Information," then scroll down to the Local Transportation Expense Standards drop-down menu and choose your region. The ownership figure is near the bottom of the page.

On Line 23b, enter your average monthly payment (over the next five years) for all debts secured by your first car. For example, assume you have three years left to pay on the car and the monthly payment is $350. The total amount you will owe in the next five years is $12,600 (36 months times $350). If you spread that amount over the next five years—by dividing the total by 60, the number of months in five years—you'll see that you have an average monthly payment of $210.

On Line 23c, subtract Line b from Line a and enter the result in the column on the right. Later on, if necessary, you will be able to deduct your car payments to figure out whether you have disposable income for a Chapter 13 plan.

Line 24. Complete this item only if you have a second car (and checked the second car box in Line 23). Follow the instructions for Line 23 to enter the required figures for your second car.

Line 25. Enter the total average monthly expense that you actually incur for all taxes *other than real estate or sales taxes*. Examples of taxes that you enter here are income taxes, self-employment taxes, Social Security taxes, and Medicare taxes. In some cases, these taxes will show up on your wage stub. You'll need to convert the period covered by your wage stub to a monthly figure. Once you have figured out how much you pay each month for each type of tax, add them all together and enter them in the column on the right.

Converting Taxes to a Monthly Figure

If you are paid weekly, biweekly, or twice a month, you will have to convert the tax amounts on your pay stubs to a monthly amount. And, if you pay quarterly taxes (estimated income taxes, for example), you'll need to convert that figure as well. Here's how to do it:

- Weekly taxes: multiply by 4.6 to get a monthly amount.
- Biweekly taxes: divide by 2 to get a weekly amount, then multiply by 4.6.
- Bimonthly taxes: divide by 2.
- Quarterly taxes: divide by 3.

Line 26. Enter all of your mandatory payroll deductions here. Use the conversion rules set out in the sidebar above to arrive at average monthly deductions. Make sure you deduct only mandatory deductions. (such as mandatory retirement contributions, union dues, and uniform costs). Contributions to a 401(k) should not be included, because they are voluntary.

Line 27. Enter any monthly payments you make for term life insurance. Do not enter payments for any other type of insurance, such as credit insurance, car insurance, renter's insurance, insurance on the lives of your dependents, or whole life insurance on your own life. (Whole life insurance is the type that allows you to borrow against the policy.)

Line 28. Enter the amount of any payments you make pursuant to a court order. Child support and alimony are the most common examples, but you may also have to pay to satisfy a court money judgment or a criminal fine. Do not include court-ordered payments towards a child support or alimony arrearage; only the payments you need to stay current should be entered here.

Line 29. Enter the total monthly amount that you pay for education required by your employer to keep your job, and the total monthly amount you pay for the education of a physically or mentally challenged dependent child for whom no public education providing similar services is available. Included in this amount would be the actual costs of after-school enrichment educational services for a physically or mentally challenged child, and the actual educational expenses you are paying in support of an individual educational plan.

Line 30. Enter the average monthly expense of childcare. If your employment (and therefore, your need for childcare) is seasonal, add your childcare costs up for the year and divide the total by 12. Do not equate education with childcare. For instance, childcare for a child who is of public education school age should only cover the hours before and after school.

Line 31. Enter the average monthly amount you pay for out-of-pocket health care expenses. Do not include health care expenses that are reimbursed by insurance or provided by an HMO or by Medicaid.

Line 32. Enter the average monthly expenses you pay for any communication devices that are necessary for the health and welfare of you or your dependents. Examples provided by the form are cell phones, pagers, call waiting, caller identification, and special long distance or Internet services. Virtually all of these devices arguably are necessary for the health and welfare of your family. However, some expenses might not be allowed (for example, a cell phone you use for your business, or broadband Internet service). When in doubt, list the expense.

Line 33. Add the expenses you entered in Lines 19 through 32 and put the total in the column at the right.

Subpart B: Additional Expense Deductions under § 707 (b)
The expenses in this subpart are allowed by the Bankruptcy Code, in addition to the IRS expenses. However, you can't list an expense twice; if you already claimed it in Subpart A, don't list it again here.

Line 34. List the average monthly amounts you spend on health insurance, disability insurance, and health savings accounts (HSAs). Add these together and put the total in the right-hand column.

Line 35. Anything you spend to care for a member of your household or immediate family because of his or her age, illness, or disability can be deducted here. If your contributions are episodic—a wheelchair here, a vacation with a companion there—estimate your average monthly expense and enter it here.

Your response here could affect eligibility for government benefits. Expenses you list here could render the person you are assisting ineligible for Social Security or other government benefits. For example, if you state that you are spending $500 a month for the care of a relative, and that relative is receiving SSI, your relative might receive a lower benefit amount each month, to reflect your contribution. On the other hand, if you are making such expenditures, you are required to disclose them here. If you find yourself in this predicament, talk to a lawyer.

Line 36. The average monthly expense of security systems and any other method of protecting your family should be entered here.

Line 37. If your actual housing expenses, other than your mortgage or rent payment, exceed the figure you entered on Line 20A, enter it here. As the form indicates, you may need to prove this extra expense to the trustee. Whether you need to prove this extra expense will depend on the results of this means test. If the amount you enter here is the deciding factor in determining that you don't have enough disposable income to fund a Chapter 13 plan, proof will definitely be required.

Line 38. This item is for people who provide their children with private education. If your average monthly expense is $125 or more, put $125 in this blank; that's the maximum you can deduct. Remember not to list an amount twice; if you already listed an expense on Line 29 or 30, for example, don't repeat it here.

Line 39. Here, you can list the amount by which your actual expenses for food and clothing exceed the IRS allowance for these items as entered in Line 19. However, you cannot list more than 5% over the IRS allowance.

Line 40. If you have been making charitable contributions to an organization before your bankruptcy filing date, you can enter them here as long as the group organized and operated exclusively for religious, charitable, scientific, literary, or educational purposes; to foster national or international amateur sports competition (but only if no part of its activities involve the provision of athletic facilities or equipment); or for the prevention of cruelty to children or animals. The organization also can't be disqualified from tax exemption status because of its political activities.

Line 41. Enter the total of Lines 34 through 40 in the column on the right.

Subpart C: Deductions for Debt Payment

Here, you deduct average monthly payments you will have to make over the next five years. Once you complete this section, you can put all the numbers together to figure out whether you pass the means test.

Line 42. List the average monthly payment you will have to make over the next five years to creditors that hold a secured interest in your property (for example, the mortgage holder on your house, or the creditor that holds your car note). As explained in the instructions for Line 23, you can calculate this amount by figuring out the total amount you will owe over the next five years, then dividing that total by 60.

Line 43. Here, list the average monthly payment you would have to make to cure what you owe to creditors on property that you must keep for your support or support of your dependents. That would typically include a car, your home, and any property you need for your employment. (Come up with the monthly figure by dividing the total amount you would have to pay back by 60.)

Line 44. List the average monthly amount you will have to pay for priority claims over the next five years. Your priority claims are all claims you listed earlier in Schedule E. You divide by 60 to arrive at the monthly average.

Line 45. Here, you must calculate the fee that the trustee would charge if you ended up in Chapter 13 bankruptcy. That fee would depend on how much you would be paying, through the trustee, to your secured and unsecured creditors. It's impossible to come up with a figure at this point in the form, so leave it blank for now. If you don't pass the means test with this line left blank, come back here when you've complete Part VI and follow these instructions to come up with a figure:

- Add Lines 42, 43, and 44.
- Divide the total on Line 54 by 60 (for the average monthly payment you would have to make to pay down 25% of your unsecured debt over five years).
- Add this number to the total of Lines 42, 43, and 44, and put the result on Line 45a. This is the average amount you would have to pay into a Chapter 13 plan to cover your secured debts, arrearages on those debts, priority debts, and 25% of your unsecured debts.

- On Line 45b, enter the multiplier percentage from the U.S. Trustee's website for your state and district. Go to www.usdoj.gov/ust, click "Means Testing Information," scroll down to the section called "Administrative Expenses Multiplier" and click "Schedules," then scroll down to your district to get the percentage.
- Multiply Line 45a by Line 45b and enter the result in the column on the right.

Line 46. Add Lines 42 through 45, and enter the total in the column on the right.

Subpart D: Total Deductions Allowed under § 707(b)(2)

Line 47: Enter the total of Lines 33, 41, and 46 in the column at the right. This is the total amount you can subtract from your current monthly expenses to arrive at your disposable income.

Part VI: Determination of §707(b)(2) Presumption

This is where you find out whether you received a passing grade on the means test.

Line 48. Enter the amount from Line 18 in the column at the right.

Line 49. Enter the amount from Line 47 in the column at the right

Line 50. Subtract Line 49 from Line 48 and enter the result in the column at the right.

Line 51. Multiply the total from Line 50 by 60 (to find out how much disposable income you will have over the next five years, according to these figures). Enter the result in the column at the right.

Line 52. Here you must check one of three boxes. If the amount on Line 51 is less than $6,000, check the top box. This means that you don't have enough money left over to make a Chapter 13 plan feasible, so you can file for Chapter 7. If the total on Line 51 is more than $10,000, you have enough income to make a Chapter 13 plan feasible, and you probably won't be allowed to stay in Chapter 7. If your total is at least $6,000 but no more than $10,000, you will have to do a few more calculations to figure out where you fall.

If you checked the top box, go back to the first page and check the bottom box at the top, right-hand side of the page ("The presumption does not arise"). Then, complete the verification in Part VIII below.

If you checked the middle box, go back to Page One, check the top box ("The presumption arises"), and complete the verification in Part VIII.

If you checked the bottom box, continue on to Line 53.

Line 53. Enter the total nonpriority, unsecured debt that you entered in your Schedule F, above.

⚠️ **Don't double a debt for duplicate creditors.** To get an accurate result here, you must make sure that you didn't duplicate the amount of any debt for which you have more than one creditor on Schedule F. If you did, go back and retotal your schedule F, putting in each debt only one time even though you are adding two or more creditors for a specific debt (for instance the original debtor, a collection agency, and an attorney).

Line 54. Multiply the amount on Line 53 by the number 0.25 and enter the result in the box on the right. This is equal to 25% of your total nonpriority, unsecured debt.

Line 55. Here, you determine whether the income you have left over (listed on Line 51) is sufficient to pay 25% of your unsecured, nonpriority debt (listed on Line 54). If Line 51 is less than Line 54, congratulations: You have passed the means test. Go back to the first page, check the bottom box at the top right-hand side of the page ("The presumption does not arise") and complete the verification in Part VIII below.

If Line 51 is greater than Line 54, you have failed the means test. The form instructs you to go back to the first page, check the top box at the top right-hand side of the page ("The presumption arises"), and complete the verification.

If you don't pass the means test, you can complete Part VII, in which you list additional expenses that were somehow not included in the earlier parts of the form. Those expenses will be taken into account by the U.S. Trustee as long as they don't duplicate earlier expenses and are reasonably necessary for the support of you and your family.

If you have to check the "presumption arises" box, the U.S. Trustee will issue a notice and schedule a hearing at which the judge will be asked either to dismiss your case or convert it to Chapter 13. This is something that you probably don't want. What to do? Before completing Part VIII, we suggest that you go back over the form and carefully examine the expense items that aren't mandated by the IRS. Often people underestimate their actual expenses. If you find that you underestimated one or more expenses, or left an expense out that is provided for in the form, make the adjustments and see whether you can get a passing grade. Because this form is so complex, we recommend that you go through it at least twice before arriving at your final figures.

See a lawyer if the presumption arises and you want to stay in Chapter 7. If you have to check the box stating that the presumption (of abuse) arises, your Chapter 7 filing is in trouble. Unless you are willing to proceed under Chapter 13, or have your bankruptcy dismissed, we strongly suggest that you find a bankruptcy lawyer to help you

K. Form B201: Notice to Individual Consumer Debtor Under § 342(b) of the Bankruptcy Code

This form, required by the new bankruptcy law, gives you some information about credit counseling and the various chapters of bankruptcy available. It also warns you sternly of the consequences of lying on your bankruptcy papers, concealing assets, and failing to file the required forms on time.

You can find a blank copy of the form in Appendix 3. Sign and date it in the space provided. If a bankruptcy petition preparer assisted you with your paperwork, have that person fill in the requested information.

L. Mailing Matrix

As part of your bankruptcy filing, you are required to submit a list of all of your creditors, so the court can give them official notice of your bankruptcy. Called the mailing "matrix," this list must be prepared in a specific format prescribed by your local bankruptcy court. Your court may also require you to submit a declaration, or "verification," stating that your list is correct (as ever, be sure to check your court's local rules). In a few courts, the form consists of boxes on a page in which you enter the names and addresses of your creditors. This is an artifact from the time when the trustee would use the form to prepare mailing labels.

Now, however, most courts ask you to submit the list on a computer disk in a particular word processing format, or at least submit a computer printout of the names so that they may be scanned. You should check with the bankruptcy court clerk or the court's local rules to learn the precise format. Once you understand the format, take these steps:

Step 1: Make a list of all of your creditors, in alphabetical order. You can copy them from Schedules D, E, F, and H. Be sure to include cosigners and joint debtors. If you and your spouse jointly incurred a debt and are filing jointly, however, don't include your spouse. Also include collection agencies, sheriffs, and attorneys who either have sued you or are trying to collect the debt. And, if you're seeking to discharge marital debts you assumed during a divorce, include both your ex-spouse and the creditors. Finally, if you have two or more debts owed to the same creditor at the same address, you can just list one.

Step 2: Make several copies of the Mailing Matrix form in Appendix 3.

Step 3: If you are using the "box" format, enter your name and address in the top left-hand box on the sheet you designate as the first page. Then enter the names and addresses of each creditor, one per box and in alphabetical order (or in the order required by your local bankruptcy court). Use as many sheets as you need.

It is very important to be complete when preparing the matrix. If you leave a creditor off the matrix and the creditor does not find out about your bankruptcy by some other means, that debt may survive your bankruptcy—and you will have to pay it down the line.

M. How to File Your Papers

Gather up all of the forms you have completed, as well as the documents you gathered in Section A. Make sure you have everything on the Bankruptcy Form Checklist and Bankruptcy Documents Checklist.

Using a bankruptcy petition preparer increases the paperwork. If you use a petition preparer, there will be several additional forms to file.

1. Basic Filing Procedures

Once you've got all of your papers together, follow these filing instructions.

Step 1: Put all your bankruptcy forms in the proper order. (See Section B, above, for information on finding out what order your court requires.)

Step 2: Check that you, and your spouse if you're filing a joint petition, have signed and dated each form where required.

Step 3: Make the required number of copies, plus one additional copy for you to keep just in case your papers are lost in the mail (if you file by mail). In addition, make:

- one extra copy of the Statement of Intention for each person listed on that form, and
- one extra copy of the Statement of Intention for the trustee.

Step 4: Unless the court clerk will hole-punch your papers when you file them, use a standard two-hole punch (copy centers have them) to punch the top center of your original set of bankruptcy papers. Don't staple any forms together.

Step 5: If you plan to mail your documents to the court, address a 9" by 12" envelope to yourself and affix adequate postage to handle one copy of all the paperwork. Although many people prefer to file by mail, we recommend that you personally take your papers to the bankruptcy court clerk if at all possible. Going to the court will give you a chance to correct minor mistakes on the spot.

Step 6: If you can pay the filing and administrative fees when you file, clip or staple a money order (courts don't accept checks), payable to "U.S. Bankruptcy Court," to your original set of papers. If you want to pay in installments, attach a filled-in Application and Order to Pay Filing Fee in Installments, plus any additional papers required by local rules. (See Section 2, below.)

Step 7: Take or mail the original and copies of all forms to the correct bankruptcy court. (See Section B, above, for more on finding the right court.)

Step 8: The bankruptcy rules require you to serve (by mail) the Statement of Intention on each creditor listed on the statement. You have between 30 and 45 days to do this. We recommend you do it immediately so you don't forget. If you don't serve your Statement

of Intention on time, the creditor can repossess the collateral. The trustee must also be served. The trustee's contact information will be provided on the copy of your papers that the clerk returns to you.

Have a friend or relative (other than your spouse, if you are filing jointly) over the age of 18 mail, by first class, a copy of your Statement of Intention to the bankruptcy trustee and to all the creditors listed on that form. Be sure to keep the original.

Step 9: On a Proof of Service by Mail (a copy is in Appendix 3), enter the name and complete address of the trustee and all creditors to whom your friend or relative sent your Statement of Intention. Have that person sign and date the Proof of Service.

2. Paying in Installments

You can pay in up to four installments over 120 days. You can ask the judge to give you extra time for a particular installment, but all installments ultimately must be paid within 180 days after you file. (Federal Rule of Civil Procedure 1006(b).) Some courts will require you to appear at a separate hearing a couple of weeks after you file to make your case for installment payments before the bankruptcy judge. If the judge refuses your request, you will be given some time to come up with the fees (probably 10 days, perhaps longer). Because of this "appearance before the judge" requirement, many debtors prefer to raise the whole fee before filing and hopefully get through their entire bankruptcy without ever meeting up with the judge.

If you are applying to pay in installments, you must file a completed Form B3A (Application and Order to Pay Filing Fee in Installments) when you file your petition. You can find a blank copy of this form in Appendix 3. Important: You cannot apply for permission to pay in installments if you've paid an attorney to help you with your bankruptcy.

The application is easy to fill out. At the top, fill in the name of the court (this is on Form 1—Voluntary Petition), your name (and your spouse's name if you're filing jointly), and "7" following the blank "Chapter." Leave the Case No. space blank. Then enter:

- the total filing fee you must pay: $299 (Item 1)
- the amount you propose to pay when you file the petition (Item 4, first blank)

- the number of additional installments you need (the maximum is four), and
- the amount and date you propose for each installment payment (Item 4, second, third, and fourth blanks).

You (and your spouse, if you're filing jointly) must sign and date the application. Leave the rest blank. As mentioned, the judge may require you to appear for a hearing at which the judge will decide whether to approve or modify your application.

Waiver of Filing Fee

You also may apply to have your fees waived altogether by filing Form B3B. This form is fairly complex and asks for a lot of the information you've provided in the schedules completed earlier in this chapter. A blank copy of this form is in Appendix 3, and on the official U.S. Courts website at www. uscourts.gov. There is some doubt as to whether the courts will grant this benefit, but there is no harm in trying.

---

3. Emergency Filing

If you want to file for bankruptcy in a hurry to get an automatic stay, you can accomplish that (in most places) by filing Form 1—Voluntary Petition, the Mailing Matrix, and Form 21 (Statement of Social Security Number). You will also have to file your certification of completion of credit counseling. Some courts also require you to file a cover sheet and an Order Dismissing Chapter 7 Case, which will be processed if you don't file the rest of your papers within 15 days. (Bankruptcy Rule 1007(c).) If the bankruptcy court for your district requires this form, you can get it from the court (possibly on its website), a local bankruptcy attorney, or a bankruptcy petition preparer.

If you don't follow up by filing the additional documents within 15 days, your bankruptcy case will be dismissed. You can file again, if necessary. However, if your case was dismissed when you opposed a creditor's request to lift the stay, you'll have to wait 180 days to refile. And even if you don't have to wait to file, you'll have to ask the court to keep the automatic

stay in effect once 30 days have passed after you file. (See Ch. 2, Section B.)

For an emergency filing, follow these steps:

Step 1: Check with the court to find out exactly what forms must be submitted for an emergency filing.

Step 2: Fill in Form 1—Voluntary Petition. (See Section E, above.)

Step 3: On a Mailing Matrix (or whatever other form is required by your court), list all your creditors, as well as collection agencies, sheriffs, attorneys, and others who are seeking to collect debts from you.

Step 4: Fill in the Statement of Social Security Number and any other papers the court requires.

Step 5: File the originals and the required number of copies, accompanied by your fee (or an application for payment of fee in installments) and a self-addressed envelope with the bankruptcy court. Keep copies of everything for your records.

Step 6: File all other required forms within 15 days. If you don't, your case will probably be dismissed.

N. After You File

Filing a bankruptcy petition has a dramatic effect on your creditors and your property.

1. The Automatic Stay

The instant you file for Chapter 7 bankruptcy, your creditors are subject to the automatic stay, as described in detail in Ch. 2. If you haven't read that chapter, now is the time to do it.

2. Property Ownership

When you file your bankruptcy papers, the trustee becomes the owner of all the property in your bankruptcy estate as of that date. (See Ch. 3, Section A, for an explanation of what's in your bankruptcy estate.) However, the trustee won't actually take physical control of the property. Most, if not all, of your property will be exempt, which means the trustee will return it to your legal possession after your bankruptcy is closed. If you have any questions about dealing with property after you file, ask the trustee or the trustee's staff.

While your bankruptcy is pending, do not throw out, give away, sell, or otherwise dispose of the property you owned as of your filing date—unless and until the bankruptcy trustee says otherwise. Even if all of your property is exempt, you are expected to hold on to it, in case the trustee challenges your exemption claims.

If some of your property is nonexempt, the trustee may ask you to turn it over. Or, the trustee may decide that the property is worth too little to bother with and abandon it. (Typically, the trustee doesn't let you know if property is abandoned, but once you receive your discharge, the property is deemed abandoned.)

If you are a sole proprietor with business inventory, the trustee takes legal control of your inventory, although you still keep physical control of it. Ask the trustee if you can continue running your business. Usually you can, but you must be prepared to account for any inventory you sell during the bankruptcy, in case the trustee wants to be reimbursed for it. If your business is a corporation or other entity, you will need to consult an attorney.

You are allowed to spend cash you had when you filed (declared on Schedule B) to make day-to-day purchases for necessities such as groceries, personal effects, and clothing. Just make sure you can account for what happened to that cash: You may need to reimburse the bankruptcy estate if the money wasn't exempt and the trustee disapproves your purchases.

In a Chapter 7 case, with a few exceptions, the trustee has no claim to property you acquire or income you earn after you file. You are free to spend it as you please. The exceptions are: property from an insurance settlement, marital settlement agreement, or inheritance that you become entitled to receive within 180 days after your filing date. (See Ch. 3, Sections A and B.)

You Can Pay Creditors After You File

You may be tempted to leave some creditors (like your doctor, dentist, or favorite electrician) off of your bankruptcy schedules, in order to stay in their good graces. That's not a good idea. You must list all of your creditors. But there is nothing to prevent you from paying a dischargeable debt after you file—as long as you don't do so with money from your bankruptcy estate.

If you plan to pay certain creditors despite your bankruptcy, let them know. This will lessen the sting from the notice of filing that they'll receive from the bankruptcy court. Although your promise is unenforceable, creditors will gladly accept your money.

Handling Your Case in Court

For most people, the Chapter 7 bankruptcy process is straightforward and proceeds pretty much on automatic pilot. The bankruptcy trustee decides whether your papers pass muster and, if not, what amendments you need to file. Ordinarily, you have few decisions to make.

This chapter tells you how to handle the routine procedures that move your bankruptcy case along, and how to deal with unexpected complications that may arise if any of the following occur:

- You or the trustee discovers an error in your papers.
- A creditor asks the court to lift the automatic stay.
- You decide to object to a creditor's claim.
- A creditor objects to the discharge of a particular debt.
- A creditor or the trustee objects to your claim that an item of property is exempt.
- You decide to dismiss your case or convert it to another type of bankruptcy, such as a Chapter 13 bankruptcy.

Some of these problems—fixing a simple error in your papers, for example—you can handle yourself. For more complicated problems, such as fighting a creditor in court about the discharge of a large debt, you'll probably need a lawyer's help.

A. Routine Bankruptcy Procedures

A routine Chapter 7 bankruptcy case takes three to six months from beginning to end and follows a series of predictable steps.

1. The Court Schedules the Meeting of Creditors

Shortly after you file for bankruptcy, the court sends an official notice to all of the creditors listed in your mailing matrix. This notice contains several crucial pieces of information.

a. Your Filing Date and Case Number

This information puts the creditors on notice that you have filed for bankruptcy and gives them a reference number to use when seeking information about your case.

b. Whether the Case Is an Asset Case or a No-Asset Case

When you filled in the bankruptcy petition, you had to check one of the following two boxes:

- ☐ Debtor estimates that funds will be available for distribution to unsecured creditors.
- ☐ Debtor estimates that, after any exempt property is excluded and administrative expenses paid, there will be no funds available for distribution to unsecured creditors.

Your choice of these boxes determines the type of notice the court sends to your creditors. If you checked the first box, your case is known as an "asset case" and your creditors will be advised to file a claim describing what you owe them. If you checked the second box, your case will be known as a "no-asset" case and your creditors will be told to not file a claim. However, they will also be informed that they will have an opportunity to file a claim later if it turns out that there are assets available after all.

c. The Date for the Creditors' Meeting

The notice also sets a date for the meeting of creditors (also called the "341 meeting"), usually several weeks later. Mark this date carefully—it is very important for several reasons.

- You must attend the creditors' meeting; if you don't, your case can be dismissed.
- Your creditors must file their claims (if it is an asset case) within 60 days after this meeting.
- Your creditors must file any objections they have to the discharge of their debts within 60 days after this meeting.

2. Your Creditors Must Cease Most Collection Actions

When the court mails your creditors official notice of your filing, the automatic stay goes into effect. The automatic stay prohibits most creditors and government support entities from taking any action to collect the debts you owe them until the court says otherwise.

How a Routine Chapter 7 Bankruptcy Proceeds

Step	Description	When It Happens
You begin your case by filing bankruptcy papers.	You file the petition and supporting schedules with the bankruptcy clerk, who scans them into the court records.	When you decide to do so. Once you file, your creditors are barred from taking collection actions.
The court notifies creditors that you have filed for bankruptcy.	A notice of your filing and a date for the creditors' meeting is mailed to everyone you list as a creditor.	A few days after you file.
The court assigns a trustee to the case.	The trustee's job is to review your paperwork and take possession of any nonexempt property.	The trustee is appointed at the same time the notice to creditors is mailed.
You file your most recent tax return.	You must file your most recent tax return but can black out sensitive information such as your Social Security number and date of birth.	Seven days prior to the creditors' meeting.
The creditors' meeting is held.	The creditors' meeting is the only personal appearance most filers make. The judge is not there and creditors seldom attend. The trustee questions you about your paperwork. Most meetings last a few minutes.	Between 20 and 40 days after the date you file.
The means test is applied in appropriate cases.	The U.S. Trustee starts a process leading to dismissal or conversion of your case to Chapter 13 if your papers show that you have adequate income to fund a repayment plan.	The U.S. Trustee must file a statement within ten days after the creditors' meeting if it appears from the paperwork or information gleaned in the creditors' meeting that your income is over the state median and you can't pass the means test.
Negotiations are held regarding nonexempt property, if any.	If you have nonexempt property, the trustee will give you a chance to buy it back. Otherwise, the trustee will require you to hand over the property so it can be sold for the benefit of the unsecured creditors.	Within 60 days after the meeting of creditors.
Secured property is dealt with.	If you owe money on property, you must either redeem or reaffirm the debt if you want to hold on to the property.	Within 30 days after the creditors' meeting.
You attend budget counseling.	You must undergo personal financial management counseling before you can get your discharge.	Within 45 days after the creditors' meeting.
The court holds a reaffirmation hearing.	If you reaffirm a debt and aren't represented by a lawyer, you must attend a court hearing where the judge reviews your decision.	Roughly 60 days after your creditors' meeting.
The court grants your discharge.	The court mails a notice of discharge that discharges all debts that can legally be discharged, unless the court has ruled otherwise in the court of your bankruptcy (very rare). The automatic stay is lifted at this time.	Roughly 90 days after you file.
Your case is closed.	The trustee distributes any property collected from you to your unsecured creditors.	A few days or weeks after your discharge.

There are some notable exceptions to the automatic stay, however. Even if you file for bankruptcy, the following proceedings can continue:

- A criminal case can proceed against you.
- A case to establish paternity or to establish, modify, or collect child support or alimony can go forward.
- A tax audit, the issuance of a tax deficiency notice, a demand for a tax return, the issuance of a tax assessment, and the demand for payment of such an assessment can all take place. The IRS cannot, however, record a lien or seize your property after you file for bankruptcy. (11 U.S.C. § 362(b).)
- Certain evictions can go forward.

Ch. 2 provides detailed information on the automatic stay, including which actions it does—and does not—prohibit.

In addition, the bankruptcy court can lift the automatic stay for a particular creditor—that is, allow the creditor to continue collection efforts. (Lifting the automatic stay is covered in Section D, below.)

Creditors won't know that they have to stop their collection efforts until they receive notice of your bankruptcy filing. The notice sent by the court may take a week or more to reach your creditors. If you need quicker results, send your own notice to creditors (and bill collectors, landlords, or sheriffs about to enforce an eviction order). A sample letter notifying your creditors is shown below. You can also call your creditors. Be prepared to give your bankruptcy case number, the date you filed, and the name of the court in which you filed.

Notice to Creditor of Filing for Bankruptcy

Lynn Adams
18 Orchard Park Blvd.
East Lansing, MI 48823

June 15, 20XX

Cottons Clothing Store
745 Main Street
Lansing, MI 48915

Dear Cottons Clothing:

On June 14, 20XX, I filed a voluntary petition under Chapter 7 of the U.S. Bankruptcy Code. The case number is 43-6736-91. I filed my case *in pro per*; no attorney is assisting me. Under 11 U.S.C. § 362(a), you may not:

- take any action against me or my property to collect any debt
- enforce any lien on my real or personal property
- repossess any property in my possession
- discontinue any service or benefit currently being provided to me, or
- take any action to evict me from where I live.

A violation of these prohibitions may be considered contempt of court and punished accordingly.

Very truly yours,

Lynn Adams

Lynn Adams

If a creditor tries to collect a debt in violation of the automatic stay, you can ask the bankruptcy court to hold the creditor in contempt of court and to award you money damages. The procedures for making this request are beyond the scope of this book.

3. Attend the Meeting of Creditors

The meeting of creditors is the place where the trustee gets information from the debtor, usually by asking a few questions, and resolves any issues he or she sees in your paperwork. Some trustees question a debtor more closely about items in the bankruptcy papers than others. The trustee may want to see documentation of some of your figures, such as the value of a house or car; if you don't have this paperwork with you, the trustee will continue the meeting to another date to give you time to find the necessary documents. Typically, you won't have to appear at another meeting, but can submit these documents by mail.

For most people, the creditors' meeting is brief. Very few, if any, creditors show up, but *you* must show up. If you don't appear and haven't notified the trustee in advance, your case will very likely be scheduled for dismissal, which means you'll have to explain yourself to the judge. Some trustees will automatically give you a second chance without seeking dismissal. Especially if you have a good excuse for not attending, the trustee is likely to reschedule.

If you're married and filing jointly. Both you and your spouse must attend the first scheduled meeting of creditors. If the meeting is continued to another date for a technical reason—to turn over certain papers to the trustee, for example—only one spouse may have to attend. Ask the trustee whether both of you have to come back, or whether one will do.

a. Preparing for the Creditors' Meeting

Before the meeting, call the regular trustee whose name and phone number appear on the notice the court sends out. Explain that you're proceeding without a lawyer ("in pro per") and ask what records you're required to bring. At a minimum, you should take a copy of every paper you've filed with the bankruptcy court.

You should also bring the following:
- evidence of your current income (if the wage stubs you already had to file don't provide this information)
- statements from financial institutions for all of your deposit and investment accounts
- your most recent tax return (you are required to give this to the trustee at least seven days before the creditors' meeting), and
- if you had to take the means test, proof of your monthly expenses.

If You Can't Appear

Sometimes, a person who has filed for bankruptcy is unable to attend the creditors' meeting because of a legitimate reason, such as a disability. If that is true in your case, contact the trustee for information on how to proceed. Here is what the U.S. Trustee's office tells the regular trustees about how to handle people who are unable to appear:

"The trustee should consult with the United States Trustee regarding the general procedures for approving a debtor's alternative appearance when extenuating circumstances prevent the debtor from appearing in person. Extenuating circumstances may include military service, serious medical condition, or incarceration. In such instances, a debtor's appearance at a § 341(a) meeting may be secured by alternative means, such as telephonically. When the debtor(s) cannot personally appear before the trustee, arrangements should be made for an independent

third party authorized to administer oaths to be present at the alternate location to administer the oath and to verify the debtor's identity and state the Social Security number on the record.... On the rare occasion when other arrangements need to be made to address a particular situation, the trustee should consult with the United States Trustee about the appropriate safeguards to follow. The trustee also may allow such debtors to provide proof of identity and Social Security numbers at the trustee's office at their convenience any time before the next scheduled meeting.

When a trustee becomes aware of a debtor's disability, including hearing impairment, the trustee must notify the United States Trustee immediately so that reasonable accommodation can be made. The United States Trustee has procedures in place to address the special needs of debtors."

If requested, bring copies of all documents that describe your debts and property, such as bills, deeds, contracts, and licenses. Some trustees also require you to bring financial records, such as tax returns (in addition to the one you filed with the court), checkbooks, and records for any business you have operated in the past six years. You have a right to redact (black out) all but the last four numbers of your Social Security number on any papers you submit. You can also redact the names of your minor children, full dates of birth, and full account numbers.

Some people become anxious at the prospect of answering a trustee's questions and consider having an attorney accompany them. But if you were completely honest in preparing your bankruptcy papers, there's no reason to have an attorney with you at the creditors' meeting. If the trustee does have tough questions, it is you, not the attorney, who will have to answer them, anyway.

If you think you've been dishonest on the forms or with a creditor, or have attempted to unload some of your property before filing, see a lawyer before you go to court.

You can visit the hearing room where your district holds creditor meetings (typically, the nearest federal building) and watch other meetings of creditors if you think that might help alleviate some anxiety. Just check with the U.S. Trustee's office in your district (see www.usdog.gov/ust for contact information) to find out when these meetings are held.

A day or so before the creditors' meeting, thoroughly review the papers you filed with the bankruptcy court. If you discover mistakes, make careful note of them. You'll probably have to correct your papers after the meeting, but that's an easy process. (Instructions are in Section B, below.)

After reviewing your papers, go over the list of questions the trustee may ask you (set out in "What Will the Trustee Ask You?," below). Use these questions as a checklist for your bankruptcy. Despite the fact that these are "required" questions, few trustees ask all of them, and many trustees ask only one or two. Still, it's a good idea to be able to answer them all, to the extent they relate to your situation.

At the beginning of the meeting, the trustee may ask you whether you have read the Statement of Information required by 11 U.S.C. § 342. If you read

Chs. 1 and 2, you have learned all the information on this form. However, we set the form out at the end of this chapter so you will be able to answer "yes" to the trustee's question.

Don't forget your ID. You'll need identification at the creditors' meeting. Bring both a photo ID (such as a driver's license, passport, or identification card) and proof of your Social Security number from a third-party source (like a wage stub, retirement account statement, or passport).

b. The Routine Creditors' Meeting

Most creditors' meetings are quick and simple. You appear in the designated meeting place at the date and time stated on the bankruptcy notice. A number of other people who have filed for bankruptcy will be there, too, for their own creditors' meetings. When your name is called, you'll be asked to sit or stand near the front of the meeting room. The trustee will swear you in and ask you for your identification. At that point, many trustees look you in the eye and sternly ask whether everything in your papers is 100% true and correct. If you are uncertain about information in your papers or you have lied, the trustee is likely to pick up on your hesitancy and follow up with more questions that may make you uncomfortable. That's why it's so important that you:

- review your papers before filing them
- file amendments before the creditors' meeting if you discover any errors after you file (refer to Section B, below)
- review your papers again shortly before the creditors' meeting, and
- volunteer any additional changes at the meeting.

Then you can confidently answer "yes" to the trustee's first question.

There is a long list of "required" questions in "What Will the Trustee Ask You?," below, but the trustee will probably be most interested in:

- how you came up with a value for big ticket items, such as your home or car
- anticipated tax refunds
- any possible right that you have to sue someone because of a recent accident or business loss
- reasons for inconsistencies in your paperwork or

omitted information (such as answering "none" to the question about clothing or bank accounts when it's obvious that you have either or both)

- recent large payments to creditors or relatives, and
- possible inheritances or insurance proceeds coming your way.

If your answer to a trustee's question is different from what you said in your bankruptcy papers, the trustee will have reason to suspect your entire case—and your bankruptcy may change from a routine procedure to an uphill battle. If you know that you have made mistakes, you should call them to the trustee's attention before the trustee raises the issue. If you are caught in a contradiction, immediately explain how it happened. But this may prove difficult. For instance, if someone else prepared your papers for you, you can't use that as an excuse. You are responsible for the information in your papers—which is why you should thoroughly review them before appearing.

When the trustee is finished questioning you, the trustee will offer any creditors who have appeared an opportunity to ask you questions. Most often, no creditors show up. If any do appear, they will probably be secured creditors who want to clarify your intentions regarding the collateral securing the debt. (For example, if you've taken out a car loan and the car

is the collateral, the creditor may ask whether you are going to reaffirm the debt or whether you might prefer to redeem the car at its replacement value.) Also, if you obtained any cash advances or ran up credit card debts shortly before filing for bankruptcy, the credit card issuers may show up to question you about the circumstances and about what you did with the proceeds. And, finally, a creditor might also ask for explanations if information in your bankruptcy papers differs from what was on your credit application. When the creditors are through asking questions, the meeting will end.

Except in highly unusual situations, the trustee and any creditors should be finished questioning you in five minutes or less. In busy courts, creditors' meetings often last no more than 90 seconds. When the trustee and creditors are done, the meeting will be concluded and you will be told you can leave. If you have no secured debts or nonexempt property, and neither you nor your creditors will be asking the court to rule on the dischargeability of a debt or the continuing effect of a lien, your case will effectively be over. No one will come to your house to inventory your property. No one will call your employer to confirm the information on your papers. Your bankruptcy case turns into a waiting game—waiting for the court to send you your notice of discharge and case closure. That should happen two to three months after your creditors' meeting.

Hold Your Head High

No matter how well you prepare for the creditors' meeting, you may feel nervous and apprehensive about coming face to face with the trustee and possibly your creditors, to whom you've disclosed the intimate details of your finances over the last several years. You may feel angry with yourself and your creditors at having to be there. You may be embarrassed. You may think you're being perceived as a failure.

Nonsense. It takes courage to face your situation and deal firmly with it. Bankruptcy, especially when you're handling your own case without a lawyer, isn't an easy out. Let yourself see this as a turning point at which you're taking positive steps to improve your life. Go to the creditors' meeting proud that you've chosen to take control over your life and legal affairs.

What Will the Trustee Ask You?

The trustee is *required* to ask the following questions at your creditors' meeting (although some don't):

1. State your name and current address for the record.
2. Have you read the Bankruptcy Information Sheet provided by the United States Trustee?
3. Did you sign the petition, schedules, statements, and related documents you filed with the court? Did you read the petition, schedules, statements, and related documents before you signed them, and is the signature your own?
4. Please provide your picture ID and Social Security number card for review.
5. Are you personally familiar with the information contained in the petition, schedules, statements, and related documents?
6. To the best of your knowledge, is the information contained in the petition, schedules, statements, and related documents true and correct?
7. Are there any errors or omissions to bring to my, or the court's, attention at this time?
8. Are all of your assets identified on the schedules?
9. Have you listed all of your creditors on the schedules?
10. Have you previously filed for bankruptcy? (If so, the trustee must obtain the case number and the discharge information to determine your discharge eligibility.)

The trustee may also ask additional questions, such as these:

1. Do you own or have any interest in any real estate?
   - Property that you own: When did you purchase the property? How much did the property cost? What are the mortgages encumbering it? What do you estimate the present value of the property to be? Is that the whole value or your share? How did you arrive at that value?
   - Property that you're renting: Have you ever owned the property in which you live? Is its owner in any way related to you?
2. Have you made any transfers of any property, or given any property away, within the last year (or a longer period if applicable under state law)? If so, what did you transfer? To whom was it transferred? What did you receive in exchange? What did you do with the funds?

3. Does anyone hold property belonging to you? If so, who holds the property, and what is it? What is its value?
4. Do you have a claim against anyone or any business? If there are large medical debts, are the medical bills from injury? Are you the plaintiff in any lawsuit? What is the status of each case, and who is representing you?
5. Are you entitled to life insurance proceeds or an inheritance as a result of someone's death? If so, please explain the details. (If you become a beneficiary of anyone's estate within six months of the date your bankruptcy petition was filed, the trustee must be advised within ten days through your counsel of the nature and extent of the property you will receive. (FRBP 1007(h).)) (See Ch. 10, Section D for a description of the Federal Rules of Bankruptcy Procedure.)
6. Does anyone owe you money? If so, is the money collectible? Why haven't you collected it? Who owes the money, and where is that person?
7. Have you made any large payments, over $600, to anyone in the past year?
8. Were your federal income tax returns filed on a timely basis? When was the last return filed? Do you have copies of the federal income tax returns? At the time of the filing of your petition, were you entitled to a tax refund from the federal or state government?
9. Do you have a bank account, either checking or savings? If so, in what banks and what were the balances as of the date you filed your petition?
10. When you filed your petition, did you have:
    - any cash on hand
    - any U.S. Savings Bonds
    - any other stocks or bonds
    - any Certificates of Deposit, or
    - a safe deposit box in your name or in anyone else's name?
11. Do you own an automobile? If so, what is the year, make, and value? Do you owe any money on it? Is it insured?
12. Are you the owner of any cash value life insurance policies? If so, state the name of the company, face amount of the policy, cash surrender value (if any), and beneficiaries.

What Will the Trustee Ask You? (continued)

13. Do you have any winning lottery tickets?

14. Do you anticipate that you might realize any property, cash or otherwise, as a result of a divorce or separation proceeding?

15. Regarding any consumer debts secured by your property, have you filed the required Statement of

Intention with respect to the exemption, retention, or surrender of that secured property? Please provide a copy of the statement to the trustee. Have you performed that intention?

16. Have you been engaged in any business during the last six years? If so, where and when? What happened to the assets of the business?

---

c. Potential Problems at the Creditors' Meeting

If you or your papers give any indication that you own valuable nonexempt property, the trustee may question you vigorously about how you arrived at the values in question. For instance if you have valued your real estate at $150,000, and the trustee thinks it's worth a lot more, you will be asked where you got your figures. Or, a creditor who's owed a lot of money may grill you about the circumstances of the debt, hoping to show that you incurred the debt without intending to pay it, or by lying on a credit application, and that therefore it should survive bankruptcy. (See Ch. 8.)

You may also be closely questioned about why you claimed certain property to be exempt. For some reason, some bankruptcy trustees, who are usually attorneys, believe that claiming exemptions requires legal expertise. If this happens to you, simply describe the process you went through in selecting your exemptions from Appendix 1. If you consulted an attorney about exemptions or other issues, mention this also. The only thing a trustee who disagrees can do is to object to your exemptions. This must be done within 30 days of the creditors' meeting. (See Section D3, below.)

Make Sure the Creditors' Meeting Is Closed

The 30-day period in which the trustee and creditors may file objections to exemptions starts running when the creditors' meeting is finished or "closed." The meeting is officially closed—and the clock starts to run on objections—only when the trustee so notes in the court's docket. The trustee's oral statement alone at the creditors' meeting isn't enough to officially close the meeting. Check the court file to make sure that the trustee closed (or adjourned) the creditors' meeting, and follow up with the trustee if you don't see an entry like that. Otherwise, the 30-day period to file objections never starts to run, and the trustee and creditors will have unlimited time to file objections.

You're responsible for your paperwork, even if you used a bankruptcy petition preparer. You must provide the property valuation and other information in your bankruptcy papers. You cannot shift responsibility for the accuracy and thoroughness of your petition to the preparer, whose job is just to enter the information you supply. If you use a preparer, check all of your paperwork carefully before signing it and filing it with the court.

4. Deal With Nonexempt Property

After the meeting of creditors, the trustee is supposed to collect all of your nonexempt property and have it sold to pay off your creditors. Normally, the trustee accepts the exemptions you claim on Schedule C and only goes after property you haven't claimed as exempt. If, however, the trustee or a creditor disagrees with an exemption you claimed and files a written objection with the bankruptcy court, the court will schedule a hearing. After listening to both sides, the judge will decide the issue. (See Section D, below.)

If you really want to keep certain nonexempt items and can borrow money from friends or relatives, or you've come into some cash since you filed for bankruptcy, you may be able to trade cash for the item. The trustee, whose sole responsibility at this stage is to maximize what your creditors get paid, is interested simply in what cash your property can produce, not in taking a particular item. So the trustee shouldn't mind taking cash in place of nonexempt property you want to keep.

> **EXAMPLE:** Maura files for Chapter 7 bankruptcy and claims her parlor grand piano as exempt. The trustee disagrees, and the judge rules that the piano is not exempt. To replace the piano on the open market might cost Maura $7,000. The trustee determines that the piano would probably sell for $4,500 at an auction, and is willing to let Maura keep the piano if she can come up with $3,750, to avoid the cost of moving the piano, storing it, and selling it at auction.

The trustee may also be willing to let you keep nonexempt property if you volunteer to trade exempt property of equal value. For instance, the trustee might be willing to let Maura keep her nonexempt piano if she gives up her car, even though Maura could claim the car as exempt. Again, the trustee is interested in squeezing as many dollars as possible from the estate and usually won't care whether the money comes from exempt or nonexempt assets.

5. Deal With Secured Property

When you filed your Statement of Intention, you told the trustee and your creditors whether you wanted to keep property that is security for a debt, or give it to the creditor in return for cancellation of the debt.

The law contradicts itself on the time limits for carrying out your intentions. Depending on which provision you believe, you have either 30 or 45 days after the date set for your first creditors' meeting to deal with your secured property. If you miss the deadline, the creditor can repossess the collateral—the automatic stay no longer applies (see Ch. 2, Section

B). Because of these serious consequences, we strongly recommend that you handle your secured property within 30 days of the meeting, just in case the court follows this earlier deadline. (Ch. 5 explains how to decide what to do with your secured property and how to carry out your intentions.)

6. Complete an Approved Financial Management Course

Within 45 days after the meeting of creditors, you must take a course in personal financial management. The court will not give you a discharge until you complete this counseling. The agencies offering these courses must be approved by the Office of the U.S. Trustee and must offer approximately two hours of required curriculum. (You can find a list of approved agencies at the U.S. Trustee's website at www.usdoj/gov.ust; click "Credit Counseling and Debtor Education.") These agencies do not have to be nonprofits, but they must offer services in person, on a sliding fee scale.

Once you complete your counseling, fill out Form 23, Debtor's Certification of Completion of Instructional Course Concerning Personal Financial Management, and file it with the court. (You can find a blank copy in Appendix 3.)

7. Attend the Discharge Hearing

You may have to attend a brief court hearing at the end of your case, called a discharge hearing. At the hearing, the judge explains the effects of discharging your debts in bankruptcy and lectures you about staying clear of debt. You should receive a discharge order from the court within four weeks of the hearing. If you don't, call the trustee.

Most courts don't schedule a discharge hearing unless you signed a Reaffirmation Agreement that was filed with the court. If you have signed and filed a Reaffirmation Agreement, the court will hold a hearing. At the hearing, the judge will determine whether reaffirmation would impose an undue hardship on you, and whether it would be in your best interest to reaffirm the debt. You can find a complete explanation of the reaffirmation process in Ch. 5.

8. Understand Your Discharge Order

About two or three months after the creditors' meeting, the court will send you a copy of your discharge order. On the back, it says that all debts you owed as of your filing date are discharged—unless they aren't. It then lists the categories of debt that are not discharged. (A sample discharge order is below.) You will notice that your order does not refer to your debts or state which of your specific debts are or aren't discharged. To get a handle on this crucial information, carefully read Ch. 9.

Make several photocopies of the discharge order and keep them in a safe place. Send them to creditors who attempt to collect their debt after your case is over, or to credit bureaus that still list you as owing a discharged debt. Refer to Ch. 5, Sections C and D, regarding postbankruptcy collection efforts.

B. Amending Your Bankruptcy Papers

One of the helpful aspects of bankruptcy procedure is that you can amend any of your papers at any time before your final discharge. This means that if you made a mistake on papers you've filed, you can correct it easily.

Despite this liberal amendment policy as stated in Bankruptcy Rule 1009, some judges will not let you amend your exemption schedule after the deadline for creditors to object to the exemptions has passed. If you run into one of these judges, consult a bankruptcy attorney.

In most courts, you will have to pay to amend your bankruptcy papers only if you are amending Schedules D, E, or F to add a new creditor or change an address, because these changes require the court to make an additional mailing. The fee for this type of amendment is $26.

If you become aware of debts or property that you should have included in your papers, amending your petition will avoid any suspicion that you're trying to conceal things from the trustee. If you don't amend your papers after discovering this kind of information, your bankruptcy petition may be dismissed or one or more of your debts may not be discharged if that new information comes to light.

Even if your bankruptcy case is already closed, you may be allowed to reopen your case and amend your papers to add an omitted creditor who tries to collect the debt. (See Ch. 8.)

⚠ Try to get it right the first time. Too many changes can make you look dishonest, which can get your case dismissed and (if it seems you were hiding assets) investigated. The Open Letter to Debtors and Their Counsel at the end of Ch. 1, Section C, gives a judge's negative view of amendments. Of course, if the facts have changed since you filed your petition, or you notice mistakes, you should amend. But the more accurate your papers are at the outset, the less likely your case will run into trouble.

1. Common Amendments

Even a simple change in one form may require changes to several other forms. Here are some of the more common reasons for amendments and the forms that you may need to amend. Exactly which forms you'll have to change depends on your court's rules. (Instructions for making the amendments are in Section B2, below.)

a. Add or Delete Exempt Property on Schedule C

If you want to add or delete property from your list of exemptions, you must file a new Schedule C. You may also need to change other schedules, depending on the omission:

- Schedule A, if the property is real estate and you didn't list it there
- Schedule B, if the property is personal property and you didn't list it there
- Schedule D and Form 8—Chapter 7 Individual Debtor's Statement of Intention, if the property is collateral for a secured debt and isn't already listed
- Form 7—Statement of Financial Affairs, if any transactions regarding the property weren't described on that form, or
- Mailing Matrix, if the exempt item is tied to a particular creditor.

b. Add or Delete Property on Schedule A or B

You may have forgotten to list some of your property on your schedules. Or, you may have received property after filing for bankruptcy. The following property must

Form 18
(10/05)

United States Bankruptcy Court

_____ District Of _____

In re _____,)
       [Set forth here all names including married,   )
       maiden, and trade names used by debtor within)
       last 8 years.]   )
                 Debtor   ) Case No. _____
)
)
Address _____)
)
_____   ) Chapter 7
)
Last four digits of Social Security No(s).: _____)
_____   )
Employer's Tax Identification No(s). *[if any]*:_____)
_____   )

DISCHARGE OF DEBTOR

    It appearing that the debtor is entitled to a discharge, **IT IS ORDERED:** The debtor is granted a discharge under section 727 of title 11, United States Code, (the Bankruptcy Code).

Dated: _____

                                    BY THE COURT

                                  _____

                                  United States Bankruptcy Judge

SEE THE BACK OF THIS ORDER FOR IMPORTANT INFORMATION.

Official Form 18 - Contd.
(10/05)

EXPLANATION OF BANKRUPTCY DISCHARGE
IN A CHAPTER 7 CASE

This court order grants a discharge to the person named as the debtor. It is not a dismissal of the case and it does not determine how much money, if any, the trustee will pay to creditors.

Collection of Discharged Debts Prohibited

The discharge prohibits any attempt to collect from the debtor a debt that has been discharged. For example, a creditor is not permitted to contact a debtor by mail, phone, or otherwise, to file or continue a lawsuit, to attach wages or other property, or to take any other action to collect a discharged debt from the debtor. *[In a case involving community property:* There are also special rules that protect certain community property owned by the debtor's spouse, even if that spouse did not file a bankruptcy case.] A creditor who violates this order can be required to pay damages and attorney's fees to the debtor.

However, a creditor may have the right to enforce a valid lien, such as a mortgage or security interest, against the debtor's property after the bankruptcy, if that lien was not avoided or eliminated in the bankruptcy case. Also, a debtor may voluntarily pay any debt that has been discharged.

Debts That are Discharged

The chapter 7 discharge order eliminates a debtor's legal obligation to pay a debt that is discharged. Most, but not all, types of debts are discharged if the debt existed on the date the bankruptcy case was filed. (If this case was begun under a different chapter of the Bankruptcy Code and converted to chapter 7, the discharge applies to debts owed when the bankruptcy case was converted.)

Debts that are Not Discharged.

Some of the common types of debts which are <u>not</u> discharged in a chapter 7 bankruptcy case are:

a. Debts for most taxes;

b. Debts incurred to pay nondischargeable taxes;

c. Debts that are domestic support obligations;

d. Debts for most student loans;

e. Debts for most fines, penalties, forfeitures, or criminal restitution obligations;

f. Debts for personal injuries or death caused by the debtor's operation of a motor vehicle, vessel, or aircraft while intoxicated;

g. Some debts which were not properly listed by the debtor;

h. Debts that the bankruptcy court specifically has decided or will decide in this bankruptcy case are not discharged;

i. Debts for which the debtor has given up the discharge protections by signing a reaffirmation agreement in compliance with the Bankruptcy Code requirements for reaffirmation of debts.

j. Debts owed to certain pension, profit sharing, stock bonus, other retirement plans, or to the Thrift Savings Plan for federal employees for certain types of loans from these plans.

This information is only a general summary of the bankruptcy discharge. There are exceptions to these general rules. Because the law is complicated, you may want to consult an attorney to determine the exact effect of the discharge in this case.

be reported to the bankruptcy trustee if you receive it, or become entitled to receive it, within 180 days after filing for bankruptcy:

- property you inherit or become entitled to inherit
- property from a marital settlement agreement or divorce decree, and
- death benefits or life insurance policy proceeds. (See Ch. 3, Section A.)

If you have new property to report for any of these reasons, you may need to file amendments to:

- Schedule A, if the property is real estate
- Schedule B, if the property is personal property
- Schedule C, if the property was claimed as exempt and it's not, or you want to claim it as exempt
- Schedule D and Form 8—Chapter 7 Individual Debtor's Statement of Intention, if the property is collateral for a secured debt
- Form 7—Statement of Financial Affairs, if any transactions regarding the property haven't been described on that form, or
- Mailing Matrix, if the item is tied to a particular creditor.

If your bankruptcy case is already closed, see Ch. 8.

c. Change Your Plans for Secured Property

If you've changed your plans for dealing with an item of secured property, you must file an amended Form 8—Chapter 7 Individual Debtor's Statement of Intention.

d. Correct Your List of Creditors

To correct your list of creditors, you may need to amend:

- Schedule C, if the debt is secured and you plan to claim the collateral as exempt
- Schedule D, if the debt is a secured debt
- Schedule E, if the debt is a priority debt (as defined in Ch. 6)
- Schedule F, if the debt is unsecured
- Form 7—Statement of Financial Affairs, if any transactions regarding the property haven't been described on that form, or
- Mailing Matrix, which contains the names and addresses of all your creditors.

If your bankruptcy case is already closed, see Ch. 8.

e. Add an Omitted Payment to a Creditor

If you didn't report a payment to a creditor made within the year before you filed for bankruptcy, you must amend your Form 7—Statement of Financial Affairs.

2. How to File an Amendment

To make an amendment, take these steps:

Step 1: Fill out the Amendment Cover Sheet in Appendix 3, if no local form is required. Otherwise, use the local form. If you use our form, here's how to fill it in:

- Put the appropriate information in the top blanks (for instance, <u>Western</u> District of <u>Tennessee</u>).
- After "In re," enter your name, the name of your spouse if you're married and filing jointly, and all other names you have used in the last six years.
- Enter your address, the last four digits of your Social Security number, and a taxpayer ID number (if you have one because of a business you own).
- On the right side, enter your case number, then put "7" in the line after Chapter.
- Check the boxes of the forms you are amending. If you are adding new creditors or changing addresses, check the box that you have enclosed the appropriate fee (currently $26).
- Sign the form.
- Continue to the declaration about the truth of the amendment.
- Enter your name (and the name of your spouse if you're filing jointly) after "I(we)."
- Enter the number of pages that will be accompanying the cover sheet.
- Enter the date you are signing the document.
- Sign (both you and your spouse, if you're filing jointly) at the bottom to swear that your amendment is true, under penalty of perjury.

Step 2: Make copies of the forms affected by your amendment.

Step 3: Check your local court rules or ask the court clerk whether you must retype the whole form to make the correction, or if you can just type the new information on another blank form. If you can't find the answer, ask a local bankruptcy lawyer or nonattorney bankruptcy petition preparer. If it's acceptable to just type the new information, precede the information you're typing with "ADD:", "CHANGE:", or "DELETE:" as appropriate. At the bottom of the form, type "AMENDED" in capital letters.

Step 4: Call or visit the court and ask what order the papers must be in and how many copies are required.

Step 5: Make the required number of copies, plus one copy for yourself, one for the trustee, and one for any creditor affected by your amendment.

Step 6: Have a friend or relative mail, first class, a copy of your amended papers to the bankruptcy trustee and to any creditor affected by your amendment.

Step 7: Enter the name and complete address of every new creditor affected by your amendment on the Proof of Service by Mail (a copy is in Appendix 3). Also enter the name and address of the bankruptcy trustee. Then have the person who mailed the amendment to the trustee and new creditors sign and date the Proof of Service.

Step 8: Mail or take the original amendment and Proof of Service and copies to the bankruptcy court. Enclose or take a money order for the filing fee, if required. If you use the mail, enclose a prepaid self-addressed envelope so the clerk can return a file-stamped set of papers to you.

If the meeting of creditors occurred before you file your amendment, the court is likely to schedule another one.

C. Filing a Change of Address

If you move while your bankruptcy case is still open, you must give your new address to the court, the trustee, and your creditors. Here's how to do it:

Step 1: Make one or two photocopies of the blank Notice of Change of Address and Proof of Service forms in Appendix 3.

Step 2: Fill in the Change of Address form.

Step 3: Make one photocopy for the trustee, one for your records, and one for each creditor listed in Schedules D, E, and F or the Mailing Matrix.

Step 4: Have a friend or relative mail a copy of the Notice of Change of Address to the trustee and to each creditor.

Step 5: Have the friend or relative complete and sign the Proof of Service by Mail form, listing the bankruptcy trustee and the names and addresses of all creditors to whom the notice was mailed.

Step 6: File the original notice and original Proof of Service with the bankruptcy court.

D. Special Problems

Sometimes, complications arise in a bankruptcy—usually when a creditor files some type of motion or objects to the discharge of a debt or the entire bankruptcy. If a creditor does this, the court will notify you by sending you a Notice of Motion or Notice of Objection. (See sample copy, below.) At that point, you may need to go to court yourself or get an attorney to help you. Here are some of the more common complications that may crop up.

1. You Failed the Means Test

If you didn't pass the means test (described in Ch. 6) but decided to file for Chapter 7 anyway, you may face a motion to dismiss or convert your case to a Chapter 13 bankruptcy.

a. Presumed Abuse

If you don't pass the means test, your Chapter 7 bankruptcy will be presumed to be abusive. This means that you won't be allowed to proceed unless you can establish that the presumption of abuse should be set aside because of special circumstances.

However, none of this is automatic. To stop your Chapter 7 bankruptcy on the grounds of abuse, someone—a creditor, the trustee, or, most likely, the U.S. Trustee—must request a court hearing to dismiss or convert your case. Under the new bankruptcy law, the U.S. Trustee must file a statement, within ten days after your meeting of creditors, indicating whether your case should be considered a presumed abuse. (This statement is required only if your income is more than the state median; see Ch. 1, Section B, for more information). Five days after the U.S. Trustee's statement is filed, the court must send it to all of your creditors, to inform them of the U.S. Trustee's decision and give them an opportunity to file a motion to dismiss or convert your case.

Within 30 days after filing this statement, the U.S. Trustee must either:

- file its own motion to dismiss or convert your case on grounds of abuse, or
- explain why a motion to convert or dismiss isn't appropriate (for example, because you passed the means test).

These duties and time limits apply only to the U.S. Trustee. If your income is more than the state median, your creditors can file a motion to dismiss or convert any time after you file, but no later than 60 days after the first date set for your meeting of creditors.

b. Defending a Motion to Dismiss or Convert

If the U.S. Trustee (or a trustee or a creditor, in some cases) files a Motion to Dismiss or Convert your case on the basis of presumed abuse, you are entitled to notice of the hearing at least 20 days in advance. You will receive papers in the mail explaining the grounds for the motion and what you need to do to respond. Because abuse is presumed, you will bear the burden of proving that your filing really isn't abusive, and that you should be allowed to proceed.

There are two basic defenses to this type of motion:

1. **You didn't fail the means test.** To defend on this basis, you must be able to show that you actually passed the means test and the party bringing the motion to dismiss or convert misinterpreted the information you provided in Form B22A or misinterpreted the applicable law (for example, by including Social Security benefits in your current monthly income).

2. **Special circumstances exist that allow you to pass the means test.** The new law gives a serious medical condition or a call to active duty in the armed forces as examples of special circumstances, but this isn't an exhaustive list.

However, it isn't enough just to show that special circumstances exist: You must also show that they justify additional expenses or adjustments to your current monthly income "for which there is no reasonable alternative."

To prove special circumstances, you must itemize each additional expense or adjustment of your income, and provide:

- documentation for the expense or adjustment, and
- a detailed explanation of the special circumstances that make the expense or adjustment necessary and reasonable.

You will win only if the additional expenses or adjustments to your income enable you to pass the means test. (Ch. 6 explains how to make this calculation.)

EXAMPLE: Maureen and Ralph have a child (Sarah) with severe autism. Sarah is making remarkable progress in her private school, for which Maureen and Ralph pay $1,000 a month. No equivalent school is available at a lower tuition. Under the means test guidelines, Maureen and Ralph are entitled to deduct only $150 a month from the income for private school expenses. If Maureen and Ralph were allowed to deduct the full $1,000 monthly tuition, they would easily pass the means test. By documenting Sarah's condition, the necessity for the extra educational expense, and the fact that moving her to a less-expensive school would greatly undermine her progress, Maureen and Ralph would have a good chance of convincing the court to allow the $1,000 expense, which would, in turn, rebut the presumption of abuse.

2. A Creditor Asks the Court to Lift the Automatic Stay

Your automatic stay lasts from the date you file your papers until the date you receive your bankruptcy discharge or the date your bankruptcy case is closed, whichever happens first. For example, assume you receive a discharge but the trustee keeps your case open because the trustee is waiting to collect your tax refund or an inheritance you are due to receive in the future. In this situation, the automatic stay would not be in effect after your discharge, even though your case would still be open.

As long as the stay is in effect, most creditors must get permission from a judge to take any action against you or your property that might affect your bankruptcy estate. (See Ch. 2 for information on which creditors are affected by the stay—and which are free to proceed with collection efforts despite the stay.) To get this permission, the creditor must file a request in writing called a Motion to Lift Stay. The court will schedule a hearing on this motion and send you written notice. You will have a certain period of time to file a written response. Even if you decide not to file a response, you may still be able to appear in court to argue that the stay shouldn't be lifted. Check your local rules on this point.

If you don't show up for the hearing—even if you filed a written response—the stay will probably be lifted as requested by the creditor, unless lifting the stay would potentially harm other creditors. For instance, if the creditor is seeking permission to repossess your car, and your equity in the car would produce some income for your unsecured creditors if sold by the trustee, the court may refuse to lift the stay whether or not you show up.

After hearing the motion, the judge will either decide the issue a decision then and there (rule "from the bench"), or "take it under submission" and mail a decision in a few days. A creditor can ask a judge to lift the stay within a week or two after you file, but a delay of several weeks to several months is more common.

a. Grounds for Lifting the Stay

The bankruptcy court may lift the automatic stay for several reasons:

- The activity being stayed is not a legitimate concern of the bankruptcy court. For instance, the court will let a child custody hearing proceed, because its outcome won't affect your economic situation.
- The activity being stayed is going to happen, no matter what the bankruptcy court does. For instance, if a lender shows the court that

a mortgage foreclosure will ultimately occur, regardless of the bankruptcy filing, the court will usually lift the stay and let the foreclosure proceed. (If you want to keep your house, you may be better off filing for Chapter 13 bankruptcy. See Ch. 4.)

- The stay is harming the creditor's interest in property you own or possess. For instance, if you've stopped making payments on a car and it's losing value, the court may lift the stay. That would allow the creditor to repossess the car now, unless you're willing and able to periodically pay the creditor an amount equal to the ongoing depreciation until your case is closed.
- You have no ownership interest in property sought by the creditor (ownership interests are explained just below). If you don't own some interest in property that a creditor wants, the court isn't interested in protecting the property—and won't hesitate to lift the stay. The most common example is when a month-to-month tenant files bankruptcy to forestall an eviction. Because the tenancy has no monetary value, it is not considered to be property of the estate, and the stay will almost always be lifted.

Official Form 20A
(12/03)

United States Bankruptcy Court

_____ District Of _____

In re _____,   )
Set forth here all names including married,   )
maiden, and trade names used by debtor within   )
last 6 years.]   )
                          Debtor   )   Case No. _____
)
Address _____   )
)
_____   )   Chapter _____
)
Employer's Tax Identification (EIN) No(s). *[if any]:* _____)
_____)
Last four digits of Social Security No(s).: _____)

NOTICE OF [MOTION TO   ] [OBJECTION TO   ]

_____has filed papers with the court to [relief sought in motion or objection].

Your rights may be affected. **You should read these papers carefully and discuss them with your attorney, if you have one in this bankruptcy case. (If you do not have an attorney, you may wish to consult one.)**

If you do not want the court to [relief sought in motion or objection], or if you want the court to consider your views on the [motion] [objection], then on or before *(date)* , you or your attorney must:

[File with the court a written request for a hearing {*or, if the court requires a written response*, an answer, explaining your position} at:

          {address of the bankruptcy clerk's office}

If you mail your {request}{response} to the court for filing, you must mail it early enough so the court will **receive** it on or before the date stated above.

You must also mail a copy to:

          {movant's attorney's name and address}

          {names and addresses of others to be served}]

[Attend the hearing scheduled to be held on __*(date)*__ , _*(year)*_ , at ____a.m./p.m. in Courtroom ____, United States Bankruptcy Court, {address}.]

[Other steps required to oppose a motion or objection under local rule or court order.]

If you or your attorney do not take these steps, the court may decide that you do not oppose the relief sought in the motion or objection and may enter an order granting that relief.

Date: _____   Signature: _____
                                                           Name:
                                                           Address:

Do You Have an Ownership Interest in the Property?

There are many kinds of ownership interests. You can own property outright. You can own the right to possess it sometime in the future. You can co-own it jointly with any number of other owners. You can own the right to possess it, while someone else actually owns legal title.

For most kinds of property, there's an easy way to tell if you have an ownership interest: If you would be entitled to receive any cash if the property were sold, you have an ownership interest.

For intangible property, however—property you can't see or touch—it may be harder to show your ownership interest. This most often arises in cases involving contracts concerning residential real estate.

For instance, if you have a lease (a type of contract) on your home when you file, most bankruptcy courts would consider it an ownership interest in the property and would not lift the stay to let a landlord go ahead with eviction, regardless of the reason. But if the lease expired by its own terms before you filed—which converted your interest from a "leasehold" to a month-to-month tenancy—most courts would rule that you have no ownership interest in the property and would lift the stay, allowing the eviction to go forward.

Another ownership interest is the contractual right to continued coverage that an insured person has under an insurance policy. This means the automatic stay prevents insurance companies from canceling insurance policies.

b. Opposing a Request to Lift the Stay

Generally, a court won't lift the stay if you can show that it's necessary to preserve your property for yourself (if it's exempt) or for the benefit of your creditors (if it's not), or to maintain your general economic condition. You may also need to convince the court that the creditor's investment in the property will be protected while the bankruptcy is pending.

Here are some possible responses you can make if a creditor tries to get the stay lifted:

- **Repossession of cars or other personal property:** If the stay is preventing a creditor from repossessing personal property pledged as collateral, such as your car, furniture, or jewelry, the creditor will probably argue that the stay should be lifted because you might damage the collateral or because the property is depreciating (declining in value) while your bankruptcy case is pending. Your response should depend on the facts. If the property is still in good shape, be prepared to prove it to the judge.

  If the property is worth more than you owe on it, you can argue that depreciation won't hurt the creditor, because the property could be repossessed later and sold for the amount of the debt or more. But if, as is common, you have little or no equity in the property, you'll need to propose a way to protect the creditor's interest while you keep the property—assuming you want it. One way to do this is to pay the creditor a cash security deposit that would offset the expected depreciation.

  If you intend to keep secured property (see Ch. 5), you can argue that lifting the stay would deprive you of your rights under the bankruptcy laws. For example, if you intend to redeem a car by paying its replacement value, the court should deny the motion to lift the stay until you have an opportunity to do so.

- **Utility disconnections:** For 20 days after you file your bankruptcy petition, a public utility—electric, gas, telephone, or water company—may not alter, refuse, or discontinue service to you, or discriminate against you in any other way, solely on the basis of an unpaid debt or your bankruptcy filing. (11 U.S.C. § 366(a).) If your service was disconnected before you filed, the utility company must restore it within 20 days after you file for bankruptcy—without requiring a deposit—if you request it.

  Twenty days after the order to continue service, the utility is entitled to discontinue service unless you provide adequate assurance that your future bills will be paid. (11 U.S.C. § 366(b).) Usually, that means you'll have to come up with a security deposit.

If you and the utility can't agree on the size of the deposit, the utility may cut off service, which means you'll need to get a lawyer and ask the bankruptcy court to have it reinstated. If the utility files a motion to lift the stay, argue at the hearing that your deposit is adequate.

- **Evictions:** Filing for bankruptcy has been a favorite tactic for some eviction defense clinics, which file a bare-bones bankruptcy petition to stop evictions even if the tenant's debts don't justify bankruptcy. Under the new bankruptcy law, the automatic stay doesn't apply if your landlord obtained a judgment for eviction before you filed for bankruptcy, or if the eviction is based on your endangerment of the property or use of illegal controlled substances on the premises. These exceptions to the general rules are explained in Ch. 2, Section C.

3. The Trustee or a Creditor Disputes a Claimed Exemption

After the creditors' meeting, the trustee and creditors have 30 days to object to the exemptions you claimed. If the deadline passes and the trustee or a creditor wants to challenge an exemption, it's usually too late, even if the exemption statutes don't support the claimed exemption. (*Taylor v. Freeland and Kronz,* 503 U.S. 638 (1992).) The objections must be in writing and filed with the bankruptcy court. Copies must be served on the trustee (that is, personally handed or mailed to the trustee), you, and, if you have one, your lawyer. (Bankruptcy Rule 4003.)

In some cases, the trustee can object to an exemption after the 30-day period has passed. For instance, in one case the debtor stated that the value of certain stock options was unknown and used a $4,000 or so wildcard exemption to cover the value, whatever it was. Eight months after the bankruptcy case was closed, the trustee asked the debtor what happened to the stock options. As it happened, they had been cashed out for nearly $100,000. The trustee sought to have the case reopened to recover the excess value. The debtor argued that the 30-day period prevented a reexamination of the exemption claim. The issue was ultimately decided in favor of the trustee—on the ground that the debtor's use of the term "unknown" meant that the trustee wasn't under an obligation to challenge the exemption claim within the 30-day limit. If, on the other hand, the debtor had listed a specific value for the options, the trustee's duty to file an objection within the deadline would have been triggered. (*In re Wick,* 276 F.3d 412 (8th Cir 2002).)

a. Reasons for Objecting

The most common grounds for objecting are:

- You aren't eligible to use the state exemptions you claimed. Under the new bankruptcy law, you may use a state's exemptions only if you have lived there for at least two years before filing. If you haven't lived in your current state for at least two years, you must use the exemptions for the state where you were living for the better part of the 180-day period ending two years before you filed for bankruptcy. (See Ch. 3, Section C, for more on these rules, and Ch. 4 for more on the stricter rules that apply to homestead exemptions.)

- The claimed item isn't exempt under the law. For example, a plumber who lives in New Jersey and selects his state exemptions might try to exempt his plumbing tools under the "goods and chattels" exemption. The trustee and creditors are likely to object on the ground that these are work tools rather than goods and chattels, and that New Jersey has no "tools of trade" exemption.

- Within ten years before you filed for bankruptcy, you sold nonexempt property and purchased exempt property to hinder, delay, or cheat your creditors. (Ways to avoid this accusation are discussed in Ch. 3, Section D.)

- Property you claimed as exempt is worth more than you say it is. If the property's true replacement value is higher than the exemption limit for that item, the item can be sold and the excess over the exemption limit distributed to your creditors (assuming you don't buy the property back from the trustee at a negotiated price).

  EXAMPLE: In Connie's state, clothing is exempt to a total of $2,000. Connie values her mink coat at $1,000 and her other clothes at $1,000, bringing her within the $2,000 exemption. A creditor objects to the $1,000 valuation of the coat, claiming that such mink coats routinely sell for $3,000 and up. If the creditor prevails, Connie would have to surrender the coat to the trustee. She'd get the first $1,000 (the exempt amount of the coat's sale price). Or, Connie could keep the coat if she gave the trustee a negotiated amount of cash ($2,000 or less) or other property of equivalent value.

- You and your spouse have doubled an exemption where doubling isn't permitted.

  EXAMPLE: David and Marylee, a married couple, file for bankruptcy using California's System 1 exemptions. Each claims a $2,300 exemption in their family car, for a total of $4,600. California bars a married couple from doubling the System 1 automobile exemption. They can only claim $2,300.

b. Responding to Objections

When objection papers are filed, the court schedules a hearing. The creditor or trustee must prove to the bankruptcy court that the exemption is improper. You don't have to prove anything. In fact, you don't have to respond to the objection or show up at the hearing unless the bankruptcy court orders—or local rules require—that you do so. Of course, you can—and probably should—either file a response or show up at the hearing to defend your claim of a legitimate exemption. If you don't show up, the bankruptcy judge will decide on the basis of the paperwork filed by the objecting party and the applicable laws, which most often means you'll lose—especially if the trustee or a bankruptcy attorney is objecting.

4. A Creditor Objects to the Discharge of a Debt

There are a variety of reasons a creditor may object to the discharge of a debt. In consumer bankrupcies, the most common reason is that the creditor believes you incurred the debt through fraudulent representations. See Ch. 9 for more on this and other potential objections.

5. You Want to Get Back Exempt Property Taken by a Creditor

You may have filed for bankruptcy after a creditor:
- repossessed collateral (such as a car) under a security agreement, or
- seized some of your property as part of a judgment collection action.

If so, you should have described the event in your Statement of Financial Affairs, which you filed along with your bankruptcy petition and schedules. Repossessions are difficult to undo, because they occur under a contract that you voluntarily entered into. However, property seized to satisfy a judgment can be pulled back into your bankruptcy estate if the seizure occurred within the three months before you filed. If the property is not exempt (or at least some of it is not exempt), the trustee may go after it so that it can be sold for the benefit of your unsecured creditors. If the property is exempt (meaning you are entitled to keep it), you can go after it yourself. However, you'll have to file a formal complaint in the bankruptcy court against the creditor.

The process for getting the bankruptcy judge to order property returned to you is a complex one; you'll probably need the assistance of an attorney. Given the cost of attorneys, it's seldom worth your while to go after this type of property unless it's valuable or an irreplaceable family heirloom. Keep in mind that most property is only exempt up to a certain value—for example, a car may be exempt up to $1,200, furnishings up to $1,000. Thus, even if you get the property back, the trustee may decide to sell it, in which case you'll receive only the exempt amount from the proceeds.

6. You Want to Dismiss Your Case

If you change your mind after you file for bankruptcy, you can ask the court to dismiss your case.

Common reasons for wanting to dismiss a case include the following:
- You discover that a major debt you thought was dischargeable isn't. You don't have enough other debts to justify your bankruptcy case.
- You realize that an item of property you thought was exempt isn't. You don't want to lose it in bankruptcy.

- You come into a sum of money and can afford to pay your debts.
- You realize that you have more property in your estate than you thought and decide that you don't have to file for bankruptcy after all.
- Your bankruptcy case turns out to be more complex than you originally thought. You need a lawyer, but you don't have the money to hire one.
- The emotional stress of bankruptcy is too much for you.

It is within the court's discretion to dismiss your case. That means the court can grant or refuse the dismissal. What the court does will vary from district to district. In some districts, dismissing a case is next to impossible if your bankruptcy estate has assets that can be sold. However, if yours is a no-asset case and no creditor objects to the dismissal, you may have better luck dismissing it.

If you want to dismiss your case, you must file a request with the court. Instructions on how to do this follow. Depending on how receptive your local bankruptcy court is to dismissal, you may need the help of a lawyer.

Step 1: Check your court's local rules for time limits, format of papers, and other requirements for voluntary dismissals. (See Ch. 10 for information on finding local rules online.) If you can't find the information you need from reading your local rules, ask the court clerk, the trustee assigned to your case, a local bankruptcy petition preparer, or a bankruptcy lawyer for help.

Step 2: Refer to the end of this chapter for a sample Petition for Voluntary Dismissal and a sample order granting voluntary dismissal. Follow along with the sample as you type your caption, inserting your own information in the blanks.

    a. Center and type (in capital letters) "UNITED STATES BANKRUPTCY COURT. "

    b. On the next line, type the district and state your case is in. Examples: "FOR THE WESTERN DISTRICT OF MICHIGAN, FOR THE DISTRICT OF MONTANA," or "FOR THE MIDDLE DISTRICT OF NORTH CAROLINA."

    c. Starting at the left margin, type the name of your case, which is: "In re [*your full name, your spouse's name (if you filed for bankruptcy jointly), and any names you or your cofiling spouse used before*]." Below that and indented, type "Debtor(s)."

    d. Type your full address.

    e. If you are an employer and you have an EIN, enter it.

    f. Type "Last four digits of Social Security No(s):" and enter your number(s).

    g. Type a column of right parentheses, which is supposed to look sort of like a box around the case name.

    h. Put your case number to the right of the column of parentheses. For example, "Case No. 05-01234-AB." (Your case number may also have a city code or may omit the dash before the judge's initials; type it the way your district does it.)

    i. Below your case number, type "Chapter 7."

Step 3: Make a few photocopies of what you have typed so far, so you can make two different documents with that one caption.

Step 4: On one copy of your caption, center and type "PETITION FOR VOLUNTARY DISMISSAL." The text of the petition will be similar to the sample but tailored to the facts of your case. In particular, you will put your filing date in Paragraph 1; in Paragraph 3 you will explain your own reason for wanting to dismiss the case.

Step 5: Sign and date the petition. If you filed together with your spouse, both of you must sign. Otherwise, leave the spouse's signature line blank.

Step 6: On another photocopy of the caption you made, center and type: "[PROPOSED] ORDER GRANTING VOLUNTARY DISMISSAL." Then type the text of the order from the sample at the end of this chapter. Include the blanks; the judge will fill them in.

Step 7: Make at least three copies of your signed petition and your blank order.

Step 8: Take your originals and copies to the bankruptcy court clerk. When you get to the court clerk, explain that you are filing a petition to dismiss your case. The clerk will take your originals and one or more of your copies. Ask the clerk the following:

- What notice to your creditors is required?
- If there is a problem, will you be contacted? If not, how will you learn of the problem?
- If the judge signs the order, when can you expect to get it?

- Once you have a signed order, who sends copies to your creditors—you or the court? If you send the copies, do you also have to file a Proof of Service?

Step 9: Once you receive the signed order, put it away for safekeeping if you don't have to notify your creditors. If you do, make copies and send one to each.

Step 10: If you have to file a Proof of Service, follow the instructions in Ch. 5.

Petition for Voluntary Dismissal

UNITED STATES BANKRUPTCY COURT

_____ DISTRICT OF _____

In re _____)

        [*Set forth here all names including*   )

        married, maiden, and trade names used   )

        by debtor within last 8 years]   )

                          Debtor(s)   )   Case No. _____

Address _____)

)

_____)   Chapter 7

)

Employer's Tax Identification (EIN) No(s). [*if any*]:   )

_____)

Last four digits of Social Security no(s). _____)

PETITION FOR VOLUNTARY DISMISSAL

The debtor in the above-mentioned case hereby moves to dismiss his/her bankruptcy case for the following reasons:

1. Debtor filed a voluntary petition under Chapter 7 of the Bankruptcy Code on _____, 20XX.

2. No complaints objecting to discharge or to determine the dischargeability of any debts have been filed in the case.

3. Debtor realizes that filing a Chapter 7 bankruptcy petition was erroneous. Debtor now realizes that a particular debt may not be dischargeable. Debtor would have to litigate this matter, and Debtor does not feel he/she has the ability to do so on his/her own nor the resources to hire an attorney to do it for him/her. Debtor intends to pursue other means of handling his/her debts.

4. No creditor has filed a claim in this case.

5. No creditor has requested relief from the automatic stay.

WHEREFORE, Debtor prays that this bankruptcy case be dismissed without prejudice.

Date: _____
                            Signature of Debtor

Date: _____
                           Signature of Debtor's Spouse

Order Granting Voluntary Dismissal

UNITED STATES BANKRUPTCY COURT

_____ DISTRICT OF _____

In re _____)
        [Set forth here all names including)
        married, maiden, and trade names used)
        by debtor within last 8 years])
                   Debtor(s)) Case No. _____
Address _____)
)
      _____) Chapter 7
)
Employer's Tax Identification (EIN) No(s). _[if any]_:)
_____)
Last four digits of Social Security no(s). _____)

[PROPOSED] ORDER GRANTING VOLUNTARY DISMISSAL

AND NOW, this _____ day of _____, 20____, the Court having found that the voluntary dismissal of this case is in the best interests of the debtor and does not prejudice the rights of any of his or her creditors, it is hereby ordered that the petition for voluntary dismissal is approved.

Dated: _____ _____
                                U.S. Bankruptcy Judge

STATEMENT OF INFORMATION REQUIRED BY 11 U.S.C. § 341

Introduction

Pursuant to the Bankruptcy Reform Act of 1994, the office of the United States Trustee, United States Department of Justice, has provided this information to help you understand some of the possible consequences of filing a bankruptcy petition under Chapter 7 of the Bankruptcy Code. This information is intended to make you aware of—

1. The potential consequences of seeking a discharge in bankruptcy, including the effects on credit history
2. The effect of receiving a discharge of debts
3. The effect of reaffirming a debt
4. Your ability to file a petition under a different chapter of the Bankruptcy Code.

There are many other provisions of the Bankruptcy Code that may affect your situation. This information contains only general principles of law and is not a substitute for legal advice. If you have questions or need further information as to how the bankruptcy laws apply to your specific case, you should consult with an attorney.

What Is a Discharge?

The filing of a Chapter 7 petition is designed to result in a discharge of most of the debts listed on bankruptcy schedules. A discharge is a court order that says you do not have to repay your debts, but there are a number of exceptions. Debts which may not be discharged in a Chapter 7 case include:

Most taxes, child support, alimony, student loans, court-ordered fines and restitution, debts obtained through fraud and deception, and personal injury debts caused by driving while intoxicated or under the influence of drugs.

Your discharge may be denied entirely if you, for example, destroy or conceal property, destroy, conceal or falsify records or make a false oath. Creditors cannot compel you to pay any debts which have been discharged. You can only receive a Chapter 7 discharge once every six years.

What Are the Potential Effects of a Discharge?

The fact that you filed bankruptcy can appear on your credit record for as long as 10 years. Thus filing a bankruptcy petition may affect your ability to obtain credit in the future. Also, you may not be excused from repaying any debts that were not listed on your bankruptcy schedules or that you incurred after you filed bankruptcy.

What Are the Effects of Reaffirming a Debt?

After you file your petition, a creditor may ask you to reaffirm a certain debt or you may seek to do so on your own. Reaffirming a debt means that you sign and file with the court a legally enforceable document, which states that you promise to repay all or a portion of the debt that may otherwise have been discharged in a bankruptcy case.

Reaffirmation agreements are strictly voluntary. REAFFIRMATION AGREEMENTS ARE NOT REQUIRED BY THE BANKRUPTCY CODE OR OTHER STATE OR FEDERAL LAW. You can voluntarily repay any debt instead of signing a reaffirmation agreement, but there may be valid reasons for wanting to reaffirm a particular debt.

Reaffirmation agreements must not impose an undue burden on you or your dependents and must be in your best interest. If you decide to sign a reaffirmation agreement, you may cancel it at any time before the court issues your discharge order or within 60 days after the reaffirmation agreement is filed with the court, whichever is later. If you reaffirm a debt and fail to make the payments required in the reaffirmation agreement, the creditor can take action against you to recover any property that was given as security for the loan and you may remain personally liable for any remaining debt.

Other Bankruptcy Options

You have a choice in deciding what chapter of the Bankruptcy Code will best suit your needs. Even if you have already filed for relief under Chapter 7, you may be eligible to convert your case to a different chapter. (See the various chapters under bankruptcy which are included in the Notice to Individual Consumer Debtor in the packet of documents, B201.)

AGAIN, PLEASE CONSULT AN ATTORNEY IF YOU NEED FURTHER INFORMATION OR EXPLANATION, INCLUDING HOW THE BANKRUPTCY LAWS RELATE TO YOUR SPECIFIC CASE.

Debtor's Signature   Date

CHAPTER

8

Life After Bankruptcy

Congratulations! After you receive your final discharge, you can get on with your life and enjoy the fresh start that bankruptcy offers. You may, however, want to rebuild your credit, and you may need to take action if:

- You receive or discover new nonexempt property.
- A creditor tries to collect a nondischargeable debt.
- A creditor tries to collect a debt that has been discharged in your bankruptcy.
- A creditor or the trustee asks the court to revoke your discharge in your bankruptcy.
- A government agency or private employer discriminates against you because of your bankruptcy.

This chapter explains how these events typically unfold, and how you can respond to them. But don't worry: Very few people face these circumstances. If you were complete and honest in your paperwork, it's very unlikely that you'll run into any post-bankruptcy problems. We provide the information in this chapter just in case you're one of the rare exceptions.

A. Newly Acquired or Discovered Property

If you omit property from your bankruptcy papers, or you acquire certain kinds of property soon after you file, the trustee may reopen your case after your discharge (if the trustee learns about the property). The trustee probably won't take action, however, unless the property is nonexempt and is valuable enough to justify the expense of reopening the case, seizing and selling the property, and distributing the proceeds among your creditors. Even if the after-discharge property you acquire or discover is of little value, however, you should still tell the trustee about it, even if you think the assets don't justify reopening the case. Whether to reopen is the trustee's decision, not yours.

1. Notifying the Trustee

It's your legal responsibility to notify the bankruptcy trustee if either of the following are true:

- Within 180 days of filing for bankruptcy, you receive or become entitled to receive property that belongs in your bankruptcy estate.
- You failed to list some of your nonexempt property in your bankruptcy papers.

a. Newly Acquired Property

If you receive, or become entitled to receive, certain property within 180 days after your bankruptcy filing date, you must report it to the trustee, even if you think the property is exempt or your case is already closed. If you don't report it and the trustee learns of your acquisition, the trustee could ask the court to revoke the discharge of your debts. (See Section E, below.) You must report:

- an inheritance (property you receive, or become entitled to receive, because of someone's death)
- property from a divorce settlement, or
- proceeds of a life insurance policy or death benefit plan. (11 U.S.C. § 541(a)(5).)

These categories of property are discussed in more detail in Ch. 3, Section A.

To report this property to the trustee, use the form called Supplemental Schedule for Property Acquired After Bankruptcy Discharge. A blank copy is in Appendix 3. The form is self-explanatory. When you've filled it out, follow these steps:

Step 1: Photocopy a Proof of Service by Mail (a blank copy is in Appendix 3) and fill it out, but don't sign it.

Step 2: Make three photocopies of the Supplemental Schedule and the Proof of Service.

Step 3: Have a friend or relative mail the original Supplemental Schedule and a copy of the Proof of Service to the trustee and the U.S. Trustee, and then sign the original Proof of Service.

Step 4: File a copy of the Supplemental Schedule and the original Proof of Service with the bankruptcy court. No additional filing fee is required.

Step 5: Keep a copy of the Supplemental Schedule and the Proof of Service for your records.

In some areas, the court may require you to file amended bankruptcy papers. If that happens, follow the instructions in Ch. 7, Section B.

b. Property Not Listed in Your Papers

If, after your bankruptcy case is closed, you discover some property that you should have listed in your bankruptcy papers, you don't need to file any documents with the court. You must, however, notify the trustee. A sample letter is shown below.

Letter to Trustee

1900 Wishbone Place
Wilkes-Barre, PA 18704

October 22, 20XX

Francine J. Chen
Trustee of the Bankruptcy Court
217 Federal Building
197 S. Main St.
Wilkes-Barre, PA 18701

Dear Ms. Chen:

I've just discovered that I own some property I didn't know of while my bankruptcy case was open. Apparently, when I was a child I inherited a bank account from my uncle, the proceeds of which were supposed to be turned over to me when I turned 21. Although I turned 21 eight years ago, for some unknown reason I never got the money.

The account, #2424-5656-08 in the Bank of New England, 1700 Minuteman Plaza, Boston, MA 02442, has a balance of $4,975.19. As you know, I opted for the federal exemptions in my case and do not own a home. I believe this property would be exempt under 11 U.S.C. § 522(d)(5). Please let me know how you intend to proceed.

Sincerely,
Ondine Wallace
Ondine Wallace

⚠ Omitting property could put your discharge at risk. If the trustee believes you were playing fast and loose with the bankruptcy court by omitting the property from your petition, the trustee can get your case reopened and attempt to cancel your discharge. If it would appear to a neutral person that your omission of valuable property from your petition likely was deliberate, consult a bankruptcy lawyer before talking to the trustee.

2. Reopening Your Bankruptcy Case

If any of the new or newly discovered property is valuable and nonexempt, the trustee may try to reopen your case, take the property, and have it sold to pay your creditors. As noted above, the trustee will probably opt to do this if it looks like the profit from selling the property will be large enough to offset the cost of reopening your bankruptcy case and administering the sale.

To get to these new assets, the trustee files a motion to reopen the case. Judges usually grant these motions, unless they think too much time has passed or the property isn't valuable enough to justify reopening. How much time constitutes "too much time" varies with the facts of the case. Once the case is reopened, the trustee asks the court for authorization to sell the new assets and distribute the proceeds.

⚠ Get help if you're fighting the trustee's attempt to reopen your case. If you can bear to lose the property, consider consenting to what the trustee wants. But if your discharge or valuable property is at stake, consult a bankruptcy lawyer. You could oppose the motion to reopen on your own, but you will need to do a lot of legal research. (See Ch. 10 for tips on lawyers and research.)

B. Newly Discovered Creditors

Perhaps you inadvertently failed to list a particular creditor on your schedule. As we pointed out in Ch. 7, you can always amend if you discover the omission while your bankruptcy case is still open. But suppose you don't become aware of your omission until your bankruptcy is closed. Does that mean that the debt survives your bankruptcy? Not at all. If the creditor had actual knowledge of your bankruptcy, then it's the same as if the creditor were actually listed in your papers.

Suppose now that the omitted creditor didn't have actual knowledge, or, as is more common than you might think, you lost track of one or more of your creditors and had no way to identify them in your bankruptcy schedules. Even then, the chances are great that the debt will be considered discharged.

If yours was a no-asset case (that is, all your property was exempt), the debt is considered discharged unless, by being left out, your creditor lost the opportunity to contest the discharge on the ground that the debt was caused by your fraudulent or embezzling behavior, or by a willful and malicious act (such as assault or libel). It is often possible to reopen the bankruptcy and let the bankruptcy judge rule on whether the debt is, in fact, dischargeable. If the creditor sues you in state court for a judgment, you could argue the issue in that forum or have the case removed to bankruptcy court.

If yours was an asset case—that is, at some point in your case, your unsecured creditors received some property from your bankruptcy estate—your situation is more difficult. Your nonexempt assets were already distributed to your other unsecured creditors, so the omitted creditor would be unfairly discriminated against if the debt were discharged. If the debt is a large one, you might want to hire a lawyer to reopen the case and argue that the debt should be discharged due to your particular circumstances. (See Ch. 10 for advice on finding and working with a lawyer.)

C. Post-Bankruptcy Attempts to Collect Debts

After bankruptcy, creditors whose debts haven't been discharged are entitled to be paid. Creditors whose debts have been discharged may not pursue the debt further. But it isn't always clear into which category a creditor falls. The bankruptcy court doesn't give you an itemized list of your discharged debts. Instead, your final discharge paper merely explains the types of debts that are discharged in general terms. Because of this lack of specificity, it can be tough to figure out whether a particular debt has been wiped out.

How do you know which debts have been discharged and which debts must still be paid? Here's the general rule: All the debts you listed in your bankruptcy papers are discharged unless a creditor successfully objected to the discharge of a particular debt in the bankruptcy court, or the debt falls in one of the following categories:

- student loans (unless the court ruled it would be an undue hardship for you to repay them)
- taxes that became due within the past three years or that were assessed within the previous 240 days
- debts you took on to pay nondischargeable taxes
- child support or alimony
- fines and penalties or court fees
- debts related to personal injury or death caused by your intoxicated driving
- debts not discharged in a previous bankruptcy because of fraud or misfeasance
- certain condominium and cooperative fees incurred after your filing date, or
- loans you took out from a retirement fund.

Ch. 9 discusses all of these categories in more detail.

In addition, if only one spouse files for bankruptcy in a community property state, the other spouse's share of the community debts (debts incurred during the marriage) is also discharged. The community property states are Alaska (if the spouses agree in writing), Arizona, California, Idaho, Louisiana, Nevada, New Mexico, Texas, Washington, and Wisconsin.

Finally, as we've seen, even if a debt is not listed in your bankruptcy papers, it will be considered discharged if yours was a no-asset case—unless the creditor could have successfully challenged the discharge in bankruptcy court if the creditor were properly notified of your case.

Even if you think some of your debts weren't discharged in bankruptcy, the creditors may never try to collect. Many creditors believe that bankruptcy cuts off their rights, period; even attorneys often don't understand that some debts can survive bankruptcy.

If a creditor does try to collect a debt after your bankruptcy discharge, write to the creditor and state that your debts were discharged. Unless you're absolutely certain that the debt wasn't discharged—for example, a student loan for which the court denied your hardship request—this is a justifiable position for you to take.

Letter to Creditor

388 Elm Street
Oakdale, WY 95439

March 18, 20XX

Bank of Wyoming
18th and "J" Streets
Cheyenne, WY 98989

To Whom It May Concern:

I've received numerous letters from your bank claiming that I owe $6,000 for charges between September of 1997 and September of 1999. I received a bankruptcy discharge of my debts on February 1, 20XX. I enclose a copy of the discharge for your reference.

Sincerely,
Brenda Woodruff
Brenda Woodruff

If the creditor ignores your letter and continues collection efforts, there are other ways to respond:

- **Amend your bankruptcy papers.** Remember that an unlisted debt is discharged in a no-asset case, unless the creditor was deprived of a chance to oppose the debt's discharge. You can reopen the bankruptcy, amend your papers to list the debt, and then see what the creditor does. See Section B, above.
- **Do nothing.** The creditor knows you've just been through bankruptcy, have little or no nonexempt property, and probably have no way to pay the debt, especially all at once. Thus, if you don't respond to collection efforts, the creditor may decide to leave you alone, at least for a while.
- **Try to get judgments wiped out.** If a creditor sued you and won before you filed for bankruptcy, the creditor may try to collect on that judgment, unless you can convince a state court that the judgment was discharged in bankruptcy. Creditors can try to enforce judgments years after they won

them, so it's a good idea for you to reopen the bankruptcy case and ask the judge to rule that the judgment is discharged.
- **Negotiate.** Try to negotiate for a lower balance or a payment schedule that works for you. Again, the creditor knows you've just been through bankruptcy and may be willing to compromise.
- **Defend in court.** If the creditor sues you for the debt, you can raise any defenses you have to the debt itself.

  EXAMPLE: The Department of Education sued Edna for failing to pay back a student loan she received. Edna refused to make the payments because the trade school she gave the money to went out of business before classes even began. Because this is a valid defense to the collection of a student loan, Edna should respond to the lawsuit and assert her defense.

- **Protest a garnishment or other judgment collection effort.** A creditor who has sued you and won a court judgment for a nondischargeable debt is likely to try to take (garnish) your wages or other property to satisfy the judgment. But the creditor can't take it all. What was exempt during bankruptcy is still exempt. (Appendix 1 lists exempt property.) Nonetheless, the creditor can still request that 25% of your wages be taken out of each paycheck. If the debt was for child support or alimony, the creditor can take even more—up to 60% if you don't currently support anyone and up to 50% if you do. Those amounts may increase by 5% if you haven't paid child support in more than 12 weeks.

  Soon after the garnishment—or, in some states, before—the state court must notify you of the garnishment, what's exempt under your state's laws, and how you can protest. You can protest a garnishment if it isn't justified or causes you hardship. To protest, you'll have to file a document in the state court. That document goes by different names in different states. In New York, for example, it's called a Discharge of Attachment; in California, it's a Claim of Exemption. If you do protest, the state court must hold a hearing within a reasonable time, where you can present evidence as to why the court should not enforce the garnishment. The court may not agree, but it's certainly worth a try.

Protesting a wage garnishment is usually a relatively straightforward procedure. Because states are required to tell you how to proceed, you'll probably be able to handle it without the assistance of a lawyer.

Most states also have procedures for objecting to other types of property garnishments, such as a levy of a bank account. You'll have to do a bit of research at a law library to learn the exact protest procedure, which is generally similar to the one for protesting a wage garnishment. (See Ch. 10 for tips on doing your own research.)

Dealing With Difficult Debts After Bankruptcy

For some debts, such as taxes, child support, or alimony, exempt property may be taken and a garnishment protest will do little good. Don't be surprised if the U.S. Treasury Department garnishes nearly 100% of your wages to pay back federal income taxes. The best strategy here is to attempt to negotiate the amount down, not to fight the creditor's right to garnish in the first place.

Debt resources. For tips on "doing nothing," negotiating with your creditors, defending against a lawsuit, or protesting a garnishment, see *Solve Your Money Troubles: Get Debt Collectors Off Your Back & Regain Financial Freedom*, by Robin Leonard (Nolo). For specific help in dealing with tax debts, see *Stand Up to the IRS*, by Frederick W. Daily (Nolo).

D. Attempts to Collect Clearly Discharged Debts

If a creditor tries to collect a debt that clearly was discharged in your bankruptcy, you should respond at once with a letter like the one shown below. Again, you can assume a debt was discharged if you listed it in your bankruptcy papers, the creditor didn't successfully object to its discharge, and it doesn't fall into one of the

nondischargeable categories cited in Section C, above. Also, if yours was a no-asset case, you can assume the debt was discharged even if the debt wasn't listed. If you live in a community property state and your spouse filed alone, your share of the community debts is also discharged.

If a debt was discharged, the law prohibits creditors from filing a lawsuit, sending you collection letters, calling you, withholding credit, and threatening to file or actually filing a criminal complaint against you. (11 U.S.C. § 524.)

Letter to Creditor

1905 Fifth Road
N. Miami Beach, FL 35466

March 18, 20XX

Bank of Miami
2700 Finances Hwy
Miami, FL 36678

To Whom It May Concern:

I've been contacted once by letter and once by phone by Rodney Moore of your bank. Mr. Moore claims that I owe $4,812 on Visa account number 1234 567 890 123.

As you're well aware, this debt was discharged in bankruptcy on February 1, 20XX. Thus, your collection efforts violate federal law, 11 U.S.C. § 524. If they continue, I won't hesitate to pursue my legal rights, including bringing a lawsuit against you for harassment.

Sincerely,
Dawn Schaffer
Dawn Schaffer

If the collection efforts don't immediately stop, you'll likely need the assistance of a lawyer to write the creditor again and, if that doesn't work, to sue the creditor for harassment. If the creditor sues you over the debt, you'll want to raise the discharge as a defense and sue the creditor yourself to stop the illegal collection efforts. The court has the power to hold the creditor in contempt of court. The court may also fine the creditor for the humiliation, inconvenience, and anguish you suffered, and order the creditor to pay your attorneys' fees. (See, for example, *In re Barbour*, 77 B.R. 530 (E.D. N.C. 1987), where the court fined a creditor $900 for attempting to collect a discharged debt.)

You can bring a lawsuit to stop collection efforts in state court or in the bankruptcy court. Bankruptcy courts are often more familiar with the prohibitions against collection and may be more sympathetic to you. If the creditor sues you (almost certainly in state court), you or your attorney can file papers requesting that the case be transferred to the bankruptcy court.

E. Attempts to Revoke Your Discharge

In rare instances, a trustee or creditor may ask the bankruptcy court to revoke the discharge of *all* your debts. If the trustee or a creditor attempts to revoke your discharge, consult a bankruptcy attorney. (See Ch. 10 for tips on finding a lawyer.)

Your discharge can be revoked only if the creditor or trustee proves any of the following:

- You obtained the discharge through fraud that the trustee or creditor discovered after your discharge.
- You intentionally didn't tell the trustee that you acquired property from an inheritance, a divorce settlement, or a life insurance policy or death benefit plan within 180 days after you filed for bankruptcy.
- Before your case was closed, you refused to obey an order of the bankruptcy court or, for a reason other than the privilege against self-incrimination, you refused to answer an important question asked by the court.

For the court to revoke your discharge on the basis of fraud, the trustee or creditor must file a complaint within one year of your discharge. For the court to revoke your discharge on the basis of your fraudulent failure to report property or your refusal to obey an order or answer a question, the complaint must be filed either within one year of your discharge or before your case is closed, whichever is later. You're entitled to receive a copy of the complaint and to

respond, and the court must hold a hearing on the matter before deciding whether to revoke your discharge.

If your discharge is revoked, you'll owe your debts, just as if you'd never filed for bankruptcy. Any payment your creditors received from the trustee, however, will be credited against what you owe.

F. Post-Bankruptcy Discrimination

Although declaring bankruptcy has serious consequences, it might not be as bad as you think. There are laws that will protect you from most types of post-bankruptcy discrimination by the government and by private employers.

1. Government Discrimination

All federal, state, and local governmental units are prohibited from denying, revoking, suspending, or refusing to renew a license, permit, charter, franchise, or other similar grant solely because you filed for bankruptcy. (11 U.S.C. § 525(a).) This part of the Bankruptcy Code provides important protections, but it does not insulate debtors from all adverse consequences of filing for bankruptcy. Lenders, for example, can consider your bankruptcy filing when reviewing an application for a government loan or extension of credit. (See, for example, *Watts v. Pennsylvania Housing Finance Co.*, 876 F.2d 1090 (3rd Cir. 1989) and *Toth v. Michigan State Housing Development Authority*, 136 F.3d 477 (6th Cir. 1998).) Still, under this provision of the Bankruptcy Code, the government cannot use your bankruptcy as a reason to:

- deny you a job or fire you
- deny you or terminate your public benefits
- evict you from public housing (although if you have a Section 8 voucher, you may not be protected)
- deny you or refuse to renew your state liquor license
- withhold your college transcript
- deny you a driver's license, or
- deny you a contract, such as a contract for a construction project.

In addition, the Bankruptcy Code bars lenders from excluding you from government-guaranteed student loan programs. (11 U.S.C. §525(c).)

In general, once any government-related debt has been discharged, all acts against you that arise out of that debt also must end. If, for example, you lost your driver's license because you didn't pay a court judgment that resulted from a car accident, you must be granted a license once the debt is discharged. If your license was also suspended because you didn't have insurance, you may not get your license back until you meet the requirements set forth in your state's financial responsibility law.

If, however, the judgment wasn't discharged, you can still be denied your license until you pay up. If you and the government disagree about whether or not the debt was discharged, see Section C, above.

Keep in mind that only government denials based on your bankruptcy are prohibited. You may be denied a loan, job, or apartment for reasons unrelated to the bankruptcy. This includes denials for reasons related to your future creditworthiness—for example, because the government concludes you won't be able to repay a Small Business Administration loan.

2. Nongovernment Discrimination

Private employers may not fire you or otherwise discriminate against you solely because you filed for bankruptcy. (11 U.S.C. § 525(b).) While the Bankruptcy Act expressly prohibits employers from firing you, it is unclear whether the act prohibits employers from refusing to hire you because you went through bankruptcy.

Unfortunately, other forms of discrimination in the private sector aren't illegal. If you seek to rent an apartment and the landlord does a credit check, sees your bankruptcy, and refuses to rent to you, there's not much you can do other than try to show that you'll pay your rent and be a responsible tenant. It's often helpful if you can prepay your rent for a few months, or, if it is permitted under your state's laws, provide a bigger security deposit. (However, if you file for bankruptcy in the midst of a lease, your landlord cannot use this as grounds to evict you before the lease term is up.)

If a private employer refuses to hire you because of a poor credit history—not because you filed for bankruptcy—you may have little recourse.

If you suffer illegal discrimination because of your bankruptcy, you can sue in state court or in the bankruptcy court. You'll probably need the assistance of an attorney.

G. Rebuilding Credit

Although a bankruptcy filing can remain on your credit record for up to ten years after your discharge, you can probably rebuild your credit in about three years to the point that you won't be turned down for a major loan. Most creditors look for steady employment and a history, since bankruptcy, of making and paying for purchases on credit. And many creditors disregard a bankruptcy completely after about five years.

Rebuilding your credit. For more information on rebuilding your credit, see *Credit Repair*, by Robin Leonard (Nolo).

Should You Rebuild Your Credit?

Habitual overspending can be just as hard to overcome as excessive gambling or drinking. If you think you may be a compulsive spender, one of the worst things you might do is rebuild your credit. You need to get a handle on your spending habits, not give yourself more opportunities to indulge them.

Debtors Anonymous is a 12-step support program similar to Alcoholics Anonymous. It has programs nationwide. If a Debtors Anonymous group or a therapist recommends that you stay out of the credit system for a while, follow that advice. Even if you don't feel you're a compulsive spender, paying as you go may still be the best strategy.

Debtors Anonymous meets all over the country. Take a look at their website, which is extremely informative, at www.debtorsanonymous.org. To find a meeting near you, consult the website, call directory assistance, or send a self-addressed stamped envelope to Debtors Anonymous, General Services Board, P.O. Box 920888, Needham, MA 02492-0009. Or call and speak to a volunteer or leave a message at 781-453-2743.

1. Create a Budget

The first step to rebuilding your credit is to create a budget. Making a budget will help you control impulses to overspend and help you start saving money—an essential part of rebuilding your credit.

Before you put yourself on a budget that limits how much you spend, take some time to find out exactly how much money you spend right now. Write down every cent you spend for the next 30 days: 50¢ for the paper, $2 for your morning coffee and muffin, $5 for lunch, $3 for the bridge or tunnel toll, and so on. If you omit any money spent, your picture of how much you spend, and your budget, will be inaccurate.

At the end of the 30 days, review your ledger. Are you surprised? Are you impulsively buying things, or do you tend to buy the same types of things consistently? If the latter, you'll have an easier time planning a budget than if your spending varies tremendously from day to day.

Think about the changes you need to make to put away a few dollars at the end of every week. Even if you think there's nothing to spare, try to set a small goal—even $5 a week. It will help. If you spend $2 per day on coffee and a muffin, that adds up to $10 per week and at least $40 per month. Eating breakfast at home might save you most of that amount. If you buy the newspaper at the corner store every day, consider subscribing. A subscription doesn't involve extending credit; if you don't pay, they simply stop delivering.

Once you understand your spending habits and identify the changes you need to make, you're ready to make a budget. At the top of a sheet of paper, write down your monthly net income—that is, the amount you bring home after taxes and other mandatory deductions. At the left, list everything you spend money on in a month. Include any bank or other deposit accounts you use or plan to use for saving money and any nondischarged, reaffirmed, or other debts you make payments on. To the right of each item, write down the amount of money you spend, deposit, or pay each month. Finally, total up the amount. If it exceeds your monthly income, make some changes—by eliminating or reducing unnecessary expenditures—and start over. Once your budget is final, stick to it.

Avoiding Financial Problems

These nine rules, suggested by people who have been through bankruptcy, will help you stay out of financial hot water.

1. **Create a realistic budget and stick to it.**

2. **Don't buy on impulse.** When you see something you hadn't planned to purchase, go home and think it over. It's unlikely you'll decide to return to the store and buy it.

3. **Avoid sales.** Buying a $500 item on sale for $400 isn't a $100 savings if you didn't need the item in the first place.

4. **Get medical insurance.** Because you can't avoid medical emergencies, living without medical insurance is an invitation to financial ruin.

5. **Charge items only if you could pay for them now.** Don't charge based on future income—sometimes future income doesn't materialize.

6. **Avoid large house payments.** Obligate yourself only for what you can now afford and increase your mortgage payments only as your income increases. Again, don't obligate yourself based on future income that you might not have.

7. **Think long and hard before agreeing to cosign or guarantee a loan for someone.** Your signature obligates you as if you were the primary borrower. You can't be sure that the other person will pay.

8. **Avoid joint obligations with people who have questionable spending habits**—even your spouse or significant other. If you incur a joint debt, you're probably liable for it all if the other person defaults.

9. **Avoid high-risk investments,** such as speculative real estate, penny stocks, and junk bonds. Invest conservatively in things such as certificates of deposit, money market funds, and government bonds. And never invest more than you can afford to lose.

2. Keep Your Credit File Accurate

Rebuilding your credit requires you to keep incorrect information out of your credit file.

Start by obtaining a copy of your file from one of the "big three" credit reporting agencies:

- Equifax, P.O. Box 740241, Atlanta, GA 30374; 800-685-1111; www.equifax.com
- Experian, P.O. Box 2104, Allen, TX 75013-2104; 888-EXPERIAN; www.experian.com, and
- TransUnion, Consumer Disclosure Center, P.O. Box 2000, Chester, PA 19022; 800-888-4213; www.tuc.com.

You can request a report from one or more of these agencies by contacting the Annual Credit Report Request Service, P.O. Box 105281, Atlanta, GA 30348-5281; 877-322-8228; www.annualcreditreport.com.

You will need to provide your name and any previous names, addresses for the last two years, telephone number, year or date of birth, employer, and Social Security number.

You are entitled to a free copy of your credit report once a year, thanks to an amendment to the Fair Credit Reporting Act (FCRA). For more information, follow the links at www.ftc.gov.

You can also get a free copy of your report once a year if, within the past 60 days, you were denied credit based on something in your credit report. You are entitled to a free copy if you are on public assistance or if you're unemployed and planning to look for work in the next 60 days. In addition, you can have a free copy if you believe that your file contains errors due to identity theft (fraudulent use of your name, Social Security number, and so on). If you are not entitled to a free copy of your report, expect to pay no more than $9 for a copy from one of the credit-reporting bureaus.

Don't pay for a credit score. The credit bureau might offer to tell you your credit *score,* for a fee. You don't need that now. Your goal is to check your credit *report* to make sure the information in it is accurate.

In addition to your credit history, your credit report will tell you the sources of the information it contains and the names of people or institutions that have received your file within the last year, or within the last two years if they sought your file for employment reasons.

Credit files can contain negative information for up to seven years, except for bankruptcy filings, which can remain in your file for ten years. You will want to challenge outdated entries as well as incorrect or incomplete information. The bureau must investigate the accuracy of anything you challenge within 30 days, and either correct it or, if it can't verify the item, remove it.

If, after the investigation, the bureau keeps information in your file that you still believe is wrong, you are entitled to write a statement of up to 100 words giving your version, to be included in your file. Be sure the statement is tied to a particular item in your file. When the item eventually is removed from your file, the statement will be also. If you write a general "my life was a mess and I got into debt" statement, however, it will stay for a full seven years from the date you submit it, even if the negative items come out sooner. An example of a statement is shown below.

Letter to Credit Bureau

74 Ash Avenue
Hanover, NH 03222

March 18, 20xx

Credit Reporters of New England
4118 Main Blvd.
Manchester, NH 03101

To Whom It May Concern:

Your records show that I am unemployed. That's incorrect. I am a self-employed cabinetmaker and carpenter. I work out of my home and take orders from people who are referred to me through various sources. My work is known in the community and that's how I earn my living.

Sincerely,
Denny Porter
Denny Porter

Your statement, or a summary of it, must be given to anyone who receives your credit file. In addition, if you request it, the bureau must pass on a copy or summary of your statement to any person who received your report within the past year, or two years if your report was requested for employment-related reasons.

You also want to keep new negative information out of your file. To do this, remain current on your bills. What you owe, as well as how long it takes you to pay, will show up in that file.

In addition to information about credit accounts, credit reports also contain information from public records, including arrests and lawsuits.

After receiving your bankruptcy discharge, be sure to modify public records to reflect what occurred in the bankruptcy, so wrong information won't appear in your credit file. For example, if a court case was pending against you at the time you filed for bankruptcy and, as part of the bankruptcy, the potential judgment against you was discharged, be sure the court case is formally dismissed. You may need the help of an attorney. (See Ch. 10 for information on finding a lawyer.)

Avoid Credit Repair Agencies

You've probably seen ads for companies that claim they can fix your credit, qualify you for a loan, and get you a credit card. Stay clear of these companies. Their practices are almost always deceptive and sometimes illegal. Some steal the credit files or Social Security numbers of people who have died or live in places like Guam or the U.S. Virgin Islands, and then replace your file with these other files. Others create new identities for debtors by applying to the IRS for a taxpayer I.D. number and telling debtors to use it in place of their Social Security number.

But even the legitimate companies can't do anything for you that you can't do yourself. If items in your credit file are correct, these companies cannot get them removed. About the only difference between using a legitimate credit repair agency and doing it yourself is the money you will save by going it alone.

3. Negotiate With Some Creditors

If you owe any debts that show up as past due on your credit file (perhaps the debt wasn't discharged in bankruptcy, was reaffirmed in bankruptcy, or was incurred after you filed), you can take steps to make them current. Contact the creditor and ask that the item be removed in exchange for either full or partial payment. On a revolving account (such as a department store), ask the creditor to "re-age" the account—that is, to make the current month the first repayment month and show no late payments on the account.

4. Stabilize Your Income and Employment

Your credit history is not the only thing lenders will consider in deciding whether to give you credit. They also look carefully at the stability of your income and employment. Plus, if you start getting new credit before you're back on your feet financially, you'll end up in the same mess that led you to file for bankruptcy in the first place.

5. Get a Credit Card

Once you have your budget and some money saved, you can begin to get some positive information in your credit file. One way to do this is by getting a secured credit card.

Some banks will give you a credit card and a line of credit if you deposit money into a savings account. In exchange, you cannot remove the money from your account. Because it's difficult to guarantee a hotel reservation or rent a car without presenting at least one major credit card, get such a card if you truly believe you'll control any impulses to overuse—or even use—it.

Another reason to have these cards is that, in a few years, banks and other large creditors will be more apt to grant you credit if, since your bankruptcy, you've made and paid for purchases on credit. A major drawback with these cards, however, is that they often have extremely high interest rates. So use the card only to buy inexpensive items you can pay for when the bill arrives. Otherwise, you're going to pay a bundle in interest and may end up back in financial trouble.

Be sure to shop around before signing up for a secured credit card. Even though you just filed for bankruptcy, you'll probably still get lots of offers for unsecured cards in the mail. Often, these cards have better terms than do secured cards. If you do choose a secured credit card, be sure it isn't secured by your home.

⚠️ **Avoid credit card look-alikes.** Some cards allow you to make purchases only from the issuing company's own catalogues. The items in the catalogue tend to be overpriced and of mediocre quality. And your use of the card isn't reported to credit bureaus, so you won't be rebuilding your credit.

6. Work With a Local Merchant

Another step to consider in rebuilding your credit is to approach a local merchant (such as a jewelry or furniture store) about purchasing an item on credit. Many local stores will work with you in setting up a payment schedule, but be prepared to put down a deposit of up to 30%, pay a high rate of interest, or find someone to cosign the loan.

7. Borrow From a Bank

Bank loans provide an excellent way to rebuild credit. A few banks offer something called a passbook savings loan. But, in most cases, you'll have to apply for a standard bank loan. You probably won't qualify for a standard bank loan unless you bring in a cosigner, offer some property as collateral, or agree to a very high rate of interest.

The amount you can borrow will depend on how much the bank requires you to deposit (in the case of a passbook loan) or its general loan term limits.

Banks that offer passbook loans typically give you one to three years to repay the loan. But don't pay the loan back too soon—give it about six to nine months to appear on your credit file. Standard bank loans are paid back on a monthly schedule.

Before you take out any loan, be sure to understand the terms:

- **Interest rate.** The interest rate on your loan will probably be between two and six percentage points more than what the bank charges its customers with the best credit.
- **Prepayment penalties.** Usually, you can pay the loan back as soon as you want without incurring any prepayment penalties. Prepayment penalties are fees banks sometimes charge if you pay back a loan early and the bank doesn't collect as much interest from you as it had expected. The penalty is usually a small percentage of the loan amount.
- **Whether the bank reports the loan to a credit bureau.** This is key; the whole reason you want to take out the loan is to rebuild your credit, which means you want the loan to appear in your file. You may have to make several calls to find a bank that reports the loan. ■

Which Debts Are Discharged

Not all debts can be discharged in a Chapter 7 bankruptcy. Some debts survive the bankruptcy process—they remain valid and collectable, just as they were before you filed for bankruptcy. To understand exactly what bankruptcy will do for you, you need to know which, if any, of your debts you will still owe after your bankruptcy case is over.

When granting your final discharge, the bankruptcy court won't specify which of your debts have been discharged. Instead, you'll receive a nonspecific form from the court stating that you have received a discharge. (A copy is in Ch. 7, Section A.) This chapter helps you figure out exactly which of your debts are discharged, and which debts may survive.

Here's the lay of the land:

- Certain kinds of debts are always discharged in bankruptcy, except in rare circumstances. These debts are covered in Section A, below.
- Nine types of debts are never discharged in bankruptcy. Section B1, below, covers these debts.
- Student loan and income tax debts are not discharged unless you can prove that your situation is an exception to the rule. For more information, see Section B2, below.
- Four types of debts are discharged unless the creditor comes to court and successfully objects to the discharge. These debts are covered in Section B3, below.

Debts Your Creditors Claim Are Nondischargeable

Some of your creditors may claim that the debts you owe them cannot be wiped out in bankruptcy. For example, computer leases—for software and hardware—often contain clauses stating that if you're unable to complete the lease period, you can't eliminate the balance of the debt in bankruptcy.

Don't fall for these arguments. The only debts you can't discharge in bankruptcy are the ones specifically listed in the Bankruptcy Code as nondischargeable—and we'll describe them in this chapter. Don't let your creditors intimidate you into thinking otherwise.

A. Debts That Will Be Discharged in Bankruptcy

Certain types of debts will be discharged—that is, you will no longer be responsible for repaying them—when you receive your Chapter 7 discharge. The bankruptcy trustee will divide your nonexempt assets (if you have any) among your creditors, then the court will discharge any amount that remains unpaid at the end of your case.

1. Credit Card Debts

Without a doubt, the vast majority of those who file for bankruptcy are trying to get rid of credit card debts. Happily for these filers, most bankruptcies succeed in this mission. With a few rare exceptions for cases involving fraud or luxury purchases immediately prior to your bankruptcy (outlined in Section B, below), you can expect to get rid of your credit card debt by filing for bankruptcy.

2. Medical Bills

Many people who file for bankruptcy got into financial trouble because of medical bills. Some 40 million Americans have no medical insurance or other access to affordable medical care and must rely on emergency rooms for their primary care. Many more millions of working Americans either have inadequate insurance from their employer or can't afford the plans that are available to them.

Luckily, bankruptcy provides an out: Your medical bills will be discharged at the end of your bankruptcy case. In fact, billions of dollars in medical bills are discharged in bankruptcy every year.

3. Lawsuit Judgments

Most civil court cases are about money. If someone wins one of these lawsuits against you, the court issues a judgment ordering you to pay. If you don't come up with the money voluntarily, the judgment holder is entitled to collect it by, for example, grabbing your bank account, levying your wages, or placing a lien on your home.

Money judgments are almost always dischargeable in bankruptcy, regardless of the facts that led to the lawsuit in the first place. There are a couple of exceptions (discussed in Section B, below), but in the vast majority of cases, money judgments are discharged. Even liens on your home arising from a court money judgment can be cancelled if they interfere with your homestead exemption. (See Ch. 6 for more on how bankruptcy affects a judicial lien on your home.)

4. Obligations Under Leases and Contracts

Increasingly in our society, things are leased rather than owned. And most leases have severe penalty clauses that kick in if, for some reason, you are unable to make the monthly payment or do whatever else the lease requires you to do.

Some debtors also have obligations under a contract, such as a contract to sell real estate, buy a business, deliver merchandise, or perform in a play. The other party may want to force you to hold up your end of the deal, even if you don't want (or are unable) to, and sue you for breach of contract damages.

Obligations and liabilities under these types of agreements can also be discharged in bankruptcy. Almost always, filing for bankruptcy will convert your lease or contractual obligation into a dischargeable debt—unless the trustee believes the lease or contract will produce money to pay your unsecured creditors or the court finds that you've filed for bankruptcy precisely for the purpose of getting out of a personal services contract (such as a recording contract).

5. Personal Loans and Promissory Notes

Money you borrow in exchange for a promissory note (or even a handshake and an oral promise to pay the money back) is almost always dischargeable in bankruptcy. As with any debt, however, the court may refuse to discharge a loan debt if the creditor can prove that you acted fraudulently. (See Section B3, below.) But that almost never happens.

6. Other Obligations

The sections above outline the most common debts that are discharged in bankruptcy, but this isn't an exhaustive list. Any obligation or debt will be discharged unless it fits within one of the exceptions discussed in Section B, below.

B. Debts That Survive Chapter 7 Bankruptcy

Under bankruptcy law, there are several categories of debt that are "not dischargeable" in Chapter 7 (that is, you will still owe them after your bankruptcy is final):

- Some debts can't be discharged under any circumstances (see Subsection 1, below).
- Some will not be discharged unless you convince the court that the debts fit within a narrow exception to the rule (see Subsection 2, below).
- Some will not be discharged, but only if the creditor convinces the court that they shouldn't be (see Subsection 3, below).

Are Secured Debts Dischargeable?

Some types of secured debts are contractually linked to specific items of property, called collateral. If you don't pay the debt, the creditor can take the collateral. The most common secured debts include loans for cars and homes. If you have a debt secured by collateral, bankruptcy eliminates your personal liability for the underlying debt—that is, the creditor can't sue you to collect the debt itself. But bankruptcy doesn't eliminate the creditor's hold, or "lien," on the property that served as collateral under the contract. Other types of secured debts arise involuntarily, often as a result of a lawsuit judgment or an enforcement action by the IRS on taxes that are old enough to be discharged (see Section 2, below). In these cases, too, bankruptcy gets rid of the underlying debt, but may not eliminate a lien placed on your property by the IRS or a judgment creditor.

Chapter 7 bankruptcy offers several options for dealing with secured debts, ranging from buying the property from the creditor for its replacement value, reaffirming the contract, or surrendering the property. Secured debts and options for dealing with them are discussed in Ch. 5.

1. Debts Not Dischargeable Under Any Circumstances

There are certain debts that bankruptcy doesn't affect at all: You will continue to owe them just as if you had never filed.

a. Domestic Support Obligations

Debts defined as "domestic support obligations" are not dischargeable. Domestic support obligations are child support, alimony, and any other debt that is in the nature of alimony, maintenance, or support. For example, one spouse may have agreed to pay some of the other spouse's or the children's future living expenses (shelter, clothing, health insurance, and transportation) in exchange for a lower support obligation. The obligation to pay future living expenses may be treated as support owed to the other spouse (and considered nondischargeable), even though no court ordered it.

To be nondischargeable under this section, a domestic support obligation must have been established—or must be capable of becoming established—in:

- a separation agreement, divorce decree, or property settlement agreement
- an order of a court that the law authorizes to impose support obligations, or
- a determination by a child support enforcement agency (or other government unit) that is legally authorized to impose support obligations.

A support obligation that has been assigned to a private entity for reasons other than collection (for example, as collateral for a loan) is dischargeable. This exception rarely applies, however: Almost all assignments of support to government or private entities are made for the purpose of collecting the support.

b. Other Debts Owed to a Spouse, Former Spouse, or Child

Under the old bankruptcy law, debts owed to a spouse or child, other than support that arose from a divorce or separation, were discharged unless the spouse or child appeared in court to contest the debt. Under the new bankruptcy law, this category of debt is now automatically nondischargeable. The most common

of these types of debts is when one spouse agrees to assume responsibility for marital debt or promises to pay the other spouse in exchange for his or her share of the family home. These types of obligations will now be nondischargeable if they are owed to a spouse, former spouse, or child, and arose out of "a divorce or separation or in connection with a separation agreement, divorce decree, or other order of a court or record, or a determination made in accordance with State or territorial law by a governmental unit." (11 U. S.C. Section 523 (15).)

Note that this rule doesn't apply to debts arising from a separation agreement between domestic partners. This is one example of many as to why civil unions do not provide the same benefits as marriage.

c. Fines, Penalties, and Restitution

You can't discharge fines, penalties, or restitution that a federal, state, or local government has imposed to punish you for violating a law. Examples include:

- fines or penalties imposed under federal election law
- fines for infractions, misdemeanors, or felonies
- fines imposed by a judge for contempt of court
- fines imposed by a government agency for violating agency regulations
- surcharges imposed by a court or agency for enforcement of a law, and
- restitution you are ordered to pay to victims in federal criminal cases.

d. Certain Tax Debts

While regular income tax debts are dischargeable if they are old enough and meet some other requirements (see Section 2, below), other types of taxes are frequently not dischargeable. The specific rules depend on the type of tax.

Fraudulent income taxes. You cannot discharge debts for income taxes if you didn't file a return or you were intentionally avoiding your tax obligations. Returns filed on your behalf by the IRS are not considered returns and therefore don't make you eligible for a discharge of income tax debt.

Property taxes. Property taxes aren't dischargeable unless they became due more than a year before you file for bankruptcy. Even if your personal liability to pay the property tax is discharged, however, the tax lien on your property will remain. From a practical standpoint, this discharge won't help you much, because you'll have to pay off the lien before you can transfer the property with clear title. In fact, you may even face a foreclosure action by the property tax creditor if you take too long to come up with the money.

Other taxes. Other types of taxes that aren't dischargeable are mostly business related: payroll taxes, excise taxes, and customs duties. Sales, use, and poll taxes are also probably not dischargeable.

Get help for business tax debts. If you owe any of these nondischargeable tax debts, see a bankruptcy attorney before you file.

e. Court Fees

If you are a prisoner, you can't discharge a fee imposed by a court for filing a case, motion, complaint, or appeal, or for other costs and expenses assessed for that court filing, even if you claimed that you were unable to afford the fees. (You can discharge these types of fees in Chapter 13, however.)

f. Intoxicated Driving Debts

If you kill or injure someone while you are driving and are illegally intoxicated by alcohol or drugs, any debts resulting from the incident aren't dischargeable. Even if a judge or jury finds you liable but doesn't specifically find that you were intoxicated, the debt may still be nondischargeable. The judgment against you won't be discharged if the bankruptcy court (or a state court in a judgment collection action) determines that you were, in fact, intoxicated.

Note that this rule applies only to personal injuries: Debts for property damage resulting from your intoxicated driving are dischargeable.

EXAMPLE: Christopher was in a car accident in which he injured Ellen and damaged her car. He was convicted of driving under the influence. Several months later, Christopher filed for bankruptcy and listed Ellen as a creditor. After the bankruptcy case was over, Ellen sued Christopher, claiming that the debt wasn't discharged because Christopher

was driving while intoxicated. If Ellen shows that Christopher was illegally intoxicated under his state's laws, she will be able to pursue her personal injury claim against him. She doesn't have to file anything in the bankruptcy proceeding. She is barred, however, from trying to collect for the damage to her car.

g. Condominium, Cooperative, and Homeowners' Association Fees

You cannot discharge fees assessed after your bankruptcy filing date by a membership association for a condominium, housing cooperative, or lot in a homeownership association if you or the trustee have an ownership interest in the condominium, cooperative, or lot. As a practical matter, this means that any fees that become due after you file for Chapter 7 bankruptcy will survive the bankruptcy, but fees you owed prior to filing will be discharged.

h. Debts for Loans From a Retirement Plan

If you've borrowed from your 401(k) or other retirement plan that is qualified under IRS rules for tax-deferred status, you'll be stuck with that debt. (You can, however, discharge a loan from a retirement plan in Chapter 13.)

i. Debts You Couldn't Discharge in a Previous Bankruptcy

If a bankruptcy court dismissed a previous bankruptcy case because of your fraud or other bad acts (for instance, misfeasance or failure to cooperate with the trustee), you cannot discharge any debts that you tried to discharge in that earlier bankruptcy. (This rule doesn't affect debts you incurred after filing the earlier bankruptcy case.)

EXAMPLE: You filed for Chapter 7 bankruptcy in 2001, during a really rough time in your life. You had received a Chapter 7 discharge in 1998, which made you ineligible to file for Chapter 7 again before 2004, so you used a phony Social Security number when you filed in 2001. The court quickly discovered your ruse and dismissed your case. Luckily for you, you were not prosecuted for fraud. In 2007, you want to file a Chapter 7 case again. You can, because eight years have passed since you received your 1998 discharge. Because of your dishonesty, however, you won't be able to discharge any of the debts you listed in your 2001 case.

2. Debts Not Dischargeable Unless You Can Prove That an Exception Applies

Some debts cannot be discharged in Chapter 7 unless you show the bankruptcy court that the debt really is dischargeable because it falls within an exception. To get a debt in one of these categories discharged, you can take one of two courses of action:

- While your case is open, ask the bankruptcy court to rule that the debt should be discharged. To do this, you have to file and serve a Complaint to Determine Dischargeability of a Debt and then show, in court, that your debt isn't covered by the general rule. (The grounds and procedures for getting such debts discharged are discussed in Section C, below.) If you succeed, the court will rule that the debt is discharged, and the creditor won't be allowed to collect it after bankruptcy.

- In the alternative, you may decide not to take any action during your bankruptcy. If the creditor attempts to collect after your case is closed, you can try to reopen your bankruptcy and raise the issue then (by bringing a contempt motion or by filing a Complaint to Determine Dischargeability). Or, you can wait until the creditor sues you over the debt (or, if you've already lost a lawsuit, until the creditor tries to collect on the judgment), then argue in state court that the debt has been discharged.

The advantage of not raising the issue in the bankruptcy court is that you avoid the hassle of litigating the issue. And the problem may never come up again if the creditor doesn't sue you. The down side to this strategy is that questions about whether the debt has been discharged will be left hanging over your head after the bankruptcy case is over.

As a general rule, you are better off litigating issues of dischargeability in the bankruptcy court—either during or after your bankruptcy—because bankruptcy courts tend to tilt in the interest of giving the debtor a fresh start, and may be more willing to give you the benefit of the doubt.

If your creditor is a federal or state taxing agency or a student loan creditor, you are probably better off raising the issue during your bankruptcy. However, you might be better off not raising the issue in your bankruptcy case if you're up against an individual creditor whose claim is not big enough to justify hiring a lawyer. These creditors are probably less likely to pursue you—or even know that they can—after your bankruptcy is over.

a. Student Loans

Under the old law, student loans made by nonprofit organizations were not dischargeable unless the debtor could show undue hardship. Under the new law, this rule extends to virtually all student loans, whether made by nonprofit or commercial entities.

Specifically, in addition to loans provided by a nonprofit or government institution, the new law provides that any other "qualified educational loan" (as defined by the Internal Revenue Code) will not be discharged in bankruptcy unless the debtor shows undue hardship. The Internal Revenue Code (Section 221(d)(1) defines a qualified educational loan as:

"any indebtedness incurred by the taxpayer solely to pay qualified higher education expenses—

(A) which are incurred on behalf of the taxpayer, the taxpayer's spouse, or any dependent of the taxpayer as of the time the indebtedness was incurred,

(B) which are paid or incurred within a reasonable period of time before or after the indebtedness is incurred, and

(C) which are attributable to education furnished during a period during which the recipient was an eligible student.

Such term includes indebtedness used to refinance indebtedness which qualifies as a qualified education loan."

There may be some legal developments as courts interpret this new language, but generally it means that just about any type of debt incurred for higher education expenses will be nondischargeable absent undue hardship.

To discharge your student loan on the basis of undue hardship, you must file a separate action in the bankruptcy court (Complaint to Determine Dischargeability) and obtain a court ruling in your favor on this issue. An action to discharge a student loan debt typically requires the services of an attorney, although it's possible to do it yourself if you're willing to put in the time. (See Section C, below.)

In determining undue hardship, most bankruptcy courts look at three factors listed below. The main case establishing the three-factor approach is *Brunner v. New York State Higher Education Services Inc.,* 46 B.R. 752 (S.D. N.Y. 1985), aff'd, 831 F.2d 395 (2nd Cir. 1987). If you can show that all three factors are present, the court is likely to grant you an undue hardship discharge of your student loan. These factors are:

- **Poverty.** Based on your current income and expenses, you cannot maintain a minimal living standard and repay the loan. The court must consider your current and future employment and income (or employment and income potential), education, and skills; the marketability of your skills; and your health and family support obligations.
- **Persistence.** It is not enough that you can't currently pay your loan. You must also demonstrate to the court that your current financial condition is likely to continue for a significant portion of the repayment period.
- **Good faith.** You must prove to the court that you've made a good-faith effort to repay your debt. Someone who files for bankruptcy immediately after getting out of school or after the period for paying back the loan begins will not fall into good favor with the court. Nor will someone who hasn't looked extensively for employment. And, if you haven't made any payments, you should be able to show the court that you thought enough of your obligation to obtain a deferment or forbearance.

Courts have rarely allowed student loans to be discharged. They take the position that Congress wants student loans to be repaid, absent exceptional circumstances. Courts also recognize that federal student loan regulations require a lot of flexibility on the creditor's part, including moratoriums on payments, temporary reductions in payments, and extensions of the repayment period that lower the monthly payments to an affordable amount. These options give debtors other ways (short of filing for bankruptcy) to seek relief from student loan debt. However, because the new law makes virtually all student loans nondischargeable, including commercial loans with conventional repayment terms (and without much flexibility for the debtor), courts may not be as willing to assume that the debtor had other options.

In some cases, courts have found that it would be an undue hardship to repay the entire loan and relieved the debtor of a portion of the debt. Other courts take the position that it's an all-or-nothing proposition—either the entire loan is discharged or none of it is discharged. Ask a local bankruptcy attorney how courts in your area handle student loans.

Special Rules for HEAL and PLUS Loans

The federal Health Education Assistance Loans (HEAL) Act, not bankruptcy law, governs HEAL loans. Under the HEAL Act, to discharge a loan, you must show that the loan became due more than seven years ago, and that repaying it would not merely be a hardship, but would impose an "unconscionable burden" on your life.

Parents can get Parental Loans for Students (PLUS Loans) to finance a child's education. Even though the parent does not receive the education, the loan is treated like any other student loan if the parent files for bankruptcy. The parents must meet the undue hardship test to discharge the loan.

Getting Your Transcript

If you don't pay back loans obtained directly from your college, the school can withhold your transcript. But if you file for bankruptcy and receive a discharge of the loan, the school can no longer withhold your records. (*In re Gustafson,* 111 B.R. 282 (9th Cir. BAP 1990).) In addition, while your bankruptcy case is pending, the school cannot withhold your transcript, even if the court eventually rules your school loan nondischargeable. (*Loyola University v. McClarty,* 234 B.R. 386 (E.D. La. 1999).)

b. Regular Income Taxes

People who are considering bankruptcy because of tax problems are almost always concerned about income taxes they owe to the IRS or the state equivalent. There is a myth afoot that income tax debts can never be discharged in bankruptcy. This is not true, however, if the debt is relatively old and you can meet several other conditions. Tax debts that qualify under these rules are technically discharged; however, you may have to go to court (by filing a complaint to determine dischargeability of the debt) and have the judge order the IRS to honor the discharge.

Income tax debts are dischargeable if you meet all of these conditions:

- You filed a legitimate (nonfraudulent) tax return for the tax year or years in question. If the IRS completes a Substitute for Return on your behalf that you neither sign nor consent to, your return is not considered filed. (See *In re Bergstrom,* 949 F.2d 341 (10th Cir. 1991).)
- The liability you wish to discharge is for a tax return (not a Substitute for Return) that you actually filed at least two years before you filed for bankruptcy.
- The tax return for the liability you wish to discharge was due at least three years before you filed for bankruptcy.
- The IRS has not assessed your liability for the taxes within the 240 days (eight months) before you filed for bankruptcy. You're probably safe if you do not receive a formal notice of assessment of federal taxes from the IRS within that 240-day period. If you're unsure of the assessment date, consider seeing a tax lawyer—but don't rely on the IRS for the date. If the IRS gives you the wrong date—telling you that the 240 days have elapsed—the IRS won't be held to it if it turns out to be wrong. See, for example, *In re Howell,* 120 B.R. 137 (9th Cir. BAP 1990). Under the new bankruptcy law, the 240-day period is extended by the period of time collections were suspended because you were negotiating with the IRS for an offer in compromise or because of a previous bankruptcy.

EXAMPLE: Fred filed a tax return in August 2003 for the 2002 tax year. In March 2005, the IRS audited Fred's 2002 return and assessed a tax due of $8,000. In May 2006, Fred files for bankruptcy. The taxes that Fred wishes to discharge were for tax year 2002. The return for those taxes was due on April 15, 2003, more than three years prior to Fred's filing date. The tax return was filed in August 2003, more than two years before Fred's bankruptcy filing date, and the assessment date of March 2005 was more than 240 days before the filing date. Fred can discharge those taxes.

If you meet each of these four requirements, your personal liability for the taxes should be discharged. However, any lien placed on your property by the taxing authority will remain after your bankruptcy. The result is that the taxing authority can't go after your bank account or wages, but you'll have to pay off the lien before you can sell your real estate with a clear title.

Penalties on taxes that are dischargeable are also dischargeable. If the underlying tax debt is nondischargeable, courts are split as to whether you can discharge the penalties or not.

EXAMPLE: Jill failed to file a tax return for 1999. In 2004, the IRS discovers Jill's failure and in January 2005 assesses taxes of $5,000 and penalties and interest of $12,000. Jill files for bankruptcy in January 2006. Because Jill didn't file a return for 1999, she can't discharge the tax, even though it became due more than three years past (and more than 240 days have elapsed since the taxes were assessed). Jill may be able to discharge the IRS penalties for failure to file a tax return and failure to pay the tax. Or course, the IRS is likely to argue that she cannot discharge the penalties, and some courts will agree.

⚠ **Debts incurred to pay nondischargeable taxes will also be nondischargeable.** If you borrowed money or used your credit card to pay taxes that would otherwise not be discharged, you can't eliminate that loan or credit card debt in a Chapter 7 bankruptcy. In other words, you can't turn a nondischargeable tax debt into a dischargeable tax debt by paying it on your credit card. This is true for any type of nondischargeable tax owed to a governmental agency.

3. Debts Not Dischargeable in Bankruptcy If the Creditor Successfully Objects

Four types of debts may survive Chapter 7 bankruptcy if, and only if:

- the creditor files a formal objection—called a Complaint to Determine Dischargeability—during the bankruptcy proceedings, and
- the creditor proves that the debt fits into one of the categories discussed below.

Creditors might not bother to object. Even though bankruptcy rules give creditors the right to object to the discharge of certain debts, many creditors—and their attorneys—don't fully understand this right. Even a creditor who knows the score might sensibly decide to write off the debt rather than contesting it. It can cost a lot to bring a "dischargeability action" (as this type of case is known). If the debt isn't huge, a cost benefit analysis might show that it will be cheaper to forego collecting the debt than to fight about it in court.

a. Debts Arising From Fraud

In order for a creditor to prove that one of your debts should survive bankruptcy because you incurred it through fraud, the debt must fit one of the categories below.

Debts from intentionally fraudulent behavior. If a creditor can show that a debt arose because of your dishonest act, and that the debt wouldn't have arisen had you been honest, the court probably will not let you discharge the debt. Here are some common examples:

- You wrote a check for something and stopped payment on it, even though you kept the item.
- You wrote a check against insufficient funds but assured the merchant that the check was good.
- You rented or borrowed an expensive item and claimed it was yours, in order to use it as collateral to get a loan.
- You got a loan by telling the lender you'd pay it back, when you had no intention of doing so.

For this type of debt to be nondischargeable, your deceit must be intentional, and the creditor must have relied on your deceit in extending credit. Again, these are facts that the creditor has to prove before the debt will be ruled nondischargeable by the court.

Debts from a false written statement about your financial condition. If a creditor proves that you incurred a debt by making a false written statement, the debt isn't dischargeable. Here are the rules:

- The false statement must be written—for instance, made in a credit application, rental application, or resume.
- The false statement must have been "material"— that is, it was a potentially significant factor in the creditor's decision to extend you credit. The two most common materially false statements are omitting debts and overstating income.
- The false statement must relate to your financial condition or the financial condition of an "insider"—a person close to you or a business entity with which you're associated.
- The creditor must have relied on the false statement, and the reliance must have been reasonable.
- You must have intended to deceive the creditor. This is extremely hard for the creditor to prove based simply on your behavior. The creditor would have to show outrageous behavior on your part, such as adding a "0" to your income (claiming you make $180,000 rather than $18,000) on a credit application.

Recent debts for luxuries. If you run up more than $500 in debt to any one creditor for luxury goods or services within the 90 days before you file for bankruptcy, the law presumes that your intent was fraudulent regarding those charges; all the charges will survive your bankruptcy unless you prove that your intent wasn't fraudulent. The term "luxury goods and services" does not include things that are reasonably necessary for the support and maintenance of you and your dependents (what that means will be decided on a case-by-case basis).

Recent cash advances. If you get cash advances from any one creditor totaling more than $750 under an open-ended consumer credit plan within the 70 days before you file for bankruptcy, the debt is nondischargeable. "Open-ended" means there's no date when the debt must be repaid, but rather, as with most credit cards, you may take forever to repay the debt as long as you pay a minimum amount each month.

b. Debts Arising From Debtor's Willful and Malicious Acts

If the act that caused the debt was willful *and* malicious (that is, you intended to inflict a specific injury to person or property), the debt isn't dischargeable if the creditor successfully objects. However, for reasons probably related to ignorance of their rights, creditors don't often object in this situation.

Generally, crimes involving the intentional injury to people or damage to property are considered willful and malicious acts. Examples are assaults, rape, intentionally setting fire to a house (arson), or vandalism.

Your liability for the personal injury or property damage to the victim sustained in these types of cases will almost always be ruled nondischargeable—but (once again) only if the victim-creditor objects during your bankruptcy case. Other acts that would typically be considered to be willful and malicious include:

- kidnapping
- deliberately causing extreme anxiety, fear, or shock
- libel or slander, and
- illegal acts by a landlord to evict a tenant, such as removing a door or changing the locks.

c. Debts From Embezzlement, Larceny, or Breach of Fiduciary Duty

A debt incurred as a result of embezzlement, larceny, or breach of fiduciary duty is not dischargeable if the creditor successfully objects to its discharge.

"Embezzlement" means taking property entrusted to you for another and using it for yourself. "Larceny" is another word for theft. "Breach of fiduciary duty" is the failure to live up to a duty of trust you owe someone, based on a relationship where you're required to manage property or money for another, or where your relationship is a close and confidential one. Common fiduciary relationships include those between:

- business partners
- attorney and client
- estate executor and beneficiary
- in-home caregiver and recipient of services
- guardian and ward, and
- husband and wife.

d. Debts or Creditors You Don't List

Bankruptcy requires you to list all of your creditors on your bankruptcy papers and provide their most current addresses. This gives the court some assurance that everyone who needs to know about your bankruptcy will receive notice. As long as you do your part, the debt will be discharged (as long as it's otherwise dischargeable under the rules), even if the official notice fails to reach the creditor for some reason beyond your control—for example, because the post office errs, or the creditor moves without leaving a forwarding address.

Suppose, however, that you forget to list a creditor on your bankruptcy papers or carelessly misstate a creditor's identity or address. In that situation, the court's notice may not reach the creditor and the debt may not be discharged. Here are the rules:

- If the creditor knew or should have known of your bankruptcy through other means, such as a letter or phone call from you, the debt will be discharged even though the creditor wasn't listed. In this situation, the creditor should have taken steps to protect its interests, even though it didn't receive formal notice from the court.
- If all of your assets are exempt—that is, you have a no-asset case—the debt will be discharged unless the debt is nondischargeable in any circumstances (see Section B1, above). In this situation, the creditor wouldn't have benefited from receiving notice, anyway, because there is no property to distribute. However, if the lack of notice deprives a creditor of the opportunity to successfully object to the discharge by filing a complaint in the bankruptcy court (such as for a fraudulent debt), the debt may survive your bankruptcy.

If an Unknown Creditor Pops Up After Bankruptcy

If a creditor comes out of the woodwork after your bankruptcy case is closed, you can always reopen your case, name the creditor, and then seek an amended discharge. (See Ch. 7 for more information.) If it's the kind of debt that will be discharged anyway, many courts won't let you reopen because there is no need to. The debt is discharged by law and most creditors know this. However, if the creditor continues to try to collect the debt, you can haul the creditor into the bankruptcy court on a contempt charge.

C. Disputes Over Dischargeability

If your debt falls into one of the categories described in Sections B2 or B3, above, there may be a dispute over whether the debt should be discharged. For example, if the debt is one that you have to prove should be discharged, you may have to file a complaint to determine dischargeability. Or, if the creditor must prove that the debt should not be discharged, you might have to defend yourself in court against the creditor's claims.

1. Complaints to Determine Dischargeability

If you want to have a student loan or tax debt wiped out, you will have to prove to the court that you meet all of the requirements for discharge. To do this, you must file a formal complaint with the bankruptcy court. Generally, you can file your complaint any time after you file for bankruptcy. Some courts may impose their own deadlines, however, so check your court's local rules.

Suppose, for example, that you want to have a student loan discharged. As discussed in Section B2, above, you will have to prove that it would be an undue hardship to repay the loan. You will file at least two forms: a complaint, stating the facts that make repayment an undue hardship, and a proof of service, showing that you served the complaint on the affected creditor and the trustee. We provide sample forms below; depending on your court's rules, you may have to file more or different forms. These are intended only to give you an idea of what this type of complaint might look like.

Get help from a lawyer, if you need it. Before you charge off into court, here is a heartfelt warning: Embarking upon federal litigation in the bankruptcy court can be quite a challenge if you don't have substantial coaching from someone who has experience in the field. At the very least, you'll want to obtain a copy of *Represent Yourself in Court* by Paul Bergman and Sarah Berman-Barrett (Nolo) and maybe consult with a bankruptcy lawyer from time to time to get your bearings. If your case is fairly straightforward—for example, a medical or similar condition is keeping you from working enough to pay your student loan—you may be able to proceed on your own. However, some people find it stressful or uncomfortable to discuss their own medical or other problems in court. If you think this might be difficult for you, consider filing your own bankruptcy and then hiring a lawyer to handle only this procedure.

Complaint to Determine Dischargeability of Student Loan

UNITED STATES BANKRUPTCY COURT

_____ DISTRICT OF _____

In re _____

[Set forth here all names including married, maiden, and trade names used by debtor within last 8 years]

_____ Debtor(s)

Address _____

Case No. _____

Chapter 7

Employer's Tax Identification (EIN) No(s). [if any]: _____

Last four digits of Social Security no(s). _____

COMPLAINT TO DETERMINE DISCHARGEABILITY OF STUDENT LOAN

1. Debtor(s) filed this case under Chapter 7 of the Bankruptcy Code on [insert the date you filed your petition]. This Court thus has jurisdiction over this action under 28 U.S.C. § 1334. This proceeding is a core proceeding.

2. One of the unsecured debts owing by the Debtor(s) and listed on Schedule F—Creditors Holding Unsecured Nonpriority Claims—is a student loan owing to [insert the name of the holder of your loan].

3. This loan was incurred to pay expenses at [insert the name of the school(s) you attended].

4. Based on the Debtor(s)' current income and expenses, the Debtor(s) cannot maintain a minimal living standard and repay off loan. [insert information about your current and future employment, your income and income potential, education, skills and the marketability of your skills, health, and family support obligations].

5. The Debtor(s)' current financial condition is likely to continue for a significant portion of the repayment period of the loan. [insert information about your health including any life-threatening, debilitating or chronic conditions you have].

6. The Debtor(s) have made a good-faith effort to repay their debt.

7. The Debtor(s) have filed for bankruptcy for reasons other than just to discharge their student loan.

Dated: _____   Debtor in Propria Persona

Dated: _____   Debtor in Propria Persona

repayment period of the loan. [insert explanation, such as information about your health including any life-threatening, debilitating, or chronic conditions you have].

6. The Debtor(s) have made a good-faith effort to repay their debt as follows: [insert information about your payment history or other attempts to pay back the loan].

7. The Debtor(s) have filed for bankruptcy for reasons other than just to discharge their student loan.

WHEREFORE, the Debtor(s) ask this court to enter an Order declaring the student loan debt to be dischargeable.

Dated: _____   Debtor in Propria Persona

Dated: _____   Debtor in Propria Persona

_____ Address

Proof of Service by Mail

UNITED STATES BANKRUPTCY COURT

_____ DISTRICT OF _____

In re _____

[Set forth here all names including married, maiden, and trade names used by debtor within last 8 years]

_____ Debtor(s)

Case No. _____

Chapter 7

Address _____

Employer's Tax Identification (EIN) No(s). [if any]: _____

Last four digits of Social Security no(s): _____

PROOF OF SERVICE BY MAIL

I, *[friend's name]*, declare that : I am a resident or employed in the County of *[the county where friend lives or works]*, State of *[state where friend lives or works]*. My residence/business address is *[friend's address]*. I am over the age of eighteen years and not a party to this case.

On *[leave blank]*, 20___. I served the Notice of Motion and Motion to Avoid Judicial Lien on *[creditor's name]*, by placing true and correct copies thereof enclosed in a sealed envelope with postage thereon fully prepaid in the United States Mail at *[city of post office where papers will be mailed]* address as follows:

[address of affected creditor's and trustee]

I declare under penalty of perjury that the foregoing is true and correct, and that this declaration was executed on.

Dated: _____*[leave blank]*_____, 20___ at _____*[leave blank]*_____
City and State

_____*[leave blank]*
Signature

2. Creditor Objections to Discharges

To object formally to the discharge of a debt, the creditor must file a document called a Complaint to Determine Dischargeability of a Debt. The creditor must give you and the trustee a copy of the complaint. To defend against the objection, you must file a written response within a specified time limit and be prepared to argue your case in court.

If the creditor's debt is one of the types that will be discharged unless the creditor objects, the creditor has the burden of proving that the debt fits within the specified category. For instance, if the creditor claims that the debt arose from a "willful and malicious injury" you caused, the creditor will have to prove that your actions were willful and malicious. Similarly, if the creditor is arguing that a particular debt arose from your fraudulent acts, the creditor will have to prove that all the required elements of fraud were present. Absent this proof, the bankruptcy court will reject the creditor's lawsuit and maybe even award you attorneys' fees (if you use an attorney).

Keep in mind, however, that if you plead guilty to a criminal charge involving fraud, a document from the court showing your conviction may be all that's necessary to convince the judge to rule the debt nondischargeable. A no-contest plea, on the other hand, would not have the same effect, because that type of plea can't be used as evidence in a later civil case (such as a bankruptcy case).

The fact that the creditor has the burden of proof doesn't mean that you should sit back and do nothing. You should be prepared with proof of your own to show that the creditor's allegations in the complaint are not true (unless, of course, you already admitted your guilt in a prior case by pleading guilty or being convicted after trial).

3. Objections on the Basis of Credit Card Fraud

Increasingly, the creditors most likely to object to the discharge of a debt are credit card issuers. Except for charges made shortly before filing for bankruptcy (see Section B3, above), there are few specific rules about what constitutes credit card fraud in bankruptcy. But courts are increasingly looking to the following factors to determine fraud:

- **Timing.** A short time between incurring the charges and filing for bankruptcy may suggest a fraudulent intent.
- **Manipulation of the system.** Incurring more debt after consulting an attorney may lead a judge to conclude that you ran up your debts in anticipation of your bankruptcy filing.
- **Amount.** As mentioned earlier, recent charges over $500 for luxuries will be presumed to be fraudulent.
- **Crafty use of the card.** Multiple charges under $50 (to avoid preclearance of the charge by the credit card issuer) when you've reached your credit limit will start to look a lot like fraud.
- **Deliberate misuse.** Charges after the card issuer has ordered you to return the card or sent several "past due" notices.
- **Last-minute sprees.** Charges in your pattern of use of the card (for instance, much travel after a sedentary life), charges for luxuries, and multiple charges on the same day.
- **Bad-faith use.** Charges made when you were clearly insolvent and wouldn't be able to make the required minimum payment (for instance, you had lost your job and had no other income or savings).

Banks claim that insolvency is evidenced by any of the following:

- A notation in the customer's file that the customer has met with an attorney (perhaps because the customer told the creditor he or she was considering bankruptcy and had talked to an attorney about it).
- A rapid increase in spending, followed by 60–90 days without activity.
- The date noted on any attorney's fee statement, if the customer consults a lawyer for help with a bankruptcy.

Of course, the mere fact that a creditor challenges your discharge of a credit card debt doesn't mean the creditor will win in court. In most of these cases, the creditor files a standard 15- to 20-paragraph form complaint, which states conclusions without supporting facts. The creditor rarely attaches statements for the account, but only a printout of the charges to which it is objecting.

Some very sophisticated debtors may be able to represent themselves in this type of case. If you decide to do this, you'll need lots of time to familiarize yourself with general litigation procedures and strategies, as well as the bankruptcy cases in your district that deal with this issue. Start by getting a copy of *Represent Yourself in Court*, by Paul Bergman and Sara Berman-Barrett (Nolo).

Consider getting help from a lawyer. Allegations of fraud should make you seriously consider consulting an attorney. If a creditor challenges discharge of a debt by claiming you engaged in fraud, but the judge finds in your favor, the judge may order the creditor to reimburse you for the money you spent on attorneys' fees.

Questions for Credit Card Companies

If you find yourself facing a dischargeability action over a credit card debt, you'll have an opportunity to send questions (called interrogatories) to the company, to be answered under oath. Here are some you might considering asking:

- You (the card issuer) have alleged that the debtor obtained funds from you by false pretenses and false representations. Please state with particularity the nature of the false pretenses and false representations.
- State all steps taken by you, the card issuer, to determine the creditworthiness of the debtor.
- Identify all means that you, the card issuer, used to verify the debtor's income, expenses, assets, or liabilities. Identify any documents obtained in the verification process.
- Identify your general policies concerning the decision to grant credit and how those policies were applied to the debtor.
- You have alleged that at the time the debtor obtained credit from you, the debtor did not intend to repay it. State all facts in your possession to support this allegation.

- Identify all credit policies you allege were violated by the debtor. State how such policies were communicated to the debtor, and identify all documents that contained those policies.
- Identify the dates on which you claim any of the following events occurred:
  - The debtor consulted a bankruptcy attorney.
  - The debtor had a reduction in income.
  - The debtor formed the intent not to repay this debt.
  - The debtor violated the terms of the credit agreement.
- State whether you believe that every user of a credit card who does not later repay the debt has committed fraud.
- If the answer to the preceding question is no, state all facts that give rise to fraud in this debtor's use of the card.

After receiving a list of questions like these, the credit card issuer is likely to conclude that you are serious about defending yourself. It might even withdraw its complaint

Research Tips

If you want to read cases supporting the debtor's position when a credit card issuer claims fraud, visit a law library (Ch. 10, Section D) or search the Internet for some of these cases:

- *In re Hearn,* 211 B.R. 774 (Bankr. N.D. Ga. 1997)
- *In re Etto,* 210 B.R. 734 (Bankr. N.D. Ohio 1997)
- *In re Hunter,* 210 B.R. 212 (Bankr. M.D. Fla. 1997)
- *In re Davis,* 176 B.R. 118 (Bankr. W.D. N.Y. 1994)
- *In re Kitzmiller,* 206 B.R. 424 (Bankr. N.D. W.Va. 1997)
- *In re Christensen,* 193 B.R. 863 (N.D. Ill. 1996)
- *In re Chinchilla,* 202 B.R. 1010 (Bankr. S.D. Fla. 1996)
- *In re Grayson,* 199 B.R. 397 (Bankr. W.D. Mo. 1996), and
- *In re Vianese,* 195 B.R. 572 (Bankr. N.D. N.Y. 1995).

An excellent resource that will help you sort out credit card discharge issues, should they arise in your case, is *Discharging Credit Card Debts in Bankruptcy,* by James P. Caher (LRP Publications). You can contact LRP Publications at: www.lrp.com, 800-341-7874 (phone), 215-784-9639 (fax), 215-658-0938 (TYY), or custserve@LRP.com (email). The cost of the book is about $30.

CHAPTER

10

Help Beyond the Book

Although this book covers routine bankruptcy procedures in some detail, it doesn't come close to covering everything. That would require a 1,000-page treatise, most of which would be irrelevant for nearly all readers. That said, here are some suggestions if you need more information or advice than this book provides.

The major places to go for follow-up help are:

- **Bankruptcy petition preparers.** When you're ready to file for bankruptcy, but need assistance in typing the forms and organizing them for filing in your district
- **Lawyers.** When you want information, advice, or legal representation, and
- **Law libraries and the Internet.** When you want to do your own research on issues raised in the course of your bankruptcy.

Before we discuss each of these resources in more detail, here's a general piece of advice: Maintain control of your case whenever possible. By getting this book and filing for Chapter 7 bankruptcy, you've taken responsibility for your own legal affairs. If you decide to get help from others, shop around until you find someone who respects your efforts as a self-helper and recognizes your right to participate in the case as a valuable partner.

A. Debt Relief Agencies

Under the new bankruptcy law, any person, business, or organization that you pay or otherwise compensate for help with your bankruptcy is considered a debt relief agency—and must identify itself as such. The two main types of debt relief agencies are lawyers and bankruptcy petition preparers (BPPs). Credit counseling agencies and budget counseling agencies are not debt relief agencies. Nor are any of the following:

- employers or employees of debt relief agencies (for instance, legal secretaries)
- nonprofit organizations that have federal 501(c)(3) tax-exempt status
- any creditor who works with you to restructure your debt
- banks, credit unions, and other deposit institutions, or
- an author, publisher, distributor, or seller of works subject to copyright protection when acting in that capacity (in other words, Nolo Press and the stores that sell its books aren't debt relief agencies).

BPPs and lawyers are covered separately in Sections B and C, below. This section explains what the new bankruptcy law requires of debt relief agencies generally, so you'll know what you can expect for your money.

1. Mandatory Contract

Within five days after a debt relief agency assists you, it (or he or she) must enter into a contract with you that explains, clearly and conspicuously:

- what services the agency will provide
- what the agency will charge for the services, and
- the terms of payment.

The agency must give you a copy of the completed, signed contract.

2. Mandatory Disclosures and Notices

Debt relief agencies must inform you, in writing, that:

- All information you are required to provide in your bankruptcy papers must be complete, accurate, and truthful.
- You must completely and accurately disclose your assets and liabilities in the documents you file to begin your case.
- You must undertake a reasonable inquiry to establish the replacement value of any item you plan to keep, before you provide that value on your forms.
- Your current monthly income, the amounts you provide in the means test, and your computation of projected disposable income (in a Chapter 13 case), as stated in your bankruptcy papers, must be based on a reasonable inquiry into their accuracy.
- Your case may be audited, and your failure to cooperate in the audit may result in dismissal of your case or some other sanction, including a possible criminal penalty.

In addition to these stark warnings—which most debt relief agencies would rather not have to give—a debt relief agency must also give you a general notice regarding some basic bankruptcy requirements and your options for help in filing and pursuing your case. Here is the notice that you can expect to receive from any debt relief agency within three business days after the agency first offers to provide you with services. Failure to give you this notice—in a timely manner—can land the agency in big trouble.

Sample Notice From Debt Relief Agency

IMPORTANT INFORMATION ABOUT BANKRUPTCY ASSISTANCE SERVICES FROM AN ATTORNEY OR BANKRUPTCY PETITION PREPARER.

If you decide to seek bankruptcy relief, you can represent yourself, you can hire an attorney to represent you, or you can get help in some localities from a bankruptcy petition preparer who is not an attorney. THE LAW REQUIRES AN ATTORNEY OR BANKRUPTCY PETITION PREPARER TO GIVE YOU A WRITTEN CONTRACT SPECIFYING WHAT THE ATTORNEY OR BANKRUPTCY PETITION PREPARER WILL DO FOR YOU AND HOW MUCH IT WILL COST. Ask to see the contract before you hire anyone.

The following information helps you understand what must be done in a routine bankruptcy case to help you evaluate how much service you need. Although bankruptcy can be complex, many cases are routine. Before filing a bankruptcy case, either you or your attorney should analyze your eligibility for different forms of debt relief available under the Bankruptcy Code and which form of relief is most likely to be beneficial for you. Be sure you understand the relief you can obtain and its limitations.

To file a bankruptcy case, documents called a Petition, Schedules and Statement of Financial Affairs, as well as in some cases a Statement of Intention need to be prepared correctly and filed with the bankruptcy court. You will have to pay a filing fee to the bankruptcy court. Once your case starts, you will have to attend the required first meeting of creditors where you may be questioned by your creditors.

If you choose to file a chapter 7 case, you may be asked by a creditor to reaffirm a debt. You may want help deciding whether to do so. A creditor is not permitted to coerce you into reaffirming your debts.

If you choose to file a chapter 13 case in which you repay your creditors what you can afford over 3 to 5 years, you may also want help with preparing your chapter 13 plan and with the confirmation hearing on your plan which will be before a bankruptcy judge.

If you select another type of relief under the Bankruptcy Code other than chapter 7 or chapter 13, you will want to find out what should be done from someone familiar with that type of relief.

Your bankruptcy case may also involve litigation. You are generally permitted to represent yourself in litigation in bankruptcy court, but only attorneys, not bankruptcy petition preparers, can give you legal advice.

Finally, every debt relief agency has to give you some plain-English written information about the basic tasks associated with most bankruptcies, such as how to deal with secured debts and choose exemptions. Ideally, debt relief agencies would freely distribute this book, which has all of the information required (and much more, of course).

3. Restrictions on Debt Relief Agencies

Under the new law, a debt relief agency may not:

- fail to perform any service that the agency informed you it would perform in connection with your bankruptcy case
- counsel you to make any statement in a document that is untrue and misleading or that the agency should have known was untrue or misleading, or
- advise you to incur more debt in order to pay for the agency's services (for instance, accepting a credit card or steering you to a cash advance business).

Any contract that doesn't comply with the new requirements on debt relief agencies may not be enforced against you. A debt relief agency is liable to you for costs and fees, including legal fees, if the agency negligently or intentionally:

- fails to comply with the new law's restrictions on debt relief agencies, or
- fails to file a document that results in dismissal of your case or conversion to another bankruptcy chapter.

In sum, debt relief agencies are on the hook if they are negligent in performing the services required by the bankruptcy law or other services they have agreed to provide.

B. Bankruptcy Petition Preparers

Even though you should be able to handle routine bankruptcy procedures yourself, you may want someone familiar with the bankruptcy forms and courts in your area to use a computer to enter your data in the official forms and print them out for filing with the court. For this level of assistance—routine form preparation and organization—consider using a bankruptcy petition preparer (BPP).

1. What a Bankruptcy Petition Preparer Can Do for You

BPPs are very different from lawyers. BPPs are legally prohibited from giving you legal advice, which includes a lot of the information in this book, such as:

- whether to file a bankruptcy petition or which chapter (7, 11, 12, or 13) is appropriate
- whether your debts will be discharged under a particular chapter
- whether you will be able to hang on to your home or other property if you file under a particular chapter (that is, which exemptions you should choose)
- information about the tax consequences of a case brought under a particular chapter or whether tax claims in your case can be discharged
- whether you should offer to repay or agree to reaffirm a debt
- how to characterize the nature of your interest in property or debts, and
- information about bankruptcy procedures and rights.

2. Fees

All fees charged by debt relief agencies are reviewed by the U.S. Trustee for reasonableness. However, unlike lawyers' fees, which can vary widely according to the circumstances, a BPP's fees are subject to a strict cap, somewhere between $100 and $200, depending on the district. The rationale offered by the U.S. Trustee for this cap—and by the courts that have upheld it—is that BPP fees can be set according to what general typists charge per page in the community. Because BPPs aren't supposed to be doing anything other than "typing" the forms, the argument goes, they shouldn't be able to charge rates for professional services.

Rates allowed for BPPs are far less than lawyers charge—see Section C, below. For that reason, BPPs are a good choice for people who want some help getting their forms typed and organized in a way that will please the court clerk.

3. How Bankruptcy Petition Preparers Are Regulated

Anyone can be a BPP. Yes, anyone. There is nothing in the bankruptcy code that requires BPPs to have any particular level of education, training, or experience. Unlike most other jobs, a prison record is no handicap to becoming a BPP. How, then, are BPPs regulated? Regulation is provided by the U.S. Trustee's office, which reviews all bankruptcy petitions prepared by a BPP. BPPs must provide their name, address, telephone number, and Social Security number on the bankruptcy petition, as well as on every other bankruptcy document they prepare. The U.S. Trustee uses this information to keep tabs on BPPs.

BPPs are also regulated at the creditors' meeting, where the bankruptcy trustee can ask you about the manner in which the BPP conducts his or her business. For instance, if you are representing yourself, the trustee might ask how you got the information necessary to choose your exemptions (see Ch. 3) or decide which bankruptcy chapter to use.

If the BPP provided you with this information, the trustee may refer the case to the U.S. Trustee's office and the BPP will be hauled into court to explain why he or she violated the rules against giving legal advice. The BPP may be forced to return the fee you paid and may even be banned from practicing as a BPP, if it's not the first offense. None of this will have any effect on your case, however, other than the inconvenience of being dragged into court.

Can BPPs Give You Written Information?

Under the Bankruptcy Code, BPPs are supposed to prepare your bankruptcy forms under your direction. This means you are supposed to tell the BPP what exemptions to choose, whether to file under Chapter 7 or Chapter 13, what approach to take in respect to your secured debts (car note, mortgage) and what values to place on your property. That's fine in theory, but unless you have the benefit of this book or another source of legal information, there is no way you would have adequate bankruptcy expertise to tell the BPP how to proceed. In an attempt to bridge this gap, many BPPs hand their customers written materials that contain all the information their customers need to direct the case. Unfortunately, providing a customer with written legal information about bankruptcy has itself been held to be the unauthorized practice of law in many states (California is an important exception.) Whether these holdings will continue under the new bankruptcy law remains to be seen.

BPPs can be fined for certain actions and inactions spelled out in the Bankruptcy Code (11 U.S.C. § 110). These are:

- failing to put their name, address, and Social Security number on your bankruptcy petition
- failing to give you a copy of your bankruptcy documents when you sign them
- using the word "legal" or any similar term in advertisements, or advertising under a category that includes such terms, and
- accepting court filing fees from you—you must pay the filing fee to the court yourself or, in some districts, give the BPP a cashier's check made out to the court.

Finally, under the new law, BPPs must submit a statement under oath with each petition they prepare stating how much you paid them in the previous 12 months and any fees that you owe them but haven't yet paid them. If they charge more than they are permitted, they will be ordered to return the excess fees to you.

If a BPP engages in any fraudulent act in regard to your case or fails to comply with the rules governing their behavior listed above, they may be required to return your entire fee as well as pay a $500 fine for each transgression. If they engage in serious fraud, they may be fined up to $2,000 and triple your fee, and even be ordered to cease providing BPP services. Simply put, fraudulent BPPs (those who would take your money without providing promised services or counsel you to play fast and loose with the bankruptcy system) are likely to be weeded out in a hurry.

4. How to Find Bankruptcy Petition Preparers

BPP services are springing up all over the country to help people who don't want or can't afford to hire a lawyer, but you're still more likely to find a BPP if you live on the West Coast. The best way to find a reputable BPP in your area is to get a recommendation from someone who has used a particular BPP and been satisfied with his or her work.

BPPs sometimes advertise in classified sections of local newspapers and in the yellow pages. You may have to look hard to spot their ads, however, because they go by different names in different states. In California, your best bet is to find a legal document assistant (the official name given to independent paralegals in California) who also provide BPP services. Check the website maintained by the California Association of Legal Document Assistants (www.calda.org). In Arizona, hunt for a legal document preparer. In other states, especially Florida, search for paralegals who directly serve the public (often termed independent paralegals or legal technicians). In many states, an independent paralegal franchise called We the People offers BPP services. Finally, the National Bankruptcy Law Project maintains a registry of BPPs on its website at www.bankruptcylawproject.com.

5. Combining Lawyers and Bankruptcy Petition Preparers

In California and some other parts of the country, it is possible to use a BPP to grind out your paperwork and a lawyer to provide you with all the legal savvy you need to direct your own case. Under this arrangement, you are still representing yourself, but you are combining legal and secretarial resources to get the job done. This is what is known as unbundled legal service, where you hire an attorney for a discrete task (legal advice in this case) rather

than for the whole enchilada we know as "legal representation." For example, the National Bankruptcy Law Project offers folks using a BPP the services of a knowledgeable lawyer for a flat fee for all questions related to the bankruptcy. This works a little like prepaid insurance. However, you don't pay for the service until it is clear that you need an attorney, and the service is very specialized. For more information on how this type of service works, see Section C2, below. For information on the services offered by the National Bankruptcy Law Project, go to www.bankruptcylawproject.com/Pagestelephone.html.

6. A Bankruptcy Petition Preparer Cannot Represent You

If you decide to use a BPP, remember that you are representing yourself and are responsible for the outcome of your case. This means not only learning about your rights under the bankruptcy law and understanding the proper procedures to be followed, but also accepting responsibility for correctly and accurately filling in the bankruptcy petition and schedules. If, for example, you lose your home because it turned out to be worth much more than you thought, and the homestead exemption available to you didn't cover your equity, you can't blame the BPP. Nor can you blame the BPP if other property is taken from you because you didn't get the necessary information—from a lawyer or from this book—to properly claim your exemptions. The point is, unless you hire a lawyer to represent you, you are solely responsible for acquiring the information necessary to competently pursue your case. (See Section C, below, for more on what it means to be represented by an attorney.)

C. Bankruptcy Lawyers

Bankruptcy lawyers (a type of debt relief agency under the new law) are regular lawyers who specialize in handling bankruptcy cases. Under the old law, it was usually possible to find an affordable bankruptcy lawyer who would provide at least a minimal level of representation throughout your case. However, for the reasons discussed below, lawyers are charging a lot more to represent clients in bankruptcies filed under the new law.

If you aren't represented by a lawyer, but want to file for bankruptcy, you will need to represent yourself. While this will involve a fair amount of work—much more than under the old law—it is certainly possible. And there is help available for you. In addition to books published by Nolo, you can use a combination of bankruptcy petition preparers and telephone legal advice from a lawyer to help you over the clerical and legal humps and get you through the process in reasonably good shape—for far less than a lawyer would charge to represent you. (See Sections B, above, and D, below, for more information about the help available for people representing themselves.)

1. Full-Service Lawyer Representation

In a general sense, you are represented by a lawyer if you contract with the lawyer to handle some or all of your bankruptcy case for you. More specifically, there are two types of representation—the type where you hire a lawyer to assume complete responsibility for your bankruptcy, and the type where you represent yourself but hire a lawyer to handle one particular aspect of your bankruptcy case. We refer to the first type of representation as "full-service representation" and the second type of representation as unbundled services (discussed in Section 2, below).

When providing full-service representation, a bankruptcy lawyer is responsible for making sure that all of your paperwork is filed on time and that the information in your paperwork is accurate. These duties require the lawyer to review various documents—for instance, your credit report, tax returns, and home value appraisal—both to assure the accuracy of your paperwork and to make sure that you are filing for bankruptcy under the appropriate chapter. Under the new law, if your paperwork is inaccurate or you filed under Chapter 7 when you should have filed under Chapter 13, the lawyer can be fined a hefty amount and be required to return your fees.

In exchange for their basic fee, full-service bankruptcy lawyers also are typically responsible for appearing on your behalf at the creditors' meeting (see Ch. 7, Section A), representing you if a creditor opposes the discharge of a debt (see Ch. 9), and eliminating any liens that the bankruptcy laws allow to be stripped from your property (see Ch. 5).

Often, it will be very clear from the start that you should use Chapter 7 and that there are no complications—such as a lien that must be stripped from your property—that require the skills of a lawyer. In this situation, you can get by with the help of this book and, if you wish, other support resources described in this chapter. That's because the standard Chapter 7 bankruptcy case only requires one out-of-court appearance before a trustee.

In some cases, however, the opposite is true: You can tell from the very beginning that you—or an attorney representing you—will have to appear before a bankruptcy judge to keep your bankruptcy on track and fully assert your rights under the bankruptcy laws. And that can be intimidating. For instance, if you want to discharge a student loan, you might want to hire a full-service attorney at the very beginning of your case. As a general rule, you might also consider hiring a full-service lawyer at the beginning of your case if you know that you will need to prepare custom-made court papers (for which there aren't any official forms) or to negotiate with creditors in situations where a lot is at stake and you don't have confidence in your own negotiating skills.

Sometimes, a case appears to be simple at the beginning but turns out to be complicated later on. In that event, you might start out representing yourself but later decide to hire an attorney to handle a tricky issue that arises. (See Section 2, below.)

Because full-service lawyer duties for even a simple bankruptcy case have drastically increased under the new bankruptcy law, typical lawyer fees have gone way up. (See Section 5, below.) For this reason, many people who would have used lawyers in the past will now be forced to represent themselves—with or without the help of outside resources. And many readers of this book are likely to find themselves in this boat.

2. Unbundled Services

As mentioned earlier, the recent changes in bankruptcy law means that many people who would have hired a full-service lawyer in the past will now have to represent themselves. However, this doesn't mean that they can't get a lawyer to help out with some aspect of the case. Since the 1990s, lawyers have been increasingly willing to offer their services on a piecemeal basis and provide legal advice over the telephone and Internet to help people who are representing themselves. In bankruptcy cases, lawyers are increasingly willing to step in and handle a particular matter, such as stripping liens from your property or handling a dischargeability action brought by you or a creditor.

When lawyers do specific jobs at a client's request but don't contract for full-service representation in the underlying case, they are said to be providing an unbundled service. For example, you may be able to hire an attorney to handle a specific procedure—such as to defend against a motion for relief from stay—while you handle the main part of the bankruptcy yourself.

Few cases discuss the boundaries of unbundled services. Some courts have held that attorneys can't "ghostwrite" legal documents for nonlawyers—because that would be a type of fraud on the court—but the issue has not been decided by most courts. Also, nothing prevents a lawyer from appearing for you in a limited capacity and putting his or her own name on associated documents.

Lawyers providing unbundled services usually charge an hourly fee. As a general rule, you should bring an attorney into the case for an unbundled service only if a dispute involves something valuable enough to justify the attorney's fees. If a creditor objects to the discharge of a $500 debt, and it will cost you $400 to hire an attorney, you may be better off trying to handle the matter yourself, even though this increases the risk that the creditor will win. If, however, the dispute is worth $1,000 and the attorney will cost you $200, hiring the attorney makes better sense.

Unfortunately, many bankruptcy attorneys do not like to appear or do paperwork on a piecemeal basis. Justified or not, these attorneys believe that by doing a little work for you, they might be on the hook if something goes wrong in another part of your case—that is, if they are in for a penny, they are in for a pound. Also, the bar associations of some states frown on unbundled services on ethical grounds. On the other hand, a number of other state bar associations are starting to encourage their attorneys to offer unbundled services simply because so many people—even middle income people—are unable to afford full representation.

3. Bankruptcy Consultants

Under the old bankruptcy law, many people were able to represent themselves with a Nolo book as their main source of information. Bankruptcy under the new law is more complex, but in many cases, it's still just a matter of knowing what to put in the forms and what forms to file. For many people, however, a book just won't do the trick, no matter how well written and complete: You want to talk to a human being. Because of unauthorized practice laws and restrictions in the bankruptcy law, however, there is only one kind of human being who is authorized to answer your questions about bankruptcy law and procedure—a lawyer.

Fortunately, there are lawyers who provide bankruptcy consultations (a category of unbundled service) for a transaction fee (for example, a $39.95 flat rate) or a fee based on the amount of time your call takes (for example, $3 a minute). There are also free consultations offered by private attorneys and bar associations. Similar services—free and paid—are available on the Internet. To find a telephonic or online consultation service, in addition to those mentioned here, go to Google or another search engine and look for "bankruptcy legal advice telephone or Internet."

Even if you use a BPP to prepare your paperwork, and are using this book, you may wish to talk to a lawyer to get the information you need to make your own choices and tell the BPP what you want in your papers. For instance, a BPP can't choose your exemptions for you, because that would be considered the practice of law—something only lawyers can do. However, a lawyer can help you decide which exemptions to pick so you can tell the BPP what to put in the form that lists your exemptions.

As with other debt relief agencies, lawyers offering telephonic services are considered debt relief agencies and will have to offer you a contract detailing their services and provide the other notices described in Section A, above.

4. How to Find a Bankruptcy Lawyer

Where there's a bankruptcy court, there are bankruptcy lawyers. They're listed in the yellow pages under "Attorneys," and often advertise in newspapers. You should use an experienced bankruptcy lawyer, not a general practitioner, to advise you or handle matters associated with bankruptcy.

There are several ways to find the best bankruptcy lawyer for your job:

- **Personal referrals.** This is your best approach. If you know someone who was pleased with the services of a bankruptcy lawyer, call that lawyer first.

- **Bankruptcy petition preparers.** If there's a BPP in your area, he or she may know some bankruptcy attorneys who are both competent and sympathetic to self-helpers. It is here that you are most likely to find a good referral to attorneys who are willing to deliver unbundled services, including advice over the telephone.

- **Legal Aid.** Legal Aid offices are partially funded by the federal Legal Services Corporation and offer legal assistance in many areas. A few offices may do bankruptcies, although most do not. To qualify for Legal Aid, you must have a very low income.

- **Legal clinic.** Many law schools sponsor legal clinics and provide free legal advice to consumers. Some legal clinics have the same income requirements as Legal Aid; others offer free services to low- and moderate-income people.

- **Group legal plans.** If you're a member of a plan that provides free or low-cost legal assistance and the plan covers bankruptcies, make that your first stop in looking for a lawyer.

- **Lawyer-referral panels.** Most county bar associations will give you the names of bankruptcy attorneys who practice in your area. But bar associations may not provide much screening. Take the time to check out the credentials and experience of the person to whom you're referred.

- **Internet directories.** Both bar associations and private companies provide lists of bankruptcy lawyers on the Internet, with a lot more information about the lawyer than you're likely to get in a yellow pages ad. One good place to start is the online lawyer directory at http://lawyers .findlaw.com.

5. Fees

For a routine Chapter 7 bankruptcy, a full-service lawyer will likely charge you somewhere between $1,000 and $2,000 (plus the $299 filing fee). In most situations, you will have to pay the attorney in full before the attorney will file your case. Once you file your Chapter 7 bankruptcy, any money you owe the attorney is discharged along with your other dischargeable unsecured debts.

On your bankruptcy papers, you must state the amount you are paying your bankruptcy lawyer. Because every penny you pay to a bankruptcy lawyer is a penny not available to your creditors (at least in theory), the court has the legal authority to make the attorney justify his or her fee. This rarely happens, however, because attorneys know the range of fees generally allowed by local bankruptcy judges, and set their fees accordingly. This means that you probably won't find much variation in the amounts charged by lawyers in your area (although it never hurts to shop around).

The scope and range of services that the attorney promises you in return for your initial fee will be listed in what's called a "Rule 2016 Attorney Fee Disclosure Form." This form is filed as part of your bankruptcy papers. In the typical Chapter 7 case, the attorney's fee will include the routine tasks associated with a bankruptcy filing: counseling, preparing bankruptcy and reaffirmation forms, and attendance at the creditors' meeting. Any task not included in the Rule 2016 disclosure form is subject to a separate fee.

If your case will likely require more attorney time, you may—and probably will—be charged extra, according to the attorney's hourly fee or other criteria he or she uses. A typical bankruptcy attorney charges between $200 and $300 an hour (rural and urban) and would charge a minimum of roughly $400 to $600 for a court appearance. Some attorneys will add these fees to their standard fee and require you to pay it all in advance. For instance, if the attorney's standard fee is $1,000, but the attorney sees extra work down the line, you may be charged $1,500 or even $2,000 in anticipation of the extra work.

Other attorneys will happily just charge you their standard fee up front and wait until after you file to charge you for the extra work. Because these fees are earned after your bankruptcy filing, they won't be discharged in your bankruptcy and the attorney need not collect them up front. However the attorney charges you, you are protected against fee gouging. An attorney must file a supplemental Rule 2016 form to obtain the court's permission for any postfiling fees.

6. What to Look for in a Lawyer

No matter how you find a lawyer, these three suggestions will help you make sure you have the best possible working relationship.

First, fight any urge you may have to surrender to, or be intimidated by, the lawyer. You should be the one who decides what you feel comfortable doing about your legal and financial affairs. Keep in mind that you're hiring the lawyer to perform a service for you, so shop around if the price or personality isn't right.

Second, make sure you have good "chemistry" with any lawyer you hire. When making an appointment, ask to talk directly to the lawyer. If you can't, this may give you a hint as to how accessible he or she is. Of course, if you're told that a paralegal will be handling the routine aspects of your case under the supervision of a lawyer, you may be satisfied with that arrangement. If you do talk directly, ask some specific questions. Do you get clear, concise answers? If not, try someone else. Also pay attention to how the lawyer responds to your knowledge. If you've read this book, you're already better informed than most clients (and some lawyers are threatened by clients who have done their homework).

Finally, once you find a lawyer you like, make an hour-long appointment to discuss your situation fully. The lawyer or a paralegal in the lawyer's office will tell you what to bring to the meeting, if anything (if not, be sure to ask ahead of time). Some lawyers will want to see a recent credit report and tax return, while others will send you a questionnaire to complete prior to your visit. Depending on the circumstances, you may also be asked to bring your bills and documents pertaining to your home and other real estate you own. Some lawyers prefer not to deal with details during the first visit, and will simply ask you to come as you are.

Your main goal at the initial conference is to find out what the lawyer recommends in your particular case and how much it will cost. Go home and think about the lawyer's suggestions. If they don't make sense or you have other reservations, call someone else.

 Look for a member of the National Association of Consumer Bankruptcy Attorneys. Because of the massive changes enacted by the new bankruptcy law, you will want to find an attorney who has a means of keeping up to date and communicating with other bankruptcy lawyers. Membership in the National Association of Consumer Bankruptcy Attorneys (NACBA) is a good sign that your lawyer will be tuned in to the nuances of the new law and the court interpretations of the law that are sure to come.

D. Legal Research

Legal research can vary from the very simple to the hopelessly complex. In this section, we are staying on the simple side. If you would like to learn more about legal research or if you find that our suggestions come up a bit short in your particular case, we recommend that you obtain a copy of *Legal Research: How to Find & Understand the Law*, by Stephen Elias and Susan Levinkind (Nolo), which provides a plain-English tutorial on legal research in the law library and on the Internet.

1. Sources of Bankruptcy Law

Bankruptcy law comes from a variety of sources:
- federal bankruptcy statutes passed by Congress
- federal rules about bankruptcy procedure issued by a federal judicial agency
- local rules issued by individual bankruptcy courts
- federal and bankruptcy court cases applying bankruptcy laws to specific disputes
- laws (statutes) passed by state legislatures that define the property you can keep in bankruptcy, and
- state court cases interpreting state exemption statutes.

Not so long ago, you would have had to visit a law library to find these resources. Now you can find most of them on the Internet. However, if you are able to visit a decent-sized law library, your research will be the better for it. Using actual books allows you to more easily find and read relevant court interpretations of the underlying statutes and rules—which are crucial to getting a clear picture of what the laws and rules really mean.

There is another important reason to visit the law library, if possible. While you can find superficial discussions and overviews of various aspects of bankruptcy on the Internet, you'll find in-depth encyclopedias and treatises in the law library that delve into every aspect of bankruptcy. In other words, you can find not only the law itself in the law library, but also what the experts have to say about all the picky little issues that have arisen over the years. Also, books in a law library are almost always subjected to a rigorous quality control process—as is this book— whereas you never know what you're getting on the Internet. To avoid getting lost in cyberspace, follow our suggestions below for researching bankruptcy law online and avoid the temptation to settle for the first hit in a Google search.

Below, we show you how to get to the resources you'll most likely be using, whether you are doing your research on the Internet or in the law library.

How to Use Law Libraries

Law libraries that are open to the public are most often found in and around courthouses. Law schools also frequently admit the public at least some of the time (not, typically during exam time, over the summer, or during other breaks in the academic year).

If you're using a library as a member of the public, find a way to feel at home, even if it seems that the library is run mostly to serve members of the legal community: law students, judges, lawyers, and paralegals. Almost without exception, law libraries come with law librarians. The law librarians will be helpful as long as you ask them the right questions. For example, the law librarians will help you find specific library resources (for instance, where you can find the federal bankruptcy statutes or rules), but they normally won't teach you the ins and outs of legal research. Nor will they give an opinion about what a law means, how you should deal with the court, or how your particular question should be answered. For instance, if you want to find a state case interpreting a particular exemption, the law librarian will show you where your state code is located on the shelves and may even point out the volumes that contain the exemptions. The librarian won't, however, help you interpret the exemption, apply the exemption to your specific facts, or tell you how to raise the exemption in your bankruptcy case. Nor is the librarian likely to tell you what additional research steps you can or should take. When it comes to legal research in the law library, self help is the order of the day.

---

2. Bankruptcy Background Materials: Overviews, Encyclopedias, and Treatises

Before digging into the primary law sources (statutes, rules, cases, and so on that we discuss below), you may want to do some background reading to get a firm grasp of your issue or question.

a. The Internet

A number of Internet sites contain large collections of articles written by experts about various aspects of bankruptcy. A good starting place is Nolo's website, at www.nolo.com (click the "Property and Money" tab to get started). Our next favorite jumping-off site for this type of research is The Bankruptcy Law Trove page at www.lawtrove.com/bankruptcy. You might also want to visit www.bankruptcyfinder.com, a comprehensive site that provides links to hundreds of bankruptcy articles, reference materials, statutes, and more.

b. The Law Library

Providing you with a good treatise or encyclopedia discussion of bankruptcy is where the law library shines. This type of resource is not typically available online unless you find a way to access the expensive legal databases—Westlaw and Lexis—marketed almost exclusively to lawyers.

i. *Collier on Bankruptcy*

It's a good idea to get an overview of your subject before trying to find a precise answer to a precise question. The best way to do this is to find a general commentary on your subject by a bankruptcy expert. For example, if you want to find out whether a particular debt is nondischargeable, you should start by reading a general discussion about the type of debt you're dealing with. Or, if you don't know whether you're entitled to claim certain property as exempt, a good overview of your state's exemptions would get you started on the right track.

The most complete source of this type of background information is a set of books known as *Collier on Bankruptcy*, by Lawrence P. King, et al. (Matthew Bender). It's available in virtually all law libraries. *Collier* is both incredibly thorough and meticulously up to date; semiannual supplements, with all the latest developments, are in the front of each volume. In addition to comments on every aspect of bankruptcy law, *Collier* contains the bankruptcy statutes, rules, and exemption lists for every state.

Collier is organized according to the bankruptcy statutes. This means that the quickest way to find information in it is to know what statute you're looking for. See the Bankruptcy Code sections set out in the sidebar below. If you still can't figure out the governing statute, start with the *Collier* subject matter index. Be

warned, however, that the index can be difficult to use because it contains a lot of bankruptcy jargon you may be unfamiliar with. A legal dictionary will be available in the library.

ii. Other Background Resources

For general discussions of bankruptcy issues, there are several other good places to start. An excellent all-around resource is called *Consumer Bankruptcy Law and Practice*. This volume, published by the National Consumer Law Center, is updated every year. It contains a complete discussion of Chapter 7 bankruptcy procedures, the official bankruptcy forms, and a marvelous bibliography.

Another good treatise is a legal encyclopedia called *American Jurisprudence*, 2nd Series. Almost all law libraries carry it. The article on bankruptcy has an extensive table of contents, and the entire encyclopedia has an index. Between these two tools, you should be able to zero in on helpful material. Finally, some large and well-stocked law libraries carry a looseleaf publication known as the Commerce Clearing House (CCH) *Bankruptcy Law Reporter* (BLR). In this publication, you can find all three primary source materials relating to bankruptcy: statutes, rules, and cases.

If you are looking for information on adversary proceedings (such as how to defend against a creditor's challenge to the dischargeability of a debt), turn to *Represent Yourself in Court,* by Paul Bergman and Sara J. Berman-Barrett (Nolo). It has an entire chapter on representing yourself in adversary proceedings in bankruptcy court. If you need information on court procedures or the local rules of a specific court, consult the *Collier Bankruptcy Practice Manual.*

3. Finding Federal Bankruptcy Statutes

Title 11 of the United States Code contains all the statutes that govern your bankruptcy.

a. The Internet

If you are using the Internet, click www.lawtrove.com/bankruptcy or go to the Legal Information Institute of Cornell University Law School, www.law.cornell.edu. Cornell lets you browse laws by subject matter and also offers a key word search. To help you in your browsing, here is a table setting out the various subject matter sections of the U.S. Code that apply to bankruptcy.

Bankruptcy Code Sections (11 U.S.C.)

§ 101 Definitions

§ 109 Who May File for Which Type of Bankruptcy; Credit Counseling Requirements

§ 110 Rules for Bankruptcy Petition Preparers

§ 111 Budget and Credit Counseling Agencies

§ 302 Who Can File Joint Cases

§ 326 How Trustees Are Compensated

§ 332 Consumer Privacy Ombudsmen

§ 341 Meeting of Creditors

§ 342 Notice of Creditors' Meeting; Informational Notice to Debtors; Requirements for Notice By Debtors

§ 343 Examination of Debtor at Creditors' Meeting

§ 348 Converting From One Type of Bankruptcy to Another

§ 349 Dismissing a Case

§ 350 Closing and Reopening a Case

§ 362 The Automatic Stay

§ 365 How Leases and Executory Contracts Are Treated in Bankruptcy

§ 366 Continuing or Reconnecting Utility Service

§ 501 Filing of Creditors' Claims

§ 506 Allowed Secured Claims and Lien Avoidance

§ 507 Priority Claims

§ 521 Paperwork Requirements and Deadlines

§ 522 Exemptions; Residency Requirements for Homestead Exemption; Stripping Liens from Property

§ 523 Nondischargeable Debts

§ 524 Effect of Discharge and Reaffirmation of Debts

§ 525 Prohibited Post-Bankruptcy Discrimination

§ 526 Restrictions on Debt Relief Agencies

§ 527 Required Disclosures by Debt Relief Agencies

§ 528 Requirements for Debt Relief Agencies

§ 541 What Property Is Part of the Bankruptcy Estate

§ 547 Preferences

§ 548 Fraudulent Transfers

§ 554 Trustee's Abandonment of Property in the Bankruptcy Estate

§ 707 The Means Test; Dismissal for Abuse; Conversion From Chapter 7 to Chapter 13

§ 722 Redemption of Liens on Personal Property

§ 727 Chapter 7 Discharge; Financial Management Counseling Requirements

b. The Law Library

Virtually every law library has at least one complete set of the annotated United States Code ("annotated" means that each statute is followed by citations and summaries of cases interpreting that provision). If you already have a citation to the statute you are seeking, you can use the citation to find the statute. However, if you have no citation—which is frequently the case— you can use either the index to Title 11 (the part of the Code that applies to bankruptcy) or the table we set out just above, which matches various issues that are likely to interest you with specific sections of Title 11.

Once you have found and read the statute, you can browse the one-paragraph summaries of written opinions issued by courts that have interpreted that particular statute. You will be looking to see whether a court has addressed your particular issue. If so, you can find and read the entire case in the law library. Reading what a judge has had to say about the statute regarding facts similar to yours is an invaluable guide to understanding how a judge is likely to handle the issue in your case, although when and where the case was decided may be important.

4. Finding the Federal Rules of Bankruptcy Procedure (FRBP)

The Federal Rules of Bankruptcy Procedure govern what happens if an issue is contested in the bankruptcy court. They also apply to certain routine bankruptcy procedures, such as deadlines for filing paperwork. Because most cases sail through the court without any need for the bankruptcy judge's intervention, you may not need to be familiar with these rules. However, certain types of creditor actions in the bankruptcy court must proceed by way of a regular lawsuit conducted under both these rules and the Federal Rules of Civil Procedure—for example, complaints to determine dischargeability of a debt. If you are representing yourself in such a lawsuit, you'll want to know these rules and look at the cases interpreting them. Any law library will have these rules. Your bankruptcy court's website will have a link to the rules, as does www.law .cornell.edu.

5. Finding Local Court Rules

Every bankruptcy court operates under a set of local rules that govern how it does business and what is expected of the parties who use it. Throughout this book, we have cautioned you to read the rules for your particular court so that your dealings with the court will go smoothly—and so you won't end up getting tossed out of court if you become involved in litigation, such as an action to determine the dischargeability of a debt or a creditor's motion to lift the automatic stay.

Your bankruptcy court clerk's office will have the local rules available for you. Most courts also post their local rules on their own websites. To find the website for your court, take these steps:

Step 1: Go to www.uscourts.gov/links.html.

Step 2: Click the number on the map that is closest to where you live.

Step 3: Browse the list until you find your court and click on it.

Step 4: Click on the local rules link.

These court websites usually contain other helpful information as well, including case information, official and local bankruptcy forms, court guidelines (in addition to the local rules), information for lawyers and BPPs, information about the court and its judges, and the court calendar.

At the law library, the *Collier Bankruptcy Practice Manual* has the local rules for most (if not all) of the nation's bankruptcy courts.

6. Finding Federal Court Bankruptcy Cases

Court opinions are vital to understanding how a particular law might apply to your individual case. The following levels of federal courts issue bankruptcy-related opinions:

- the U.S. Supreme Court
- the U.S. Courts of Appeals
- the Bankruptcy Appellate Panels
- the U.S. District Courts, and
- the bankruptcy courts.

Most bankruptcy-related opinions are, not surprisingly, issued by the bankruptcy courts. By comparison, very few bankruptcy opinions come out of the U.S. Supreme Court. The other courts are somewhere in the middle.

a. The Internet

Depending on the date the case was decided, U.S. Supreme Court decisions and U.S. Court of Appeals decisions are available for free on the Internet. For $13.95 a month you can also subscribe to VersusLaw (at www.versuslaw.com), which provides U.S. Court of Appeals cases for an earlier period than you can get for free—often back to 1950. VersusLaw doesn't require you to sign a long-term contract. So, one payment of $13.95 gets you a month's worth of research. Not too shabby. VersusLaw also publishes many U.S. District Court cases on its website. Opinions by the bankruptcy courts are generally not yet available over the Internet, unless you subscribe to Lexis or Westlaw, both of which are extremely pricey.

U.S. Supreme Court. To find a Supreme Court case, go to www.findlaw.com/casecode/supreme.html. Use one of the search options to locate a particular case. If you don't know the case name and you don't have a citation, enter some relevant words relating to your issue and see what you pull up. You can search cases all the way back to 1893.

U.S. Court of Appeals. You can find a U.S Circuit Court of Appeals case back to roughly 1996. Follow these steps:

Step 1: Go to www.findlaw.com/casecode/index.html.

Step 2: Scroll down to U.S Courts of Appeals—Opinions and Websites.

Step 3: Click on the link that contains your state's abbreviation.

Step 4: Use one of the search options to find the case.

Again, if you are looking for a case decided prior to 1996, your best bet is to sign up for VersusLaw, described just above.

U.S. District Court and Bankruptcy Court. Cases reported by the bankruptcy courts are generally not available online unless you subscribe to Westlaw or Lexis. However, if you know the name of a particular case, a Google search might lead you to a court's website, where some judges post their decisions. You will probably have to take a trip to a law library if you want to know what the judges are doing in these courts—where the legal rubber meets the judicial road.

b. The Law Library

U.S. Supreme Court cases are published in three different book series:

- Supreme Court Reports
- Supreme Court Reporter, and
- Supreme Court Lawyer's Edition.

Some law libraries carry all three of these publications; others have only one. The cases are the same, but each series has different editorial enhancements.

U.S. Court of Appeals cases are published in the Federal Reporter (abbreviated simply as "F."). Most law libraries, large and small, carry this series.

Many U.S. District Court cases are published in the Federal Supplement (F.Supp), a series available in most law libraries.

Written opinions of bankruptcy judges, and related appeals, are published in the Bankruptcy Reporter (B.R.), available in most mid- to large-sized libraries. To accurately understand how your bankruptcy court is likely to interpret the laws in your particular case, sooner or later you will need access to the Bankruptcy Reporter.

7. State Statutes

The secret to understanding what property you can keep frequently lies in the exemptions that your state allows you to claim. These exemptions are found in your state's statutes.

a. The Internet

Every state has its statutes online, including its exemption statutes. This means that you can read your state's exemption statutes for yourself. Follow these steps:

Step 1: Go to Appendix 1. At the top of your state's exemption table, you'll see a general reference to the collection of state laws for your state that contain the exemption statutes.

Step 2: Go to www.nolo.com.

Step 3: Click "Site Map" at the bottom of the page.

Step 4: Select "State Laws" under the "Legal Research" heading.

Step 5: Click on your state.

Step 6: Locate the collection of statutes mentioned in Appendix 1.

Step 7: Use the exemption citation to the far right of your state's exemption table to search for the statute.

b. The Law Library

Your law library will have your state's statutes in book form, usually referred to as your state's code, annotated statutes, or compiled laws. Use Appendix 1 in this book to find a reference to the exemption statute you want to read, then use that reference to locate the exemption statute in the code. Once you find and read the statute, you can browse the summaries of court opinions interpreting the statute and, if you wish, read the cases in their entirety.

Alternatively, if your library has a copy of *Colliers on Bankruptcy* (see Section 2b, above), you can find the exemptions for your state, accompanied by annotations summarizing state court interpretations.

8. State Court Cases

State courts are sometimes called on to interpret exemption statutes. If a court has interpreted the statute in which you are interested, you'll definitely want to chase down the relevant case and read it for yourself.

a. The Internet

All states make their more recent cases available free on the Internet—usually back to about 1996. To find these cases for your state:

Step 1: Go to www.law.cornell.edu/opinions .html#state.

Step 2: Click on your state.

Step 3: Locate the link to the court opinions for your state. This may be one link, or there may be separate links for your state's supreme court and your state's courts of appeal (the lower trial courts seldom publish their opinions, so you probably won't be able to find them).

If you want to go back to an earlier case, consider subscribing to VersusLaw at www.versuslaw.com. As mentioned earlier, you don't have to sign a long-term contract.

b. The Law Library

Your law library will have a collection of books that contain opinions issued by your state's courts. If you have a citation, you can go right to the case. If you don't have a citation, you'll need to use a digest to find relevant bankruptcy cases. Finding cases by subject matter is a little too advanced for this brief summary. See *Legal Research: How to Find & Understand the Law,* by Stephen Elias and Susan Levinkind (Nolo), for more help.

9. Other Helpful Resources

Probably the most helpful bankruptcy website is maintained by the Office of the United States Trustee, at www.usdoj.gov/ust. This site provides lists of approved credit and financial management counseling agencies, median income figures for every state, the IRS national, regional, and local expenses you will need to complete the means test, and all of the forms you will need to file, in fill-in-the-blanks, PDF format. You can also download official bankruptcy forms from www.uscourts.gov/bkforms/index.html. However, this site doesn't include required local forms; for those, you'll have to visit your court or its website.

If you're looking for a software program to help you complete your bankruptcy forms, check out Blankrupter 4.0, from Blumberg's Excelsior at www.blumberg.com. (You can download and try the program free, but you must pay the piper—to the tune of $49.95—to print your completed forms for filing.) Using this program allows you to fill out the forms on your computer and save your entries, so you don't have to complete and print an entire form in one sitting. The program also saves you time by putting your information in the appropriate spots on every form to which it applies. And the program will do your math for you, using IRS and Census Bureau data if you have to take the means test. If you edit your entries, the program will automatically revise the means test presumption and fill out the appropriate forms; you won't have to re-enter data.

As part of the bankruptcy process, you are required to give the replacement (retail) value for all of the property you list in Schedule A (real property) and Schedule B (personal property). These figures are also the key to figuring out which of your property is

Our Websites

Nolo's website, www.nolo.com, offers lots of free information on bankruptcy, credit repair, student loans, and much more. (Click the "Property and Money" tab to get started.) You can also view information on the Nolo products mentioned in this book, including links to legal updates highlighting important developments that occurred after this book went to press.

In addition, two of the authors of this book maintain their own websites, both of which provide plenty of free information on a variety of bankruptcy topics:

- www.bankruptcylawproject.com, created by Stephen Elias, provides information on bankruptcy, a registry of bankruptcy petition preparers, and unlimited legal advice by telephone, at a flat rate (currently $100).
- www.how-to-file-bankruptcy.com, created by Albin Renauer, provides free bankruptcy information and resources organized by the user's zip code. The site offers a means test calculator, state and federal exemption laws, contact information for your local bankruptcy court, links to official court forms and instructions, links to other resources, and more.

exempt. Here are some tips on finding these values:

- Cars: Use the Kelley Blue Book, at www.kbb.com, or the website of the National Auto Dealers Association, www.nada.com.
- Other personal property: Check prices on eBay, www.ebay.com.
- Homes: Check the prices for which comparable homes have sold in the recent past. For a modest fee, you can get details on comparable homes, including sales history, number of bedrooms and baths, square footage, and property tax information, at www.smarthomebuy.com. Less-detailed information (purchase price, sales date, and address) is available free from sites like www.homevalues.com, www.domania.com, www.homeradar.com, and http://list.realestate.yahoo.com/re/homevalues. ■

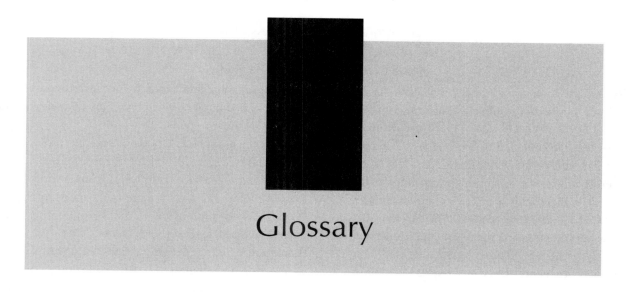

Glossary

341 meeting. See "meeting of creditors."

341 notice. A notice sent to the debtor and the debtor's creditors announcing the date, time, and place for the first meeting of creditors. The 341 notice is sent along with the notice of bankruptcy filing and information about important deadlines by which creditors have to take certain actions, such as filing objections.

342 notice. A notice that the court clerk is required to give to debtors pursuant to Section 342 of the Bankruptcy Code, to inform them of their obligations as bankruptcy debtors and the consequences of not being completely honest in their bankruptcy case.

707(b) action. An action taken by the U.S. Trustee, the regular trustee, or any creditor, under authority of Section 707(b) of the Bankruptcy Code, to dismiss a debtor's Chapter 7 filing on the ground of abuse.

Abuse. Misuse of the Chapter 7 bankruptcy remedy. This term is typically applied to Chapter 7 bankruptcy filings that should have been filed under Chapter 13 because the debtor appears to have enough disposable income to fund a Chapter 13 repayment plan.

Accounts receivable. Money or other property that one person or business owes to another for goods or services. Accounts receivable most often refer to the debts owed to a business by its customers.

Administrative expenses. The trustee's fee, the debtor's attorney fee, and other costs of bringing a bankruptcy case that a debtor must pay in full in a Chapter 13 repayment plan. Administrative costs are typically 10% of the debtor's total payments under the plan.

Administrative Office of the United States Courts. The federal government agency that issues court rules and forms to be used by the federal courts, including bankruptcy courts.

Adversary action. Any lawsuit that begins with the filing of a formal complaint and formal service of process on the parties being sued. In a bankruptcy case, adversary actions are often brought to determine the dischargeability of a debt or to recover property transferred by the debtor shortly before filing for bankruptcy.

Affidavit. A written statement of facts, signed under oath in front of a notary public.

Allowed secured claim. A debt that is secured by collateral or a lien against the debtor's property, for which the creditor has filed a proof of claim with the bankruptcy court. The claim is secured only to the extent of the value of the property—for example, if a debtor owes $5,000 on a note for a car that is worth only $3,000, the remaining $2,000 is an unsecured claim.

Amendment. A document filed by the debtor that changes one or more documents previously filed with the court. A debtor often files an amendment because the trustee requires changes to the debtor's paperwork based on the testimony at the meeting of creditors.

Animals. An exemption category in many states. Some states specifically exempt pets or livestock and poultry. If your state simply allows you to exempt "animals," you may include livestock, poultry, or pets. Some states exempt only domestic animals, which are usually considered to be all animals except pets.

Annuity. A type of insurance policy that pays out during the life of the insured, unlike life insurance, which pays out at the insured's death. Once the insured reaches the age specified in the policy, he or she receives monthly payments until death.

Appliance. A household apparatus or machine, usually operated by electricity, gas, or propane. Examples include refrigerators, stoves, washing machines, dishwashers, vacuum cleaners, air conditioners, and toasters.

Arms and accoutrements. Arms are weapons (such as pistols, rifles, and swords); accoutrements are the furnishings of a soldier's outfit, such as a belt or pack, but not clothes or weapons.

Arms-length creditor. A creditor with whom the debtor deals in the normal course of business, as opposed to an insider (a friend, relative, or business partner).

Articles of adornment. See "jewelry."

Assessment benefits. See "stipulated insurance."

Assisted person. Any person contemplating or filing for bankruptcy who receives bankruptcy assistance, whose debts are primarily consumer debts, and whose nonexempt property is valued at less than $150,000. A person or entity that offers help to an assisted person is called a "debt relief agency."

Automatic stay. An injunction automatically issued by the bankruptcy court when a debtor files for bankruptcy. The automatic stay prohibits most creditor collection activities, such as filing or continuing lawsuits, making written requests for payment, or notifying credit reporting bureaus of an unpaid debt.

Avails. Any amount available to the owner of an insurance policy other than the actual proceeds of the policy. Avails include dividend payments, interest, cash or surrender value (the money you'd get if you sold your policy back to the insurance company), and loan value (the amount of cash you can borrow against the policy).

Bankruptcy Abuse Prevention and Reform Act of 2005. The formal name of the new bankruptcy law that took effect on October 17, 2005.

Bankruptcy administrator. The official responsible for supervising the administration of bankruptcy cases, estates, and trustees in Alabama and North Carolina, where there is no U.S. Trustee.

Bankruptcy Appellate Panel. A specialized court that hears appeals of bankruptcy court decisions (available only in some regions).

Bankruptcy assistance. Goods or services provided to an "assisted person" for the purpose of providing information, advice, counsel, document preparation or filing, or attendance at a creditors' meeting; appearing in a case or proceeding on behalf of another person; or providing legal representation.

Bankruptcy Code. The federal law that governs the creation and operation of the bankruptcy courts and establishes bankruptcy procedures. (You can find the Bankruptcy Code in Title 11 of the United States Code.)

Bankruptcy estate. All of the property you own when you file for bankruptcy, except for most pensions and educational trusts. The trustee technically takes control of your bankruptcy estate for the duration of your case.

Bankruptcy lawyer. A lawyer who specializes in bankruptcy and is licensed to practice law in the federal courts.

Bankruptcy petition preparer. Any nonlawyer who helps someone with his or her bankruptcy. Bankruptcy petition preparers (BPPs) are a special type of debt relief agency, regulated by the U.S. Trustee. Because they are not lawyers, BPPs can't represent anyone in bankruptcy court or provide legal advice.

Bankruptcy Petition Preparer Fee Declaration. An official form bankruptcy petition preparers must file with the bankruptcy court to disclose their fees.

Bankruptcy Petition Preparer Notice to Debtor. A written notice that bankruptcy petition preparers must provide to debtors who use their services. The notice explains that bankruptcy petition preparers aren't attorneys and that they are permitted to perform only certain acts, such as entering information in the bankruptcy petition and schedules under the direction of their clients.

Benefit or benevolent society benefits. See "fraternal benefit society benefits."

Building materials. Items, such as lumber, brick, stone, iron, paint, and varnish, that are used to build or improve a structure.

Burial plot. A cemetery plot.

Business bankruptcy. A bankruptcy in which the debts arise primarily from the operation of a business, including bankruptcies filed by corporations, limited liability companies, and partnerships.

Certification. The act of signing a document under penalty of perjury. (The document that is signed is also called a certification.)

Chapter 7 bankruptcy. A liquidation bankruptcy, in which the trustee sells the debtor's nonexempt property and distributes the proceeds to the debtor's creditors. At the end of the case, the debtor receives a discharge of all remaining debts, except those that cannot legally be discharged.

Chapter 9 bankruptcy. A type of bankruptcy restricted to governmental units.

Chapter 11 bankruptcy. A type of bankruptcy intended to help businesses reorganize their debt load in order to remain in business. A Chapter 11 bankruptcy is typically much more expensive than a Chapter 7 or 13 bankruptcy because all of the lawyers must be paid out of the bankruptcy estate.

Chapter 12 bankruptcy. A type of bankruptcy designed to help small farmers reorganize their debts.

Chapter 13 bankruptcy. A type of consumer bankruptcy designed to help individuals reorganize their debts and pay all or a portion of them over three to five years.

Chapter 13 plan. A document filed in a Chapter 13 bankruptcy in which the debtor shows how all of his or her projected disposable income will be used over a three- to five-year period to pay all mandatory debts—for example, back child support, taxes, and mortgage arrearages—as well as some or all unsecured, nonpriority debts, such as medical and credit card bills.

Claim. A creditor's assertion that the bankruptcy filer owes it a debt or obligation.

Clothing. As an exemption category, the everyday clothes you and your family need for work, school, household use, and protection from the elements. In many states, luxury items and furs are not included in the clothing exemption category.

Codebtor. A person who assumes an equal responsibility, along with the debtor, to repay a debt or loan.

Collateral. Property pledged by a borrower as security for a loan.

Common law property states. States that don't use a community property system to classify marital property.

Community property. Certain property owned by married couples in Arizona, California, Idaho, Louisiana, New Mexico, Nevada, Texas, Washington, Wisconsin, and, if both spouses agree, Alaska. Very generally, all property acquired during the marriage is considered community property, belonging equally to both spouses, except for gifts and inheritances by one spouse. Similarly, all debts incurred during the marriage are considered community debts, owed equally by both spouses, with limited exceptions.

Complaint. A formal document that initiates a lawsuit.

Complaint to determine dischargeablity. A complaint initiating an adversary action in bankruptcy court that asks the court to decide whether a particular debt should be discharged at the end of the debtor's bankruptcy case.

Condominium. A building or complex in which separate units, such as townhouses or apartments, are owned by individuals, and the common areas (lobby, hallways, stairways, and so on) are jointly owned by the unit owners.

Confirmation. The bankruptcy judge's ruling approving a Chapter 13 plan.

Confirmation hearing. A court hearing conducted by a bankruptcy judge in which the judge decides whether a debtor's proposed Chapter 13 plan appears to be feasible and meets all applicable legal requirements.

Consumer bankruptcy. A bankruptcy in which a preponderance of the debt was incurred for personal, family, or household purposes.

Consumer debt. A debt incurred by an individual for personal, family, or household purposes.

Contingent debts. Debts that may be owed if certain events happen or conditions are satisfied.

Contingent interests in the estate of a decedent. The right to inherit property if one or more conditions to the inheritance are satisfied. For example, a debtor who will inherit property only if he survives his brother has a contingent interest.

Conversion. When a debtor who has filed one type of bankruptcy switches to another type—as when a Chapter 7 debtor converts to a Chapter 13 bankruptcy, or vice versa.

Cooperative housing. A building or other residential structure that is owned by a corporation formed by the residents. In exchange for purchasing stock in the corporation, the residents have the right to live in particular units.

Cooperative insurance. Compulsory employment benefits provided by a state or federal government, such as old age, survivors, disability, and health insurance, to assure a minimum standard of living for lower- and middle-income people. Also called social insurance.

Court clerk. The court employee who is responsible for accepting filings and other documents, and generally maintaining an accurate and efficient flow of paper and information in the court.

Cramdown. In a Chapter 13 bankruptcy, the act of reducing a secured debt to the replacement value of the collateral securing the debt.

Credit and debt counseling. Counseling that explores the possibility of repaying debts outside of bankruptcy and educates the debtor about credit, budgeting, and financial management. Under the new bankruptcy law, a debtor must undergo credit counseling with an approved provider before filing for bankruptcy.

Credit insurance. An insurance policy that covers a borrower for an outstanding loan. If the borrower dies or becomes disabled before paying off the loan, the policy will pay off the balance due.

Creditor. A person or institution to whom money is owed.

Creditor committee. In a Chapter 11 bankruptcy, a committee that represents the unsecured debtors in reorganization proceedings.

Creditor matrix. A specially formatted list of creditors that a debtor must file with the bankruptcy petition. The matrix helps the court notify creditors of the bankruptcy filing and the date and time set for the first meeting of creditors.

Creditors' meeting. See "meeting of creditors."

Crops. Products of the soil or earth that are grown and raised annually and gathered in a single season. Thus, oranges (on the tree or harvested) are crops; an orange tree isn't.

Current market value. What property could be sold for. This is how a debtor's property was previously valued for purposes of determining whether the property is protected by an applicable exemption. Under the new bankruptcy law, property must be valued at its "replacement cost."

Current monthly income. As defined by the new bankruptcy law, a bankruptcy filer's total gross income (whether taxable or not), averaged over the six-month period immediately preceding the month in which the bankruptcy is filed. The current monthly income is used to determine whether the debtor can file for Chapter 7 bankruptcy, among other things.

Debt. An obligation of any type, including a loan, credit, or promise to perform a contract or lease.

Debt relief agency. An umbrella term for any person or agency—including lawyers and bankruptcy petition preparers, but excluding banks, nonprofit and government agencies, and employees of debt relief agencies—that provides "bankruptcy assistance" to an "assisted person."

Debtor. Someone who owes money to another person or business. Also, the generic term used to refer to anyone who files for bankruptcy.

Declaration. A written statement that is made under oath but not witnessed by a notary public.

Declaration of homestead. A form filed with the county recorder's office to put on record your right to a homestead exemption. In most states, the homestead exemption is automatic—that is, you are not required to record a homestead declaration in order to claim the homestead exemption. A few states do require such a recording, however.

Disability benefits. Payments made under a disability insurance or retirement plan when the insured is unable to work (or retires early) because of disability, accident, or sickness.

Discharge. A court order, issued at the conclusion of a Chapter 7 or Chapter 13 bankruptcy case, which legally relieves the debtor of personal liability for debts that can be discharged in that type of bankruptcy.

Discharge exceptions. Debts that are not discharged in a bankruptcy case. The debtor continues to owe these debts even after the bankruptcy is concluded.

Discharge hearing. A hearing conducted by a bankruptcy court to explain the discharge, urge the debtor to stay out of debt, and review reaffirmation agreements to make sure they are feasible and fair.

Dischargeability action. An adversary action brought by a party who asks the court to determine whether a particular debt qualifies for discharge.

Dischargeable debt. A debt that is wiped out at the conclusion of a bankruptcy case, unless the judge decides that it should not be.

Dismissal. When the court orders a case to be closed without providing the relief available under the bankruptcy laws. For example, a Chapter 13 case might be dismissed because the debtor fails to propose a feasible plan; a Chapter 7 case might be dismissed for abuse.

Disposable income. The difference between a debtor's "current monthly income" and allowable expenses. This is the amount that the bankruptcy law deems available to pay into a Chapter 13 plan.

Domestic animals. See "animals."

Domestic support obligation. An obligation to pay alimony or child support to a spouse, child, or government entity pursuant to an order by a court or other governmental unit.

Doubling. The ability of married couples to double the amount of certain property exemptions when filing for bankruptcy together. The federal bankruptcy exemptions allow doubling. State laws vary—some permit doubling and some do not.

Education Individual Retirement Account. A type of account to which a person can contribute a certain amount of tax-deferred funds every year for the educational benefit of the debtor or certain relatives. Such an account is not part of the debtor's bankruptcy estate.

Emergency bankruptcy filing. An initial bankruptcy filing that includes only the petition and the creditor matrix, filed right away because the debtor needs the protection of the automatic stay to prevent a creditor from taking certain action, such as a foreclosure. An emergency filing case will be dismissed if the other required documents and forms are not filed in a timely manner.

Endowment insurance. An insurance policy that gives an insured who lives for a specified time (the endowment period) the right to receive the face value of the policy (the amount paid at death). If the insured dies sooner, the beneficiary named in the policy receives the proceeds.

Equity. The amount you get to keep if you sell property—typically the property's market value, less the costs of sale and the value of any liens on the property.

ERISA-qualified benefits. Pensions that meet the requirements of the Employee Retirement Income Security Act (ERISA), a federal law that sets minimum standards for such plans and requires beneficiaries to receive certain notices.

Executory contract. A contract in which one or both parties still have a duty to carry out one or more of the contract's terms.

Exempt property. Property described by state and federal laws (exemptions) that a debtor is entitled to keep in a Chapter 7 bankruptcy. Exempt property cannot be taken and sold by the trustee for the benefit of the debtor's unsecured creditors.

Exemptions. State and federal laws specifying the types of property creditors are not entitled to take to satisfy a debt, and the bankruptcy trustee is not entitled to take and sell for the benefit of the debtor's unsecured creditors.

Farm tools. Tools used by a person whose primary occupation is farming. Some states limit farm tools of the trade to items that can be held in the hand, such as hoes, axes, pitchforks, shovels, scythes, and the like. In other states, farm tools also include plows, harnesses, mowers, reapers, and so on.

Federal exemptions. A list of exemptions contained in the federal Bankruptcy Code. Some states give debtors the option of using the federal exemptions rather than the state exemptions.

Federal Rules of Bankruptcy Procedure. A set of rules issued by the Administrative Office of the United States Courts, which govern bankruptcy court procedures.

Filing date. The date a bankruptcy petition in a particular case is filed. With few exceptions, debts incurred after the filing date are not discharged. Similarly, property owned before the filing date is part of the bankruptcy estate, while property acquired after the filing date is not.

Fines, penalties, and restitution. Debts owed to a court or a victim as a result of a sentence in a criminal matter. These debts are generally not dischargeable in bankruptcy.

Foreclosure. The process by which a creditor with a lien on real estate forces a sale of the property in order to collect on the lien. Foreclosure typically occurs when a homeowner defaults on a mortgage.

Fraternal benefit society benefits. Benefits, often group life insurance, paid for by fraternal societies, such as the Elks, Masons, Knights of Columbus, or the Knights of Maccabees, for their members. Also called benefit society, benevolent society, or mutual aid association benefits.

Fraud. Generally, an act that is intended to mislead another for the purpose of financial gain. In a bankruptcy case, fraud is any writing or representation intended to mislead creditors for the purpose of obtaining a loan or credit, or any act intended to mislead the bankruptcy court or the trustee.

Fraudulent transfer. In a bankruptcy case, a transfer of property to another for less than the property's value for the purpose of hiding the property from the bankruptcy trustee—for instance, when a debtor signs a car over to a relative to keep it out of the bankruptcy estate. Fraudulently transferred property can be recovered and sold by the trustee for the benefit of the creditors.

Fraudulently concealed assets. Property that a bankruptcy debtor deliberately fails to disclose as required by the bankruptcy rules.

Furnishings. An exemption category recognized in many states, which includes furniture, fixtures in your home (such as a heating unit, furnace, or built-in lighting), and other items with which a home is furnished, such as carpets and drapes.

Good faith. In a Chapter 13 case, when a debtor files for bankruptcy with the sincere purpose of paying off debts over the period of time required by law rather than for manipulative purposes—such as to prevent a foreclosure that by all rights should be allowed to proceed.

Goods and chattels. See "personal property."

Group life or group health insurance. A single insurance policy covering individuals in a group (for example, employees) and their dependents.

Head of household. A person who supports and maintains, in one household, one or more people who are closely related to the person by blood, marriage, or adoption. Also referred to as "head of family."

Health aids. Items needed to maintain their owner's health, such as a wheelchair, crutches, prosthesis, or a hearing aid. Many states require that health aids be prescribed by a physician.

Health benefits. Benefits paid under health insurance plans, such as Blue Cross/Blue Shield, to cover the costs of health care.

Heirloom. An item with special monetary or sentimental value, which is passed down from generation to generation.

Home equity loan. A loan made to a homeowner on the basis of the equity in the home—and secured by the home in the same manner as a mortgage.

Homestead. A state or federal exemption applicable to property where the debtor lives when he or she files bankruptcy—usually including boats and mobile homes.

Homestead declaration. See "declaration of homestead."

Household good. As an exemption category, an item of permanent nature (as opposed to items consumed, like food or cosmetics) used in or about the house. This includes linens, dinnerware, utensils, pots and pans, and small electronic equipment like radios. Many state laws specifically list the types of household goods that fall within this exemption, as do the federal bankruptcy laws.

Householder. A person who supports and maintains a household, with or without other people. Also called a "housekeeper."

Impairs an exemption. When a lien, in combination with any other liens on the property and the amount the debtor is entitled to claim as exempt, exceeds the value of the property the debtor could claim in the absence of any liens. For example, if property is worth $15,000, there are $5,000 worth of liens on the property, and the debtor is entitled to a $5,000 exemption in the property, a lien that exceeded $5,000 would impair the debtor's exemption. Certain types of liens that impair an exemption may be removed (avoided) by the debtor if the court so orders.

Implement. As an exemption category, an instrument, tool, or utensil used by a person to accomplish his or her job.

In lieu of homestead (or burial) exemption. Designates an exemption that is available only if you don't claim the homestead (or burial) exemption.

Individual Debtor's Statement of Intention. An official bankruptcy form that debtors with secured debts must file to indicate what they want to do with the property that secures the debt. For instance, a debtor with a car note must indicate whether he or she wants to keep the car and continue the debt (reaffirmation), pay off the car note at a reduced price (redemption), or give the car back to the creditor and cancel the debt.

Injunction. A court order prohibiting a person or entity from taking specified actions—for example, the automatic stay (in reality an automatic injunction), which prevents most creditors from trying to collect their debts.

Insider creditor. A creditor with whom the debtor has a personal relationship, such as a relative, friend, or business partner.

Intangible property. Property that cannot be physically touched, such as an ownership share in a corporation or a copyright. Documents—such as a stock certificate—may provide evidence of intangible property.

Involuntary dismissal. When a bankruptcy judge dismisses a case because the debtor fails to carry out his or her duties—such as filing papers in a timely manner and cooperating with the trustee—or because the debtor files the bankruptcy in bad faith or engages in abuse by wrongfully filing for Chapter 7 when he or she should have filed for Chapter 13.

Involuntary lien. A lien that is placed on the debtor's property without the debtor's consent—for instance, when the IRS places a lien on property for back taxes.

IRS expenses. A table of national and regional expense estimates published by the IRS. Debtors whose "current monthly income" is more than their state's "median family income" must use the IRS expenses to calculate their average net income in a Chapter 7 case, or their disposable income in a Chapter 13 case.

Jewelry. Items created for personal adornment; usually includes watches. Also called "articles of adornment."

Joint debtors. Married people who file for bankruptcy together and pay a single filing fee.

Judgment proof. A description of a person whose income and property are such that a creditor can't (or won't) seize them to enforce a money judgment—for example, a dwelling protected by a homestead exemption or a bank account containing only a few dollars.

Judicial lien. A lien created by the recording of a court money judgment against the debtor's property—usually real estate.

Lease. A contract that governs the relationship between an owner of property and a person who wishes to use the property for a specific period of time—as in car and real estate leases.

Lien. A legal claim against property that must be paid before title to the property can be transferred. Liens can also often be collected through repossession (personal property) or foreclosure (real estate), depending on the type of lien.

Lien avoidance. A bankruptcy procedure in which certain types of liens can be removed from certain types of property. Liens that are not avoided survive the bankruptcy even though the underlying debt may be cancelled—for instance, a lien remains on a car even if the debt evidenced by the car note is discharged in the bankruptcy.

Life estate. The right to live in, but not own, a specific home until your death.

Life insurance. A policy that provides for the payment of money to an individual (called the beneficiary) in the event of the death of another (called the insured). The policy matures (becomes payable) only when the insured dies.

Lifting the stay. When a bankruptcy court allows a creditor to continue with debt collection or other activities that are otherwise banned by the automatic stay. For instance, the court might allow a landlord to proceed with an eviction or a lender to repossess a car because the debtor has defaulted on the note.

Liquid assets. Cash or items that are easily convertible into cash, such as a money market account, stock, U.S. Treasury bill, or bank deposit.

Liquidated debt. An existing debt for a specified amount arising out of a contract or court judgment. In contrast, an unliquidated debt is a claim for an as-yet uncertain amount, such as for injuries suffered in a car accident before the case goes to court.

Lost future earnings. The portion of a lawsuit judgment intended to compensate an injured person for the money he or she won't be able to earn in the future because of the injury. Also called lost earnings payments or recoveries.

Luxuries. In bankruptcy, goods or services purchased by the debtor that a court decides were not appropriate in light of the debtor's insolvency. This might include vacations, jewelry, costly cars, or frequent meals at expensive restaurants.

Mailing matrix. See "creditor matrix."

Marital debts. Debts owed jointly by a married couple.

Marital property. Property owned jointly by a married couple.

Marital settlement agreement. An agreement between a divorcing couple that sets out who gets what percentage (or what specific items) of the marital property, who pays what marital debts, and who gets custody and pays child support if there are children of the marriage.

Materialmen's and mechanics' liens. Liens imposed by statute on real estate when suppliers of materials, labor, and contracting services used to improve the real estate are not properly compensated.

Matured life insurance benefits. Insurance benefits that are currently payable because the insured person has died.

Means test. A formula that uses predefined income and expense categories to determine whether a debtor whose income is more than the median family income for his or her state should be allowed to file a Chapter 7 bankruptcy.

Median family income. An annual income figure for which there are as many families with incomes below that level as there are above that level. The U.S. Census Bureau publishes median family income figures for each state and for different family sizes. In bankruptcy, the median family income is used as a basis for determining whether a debtor must pass the means test to file Chapter 7 bankruptcy, and whether a debtor filing a Chapter 13 bankruptcy must commit all his or her projected disposable income to a five-year repayment plan.

Meeting of creditors. A meeting that the debtor is required to attend in a bankruptcy case, at which the trustee and creditors may ask the debtor questions about his or her property, information in the documents and forms he or she filed, and his or her debts.

Mortgage. A contract in which a loan to purchase real estate is secured by the real estate as collateral. If the borrower defaults on loan payments, the lender can foreclose on the property.

Motion. A formal legal procedure in which the bankruptcy judge is asked to rule on a dispute in the bankruptcy case. To bring a motion, a party must file a document explaining what relief is requested, the facts of the dispute, and the legal reasons why the court should grant the relief. The party bringing the motion must mail these documents to all affected parties and let them know when the court will hear argument on the motion.

Motion to avoid judicial lien on real estate. A motion brought by a bankruptcy debtor that asks the bankruptcy court to remove a judicial lien on real estate because the lien impairs the debtor's homestead exemption.

Motion to lift stay. A motion in which a creditor asks the court for permission to continue a court action or collection activities in spite of the automatic stay.

Motor vehicle. A self-propelled vehicle suitable for use on a street or road. This includes a car, truck, motorcycle, van, and moped. See also "tools of the trade."

Musical instrument. An instrument having the capacity, when properly operated, to produce a musical sound. Pianos, guitars, drums, drum machines, synthesizers, and harmonicas are all musical instruments.

Mutual aid association benefits. See "fraternal benefit society benefits."

Mutual assessment or mutual life. See "stipulated insurance."

Necessities. Articles needed to sustain life, such as food, clothing, medical care, and shelter.

Newly discovered creditors. Creditors who the debtor discovers after the bankruptcy is filed. If the case is still open, the debtor can amend the list to include the creditor; if the case is closed, it usually can be reopened to accommodate the amendment.

Nonbankruptcy federal exemptions. Federal laws that allow a debtor who has not filed for bankruptcy to keep creditors away from certain property. The debtor can also use these exemptions in bankruptcy if the debtor is using a state exemption system.

Nondischargeable debt. Debt that survives bankruptcy, such as back child support and most student loans.

Nonexempt property. Property in the bankruptcy estate that is unprotected by the exemption system available to the debtor (this is typically—but not always—the exemption system in the state where the debtor files bankruptcy). In a Chapter 7 bankruptcy, the trustee may sell it for the benefit of the debtor's unsecured creditors. In a Chapter 13 bankruptcy, debtors must propose a plan that pays their unsecured creditors at least the value of their unsecured property.

Nonpossessory, nonpurchase-money lien. A lien placed on property that is already owned by the debtor and is used as collateral for the loan without being possessed by the lender. In contrast, a nonpurchase-money, possessory lien exists on collateral that is held by a pawnshop.

Nonpriority debt. A type of debt that is not entitled to be paid first in bankruptcy, as priority debts are. Nonpriority debts do not have to be paid in full in a Chapter 13 case.

Nonpriority, unsecured claim. A claim that is not for a priority debt (such as child support) and is not secured by collateral or other property. Typical examples include credit card debt, medical bills, and student loans. In a Chapter 13 repayment plan, nonpriority, unsecured claims are paid only after all other debts are paid.

Notice of appeal. A form that must be filed with a court when a party wishes to appeal a judgment or order issued by the court. Often, the notice of appeal must be filed within ten days of the date the order or judgment is entered in the court's records.

Objection. A document one party files to oppose a proposed action by another party—for instance, when a creditor or trustee files an objection to a bankruptcy debtor's claim of exemption.

Order for relief. The court's automatic injunction against certain collection and other activities that might negatively affect the bankruptcy estate. Another name for the "automatic stay."

Oversecured debt. A debt that is secured by collateral that is worth more than the amount of the debt.

PACER. An online, fee-based database containing bankruptcy court dockets (records of proceedings in bankruptcy cases) and federal court documents, such as court rules and recent appellate court decisions.

Pain and suffering damages. The portion of a court judgment intended to compensate for past, present, and future mental and physical pain, suffering, impairment of ability to work, and mental distress caused by an injury.

Partially secured debt. A debt secured by collateral that is worth less than the debt itself—for instance, when a person owes $15,000 on a car that is worth only $10,000.

Party in interest. Any person or entity that has a financial interest in the outcome of a bankruptcy case, including the trustee, the debtor, and all creditors.

Pension. A fund into which payments are made to provide an employee income after retirement. Typically, the beneficiary can't access the account without incurring a significant penalty, usually a tax. There are many types of pensions, including defined benefit pensions provided by many large corporations and individual pensions (such as 401(k) and IRA accounts). In bankruptcy, most pensions are not considered part of the bankruptcy estate and are therefore not affected by a bankruptcy filing.

Personal financial responsibility counseling. Under the new bankruptcy law, a two-hour class intended to teach good budget management. Every consumer bankruptcy filer must attend such a class in order to obtain a discharge in Chapter 7, Chapter 12, or Chapter 13 bankruptcy.

Personal injury cause of action. The right to seek compensation for physical and mental suffering, including injury to body, reputation, or both. For example, someone who is hit and injured by a car might have a personal injury cause of action against the driver.

Personal injury recovery. The portion of a lawsuit judgment or insurance settlement that is intended to compensate someone for physical and mental suffering, including physical injury, injury to reputation, or both. Bankruptcy exemptions usually do not apply to compensation for pain or suffering or punitive damages—in other words, that part of the recovery can be taken by the trustee in a Chapter 7 case.

Personal property. All property not classified as real property, including tangible items such as cars and jewelry, and intangible property such as stocks and pensions.

Petition. The document a debtor files to officially begin a bankruptcy case and ask for relief. Other documents and schedules must be filed to support the petition at the time it is filed, or shortly afterwards.

Pets. See "animals."

Preference. A payment made by a debtor to a creditor within a defined period prior to filing for bankruptcy—within three months for arms-length creditors (regular commercial creditors) and one year for insider creditors (friends, family, business associates). Because a preference gives that debtor an edge over other debtors in the bankruptcy case, the trustee can recover the preference and distribute it among all of the creditors.

Pre-petition. Any time prior to the moment the bankruptcy petition is filed.

Pre-petition counseling. Debt or credit counseling that occurs before the bankruptcy petition is filed—as opposed to personal financial management counseling, which occurs after the petition is filed.

Presumed abuse. In a Chapter 7 bankruptcy, when the debtor has a current monthly income in excess of the family median income for the state where the debtor lives, and has sufficient income to propose a Chapter 13 plan under the "means test." If abuse is presumed, the debtor has to prove that his or her Chapter 7 filing is not abusive in order to proceed further.

Primarily business debts. When the majority of debt owed by a bankruptcy debtor—in dollar terms—arises from debts incurred to operate a business.

Primarily consumer debts. When the majority of debt owed by a bankruptcy debtor—in dollar terms—arises from debts incurred for personal or family purposes.

Priority claim. See "priority debt."

Priority creditor. A creditor who has filed a Proof of Claim showing that the debtor owes it a priority debt.

Priority debt. A type of debt that is paid first if there are distributions to be made from the bankruptcy estate. Priority debts include alimony and child support, fees owed to the trustee and attorneys in the case, and wages owed to employees. With one exception (back child support obligations assigned to government entities), priority claims must be paid in full in a Chapter 13 bankruptcy.

Proceeds for damaged exempt property. Money received through insurance coverage, arbitration, mediation, settlement, or a lawsuit to pay for exempt property that has been damaged or destroyed. For example, if a debtor had the right to use a $30,000 homestead exemption, but his or her home was destroyed by fire, the debtor can instead exempt $30,000 of the insurance proceeds.

Projected disposable income. The amount of income a debtor will have left over each month, after deducting allowable expenses, payments on mandatory debts, and administrative expenses from his or her current monthly income. This is the amount the debtor must pay towards his or her unsecured nonpriority debts in a Chapter 13 plan.

Proof of Claim. A formal document filed by bankruptcy creditors in a bankruptcy case to assert their right to payments from the bankruptcy estate, if any payments are made.

Proof of service. A document signed under penalty of perjury by the person serving a document showing how the service was made, who made it, and when.

Property of the estate. See "bankruptcy estate."

Purchase-money loans. Loans that are made to purchase specific property items, and that use the property as collateral to assure repayment, such as car loans and mortgages.

Purchase-money security interest. A claim on property owned by the holder of a loan that was used to purchase the property and that is secured by the property (as collateral).

Reaffirmation. An agreement entered into after a bankruptcy filing (post-petition) between the debtor and a creditor in which the debtor agrees to repay all or part of a pre-petition debt after the bankruptcy is over. For instance, a debtor makes an agreement with the holder of a car note that the debtor can keep the car and must continue to pay the debt after bankruptcy.

Real property. Real estate (land and buildings on the land, usually including mobile homes attached to a foundation).

Reasonable investigation. A bankruptcy attorney's obligation, under the new bankruptcy law, to look into the information provided to them by their clients.

Redemption. In a Chapter 7 bankruptcy, when the debtor obtains legal title to collateral for a secured debt by paying the secured creditor the replacement value of the collateral in a lump sum. For example, a debtor may redeem a car note by paying the lender the replacement value of the car (what a retail vendor would charge for the car, considering its age and condition).

Reopen a case. To open a closed bankruptcy case— usually for the purpose of adding an overlooked creditor or filing a motion to avoid an overlooked lien. A debtor must request that the court reopen the case.

Repayment plan. An informal plan to repay creditors most or all of what they are owed outside of bankruptcy. Also refers to the plan proposed by a debtor in a Chapter 13 case.

Replacement cost. What it would cost to replace a particular item by buying it from a retail vendor, considering its age and condition—for instance, when buying a car from a used car dealer, furniture from a used furniture shop, or electronic equipment on eBay.

Repossession. When a secured creditor takes property used as collateral because the debtor has defaulted on the loan secured by the collateral.

Request to lift the stay. A written request filed in bankruptcy court by a creditor, which seeks permission to engage in debt collection activity otherwise prohibited by the automatic stay.

Schedule A. The official bankruptcy form a debtor must file to describe all of his or her real property.

Schedule B. The official bankruptcy form a debtor must file to describe all personal property owned by the debtor, including tangible property, such as jewelry and vehicles, and intangible property, such as investments and accounts receivable.

Schedule C. The official bankruptcy form a debtor must file to describe the property the debtor is claiming as exempt, and the legal basis for the claims of exemption.

Schedule D. The official bankruptcy form a debtor must file to describe all secured debts owed by the debtor, such as car notes and mortgages.

Schedule E. The official bankruptcy form a debtor must file to describe all priority debts owed by the debtor, such as back child support and taxes.

Schedule F. The official bankruptcy form a debtor must file to describe all nonpriority, unsecured debts owed by the debtor, such as most credit card and medical bills.

Schedule G. The official bankruptcy form a debtor must file to describe any leases and executory contracts (contracts under which one or both parties still have obligations) to which the debtor is a party.

Schedule H. The official bankruptcy form a debtor must file to describe all codebtors that might be affected by the bankruptcy.

Schedule I. The official bankruptcy form a debtor must file to describe the debtor's income.

Schedule J. The official bankruptcy form a debtor must file to describe the debtor's actual monthly expenses.

Schedules. Official bankruptcy forms a debtor must file, detailing the debtor's property, debts, income, and expenses.

Second deed of trust. A loan against real estate made after the original mortgage (or first deed of trust). Most home equity loans are second deeds of trust.

Secured claim. A debt secured by collateral under a written agreement (for instance, a mortgage or car note) or by operation of law—such as a tax lien.

Secured creditor. The owner of a secured claim.

Secured debt. A debt secured by collateral.

Secured interest. A claim to property used as collateral. For instance, a lender on a car note retains legal title to the car until the loan is paid off.

Secured property. Property that is collateral for a secured debt.

Serial bankruptcy filing. A practice used by some debtors to file and dismiss one bankruptcy after another to obtain the protection of the automatic stay, even though the bankruptcies themselves offer no debt relief—for instance, when a debtor files successive Chapter 13 cases to prevent foreclosure of his or her home even though there are no debts to repay.

Sickness benefits. See "disability benefits."

State exemptions. State laws that specify the types of property creditors are not entitled to take to satisfy a debt, and the bankruptcy trustee is not entitled to take and sell for the benefit of the debtor's unsecured creditors.

Statement of Affairs. The official bankruptcy form a debtor must file to describe the debtor's legal, economic, and business transactions for the several years prior to filing, including gifts, preferences, income, closing of deposit accounts, lawsuits, and other information that the trustee needs to assess the legitimacy of the bankruptcy and the true extent of the bankruptcy estate.

Statement of Current Monthly Income and Disposable Income Calculation. The official bankruptcy form a debtor must file in a Chapter 13 case, setting out the debtor's current monthly income and calculating the debtor's projected disposable income that will determine how much will be paid to the debtor's unsecured creditors.

Statement of Current Monthly Income and Means Test Calculation. The official bankruptcy form a debtor must file in a Chapter 7 filing that shows the debtor's current monthly income, calculates whether the debtor's income is higher than the state's median family income, and, if so, uses the means test to determine whether a Chapter 7 bankruptcy would constitute abuse.

Statement of Intention. The official bankruptcy form a debtor must file in a Chapter 7 case to tell the court and secured creditors how the debtor plans to treat his or her secured debts—that is, reaffirm the debt, redeem the debt, or surrender the property and discharge the debt.

Statement of Social Security Number. The official bankruptcy form a debtor must file to disclose the debtor's complete Social Security number.

Statutory lien. A lien imposed on property by law, such as tax liens and mechanics' liens, as opposed to voluntary liens (such as mortgages) and liens arising from court judgments (judicial liens).

Stay. See "automatic stay."

Stipulated insurance. An insurance policy that allows the insurance company to assess an amount on the insured, above the standard premium payments, if the company experiences losses worse than had been calculated into the standard premium. Also called assessment, mutual assessment, or mutual life insurance.

Stock options. A contract between a corporation and an employee that gives the employee the right to purchase corporate stock at a specific price mentioned in the contract (the strike price).

Strip down of lien. In a Chapter 13 bankruptcy, when the amount of a lien on collateral is reduced to the collateral's replacement value. See "cramdown."

Student loan. A type of loan made for educational purposes by nonprofit or commercial lenders with repayment and interest terms dictated by federal law. Student loans are not dischargeable in bankruptcy unless the debtor can show that repaying the loan would impose an "undue hardship."

Substantial abuse. Under the old bankruptcy law, filing a Chapter 7 bankruptcy when a Chapter 13 bankruptcy was feasible.

Suits, executions, garnishments, and attachments. Activities engaged in by creditors to enforce money judgments, typically involving the seizure of wages and bank accounts.

Summary of Schedules. The official bankruptcy form a debtor must file to summarize the property and debt information contained in a debtor's schedules

Surrender value. See "avails."

Surrendering collateral. In Chapter 7 bankruptcy, the act of returning collateral to a secured lender in order to discharge the underlying debt—for example, returning a car to discharge the car note.

Tangible personal property. See "tangible property" and "personal property."

Tangible property. Property that may be physically touched. Examples include money, furniture, cars, jewelry, artwork, and houses. Compare "intangible property."

Tax lien. A statutory lien imposed on property to secure payment of back taxes—typically income and property taxes.

Tenancy by the entirety. A way that married couples can hold title to property in about half of the states. When one spouse dies, the surviving spouse automatically owns 100% of the property. In most cases, this type of property is not part of the bankruptcy estate if only one spouse files.

To ___ acres. A limitation on the size of a homestead that may be exempted.

Tools of the trade. Items needed to perform a line of work that you are currently doing and relying on for support. For a mechanic, plumber, or carpenter, for example, tools of trade are the implements used to repair, build, and install. Traditionally, tools of the trade were limited to items that could be held in the hand. Most states, however, now embrace a broader definition, and a debtor may be able to fit many items under a tool of trade exemption.

Transcript of tax return. A summary of a debtor's tax return provided by the IRS upon the debtor's request, usually acceptable as a substitute for the return in the instances when a return must be filed under the new bankruptcy law.

Trustee. An official appointed by the bankruptcy court to carry out the administrative tasks associated with a bankruptcy and to seize and sell nonexempt property in the bankruptcy estate for the benefit of the debtor's unsecured creditors.

U.S. Trustee. An official employed by Office of the U.S. Trustee (a division of the U.S. Department of Justice) who is responsible for overseeing the bankruptcy trustees, regulating credit and personal financial management counselors, regulating bankruptcy petition preparers, auditing bankruptcy cases, ferreting out fraud, and generally making sure that the bankruptcy laws are obeyed.

Undersecured debt. A debt secured by collateral that is worth less than the debt.

Undue hardship. The conditions under which a debtor may discharge a student loan—for example, when the debtor has no income and little chance of earning enough to repay the loan in the future.

Unexpired lease. A lease that is still in effect.

Unmatured life insurance. A policy that is not yet payable because the insured is still alive.

Unscheduled debt. A debt that is not included in the schedules accompanying a bankruptcy filing, perhaps because it was overlooked or intentionally left out.

Unsecured priority claims. Priority claims that aren't secured by collateral, such as back child support or taxes for which no lien has been placed on the debtor's property.

Valuation of property. The act of determining the replacement value of property for the purpose of describing it in the bankruptcy schedules, determining whether it is protected by an applicable exemption, redeeming secured property, or cramming down a lien in Chapter 13 bankruptcy.

Voluntary dismissal. When a bankruptcy debtor dismisses his or her Chapter 7 or Chapter 13 case on his or her own, without coercion by the court.

Voluntary lien. A lien agreed to by the debtor, as when the debtor signs a mortgage, car note, or second deed of trust.

Weekly net earnings. The earnings a debtor has left after mandatory deductions, such as income tax, mandatory union dues, and Social Security contributions, have been subtracted from his or her gross income.

Wildcard exemption. A dollar value that the debtor can apply to any type of property to make it—or more of it—exempt. In some states, filers may use the unused portion of a homestead exemption as a wildcard exemption.

Willful and malicious act. An act done with the intent to cause harm. In a Chapter 7 bankruptcy, a debt arising from the debtor's willful and malicious act is not discharged if the victim proves to the bankruptcy court's satisfaction that the act occurred.

Willful or malicious act resulting in a civil judgment. A bad act that was careless or reckless, but was not necessarily intended to cause harm. In a Chapter 13 case, a debt arising from the debtor's act that was either willful or malicious is not discharged if it is part of a civil judgment.

Wrongful death cause of action. The right to seek compensation for having to live without a deceased person. Usually only the spouse and children of the deceased have a wrongful death cause of action.

Wrongful death recoveries. The portion of a lawsuit judgment intended to compensate a plaintiff for having to live without a deceased person. The compensation is intended to cover the earnings and the emotional comfort and support the deceased would have provided. ■

State and Federal Exemptions Tables

The charts in this appendix summarize the laws that determine how much property people can keep when they file for Chapter 7 bankruptcy. As you will see, the charts are divided into categories of property, such as insurance, personal property, and wages. Following each exemption, we list the numerical citation to the state statute that includes the exemption. You'll need this information to complete your bankruptcy forms, as explained in Ch. 6.

The states are listed alphabetically, followed by the federal bankruptcy exemptions. (We also note the states that allow you to choose between the federal and state bankruptcy exemptions—see Ch. 3 for more information.)

Need help understanding a term? Many of the categories, types of property, and other terms used in these charts are defined in the Glossary, which you'll find right before this appendix.

A. Doubling

When married couples file for bankruptcy jointly, federal law and the laws of some states allow them each to claim the full amount of an exemption. (11 U.S.C. § 522.) Because these couples get to claim twice the amount available to those who file alone, this practice is informally known as "doubling."

Not all states allow doubling, however. And some states allow married filers to double only certain exemptions (for example, they can double personal property exemptions but not the homestead exemption). In the charts that follow, we indicate exemptions that cannot be doubled (and states that don't allow doubling at all). Unless you see a note stating that you cannot double, assume that you can.

These charts provide general information only. There are exceptions to state exemption laws that are much too detailed to include here. For example, even if an item is listed as exempt in one of these charts, you might have to give it up to pay a child support or tax debt. Consider doing further legal research or consulting an attorney about the exemptions you plan to claim, particularly if you anticipate—or are facing—a challenge to the value or types of property you want to keep. And, if valuable or cherished property is at stake, you may want to consult a local lawyer or accountant who is experienced in asset protection strategies.

B. Residency Requirements for Claiming State Exemptions

Prior to the new bankruptcy law, filers could use the exemptions of the state where they lived when they filed for bankruptcy. Under the new rules, however, some filers will have to use the exemptions of the state where they *used* to live. Congress was concerned about people gaming the system by moving to states with liberal exemptions just to file for bankruptcy. As a result, filers must now meet certain residency requirements before they can use a state's exemption system.

Here is a summary of these new rules:
- If you have lived or made your residence in your current state for at least two years, you can use that state's exemptions.
- If you have lived or made your residence in your current state for more than 91 days but less than two years, you must use the exemptions of the state where you lived for the greater part of the 180-day period immediately prior to the two-year period preceding your filing.
- If you have lived or made your residence in your current state for fewer than 91 days, you can either file in the state where you lived immediately before (as long as you lived there for at least 91 days) or wait until you have logged 91 days in your new home and file in your current state. Once you figure out where you can file, you'll need to use whatever exemptions are available to you according to the rules set out above.
- If the state you are filing in offers a choice between the state and federal bankruptcy exemptions, you can use the federal exemption list regardless of how long you've been living in the state.
- If these rules deprive you of the right to use *any* state's exemptions, you can use the federal exemption list. For example, some states allow their exemptions to be used only by current state residents, which might leave former residents who haven't lived in their new home state for at least two years without any available state exemptions.

For more detailed information and examples, see Ch. 3.

A longer residency requirement applies to homestead exemptions: If you acquired a home in your current state within the 40 months before you file for bankruptcy (and you didn't purchase it with the proceeds from selling another home in that state), your homestead exemption will be subject to a cap of $125,000, even if the state homestead exemption available to you is larger. For detailed information on homestead exemptions, see Ch. 4.

C. New Exemptions for Retirement Accounts

Under the new bankruptcy law, virtually all types of tax-exempt retirement accounts are exempt in bankruptcy, whether you use the state or federal exemptions. You can exempt 401(k)s, 403(b)s, profit-sharing and money purchase plans, IRAs (including Roth, SEP, and SIMPLE IRAs), and defined-benefit plans.

These exemptions are unlimited—that is, the entire account is exempt, regardless of how much money is in it—except in the case of traditional and Roth IRAs. For these types of IRAs only, the exemption is limited to a total value of $1 million per person (this figure will be adjusted every three years for inflation). If you have more than one traditional or Roth IRA, you don't get to exempt $1 million per account; your total exemption, no matter how many accounts you have, is $1 million.

If you are using the federal bankruptcy exemptions, you can find this new retirement account provision at 11 U.S.C. § 522(d)(12). If you are using state exemptions, cite 11 U.S.C. § 522(b)(3)(C) as the applicable exemption when you complete your bankruptcy papers.

Alabama

Federal bankruptcy exemptions not available. All law references are to Alabama Code unless otherwise noted.

ASSET	EXEMPTION	LAW
homestead	Real property or mobile home to $5,000; property cannot exceed 160 acres	6-10-2
	Must record homestead declaration before attempted sale of home	6-10-20
insurance	Annuity proceeds or avails to $250 per month	27-14-32
	Disability proceeds or avails to an average of $250 per month	27-14-31
	Fraternal benefit society benefits	27-34-27
	Life insurance proceeds or avails	6-10-8; 27-14-29
	Life insurance proceeds or avails if clause prohibits proceeds from being used to pay beneficiary's creditors	27-15-26
	Mutual aid association benefits	27-30-25
pensions	Tax-exempt retirement accounts, including 401(k)s, 403(b)s, profit-sharing and money purchase plans, SEP and SIMPLE IRAs, and defined-benefit plans	11 U.S.C. § 522(b)(3)(C)
	Traditional and Roth IRAs to $1,000,000 per person	11 U.S.C. § 522(b)(3)(C); (n)
	IRAs & other retirement accounts	19-3-1
	Judges (only payments being received)	12-18-10(a),(b)
	Law enforcement officers	36-21-77
	State employees	36-27-28
	Teachers	16-25-23
personal property	Books of debtor & family	6-10-6
	Burial place for self & family	6-10-5
	Church pew for self & family	6-10-5
	Clothing of debtor & family	6-10-6
	Family portraits or pictures	6-10-6
public benefits	Aid to blind, aged, disabled; & other public assistance	38-4-8
	Crime victims' compensation	15-23-15(e)
	Southeast Asian War POWs' benefits	31-7-2
	Unemployment compensation	25-4-140
	Workers' compensation	25-5-86(b)
tools of trade	Arms, uniforms, equipment that state military personnel are required to keep	31-2-78
wages	With respect to consumer loans, consumer credit sales, & consumer leases, 75% of weekly net earnings or 30 times the federal minimum hourly wage; all other cases, 75% of earned but unpaid wages; bankruptcy judge may authorize more for low-income debtors	5-19-15; 6-10-7
wildcard	$3,000 of any personal property, except wages	6-10-6

Alaska

Alaska law states that only the items found in Alaska Statutes §§ 9.38.010, 9.38.015(a), 9.38.017, 9.38.020, 9.38.025, and 9.38.030 may be exempted in bankruptcy. In *In re McNutt,* 87 B.R. 84 (9th Cir. 1988), however, an Alaskan debtor used the federal bankruptcy exemptions. All law references are to Alaska Statutes unless otherwise noted.

Alaska exemption amounts are adjusted regularly by administrative order. Current amounts are found at 8 Alaska Admin. Code tit. 8, § 95.030.

ASSET	EXEMPTION	LAW
homestead	$67,500 (joint owners may each claim a portion, but total can't exceed $67,500)	09.38.010(a)
insurance	Disability benefits	09.38.015(b); 09.38.030(e)(1),(5)
	Fraternal benefit society benefits	21.84.240
	Life insurance or annuity contracts, total avails to $12,500	09.38.025
	Medical, surgical, or hospital benefits	09.38.015(a)(3)
miscellaneous	Alimony, to extent wages exempt	09.38.030(e)(2)
	Child support payments made by collection agency	09.38.015(b)
	Liquor licenses	09.38.015(a)(7)
	Property of business partnership	09.38.100(b)
pensions	Tax-exempt retirement accounts, including 401(k)s, 403(b)s, profit-sharing and money purchase plans, SEP and SIMPLE IRAs, and defined-benefit plans	11 U.S.C. § 522(b)(3)(C)
	Traditional and Roth IRAs to $1,000,000 per person	11 U.S.C. § 522(b)(3)(C); (n)
	Elected public officers (only benefits building up)	09.38.015(b)
	ERISA-qualified benefits deposited more than 120 days before filing bankruptcy	09.38.017
	Judicial employees (only benefits building up)	09.38.015(b)
	Public employees (only benefits building up)	09.38.015(b); 39.35.505
	Roth & traditional IRAs, medical savings accounts	09.38.017(e)(3)
	Teachers (only benefits building up)	09.38.015(b)
	Other pensions, to extent wages exempt (only payments being received)	09.38.030(e)(5)
personal property	Books, musical instruments, clothing, family portraits, household goods, & heirlooms to $3,750 total	09.38.020(a)
	Building materials	34.35.105
	Burial plot	09.38.015(a)(1)
	Cash or other liquid assets to $1,750; for sole wage earner in household, $2,750 (restrictions apply—see *wages*)	09.38.030(b)
	Deposit in apartment or condo owners' association	09.38.010(e)
	Health aids needed	09.38.015(a)(2)
	Jewelry to $1,250	09.38.020(b)
	Motor vehicle to $3,750; vehicle's market value can't exceed $25,000	09.38.020(e)
	Personal injury recoveries, to extent wages exempt	09.38.030(e)(3)
	Pets to $1,250	09.38.020(d)
	Proceeds for lost, damaged, or destroyed exempt property	09.38.060
	Tuition credits under an advance college tuition payment contract	09.38.015(a)(8)
	Wrongful death recoveries, to extent wages exempt	09.38.030(e)(3)
public benefits	Adult assistance to elderly, blind, disabled	47.25.550
	Alaska longevity bonus	09.38.015(a)(5)
	Crime victims' compensation	09.38.015(a)(4)
	Federally exempt public benefits paid or due	09.38.015(a)(6)
	General relief assistance	47.25.210
	Senior care (prescription drug) benefits	09.38.015(a)(10)
	20% of permanent fund dividends	43.23.065
	Unemployment compensation	09.38.015(b); 23.20.405
	Workers' compensation	23.30.160

tools of trade	Implements, books & tools of trade to $3,500	09.38.020(c)
wages	Weekly net earnings to $438; for sole wage earner in a household, $688; if you don't receive weekly or semi-monthly pay, can claim $1,750 in cash or liquid assets paid any month; for sole wage earner in household, $2,750	9.38.030(a),(b); 9.38.050(b)
wildcard	None	

Arizona

Federal bankruptcy exemptions not available. All law references are to Arizona Revised Statutes unless otherwise noted.

ASSET	EXEMPTION	LAW
homestead	Real property, an apartment, or mobile home you occupy to $150,000; sale proceeds exempt 18 months after sale or until new home purchased, whichever occurs first (husband & wife may not double)	33-1101(A)
	May record homestead declaration to clarify which one of multiple eligible parcels is being claimed as homestead	33-1102
insurance	Fraternal benefit society benefits	20-877
	Group life insurance policy or proceeds	20-1132
	Health, accident, or disability benefits	33-1126(A)(4)
	Life insurance cash value or proceeds, or annuity contract if owned at least two years and beneficiary is dependent family member	33-1126(A)(6); 20-1131(D)
	Life insurance proceeds to $20,000 if beneficiary is spouse or child	33-1126(A)(1)
miscellaneous	Alimony, child support needed for support	33-1126(A)(3)
	Minor child's earnings, unless debt is for child	33-1126(A)(2)
pensions *see also wages*	Tax-exempt retirement accounts, including 401(k)s, 403(b)s, profit-sharing and money purchase plans, SEP and SIMPLE IRAs, and defined-benefit plans	11 U.S.C. § 522(b)(3)(C)
	Traditional and Roth IRAs to $1,000,000 per person	11 U.S.C. § 522(b)(3)(C); (n)
	Board of regents members, faculty & administrative officers under board's jurisdiction	15-1628(I)
	District employees	48-227
	ERISA-qualified benefits deposited over 120 days before filing	33-1126(B)
	IRAs & Roth IRAs	33-1126(B) *In re Herrscher,* 121 B.R. 29 (D. Ariz. 1989)
	Firefighters	9-968
	Police officers	9-931
	Rangers	41-955
	State employees retirement & disability	38-792; 38-797.11
personal property *husband & wife may double all personal property*	2 beds & bedding; 1 living room chair per person; 1 dresser, table, lamp; kitchen table; dining room table & 4 chairs (1 more per person); living room carpet or rug; couch; 3 lamps; 3 coffee or end tables; pictures, paintings, personal drawings, family portraits; refrigerator, stove, washer, dryer, vacuum cleaner; TV, radio, stereo, alarm clock to $4,000 total	33-1123
	Bank deposit to $150 in one account	33-1126(A)(9)
	Bible; bicycle; sewing machine; typewriter; burial plot; rifle, pistol, or shotgun to $500 total	33-1125
	Books to $250; clothing to $500; wedding & engagement rings to $1,000; watch to $100; pets, horses, milk cows, & poultry to $500; musical instruments to $250	33-1125
	Food & fuel to last 6 months	33-1124
	Funeral deposits to $5,000	32-1391.05(4)
	Health aids	33-1125(9)
	Motor vehicle to $5,000 ($10,000, if disabled)	33-1125(8)
	Prepaid rent or security deposit to $1,000 or 1-1/2 times your rent, whichever is less, in lieu of homestead	33-1126(C)
	Proceeds for sold or damaged exempt property	33-1126(A)(5),(8)
	Wrongful death awards	12-592
public benefits	Unemployment compensation	23-783(A)
	Welfare benefits	46-208
	Workers' compensation	23-1068(B)
tools of trade *husband & wife may double*	Arms, uniforms, & accoutrements of profession or office required by law	33-1130(3)
	Farm machinery, utensils, seed, instruments of husbandry, feed, grain, & animals to $2,500 total	33-1130(2)
	Library & teaching aids of teacher	33-1127
	Tools, equipment, instruments, & books to $2,500	33-1130(1)

| wages | 75% of earned but unpaid weekly net earnings or 30 times the federal minimum hourly wage; 50% of wages for support orders; bankruptcy judge may authorize more for low-income debtors | 33-1131 |
| wildcard | None | |

Arkansas

Federal bankruptcy exemptions available. All law references are to Arkansas Code Annotated unless otherwise noted.

Note: *In re Holt*, 894 F.2d 1005 (8th Cir. 1990) held that Arkansas residents are limited to exemptions in the Arkansas Constitution. Statutory exemptions can still be used within Arkansas for nonbankruptcy purposes, but they cannot be claimed in bankruptcy

ASSET	EXEMPTION	LAW
homestead *choose Option 1 or 2*	1. For married person or head of family: unlimited exemption on real or personal property used as residence to 1/4 acre in city, town, or village, or 80 acres elsewhere; if property is between 1/4–1 acre in city, town, or village, or 80-160 acres elsewhere, additional limit is $2,500; homestead may not exceed 1 acre in city, town, or village, or 160 acres elsewhere (husband & wife may not double)	Constitution 9-3; 9-4, 9-5; 16-66-210; 16-66-218(b)(3), (4) *In re Stevens*, 829 F.2d 693 (8th Cir. 1987)
	2. Real or personal property used as residence to $800 if single; $1,250 if married	16-66-218(a)(1)
insurance	Annuity contract	23-79-134
	Disability benefits	23-79-133
	Fraternal benefit society benefits	23-74-403
	Group life insurance	23-79-132
	Life, health, accident, or disability cash value or proceeds paid or due to $500	16-66-209; Constitution 9-1, 9-2; *In re Holt*, 894 F. 2d 1005 (7th Cir. 1990)
	Life insurance proceeds if clause prohibits proceeds from being used to pay beneficiary's creditors	23-79-131
	Life insurance proceeds or avails if beneficiary isn't the insured	23-79-131
	Mutual assessment life or disability benefits to $1,000	23-72-114
	Stipulated insurance premiums	23-71-112
miscellaneous	Property of business partnership (will be repealed in 2005)	4-42-502
pensions	Tax-exempt retirement accounts, including 401(k)s, 403(b)s, profit-sharing and money purchase plans, SEP and SIMPLE IRAs, and defined-benefit plans	11 U.S.C. § 522(b)(3)(C)
	Traditional and Roth IRAs to $1,000,000 per person	11 U.S.C. § 522(b)(3)(C); (n)
	Disabled firefighters	24-11-814
	Disabled police officers	24-11-417
	Firefighters	24-10-616
	IRA deposits to $20,000 if deposited over 1 year before filing for bankruptcy	16-66-218(b)(16)
	Police officers	24-10-616
	School employees	24-7-715
	State police officers	24-6-205; 24-6-223
personal property	Burial plot to 5 acres, if choosing federal homestead exemption (Option 2)	16-66-207; 16-66-218(a)(1)
	Clothing	Constitution 9-1, 9-2
	Motor vehicle to $1,200	16-66-218(a)(2)
	Prepaid funeral trusts	23-40-117
	Wedding rings	16-66-219
public benefits	Crime victims' compensation	16-90-716(e)
	Unemployment compensation	11-10-109
	Workers' compensation	11-9-110
tools of trade	Implements, books, & tools of trade to $750	16-66-218(a)(4)
wages	Earned but unpaid wages due for 60 days; in no event less than $25 per week	16-66-208; 16-66-218(b)(6)
wildcard	$500 of any personal property if married or head of family; $200 if not married	Constitution 9-1, 9-2; 16-66-218(b)(1),(2)

California—System 1

Federal bankruptcy exemptions not available. California has two systems; you must select one or the other. All law references are to California Code of Civil Procedure unless otherwise noted. Many exemptions do not apply to claims for child support.

Note: California's exemption amounts are no longer updated in the statutes themselves. California Code of Civil Procedure section 740.150 deputized the California Judicial Council to update the exemption amounts every three years. (The next revision will be in 2007.) As a result, the amounts listed in this chart will not match the amounts that appear in the cited statutes. The current exemption amounts can be found on the California Judicial Council website, www.courtinfo.ca.gov/forms/exemptions.htm.

ASSET	EXEMPTION	LAW
homestead	Real or personal property you occupy including mobile home, boat, stock cooperative, community apartment, planned development, or condo to $50,000 if single & not disabled; $75,000 for families if no other member has a homestead (if only one spouse files, may exempt one-half of amount if home held as community property & all of amount if home held as tenants in common); $150,000 if 65 or older, or physically or mentally disabled; $150,000 if 55 or older, single, & earn under $15,000 or married & earn under $20,000 & creditors seek to force the sale of your home; forced sale proceeds received exempt for 6 months after (husband & wife may not double)	704.710; 704.720; 704.730 *In re McFall,* 112 B.R. 336 (9th Cir. B.A.P. 1990)
	May file homestead declaration to protect exemption amount from attachment of judicial liens and to protect proceeds of voluntary sale for 6 months	704.920
insurance	Disability or health benefits	704.130
	Fidelity bonds	Labor 404
	Fraternal benefit society benefits	704.170
	Fraternal unemployment benefits	704.120
	Homeowners' insurance proceeds for 6 months after received, to homestead exemption amount	704.720(b)
	Life insurance proceeds if clause prohibits proceeds from being used to pay beneficiary's creditors	Ins. 10132; Ins. 10170; Ins. 10171
	Matured life insurance benefits needed for support	704.100(c)
	Unmatured life insurance policy cash surrender value completely exempt. Loan value exempt to $9,700	704.100(b)
miscellaneous	Business or professional licenses	695.060
	Inmates' trust funds to $1,225 (husband & wife may not double)	704.090
	Property of business partnership	Corp. 16501-04
pensions	Tax-exempt retirement accounts, including 401(k)s, 403(b)s, profit-sharing and money purchase plans, SEP and SIMPLE IRAs, and defined-benefit plans	11 U.S.C. § 522(b)(3)(C)
	Traditional and Roth IRAs to $1,000,000 per person	11 U.S.C. § 522(b)(3)(C); (n)
	County employees	Gov't 31452
	County firefighters	Gov't 32210
	County peace officers	Gov't 31913
	Private retirement benefits, including IRAs & Keoghs	704.115
	Public employees	Gov't 21255
	Public retirement benefits	704.110
personal property	Appliances, furnishings, clothing, & food	704.020
	Bank deposits from Social Security Administration to $2,425 ($3,650 for husband & wife); unlimited if SS funds are not commingled with other funds Bank deposits of other public benefits to $1,225 ($1,825 for husband & wife)	704.080
	Building materials to repair or improve home to $2,425 (husband & wife may not double)	704.030
	Burial plot	704.200
	Funds held in escrow	Fin. 17410
	Health aids	704.050
	Jewelry, heirlooms, & art to $6,075 total (husband & wife may not double)	704.040
	Motor vehicles to $2,300, or $2,300 in auto insurance for loss or damages (husband & wife may not double)	704.010
	Personal injury & wrongful death causes of action	704.140(a); 704.150(a)
	Personal injury & wrongful death recoveries needed for support; if receiving installments, at least 75%	704.140(b),(c),(d); 704.150(b),(c)

ASSET	EXEMPTION	LAW
public benefits	Aid to blind, aged, disabled; public assistance	704.170
	Financial aid to students	704.190
	Relocation benefits	704.180
	Unemployment benefits	704.120
	Union benefits due to labor dispute	704.120(b)(5)
	Workers' compensation	704.160
tools of trade	Tools, implements, materials, instruments, uniforms, books, furnishings, & equipment to $6,075 total ($12,150 total if used by both spouses in same occupation)	704.060
	Commercial vehicle (Vehicle Code § 260) to $4,850 ($9,700 total if used by both spouses in same occupation)	704.060
wages	Minimum 75% of wages paid within 30 days prior to filing	704.070
	Public employees' vacation credits; if receiving installments, at least 75%	704.113
wildcard	None	

California—System 2

Refer to the notes for California—System 1, above.

Note: Married couples may not double any exemptions. (*In re Talmadge,* 832 F.2d 1120 (9th Cir. 1987); *In re Baldwin,* 70 B.R. 612 (9th Cir. B.A.P. 1987).)

ASSET	EXEMPTION	LAW
homestead	Real or personal property, including co-op, used as residence to $18,675; unused portion of homestead may be applied to any property	703.140(b)(1)
insurance	Disability benefits	703.140(b)(10)(C)
	Life insurance proceeds needed for support of family	703.140(b)(11)(C)
	Unmatured life insurance contract accrued avails to $9,975	703.140(b)(8)
	Unmatured life insurance policy other than credit	703.140(b)(7)
miscellaneous	Alimony, child support needed for support	703.140(b)(10)(D)
pensions	Tax-exempt retirement accounts, including 401(k)s, 403(b)s, profit-sharing and money purchase plans, SEP and SIMPLE IRAs, and defined-benefit plans	11 U.S.C. § 522(b)(3)(C)
	Traditional and Roth IRAs to $1,000,000 per person	11 U.S.C. § 522(b)(3)(C); (n)
	ERISA-qualified benefits needed for support	703.140(b)(10)(E)
personal property	Animals, crops, appliances, furnishings, household goods, books, musical instruments, & clothing to $475 per item	703.140(b)(3)
	Burial plot to $18,675, in lieu of homestead	703.140(b)(1)
	Health aids	703.140(b)(9)
	Jewelry to $1,225	703.140(b)(4)
	Motor vehicle to $2,975	703.140(b)(2)
	Personal injury recoveries to $18,675 (not to include pain & suffering; pecuniary loss)	703.140(b)(11)(D),(E)
	Wrongful death recoveries needed for support	703.140(b)(11)(B)
public benefits	Crime victims' compensation	703.140(b)(11)(A)
	Public assistance	703.140(b)(10)(A)
	Social Security	703.140(b)(10)(A)
	Unemployment compensation	703.140(b)(10)(A)
	Veterans' benefits	703.140(b)(10)(B)
tools of trade	Implements, books, & tools of trade to $1,875	703.140(b)(6)
wages	None (use federal nonbankruptcy wage exemption)	
wildcard	$1,000 of any property	703.140(b)(5)
	Unused portion of homestead or burial exemption of any property	703.140(b)(5)

Colorado

Federal bankruptcy exemptions not available. All law references are to Colorado Revised Statutes unless otherwise noted.

ASSET	EXEMPTION	LAW
homestead	Real property, mobile home, manufactured home, or house trailer you occupy to $45,000; sale proceeds exempt 1 year after received	38-41-201; 38-41-201.6; 38-41-203; 38-41-207; *In re Pastrana,* 216 B.R. 948 (Colo., 1998)
	Spouse or child of deceased owner may claim homestead exemption	38-41-204
insurance	Disability benefits to $200 per month; if receive lump sum, entire amount exempt	10-16-212
	Fraternal benefit society benefits	10-14-403
	Group life insurance policy or proceeds	10-7-205
	Homeowners' insurance proceeds for 1 year after received, to homestead exemption amount	38-41-209
	Life insurance cash surrender value to $50,000, except contributions to policy within past 48 months	13-54-102(1)(l)
	Life insurance proceeds if clause prohibits proceeds from being used to pay beneficiary's creditors	10-7-106
miscellaneous	Child support	13-54-102.5
	Property of business partnership	7-60-125
pensions *see also wages*	Tax-exempt retirement accounts, including 401(k)s, 403(b)s, profit-sharing and money purchase plans, SEP and SIMPLE IRAs, and defined-benefit plans	11 U.S.C. § 522(b)(3)(C)
	Traditional and Roth IRAs to $1,000,000 per person	11 U.S.C. § 522(b)(3)(C); (n)
	ERISA-qualified benefits, including IRAs & Roth IRAs	13-54-102(1)(s)
	Firefighters & police officers	31-30.5-208; 31-31-203
	Public employees' pensions & defined contribution plans as of 2006	24-51-212
	Public employees' deferred compensation	24-52-105
	Teachers	22-64-120
	Veteran's pension for veteran, spouse, or dependents if veteran served in war or armed conflict	13-54-102(1)(h); 13-54-104
personal property	1 burial plot per family member	13-54-102(1)(d)
	Clothing to $1,500	13-54-102(1)(a)
	Food & fuel to $600	13-54-102(1)(f)
	Health aids	13-54-102(1)(p)
	Household goods to $3,000	13-54-102(1)(e)
	Jewelry & articles of adornment to $1,000	13-54-102(1)(b)
	Motor vehicles or bicycles used for work to $3,000; to $6,000 if used by a debtor or by a dependent who is disabled or 65 or over	13-54-102(j)(I), (II)
	Personal injury recoveries	13-54-102(1)(n)
	Family pictures & books to $1,500	13-54-102(1)(c)
	Proceeds for damaged exempt property	13-54-102(1)(m)
	Security deposits	13-54-102(1)(r)
public benefits	Aid to blind, aged, disabled; public assistance	26-2-131
	Crime victims' compensation	13-54-102(1)(q); 24-4.1-114
	Earned income tax credit	13-54-102(1)(o)
	Unemployment compensation	8-80-103
	Veteran's benefits for veteran, spouse, or child if veteran served in war or armed conflict	13-54-102(1)(h)
	Workers' compensation	8-42-124
tools of trade	Livestock or other animals, machinery, tools, equipment, & seed of person engaged in agriculture, to $25,000 total	13-54-102(1)(g)
	Professional's library to $3,000 (if not claimed under other tools of trade exemption)	13-54-102(1)(k)
	Stock in trade, supplies, fixtures, tools, machines, electronics, equipment, books, & other business materials, to $10,000 total	13-54-102(1)(i)
	Military equipment personally owned by members of the national guard	13-54-102(1)(h.5)
wages	Minimum 75% of weekly net earnings or 30 times the federal minimum wage, whichever is greater, including pension & insurance payments	13-54-104
wildcard	None	

Connecticut

Federal bankruptcy exemptions available. All law references are to Connecticut General Statutes Annotated unless otherwise noted.

ASSET	EXEMPTION	LAW
homestead	Real property, including mobile or manufactured home, to $75,000; applies only to claims arising after 1993, but to $125,000 in the case of a money judgment arising out of services provided at a hospital.	52-352a(e); 52-352b(t)
insurance	Disability benefits paid by association for its members	52-352b(p)
	Fraternal benefit society benefits	38a-637
	Health or disability benefits	52-352b(e)
	Life insurance proceeds if clause prohibits proceeds from being used to pay beneficiary's creditors	38a-454
	Life insurance proceeds or avails	38a-453
	Unmatured life insurance policy avails to $4,000 if beneficiary is dependent	52-352b(s)
miscellaneous	Alimony, to extent wages exempt	52-352b(n)
	Child support	52-352b(h)
	Farm partnership animals & livestock feed reasonably required to run farm where at least 50% of partners are members of same family	52-352d
pensions	Tax-exempt retirement accounts, including 401(k)s, 403(b)s, profit-sharing and money purchase plans, SEP and SIMPLE IRAs, and defined-benefit plans	11 U.S.C. § 522(b)(3)(C)
	Traditional and Roth IRAs to $1,000,000 per person	11 U.S.C. § 522(b)(3)(C); (n)
	ERISA-qualified benefits, including IRAs, Roth IRAs, & Keoghs, to extent wages exempt	52-321a; 52-352b(m)
	Medical savings account	52-321a
	Municipal employees	7-446
	State employees	5-171; 5-192w
	Teachers	10-183q
personal property	Appliances, food, clothing, furniture, bedding	52-352b(a)
	Burial plot	52-352b(c)
	Health aids needed	52-352b(f)
	Motor vehicle to $1,500	52-352b(j)
	Proceeds for damaged exempt property	52-352b(q)
	Residential utility & security deposits for 1 residence	52-3252b(l)
	Spendthrift trust funds required for support of debtor & family	52-321(d)
	Transfers to a nonprofit debt adjuster	52-352b(u)
	Wedding & engagement rings	52-352b(k)
public benefits	Crime victims' compensation	52-352b(o); 54-213
	Public assistance	52-352b(d)
	Social Security	52-352b(g)
	Unemployment compensation	31-272(c); 52-352b(g)
	Veterans' benefits	52-352b(g)
	Workers' compensation	52-352b(g)
tools of trade	Arms, military equipment, uniforms, musical instruments of military personnel	52-352b(i)
	Tools, books, instruments, & farm animals needed	52-352b(b)
wages	Minimum 75% of earned but unpaid weekly disposable earnings, or 40 times the state or federal hourly minimum wage, whichever is greater	52-361a(f)
wildcard	$1,000 of any property	52-352b(r)

Delaware

Federal bankruptcy exemptions not available. All law references are to Delaware Code Annotated (in the form title number-section number) unless otherwise noted.

Note: A single person may exempt no more than $25,000 total in all exemptions (not including retirement plans); a husband & wife may exempt no more than $50,000 total (10-4914).

ASSET	EXEMPTION	LAW
homestead	Real property or manufactured home used as principal residence to $50,000 (spouses may not double)	10-4914(c)
	Property held as tenancy by the entirety may be exempt against debts owed by only one spouse	*In re Kelley,* 289 B.R. 38 (Bankr. D. Del. 2003)
insurance	Annuity contract proceeds to $350 per month	18-2728
	Fraternal benefit society benefits	18-6218
	Group life insurance policy or proceeds	18-2727
	Health or disability benefits	18-2726
	Life insurance proceeds if clause prohibits proceeds from being used to pay beneficiary's creditors	18-2729
	Life insurance proceeds or avails	18-2725
pensions	Tax-exempt retirement accounts, including 401(k)s, 403(b)s, profit-sharing and money purchase plans, SEP and SIMPLE IRAs, and defined-benefit plans	11 U.S.C. § 522(b)(3)(C)
	Traditional and Roth IRAs to $1,000,000 per person	11 U.S.C. § 522(b)(3)(C); (n)
	IRAs, Roth IRAs, & any other retirement plans	*In re Yuhas,* 104 F.3d 612 (3rd Cir. 1997)
	Kent County employees	9-4316
	Police officers	11-8803
	State employees	29-5503
	Volunteer firefighters	16-6653
personal property	Bible, books, & family pictures	10-4902(a)
	Burial plot	10-4902(a)
	Church pew or any seat in public place of worship	10-4902(a)
	Clothing, includes jewelry	10-4902(a)
	College investment plan account (limit for year before filing is $5,000 or average of past two years' contribution, whichever is more)	10-4916
	Principal and income from spendthrift trusts	12-3536
	Pianos & leased organs	10-4902(d)
	Sewing machines	10-4902(c)
public benefits	Aid to blind	31-2309
	Aid to aged, disabled, general assistance	31-513
	Crime victims' compensation	11-9011
	Unemployment compensation	19-3374
	Workers' compensation	19-2355
tools of trade	Tools of trade and/or vehicle necessary for employment to $15,000 each	10-4914(c)
	Tools, implements, & fixtures to $75 in New Castle & Sussex Counties; to $50 in Kent County	10-4902(b)
wages	85% of earned but unpaid wages	10-4913
wildcard	$500 of any personal property, except tools of trade, if head of family	10-4903

District of Columbia

Federal bankruptcy exemptions available. All law references are to District of Columbia Code unless otherwise noted.

ASSET	EXEMPTION	LAW
homestead	Any property used as a residence or co-op that debtor or debtor's dependent uses as a residence	15-501(a)(14)
	Property held as tenancy by the entirety may be exempt against debts owed by only one spouse	*Estate of Wall*, 440 F.2d 215 (D.C. Cir. 1971)
insurance	Disability benefits	15-501(a)(7); 31-4716.01
	Fraternal benefit society benefits	31-5315
	Group life insurance policy or proceeds	31-4717
	Life insurance payments	15-501(a)(11)
	Life insurance proceeds if clause prohibits proceeds from being used to pay beneficiary's creditors	31-4719
	Life insurance proceeds or avails	31-4716
	Other insurance proceeds to $200 per month, maximum 2 months, for head of family; else $60 per month	15-503
	Unmatured life insurance contract other than credit life insurance	15-501(a)(5)
miscellaneous	Alimony or child support	15-501(a)(7)
pensions *see also wages*	Tax-exempt retirement accounts, including 401(k)s, 403(b)s, profit-sharing and money purchase plans, SEP and SIMPLE IRAs, and defined-benefit plans	11 U.S.C. § 522(b)(3)(C)
	Traditional and Roth IRAs to $1,000,000 per person	11 U.S.C. § 522(b)(3)(C); (n)
	ERISA-qualified benefits, IRAs, Keoghs, etc. to maximum deductible contribution	15-501(b)(9)
	Any stock bonus, annuity, pension, or profit-sharing plan	15-501(a)(7)
	Judges	11-1570(f)
	Public school teachers	38-2001.17; 38-2021.17
personal property	Appliances, books, clothing, household furnishings, goods, musical instruments, pets to $425 per item or $8,625 total	15-501(a)(2)
	Cemetery & burial funds	43-111
	Cooperative association holdings to $50	29-928
	Food for 3 months	15-501(a)(12)
	Health aids	15-501(a)(6)
	Higher education tuition savings account	47-4510
	Residential condominium deposit	42-1904.09
	All family pictures; & all the family library, to $400	15-501(a)(8)
	Motor vehicle to $2,575	15-501(a)(1)
	Payment including pain & suffering for loss of debtor or person depended on	15-501(a)(11)
	Uninsured motorist benefits	31-2408.01(h)
	Wrongful death damages	15-501(a)(11); 16-2703
public benefits	Aid to blind, aged, disabled; general assistance	4-215.01
	Crime victims' compensation	4-507(e); 15-501(a)(11)
	Social Security	15-501(a)(7)
	Unemployment compensation	51-118
	Veterans' benefits	15-501(a)(7)
	Workers' compensation	32-1517
tools of trade	Library, furniture, tools of professional or artist to $300	15-501(a)(13)
	Tools of trade or business to $1,625	15-501(a)(5)
	Mechanic's tools to $200	15-503(b)
	Seal & documents of notary public	1-1206

wages	Minimum 75% of earned but unpaid wages, pension payments; bankruptcy judge may authorize more for low-income debtors	16-572
	Nonwage (including pension & retirement) earnings to $200/mo for head of family; else $60/mo for a maximum of two months	15-503
	Payment for loss of future earnings	15-501(e)(11)
wildcard	Up to $850 in any property, plus up to $8,075 of unused homestead exemption	15-501(a)(3)

Florida

Federal bankruptcy exemptions not available. All law references are to Florida Statutes Annotated unless otherwise noted.

ASSET	EXEMPTION	LAW
homestead	Real or personal property including mobile or modular home to unlimited value; cannot exceed half acre in municipality or 160 acres elsewhere; spouse or child of deceased owner may claim homestead exemption	222.01; 222.02; 222.03; 222.05; Constitution 10-4 *In re Colwell,* 196 F.3d 1225 (11th Cir. 1999)
	May file homestead declaration	222.01
	Property held as tenancy by the entirety may be exempt against debts owed by only one spouse	*Havoco of America, Ltd. v. Hill,* 197 F.3d 1135 (11th Cir Fla.,1999)
insurance	Annuity contract proceeds; does not include lottery winnings	222.14; *In re Pizzi,* 153 B.R. 357 (S.D. Fla. 1993)
	Death benefits payable to a specific beneficiary, not the deceased's estate	222.13
	Disability or illness benefits	222.18
	Fraternal benefit society benefits	632.619
	Life insurance cash surrender value	222.14
miscellaneous	Alimony, child support needed for support	222.201
	Damages to employees for injuries in hazardous occupations	769.05
pensions *see also wages*	Tax-exempt retirement accounts, including 401(k)s, 403(b)s, profit-sharing and money purchase plans, SEP and SIMPLE IRAs, and defined-benefit plans	11 U.S.C. § 522(b)(3)(C)
	Traditional and Roth IRAs to $1,000,000 per person	11 U.S.C. § 522(b)(3)(C); (n)
	County officers, employees	122.15
	ERISA-qualified benefits, including IRAs & Roth IRAs	222.21(2)
	Firefighters	175.241
	Police officers	185.25
	State officers, employees	121.131
	Teachers	238.15
personal property	Any personal property to $1,000 (husband & wife may double)	Constitution 10-4 *In re Hawkins,* 51 B.R. 348 (S.D. Fla. 1985)
	Federal income tax refund or credit	222.25
	Health aids	222.25
	Motor vehicle to $1,000	222.25
	Pre-need funeral contract deposits	497.56(8)
	Prepaid college education trust deposits	222.22(1)
	Prepaid hurricane savings accounts	222.22(4)
	Prepaid medical savings account deposits	222.22(2)
public benefits	Crime victims' compensation, unless seeking to discharge debt for treatment of injury incurred during the crime	960.14
	Public assistance	222.201
	Social Security	222.201
	Unemployment compensation	222.201; 443.051(2),(3)
	Veterans' benefits	222.201; 744.626
	Workers' compensation	440.22
tools of trade	None	
wages	100% of wages for heads of family up to $500 per week either unpaid or paid & deposited into bank account for up to 6 months	222.11
	Federal government employees' pension payments needed for support & received 3 months prior	222.21
wildcard	See personal property	

Georgia

Federal bankruptcy exemptions not available. All law references are to the Official Code of Georgia Annotated unless otherwise noted.

ASSET	EXEMPTION	LAW
homestead	Real or personal property, including co-op, used as residence to $10,000 (to $20,000 if married, whether or not spouse is filing); up to $5,000 of unused portion of homestead may be applied to any property	44-13-100(a)(1); 44-13-100(a)(6); *In re Burnett,* 303 B.R. 684 (M.D. Ga. 2003)
insurance	Annuity & endowment contract benefits	33-28-7
	Disability or health benefits to $250 per month	33-29-15
	Fraternal benefit society benefits	33-15-62
	Group insurance	33-30-10
	Proceeds & avails of life insurance	33-26-5; 33-25-11
	Life insurance proceeds if policy owned by someone you depended on, needed for support	44-13-100(a)(11)(C)
	Unmatured life insurance contract	44-13-100(a)(8)
	Unmatured life insurance dividends, interest, loan value, or cash value to $2,000 if beneficiary is you or someone you depend on	44-13-100(a)(9)
miscellaneous	Alimony, child support needed for support	44-13-100(a)(2)(D)
pensions	Tax-exempt retirement accounts, including 401(k)s, 403(b)s, profit-sharing and money purchase plans, SEP and SIMPLE IRAs, and defined-benefit plans	11 U.S.C. § 522(b)(3)(C)
	Traditional and Roth IRAs to $1,000,000 per person	11 U.S.C. § 522(b)(3)(C); (n)
	Employees of nonprofit corporations	44-13-100(a)(2.1)(B)
	ERISA-qualified benefits & IRAs	18-4-22
	Public employees	44-13-100(a)(2.1)(A); 47-2-332
	Payments from IRA necessary for support	44-13-100(a)(2)(F)
	Other pensions needed for support	18-4-22; 44-13-100(a)(2)(E); 44-13-100(a)(2.1)(C)
personal property	Animals, crops, clothing, appliances, books, furnishings, household goods, musical instruments to $300 per item, $5,000 total	44-13-100(a)(4)
	Burial plot, in lieu of homestead	44-13-100(a)(1)
	Compensation for lost future earnings needed for support to $7,500	44-13-100(a)(11)(E)
	Health aids	44-13-100(a)(10)
	Jewelry to $500	44-13-100(a)(5)
	Motor vehicles to $3,500	44-13-100(a)(3)
	Personal injury recoveries to $10,000	44-13-100(a)(11)(D)
	Wrongful death recoveries needed for support	44-13-100(a)(11)(B)
public benefits	Aid to blind	49-4-58
	Aid to disabled	49-4-84
	Crime victims' compensation	44-13-100(a)(11)(A)
	Local public assistance	44-13-100(a)(2)(A)
	Old age assistance	49-4-35
	Social Security	44-13-100(a)(2)(A)
	Unemployment compensation	44-13-100(a)(2)(A)
	Veterans' benefits	44-13-100(a)(2)(B)
	Workers' compensation	34-9-84
tools of trade	Implements, books, & tools of trade to $1,500	44-13-100(a)(7)
wages	Minimum 75% of earned but unpaid weekly disposable earnings, or 40 times the state or federal hourly minimum wage, whichever is greater, for private & federal workers; bankruptcy judge may authorize more for low-income debtors	18-4-20; 18-4-21
wildcard	$600 of any property	44-13-100(a)(6)
	Unused portion of homestead exemption to $5,000	44-13-100(a)(6)

Hawaii

Federal bankruptcy exemptions available. All law references are to Hawaii Revised Statutes unless otherwise noted.

ASSET	EXEMPTION	LAW
homestead	Head of family or over 65 to $30,000; all others to $20,000; property cannot exceed 1 acre; sale proceeds exempt for 6 months after sale (husband & wife may not double)	651-91; 651-92; 651-96
	Property held as tenancy by the entirety may be exempt against debts owed by only one spouse	*Security Pacific Bank v. Chang*, 818 F.Supp. 1343 (D. Haw. 1993)
insurance	Annuity contract or endowment policy proceeds if beneficiary is insured's spouse, child, or parent	431:10-232(b)
	Accident, health, or sickness benefits	431:10-231
	Fraternal benefit society benefits	432:2-403
	Group life insurance policy or proceeds	431:10-233
	Life insurance proceeds if clause prohibits proceeds from being used to pay beneficiary's creditors	431:10D-112
	Life or health insurance policy for spouse or child	431:10-234
miscellaneous	Property of business partnership	425-125
pensions	Tax-exempt retirement accounts, including 401(k)s, 403(b)s, profit-sharing and money purchase plans, SEP and SIMPLE IRAs, and defined-benefit plans	11 U.S.C. § 522(b)(3)(C)
	Traditional and Roth IRAs to $1,000,000 per person	11 U.S.C. § 522(b)(3)(C); (n)
	IRAs, Roth IRAs, and ERISA-qualified benefits deposited over 3 years before filing bankruptcy	651-124
	Firefighters	88-169
	Police officers	88-169
	Public officers & employees	88-91; 653-3
personal property	Appliances & furnishings	651-121(1)
	Books	651-121(1)
	Burial plot to 250 sq. ft. plus tombstones, monuments, & fencing	651-121(4)
	Clothing	651-121(1)
	Jewelry, watches, & articles of adornment to $1,000	651-121(1)
	Motor vehicle to wholesale value of $2,575	651-121(2)
	Proceeds for sold or damaged exempt property; sale proceeds exempt for 6 months after sale	651-121(5)
public benefits	Crime victims' compensation & special accounts created to limit commercial exploitation of crimes	351-66; 351-86
	Public assistance paid by Dept. of Health Services for work done in home or workshop	346-33
	Temporary disability benefits	392-29
	Unemployment compensation	383-163
	Unemployment work relief funds to $60 per month	653-4
	Workers' compensation	386-57
tools of trade	Tools, implements, books, instruments, uniforms, furnishings, fishing boat, nets, motor vehicle, & other property needed for livelihood	651-121(3)
wages	Prisoner's wages held by Dept. of Public Safety (except for restitution, child support, & other claims)	353-22.5
	Unpaid wages due for services of past 31 days	651-121(6)
wildcard	None	

Idaho

Federal bankruptcy exemptions not available. All law references are to Idaho Code unless otherwise noted.

ASSET	EXEMPTION	LAW
homestead	Real property or mobile home to $50,000; sale proceeds exempt for 6 months (husband & wife may not double)	55-1003; 55-1113
	Must record homestead exemption for property that is not yet occupied	55-1004
insurance	Annuity contract proceeds to $1,250 per month	41-1836
	Death or disability benefits	11-604(1)(a); 41-1834
	Fraternal benefit society benefits	41-3218
	Group life insurance benefits	41-1835
	Homeowners' insurance proceeds to amount of homestead exemption	55-1008
	Life insurance proceeds if clause prohibits proceeds from being used to pay beneficiary's creditors	41-1930
	Life insurance proceeds or avails for beneficiary other than the insured	11-604(d); 41-1833
	Medical, surgical, or hospital care benefits	11-603(5)
	Unmatured life insurance contract, other than credit life insurance, owned by debtor	11-605(8)
	Unmatured life insurance contract interest or dividends to $5,000 owned by debtor or person debtor depends on	11-605(9)
miscellaneous	Alimony, child support	11-604(1)(b)
	Liquor licenses	23-514
pension *see also wages*	Tax-exempt retirement accounts, including 401(k)s, 403(b)s, profit-sharing and money purchase plans, SEP and SIMPLE IRAs, and defined-benefit plans	11 U.S.C. § 522(b)(3)(C)
	Traditional and Roth IRAs to $1,000,000 per person	11 U.S.C. § 522(b)(3)(C); (n)
	ERISA-qualified benefits	55-1011
	Firefighters	72-1422
	Government & private pensions, retirement plans, IRAs, Roth IRAs, Keoghs, etc.	11-604A
	Police officers	50-1517
	Public employees	59-1317
personal property	Appliances, furnishings, books, clothing, pets, musical instruments, 1 firearm, family portraits, & sentimental heirlooms to $500 per item, $5,000 total	11-605(1)
	Building materials	45-514
	Burial plot	11-603(1)
	College savings program account	11-604A(4)(b)
	Crops cultivated on maximum of 50 acres, to $1,000; water rights to 160 inches	11-605(6)
	Health aids	11-603(2)
	Jewelry to $1,000	11-605(2)
	Motor vehicle to $3,000	11-605(3)
	Personal injury recoveries	11-604(1)(c)
	Proceeds for damaged exempt property for 3 months after proceeds received	11-606
	Wrongful death recoveries	11-604(1)(c)
public benefits	Aid to blind, aged, disabled	56-223
	Federal, state, & local public assistance	11-603(4)
	General assistance	56-223
	Social Security	11-603(3)
	Unemployment compensation	11-603(6)
	Veterans' benefits	11-603(3)
	Workers' compensation	72-802
tools of trade	Arms, uniforms, & accoutrements that peace officer, National Guard, or military personnel is required to keep	11-605(5)
	Implements, books, & tools of trade to $1,500	11-605(3)
wages	Minimum 75% of earned but unpaid weekly disposable earnings, or 30 times the federal hourly minimum wage, whichever is greater; pension payments; bankruptcy judge may authorize more for low-income debtors	11-207
wildcard	$800 in any tangible personal property	11-605(10)

Illinois

Federal bankruptcy exemptions not available. All law references are to Illinois Compiled Statutes Annotated unless otherwise noted.

ASSET	EXEMPTION	LAW
homestead	Real or personal property including a farm, lot, & buildings, condo, co-op, or mobile home to $15,000; sale proceeds exempt for 1 year	735-5/12-901; 735-5/12-906
	Spouse or child of deceased owner may claim homestead exemption	735-5/12-902
	Illinois recognizes tenancy by the entirety, with limitations	750-65/22; 765-1005/1c; *In re Gillissie*, 215 B.R. 370 (Bankr. N.D. Ill. 1998); *Great Southern Co. v. Allard*, 202 B.R. 938 (N.D. Ill. 1996).
insurance	Fraternal benefit society benefits	215-5/299.1a
	Health or disability benefits	735-5/12-1001(g)(3)
	Homeowners' proceeds if home destroyed, to $15,000	735-5/12-907
	Life insurance, annuity proceeds, or cash value if beneficiary is insured's child, parent, spouse, or other dependent	215-5/238; 735-5/12-1001(f)
	Life insurance proceeds to a spouse or dependent of debtor to extent needed for support	735-5/12-1001(f),(g)(3)
miscellaneous	Alimony, child support	735-5/12-1001(g)(4)
	Property of business partnership	805-205/25
pensions	Tax-exempt retirement accounts, including 401(k)s, 403(b)s, profit-sharing and money purchase plans, SEP and SIMPLE IRAs, and defined-benefit plans	11 U.S.C. § 522(b)(3)(C)
	Traditional and Roth IRAs to $1,000,000 per person	11 U.S.C. § 522(b)(3)(C); (n)
	Civil service employees	40-5/11-223
	County employees	40-5/9-228
	Disabled firefighters; widows & children of firefighters	40-5/22-230
	IRAs and ERISA-qualified benefits	735-5/12-1006
	Firefighters	40-5/4-135; 40-5/6-213
	General assembly members	40-5/2-154
	House of correction employees	40-5/19-117
	Judges	40-5/18-161
	Municipal employees	40-5/7-217(a); 40-5/8-244
	Park employees	40-5/12-190
	Police officers	40-5/3-144.1; 40-5/5-218
	Public employees	735-5/12-1006
	Public library employees	40-5/19-218
	Sanitation district employees	40-5/13-805
	State employees	40-5/14-147
	State university employees	40-5/15-185
	Teachers	40-5/16-190; 40-5/17-151
personal property	Bible, family pictures, schoolbooks, & clothing	735-5/12-1001(a)
	Health aids	735-5/12-1001(e)
	Motor vehicle to $2,400	735-5/12-1001(c)
	Personal injury recoveries to $15,000	735-5/12-1001(h)(4)
	Pre-need cemetery sales funds, care funds, & trust funds	235-5/6-1; 760-100/4; 815-390/16
	Prepaid tuition trust fund	110-979/45(g)
	Proceeds of sold exempt property	735-5/12-1001
	Wrongful death recoveries	735-5/12-1001(h)(2)
public benefits	Aid to aged, blind, disabled; public assistance	305-5/11-3
	Crime victims' compensation	735-5/12-1001(h)(1)
	Restitution payments on account of WWII relocation of Aleuts & Japanese Americans	735-5/12-1001(12)(h)(5)
	Social Security	735-5/12-1001(g)(1)
	Unemployment compensation	735-5/12-1001(g)(1),(3)
	Veterans' benefits	735-5/12-1001(g)(2)
	Workers' compensation	820-305/21
	Workers' occupational disease compensation	820-310/21
tools of trade	Implements, books, & tools of trade to $1,500	735-5/12-1001(d)
wages	Minimum 85% of earned but unpaid weekly wages or 45 times the federal minimum hourly wage (or state minimum hourly wage, if higher); bankruptcy judge may authorize more for low-income debtors	740-170/4
wildcard	$4,000 of any personal property (does not include wages)	735-5/12-1001(b)

Indiana

Federal bankruptcy exemptions not available. All law references are to Indiana Statutes Annotated unless otherwise noted.

ASSET	EXEMPTION	LAW
homestead *see also wildcard*	Real or personal property used as residence to $15,000	34-55-10-2(c)(1);
	Property held as tenancy by the entirety may be exempt against debts incurred by only one spouse	34-55-10-2(c)(5); 32-17-3-1
insurance	Employer's life insurance policy on employee	27-1-12-17.1
	Fraternal benefit society benefits	27-11-6-3
	Group life insurance policy	27-1-12-29
	Life insurance policy, proceeds, cash value, or avails if beneficiary is insured's spouse or dependent	27-1-12-14
	Life insurance proceeds if clause prohibits proceeds to be used to pay beneficiary's creditors	27-2-5-1
	Mutual life or accident proceeds	27-8-3-23
miscellaneous	Property of business partnership	23-4-1-25
pensions	Tax-exempt retirement accounts, including 401(k)s, 403(b)s, profit-sharing and money purchase plans, SEP and SIMPLE IRAs, and defined-benefit plans	11 U.S.C. § 522(b)(3)(C)
	Traditional and Roth IRAs to $1,000,000 per person	11 U.S.C. § 522(b)(3)(C); (n)
	Firefighters	36-8-7-22 36-8-8-17
	Police officers	36-8-8-17; 10-12-2-10
	Public employees	5-10.3-8-9
	Public or private retirement benefits & contributions	34-55-10-2(c)(6)
	Sheriffs	36-8-10-19
	State teachers	21-6.1-5-17
personal property	Health aids	34-55-10-2(c)(4)
	Money in medical care savings account	34-55-10-2(c)(7)
	Spendthrift trusts	30-4-3-2
	$300 of any intangible personal property, except money owed to you	34-55-10-2(c)(3)
public benefits	Crime victims' compensation, unless seeking to discharge the debts for which the victim was compensated	5-2-6.1-38
	Unemployment compensation	22-4-33-3
	Workers' compensation	22-3-2-17
tools of trade	National guard uniforms, arms, & equipment	10-16-10-3
wages	Minimum 75% of earned but unpaid weekly disposable earnings, or 30 times the federal hourly minimum wage; bankruptcy judge may authorize more for low-income debtors	24-4.5-5-105
wildcard	$8,000 of any real estate or tangible personal property	34-55-10-2(c)(2)

Iowa

Federal bankruptcy exemptions not available. All law references are to Iowa Code Annotated unless otherwise noted.

ASSET	EXEMPTION	LAW
homestead	May record homestead declaration	561.4
	Real property or an apartment to an unlimited value; property cannot exceed 1/2 acre in town or city, 40 acres elsewhere (husband & wife may not double)	499A.18; 561.2; 561.16
insurance	Accident, disability, health, illness, or life proceeds or avails	627.6(6)
	Disability or illness benefit	627.6(8)(c)
	Employee group insurance policy or proceeds	509.12
	Fraternal benefit society benefits	512B.18
	Life insurance proceeds if clause prohibits proceeds from being used to pay beneficiary's creditors	508.32
	Life insurance proceeds paid to spouse, child, or other dependent (limited to $10,000 if acquired within 2 years of filing for bankruptcy)	627.6(6)
	Upon death of insured, up to $15,000 total proceeds from all matured life, accident, health, or disability policies exempt from beneficiary's debts contracted before insured's death	627.6(6)
miscellaneous	Alimony, child support needed for support	627.6(8)(d)
	Liquor licenses	123.38
pensions *see also wages*	Tax-exempt retirement accounts, including 401(k)s, 403(b)s, profit-sharing and money purchase plans, SEP and SIMPLE IRAs, and defined-benefit plans	11 U.S.C. § 522(b)(3)(C)
	Traditional and Roth IRAs to $1,000,000 per person	11 U.S.C. § 522(b)(3)(C); (n)
	Disabled firefighters, police officers (only payments being received)	410.11
	Federal government pension	627.8
	Firefighters	411.13
	Other pensions, annuities, & contracts fully exempt; however, contributions made within 1 year prior to filing for bankruptcy not exempt to the extent they exceed normal & customary amounts	627.6(8)(e)
	Peace officers	97A.12
	Police officers	411.13
	Public employees	97B.39
	Retirement plans, Keoghs, IRAs, Roth IRAs, ERISA-qualified benefits	627.6(8)(f)
personal property	Appliances, furnishings, & household goods to $2,000 total	627.6(5)
	Bibles, books, portraits, pictures, & paintings to $1,000 total	627.6(3)
	Burial plot to 1 acre	627.6(4)
	Clothing & its storage containers to $1,000	627.6(1)
	Health aids	627.6(7)
	Motor vehicle, musical instruments, tax refund, & accrued wages to $5,000 total; no more than $1,000 from tax refunds & accrued wages	627.6(9)
	Residential security or utility deposit, or advance rent, to $500	627.6(14)
	Rifle or musket; shotgun	627.6(2)
	Wedding or engagement rings	627.6(1)
public benefits	Adopted child assistance	627.19
	Aid to dependent children	239B.6
	Any public assistance benefit	627.6(8)(a)
	Social Security	627.6(8)(a)
	Unemployment compensation	627.6(8)(a)
	Veterans' benefits	627.6(8)(b)
	Workers' compensation	627.13
tools of trade	Farming equipment; includes livestock, feed to $10,000	627.6(11)
	Nonfarming equipment to $10,000	627.6(10)

ASSET	EXEMPTION		LAW
wages	Expected annual earnings	Amount NOT exempt per year	642.21
	$0 to $12,000	$250	
	$12,000 to $16,000	$400	
	$16,000 to $24,000	$800	
	$24,000 to $35,000	$1,000	
	$35,000 to $50,000	$2,000	
	More than $50,000	10%	
	Not exempt from spousal or child support		
	Wages or salary of a prisoner		356.29
wildcard	$100 of any personal property, including cash		627.6(13)

Kansas

Federal bankruptcy exemptions not available. All law references are to Kansas Statutes Annotated unless otherwise noted.

ASSET	EXEMPTION	LAW
homestead	Real property or mobile home you occupy or intend to occupy to unlimited value; property cannot exceed 1 acre in town or city, 160 acres on farm	60-2301; Constitution 15-9
insurance	Cash value of life insurance; not exempt if obtained within 1 year prior to bankruptcy with fraudulent intent.	60-2313(a)(7); 40-414(b)
	Disability & illness benefits	60-2313(a)(1)
	Fraternal life insurance benefits	60-2313(a)(8)
	Life insurance proceeds	40-414(a)
miscellaneous	Alimony, maintenance, & support	60-2312(b)
	Liquor licenses	60-2313(a)(6); 41-326
pensions	Tax-exempt retirement accounts, including 401(k)s, 403(b)s, profit-sharing and money purchase plans, SEP and SIMPLE IRAs, and defined-benefit plans	11 U.S.C. § 522(b)(3)(C)
	Traditional and Roth IRAs to $1,000,000 per person	11 U.S.C. § 522(b)(3)(C); (n)
	Elected & appointed officials in cities with populations between 120,000 & 200,000	13-14a10
	ERISA-qualified benefits	60-2308(b)
	Federal government pension needed for support & paid within 3 months of filing for bankruptcy (only payments being received)	60-2308(a)
	Firefighters	12-5005(e); 14-10a10
	Judges	20-2618
	Police officers	12-5005(e); 13-14a10
	Public employees	74-4923; 74-49,105
	State highway patrol officers	74-4978g
	State school employees	72-5526
	Payment under a stock bonus, pension, profit-sharing, annuity, or similar plan or contract on account of illness, disability, death, age, or length of service, to the extent reasonably necessary for support	60-2312(b)
personal property	Burial plot or crypt	60-2304(d)
	Clothing to last 1 year	60-2304(a)
	Food & fuel to last 1 year	60-2304(a)
	Funeral plan prepayments	60-2313(a)(10); 16-310(d)
	Furnishings & household equipment	60-2304(a)
	Jewelry & articles of adornment to $1,000	60-2304(b)
	Motor vehicle to $20,000; if designed or equipped for disabled person, no limit	60-2304(c)
public benefits	Crime victims' compensation	60-2313(a)(7); 74-7313(d)
	General assistance	39-717(c)
	Social Security	60-2312(b)
	Unemployment compensation	60-2313(a)(4); 44-718(c)
	Veterans' benefits	60-2312(b)
	Workers' compensation	60-2313(a)(3); 44-514
tools of trade	Books, documents, furniture, instruments, equipment, breeding stock, seed, grain, & stock to $7,500 total	60-2304(e)
	National Guard uniforms, arms, & equipment	48-245
wages	Minimum 75% of disposable weekly wages or 30 times the federal minimum hourly wage per week, whichever is greater; bankruptcy judge may authorize more for low-income debtors	60-2310
wildcard	None	

Kentucky

Federal bankruptcy exemptions not available. All law references are to Kentucky Revised Statutes unless otherwise noted.

ASSET	EXEMPTION	LAW
homestead	Real or personal property used as residence to $5,000; sale proceeds exempt	427.060; 427.090
insurance	Annuity contract proceeds to $350 per month	304.14-330
	Cooperative life or casualty insurance benefits	427.110(1)
	Fraternal benefit society benefits	427.110(2)
	Group life insurance proceeds	304.14-320
	Health or disability benefits	304.14-310
	Life insurance policy if beneficiary is a married woman	304.14-340
	Life insurance proceeds if clause prohibits proceeds from being used to pay beneficiary's creditors	304.14-350
	Life insurance proceeds or cash value if beneficiary is someone other than insured	304.14-300
miscellaneous	Alimony, child support needed for support	427.150(1)
	Property of business partnership	362.270
pensions	Tax-exempt retirement accounts, including 401(k)s, 403(b)s, profit-sharing and money purchase plans, SEP and SIMPLE IRAs, and defined-benefit plans	11 U.S.C. § 522(b)(3)(C)
	Traditional and Roth IRAs to $1,000,000 per person	11 U.S.C. § 522(b)(3)(C); (n)
	ERISA-qualified benefits, including IRAs, SEPs, & Keoghs deposited more than 120 days before filing	427.150
	Firefighters	67A.620; 95.878
	Police officers	427.120; 427.125
	State employees	61.690
	Teachers	161.700
	Urban county government employees	67A.350
personal property	Burial plot to $5,000, in lieu of homestead	427.060
	Clothing, jewelry, articles of adornment, & furnishings to $3,000 total	427.010(1)
	Health aids	427.010(1)
	Lost earnings payments needed for support	427.150(2)(d)
	Medical expenses paid & reparation benefits received under motor vehicle reparation law	304.39-260
	Motor vehicle to $2,500	427.010(1)
	Personal injury recoveries to $7,500 (not to include pain & suffering or pecuniary loss)	427.150(2)(c)
	Prepaid tuition payment fund account	164A.707(3)
	Wrongful death recoveries for person you depended on, needed for support	427.150(2)(b)
public benefits	Aid to blind, aged, disabled; public assistance	205.220(c)
	Crime victims' compensation	427.150(2)(a)
	Unemployment compensation	341.470(4)
	Workers' compensation	342.180
tools of trade	Library, office equipment, instruments, & furnishings of minister, attorney, physician, surgeon, chiropractor, veterinarian, or dentist to $1,000	427.040
	Motor vehicle of auto mechanic, mechanical, or electrical equipment servicer, minister, attorney, physician, surgeon, chiropractor, veterinarian, or dentist to $2,500	427.030
	Tools, equipment, livestock, & poultry of farmer to $3,000	427.010(1)
	Tools of nonfarmer to $300	427.030
wages	Minimum 75% of disposable weekly earnings or 30 times the federal minimum hourly wage per week, whichever is greater; bankruptcy judge may authorize more for low-income debtors	427.010(2),(3)
wildcard	$1,000 of any property	427.160

Louisiana

Federal bankruptcy exemptions not available. All law references are to Louisiana Revised Statutes Annotated unless otherwise noted.

ASSET	EXEMPTION	LAW
homestead	Property you occupy to $25,000 (if debt is result of catastrophic or terminal illness or injury, limit is full value of property as of 1 year before filing); cannot exceed 5 acres in city or town, 200 acres elsewhere (husband & wife may not double)	20:1(A)(1),(2),(3)
	Spouse or child of deceased owner may claim homestead exemption; spouse given home in divorce gets homestead	20:1(B)
insurance	Annuity contract proceeds & avails	22:647
	Fraternal benefit society benefits	22:558
	Group insurance policies or proceeds	22:649
	Health, accident, or disability proceeds or avails	22:646
	Life insurance proceeds or avails; if policy issued within 9 months of filing, exempt only to $35,000	22:647
miscellaneous	Property of minor child	13:3881(A)(3); Civil Code Art. 223
pensions	Tax-exempt retirement accounts, including 401(k)s, 403(b)s, profit-sharing and money purchase plans, SEP and SIMPLE IRAs, and defined-benefit plans	11 U.S.C. § 522(b)(3)(C)
	Traditional and Roth IRAs to $1,000,000 per person	11 U.S.C. § 522(b)(3)(C); (n)
	Assessors	11:1403
	Court clerks	11:1526
	District attorneys	11:1583
	ERISA-qualified benefits, including IRAs, Roth IRAs, & Keoghs, if contributions made over 1 year before filing for bankruptcy	13:3881(D)(1); 20:33(1)
	Firefighters	11:2263
	Gift or bonus payments from employer to employee or heirs whenever paid	20:33(2)
	Judges	11:1378
	Louisiana University employees	11:952.3
	Municipal employees	11:1735
	Parochial employees	11:1905
	Police officers	11:3513
	School employees	11:1003
	Sheriffs	11:2182
	State employees	11:405
	Teachers	11:704
	Voting registrars	11:2033
personal property	Arms, military accoutrements; bedding; dishes, glassware, utensils, silverware (nonsterling); clothing, family portraits, musical instruments; bedroom, living room, & dining room furniture; poultry, 1 cow, household pets; heating & cooling equipment, refrigerator, freezer, stove, washer & dryer, iron, sewing machine	13:3881(A)(4)
	Cemetery plot, monuments	8:313
	Engagement & wedding rings to $5,000	13:3881(A)(5)
	Spendthrift trusts	9:2004
public benefits	Aid to blind, aged, disabled; public assistance	46:111
	Crime victims' compensation	46:1811
	Earned Income tax credit	13:3881 (A)(6)
	Unemployment compensation	23:1693
	Workers' compensation	23:1205
tools of trade	Tools, instruments, books, $7,500 of equity in a motor vehicle, one firearm to $500, needed to work	13:3881(A)(2)
wages	Minimum 75% of disposable weekly earnings or 30 times the federal minimum hourly wage per week, whichever is greater; bankruptcy judge may authorize more for low-income debtors	13:3881(A)(1)
wildcard	None	

Maine

Federal bankruptcy exemptions not available. All law references are to Maine Revised Statutes Annotated, in the form title number-section number, unless otherwise noted.

ASSET	EXEMPTION	LAW
homestead	Real or personal property (including cooperative) used as residence to $35,000; if debtor has minor dependents in residence, to $70,000; if debtor over age 60 or physically or mentally disabled, $70,000; proceeds of sale exempt for six months	14-4422(1)
insurance	Annuity proceeds to $450 per month	24-A-2431
	Death benefit for police, fire, or emergency medical personnel who die in the line of duty	25-1612
	Disability or health proceeds, benefits, or avails	14-4422(13)(A),(C); 24-A-2429
	Fraternal benefit society benefits	24-A-4118
	Group health or life policy or proceeds	24-A-2430
	Life, endowment, annuity, or accident policy, proceeds or avails	14-4422(14)(C); 24-A-2428
	Life insurance policy, interest, loan value, or accrued dividends for policy from person you depended on, to $4,000	14-4422(11)
	Unmatured life insurance policy, except credit insurance policy	14-4422(10)
miscellaneous	Alimony & child support needed for support	14-4422(13)(D)
	Property of business partnership	31-305
pensions	Tax-exempt retirement accounts, including 401(k)s, 403(b)s, profit-sharing and money purchase plans, SEP and SIMPLE IRAs, and defined-benefit plans	11 U.S.C. § 522(b)(3)(C)
	Traditional and Roth IRAs to $1,000,000 per person	11 U.S.C. § 522(b)(3)(C); (n)
	ERISA-qualified benefits	14-4422(13)(E)
	Judges	4-1203
	Legislators	3-703
	State employees	5-17054
personal property	Animals, crops, musical instruments, books, clothing, furnishings, household goods, appliances to $200 per item	14-4422(3)
	Balance due on repossessed goods; total amount financed can't exceed $2,000	9-A-5-103
	Burial plot in lieu of homestead exemption	14-4422(1)
	Cooking stove; furnaces & stoves for heat	14-4422(6)(A),(B)
	Food to last 6 months	14-4422(7)(A)
	Fuel not to exceed 10 cords of wood, 5 tons of coal, or 1,000 gal. of heating oil	14-4422(6)(C)
	Health aids	14-4422(12)
	Jewelry to $750; no limit for one wedding & one engagement ring	14-4422(4)
	Lost earnings payments needed for support	14-4422(14)(E)
	Military clothes, arms, & equipment	37-B-262
	Motor vehicle to $5,000	14-4422(2)
	Personal injury recoveries to $12,500	14-4422(14)(D)
	Seeds, fertilizers, & feed to raise & harvest food for 1 season	14-4422(7)(B)
	Tools & equipment to raise & harvest food	14-4422(7)(C)
	Wrongful death recoveries needed for support	14-4422(14)(B)
public benefits	Maintenance under the Rehabilitation Act	26-1411-H
	Crime victims' compensation	14-4422(14)(A)
	Public assistance	22-3180, 22-3766
	Social Security	14-4422(13)(A)
	Unemployment compensation	14-4422(13)(A),(C)
	Veterans' benefits	14-4422(13)(B)
	Workers' compensation	39-A-106
tools of trade	Books, materials, & stock to $5,000	14-4422(5)
	Commercial fishing boat, 5-ton limit	14-4422(9)
	One of each farm implement (& its maintenance equipment needed to harvest & raise crops)	14-4422(8)

wages	None (use federal nonbankruptcy wage exemption)	
wildcard	Unused portion of exemption in homestead to $6,000; or unused exemption in animals, crops, musical instruments, books, clothing, furnishings, household goods, appliances, tools of the trade, & personal injury recoveries	14-4422(15)
	$400 of any property	14-4422(15)

Maryland

Federal bankruptcy exemptions not available. All law references are to Maryland Code of Courts & Judicial Proceedings unless otherwise noted.

ASSET	EXEMPTION	LAW
homestead	None; however, property held as tenancy by the entirety is exempt against debts owed by only one spouse	In re Birney, 200 F.3d 225 (4th Cir. 1999)
insurance	Disability or health benefits, including court awards, arbitrations, & settlements	11-504(b)(2)
	Fraternal benefit society benefits	Ins. 8-431; Estates & Trusts 8-115
	Life insurance or annuity contract proceeds or avails if beneficiary is insured's dependent, child, or spouse	Ins. 16-111(a); Estates & Trusts 8-115
	Medical insurance benefits deducted from wages plus medical insurance payments to $145 per week or 75% of disposable wages	Commercial Law 15-601.1(3)
pensions	Tax-exempt retirement accounts, including 401(k)s, 403(b)s, profit-sharing and money purchase plans, SEP and SIMPLE IRAs, and defined-benefit plans	11 U.S.C. § 522(b)(3)(C)
	Traditional and Roth IRAs to $1,000,000 per person	11 U.S.C. § 522(b)(3)(C); (n)
	ERISA-qualified benefits, including IRAs, Roth IRAs, & Keoghs	11-504(h)(1), (4)
	State employees	State Pers. & Pen. 21-502
personal property	Appliances, furnishings, household goods, books, pets, & clothing to $1,000 total	11-504(b)(4)
	Burial plot	Bus. Reg. 5-503
	Health aids	11-504(b)(3)
	Perpetual care trust funds	Bus. Reg. 5-602
	Prepaid college trust funds	Educ. 18-1913
	Lost future earnings recoveries	11-504(b)(2)
public benefits	Baltimore Police death benefits	Code of 1957 art. 24, 16-103
	Crime victims' compensation	Crim. Proc. 11-816(b)
	General assistance	Code of 1957 88A-73
	Unemployment compensation	Labor & Employment 8-106
	Workers' compensation	Labor & Employment 9-732
tools of trade	Clothing, books, tools, instruments, & appliances to $5,000	11-504(b)(1)
wages	Earned but unpaid wages, the greater of 75% or $145 per week; in Kent, Caroline, & Queen Anne's of Worcester Counties, the greater of 75% or 30 times federal minimum hourly wage	Commercial Law 15-601.1
wildcard	$6,000 in cash or any property, if claimed within 30 days of attachment or levy	11-504(b)(5)
	An additional $5,000 in real or personal property	11-504(f)

Massachusetts

Federal bankruptcy exemptions available. All law references are to Massachusetts General Laws Annotated, in the form title number-section number, unless otherwise noted.

ASSET	EXEMPTION	LAW
homestead	If statement of homestead is not in title to property, must record homestead declaration before filing bankruptcy	188-2
	Property held as tenancy by the entirety may be exempt against debt for nonnecessity owed by only one spouse.	209-1
	Property you occupy or intend to occupy (including mobile home) to $500,000 (special rules if over 65 or disabled)	188-1; 188-1A
	Spouse or children of deceased owner may claim homestead exemption	188-4
insurance	Disability benefits to $400 per week	175-110A
	Fraternal benefit society benefits	176-22
	Group annuity policy or proceeds	175-132C
	Group life insurance policy	175-135
	Life insurance or annuity contract proceeds if clause prohibits proceeds from being used to pay beneficiary's creditors	175-119A
	Life insurance policy if beneficiary is married woman	175-126
	Life or endowment policy, proceeds, or cash value	175-125
	Medical malpractice self-insurance	175F-15
miscellaneous	Property of business partnership	108A-25
pensions *see also wages*	Tax-exempt retirement accounts, including 401(k)s, 403(b)s, profit-sharing and money purchase plans, SEP and SIMPLE IRAs, and defined-benefit plans	11 U.S.C. § 522(b)(3)(C)
	Traditional and Roth IRAs to $1,000,000 per person	11 U.S.C. § 522(b)(3)(C); (n)
	Credit union employees	171-84
	ERISA-qualified benefits, including IRAs & Keoghs to specified limits.	235-34A; 246-28
	Private retirement benefits	32-41
	Public employees	32-19
	Savings bank employees	168-41; 168-44
personal property	Bank deposits to $125	235-34
	Beds & bedding; heating unit; clothing	235-34
	Bibles & books to $200 total; sewing machine to $200	235-34
	Burial plots, tombs, & church pew	235-34
	Cash for fuel, heat, water, or light to $75 per month	235-34
	Cash to $200/month for rent, in lieu of homestead	235-34
	Cooperative association shares to $100	235-34
	Food or cash for food to $300	235-34
	Furniture to $3,000; motor vehicle to $700	235-34
	Moving expenses for eminent domain	79-6A
	Trust company, bank, or credit union deposits to $500	246-28A
	2 cows, 12 sheep, 2 swine, 4 tons of hay	235-34
public benefits	Aid to families with dependent children	118-10
	Public assistance	235-34
	Unemployment compensation	151A-36
	Veterans' benefits	115-5
	Workers' compensation	152-47
tools of trade	Arms, accoutrements, & uniforms required	235-34
	Fishing boats, tackle, & nets to $500	235-34
	Materials you designed & procured to $500	235-34
	Tools, implements, & fixtures to $500 total	235-34
wages	Earned but unpaid wages to $125 per week	246-28
wildcard	None	

Michigan

Federal bankruptcy exemptions available. All law references are to Michigan Compiled Laws Annotated unless otherwise noted.

Under Michigan law, bankruptcy exemption amounts are adjusted for inflation every three years (starting in 2005) by the Michigan Department of Treasury. These amounts have already been adjusted, so the amounts listed in the statutes are not current. You can find the current amounts at www.michigan.gov/documents/BankruptcyExemptions2005_141050_7.pdf or by going to www.michigan.gov/treasury and typing "bankruptcy exemptions" in the search box.

ASSET	EXEMPTION	LAW
homestead	Property held as tenancy by the entirety may be exempt against debts owed by only one spouse	600.5451(1)(o)
	Real property including condo to $31,900 ($47,825 if over 65 or disabled); property cannot exceed 1 lot in town, village, city, or 40 acres elsewhere; spouse or children of deceased owner may claim homestead exemption	600.5451(1)(n); (5)(d)
insurance	Disability, mutual life, or health benefits	600.5451(1)(j)
	Employer-sponsored life insurance policy or trust fund	500.2210
	Fraternal benefit society benefits	500.8181
	Life, endowment, or annuity proceeds if clause prohibits proceeds from being used to pay beneficiary's creditors	500.4054
	Life insurance	500.2207
miscellaneous	Property of business partnership	449.25
pensions	Tax-exempt retirement accounts, including 401(k)s, 403(b)s, profit-sharing and money purchase plans, SEP and SIMPLE IRAs, and defined-benefit plans	11 U.S.C. § 522(b)(3)(C)
	Traditional and Roth IRAs to $1,000,000 per person	11 U.S.C. § 522(b)(3)(C); (n)
	ERISA-qualified benefits, except contributions within last 120 days	600.5451(1)(m)
	Firefighters, police officers	38.559(6); 38.1683
	IRAs & Roth IRAs, except contributions within last 120 days	600.5451(1)(l)
	Judges	38.2308; 38.1683
	Legislators	38.1057; 38.1683
	Probate judges	38.2308; 38.1683
	Public school employees	38.1346; 38.1683
	State employees	38.40; 38.1683
personal property	Appliances, utensils, books, furniture, & household goods to $475 each, $3,200 total	600.5451(1)(c)
	Building & loan association shares to $1,075 par value, in lieu of homestead	600.5451(1)(k)
	Burial plots, cemeteries	600.5451(1)(a)
	Church pew, slip, seat for entire family to $525	600.5451(1)(d)
	Clothing; family pictures	600.5451(1)(a)
	Food & fuel to last family for 6 months	600.5451(1)(b)
	Crops, animals and feed to $2,125	600.5451(1)(d)
	1 motor vehicle to $2,950	600.5451(1)(g)
	Computer & accessories to $525	600.5451(1)(h)
	Household pets to $525	600.5451(1)(f)
	Professionally prescribed health aids	600.5451(a)
public benefits	Crime victims' compensation	18.362
	Social welfare benefits	400.63
	Unemployment compensation	421.30
	Veterans' benefits for Korean War veterans	35.977
	Veterans' benefits for Vietnam veterans	35.1027
	Veterans' benefits for WWII veterans	35.926
	Workers' compensation	418.821
tools of trade	Arms & accoutrements required	600.6023(1)(a)
	Tools, implements, materials, stock, apparatus, team, motor vehicle, horse, & harness to $1,000 total	600.6023(1)(e)

wages	Head of household may keep 60% of earned but unpaid wages (no less than $15/week), plus $2/week per nonspouse dependent; if not head of household may keep 40% (no less than $10/week)	600.5311
wildcard	None	

Minnesota

Federal bankruptcy exemptions available. All law references are to Minnesota Statutes Annotated, unless otherwise noted.

NOTE: Section 550.37(4)(a) requires certain exemptions to be adjusted for inflation on July 1 of even-numbered years; this table includes all changes made through July 1, 2004. Exemptions are published in the May 1 issue of the Minnesota State Register, www.comm.media.state.mn.us/bookstore/stateregister.asp, or call the Minnesota Dept. of Commerce at 651-296-7977.

ASSET	EXEMPTION	LAW
homestead	Home & land on which it is situated to $200,000; if homestead is used for agricultural purposes, $500,000; cannot exceed 1/2 acre in city, 160 acres elsewhere (husband & wife may not double);	510.01; 510.02
	Manufactured home to an unlimited value	550.37 subd. 12
insurance	Accident or disability proceeds	550.39
	Fraternal benefit society benefits	64B.18
	Life insurance proceeds to $38,000, if beneficiary is spouse or child of insured, plus $9,500 per dependent	550.37 subd. 10
	Police, fire, or beneficiary association benefits	550.37 subd. 11
	Unmatured life insurance contract dividends, interest, or loan value to $7,600 if insured is debtor or person debtor depends on	550.37 subd. 23
miscellaneous	Earnings of minor child	550.37 subd. 15
pensions	Tax-exempt retirement accounts, including 401(k)s, 403(b)s, profit-sharing and money purchase plans, SEP and SIMPLE IRAs, and defined-benefit plans	11 U.S.C. § 522(b)(3)(C)
	Traditional and Roth IRAs to $1,000,000 per person	11 U.S.C. § 522(b)(3)(C); (n)
	ERISA-qualified benefits or needed for support, up to $57,000 in present value	550.37 subd. 24
	IRAs or Roth IRAs needed for support, up to $57,000 in present value	550.37 subd. 24
	Public employees	353.15; 356.401
	State employees	352.96 subd. 6; 356.401
	State troopers	352B.071; 356.401
personal property	Appliances, furniture, jewelry, radio, phonographs, & TV to $8,550 total	550.37 subd. 4(b)
	Bible & books	550.37 subd. 2
	Burial plot; church pew or seat	550.37 subd. 3
	Clothing, one watch, food, & utensils for family	550.37 subd. 4(a)
	Motor vehicle to $3,800 (up to $38,000 if vehicle has been modified for disability)	550.37 subd. 12(a)
	Personal injury recoveries	550.37 subd. 22
	Proceeds for damaged exempt property	550.37 subds. 9, 16
	Wedding rings to $1,225	550.37 subd. 4(c)
	Wrongful death recoveries	550.37 subd. 22
public benefits	Crime victims' compensation	611A.60
	Public benefits	550.37 subd. 14
	Unemployment compensation	268.192 subd. 2
	Veterans' benefits	550.38
	Workers' compensation	176.175
tools of trade *total (except teaching materials) can't exceed $13,000*	Farm machines, implements, livestock, produce, & crops	550.37 subd. 5
	Teaching materials of college, university, public school, or public institution teacher	550.37 subd. 8
	Tools, machines, instruments, stock in trade, furniture, & library to $9,500 total	550.37 subd. 6
wages	Minimum 75% of weekly disposable earnings or 40 times federal minimum hourly wage, whichever is greater	571.922
	Wages deposited into bank accounts for 20 days after depositing	550.37 subd. 13
	Wages, paid within 6 mos. of returning to work, after receiving welfare or after incarceration; includes earnings deposited in a financial institution in the last 60 days	550.37 subd. 14
wildcard	None	

NOTE: In cases of suspected fraud, the Minnesota constitution permits courts to cap exemptions that would otherwise be unlimited. *In re Tveten*, 402 N.W.2d 551 (Minn. 1987); *In re Medill*, 119 B.R. 685 (Bankr. D. Minn. 1990); *In re Sholdan*, 217 F.3d 1006 (8th Cir. 2000).

Mississippi

Federal bankruptcy exemptions not available. All law references are to Mississippi Code unless otherwise noted.

ASSET	EXEMPTION	LAW
homestead	May file homestead declaration	85-3-27; 85-3-31
	Mobile home does not qualify as homestead unless you own land on which it is located (see personal property)	In re Cobbins, 234 B.R. 882 (S.D. Miss. 1999)
	Property you own & occupy to $75,000; if over 60 & married or widowed may claim a former residence; property cannot exceed 160 acres; sale proceeds exempt	85-3-1(b)(i); 85-3-21; 85-3-23
insurance	Disability benefits	85-3-1(b)(ii)
	Fraternal benefit society benefits	83-29-39
	Homeowners' insurance proceeds to $75,000	85-3-23
	Life insurance proceeds if clause prohibits proceeds from being used to pay beneficiary's creditors	83-7-5; 85-3-11
miscellaneous	Property of business partnership	79-12-49
pensions	Tax-exempt retirement accounts, including 401(k)s, 403(b)s, profit-sharing and money purchase plans, SEP and SIMPLE IRAs, and defined-benefit plans	11 U.S.C. § 522(b)(3)(C)
	Traditional and Roth IRAs to $1,000,000 per person	11 U.S.C. § 522(b)(3)(C); (n)
	ERISA-qualified benefits, IRAs, Keoghs deposited over 1 yr. before filing bankruptcy	85-3-1(f)
	Firefighters (includes death benefits)	21-29-257; 45-2-1
	Highway patrol officers	25-13-31
	Law enforcement officers' death benefits	45-2-1
	Police officers (includes death benefits)	21-29-257; 45-2-1
	Private retirement benefits to extent tax-deferred	71-1-43
	Public employees retirement & disability benefits	25-11-129
	State employees	25-14-5
	Teachers	25-11-201(1)(d)
	Volunteer firefighters' death benefits	45-2-1
personal property	Mobile home to $20,000	85-3-1(e)
	Personal injury judgments to $10,000	85-3-17
	Sale or insurance proceeds for exempt property	85-3-1(b)(i)
	Tangible personal property to $10,000: any item worth less than $200; furniture, dishes, kitchenware, household goods, appliances, 1 radio & 1 TV, 1 firearm, 1 lawnmower, clothing, wedding rings, motor vehicles, tools of the trade, books, crops, health aids, domestic animals (does not include works of art, antiques, jewelry, or electronic entertainment equipment)	85-3-1(a)
public benefits	Assistance to aged	43-9-19
	Assistance to blind	43-3-71
	Assistance to disabled	43-29-15
	Crime victims' compensation	99-41-23(7)
	Social Security	25-11-129
	Unemployment compensation	71-5-539
	Workers' compensation	71-3-43
tools of trade	See personal property	
wages	Earned but unpaid wages owed for 30 days; after 30 days, minimum 75% of earned but unpaid weekly disposable earnings, or 30 times the federal hourly minimum wage, whichever is greater (bankruptcy judge may authorize more for low-income debtors)	85-3-4
wildcard	See personal property	

Missouri

Federal bankruptcy exemptions not available. All law references are to Annotated Missouri Statutes unless otherwise noted.

ASSET	EXEMPTION	LAW
homestead	Property held as tenancy by the entirety may be exempt against debts owed by only one spouse	In re Eads, 271 B.R. 371 (Bankr. W.D. Mo. 2002).
	Real property to $15,000 or mobile home to $5,000 (joint owners may not double)	513.430(6); 513.475 In re Smith, 254 B.R. 751 (Bank. W.D. Mo. 2000)
insurance	Assessment plan or life insurance proceeds	377.090
	Disability or illness benefits	513.430(10)(c)
	Fraternal benefit society benefits to $5,000, bought over 6 months before filing	513.430(8)
	Life insurance dividends, loan value, or interest to $150,000, bought over 6 months before filing	513.430(8)
	Life insurance proceeds if policy owned by a woman & insures her husband	376.530
	Life insurance proceeds if policy owned by unmarried woman & insures her father or brother	376.550
	Stipulated insurance premiums	377.330
	Unmatured life insurance policy	513.430(7)
miscellaneous	Alimony, child support to $750 per month	513.430(10)(d)
	Property of business partnership	358.250
pensions	Tax-exempt retirement accounts, including 401(k)s, 403(b)s, profit-sharing and money purchase plans, SEP and SIMPLE IRAs, and defined-benefit plans	11 U.S.C. § 522(b)(3)(C)
	Traditional and Roth IRAs to $1,000,000 per person	11 U.S.C. § 522(b)(3)(C); (n)
	Employee benefit spendthrift trust	456.014
	Employees of cities with 100,000 or more people	71.207
	ERISA-qualified benefits, IRAs, Roth IRAs, & other retirement accounts needed for support	513.430(10)(e), (f)
	Firefighters	87.090; 87.365; 87.485
	Highway & transportation employees	104.250
	Police department employees	86.190; 86.353; 86.1430
	Public officers & employees	70.695; 70.755
	State employees	104.540
	Teachers	169.090
personal property	Appliances, household goods, furnishings, clothing, books, crops, animals, & musical instruments to $3,000 total	513.430(1)
	Burial grounds to 1 acre or $100	214.190
	Health aids	513.430(9)
	Motor vehicle to $3,000	513.430(5)
	Personal injury causes of action	In re Mitchell, 73 B.R. 93 (Bankr. E.D. Mo. 1987)
	Wedding ring to $1,500, & other jewelry to $500	513.430(2)
	Wrongful death recoveries for person you depended on	513.430(11)
public benefits	Crime victim's compensation	595.025
	Public assistance	513.430(10)(a)
	Social Security	513.430(10)(a)
	Unemployment compensation	288.380(10)(l); 513.430(10)(c)
	Veterans' benefits	513.430(10)b)
	Workers' compensation	287.260

tools of trade	Implements, books, & tools of trade to $3,000	513.430(4)
wages	Minimum 75% of weekly earnings (90% of weekly earnings for head of family), or 30 times the federal minimum hourly wage, whichever is more; bankruptcy judge may authorize more for low-income debtors	525.030
	Wages of servant or common laborer to $90	513.470
wildcard	$1,250 of any property if head of family, else $600; head of family may claim additional $350 per child	513.430(3); 513.440

Montana

Federal bankruptcy exemptions not available. All law references are to Montana Code Annotated unless otherwise noted.

ASSET	EXEMPTION	LAW
homestead	Must record homestead declaration before filing for bankruptcy	70-32-105
	Real property or mobile home you occupy to $100,000; sale, condemnation, or insurance proceeds exempt for 18 months	70-32-104; 70-32-201; 70-32-213
insurance	Annuity contract proceeds to $350 per month	33-15-514
	Disability or illness proceeds, avails, or benefits	25-13-608(1)(d); 33-15-513
	Fraternal benefit society benefits	33-7-522
	Group life insurance policy or proceeds	33-15-512
	Hail insurance benefits	80-2-245
	Life insurance proceeds if clause prohibits proceeds from being used to pay beneficiary's creditors	33-20-120
	Medical, surgical, or hospital care benefits	25-13-608(1)(f)
	Unmatured life insurance contracts to $4,000	25-13-609(4)
miscellaneous	Alimony, child support	25-13-608(1)(g)
pensions	Tax-exempt retirement accounts, including 401(k)s, 403(b)s, profit-sharing and money purchase plans, SEP and SIMPLE IRAs, and defined-benefit plans	11 U.S.C. § 522(b)(3)(C)
	Traditional and Roth IRAs to $1,000,000 per person	11 U.S.C. § 522(b)(3)(C); (n)
	ERISA-qualified benefits deposited over 1 year before filing bankruptcy or up to 15% of debtor's gross annual income	31-2-106
	Firefighters	19-18-612(1)
	IRA & Roth IRA contributions & earnings made before judgment filed	25-13-608(1)(e)
	Police officers	19-19-504(1)
	Public employees	19-2-1004; 25-13-608(i)
	Teachers	19-20-706(2); 25-13-608(j)
	University system employees	19-21-212
personal property	Appliances, household furnishings, goods, animals with feed, crops, musical instruments, books, firearms, sporting goods, clothing, & jewelry to $600 per item, $4,500 total	25-13-609(1)
	Burial plot	25-13-608(1)(h)
	Cooperative association shares to $500 value	35-15-404
	Health aids	25-13-608(1)(a)
	Motor vehicle to $2,500	25-13-609(2)
	Proceeds from sale or for damage or loss of exempt property for 6 mos. after received	25-13-610
public benefits	Aid to aged, disabled needy persons	53-2-607
	Crime victims' compensation	53-9-129
	Local public assistance	25-13-608(1)(b)
	Silicosis benefits	39-73-110
	Social Security	25-13-608(1)(b)
	Subsidized adoption payments to needy persons	53-2-607
	Unemployment compensation	31-2-106(2); 39-51-3105
	Veterans' benefits	25-13-608(1)(c)
	Vocational rehabilitation to blind needy persons	53-2-607
	Workers' compensation	39-71-743
tools of trade	Implements, books, & tools of trade to $3,000	25-13-609(3)
	Uniforms, arms, accoutrements needed to carry out government functions	25-13-613(b)
wages	Minimum 75% of earned but unpaid weekly disposable earnings, or 30 times the federal hourly minimum wage, whichever is greater; bankruptcy judge may authorize more for low-income debtors	25-13-614
wildcard	None	

Nebraska

Federal bankruptcy exemptions not available. All law references are to Revised Statutes of Nebraska unless otherwise noted.

ASSET	EXEMPTION	LAW
homestead	$12,500 for married debtor or head of household; cannot exceed 2 lots in city or village, 160 acres elsewhere; sale proceeds exempt 6 months after sale (husband & wife may not double)	40-101; 40-111; 40-113
	May record homestead declaration	40-105
insurance	Fraternal benefit society benefits to $100,000 loan value unless beneficiary convicted of a crime related to benefits	44-1089
	Life insurance proceeds and avails to $100,000	44-371
pensions *see also wages*	Tax-exempt retirement accounts, including 401(k)s, 403(b)s, profit-sharing and money purchase plans, SEP and SIMPLE IRAs, and defined-benefit plans	11 U.S.C. § 522(b)(3)(C)
	Traditional and Roth IRAs to $1,000,000 per person	11 U.S.C. § 522(b)(3)(C); (n)
	County employees	23-2322
	Deferred compensation of public employees	48-1401
	ERISA-qualified benefits including IRAs & Roth IRAs needed for support	25-1563.01
	Military disability benefits	25-1559
	School employees	79-948
	State employees	84-1324
personal property	Burial plot	12-517
	Clothing	25-1556(2)
	Crypts, lots, tombs, niches, vaults	12-605
	Furniture, household goods & appliances, household electronics, personal computers, books, & musical instruments to $1,500	25-1556(3)
	Health aids	25-1556(5)
	Medical or health savings accounts to $25,000	8-1, 131(2)(b)
	Perpetual care funds	12-511
	Personal injury recoveries	25-1563.02
	Personal possessions	25-1556
public benefits	Aid to disabled, blind, aged; public assistance	68-1013
	General assistance to poor persons	68-148
	Unemployment compensation	48-647
	Workers' compensation	48-149
tools of trade	Equipment or tools including a vehicle used in/or for commuting to principal place of business to $2,400 (husband & wife may double)	25-1556(4); *In re Keller*, 50 B.R. 23 (D. Neb. 1985)
wages	Minimum 85% of earned but unpaid weekly disposable earnings or pension payments for head of family; minimum 75% of earned but unpaid weekly disposable earnings, or 30 times the federal hourly minimum wage, whichever is greater, for all others; bankruptcy judge may authorize more for low-income debtors	25-1558
wildcard	$2,500 of any personal property, except wages, in lieu of homestead	25-1552

Nevada

Federal bankruptcy exemptions not available. All law references are to Nevada Revised Statutes Annotated unless otherwise noted.

ASSET	EXEMPTION	LAW
homestead	Must record homestead declaration before filing for bankruptcy	115.020
	Real property or mobile home to $350,000	115.010; 21.090(1)(m)
insurance	Annuity contract proceeds to $350 per month	687B.290
	Fraternal benefit society benefits	695A.220
	Group life or health policy or proceeds	687B.280
	Health proceeds or avails	687B.270
	Life insurance policy or proceeds if annual premiums not over $1,000	21.090(1)(k); *In re Bower*, 234 B.R. 109 (Nev. 1999)
	Life insurance proceeds if you're not the insured	687B.260
miscellaneous	Alimony & child support	21.090(1)(r)
	Property of business partnership	87.250
pensions	Tax-exempt retirement accounts, including 401(k)s, 403(b)s, profit-sharing and money purchase plans, SEP and SIMPLE IRAs, and defined-benefit plans	11 U.S.C. § 522(b)(3)(C)
	Traditional and Roth IRAs to $1,000,000 per person	11 U.S.C. § 522(b)(3)(C); (n)
	ERISA-qualified benefits, deferred compensation, SEP IRA, Roth IRA, or IRA to $500,000	21.090(1)(q)
	Public employees	286.670
personal property	Appliances, household goods, furniture, home & yard equipment to $12,000 total	21.090(1)(b)
	Books, works of art, musical instruments, & jewelry to $5,000	21.090(1)(a)
	Burial plot purchase money held in trust	689.700
	Funeral service contract money held in trust	689.700
	Health aids	21.090(1)(p)
	Keepsakes & pictures	21.090(1)(a)
	Metal-bearing ores, geological specimens, art curiosities, or paleontological remains; must be arranged, classified, catalogued, & numbered in reference books	21.100
	Mortgage impound accounts	645B.180
	Motor vehicle to $15,000; no limit on vehicle equipped for disabled person	21.090(1)(f),(o)
	One gun	21.090(1)(i)
	Personal injury compensation to $16,500	21.090(t)
	Restitution received for criminal act	21.090(w)
	Wrongful death awards to survivors	21.090(u)
public benefits	Aid to blind, aged, disabled; public assistance	422.291
	Crime victim's compensation	21.090
	Industrial insurance (workers' compensation)	616C.205
	Public assistance for children	432.036
	Unemployment compensation	612.710
	Vocational rehabilitation benefits	615.270
tools of trade	Arms, uniforms, & accoutrements you're required to keep	21.090(1)(j)
	Cabin or dwelling of miner or prospector; mining claim, cars, implements, & appliances to $4,500 total (for working claim only)	21.090(1)(e)
	Farm trucks, stock, tools, equipment, & seed to $4,500	21.090(1)(c)
	Library, equipment, supplies, tools, inventory, & materials to $10,000	21.090(1)(d)
wages	Minimum 75% of disposable weekly earnings or 30 times the federal minimum hourly wage per week, whichever is more; bankruptcy judge may authorize more for low-income debtors	21.090(1)(g)
wildcard	None	

New Hampshire

Federal bankruptcy exemptions available. All law references are to New Hampshire Revised Statutes Annotated unless otherwise noted.

ASSET	EXEMPTION	LAW
homestead	Real property or manufactured housing (& the land it's on if you own it) to $100,000	480:1
insurance	Firefighters' aid insurance	402:69
	Fraternal benefit society benefits	418:17
	Homeowners' insurance proceeds to $5,000	512:21(VIII)
miscellaneous	Jury, witness fees	512:21(VI)
	Property of business partnership	304-A:25
	Wages of minor child	512:21(III)
pensions	Tax-exempt retirement accounts, including 401(k)s, 403(b)s, profit-sharing and money purchase plans, SEP and SIMPLE IRAs, and defined-benefit plans	11 U.S.C. § 522(b)(3)(C)
	Traditional and Roth IRAs to $1,000,000 per person	11 U.S.C. § 522(b)(3)(C); (n)
	ERISA-qualified retirement accounts including IRAs & Roth IRAs	512:2 (XIX)
	Federally created pension (only benefits building up)	512:21(IV)
	Firefighters	102:23
	Police officers	103:18
	Public employees	100-A:26
personal property	Beds, bedding, & cooking utensils	511:2(II)
	Bibles & books to $800	511:2(VIII)
	Burial plot, lot	511:2(XIV)
	Church pew	511:2(XV)
	Clothing	511:2(I)
	Cooking & heating stoves, refrigerator	511:2(IV)
	Domestic fowl to $300	511:2(XIII)
	Food & fuel to $400	511:2(VI)
	Furniture to $3,500	511:2(III)
	Jewelry to $500	511:2(XVII)
	Motor vehicle to $4,000	511:2(XVI)
	Proceeds for lost or destroyed exempt property	512:21(VIII)
	Sewing machine	511:2(V)
	1 cow, 6 sheep & their fleece, 4 tons of hay	511:2(XI); (XII)
	1 hog or pig or its meat (if slaughtered)	511:2(X)
public benefits	Aid to blind, aged, disabled; public assistance	167:25
	Unemployment compensation	282-A:159
	Workers' compensation	281-A:52
tools of trade	Tools of your occupation to $5,000	511:2(IX)
	Uniforms, arms, & equipment of military member	511:2(VII)
	Yoke of oxen or horse needed for farming or teaming	511:2(XII)
wages	50 times the federal minimum hourly wage per week	512:21(II)
	Deposits in any account designated a payroll account.	512:21(XI)
	Earned but unpaid wages of spouse	512:21(III)
wildcard	$1,000 of any property	511:2(XVIII)
	Unused portion of bibles & books, food & fuel, furniture, jewelry, motor vehicle, & tools of trade exemptions to $7,000	511:2(XVIII)

New Jersey

Federal bankruptcy exemptions available. All law references are to New Jersey Statutes Annotated unless otherwise noted.

ASSET	EXEMPTION	LAW
homestead	None, but survivorship interest of a spouse in property held as tenancy by the entirety is exempt from creditors of a single spouse	*Freda v. Commercial Trust Co. of New Jersey*, 570 A.2d 409 (N.J.,1990)
insurance	Annuity contract proceeds to $500 per month	17B:24-7
	Disability benefits	17:18-12
	Disability, death, medical, or hospital benefits for civil defense workers	App. A:9-57.6
	Disability or death benefits for military member	38A:4-8
	Group life or health policy or proceeds	17B:24-9
	Health or disability benefits	17:18-12; 17B:24-8
	Life insurance proceeds if clause prohibits proceeds from being used to pay beneficiary's creditors	17B:24-10
	Life insurance proceeds or avails if you're not the insured	17B:24-6b
pensions	Tax-exempt retirement accounts, including 401(k)s, 403(b)s, profit-sharing and money purchase plans, SEP and SIMPLE IRAs, and defined-benefit plans	11 U.S.C. § 522(b)(3)(C)
	Traditional and Roth IRAs to $1,000,000 per person	11 U.S.C. § 522(b)(3)(C); (n)
	Alcohol beverage control officers	43:8A-20
	City boards of health employees	43:18-12
	Civil defense workers	App. A:9-57.6
	County employees	43:10-57; 43:10-105
	ERISA-qualified benefits for city employees	43:13-9
	Firefighters, police officers, traffic officers	43:16-7; 43:16A-17
	IRAs	*In re Yuhas*, 104 F.3d 612 (3rd Cir. 1997)
	Judges	43:6A-41
	Municipal employees	43:13-44
	Prison employees	43:7-13
	Public employees	43:15A-53
	School district employees	18A:66-116
	State police	53:5A-45
	Street & water department employees	43:19-17
	Teachers	18A:66-51
	Trust containing personal property created pursuant to federal tax law, including 401(k) plans, IRAs, Roth IRAs, & higher education (529) savings plans	25:2-1; *In re Yuhas*, 104 F.3d 612 (3d Cir. 1997)
personal property	Burial plots	45:27-21
	Clothing	2A:17-19
	Furniture & household goods to $1,000	2A:26-4
	Personal property & possessions of any kind, stock or interest in corporations to $1,000 total	2A:17-19
public benefits	Old age, permanent disability assistance	44:7-35
	Unemployment compensation	43:21-53
	Workers' compensation	34:15-29
tools of trade	None	
wages	90% of earned but unpaid wages if annual income is less than 250% of federal poverty level; 75% if annual income is higher	2A:17-56
	Wages or allowances received by military personnel	38A:4-8
wildcard	None	

New Mexico

Federal bankruptcy exemptions available. All law references are to New Mexico Statutes Annotated unless otherwise noted.

ASSET	EXEMPTION	LAW
homestead	$30,000	42-10-9
insurance	Benevolent association benefits to $5,000	42-10-4
	Fraternal benefit society benefits	59A-44-18
	Life, accident, health, or annuity benefits, withdrawal or cash value, if beneficiary is a New Mexico resident	42-10-3
	Life insurance proceeds	42-10-5
miscellaneous	Ownership interest in unincorporated association	53-10-2
	Property of business partnership	54-1A-501
pensions	Tax-exempt retirement accounts, including 401(k)s, 403(b)s, profit-sharing and money purchase plans, SEP and SIMPLE IRAs, and defined-benefit plans	11 U.S.C. § 522(b)(3)(C)
	Traditional and Roth IRAs to $1,000,000 per person	11 U.S.C. § 522(b)(3)(C); (n)
	Pension or retirement benefits	42-10-1; 42-10-2
	Public school employees	22-11-42A
personal property	Books & furniture	42-10-1; 42-10-2
	Building materials	48-2-15
	Clothing	42-10-1; 42-10-2
	Cooperative association shares, minimum amount needed to be member	53-4-28
	Health aids	42-10-1; 42-10-2
	Jewelry to $2,500	42-10-1; 42-10-2
	Materials, tools, & machinery to dig, drill, complete, operate, or repair oil line, gas well, or pipeline	70-4-12
	Motor vehicle to $4,000	42-10-1; 42-10-2
public benefits	Crime victims' compensation (will be repealed in 2006)	31-22-15
	General assistance	27-2-21
	Occupational disease disablement benefits	52-3-37
	Unemployment compensation	51-1-37
	Workers' compensation	52-1-52
tools of trade	$1,500	42-10-1; 42-10-2
wages	Minimum 75% of disposable earnings or 40 times the federal hourly minimum wage, whichever is more; bankruptcy judge may authorize more for low-income debtors	35-12-7
wildcard	$500 of any personal property	42-10-1
	$2,000 of any real or personal property, in lieu of homestead	42-10-10

New York

Federal bankruptcy exemptions not available. All references are to Consolidated Laws of New York unless otherwise noted; Civil Practice Law & Rules are abbreviated C.P.L.R.

ASSET	EXEMPTION	LAW
homestead	Real property including co-op, condo, or mobile home, to $50,000	C.P.L.R. 5206(a); In re Pearl, 723 F.2d 193 (2nd Cir. 1983)
insurance	Annuity contract benefits due the debtor, if debtor paid for the contract; $5,000 limit if purchased within 6 mos. prior to filing & not tax-deferred	Ins. 3212(d); Debt. & Cred. 283(1)
	Disability or illness benefits to $400/month	Ins. 3212(c)
	Life insurance proceeds & avails if the beneficiary is not the debtor, or if debtor's spouse has taken out policy	Ins. 3212(b)
	Life insurance proceeds left at death with the insurance company, if clause prohibits proceeds from being used to pay beneficiary's creditors	Est. Powers & Trusts 7-1.5(a)(2)
miscellaneous	Alimony, child support	C.P.L.R. 5205 (d)(3); Debt. & Cred. 282(2)(d)
	Property of business partnership	Partnership 51
pensions	Tax-exempt retirement accounts, including 401(k)s, 403(b)s, profit-sharing and money purchase plans, SEP and SIMPLE IRAs, and defined-benefit plans	11 U.S.C. § 522(b)(3)(C)
	Traditional and Roth IRAs to $1,000,000 per person	11 U.S.C. § 522(b)(3)(C); (n)
	ERISA-qualified benefits, IRAs, Roth IRAs, & Keoghs & income needed for support	C.P.L.R. 5205(c); Debt. & Cred. 282(2)(e)
	Public retirement benefits	Ins. 4607
	State employees	Ret. & Soc. Sec. 10
	Teachers	Educ. 524
	Village police officers	Unconsolidated 5711-o
	Volunteer ambulance workers' benefits	Vol. Amb. Wkr. Ben. 23
	Volunteer firefighters' benefits	Vol. Firefighter Ben. 23
personal property	Bible, schoolbooks, other books to $50; pictures; clothing; church pew or seat; sewing machine, refrigerator, TV, radio; furniture, cooking utensils & tableware, dishes; food to last 60 days; stoves with fuel to last 60 days; domestic animal with food to last 60 days, to $450; wedding ring; watch to $35; exemptions may not exceed $5,000 total (including tools of trade & limited annuity)	C.P.L.R. 5205(a)(1)-(6); Debt. & Cred. 283(1)
	Burial plot without structure to 1/4 acre	C.P.L.R. 5206(f)
	Cash (including savings bonds, tax refunds, bank & credit union deposits) to $2,500, or to $5,000 after exemptions for personal property taken, whichever amount is less (for debtors who do not claim homestead)	Debt. & Cred. 283(2)
	College tuition savings program trust fund	C.P.L.R. 5205(j)
	Health aids, including service animals with food	C.P.L.R. 5205(h)
	Lost future earnings recoveries needed for support	Debt. & Cred. 282(3)(iv)
	Motor vehicle to $2,400	Debt. & Cred. 282(1); In re Miller, 167 B.R. 782 (S.D. N.Y. 1994)
	Personal injury recoveries up to 1 year after receiving	Debt. & Cred. 282(3)(iii)
	Recovery for injury to exempt property up to 1 year after receiving	C.P.L.R. 5205(b)
	Savings & loan savings to $600	Banking 407
	Security deposit to landlord, utility company	C.P.L.R. 5205(g)
	Spendthrift trust fund principal, 90% of income if not created by debtor	C.P.L.R. 5205(c),(d)
	Wrongful death recoveries for person you depended on	Debt. & Cred. 282(3)(ii)

public benefits	Aid to blind, aged, disabled	Debt. & Cred. 282(2)(c)
	Crime victims' compensation	Debt. & Cred. 282(3)(i)
	Home relief, local public assistance	Debt. & Cred. 282(2)(a)
	Public assistance	Soc. Serv. 137
	Social Security	Debt. & Cred. 282(2)(a)
	Unemployment compensation	Debt. & Cred. 282(2)(a)
	Veterans' benefits	Debt. & Cred. 282(2)(b)
	Workers' compensation	Debt. & Cred. 282(2)(c); Work. Comp. 33, 218
tools of trade	Farm machinery, team, & food for 60 days; professional furniture, books, & instruments to $600 total	C.P.L.R. 5205(a),(b)
	Uniforms, medal, emblem, equipment, horse, arms, & sword of member of military	C.P.L.R. 5205(e)
wages	90% of earned but unpaid wages received within 60 days before & anytime after filing	C.P.L.R. 5205(d)
	90% of earnings from dairy farmer's sales to milk dealers	C.P.L.R. 5205(f)
	100% of pay of noncommissioned officer, private, or musician in U.S. or N.Y. state armed forces	C.P.L.R. 5205(e)
wildcard	None	

North Carolina

Federal bankruptcy exemptions not available. All law references are to General Statutes of North Carolina unless otherwise noted.

ASSET	EXEMPTION	LAW
homestead	Property held as tenancy by the entirety may be exempt against debts owed by only one spouse	In re Chandler, 148 B.R. 13 (E.D. N.C., 1992)
	Real or personal property, including co-op, used as residence to $18,500; up to $5,000 of unused portion of homestead may be applied to any property	1C-1601(a)(1),(2)
insurance	Employee group life policy or proceeds	58-58-165
	Fraternal benefit society benefits	58-24-85
	Life insurance on spouse or children	1C-1601(a)(6); Const. Art. X § 5
miscellaneous	Alimony, support, separate maintenance, and child support necessary for support of debtor and dependents	1C-1601(a)(12)
	Property of business partnership	59-55
	Support received by a surviving spouse for 1 year, up to $10,000	30-15
pensions	Tax-exempt retirement accounts, including 401(k)s, 403(b)s, profit-sharing and money purchase plans, SEP and SIMPLE IRAs, and defined-benefit plans	11 U.S.C. § 522(b)(3)(C)
	Traditional and Roth IRAs to $1,000,000 per person	11 U.S.C. § 522(b)(3)(C); (n)
	Firefighters & rescue squad workers	58-86-90
	IRAs & Roth IRAs	1C-1601(a)(9)
	Law enforcement officers	143-166.30(g)
	Legislators	120-4.29
	Municipal, city, & county employees	128-31
	Retirement benefits from another state to extent exempt in that state	1C-1601(a)(11)
	Teachers & state employees	135-9; 135-95
personal property	Animals, crops, musical instruments, books, clothing, appliances, household goods & furnishings to $5,000 total; may add $1,000 per dependent, up to $4,000 total additional (all property must have been purchased at least 90 days before filing)	1C-1601(a)(4),(d)
	Burial plot to $18,500, in lieu of homestead	1C-1601(a)(1)
	College savings account established under 26 U.S.C. § 529 to $25,000, excluding certain contributions within prior year	1C-1601(a)(10)
	Health aids	1C-1601(a)(7)
	Motor vehicle to $3,500	1C-1601(a)(3)
	Personal injury & wrongful death recoveries for person you depended on	1C-1601(a)(8)
public benefits	Aid to blind	111-18
	Crime victims' compensation	15B-17
	Public adult assistance under work first program	108A-36
	Unemployment compensation	96-17
	Workers' compensation	97-21
tools of trade	Implements, books, & tools of trade to $2,000	1C-1601(a)(5)
wages	Earned but unpaid wages received 60 days before filing for bankruptcy, needed for support	1-362
wildcard	$5,000 of unused homestead or burial exemption	1C-1601(a)(2)
	$500 of any personal property	Constitution Art. X § 1

North Dakota

Federal bankruptcy exemptions not available. All law references are to North Dakota Century Code unless otherwise noted.

ASSET	EXEMPTION	LAW
homestead	Real property, house trailer, or mobile home to $80,000 (husband & wife may not double)	28-22-02(10); 47-18-01
insurance	Fraternal benefit society benefits	26.1-15.1-18; 26.1-33-40
	Life insurance proceeds payable to deceased's estate, not to a specific beneficiary	26.1-33-40
	Life insurance surrender value to $100,000 per policy, if beneficiary is insured's dependent & policy was owned over 1 year before filing for bankruptcy; limit does not apply if more needed for support	28-22-03.1(3)
miscellaneous	Child support payments	14-09-09.31
pensions	Tax-exempt retirement accounts, including 401(k)s, 403(b)s, profit-sharing and money purchase plans, SEP and SIMPLE IRAs, and defined-benefit plans	11 U.S.C. § 522(b)(3)(C)
	Traditional and Roth IRAs to $1,000,000 per person	11 U.S.C. § 522(b)(3)(C); (n)
	Disabled veterans' benefits, except military retirement pay	28-22-03.1(4)(d)
	ERISA-qualified benefits, IRAs, Roth IRAs, & Keoghs to $100,000 per plan; no limit if more needed for support; total exemption (with life insurance surrender value) cannot exceed $200,000	28-22-03.1(3)
	Public employees deferred compensation	54-52.2-06
	Public employees pensions	28-22-19(1)
personal property	1. All debtors may exempt:	
	Bible, schoolbooks; other books to $100	28-22-02(4)
	Burial plots, church pew	28-22-02(2),(3)
	Clothing & family pictures	28-22-02(1),(5)
	Crops or grain raised by debtor on 160 acres where debtor resides	28-22-02(8)
	Food & fuel to last 1 year	28-22-02(6)
	Insurance proceeds for exempt property	28-22-02(9)
	Motor vehicle to $1,200 (or $32,000 for vehicle that has been modified to accommodate owner's disability)	28-22-03.1(2)
	Personal injury recoveries to $7,500	28-22-03.1(4)(b)
	Wrongful death recoveries to $7,500	28-22-03.1(4)(a)
	2. Head of household not claiming crops or grain may claim $5,000 of any personal property or:	28-22-03
	Books & musical instruments to $1,500	28-22-04(1)
	Household & kitchen furniture, beds & bedding, to $1,000	28-22-04(2)
	Library & tools of professional, tools of mechanic, & stock in trade, to $1,000	28-22-04(4)
	Livestock & farm implements to $4,500	28-22-04(3)
	3. Non-head of household not claiming crops or grain may claim $2,500 of any personal property	28-22-05
public benefits	Crime victims' compensation	28-22-19(2)
	Old age & survivor insurance program benefits	52-09-22
	Public assistance	28-22-19(3)
	Social Security	28-22-03.1(4)(c)
	Unemployment compensation	52-06-30
	Workers' compensation	65-05-29
tools of trade	See personal property, Option 2	
wages	Minimum 75% of disposable weekly earnings or 40 times the federal minimum wage, whichever is more; bankruptcy judge may authorize more for low-income debtors	32-09.1-03
wildcard	$7,500 of any property in lieu of homestead	28-22-03.1(1)

Ohio

Federal bankruptcy exemptions not available. All law references are to Ohio Revised Code unless otherwise noted.

ASSET	EXEMPTION	LAW
homestead	Property held as tenancy by the entirety may be exempt against debts owed by only one spouse	In re Pernus, 143 B.R. 856 (N.D. Ohio, 1992)
	Real or personal property used as residence to $5,000	2329.66(A)(1)(b)
insurance	Benevolent society benefits to $5,000	2329.63; 2329.66(A)(6)(a)
	Disability benefits to $600 per month	2329.66(A)(6)(e); 3923.19
	Fraternal benefit society benefits	2329.66(A)(6)(d); 3921.18
	Group life insurance policy or proceeds	2329.66(A)(6)(c); 3917.05
	Life, endowment, or annuity contract avails for your spouse, child, or dependent	2329.66(A)(6)(b); 3911.10
	Life insurance proceeds for a spouse	3911.12
	Life insurance proceeds if clause prohibits proceeds from being used to pay beneficiary's creditors	3911.14
miscellaneous	Alimony, child support needed for support	2329.66(A)(11)
	Property of business partnership	1775.24; 2329.66(A)(14)
pensions	Tax-exempt retirement accounts, including 401(k)s, 403(b)s, profit-sharing and money purchase plans, SEP and SIMPLE IRAs, and defined-benefit plans	11 U.S.C. § 522(b)(3)(C)
	Traditional and Roth IRAs to $1,000,000 per person	11 U.S.C. § 522(b)(3)(C); (n)
	ERISA-qualified benefits needed for support	2329.66(A)(10)(b)
	Firefighters, police officers	742.47
	IRAs, Roth IRAs, & Keoghs needed for support	2329.66(A)(10)(c), (a)
	Public employees	145.56
	Public safety officers' death benefit	2329.66(A)(10)(a)
	Public school employees	3309.66
	State highway patrol employees	5505.22
	Volunteer firefighters' dependents	146.13
personal property	Animals, crops, books, musical instruments, appliances, household goods, furnishings, firearms, hunting & fishing equipment to $200 per item; jewelry to $400 for 1 item, $200 for all others; $1,500 total ($2,000 if no homestead exemption claimed)	2329.66(A)(4)(b),(c),(d); In re Szydlowski, 186 B.R. 907 (N.D. Ohio 1995)
	Beds, bedding, clothing to $200 per item	2329.66(A)(3)
	Burial plot	517.09; 2329.66(A)(8)
	Cash, money due within 90 days, tax refund, bank, security, & utility deposits to $400 total	2329.66(A)(4)(a); In re Szydlowski, 186 B.R. 907 (N.D. Ohio 1995)
	Compensation for lost future earnings needed for support, received during 12 months before filing	2329.66(A)(12)(d)
	Cooking unit & refrigerator to $300 each	2329.66(A)(3)
	Health aids (professionally prescribed)	2329.66(A)(7)
	Motor vehicle to $1,000	2329.66(A)(2)(b)
	Personal injury recoveries to $5,000, received during 12 months before filing	2329.66(A)(12)(c)
	Tuition credit or payment	2329.66(A)(16)
	Wrongful death recoveries for person debtor depended on, needed for support, received during 12 months before filing	2329.66(A)(12)(b)
public benefits	Crime victim's compensation, received during 12 months before filing	2329.66(A)(12)(a); 2743.66(D)
	Disability assistance payments	2329.66(A)(9)(f); 5115.07
	Public assistance	2329.66(A)(9)(d); 5107.12, 5108.08
	Unemployment compensation	2329.66(A)(9)(c); 4141.32
	Vocational rehabilitation benefits	2329.66(A)(9)(a); 3304.19
	Workers' compensation	2329.66(A)(9)(b); 4123.67

tools of trade	Implements, books, & tools of trade to $750	2329.66(A)(5)
wages	Minimum 75% of disposable weekly earnings or 30 times the federal hourly minimum wage, whichever is higher; bankruptcy judge may authorize more for low-income debtors	2329.66(A)(13)
wildcard	$400 of any property	2329.66(A)(18)

Oklahoma

Federal bankruptcy exemptions not available. All law references are to Oklahoma Statutes Annotated (in the form title number-section number), unless otherwise noted.

ASSET	EXEMPTION	LAW
homestead	Real property or manufactured home to unlimited value; property cannot exceed 1 acre in city, town, or village, or 160 acres elsewhere; $5,000 limit if more than 25% of total sq. ft. area used for business purposes; okay to rent homestead as long as no other residence is acquired	31-1(A)(1); 31-1(A)(2); 31-2
insurance	Annuity benefits & cash value	36-3631.1
	Assessment or mutual benefits	36-2410
	Fraternal benefit society benefits	36-2718.1
	Funeral benefits prepaid & placed in trust	36-6125
	Group life policy or proceeds	36-3632
	Life, health, accident, & mutual benefit insurance proceeds & cash value, if clause prohibits proceeds from being used to pay beneficiary's creditors	36-3631.1
	Limited stock insurance benefits	36-2510
miscellaneous	Alimony, child support	31-1(A)(19)
	Beneficiary's interest in a statutory support trust	6-3010
	Liquor license	37-532
	Property of business partnership	54-1-504
pensions	Tax-exempt retirement accounts, including 401(k)s, 403(b)s, profit-sharing and money purchase plans, SEP and SIMPLE IRAs, and defined-benefit plans	11 U.S.C. § 522(b)(3)(C)
	Traditional and Roth IRAs to $1,000,000 per person	11 U.S.C. § 522(b)(3)(C); (n)
	County employees	19-959
	Disabled veterans	31-7
	ERISA-qualified benefits, IRAs, Roth IRAs, Education IRAs, & Keoghs	31-1(A)(20),(23),(24)
	Firefighters	11-49-126
	Judges	20-1111
	Law enforcement employees	47-2-303.3
	Police officers	11-50-124
	Public employees	74-923
	Tax-exempt benefits	60-328
	Teachers	70-17-109
personal property	Books, portraits, & pictures	31-1(A)-7
	Burial plots	31-1(A)(4); 8-7
	Clothing to $4,000	31-1(A)(8)
	College savings plan interest	31-1(24)
	Deposits in an IDA (Individual Development Account)	31-1(22)
	Federal earned income tax credit	31-1(A)(25)
	Food & seed for growing to last 1 year	31-1(A)(17)
	Health aids (professionally prescribed)	31-1(A)(9)
	Household & kitchen furniture	31-1(A)(3)
	Livestock for personal or family use: 5 dairy cows & calves under 6 months; 100 chickens; 20 sheep; 10 hogs; 2 horses, bridles, & saddles; forage & feed to last 1 year	31-1(A)(10),(11),(12),(15),(16),(17)
	Motor vehicle to $3,000	31-1(A)(13)
	Personal injury & wrongful death recoveries to $50,000	31-1(A)(21)
	Prepaid funeral benefits	36-6125(H)
	War bond payroll savings account	51-42
	1 gun	31-1(A)(14)
public benefits	Crime victims' compensation	21-142.13
	Public assistance	56-173
	Social Security	56-173
	Unemployment compensation	40-2-303
	Workers' compensation	85-48

tools of trade	Implements needed to farm homestead, tools, books, & apparatus to $5,000 total	31-1(A)(5),(6); 31-1(C)
wages	75% of wages earned in 90 days before filing bankruptcy; bankruptcy judge may allow more if you show hardship	12-1171.1; 31-1(A)(18); 31-1.1
wildcard	None	

Oregon

Federal bankruptcy exemptions not available. All law references are to Oregon Revised Statutes unless otherwise noted.

ASSET	EXEMPTION	LAW
homestead	Prepaid rent & security deposit for renters dwelling *In re Casserino*	379 F.3d 1069 (9th cir. 2004)
	Real property of a soldier or sailor during time of war	408.440
	Real property you occupy or intend to occupy to $30,000 ($39,600 for joint owners); mobile home on property you own or houseboat to $23,000 ($30,000 for joint owners); mobile home not on your land to $20,000 ($27,000 for joint owners); property cannot exceed 1 block in town or city or 160 acres elsewhere; sale proceeds exempt 1 year from sale, if you intend to purchase another home	18.428; 18.395; 18.402
	Tenancy by entirety not exempt, but subject to survivorship rights of nondebtor spouse	*In re Pletz*, 225 B.R. 206 (D. Or., 1997)
insurance	Annuity contract benefits to $500 per month	743.049
	Fraternal benefit society benefits to $7,500	748.207; 18.348
	Group life policy or proceeds not payable to insured	743.047
	Health or disability proceeds or avails	743.050
	Life insurance proceeds or cash value if you are not the insured	743.046, 743.047
miscellaneous	Alimony, child support needed for support	18.345(1)(i)
	Liquor licenses	471.292 (1)
pensions	Tax-exempt retirement accounts, including 401(k)s, 403(b)s, profit-sharing and money purchase plans, SEP and SIMPLE IRAs, and defined-benefit plans	11 U.S.C. § 522(b)(3)(C)
	Traditional and Roth IRAs to $1,000,000 per person	11 U.S.C. § 522(b)(3)(C); (n)
	ERISA-qualified benefits, including IRAs & SEPs; & payments to $7,500	18.358; 18.348
	Public officers, employees pension payments to $7,500	237.980; 238.445; 18.348 (2)
personal property	Bank deposits to $7,500; cash for sold exempt property	18.348; 18.345(2)
	Books, pictures, & musical instruments to $600 total	18.345(1)(a)
	Building materials for construction of an improvement	87.075
	Burial plot	65.870
	Clothing, jewelry, & other personal items to $1,800 total	18.345(1)(b)
	Compensation for lost earnings payments for debtor or someone debtor depended on, to extent needed	18.345(1)(L),(3)
	Domestic animals, poultry, & pets to $1,000 plus food to last 60 days	18.345(1)(e)
	Federal earned income tax credit	18.345(1)(n)
	Food & fuel to last 60 days if debtor is householder	18.345(1)(f)
	Furniture, household items, utensils, radios, & TVs to $3,000 total	18.345(1)(f)
	Health aids	18.345(1)(h)
	Higher education savings account to $7,500	348.863; 18.348(1)
	Motor vehicle to $2,150	18.345(1)(d),(3)
	Personal injury recoveries to $10,000	18.345(1)(k),(3)
	Pistol; rifle or shotgun (owned by person over 16) to $1,000	18.362
public benefits	Aid to blind to $7,500	412.115; 18.348
	Aid to disabled to $7,500	412.610; 18.348
	Civil defense & disaster relief to $7,500	401.405; 18.348
	Crime victims' compensation	18.345(1)(j)(A),(3); 147.325
	General assistance to $7,500	411.760; 18.348
	Injured inmates' benefits to $7,500	655.530; 18.348
	Medical assistance to $7,500	414.095; 18.348
	Old-age assistance to $7,500	413.130; 18.348
	Unemployment compensation to $7,500	657.855; 18.348
	Veterans' benefits & proceeds of Veterans loans	407.125; 407.595; 18.348(m)
	Vocational rehabilitation to $7,500	344.580; 18.348
	Workers' compensation to $7,500	656.234; 18.348
tools of trade	Tools, library, team with food to last 60 days, to $3,000	18.345(1)(c),(3)

wages	75% of disposable wages or $170 per week, whichever is greater; bankruptcy judge may authorize more for low-income debtors	18.385
	Wages withheld in state employee's bond savings accounts	292.070
wildcard	$400 of any personal property not already covered by existing exemption	18.348(1)(o)

Pennsylvania

Federal bankruptcy exemptions available. All law references are to Pennsylvania Consolidated Statutes Annotated unless otherwise noted.

ASSET	EXEMPTION	LAW
homestead	None; however, property held as tenancy by the entirety may be exempt against debts owed by only one spouse	In re Martin, 259 B.R. 119 (M.D. Pa. 2001)
insurance	Accident or disability benefits	42-8124(c)(7)
	Fraternal benefit society benefits	42-8124(c)(1),(8)
	Group life policy or proceeds	42-8124(c)(5)
	Insurance policy or annuity contract payments, where insured is the beneficiary, cash value or proceeds to $100 per month	42-8124(c)(3)
	Life insurance & annuity proceeds if clause prohibits proceeds from being used to pay beneficiary's creditors	42-8214(c)(4)
	Life insurance annuity policy cash value or proceeds if beneficiary is insured's dependent, child or spouse	42-8124(c)(6)
	No-fault automobile insurance proceeds	42-8124(c)(9)
miscellaneous	Property of business partnership	15-8342
pensions	Tax-exempt retirement accounts, including 401(k)s, 403(b)s, profit-sharing and money purchase plans, SEP and SIMPLE IRAs, and defined-benefit plans	11 U.S.C. § 522(b)(3)(C)
	Traditional and Roth IRAs to $1,000,000 per person	11 U.S.C. § 522(b)(3)(C); (n)
	City employees	53-13445; 53-23572; 53-39383; 42-8124(b)(1)(iv)
	County employees	16-4716
	Municipal employees	53-881.115; 42-8124(b)(1)(vi)
	Police officers	53-764; 53-776; 53-23666; 42-8124(b)(1)(iii)
	Private retirement benefits to extent tax-deferred, if clause prohibits proceeds from being used to pay beneficiary's creditors; exemption limited to deposits of $15,000 per year made at least 1 year before filing (limit does not apply to rollovers from other exempt funds or accounts)	42-8124(b)(1)(vii), (viii),(ix)
	Public school employees	24-8533; 42-8124(b)(1)(i)
	State employees	71-5953; 42-8124(b)(1)(ii)
personal property	Bibles & schoolbooks	42-8124(a)(2)
	Clothing	42-8124(a)(1)
	Military uniforms & accoutrements	42-8124(a)(4); 51-4103
	Sewing machines	42-8124(a)(3)
public benefits	Crime victims' compensation	18-11.708
	Korean conflict veterans' benefits	51-20098
	Unemployment compensation	42-8124(a)(10); 43-863
	Veterans' benefits	51-20012; 20048; 20098; 20127
	Workers' compensation	42-8124(c)(2)
tools of trade	Seamstress's sewing machine	42-8124(a)(3)
wages	Earned but unpaid wages	42-8127
	Prison inmates wages	61-1054
	Wages of victims of abuse	42-8127(f)
wildcard	$300 of any property, including cash, real property, securities, or proceeds from sale of exempt property	42-8123

Rhode Island

Federal bankruptcy exemptions available. All law references are to General Laws of Rhode Island unless otherwise noted.

ASSET	EXEMPTION	LAW
homestead	$200,000 in land & buildings you occupy or intend to occupy as a principal residence (husband & wife may not double)	9-26-4.1
insurance	Accident or sickness proceeds, avails, or benefits	27-18-24
	Fraternal benefit society benefits	27-25-18
	Life insurance proceeds if clause prohibits proceeds from being used to pay beneficiary's creditors	27-4-12
	Temporary disability insurance	28-41-32
miscellaneous	Earnings of a minor child	9-26-4(9)
	Property of business partnership	7-12-36
pensions	Tax-exempt retirement accounts, including 401(k)s, 403(b)s, profit-sharing and money purchase plans, SEP and SIMPLE IRAs, and defined-benefit plans	11 U.S.C. § 522(b)(3)(C)
	Traditional and Roth IRAs to $1,000,000 per person	11 U.S.C. § 522(b)(3)(C); (n)
	ERISA-qualified benefits	9-26-4(12)
	Firefighters	9-26-5
	IRAs & Roth IRAs	9-26-4(11)
	Police officers	9-26-5
	Private employees	28-17-4
	State & municipal employees	36-10-34
personal property	Beds, bedding, furniture, household goods, & supplies, to $8,600 total (husband & wife may not double)	9-26-4(3); *In re Petrozella*, 247 B.R. 591 (R.I. 2000)
	Bibles & books to $300	9-26-4(4)
	Burial plot	9-26-4(5)
	Clothing	9-26-4(1)
	Consumer cooperative association holdings to $50	7-8-25
	Debt secured by promissory note or bill of exchange	9-26-4(7)
	Jewelry to $1,000	9-26-4 (14)
	Motor vehicles to $10,000	9-26-4 (13)
	Prepaid tuition program or tuition savings account	9-26-4 (15)
public benefits	Aid to blind, aged, disabled; general assistance	40-6-14
	Crime victims' compensation	12-25.1-3(b)(2)
	Family assistance benefits	40-5.1-15
	State disability benefits	28-41-32
	Unemployment compensation	28-44-58
	Veterans' disability or survivors' death benefits	30-7-9
	Workers' compensation	28-33-27
tools of trade	Library of practicing professional	9-26-4(2)
	Working tools to $1,200	9-26-4(2)
wages	Earned but unpaid wages due military member on active duty	30-7-9
	Earned but unpaid wages due seaman	9-26-4(6)
	Earned but unpaid wages to $50	9-26-4(8)(iii)
	Wages of any person who had been receiving public assistance are exempt for 1 year after going off of relief	9-26-4(8)(ii)
	Wages of spouse & minor children	9-26-4(9)
	Wages paid by charitable organization or fund providing relief to the poor	9-26-4(8)(i)
wildcard	None	

South Carolina

Federal bankruptcy exemptions not available. All law references are to Code of Laws of South Carolina unless otherwise noted.

ASSET	EXEMPTION	LAW
homestead	Real property, including co-op, to $5,000	15-41-30(1)
insurance	Accident & disability benefits	38-63-40(D)
	Benefits accruing under life insurance policy after death of insured, where proceeds left with insurance company pursuant to agreement; benefits not exempt from action to recover necessaries if parties agree	38-63-50
	Disability or illness benefits	15-41-30(10)(C)
	Fraternal benefit society benefits	38-38-330
	Group life insurance proceeds; cash value to $50,000	38-63-40(C); 38-65-90
	Life insurance avails from policy for person you depended on to $4,000	15-41-30(8)
	Life insurance proceeds from policy for person you depended on, needed for support	15-41-30(11)(C)
	Proceeds & cash surrender value of life insurance payable to beneficiary other than insured's estate & for the express benefit of insured's spouse, children, or dependents (must be purchased 2 years before filing)	38-63-40(A)
	Proceeds of life insurance or annuity contract	38-63-40(B)
	Unmatured life insurance contract, except credit insurance policy	15-41-30(7)
miscellaneous	Alimony, child support	15-41-30(10)(D)
	Property of business partnership	33-41-720
pensions	Tax-exempt retirement accounts, including 401(k)s, 403(b)s, profit-sharing and money purchase plans, SEP and SIMPLE IRAs, and defined-benefit plans	11 U.S.C. § 522(b)(3)(C)
	Traditional and Roth IRAs to $1,000,000 per person	11 U.S.C. § 522(b)(3)(C); (n)
	ERISA-qualified benefits; your share of the pension plan fund	15-41-30(10)(E),(13)
	Firefighters	9-13-230
	General assembly members	9-9-180
	IRAs & Roth IRAs needed for support	15-41-30(12)
	Judges, solicitors	9-8-190
	Police officers	9-11-270
	Public employees	9-1-1680
personal property	Animals, crops, appliances, books, clothing, household goods, furnishings, musical instruments to $2,500 total	15-41-30(3)
	Burial plot to $5,000, in lieu of homestead	15-41-30(1)
	Cash & other liquid assets to $1,000, in lieu of burial or homestead exemption	15-41-30(5)
	College investment program trust fund	59-2-140
	Health aids	15-41-30(9)
	Jewelry to $500	15-41-30(4)
	Motor vehicle to $1,200	15-41-30(2)
	Personal injury & wrongful death recoveries for person you depended on for support	15-41-30(11)(B)
public benefits	Crime victims' compensation	15-41-30(11)(A); 16-3-1300
	General relief; aid to aged, blind, disabled	43-5-190
	Local public assistance	15-41-30(10)(A)
	Social Security	15-41-30(10)(A)
	Unemployment compensation	15-41-30(10)(A)
	Veterans' benefits	15-41-30(10)(B)
	Workers' compensation	42-9-360
tools of trade	Implements, books, & tools of trade to $750	15-41-30(6)
wages	None (use federal nonbankruptcy wage exemption)	
wildcard	None	

South Dakota

Federal bankruptcy exemptions not available. All law references are to South Dakota Codified Law unless otherwise noted.

ASSET	EXEMPTION	LAW
homestead	Gold or silver mine, mill, or smelter not exempt	43-31-5
	May file homestead declaration	43-31-6
	Real property to unlimited value or mobile home (larger than 240 sq. ft. at its base & registered in state at least 6 months before filing) to unlimited value; property cannot exceed 1 acre in town or 160 acres elsewhere; sale proceeds to $30,000 ($170,000 if over age 70 or widow or widower who hasn't remarried) exempt for 1 year after sale (husband & wife may not double)	43-31-1; 43-31-2; 43-31-3; 43-31-4 43-45-3
	Spouse or child of deceased owner may claim homestead exemption	43-31-13
insurance	Annuity contract proceeds to $250 per month	58-12-6; 58-12-8
	Endowment, life insurance, policy proceeds to $20,000; if policy issued by mutual aid or benevolent society, cash value to $20,000	58-12-4
	Fraternal benefit society benefits	58-37A-18
	Health benefits to $20,000	58-12-4
	Life insurance proceeds, if clause prohibits proceeds from being used to pay beneficiary's creditors	58-15-70
	Life insurance proceeds to $10,000, if beneficiary is surviving spouse or child	43-45-6
pensions	Tax-exempt retirement accounts, including 401(k)s, 403(b)s, profit-sharing and money purchase plans, SEP and SIMPLE IRAs, and defined-benefit plans	11 U.S.C. § 522(b)(3)(C)
	Traditional and Roth IRAs to $1,000,000 per person	11 U.S.C. § 522(b)(3)(C); (n)
	City employees	9-16-47
	ERISA-qualified benefits, limited to income & distribution on $250,000	43-45-16
	Public employees	3-12-115
personal property	Bible, schoolbooks; other books to $200	43-45-2(4)
	Burial plots, church pew	43-45-2(2),(3)
	Cemetery association property	47-29-25
	Clothing	43-45-2(5)
	Family pictures	43-45-2(1)
	Food & fuel to last 1 year	43-45-2(6)
public benefits	Crime victim's compensation	23A-28B-24
	Public assistance	28-7A-18
	Unemployment compensation	61-6-28
	Workers' compensation	62-4-42
tools of trade	None	
wages	Earned wages owed 60 days before filing bankruptcy, needed for support of family	15-20-12
	Wages of prisoners in work programs	24-8-10
wildcard	Head of family may claim $6,000, or non-head of family may claim $4,000 of any personal property	43-45-4

Tennessee

Federal bankruptcy exemptions not available. All law references are to Tennessee Code Annotated unless otherwise noted.

ASSET	EXEMPTION	LAW
homestead	$5,000; $7,500 for joint owners (if 62 or older, $12,500 if single; $20,000 if married; $25,000 if spouse is also 62 or older)	26-2-301
	2–15 year lease	26-2-303
	Life estate	26-2-302
	Property held as tenancy by the entirety may be exempt against debts owed by only one spouse, but survivorship right is not exempt	*In re Arango,* 136 B.R. 740 aff'd, 992 F.2d 611 (6th Cir. 1993); *In re Arwood,* 289 B.R. 889 (Bankr. E.D. Ten. 2003)
	Spouse or child of deceased owner may claim homestead exemption	26-2-301
insurance	Accident, health, or disability benefits for resident & citizen of Tennessee	26-2-110
	Disability or illness benefits	26-2-111(1)(C)
	Fraternal benefit society benefits	56-25-1403
	Life insurance or annuity	56-7-203
miscellaneous	Alimony, child support owed for 30 days before filing for bankruptcy	26-2-111(1)(E)
	Educational scholarship trust funds & pre-payment plans	49-4-108; 49-7-822
pensions	Tax-exempt retirement accounts, including 401(k)s, 403(b)s, profit-sharing and money purchase plans, SEP and SIMPLE IRAs, and defined-benefit plans	11 U.S.C. § 522(b)(3)(C)
	Traditional and Roth IRAs to $1,000,000 per person	11 U.S.C. § 522(b)(3)(C); (n)
	ERISA-qualified benefits, IRAs, & Roth IRAs	26-2-111(1)(D)
	Public employees	8-36-111
	State & local government employees	26-2-105
	Teachers	49-5-909
personal property	Bible, schoolbooks, family pictures, & portraits	26-2-104
	Burial plot to 1 acre	26-2-305; 46-2-102
	Clothing & storage containers	26-2-104
	Health aids	26-2-111(5)
	Lost future earnings payments for you or person you depended on	26-2-111(3)
	Personal injury recoveries to $7,500; wrongful death recoveries to $10,000 ($15,000 total for personal injury, wrongful death, & crime victims' compensation)	26-2-111(2)(B),(C)
	Wages of debtor deserting family, in hands of family	26-2-109
public benefits	Aid to blind	71-4-117
	Aid to disabled	71-4-1112
	Crime victims' compensation to $5,000 (*see* personal property)	26-2-111(2)(A); 29-13-111
	Local public assistance	26-2-111(1)(A)
	Old-age assistance	71-2-216
	Relocation assistance payments	13-11-115
	Social Security	26-2-111(1)(A)
	Unemployment compensation	26-2-111(1)(A)
	Veterans' benefits	26-2-111(1)(B)
	Workers' compensation	50-6-223
tools of trade	Implements, books, & tools of trade to $1,900	26-2-111(4)
wages	Minimum 75% of disposable weekly earnings or 30 times the federal minimum hourly wage, whichever is more, plus $2.50 per week per child; bankruptcy judge may authorize more for low-income debtors	26-2-106,107
wildcard	$4,000 of any personal property including deposits on account with any bank or financial institution	26-2-103

Texas

Federal bankruptcy exemptions available. All law references are to Texas Revised Civil Statutes Annotated unless otherwise noted.

ASSET	EXEMPTION	LAW
homestead	Unlimited; property cannot exceed 10 acres in town, village, city or 100 acres (200 for families) elsewhere; sale proceeds exempt for 6 months after sale (renting okay if another home not acquired, Prop. 41.003)	Prop. 41.001; 41.002; Const. Art. 16 §§ 50, 51
	Must file homestead declaration, or court will file it for you & charge you for doing so	Prop. 41.005(f); 41.021 to 41.023
insurance	Church benefit plan benefits	1407a (6)
	Fraternal benefit society benefits	Ins. 885.316
	Life, health, accident, or annuity benefits, monies, policy proceeds, & cash values due or paid to beneficiary or insured	Ins. 1108.051
	Texas employee uniform group insurance	Ins. 1551.011
	Texas public school employees group insurance	Ins. 1575.006
	Texas state college or university employee benefits	Ins. 1601.008
miscellaneous	Alimony & child support	Prop. 42.001(b)(3)
	Higher education savings plan trust account	Educ. 54.709(e)
	Liquor licenses & permits	Alco.Bev.Code 11.03
	Prepaid tuition plans	Educ. 54.639
	Property of business partnership	6132b-5.01
pensions	Tax-exempt retirement accounts, including 401(k)s, 403(b)s, profit-sharing and money purchase plans, SEP and SIMPLE IRAs, and defined-benefit plans	11 U.S.C. § 522(b)(3)(C)
	Traditional and Roth IRAs to $1,000,000 per person	11 U.S.C. § 522(b)(3)(C); (n)
	County & district employees	Gov't. 811.006
	ERISA-qualified government or church benefits, including Keoghs & IRAs	Prop. 42.0021
	Firefighters	6243e(5); 6243a-1(8.03); 6243b(15); 6243e(5); 6243e.1(1.04)
	Judges	Gov't. 831.004
	Law enforcement officers, firefighters, emergency medical personnel survivors	Gov't. 615.005
	Municipal employees & elected officials, state employees	6243h(22); Gov't. 811.005
	Police officers	6243d-1(17); 6243j(20); 6243a-1(8.03); 6243b(15); 6243d-1(17)
	Retirement benefits to extent tax-deferred	Prop. 42.0021
	Teachers	Gov't. 821.005
personal property to $60,000 total for family, $30,000 for single adult (see also tools of trade)	Athletic & sporting equipment, including bicycles	Prop. 42.002(a)(8)
	Burial plots (exempt from total)	Prop. 41.001
	Clothing & food	Prop. 42.002(a)(2),(5)
	Health aids (exempt from total)	Prop. 42.001(b)(2)
	Health savings accounts	Prop. 42.0021
	Home furnishings including family heirlooms	Prop. 42.002(a)(1)
	Jewelry (limited to 25% of total exemption)	Prop. 42.002(a)(6)
	Pets & domestic animals plus their food: 2 horses, mules, or donkeys & tack; 12 head of cattle; 60 head of other livestock; 120 fowl	Prop. 42.002(a)(10),(11)
	1 two-, three- or four-wheeled motor vehicle per family member or per single adult who holds a driver's license; or, if not licensed, who relies on someone else to operate vehicle	Prop. 42.002(a)(9)
	2 firearms	Prop. 42.002(a)(7)
public benefits	Crime victims' compensation	Crim. Proc. 56.49
	Medical assistance	Hum. Res. 32.036
	Public assistance	Hum. Res. 31.040
	Unemployment compensation	Labor 207.075
	Workers' compensation	Labor 408.201
tools of trade included in aggregate dollar limits for personal property	Farming or ranching vehicles & implements	Prop. 42.002(a)(3)
	Tools, equipment (includes boat & motor vehicles used in trade), & books	Prop. 42.002(a)(4)
wages	Earned but unpaid wages	Prop. 42.001(b)(1)
	Unpaid commissions not to exceed 25% of total personal property exemptions	Prop. 42.001(d)
wildcard	None	

Utah

Federal bankruptcy exemptions not available. All law references are to Utah Code unless otherwise noted.

ASSET	EXEMPTION	LAW
homestead	Must file homestead declaration before attempted sale of home	78-23-4
	Real property, mobile home, or water rights to $20,000 if primary residence; $5,000 if not primary residence	78-23-3(1),(2),(4)
	Sale proceeds exempt for 1 year	78-23-3(5)(b)
insurance	Disability, illness, medical, or hospital benefits	78-23-5(1)(a)(iii)
	Fraternal benefit society benefits	31A-9-603
	Life insurance policy cash surrender value, excluding payments made on the contract within the prior year	78-23-5(a)(xiii)
	Life insurance proceeds if beneficiary is insured's spouse or dependent, as needed for support	78-23-5(a)(xi)
	Medical, surgical, & hospital benefits	78-23-5(1)(a)(iv)
miscellaneous	Alimony needed for support	78-23-5(1)(a)(vi)
	Child support	78-23-5(1)(a)(vi), (f),(k)
	Property of business partnership	48-1-22
pensions	Tax-exempt retirement accounts, including 401(k)s, 403(b)s, profit-sharing and money purchase plans, SEP and SIMPLE IRAs, and defined-benefit plans	11 U.S.C. § 522(b)(3)(C)
	Traditional and Roth IRAs to $1,000,000 per person	11 U.S.C. § 522(b)(3)(C); (n)
	ERISA-qualified benefits, IRAs, Roth IRAs, & Keoghs (benefits that have accrued & contributions that have been made at least 1 year prior to filing)	78-23-5(1)(a)(xiv)
	Other pensions & annuities needed for support	78-23-6(3)
	Public employees	49-11-612
personal property	Animals, books, & musical instruments to $500	78-23-8(1)(c)
	Artwork depicting, or done by, a family member	78-23-5(1)(a)(ix)
	Bed, bedding, carpets	78-23-5(1)(a)(viii)
	Burial plot	78-23-5(1)(a)(i)
	Clothing (cannot claim furs or jewelry)	78-23-5(1)(a)(viii)
	Dining & kitchen tables & chairs to $500	78-23-8(1)(b)
	Food to last 12 months	78-23-5(1)(a)(viii)
	Health aids	78-23-5(1)(a)(ii)
	Heirlooms to $500	78-23-8(1)(d)
	Motor vehicle to $2,500	78-23-8(3)
	Personal injury, wrongful death recoveries for you or person you depended on	78-23-5(1)(a)(x)
	Proceeds for sold, lost, or damaged exempt property	78-23-9
	Refrigerator, freezer, microwave, stove, sewing machine, washer & dryer	78-23-5(1)(a)(viii)
	Sofas, chairs, & related furnishings to $500	78-23-8(1)(a)
public benefits	Crime victims' compensation	63-25a-421(4)
	General assistance	35A-3-112
	Occupational disease disability benefits	34A-3-107
	Unemployment compensation	35A-4-103(4)(b)
	Veterans' benefits	78-23-5(1)(a)(v)
	Workers' compensation	34A-2-422
tools of trade	Implements, books, & tools of trade to $3,500	78-23-8(2)
	Military property of National Guard member	39-1-47
wages	Minimum 75% of disposable weekly earnings or 30 times the federal hourly minimum wage, whichever is more; bankruptcy judge may authorize more for low-income debtors	70C-7-103
wildcard	None	

Vermont

Federal bankruptcy exemptions available. All law references are to Vermont Statutes Annotated unless otherwise noted.

ASSET	EXEMPTION	LAW
homestead	Property held as tenancy by the entirety may be exempt against debts owed by only one spouse	In re McQueen, 21 B.R. 736 (D. Ver. 1982)
	Real property or mobile home to $75,000; may also claim rents, issues, profits, & outbuildings	27-101
	Spouse of deceased owner may claim homestead exemption	27-105
insurance	Annuity contract benefits to $350 per month	8-3709
	Disability benefits that supplement life insurance or annuity contract	8-3707
	Disability or illness benefits needed for support	12-2740(19)(C)
	Fraternal benefit society benefits	8-4478
	Group life or health benefits	8-3708
	Health benefits to $200 per month	8-4086
	Life insurance proceeds for person you depended on	12-2740(19)(H)
	Life insurance proceeds if clause prohibits proceeds from being used to pay beneficiary's creditors	8-3705
	Life insurance proceeds if beneficiary is not the insured	8-3706
	Unmatured life insurance contract other than credit	12-2740(18)
miscellaneous	Alimony, child support	12-2740(19)(D)
pensions	Tax-exempt retirement accounts, including 401(k)s, 403(b)s, profit-sharing and money purchase plans, SEP and SIMPLE IRAs, and defined-benefit plans	11 U.S.C. § 522(b)(3)(C)
	Traditional and Roth IRAs to $1,000,000 per person	11 U.S.C. § 522(b)(3)(C); (n)
	Municipal employees	24-5066
	Other pensions	12-2740(19)(J)
	Self-directed accounts (IRAs, Roth IRAs, Keoghs); contributions must be made 1 year before filing	12-2740(16)
	State employees	3-476
	Teachers	16-1946
personal property	Appliances, furnishings, goods, clothing, books, crops, animals, musical instruments to $2,500 total	12-2740(5)
	Bank deposits to $700	12-2740(15)
	Cow, 2 goats, 10 sheep, 10 chickens, & feed to last 1 winter; 3 swarms of bees plus honey; 5 tons coal or 500 gal. heating oil, 10 cords of firewood; 500 gal. bottled gas; growing crops to $5,000; yoke of oxen or steers; plow & ox yoke; 2 horses with harnesses, halters, & chains	12-2740(6),(9)-(14)
	Health aids	12-2740(17)
	Jewelry to $500; wedding ring unlimited	12-2740(3),(4)
	Motor vehicles to $2,500	12-2740(1)
	Personal injury, lost future earnings, wrongful death recoveries for you or person you depended on	12-2740(19)(F), (G),(I)
	Stove, heating unit, refrigerator, freezer, water heater, & sewing machines	12-2740(8)
public benefits	Aid to blind, aged, disabled; general assistance	33-124
	Crime victims' compensation needed for support	12-2740(19)(E)
	Social Security needed for support	12-2740(19)(A)
	Unemployment compensation	21-1367
	Veterans' benefits needed for support	12-2740(19)(B)
	Workers' compensation	21-681
tools of trade	Books & tools of trade to $5,000	12-2740(2)

wages	Entire wages, if you received welfare during 2 months before filing	12-3170
	Minimum 75% of weekly disposable earnings or 30 times the federal minimum hourly wage, whichever is greater; bankruptcy judge may authorize more for low-income debtors	12-3170
wildcard	Unused exemptions for motor vehicle, tools of trade, jewelry, household furniture, appliances, clothing, & crops to $7,000	12-2740(7)
	$400 of any property	12-2740(7)

Virginia

Federal bankruptcy exemptions not available. All law references are to Code of Virginia unless otherwise noted.

ASSET	EXEMPTION	LAW
homestead	$5,000 plus $500 per dependent; rents & profits; sale proceeds exempt to $5,000 (unused portion of homestead may be applied to any personal property)	*Cheeseman v. Nachman*, 656 F.2d 60 (4th Cir. 1981); 34-4; 34-18; 34-20
	May include mobile home	*In re Goad*, 161 B.R. 161 (W.D. Va. 1993)
	Must file homestead declaration before filing for bankruptcy	34-6
	Property held as tenancy by the entirety may be exempt against debts owed by only one spouse	*In re Bunker*, 312 F.3d 145 (4th Cir., 2002)
	Surviving spouse may claim $15,000; if no surviving spouse, minor children may claim exemption	64.1-151.3
insurance	Accident or sickness benefits	38.2-3406
	Burial society benefits	38.2-4021
	Cooperative life insurance benefits	38.2-3811
	Fraternal benefit society benefits	38.2-4118
	Group life or accident insurance for government officials	51.1-510
	Group life insurance policy or proceeds	38.2-3339
	Industrial sick benefits	38.2-3549
	Life insurance proceeds	38.2-3122
miscellaneous	Property of business partnership	50-73.108
pensions *see also wages*	Tax-exempt retirement accounts, including 401(k)s, 403(b)s, profit-sharing and money purchase plans, SEP and SIMPLE IRAs, and defined-benefit plans	11 U.S.C. § 522(b)(3)(C)
	Traditional and Roth IRAs to $1,000,000 per person	11 U.S.C. § 522(b)(3)(C); (n)
	City, town, & county employees	51.1-802
	ERISA-qualified benefits to $25,000	34-34
	Judges	51.1-300
	State employees	51.1-124.4(A)
	State police officers	51.1-200
personal property	Bible	34-26(1)
	Burial plot	34-26(3)
	Clothing to $1,000	34-26(4)
	Family portraits & heirlooms to $5,000 total	34-26(2)
	Health aids	34-26(6)
	Household furnishings to $5,000	34-26(4a)
	Motor vehicle to $2,000	34-26(8)
	Personal injury causes of action & recoveries	34-28.1
	Pets	34-26(5)
	Prepaid tuition contracts	23-38.81(E)
	Spendthrift trusts not created by debtor	55-19
	Wedding & engagement rings	34-26(1a)
public benefits	Aid to blind, aged, disabled; general relief	63.2-506
	Crime victims' compensation unless seeking to discharge debt for treatment of injury incurred during crime	19.2-368.12
	Payments to tobacco farmers	3.1-1111.1
	Unemployment compensation	60.2-600
	Workers' compensation	65.2-531
tools of trade	For farmer, pair of horses, or mules with gear; one wagon or cart, one tractor to $3,000; 2 plows & wedges; one drag, harvest cradle, pitchfork, rake; fertilizer to $1,000	34-27
	Tools, books, & instruments of trade, including motor vehicles, to $10,000, needed in your occupation or education	34-26(7)
	Uniforms, arms, equipment of military member	44-96

wages	Minimum 75% of weekly disposable earnings or 40 times the federal minimum hourly wage, whichever is greater; bankruptcy judge may authorize more for low-income debtors	34-29
wildcard	Unused portion of homestead or personal property exemption	34-13
	$2,000 of any property for disabled veterans	34-4.1

Washington

Federal bankruptcy exemptions available. All law references are to Revised Code of Washington Annotated unless otherwise noted.

ASSET	EXEMPTION	LAW
homestead	Must record homestead declaration before sale of home if property unimproved or home unoccupied	6.15.040
	Real property or mobile home to $40,000; unimproved property intended for residence to $15,000 (husband & wife may not double)	6.13.010; 6.13.030
insurance	Annuity contract proceeds to $2,500 per month	48.18.430
	Disability proceeds, avails, or benefits	48.36A.180
	Fraternal benefit society benefits	48.18.400
	Group life insurance policy or proceeds	48.18.420
	Life insurance proceeds or avails if beneficiary is not the insured	48.18.410
miscellaneous	Child support payments	6.15.010(3)(d)
pensions	Tax-exempt retirement accounts, including 401(k)s, 403(b)s, profit-sharing and money purchase plans, SEP and SIMPLE IRAs, and defined-benefit plans	11 U.S.C. § 522(b)(3)(C)
	Traditional and Roth IRAs to $1,000,000 per person	11 U.S.C. § 522(b)(3)(C); (n)
	City employees	41.28.200; 41.44.240
	ERISA-qualified benefits, IRAs, Roth IRAs, & Keoghs	6.15.020
	Judges	2.10.180; 2.12.090
	Law enforcement officials & firefighters	41.26.053
	Police officers	41.20.180
	Public & state employees	41.40.052
	State patrol officers	43.43.310
	Teachers	41.32.052
	Volunteer firefighters	41.24.240
personal property	Appliances, furniture, household goods, home & yard equipment to $2,700 total for individual ($5,400 for community)	6.15.010(3)(a)
	Books to $1,500	6.15.010(2)
	Burial ground	68.24.220
	Burial plots sold by nonprofit cemetery association	68.20.120
	Clothing, no more than $1,000 in furs, jewelry, ornaments	6.15.010(1)
	Fire insurance proceeds for lost, stolen, or destroyed exempt property	6.15.030
	Food & fuel for comfortable maintenance	6.15.010(3)(a)
	Health aids prescribed	6.15.010(3)(e)
	Keepsakes & family pictures	6.15.010(2)
	Motor vehicle to $2,500 total for individual (two vehicles to $5,000 for community)	6.15.010(3)(c)
	Personal injury recoveries to $16,150	6.15.010(3)(f)
public benefits	Child welfare	74.13.070
	Crime victims' compensation	7.68.070(10)
	General assistance	74.04.280
	Industrial insurance (workers' compensation)	51.32.040
	Old-age assistance	74.08.210
	Unemployment compensation	50.40.020
tools of trade	Farmer's trucks, stock, tools, seed, equipment, & supplies to $5,000 total	6.15.010(4)(a)
	Library, office furniture, office equipment, & supplies of physician, surgeon, attorney, clergy, or other professional to $5,000 total	6.15.010(4)(b)
	Tools & materials used in any other trade to $5,000	6.15.010(4)(c)
wages	Minimum 75% of weekly disposable earnings or 30 times the federal minimum hourly wage, whichever is greater; bankruptcy judge may authorize more for low-income debtors	6.27.150
wildcard	$2,000 of any personal property (no more than $200 in cash, bank deposits, bonds, stocks, & securities)	6.15.010(3)(b)

West Virginia

Federal bankruptcy exemptions not available. All law references are to West Virginia Code unless otherwise noted.

ASSET	EXEMPTION	LAW
homestead	Real or personal property used as residence to $25,000; unused portion of homestead may be applied to any property	38-10-4(a)
insurance	Fraternal benefit society benefits	33-23-21
	Group life insurance policy or proceeds	33-6-28
	Health or disability benefits	38-10-4(j)(3)
	Life insurance payments from policy for person you depended on, needed for support	38-10-4(k)(3)
	Unmatured life insurance contract, except credit insurance policy	38-10-4(g)
	Unmatured life insurance contract's accrued dividend, interest, or loan value to $8,000, if debtor owns contract & insured is either debtor or a person on whom debtor is dependent	38-10-4(h)
miscellaneous	Alimony, child support needed for support	38-10-4(j)(4)
pensions	Tax-exempt retirement accounts, including 401(k)s, 403(b)s, profit-sharing and money purchase plans, SEP and SIMPLE IRAs, and defined-benefit plans	11 U.S.C. § 522(b)(3)(C)
	Traditional and Roth IRAs to $1,000,000 per person	11 U.S.C. § 522(b)(3)(C); (n)
	ERISA-qualified benefits, IRAs needed for support	38-10-4(j)(5)
	Public employees	5-10-46
	Teachers	18-7A-30
personal property	Animals, crops, clothing, appliances, books, household goods, furnishings, musical instruments to $400 per item, $8,000 total	38-10-4(c)
	Burial plot to $25,000, in lieu of homestead	38-10-4(a)
	Health aids	38-10-4(i)
	Jewelry to $1,000	38-10-4(d)
	Lost earnings payments needed for support	38-10-4(k)(5)
	Motor vehicle to $2,400	38-10-4(b)
	Personal injury recoveries to $15,000	38-10-4(k)(4)
	Prepaid higher education tuition trust fund & savings plan payments	38-10-4(k)(6)
	Wrongful death recoveries for person you depended on, needed for support	38-10-4(k)(2)
public benefits	Aid to blind, aged, disabled; general assistance	9-5-1
	Crime victims' compensation	38-10-4(k)(1)
	Social Security	38-10-4(j)(1)
	Unemployment compensation	38-10-4(j)(1)
	Veterans' benefits	38-10-4(j)(2)
	Workers' compensation	23-4-18
tools of trade	Implements, books, & tools of trade to $1,500	38-10-4(f)
wages	Minimum 30 times the federal minimum hourly wage per week; bankruptcy judge may authorize more for low-income debtors	38-5A-3
wildcard	$800 plus unused portion of homestead or burial exemption, of any property	38-10-4(e)

Wisconsin

Federal bankruptcy exemptions available. All law references are to Wisconsin Statutes Annotated unless otherwise noted.

ASSET	EXEMPTION	LAW
homestead	Property you occupy or intend to occupy to $40,000; sale proceeds exempt for 2 years if you intend to purchase another home (husband & wife may not double)	815.20
insurance	Federal disability insurance benefits	815.18(3)(ds)
	Fraternal benefit society benefits	614.96
	Life insurance proceeds for someone debtor depended on, needed for support	815.18(3)(i)(a)
	Life insurance proceeds held in trust by insurer, if clause prohibits proceeds from being used to pay beneficiary's creditors	632.42
	Unmatured life insurance contract (except credit insurance contract) if debtor owns contract & insured is debtor or dependents, or someone debtor is dependent on	815.18(3)(f)
	Unmatured life insurance contract's accrued dividends, interest, or loan value to $4,000 total, if debtor owns contract & insured is debtor or dependents, or someone debtor is dependent on	815.18(3)(f)
miscellaneous	Alimony, child support needed for support	815.18(3)(c)
	Property of business partnership	178.21(3)(c)
pensions	Tax-exempt retirement accounts, including 401(k)s, 403(b)s, profit-sharing and money purchase plans, SEP and SIMPLE IRAs, and defined-benefit plans	11 U.S.C. § 522(b)(3)(C)
	Traditional and Roth IRAs to $1,000,000 per person	11 U.S.C. § 522(b)(3)(C); (n)
	Certain municipal employees	62.63(4)
	Firefighters, police officers who worked in city with population over 100,000	815.18(3)(ef)
	Military pensions	815.18(3)(n)
	Private or public retirement benefits	815.18(3)(j)
	Public employees	40.08(1)
personal property	Burial plot, tombstone, coffin	815.18(3)(a)
	College savings account or tuition trust fund	14.64(7); 14.63(8)
	Deposit accounts to $1,000	815.18(3)(k)
	Fire & casualty proceeds for destroyed exempt property for 2 years from receiving	815.18(3)(e)
	Household goods & furnishings, clothing, keepsakes, jewelry, appliances, books, musical instruments, firearms, sporting goods, animals, & other tangible personal property to $5,000 total	815.18(3)(d)
	Lost future earnings recoveries, needed for support	815.18(3)(i)(d)
	Motor vehicles to $1,200; unused portion of $5,000 personal property exemption may be added	815.18(3)(g)
	Personal injury recoveries to $25,000	815.18(3)(i)(c)
	Tenant's lease or stock interest in housing co-op, to homestead amount	182.004(6)
	Wages used to purchase savings bonds	20.921(1)(e)
	Wrongful death recoveries, needed for support	815.18(3)(i)(b)
public benefits	Crime victims' compensation	949.07
	Social services payments	49.96
	Unemployment compensation	108.13
	Veterans' benefits	45.03(8)(b)
	Workers' compensation	102.27
tools of trade	Equipment, inventory, farm products, books, & tools of trade to $7,500 total	815.18(3)(b)
wages	75% of weekly net income or 30 times the greater of the federal or state minimum hourly wage; bankruptcy judge may authorize more for low-income debtors	815.18(3)(h)
	Wages of county jail prisoners	303.08(3)
	Wages of county work camp prisoners	303.10(7)
	Wages of inmates under work-release plan	303.065(4)(b)
wildcard	None	

Wyoming

Federal bankruptcy exemptions not available. All law references are to Wyoming Statutes Annotated unless otherwise noted.

ASSET	EXEMPTION	LAW
homestead	Property held as tenancy by the entirety may be exempt against debts owed by only one spouse	*In re Anselmi,* 52 B.R. 479 (D. Wy. 1985)
	Real property you occupy to $10,000 or house trailer you occupy to $6,000	1-20-101; 102; 104
	Spouse or child of deceased owner may claim homestead exemption	1-20-103
insurance	Annuity contract proceeds to $350 per month	26-15-132
	Disability benefits if clause prohibits proceeds from being used to pay beneficiary's creditors	26-15-130
	Fraternal benefit society benefits	26-29-218
	Group life or disability policy or proceeds, cash surrender & loan values, premiums waived, & dividends	26-15-131
	Individual life insurance policy proceeds, cash surrender & loan values, premiums waived, & dividends	26-15-129
	Life insurance proceeds held by insurer, if clause prohibits proceeds from being used to pay beneficiary's creditors	26-15-133
miscellaneous	Liquor licenses & malt beverage permits	12-4-604
pensions	Tax-exempt retirement accounts, including 401(k)s, 403(b)s, profit-sharing and money purchase plans, SEP and SIMPLE IRAs, and defined-benefit plans	11 U.S.C. § 522(b)(3)(C)
	Traditional and Roth IRAs to $1,000,000 per person	11 U.S.C. § 522(b)(3)(C); (n)
	Criminal investigators, highway officers	9-3-620
	Firefighters' death benefits	15-5-209
	Game & fish wardens	9-3-620
	Police officers	15-5-313(c)
	Private or public retirement funds & accounts	1-20-110
	Public employees	9-3-426
personal property	Bedding, furniture, household articles, & food to $2,000 per person in the home	1-20-106(a)(iii)
	Bible, schoolbooks, & pictures	1-20-106(a)(i)
	Burial plot	1-20-106(a)(ii)
	Clothing & wedding rings to $1,000	1-20-105
	Medical savings account contributions	1-20-111
	Motor vehicle to $2,400	1-20-106(a)(iv)
	Prepaid funeral contracts	26-32-102
public benefits	Crime victims' compensation	1-40-113
	General assistance	42-2-113(b)
	Unemployment compensation	27-3-319
	Workers' compensation	27-14-702
tools of trade	Library & implements of profession to $2,000 or tools, motor vehicle, implements, team & stock in trade to $2,000	1-20-106(b)
wages	Earnings of National Guard members	19-9-401
	Minimum 75% of disposable weekly earnings or 30 times the federal hourly minimum wage, whichever is more	1-15-511
	Wages of inmates in adult community corrections program	7-18-114
	Wages of inmates in correctional industries program	25-13-107
	Wages of inmates on work release	7-16-308
wildcard	None	

Federal Bankruptcy Exemptions

Married couples filing jointly may double all exemptions. All references are to 11 U.S.C. § 522. These exemptions were last adjusted in 2004. Every three years ending on April 1, these amounts will be adjusted to reflect changes in the Consumer Price Index. Debtors in the following states may select the federal bankruptcy exemptions:

Arkansas	Massachusetts	New Jersey	Texas
Connecticut	Michigan	New Mexico	Vermont
District of Columbia	Minnesota	Pennsylvania	Washington
Hawaii	New Hampshire	Rhode Island	Wisconsin

ASSET	EXEMPTION	SUBSECTION
homestead	Real property, including co-op or mobile home, or burial plot to $18,450; unused portion of homestead to $9,250 may be applied to any property	(d)(1); (d)(5)
insurance	Disability, illness, or unemployment benefits	(d)(10)(C)
	Life insurance payments fropm policy for person you depended on, needed for support	(d)(11)(C)
	Life insurance policy with loan value, in accrued dividends or interest, to $9,850	(d)(8)
	Unmatured life insurance contract, except credit insurance policy	(d)(7)
miscellaneous	Alimony, child support needed for support	(d)(10)(D)
pensions	Tax exempt retirement accounts (including 401(k)s, 403(b)s, profit-sharing and money purchase plans, SEP and SIMPLE IRAs, and defined-benefit plans	(b)(3)(C)
	IRAs and Roth IRAs to $1 million per person	(b)(3)(C))
personal property	Animals, crops, clothing, appliances, books, furnishings, household goods, musical instruments to $475 per item, $9,850 total	(d)(3)
	Health aids	(d)(9)
	Jewelry to $1,225	(d)(4)
	Lost earnings payments	(d)(11)(E)
	Motor vehicle to $2,950	(d)(2)
	Personal injury recoveries to $18,450 (not to include pain & suffering or pecuniary loss)	(d)(11)(D)
	Wrongful death recoveries for person you depended on	(d)(11)(B)
public benefits	Crime victims' compensation	(d)(11)(A)
	Public assistance	(d)(10)(A)
	Social Security	(d)(10)(A)
	Unemployment compensation	(d)(10)(A)
	Veterans' benefits	(d)(10)(A)
tools of trade	Implements, books, & tools of trade to $1,850	(d)(6)
wages	None	
wildcard	$975 of any property	(d)(5)
	Up to $9,250 of unused homestead exemption amount, for any property	(d)(5)

Federal Nonbankruptcy Exemptions

These exemptions are available only if you select your state exemptions. You may use them for any exemptions in addition to those allowed by your state, but they cannot be claimed if you file using federal bankruptcy exemptions. All law references are to the United States Code.

ASSET	EXEMPTION	LAW
death & disability benefits	Government employees	5 § 8130
	Longshoremen & harbor workers	33 § 916
	War risk, hazard, death, or injury compensation	42 § 1717
retirement	Civil service employees	5 § 8346
	Foreign Service employees	22 § 4060
	Military Medal of Honor roll pensions	38 § 1562(c)
	Military service employees	10 § 1440
	Railroad workers	45 § 231m
	Social Security	42 § 407
	Veterans' benefits	38 § 5301
survivor's benefits	Judges, U.S. court & judicial center directors, administrative assistants to U.S. Supreme Court Chief Justice	28 § 376
	Lighthouse workers	33 § 775
	Military service	10 § 1450
miscellaneous	Indian lands or homestead sales or lease proceeds	25 § 410
	Klamath Indians tribe benefits for Indians residing in Oregon	25 §§ 543; 545
	Military deposits in savings accounts while on permanent duty outside U.S.	10 §§ 1035
	Military group life insurance	38 § 1970(g)
	Railroad workers' unemployment insurance	45 § 352(e)
	Seamen's clothing	46 § 11110
	Seamen's wages (while on a voyage) pursuant to a written contract	46 § 11109
	Minimum 75% of disposable weekly earnings or 30 times the federal minimum hourly wage, whichever is more; bankruptcy judge may authorize more for low-income debtors	15 § 1673

Worksheets and Charts

Current Monthly Income Worksheet

Personal Property Checklist

Property Exemption Worksheet

Homeowners' Worksheet

Judicial Lien Worksheet

Bankruptcy Forms Checklist

Bankruptcy Documents Checklist

Median Family Income Chart

Current Monthly Income Worksheet

Use this worksheet to calculate your current monthly income; use figures for you and your spouse if you plan to file jointly.

Line 1. Calculate your total income over the last six months from wages, salary, tips, bonuses, overtime, and so on.

    A. Month 1 $ _____

    B. Month 2   _____

    C. Month 3   _____

    D. Month 4   _____

    E. Month 5   _____

    F. Month 6   _____

    G. TOTAL WAGES (add Lines A–F) $ _____

Line 2. Add up all other income for the last six months.

    A. Business, profession, or farm income   _____

    B. Interest, dividends, and royalties   _____

    C. Rents and real property income   _____

    D. Pension and retirement income   _____

    E. Alimony or family support   _____

    F. Spousal contributions (if not filing jointly)   _____

    G. Unemployment compensation   _____

    H. Workers' compensation   _____

    I. State disability insurance   _____

    J. Annuity payments   _____

    K. Other   _____

    L. TOTAL OTHER INCOME $ _____

Line 3. Calculate total income over the six months prior to filing.

    A. Enter total wages (Line 1G).   _____

    B. Enter total other income (Line 2L).   _____

    C. TOTAL INCOME OVER THE SIX MONTHS PRIOR TO FILING. Add Lines A and B together. $ _____

Line 4. Average monthly income over the six months prior to filing. This is called your current monthly income.

    A. Enter total six-month income (Line 3C).   _____

    B. CURRENT MONTHLY INCOME. Divide Line A by six. $ _____

Personal Property Checklist

Cash on hand (include sources)
- [ ] In your home
- [ ] In your wallet
- [ ] Under your mattress

Deposits of money (include sources)
- [ ] Bank account
- [ ] Brokerage account (with stockbroker)
- [ ] Certificates of deposit (CDs)
- [ ] Credit union deposit
- [ ] Escrow account
- [ ] Money market account
- [ ] Money in a safe deposit box
- [ ] Savings and loan deposit

Security deposits
- [ ] Electric
- [ ] Gas
- [ ] Heating oil
- [ ] Security deposit on a rental unit
- [ ] Prepaid rent
- [ ] Rented furniture or equipment
- [ ] Telephone
- [ ] Water

Household goods, supplies, and furnishings
- [ ] Antiques
- [ ] Appliances
- [ ] Carpentry tools
- [ ] China and crystal
- [ ] Clocks
- [ ] Dishes
- [ ] Food (total value)
- [ ] Furniture (list every item; go from room to room so you don't miss anything)
- [ ] Gardening tools
- [ ] Home computer (for personal use)
- [ ] Iron and ironing board
- [ ] Lamps
- [ ] Lawn mower or tractor

- [ ] Microwave oven
- [ ] Patio or outdoor furniture
- [ ] Radios
- [ ] Rugs
- [ ] Sewing machine
- [ ] Silverware and utensils
- [ ] Small appliances
- [ ] Snow blower
- [ ] Stereo system
- [ ] Telephone and answering machines
- [ ] Televisions
- [ ] Vacuum cleaner
- [ ] Video equipment (VCR, camcorder)

Books, pictures, and other art objects; stamp, coin, and other collections
- [ ] Art prints
- [ ] Bibles
- [ ] Books
- [ ] Coins
- [ ] Collectibles (such as political buttons, baseball cards)
- [ ] Family portraits
- [ ] Figurines
- [ ] Original artworks
- [ ] Photographs
- [ ] Records, CDs, audiotapes
- [ ] Stamps
- [ ] Videotapes

Apparel
- [ ] Clothing
- [ ] Furs

Jewelry
- [ ] Engagement and wedding rings
- [ ] Gems
- [ ] Precious metals
- [ ] Watches

Firearms, sports equipment, and other hobby equipment

☐ Board games

☐ Bicycle

☐ Camera equipment

☐ Electronic musical equipment

☐ Exercise machine

☐ Fishing gear

☐ Guns (rifles, pistols, shotguns, muskets)

☐ Model or remote-controlled cars or planes

☐ Musical instruments

☐ Scuba diving equipment

☐ Ski equipment

☐ Other sports equipment

☐ Other weapons (swords and knives)

Interests in insurance policies

☐ Credit insurance

☐ Disability insurance

☐ Health insurance

☐ Homeowners' or renters' insurance

☐ Term life insurance

☐ Whole life insurance

Annuities

Pension or profit-sharing plans

☐ IRA

☐ Keogh

☐ Pension or retirement plan

☐ 401(k) plan

Stock and interests in incorporated and unincorporated companies

Interests in partnerships

☐ Limited partnership interest

☐ General partnership interest

Government and corporate bonds and other investment instruments

☐ Corporate bonds

☐ Municipal bonds

☐ Promissory notes

☐ U.S. savings bonds

Accounts receivable

☐ Accounts receivable from business

☐ Commissions already earned

Family support

☐ Alimony (spousal support, maintenance) due under court order

☐ Child support payments due under court order

☐ Payments due under divorce property settlement

Other debts for which the amount owed you is known and definite

☐ Disability benefits due

☐ Disability insurance due

☐ Judgments obtained against third parties you haven't yet collected

☐ Sick pay earned

☐ Social Security benefits due

☐ Tax refund due under returns already filed

☐ Vacation pay earned

☐ Wages due

☐ Workers' compensation due

Any special powers that you or another person can exercise for your benefit, other than those listed under "real estate"

☐ A right to receive, at some future time, cash, stock, or other personal property placed in an irrevocable trust

☐ Current payments of interest or principal from a trust

☐ General power of appointment over personal property

An interest in property due to another person's death

☐ Any interest as the beneficiary of a living trust, if the trustor has died

☐ Expected proceeds from a life insurance policy where the insured has died

☐ Inheritance from an existing estate in probate (the owner has died and the court is overseeing the distribution of the property), even if the final amount is not yet known

☐ Inheritance under a will that is contingent on one or more events occurring, but only if the owner has died

All other contingent claims and claims where the amount owed you is not known, including tax refunds, counterclaims, and rights to setoff claims (claims you think you have against a person, government, or corporation, but you haven't yet sued on)

☐ Claims against a corporation, government entity, or individual

☐ Potential tax refund on a return that is not yet filed

Patents, copyrights, and other intellectual property

☐ Copyrights

☐ Patents

☐ Trade secrets

☐ Trademarks

☐ Trade names

Licenses, franchises, and other general intangibles

☐ Building permits

☐ Cooperative association holdings

☐ Exclusive licenses

☐ Liquor licenses

☐ Nonexclusive licenses

☐ Patent licenses

☐ Professional licenses

Automobiles and other vehicles

☐ Car

☐ Minibike or motor scooter

☐ Mobile or motor home if on wheels

☐ Motorcycle

☐ Recreational vehicle (RV)

☐ Trailer

☐ Truck

☐ Van

Boats, motors, and accessories

☐ Boat (canoe, kayak, rowboat, shell, sailboat, pontoon, yacht)

☐ Boat radar, radio, or telephone

☐ Outboard motor

Aircraft and accessories

☐ Aircraft

☐ Aircraft radar, radio, and other accessories

Office equipment, furnishings, and supplies

☐ Artwork in your office

☐ Computers, software, modems, printers

☐ Copier

☐ Fax machine

☐ Furniture

☐ Rugs

☐ Supplies

☐ Telephones

☐ Typewriters

Machinery, fixtures, equipment, and supplies used in business

☐ Military uniforms and accoutrements

☐ Tools of your trade

Business inventory

Livestock, poultry, and other animals

☐ Birds

☐ Cats

☐ Dogs

☐ Fish and aquarium equipment

☐ Horses

☐ Other pets

☐ Livestock and poultry

Crops—growing or harvested

Farming equipment and implements

Farm supplies, chemicals, and feed

Other personal property of any kind not already listed

☐ Church pew

☐ Health aids (such as a wheelchair or crutches)

☐ Hot tub or portable spa

☐ Season tickets

Property Exemption Worksheet

1 Property	2 Replacement Value	3 Exemption	4 Statute No.
1. Cash on hand			
2. Checking/savings account, certificate of deposit, other bank accounts			
3. Security deposits held by utility companies, landlord			
4. Household goods, furniture, audio, video, and computer equipment			

	1 Property	2 Replacement Value	3 Exemption	4 Statute No.

5. Books, pictures, art objects, records, compact discs, collectibles

_____ _____ _____ _____

_____ _____ _____ _____

_____ _____ _____ _____

_____ _____ _____ _____

_____ _____ _____ _____

_____ _____ _____ _____

_____ _____ _____ _____

_____ _____ _____ _____

6. Clothing

_____ _____ _____ _____

_____ _____ _____ _____

_____ _____ _____ _____

_____ _____ _____ _____

_____ _____ _____ _____

_____ _____ _____ _____

_____ _____ _____ _____

_____ _____ _____ _____

_____ _____ _____ _____

_____ _____ _____ _____

7. Furs and jewelry

_____ _____ _____ _____

_____ _____ _____ _____

_____ _____ _____ _____

_____ _____ _____ _____

_____ _____ _____ _____

_____ _____ _____ _____

8. Sports, photographic, hobby equipment, firearms

_____ _____ _____ _____

_____ _____ _____ _____

_____ _____ _____ _____

_____ _____ _____ _____

_____ _____ _____ _____

	1 Property	2 Replacement Value	3 Exemption	4 Statute No.

9. Interest in insurance policies—specify refund or cancellation value

10. Annuities

11. Interests in pension or profit-sharing plans

12. Stock and interests in incorporated/unincorporated business

13. Interests in partnerships/joint ventures

14. Bonds

	1 Property	2 Replacement Value	3 Exemption	4 Statute No.
15. Accounts receivable				
16. Alimony/family support to which you are entitled				
17. Other liquidated debts owed to you, including tax refunds				
18. Equitable or future interests or life estates				
19. Interests in estate of decedent or life insurance plan or trust				
20. Other contingent/unliquidated claims, including tax refunds, counterclaims				
21. Patents, copyrights, other intellectual property				
22. Licenses, franchises				
23. Automobiles, trucks, trailers, and accessories				

	1 Property	2 Replacement Value	3 Exemption	4 Statute No.
24. Boats, motors, accessories				
25. Aircraft, accessories				
26. Office equipment, supplies				
27. Machinery, fixtures, etc., for business				
28. Inventory				
29. Animals				

	1 Property	2 Replacement Value	3 Exemption	4 Statute No.
30.	Crops—growing or harvested			
31.	Farming equipment, implements			
32.	Farm supplies, chemicals, feed			
33.	Other personal property of any kind not listed			

Homeowners' Worksheet

Part I. Do you have any equity in your home?

1. Market value of your home ....$_____
2. Costs of sale (if unsure, put 5% of market value)...........$_____
3. Amount owed on all mortgages...................................$_____
4. Amount of all liens on the property ....$_____
5. Total of Lines 2, 3, and 4 ....$_____
6. Your equity (Line 1 minus Line 5).. $_____

If Line 6 is less than zero, skip the rest of the worksheet. The trustee will have no interest in selling your home.

Part II. Is your property protected by an exemption?

7. Does the available homestead exemption protect your kind of dwelling?
   - ☐ Yes. Go on to Line 8.
   - ☐ No. Enter $0 on Line 11, then continue on to Line 12.
8. Do you have to file a "declaration of homestead" to claim the homestead exemption?
   - ☐ Yes, but I have not filed it yet. (You should. See instructions.)
   - ☐ Yes, and I have already filed it.
   - ☐ No
9. Is the homestead exemption based on lot size?
   - ☐ No, it is based on equity alone. Go to Line 10.
   - ☐ No, it is unlimited (true only of the exemptions for Washington, DC).

If you are using the D.C. exemptions, you can stop here. Your home is protected.

   - ☐ Yes. The exemption is limited to property of _____ acres.

If your property is smaller than this limit, you can stop here. Your home is protected. If your property exceeds this limit, see the instructions.

   - ☐ Yes, but there is an equity limit as well. The exemption is limited to property of ___ acres.

If your property is smaller than this limit, go on to Line 10. If your property exceeds this limit, see the instructions.

10. Do you own the property with your spouse in "tenancy by the entirety"?
    - ☐ Yes. *See the instructions and talk to a bankruptcy attorney to find out whether your house is fully protected.*
    - ☐ No. *Go on to Line 11.*
11. Is the dollar amount of the homestead exemption limited?
    - ☐ Yes. Enter the dollar limit here: $_____
    - ☐ No dollar limit. You can stop here. Your home is protected.
12. Can you protect more equity with a wildcard exemption?
    - ☐ Yes. Enter the dollar amount here: $_____
    - ☐ No.
13. How much of your equity is protected?

Total of Lines 11 and 12: $_____

If the total exceeds $125,000 and you are subject to the $125,000 cap on homestead exemptions, write "$125,000" on this line. See the instructions for more information.

14. Is your home fully protected?

Subtract Line 13 from Line 6: $_____

If this total is a negative number, your home is protected. If this total is a positive number, you have unprotected equity in your home, and the trustee might choose to sell it (or allow you to keep it in exchange for cash or exempt property roughly equal in value to your unprotected equity).

Judicial Lien Worksheet

1. Value of your home.. _____

2. Amount of first mortgage .... _____

3. Amount of other mortgages and home equity loans ..... _____

4. Amount of tax liens .... _____

5. Amount of mechanics' liens .... _____

6. Total of Lines 2 through 5.. _____
   (Total of all liens that are not judicial liens)

   If Line 6 is greater than Line 1, you can stop here—you can eliminate all judicial liens. Otherwise, go on to Line 7.

7. Line 1 minus Line 6. .... _____
   This is the amount of equity you can protect with an exemption.

8. **Exemption Amount** .... _____

   If Line 8 is greater than Line 7 you can stop here—you can eliminate all judicial liens. Otherwise, go on to Line 9.

9. Line 7 minus line 8.. _____
   This is the amount of the judicial liens that you can't eliminate.

10. **Amount of judicial liens**... _____

    If Line 9 is greater than Line 10, you can stop here—you cannot eliminate judicial liens from this property.
    Otherwise, go on to Line 11.

11. Line 10 minus line 9. ....
    _____
    This is the portion of the judicial lien that you can eliminate.
    (Line 9 is the portion of judicial lien you cannot eliminate.)

Bankruptcy Forms Checklist

- ❏ Form 1—Voluntary Petition
- ❏ Form 3—(only if you are paying your filing fee in installments)
- ❏ Form 6, which consists of:
    - ❏ Schedule A—Real Property
    - ❏ Schedule B—Personal Property
    - ❏ Schedule C—Property Claimed as Exempt
    - ❏ Schedule D—Creditors Holding Secured Claims
    - ❏ Schedule E—Creditors Holding Unsecured Priority Claims
    - ❏ Schedule F—Creditors Holding Unsecured Nonpriority Claims
    - ❏ Schedule G—Executory Contracts and Unexpired Leases
    - ❏ Schedule H—Codebtors
    - ❏ Schedule I—Current Income
    - ❏ Schedule J—Current Expenditures
    - ❏ Summary Schedules A through J
    - ❏ Declaration Concerning Debtor's Schedules
- ❏ Form 7—Statement of Financial Affairs
- ❏ Form 8—Chapter 7 Individual Debtor's Statement of Intention
- ❏ Form 21—Full Social Security Number Disclosure
- ❏ Form B22A—Statement of Current Monthly Income and Means Test Calculation
- ❏ Form B201—Notice to Individual Consumer Debtor Under § 342 of the Bankruptcy Code
- ❏ Mailing Matrix
- ❏ Required local forms, if any

Bankruptcy Documents Checklist

❑ Your most recent federal tax return (or a transcript of the return obtained from the IRS)

❑ A certificate showing that you have completed the required credit counseling

❑ Any repayment plan that was developed during your credit counseling

❑ Your pay stubs for the previous 60 days (along with an accompanying form, if your local court requires one)

Median Family Income Chart

State	Family Size			
	1 earner	2 people	3 people	4 people*
Alabama	$33,873	$41,103	$50,617	$56,180
Alaska	$45,191	$62,013	$70,450	$78,958
Arizona	$36,856	$48,003	$53,089	$60,160
Arkansas	$29,930	$38,438	$42,629	$51,478
California	$43,436	$55,320	$61,655	$70,626
Colorado	$41,401	$56,024	$60,550	$68,924
Connecticut	$54,311	$63,455	$79,100	$91,269
Delaware	$40,264	$53,716	$63,593	$74,444
District of Columbia	$39,649	$64,274	$64,274	$64,274
Florida	$37,099	$46,351	$51,294	$61,825
Georgia	$35,562	$47,327	$51,545	$60,028
Hawaii	$47,056	$56,383	$66,742	$78,354
Idaho	$33,634	$44,447	$48,891	$57,809
Illinois	$43,012	$53,320	$64,286	$72,742
Indiana	$36,572	$48,183	$52,526	$65,421
Iowa	$36,518	$48,095	$55,933	$64,051
Kansas	$37,795	$50,258	$56,386	$61,515
Kentucky	$33,263	$39,218	$47,955	$56,866
Louisiana	$31,685	$39,306	$47,282	$53,145
Maine	$37,765	$47,911	$54,209	$66,255
Maryland	$48,205	$60,541	$72,417	$88,454
Massachusetts	$48,775	$57,165	$73,837	$88,044
Michigan	$41,877	$49,052	$62,480	$70,887
Minnesota	$42,028	$56,449	$67,049	$75,990
Mississippi	$29,247	$36,940	$39,075	$51,584
Missouri	$36,696	$46,144	$51,617	$64,376
Montana	$31,640	$43,407	$46,248	$52,384
Nebraska	$37,084	$47,085	$56,087	$62,012
Nevada	$38,506	$52,095	$53,396	$54,538
New Hampshire	$52,120	$59,743	$70,677	$84,918
New Jersey	$54,273	$60,532	$78,028	$91,398
New Mexico	$31,652	$41,228	$42,824	$48,858
New York	$40,801	$50,136	$59,377	$69,854
North Carolina	$33,510	$43,532	$50,874	$56,985
North Dakota	$33,880	$47,374	$55,396	$60,274
Ohio	$37,333	$46,250	$57,268	$65,126
Oklahoma	$32,439	$42,450	$49,320	$51,572
Oregon	$37,530	$48,676	$54,633	$61,209

* add $6,300 for each individual in excess of 4

Median Family Income Chart (continued)

State	1 earner	2 people	3 people	4 people*
		Family Size		
Pennsylvania	$40,251	$45,865	$60,986	$68,826
Rhode Island	$41,835	$53,074	$59,932	$71,369
South Carolina	$33,476	$44,730	$50,203	$61,718
South Dakota	$33,171	$43,438	$53,430	$61,495
Tennessee	$34,151	$42,874	$50,679	$57,802
Texas	$34,408	$48,029	$50,408	$58,153
Utah	$42,496	$46,912	$52,955	$59,879
Vermont	$38,562	$51,181	$61,268	$68,065
Virginia	$43,195	$56,455	$63,177	$74,387
Washington	$43,891	$54,044	$59,732	$73,259
West Virginia	$33,704	$36,376	$47,176	$53,551
Wisconsin	$39,157	$49,918	$60,106	$70,170

Commonwealth or U.S. Territory	1 earner	2 people	3 people	4 people*
		Family Size		
Guam	$32,582	$38,956	$44,394	$53,722
Northern Mariana Islands	$21,879	$21,879	$25,456	$37,441
Puerto Rico	$18,107	$18,107	$19,916	$23,509
Virgin Islands	$25,851	$31,071	$33,127	$36,295

* add $6,300 for each individual in excess of 4

Form 1—Voluntary Petition

Exhibit C to Voluntary Petition

Schedule A—Real Property

Schedule B—Personal Property

Schedule C—Property Claimed as Exempt

Schedule D—Creditors Holding Secured Claims

Schedule E—Creditors Holding Unsecured Priority Claims

Schedule F—Creditors Holding Unsecured Nonpriority Claims

Schedule G—Executory Contracts and Unexpired Leases

Schedule H—Codebtors

Schedule I—Current Income of Individual Debtors(s)

Schedule J—Current Expenditures of Individual Debtor(s)

Declaration Concerning Debtor's Schedules

Summary of Schedules and Statistical Summary of Certain Liabilities

Form 3A—Application to Pay Filing Fee in Installments

Form 3B—Application for Waiver of the Chapter 7 Filing Fee

Form 7—Statement of Financial Affairs

Form 8—Chapter 7 Individual Debtor's Statement of Intention

Form 16A—Caption

Form B20A—Notice of Motion or Objection

Form B21—Statement of Social Security Number

Form B22A—Statement of Current Monthly Income and Means Test Calculation

Form B23—Debtor's Certification of Completion of Instructional Course Concerning Personal Financial Management

Form B201—Notice to Individual Consumer Debtor Under § 342(b) of the Bankruptcy Code

Form B240—Reaffirmation Agreement

Mailing Matrix

Amendment Cover Sheet

Notice of Change of Address

Supplemental Schedule for Property Acquired After Bankruptcy Discharge

Proof of Service by Mail

Pleading Paper

United States Bankruptcy Court _____District of_____	Voluntary Petition

Name of Debtor (if individual, enter Last, First, Middle):	Name of Joint Debtor (Spouse) (Last, First, Middle):
All Other Names used by the Debtor in the last 8 years (include married, maiden, and trade names):	All Other Names used by the Joint Debtor in the last 8 years (include married, maiden, and trade names):
Last four digits of Soc. Sec./Complete EIN or other Tax I.D. No. (if more than one, state all):	Last four digits of Soc. Sec./Complete EIN or other Tax I.D. No. (if more than one, state all):
Street Address of Debtor (No. & Street, City, and State): ZIPCODE	Street Address of Joint Debtor (No. & Street, City, and State): ZIPCODE
County of Residence or of the Principal Place of Business:	County of Residence or of the Principal Place of Business:
Mailing Address of Debtor (if different from street address): ZIPCODE	Mailing Address of Joint Debtor (if different from street address): ZIPCODE
Location of Principal Assets of Business Debtor (if different from street address above): ZIPCODE	

Type of Debtor (Form of Organization)
(Check **one** box.)

☐ Individual (includes Joint Debtors)
☐ Corporation (includes LLC and LLP)
☐ Partnership
☐ Other (If debtor is not one of the above entities, check this box and provide the information requested below.)

State type of entity: _____
_____

Nature of Business
(Check **all** applicable boxes.)

☐ Health Care Business
☐ Single Asset Real Estate as defined in 11 U.S.C. § 101 (51B)
☐ Railroad
☐ Stockbroker
☐ Commodity Broker
☐ Clearing Bank
☐ Nonprofit Organization qualified under 26 U.S.C. § 501(c)(3)

Chapter of Bankruptcy Code Under Which the Petition is Filed (Check one box)

☐ Chapter 7   ☐ Chapter 11   ☐ Chapter 15 Petition for Recognition of a Foreign Main Proceeding
☐ Chapter 9   ☐ Chapter 12
            ☐ Chapter 13   ☐ Chapter 15 Petition for Recognition of a Foreign Nonmain Proceeding

Nature of Debts (Check one box)

☐ Consumer/Non-Business   ☐ Business

Chapter 11 Debtors
Check one box:
☐ Debtor is a small business debtor as defined in 11 U.S.C. § 101(51D).
☐ Debtor is not a small business debtor as defined in 11 U.S.C. § 101(51D).
- -
Check if:
☐ Debtor's aggregate noncontingent liquidated debts owed to non-insiders or affiliates are less than $2 million.

Filing Fee (Check one box)

☐ Full Filing Fee attached

☐ Filing Fee to be paid in installments (Applicable to individuals only) Must attach signed application for the court's consideration certifying that the debtor is unable to pay fee except in installments. Rule 1006(b). See Official Form 3A.

☐ Filing Fee waiver requested (Applicable to chapter 7 individuals only). Must attach signed application for the court's consideration. See Official Form 3B.

Statistical/Administrative Information

☐ Debtor estimates that funds will be available for distribution to unsecured creditors.

☐ Debtor estimates that, after any exempt property is excluded and administrative expenses paid, there will be no funds available for distribution to unsecured creditors.

THIS SPACE IS FOR COURT USE ONLY

Estimated Number of Creditors

1-49	50-99	100-199	200-999	1,000-5,000	5,001-10,000	10,001-25,000	25,001-50,000	50,001-100,000	OVER 100,000
☐	☐	☐	☐	☐	☐	☐	☐	☐	☐

Estimated Assets

$0 to $50,000	$50,001 to $100,000	$100,001 to $500,000	$500,001 to $1 million	$1,000,001 to $10 million	$10,000,001 to $50 million	$50,000,001 to $100 million	More than $100 million
☐	☐	☐	☐	☐	☐	☐	☐

Estimated Debts

$0 to $50,000	$50,001 to $100,000	$100,001 to $500,000	$500,001 to $1 million	$1,000,001 to $10 million	$10,000,001 to $50 million	$50,000,001 to $100 million	More than $100 million
☐	☐	☐	☐	☐	☐	☐	☐

Voluntary Petition	Name of Debtor(s):
(This page must be completed and filed in every case)	

Prior Bankruptcy Case Filed Within Last 8 Years (If more than one, attach additional sheet)

Location Where Filed:	Case Number:	Date Filed:

Pending Bankruptcy Case Filed by any Spouse, Partner or Affiliate of this Debtor (If more than one, attach additional sheet)

Name of Debtor:	Case Number:	Date Filed:
District:	Relationship:	Judge:

Exhibit A

(To be completed if debtor is required to file periodic reports (e.g., forms 10K and 10Q) with the Securities and Exchange Commission pursuant to Section 13 or 15(d) of the Securities Exchange Act of 1934 and is requesting relief under chapter 11.)

☐ Exhibit A is attached and made a part of this petition.

Exhibit B

(To be completed if debtor is an individual whose debts are primarily consumer debts.)

I, the attorney for the petitioner named in the foregoing petition, declare that I have informed the petitioner that [he or she] may proceed under chapter 7, 11, 12, or 13 of title 11, United States Code, and have explained the relief available under each such chapter.

I further certify that I delivered to the debtor the notice required by § 342(b) of the Bankruptcy Code.

X _____
Signature of Attorney for Debtor(s)   Date

Exhibit C

Does the debtor own or have possession of any property that poses or is alleged to pose a threat of imminent and identifiable harm to public health or safety?

☐ Yes, and Exhibit C is attached and made a part of this petition.

☐ No

Certification Concerning Debt Counseling by Individual/Joint Debtor(s)

☐ I/we have received approved budget and credit counseling during the 180-day period preceding the filing of this petition.

☐ I/we request a waiver of the requirement to obtain budget and credit counseling prior to filing based on exigent circumstances. (Must attach certification describing.)

Information Regarding the Debtor (Check the Applicable Boxes)

Venue (Check any applicable box)

☐ Debtor has been domiciled or has had a residence, principal place of business, or principal assets in this District for 180 days immediately preceding the date of this petition or for a longer part of such 180 days than in any other District.

☐ There is a bankruptcy case concerning debtor's affiliate, general partner, or partnership pending in this District.

☐ Debtor is a debtor in a foreign proceeding and has its principal place of business or principal assets in the United States in this District, or has no principal place of business or assets in the United States but is a defendant in an action or proceeding [in a federal or state court] in this District, or the interests of the parties will be served in regard to the relief sought in this District.

Statement by a Debtor Who Resides as a Tenant of Residential Property
Check all applicable boxes.

☐ Landlord has a judgment against the debtor for possession of debtor's residence. (If box checked, complete the following.)

_____
(Name of landlord that obtained judgment)

_____
(Address of landlord)

☐ Debtor claims that under applicable nonbankruptcy law, there are circumstances under which the debtor would be permitted to cure the entire monetary default that gave rise to the judgment for possession, after the judgment for possession was entered, and

☐ Debtor has included in this petition the deposit with the court of any rent that would become due during the 30-day period after the filing of the petition.

Voluntary Petition	Name of Debtor(s):
(This page must be completed and filed in every case)	

Signatures

Signature(s) of Debtor(s) (Individual/Joint)

I declare under penalty of perjury that the information provided in this petition is true and correct.

[If petitioner is an individual whose debts are primarily consumer debts and has chosen to file under chapter 7] I am aware that I may proceed under chapter 7, 11, 12 or 13 of title 11, United States Code, understand the relief available under each such chapter, and choose to proceed under chapter 7.

[If no attorney represents me and no bankruptcy petition preparer signs the petition] I have obtained and read the notice required by § 342(b) of the Bankruptcy Code.

I request relief in accordance with the chapter of title 11, United States Code, specified in this petition.

X_____
  Signature of Debtor

X_____
 Signature of Joint Debtor

_____
 Telephone Number (If not represented by attorney)

_____
 Date

Signature of a Foreign Representative

I declare under penalty of perjury that the information provided in this petition is true and correct, that I am the foreign representative of a debtor in a foreign proceeding, and that I am authorized to file this petition.

(Check only one box.)

☐ I request relief in accordance with chapter 15 of title 11, United States Code. Certified copies of the documents required by § 1515 of title 11 are attached.

☐ Pursuant to § 1511 of title 11, United States Code, I request relief in accordance with the chapter of title 11 specified in this petition. A certified copy of the order granting recognition of the foreign main proceeding is attached.

X_____

(Signature of Foreign Representative)

_____

(Printed Name of Foreign Representative)

_____

Date

Signature of Attorney

X_____
 Signature of Attorney for Debtor(s)

_____
 Printed Name of Attorney for Debtor(s)

_____
 Firm Name

_____
 Address

_____

_____
 Telephone Number

_____
 Date

Signature of Non-Attorney Bankruptcy Petition Preparer

I declare under penalty of perjury that: (1) I am a bankruptcy petition preparer as defined in 11 U.S.C. § 110; (2) I prepared this document for compensation and have provided the debtor with a copy of this document and the notices and information required under 11 U.S.C. §§ 110(b), 110(h), and 342(b); and, (3) if rules or guidelines have been promulgated pursuant to 11 U.S.C. § 110(h) setting a maximum fee for services chargeable by bankruptcy petition preparers, I have given the debtor notice of the maximum amount before preparing any document for filing for a debtor or accepting any fee from the debtor, as required in that section.Official Form 19B is attached.

_____

Printed Name and title, if any, of Bankruptcy Petition Preparer

_____

Social Security number (If the bankrutpcy petition preparer is not an individual, state the Social Security number of the officer, principal, responsible person or partner of the bankruptcy petition preparer.)(Required by 11 U.S.C. § 110.)

_____

Address

X_____

_____

Date

Signature of Debtor (Corporation/Partnership)

I declare under penalty of perjury that the information provided in this petition is true and correct, and that I have been authorized to file this petition on behalf of the debtor.

The debtor requests relief in accordance with the chapter of title 11, United States Code, specified in this petition.

X_____
 Signature of Authorized Individual

_____
 Printed Name of Authorized Individual

_____
 Title of Authorized Individual

_____
 Date

Signature of Bankruptcy Petition Preparer or officer, principal, responsible person,or partner whose social security number is provided above.

Names and Social Security numbers of all other individuals who prepared or assisted in preparing this document unless the bankruptcy petition preparer is not an individual:

If more than one person prepared this document, attach additional sheets conforming to the appropriate official form for each person.

A bankruptcy petition preparer's failure to comply with the provisions of title 11 and the Federal Rules of Bankruptcy Procedure may result in fines or imprisonment or both 11 U.S.C. §110; 18 U.S.C. §156.

Exhibit "C"

[If, to the best of the debtor's knowledge, the debtor owns or has possession of property that poses or is alleged to pose a threat of imminent and identifiable harm to the public health or safety, attach this Exhibit "C" to the petition.]

[Caption as in Form 16B]

Exhibit "C" to Voluntary Petition

1. Identify and briefly describe all real or personal property owned by or in possession of the debtor that, to the best of the debtor's knowledge, poses or is alleged to pose a threat of imminent and identifiable harm to the public health or safety (attach additional sheets if necessary):

....
....
....
....

2. With respect to each parcel of real property or item of personal property identified in question 1, describe the nature and location of the dangerous condition, whether environmental or otherwise, that poses or is alleged to pose a threat of imminent and identifiable harm to the public health or safety (attach additional sheets if necessary):

....
....
....
....

In re _____,   Case No. _____
          Debtor   **(If known)**

SCHEDULE A - REAL PROPERTY

Except as directed below, list all real property in which the debtor has any legal, equitable, or future interest, including all property owned as a cotenant, community property, or in which the debtor has a life estate. Include any property in which the debtor holds rights and powers exercisable for the debtor's own benefit. If the debtor is married, state whether husband, wife, or both own the property by placing an "H," "W," "J," or "C" in the column labeled "Husband, Wife, Joint, or Community." If the debtor holds no interest in real property, write "None" under "Description and Location of Property."

Do not include interests in executory contracts and unexpired leases on this schedule. List them in Schedule G - Executory Contracts and Unexpired Leases.

If an entity claims to have a lien or hold a secured interest in any property, state the amount of the secured claim. See Schedule D. If no entity claims to hold a secured interest in the property, write "None" in the column labeled "Amount of Secured Claim."

If the debtor is an individual or if a joint petition is filed, state the amount of any exemption claimed in the property only in Schedule C - Property Claimed as Exempt.

DESCRIPTION AND LOCATION OF PROPERTY	NATURE OF DEBTOR'S INTEREST IN PROPERTY	HUSBAND, WIFE, JOINT, OR COMMUNITY	CURRENT VALUE OF DEBTOR'S INTEREST IN PROPERTY, WITHOUT DEDUCTING ANY SECURED CLAIM OR EXEMPTION	AMOUNT OF SECURED CLAIM

Total▶

(Report also on Summary of Schedules.)

Form B6B
(10/05)

In re _____,   Case No. _____
                    Debtor   **(If known)**

SCHEDULE B - PERSONAL PROPERTY

Except as directed below, list all personal property of the debtor of whatever kind. If the debtor has no property in one or more of the categories, place an "x" in the appropriate position in the column labeled "None." If additional space is needed in any category, attach a separate sheet properly identified with the case name, case number, and the number of the category. If the debtor is married, state whether husband, wife, or both own the property by placing an "H," "W," "J," or "C" in the column labeled "Husband, Wife, Joint, or Community." If the debtor is an individual or a joint petition is filed, state the amount of any exemptions claimed only in Schedule C - Property Claimed as Exempt.

Do not list interests in executory contracts and unexpired leases on this schedule. List them in Schedule G - Executory Contracts and Unexpired Leases.

If the property is being held for the debtor by someone else, state that person's name and address under "Description and Location of Property." In providing the information requested in this schedule, do not include the name or address of a minor child. Simply state "a minor child."

TYPE OF PROPERTY	N O N E	DESCRIPTION AND LOCATION OF PROPERTY	HUSBAND, WIFE, JOINT, OR COMMUNITY	CURRENT VALUE OF DEBTOR'S INTEREST IN PROPERTY, WITH-OUT DEDUCTING ANY SECURED CLAIM OR EXEMPTION
1. Cash on hand.				
2. Checking, savings or other financial accounts, certificates of deposit, or shares in banks, savings and loan, thrift, building and loan, and homestead associations, or credit unions, brokerage houses, or cooperatives.				
3. Security deposits with public utilities, telephone companies, landlords, and others.				
4. Household goods and furnishings, including audio, video, and computer equipment.				
5. Books; pictures and other art objects; antiques; stamp, coin, record, tape, compact disc, and other collections or collectibles.				
6. Wearing apparel.				
7. Furs and jewelry.				
8. Firearms and sports, photographic, and other hobby equipment.				
9. Interests in insurance policies. Name insurance company of each policy and itemize surrender or refund value of each.				
10. Annuities. Itemize and name each issuer.				
11. Interests in an education IRA as defined in 26 U.S.C. § 530(b)(1) or under a qualified State tuition plan as defined in 26 U.S.C. § 529(b)(1). Give particulars. (File separately the record(s) of any such interest(s). 11 U.S.C. § 521(c); Rule 1007(b)).				

In re _____,   Case No. _____
                        Debtor   **(If known)**

SCHEDULE B - PERSONAL PROPERTY
(Continuation Sheet)

TYPE OF PROPERTY	N O N E	DESCRIPTION AND LOCATION OF PROPERTY	HUSBAND, WIFE, JOINT, OR COMMUNITY	CURRENT VALUE OF DEBTOR'S INTEREST IN PROPERTY, WITH-OUT DEDUCTING ANY SECURED CLAIM OR EXEMPTION
12. Interests in IRA, ERISA, Keogh, or other pension or profit sharing plans. Give particulars.				
13. Stock and interests in incorporated and unincorporated businesses. Itemize.				
14. Interests in partnerships or joint ventures. Itemize.				
15. Government and corporate bonds and other negotiable and non-negotiable instruments.				
16. Accounts receivable.				
17. Alimony, maintenance, support, and property settlements to which the debtor is or may be entitled. Give particulars.				
18. Other liquidated debts owed to debtor including tax refunds. Give particulars.				
19. Equitable or future interests, life estates, and rights or powers exercisable for the benefit of the debtor other than those listed in Schedule A – Real Property.				
20. Contingent and noncontingent interests in estate of a decedent, death benefit plan, life insurance policy, or trust.				
21. Other contingent and unliquidated claims of every nature, including tax refunds, counterclaims of the debtor, and rights to setoff claims. Give estimated value of each.				

Form B6B-cont.
(10/05)

In re _____ ,   Case No. _____
                    Debtor   **(If known)**

SCHEDULE B -PERSONAL PROPERTY
(Continuation Sheet)

TYPE OF PROPERTY	N O N E	DESCRIPTION AND LOCATION OF PROPERTY	HUSBAND, WIFE, JOINT, OR COMMUNITY	CURRENT VALUE OF DEBTOR'S INTEREST IN PROPERTY, WITH- OUT DEDUCTING ANY SECURED CLAIM OR EXEMPTION
22. Patents, copyrights, and other intellectual property. Give particulars.				
23. Licenses, franchises, and other general intangibles. Give particulars.				
24. Customer lists or other compilations containing personally identifiable information (as defined in 11 U.S.C. § 101(41A)) provided to the debtor by individuals in connection with obtaining a product or service from the debtor primarily for personal, family, or household purposes.				
25. Automobiles, trucks, trailers, and other vehicles and accessories.				
26. Boats, motors, and accessories.				
27. Aircraft and accessories.				
28. Office equipment, furnishings, and supplies.				
29. Machinery, fixtures, equipment, and supplies used in business.				
30. Inventory.				
31. Animals.				
32. Crops - growing or harvested. Give particulars.				
33. Farming equipment and implements.				
34. Farm supplies, chemicals, and feed.				
35. Other personal property of any kind not already listed. Itemize.				

_____ continuation sheets attached   Total ▶ | $

(Include amounts from any continuation
sheets attached. Report total also on
Summary of Schedules.)

Form B6C
(10/05)

In re _____,   Case No. _____
            Debtor   **(If known)**

SCHEDULE C - PROPERTY CLAIMED AS EXEMPT

Debtor claims the exemptions to which debtor is entitled under:
(Check one box)
☐ 11 U.S.C. § 522(b)(2)
☐ 11 U.S.C. § 522(b)(3)

☐ Check if debtor claims a homestead exemption that exceeds
$125,000.

DESCRIPTION OF PROPERTY	SPECIFY LAW PROVIDING EACH EXEMPTION	VALUE OF CLAIMED EXEMPTION	CURRENT VALUE OF PROPERTY WITHOUT DEDUCTING EXEMPTION

Form B6D

(10/05)   In re _____,   Case No. _____
                              Debtor   **(If known)**

SCHEDULE D – CREDITORS HOLDING SECURED CLAIMS

State the name, mailing address, including zip code, and last four digits of any account number of all entities holding claims secured by property of the debtor as of the date of filing of the petition. The complete account number of any account the debtor has with the creditor is useful to the trustee and the creditor and may be provided if the debtor chooses to do so. List creditors holding all types of secured interests such as judgment liens, garnishments, statutory liens, mortgages, deeds of trust, and other security interests.

List creditors in alphabetical order to the extent practicable. If a minor child is a creditor, indicate that by stating "a minor child" and do not disclose the child's name. See 11 U.S.C. § 112; Fed. R. Bankr. P. 1007(m). If all secured creditors will not fit on this page, use the continuation sheet provided.

If any entity other than a spouse in a joint case may be jointly liable on a claim, place an "X" in the column labeled "Codebtor," include the entity on the appropriate schedule of creditors, and complete Schedule H – Codebtors. If a joint petition is filed, state whether husband, wife, both of them, or the marital community may be liable on each claim by placing an "H," "W," "J," or "C" in the column labeled "Husband, Wife, Joint, or Community."

If the claim is contingent, place an "X" in the column labeled "Contingent." If the claim is unliquidated, place an "X" in the column labeled "Unliquidated." If the claim is disputed, place an "X" in the column labeled "Disputed." (You may need to place an "X" in more than one of these three columns.)

Report the total of all claims listed on this schedule in the box labeled "Total" on the last sheet of the completed schedule. Report this total also on the Summary of Schedules.

☐   Check this box if debtor has no creditors holding secured claims to report on this Schedule D.

CREDITOR'S NAME AND MAILING ADDRESS INCLUDING ZIP CODE AND AN ACCOUNT NUMBER (See Instructions Above)	CODEBTOR	HUSBAND, WIFE, JOINT, OR COMMUNITY	DATE CLAIM WAS INCURRED, NATURE OF LIEN, AND DESCRIPTION AND VALUE OF PROPERTY SUBJECT TO LIEN	CONTINGENT	UNLIQUIDATED	DISPUTED	AMOUNT OF CLAIM WITHOUT DEDUCTING VALUE OF COLLATERAL	UNSECURED PORTION, IF ANY
ACCOUNT NO.								
			VALUE $					
ACCOUNT NO.								
			VALUE $					
ACCOUNT NO.								
			VALUE $					
ACCOUNT NO.								
			VALUE $					

_____ continuation sheets attached

Subtotal ▶
(Total of this page) $ _____

Total ▶
(Use only on last page) $ _____

(Report total also on Summary of Schedules)

Form B6D – Cont.
(10/05)

In re _____ ,   Case No. _____
                Debtor   **(If known)**

SCHEDULE D – CREDITORS HOLDING SECURED CLAIMS
(Continuation Sheet)

CREDITOR'S NAME AND MAILING ADDRESS INCLUDING ZIP CODE AND AN ACCOUNT NUMBER (*See Instructions Above*)	CODEBTOR	HUSBAND, WIFE, JOINT, OR COMMUNITY	DATE CLAIM WAS INCURRED, NATURE OF LIEN , AND DESCRIPTION AND VALUE OF PROPERTY SUBJECT TO LIEN	CONTINGENT	UNLIQUIDATED	DISPUTED	AMOUNT OF CLAIM WITHOUT DEDUCTING VALUE OF COLLATERAL	UNSECURED PORTION, IF ANY
ACCOUNT NO.								
			VALUE $					
ACCOUNT NO.								
			VALUE $					
ACCOUNT NO.								
			VALUE $					
ACCOUNT NO.								
			VALUE $					
ACCOUNT NO.								
			VALUE $					

Sheet no.___of___continuation sheets attached to Schedule of Creditors Holding Secured Claims

Subtotal ▶
(Total of this page) $

Total ▶
(Use only on last page) $

In re _____,   Case No._____
             Debtor   (if known)

SCHEDULE E - CREDITORS HOLDING UNSECURED PRIORITY CLAIMS

A complete list of claims entitled to priority, listed separately by type of priority, is to be set forth on the sheets provided. Only holders of unsecured claims entitled to priority should be listed in this schedule. In the boxes provided on the attached sheets, state the name, mailing address, including zip code, and last four digits of the account number, if any, of all entities holding priority claims against the debtor or the property of the debtor, as of the date of the filing of the petition. Use a separate continuation sheet for each type of priority and label each with the type of priority.

The complete account number of any account the debtor has with the creditor is useful to the trustee and the creditor and may be provided if the debtor chooses to do so. If a minor child is a creditor, indicate that by stating "a minor child" and do not disclose the child's name. See 11 U.S.C. § 112; Fed.R.Bankr.P. 1007(m).

If any entity other than a spouse in a joint case may be jointly liable on a claim, place an "X" in the column labeled "Codebtor," include the entity on the appropriate schedule of creditors, and complete Schedule H-Codebtors. If a joint petition is filed, state whether husband, wife, both of them or the marital community may be liable on each claim by placing an "H,""W,""J," or "C" in the column labeled "Husband, Wife, Joint, or Community."   If the claim is contingent, place an "X" in the column labeled "Contingent." If the claim is unliquidated, place an "X" in the column labeled "Unliquidated." If the claim is disputed, place an "X" in the column labeled "Disputed." (You may need to place an "X" in more than one of these three columns.)

Report the total of claims listed on each sheet in the box labeled "Subtotal" on each sheet. Report the total of all claims listed on this Schedule E in the box labeled "Total" on the last sheet of the completed schedule. Report this total also on the Summary of Schedules.

Report the total of amounts entitled to priority listed on each sheet in the box labeled "Subtotal" on each sheet. Report the total of all amounts entitled to priority listed on this Schedule E in the box labeled "Total" on the last sheet of the completed schedule. If applicable, also report this total on the Means Test form.

☐   Check this box if debtor has no creditors holding unsecured priority claims to report on this Schedule E.

TYPES OF PRIORITY CLAIMS (Check the appropriate box(es) below if claims in that category are listed on the attached sheets)

☐ **Domestic Support Obligations**

Claims for domestic support that are owed to or recoverable by a spouse, former spouse, or child of the debtor, or the parent, legal guardian, or responsible relative of such a child, or a governmental unit to whom such a domestic support claim has been assigned to the extent provided in 11 U.S.C. § 507(a)(1).

☐ **Extensions of credit in an involuntary case**

Claims arising in the ordinary course of the debtor's business or financial affairs after the commencement of the case but before the earlier of the appointment of a trustee or the order for relief. 11 U.S.C. § 507(a)(3).

☐ **Wages, salaries, and commissions**

Wages, salaries, and commissions, including vacation, severance, and sick leave pay owing to employees and commissions owing to qualifying independent sales representatives up to $10,000* per person earned within 180 days immediately preceding the filing of the original petition, or the cessation of business, whichever occurred first, to the extent provided in 11 U.S.C. § 507(a)(4).

☐ **Contributions to employee benefit plans**

Money owed to employee benefit plans for services rendered within 180 days immediately preceding the filing of the original petition, or the cessation of business, whichever occurred first, to the extent provided in 11 U.S.C. § 507(a)(5).

In re _____ ,   Case No._____
                              Debtor   (if known)

☐ **Certain farmers and fishermen**

Claims of certain farmers and fishermen, up to $4,925* per farmer or fisherman, against the debtor, as provided in 11 U.S.C. § 507(a)(6).

☐ **Deposits by individuals**

Claims of individuals up to $2,225* for deposits for the purchase, lease, or rental of property or services for personal, family, or household use, that were not delivered or provided. 11 U.S.C. § 507(a)(7).

☐ **Taxes and Certain Other Debts Owed to Governmental Units**

Taxes, customs duties, and penalties owing to federal, state, and local governmental units as set forth in 11 U.S.C. § 507(a)(8).

☐ **Commitments to Maintain the Capital of an Insured Depository Institution**

Claims based on commitments to the FDIC, RTC, Director of the Office of Thrift Supervision, Comptroller of the Currency, or Board of Governors of the Federal Reserve System, or their predecessors or successors, to maintain the capital of an insured depository institution. 11 U.S.C. § 507 (a)(9).

☐ **Claims for Death or Personal Injury While Debtor Was Intoxicated**

Claims for death or personal injury resulting from the operation of a motor vehicle or vessel while the debtor was intoxicated from using alcohol, a drug, or another substance. 11 U.S.C. § 507(a)(10).

* Amounts are subject to adjustment on April 1, 2007, and every three years thereafter with respect to cases commenced on or after the date of adjustment.

_____ continuation sheets attached

Form B6E - Cont.
(10/05)

In re _____,   Case No. _____
Debtor   (If known)

SCHEDULE E - CREDITORS HOLDING UNSECURED PRIORITY CLAIMS
(Continuation Sheet)

TYPE OF PRIORITY

CREDITOR'S NAME, MAILING ADDRESS INCLUDING ZIP CODE, AND ACCOUNT NUMBER (See instructions.)	CODEBTOR	HUSBAND, WIFE, JOINT, OR COMMUNITY	DATE CLAIM WAS INCURRED AND CONSIDERATION FOR CLAIM	CONTINGENT	UNLIQUIDATED	DISPUTED	AMOUNT OF CLAIM	AMOUNT ENTITLED TO PRIORITY
Account No.								
Account No.								
Account No.								
Account No.								
Account No.								

Sheet no. ___ of ___ sheets attached to Schedule of Creditors Holding Priority Claims

Subtotal▶ (Total of this page) $ $

Total▶
(Use only on last page of the completed Schedule E.
(Report total also on Summary of Schedules) $ $

In re _____ ,　　　Case No. _____

　　　　　　　　　Debtor　　　　　　　　　　　　　　　　　　　　　　**(If known)**

SCHEDULE F- CREDITORS HOLDING UNSECURED NONPRIORITY CLAIMS

State the name, mailing address, including zip code, and last four digits of any account number, of all entities holding unsecured claims without priority against the debtor or the property of the debtor, as of the date of filing of the petition. The complete account number of any account the debtor has with the creditor is useful to the trustee and the creditor and may be provided if the debtor chooses to do so. If a minor child is a creditor, indicate that by stating "a minor child" and do not disclose the child's name. See 11 U.S.C. § 112; Fed.R.Bankr.P. 1007(m). Do not include claims listed in Schedules D and E. If all creditors will not fit on this page, use the continuation sheet provided.

If any entity other than a spouse in a joint case may be jointly liable on a claim, place an "X" in the column labeled "Codebtor," include the entity on the appropriate schedule of creditors, and complete Schedule H - Codebtors. If a joint petition is filed, state whether husband, wife, both of them, or the marital community maybe liable on each claim by placing an "H," "W," "J," or "C" in the column labeled "Husband, Wife, Joint, or Community."

If the claim is contingent, place an "X" in the column labeled "Contingent." If the claim is unliquidated, place an "X" in the column labeled "Unliquidated." If the claim is disputed, place an "X" in the column labeled "Disputed." (You may need to place an "X" in more than one of these three columns.)

Report the total of all claims listed on this schedule in the box labeled "Total" on the last sheet of the completed schedule. Report this total also on the Summary of Schedules.

☐　Check this box if debtor has no creditors holding unsecured claims to report on this Schedule F.

CREDITOR'S NAME, MAILING ADDRESS INCLUDING ZIP CODE, AND ACCOUNT NUMBER (See instructions above.)	CODEBTOR	HUSBAND, WIFE, JOINT, OR COMMUNITY	DATE CLAIM WAS INCURRED AND CONSIDERATION FOR CLAIM. IF CLAIM IS SUBJECT TO SETOFF, SO STATE.	CONTINGENT	UNLIQUIDATED	DISPUTED	AMOUNT OF CLAIM
ACCOUNT NO.							
ACCOUNT NO.							
ACCOUNT NO.							
ACCOUNT NO.							
					Subtotal➤		$
					Total➤		$

_____continuation sheets attached

(Use only on last page of the completed Schedule F.)
(Report also on Summary of Schedules.)

In re _____ ,   Case No. _____
                    Debtor   **(If known)**

SCHEDULE F - CREDITORS HOLDING UNSECURED NONPRIORITY CLAIMS
(Continuation Sheet)

CREDITOR'S NAME, MAILING ADDRESS INCLUDING ZIP CODE, AND ACCOUNT NUMBER (See instructions above.)	CODEBTOR	HUSBAND, WIFE, JOINT, OR COMMUNITY	DATE CLAIM WAS INCURRED AND CONSIDERATION FOR CLAIM. IF CLAIM IS SUBJECT TO SETOFF, SO STATE.	CONTINGENT	UNLIQUIDATED	DISPUTED	AMOUNT OF CLAIM
ACCOUNT NO.							
ACCOUNT NO.							
ACCOUNT NO.							
ACCOUNT NO.							
ACCOUNT NO.							

Sheet no.___of___sheets attached to Schedule of
Creditors Holding Unsecured Nonpriority Claims

Subtotal➤ | $

Total➤ | $
(Use only on last page of the completed Schedule F.)
(Report also on Summary of Schedules.)

Form B6G
(10/05)

In re _____ ,   **Case No.** _____

                    Debtor   **(if known)**

SCHEDULE G - EXECUTORY CONTRACTS AND UNEXPIRED LEASES

Describe all executory contracts of any nature and all unexpired leases of real or personal property. Include any timeshare interests. State nature of debtor's interest in contract, i.e., "Purchaser," "Agent," etc. State whether debtor is the lessor or lessee of a lease. Provide the names and complete mailing addresses of all other parties to each lease or contract described. If a minor child is a party to one of the leases or contracts, indicate that by stating "a minor child" and do not disclose the child's name. See 11 U.S.C. § 112; Fed.R. Bankr. P. 1007(m).

☐ Check this box if debtor has no executory contracts or unexpired leases.

NAME AND MAILING ADDRESS, INCLUDING ZIP CODE, OF OTHER PARTIES TO LEASE OR CONTRACT.	DESCRIPTION OF CONTRACT OR LEASE AND NATURE OF DEBTOR'S INTEREST. STATE WHETHER LEASE IS FOR NONRESIDENTIAL REAL PROPERTY. STATE CONTRACT NUMBER OF ANY GOVERNMENT CONTRACT.

Form B6H
(10/05)

In re _____ ,   Case No. _____
                    Debtor   **(if known)**

SCHEDULE H - CODEBTORS

     Provide the information requested concerning any person or entity, other than a spouse in a joint case, that is also liable on any debts listed by debtor in the schedules of creditors. Include all guarantors and co-signers. If the debtor resides or resided in a community property state, commonwealth, or territory (including Alaska, Arizona, California, Idaho, Louisiana, Nevada, New Mexico, Puerto Rico, Texas, Washington, or Wisconsin) within the eight year period immediately preceding the commencement of the case, identify the name of the debtor's spouse and of any former spouse who resides or resided with the debtor in the community property state, commonwealth, or territory. Include all names used by the nondebtor spouse during the eight years immediately preceding the commencement of this case. If a minor child is a codebtor or a creditor, indicate that by stating "a minor child" and do not disclose the child's name. See 11 U.S.C. § 112; Fed. Bankr. P. 1007(m).

☐ Check this box if debtor has no codebtors.

NAME AND ADDRESS OF CODEBTOR	NAME AND ADDRESS OF CREDITOR

In re _____ ,   Case No._____
                    Debtor   **(if known)**

SCHEDULE I - CURRENT INCOME OF INDIVIDUAL DEBTOR(S)

The column labeled "Spouse" must be completed in all cases filed by joint debtors and by a married debtor in a chapter 7, 11, 12, or 13 case whether or not a joint petition is filed, unless the spouses are separated and a joint petition is not filed. Do not state the name of any minor child.

Debtor's Marital Status:	DEPENDENTS OF DEBTOR AND SPOUSE	
	RELATIONSHIP:	AGE:
Employment: Occupation	DEBTOR	SPOUSE
Name of Employer		
How long employed		
Address of Employer		

INCOME: (Estimate of average monthly income)   DEBTOR   SPOUSE

1. Current monthly gross wages, salary, and commissions $_____ $_____
       (Prorate if not paid monthly.)
2. Estimate monthly overtime $_____ $_____

3. SUBTOTAL $_____ $_____

4. LESS PAYROLL DEDUCTIONS
       a. Payroll taxes and social security $_____ $_____
       b. Insurance $_____ $_____
       c. Union dues $_____ $_____
       d. Other (Specify): _____ $_____ $_____

5. SUBTOTAL OF PAYROLL DEDUCTIONS $_____ $_____

6. TOTAL NET MONTHLY TAKE HOME PAY $_____ $_____

7. Regular income from operation of business or profession or farm. $_____ $_____
       (Attach detailed statement)
8. Income from real property $_____ $_____
9. Interest and dividends $_____ $_____
10. Alimony, maintenance or support payments payable to the debtor for $_____ $_____
       the debtor's use or that of dependents listed above.
11. Social security or government assistance
       (Specify):_____ $_____ $_____
12. Pension or retirement income $_____ $_____
13. Other monthly income
       (Specify):_____ $_____ $_____
       _____

14. SUBTOTAL OF LINES 7 THROUGH 13
15. TOTAL MONTHLY INCOME (Add amounts shown on lines 6 and 14) $_____ $_____

16. TOTAL COMBINED MONTHLY INCOME: $_____ $_____ $_____

                                                          (Report also on Summary of Schedules.)

17. Describe any increase or decrease in income reasonably anticipated to occur within the year following the filing of this document:

_____

_____

Form B6J
(10/05)

In re _____ ,   Case No._____
                    Debtor   **(if known)**

SCHEDULE J - CURRENT EXPENDITURES OF INDIVIDUAL DEBTOR(S)

Complete this schedule by estimating the average monthly expenses of the debtor and the debtor's family. Pro rate any payments made bi-weekly, quarterly, semi-annually, or annually to show monthly rate.

☐ Check this box if a joint petition is filed and debtor's spouse maintains a separate household. Complete a separate schedule of expenditures labeled "Spouse."

1. Rent or home mortgage payment (include lot rented for mobile home) $ _____

   a. Are real estate taxes included?   Yes _____   No _____

   b. Is property insurance included?   Yes _____   No _____

2. Utilities: a. Electricity and heating fuel $ _____

     b. Water and sewer $ _____

     c. Telephone $ _____

     d. Other _____ $ _____

3. Home maintenance (repairs and upkeep) $ _____

4. Food $ _____

5. Clothing $ _____

6. Laundry and dry cleaning $ _____

7. Medical and dental expenses $ _____

8. Transportation (not including car payments) $ _____

9. Recreation, clubs and entertainment, newspapers, magazines, etc. $ _____

10. Charitable contributions $ _____

11. Insurance (not deducted from wages or included in home mortgage payments)

     a. Homeowner's or renter's $ _____

     b. Life $ _____

     c. Health $ _____

     d. Auto $ _____

     e. Other _____ $ _____

12. Taxes (not deducted from wages or included in home mortgage payments)
(Specify) _____ $ _____

13. Installment payments: (In chapter 11, 12, and 13 cases, do not list payments to be included in the plan)

     a. Auto $ _____

     b. Other _____ $ _____

     c. Other _____ $ _____

14. Alimony, maintenance, and support paid to others $ _____

15. Payments for support of additional dependents not living at your home $ _____

16. Regular expenses from operation of business, profession, or farm (attach detailed statement) $ _____

17. Other _____ $ _____

18. TOTAL MONTHLY EXPENSES (Report also on Summary of Schedules) $ _____

19. Describe any increase or decrease in expenditures reasonably anticipated to occur within the year following the filing of

this document:

_____

20. STATEMENT OF MONTHLY NET INCOME

   a. Total monthly income from Line 16 of Schedule I $ _____

   b. Total monthly expenses from Line 18 above $ _____

   c. Monthly net income (a. minus b.) $ _____

In re _____ ,   Case No. _____

           Debtor   (If known)

DECLARATION CONCERNING DEBTOR'S SCHEDULES

DECLARATION UNDER PENALTY OF PERJURY BY INDIVIDUAL DEBTOR

I declare under penalty of perjury that I have read the foregoing summary and schedules, consisting of _____

(Total shown on summary page plus 1.)

sheets, and that they are true and correct to the best of my knowledge, information, and belief.

Date _____   Signature: _____
                                                                                       Debtor

Date _____   Signature: _____
                                                                            (Joint Debtor, if any)

[If joint case, both spouses must sign.]

DECLARATION AND SIGNATURE OF NON-ATTORNEY BANKRUPTCY PETITION PREPARER (See 11 U.S.C. § 110)

I declare under penalty of perjury that: (1) I am a bankruptcy petition preparer as defined in 11 U.S.C. § 110; (2) I prepared this document for compensation and have provided the debtor with a copy of this document and the notices and information required under 11 U.S.C. §§ 110(b), 110(h) and 342(b); and, (3) if rules or guidelines have been promulgated pursuant to 11 U.S.C. § 110(h) setting a maximum fee for services chargeable by bankruptcy petition preparers, I have given the debtor notice of the maximum amount before preparing any document for filing for a debtor or accepting any fee from the debtor, as required by that section.

_____   _____
Printed or Typed Name of Bankruptcy Petition Preparer   Social Security No.
                                                                                         (Required by 11 U.S.C. § 110.)

If the bankruptcy petition preparer is not an individual, state the name, title (if any), address, and social security number of the officer, principal, responsible person, or partner who signs this document.

_____

_____
Address

X _____   _____
Signature of Bankruptcy Petition Preparer   Date

Names and Social Security numbers of all other individuals who prepared or assisted in preparing this document, unless the bankruptcy petition preparer is not an individual:

If more than one person prepared this document, attach additional signed sheets conforming to the appropriate Official Form for each person.

A bankruptcy petition preparer's failure to comply with the provisions of title 11 and the Federal Rules of Bankruptcy Procedure may result in fines or imprisonment or both. 11 U.S.C. § 110; 18 U.S.C. § 156.

DECLARATION UNDER PENALTY OF PERJURY ON BEHALF OF A CORPORATION OR PARTNERSHIP

I, the _____ [the president or other officer or an authorized agent of the corporation or a member or an authorized agent of the partnership] of the _____ [corporation or partnership] named as debtor in this case, declare under penalty of perjury that I have read the foregoing summary and schedules, consisting of _____ sheets, and that they are true and correct to the best of my knowledge, information, and belief.   (Total shown on summary page plus 1.)

Date _____

            Signature: _____

            [Print or type name of individual signing on behalf of debtor.]

[An individual signing on behalf of a partnership or corporation must indicate position or relationship to debtor.]

Penalty for making a false statement or concealing property: Fine of up to $500,000 or imprisonment for up to 5 years or both. 18 U.S.C. §§ 152 and 3571.

Form 6-Summary
(10/05)

United States Bankruptcy Court

_____ District Of _____

In re _____,
               Debtor

Case No. _____

Chapter _____

SUMMARY OF SCHEDULES

Indicate as to each schedule whether that schedule is attached and state the number of pages in each. Report the totals from Schedules A, B, D, E, F, I, and J in the boxes provided. Add the amounts from Schedules A and B to determine the total amount of the debtor's assets. Add the amounts of all claims from Schedules D, E, and F to determine the total amount of the debtor's liabilities. Individual debtors must also complete the "Statistical Summary of Certain Liabilities."

AMOUNTS SCHEDULED

NAME OF SCHEDULE	ATTACHED (YES/NO)	NO. OF SHEETS	ASSETS	LIABILITIES	OTHER
A - Real Property			$		
B - Personal Property			$		
C - Property Claimed as Exempt					
D - Creditors Holding Secured Claims				$	
E - Creditors Holding Unsecured Priority Claims				$	
F - Creditors Holding Unsecured Nonpriority Claims				$	
G - Executory Contracts and Unexpired Leases					
H - Codebtors					
I - Current Income of Individual Debtor(s)					$
J - Current Expenditures of Individual Debtors(s)					$
TOTAL			$	$	

Form 6-Summ2
(10/05)

United States Bankruptcy Court

_____ District Of _____

In re _____,   Case No. _____
                         Debtor

                                                          Chapter _____

STATISTICAL SUMMARY OF CERTAIN LIABILITIES (28 U.S.C. § 159)
[Individual Debtors Only]

Summarize the following types of liabilities, as reported in the Schedules, and total them.

Type of Liability	Amount
Domestic Support Obligations (from Schedule E)	$
Taxes and Certain Other Debts Owed to Governmental Units (from Schedule E)	$
Claims for Death or Personal Injury While Debtor Was Intoxicated (from Schedule E)	$
Student Loan Obligations (from Schedule F)	$
Domestic Support, Separation Agreement, and Divorce Decree Obligations Not Reported on Schedule E	$
Obligations to Pension or Profit-Sharing, and Other Similar Obligations (from Schedule F)	$
TOTAL	$

The foregoing information is for statistical purposes only under 28 U.S.C. § 159.

United States Bankruptcy Court

_____ District Of _____

In re _____,
            Debtor

Case No. _____

Chapter _____

APPLICATION TO PAY FILING FEE IN INSTALLMENTS

1.   In accordance with Fed. R. Bankr. P. 1006, I apply for permission to pay the filing fee amounting to $_____ in installments.

2.   I am unable to pay the filing fee except in installments.

3.   Until the filing fee is paid in full, I will not make any additional payment or transfer any additional property to an attorney or any other person for services in connection with this case.

4.   I propose the following terms for the payment of the Filing Fee.*

       $ _____   Check one ☐   With the filing of the petition, or
                                            ☐   On or before _____

       $ _____   on or before _____

       $ _____   on or before _____

       $ _____   on or before _____

*   The number of installments proposed shall not exceed four (4), and the final installment shall be payable not later than 120 days after filing the petition. For cause shown, the court may extend the time of any installment, provided the last installment is paid not later than 180 days after filing the petition. Fed. R. Bankr. P. 1006(b)(2).

5.   I understand that if I fail to pay any installment when due, my bankruptcy case may be dismissed and I may not receive a discharge of my debts.

_____
Signature of Attorney   Date

_____
Name of Attorney

_____
Signature of Debtor   Date
(In a joint case, both spouses must sign.)

_____
Signature of Joint Debtor (if any)   Date

DECLARATION AND SIGNATURE OF NON-ATTORNEY BANKRUPTCY PETITION PREPARER (See 11 U.S.C. § 110)

     I declare under penalty of perjury that: (1) I am a bankruptcy petition preparer as defined in 11 U.S.C. § 110; (2) I prepared this document for compensation and have provided the debtor with a copy of this document and the notices and information required under 11 U.S.C. §§ 110(b), 110(h), and 342(b); (3) if rules or guidelines have been promulgated pursuant to 11 U.S.C. § 110(h) setting a maximum fee for services chargeable by bankruptcy petition preparers, I have given the debtor notice of the maximum amount before preparing any document for filing for a debtor or accepting any fee from the debtor, as required under that section; and (4) I will not accept any additional money or other property from the debtor before the filing fee is paid in full.

_____
Printed or Typed Name and Title, if any, of Bankruptcy Petition Preparer
If the bankruptcy petition preparer is not an individual, state the name, title (if any), address, and social security number of the officer, principal, responsible person, or partner who signs the document.

_____

Address

x_____
Signature of Bankruptcy Petition Preparer

_____
Social Security No. (Required by 11 U.S.C. § 110.)

_____
Date

Names and Social Security numbers of all other individuals who prepared or assisted in preparing this document, unless the bankruptcy petition preparer is not an individual:

If more than one person prepared this document, attach additional signed sheets conforming to the appropriate Official Form for each person.
A bankruptcy petition preparer's failure to comply with the provisions of title 11 and the Federal Rules of Bankruptcy Procedure may result in fines or imprisonment or both. 11 U.S.C. § 110; 18 U.S.C. § 156.

United States Bankruptcy Court
_____ District Of _____

In re _____,
               Debtor

Case No. _____

Chapter _____

ORDER APPROVING PAYMENT OF FILING FEE IN INSTALLMENTS

☐   IT IS ORDERED that the debtor(s) may pay the filing fee in installments on the terms proposed in the foregoing application.

☐   IT IS ORDERED that the debtor(s) shall pay the filing fee according to the following terms:

$ _____   Check one ☐ With the filing of the petition, or
                                       ☐ On or before _____

$ _____ on or before _____

$ _____ on or before _____

$ _____ on or before _____

☐   IT IS FURTHER ORDERED that until the filing fee is paid in full the debtor(s) shall not make any additional payment or transfer any additional property to an attorney or any other person for services in connection with this case.

BY THE COURT

Date: _____

_____
United States Bankruptcy Judge

Form B3B
(04/09/06)

APPLICATION FOR WAIVER OF THE CHAPTER 7 FILING FEE
FOR INDIVIDUALS WHO CANNOT PAY THE FILING FEE
IN FULL OR IN INSTALLMENTS

The court fee for filing a case under chapter 7 of the Bankruptcy Code is $299.

If you cannot afford to pay the full fee at the time of filing, you may apply to pay the fee in installments. A form, which is available from the bankruptcy clerk's office, must be completed to make that application. If your application to pay in installments is approved, you will be permitted to file your petition, completing payment of the fee over the course of four to six months.

If you cannot afford to pay the fee either in full at the time of filing or in installments, then you may request a waiver of the filing fee by completing this application and filing it with the Clerk of Court. A judge will decide whether you have to pay the fee. By law, the judge may waive the fee only if your income is less than 150 percent of the official poverty line applicable to your family size and you are unable to pay the fee in installments. You may obtain information about the poverty guidelines at www.uscourts.gov or in the bankruptcy clerk's office.

Required information. Complete all items in the application, and attach requested schedules. Then sign the application on the last page. If you and your spouse are filing a joint bankruptcy petition, you both must provide information as requested and sign the application.

United States Bankruptcy Court
_____ District of _____

In re: _____   Case No. _____
      Debtor(s)   (if known)

APPLICATION FOR WAIVER OF THE CHAPTER 7 FILING FEE
FOR INDIVIDUALS WHO CANNOT PAY THE FILING FEE IN FULL OR IN INSTALLMENTS

Part A. Family Size and Income

1. Including yourself, your spouse, and dependents you have listed or will list on Schedule I (Current Income of Individual Debtors(s)), how many people are in your family? (Do not include your spouse if you are separated AND are not filing a joint petition.) _____

2. Restate the following information that you provided, or will provide, on Line 16 of Schedule I. Attach a completed copy of Schedule I, if it is available.

   Total Combined Monthly Income (Line 16 of Schedule I): $_____

3. State the monthly net income, if any, of dependents included in Question 1 above. Do not include any income already reported in Item 2. If none, enter $0.

   $_____

4. Add the "Total Combined Monthly Income" reported in Question 2 to your dependents' monthly net income from Question 3.

   $_____

5. Do you expect the amount in Question 4 to increase or decrease by more than 10% during the next 6 months? Yes ___ No ___

   If yes, explain.

Part B: Monthly Expenses

6. EITHER (a) attach a completed copy of Schedule J (Schedule of Monthly Expenses), and state your total monthly expenses reported on Line 18 of that Schedule, OR (b) if you have not yet completed Schedule J, provide an estimate of your total monthly expenses.

   $ _____

7. Do you expect the amount in Question 6 to increase or decrease by more than 10% during the next 6 months? Yes ___ No ___
   If yes, explain.

Part C. Real and Personal Property

EITHER (1) attach completed copies of Schedules A (Real Property) and Schedule B (Personal Property), OR (2) if you have not yet completed those schedules, answer the following questions.

8. State the amount of cash you have on hand: $ _____

9. State below any money you have in savings, checking, or other accounts in a bank or other financial institution.

Bank or Other Financial Institution:	Type of Account such as savings, checking, CD:	Amount:
_____	_____	$ _____
_____	_____	$ _____

10. State below the assets owned by you. **Do not list ordinary household furnishings and clothing**.

Home   Address:

_____   Value: $ _____

_____   Amount owed on mortgages and liens: $ _____

Other real estate   Address:

_____   Value: $ _____

_____   Amount owed on mortgages and liens: $ _____

Motor vehicle   Model/Year: _____   Value: $ _____

_____   Amount owed: $ _____

Motor vehicle   Model/Year: _____   Value: $ _____

_____   Amount owed: $ _____

Other   Description_____   Value: $ _____

_____   Amount owed: $ _____

11. State below any person, business, organization, or governmental unit that owes you money and the amount that is owed.

Name of Person, Business, or Organization that Owes You Money	Amount Owed
_____	$ _____
_____	$ _____

Part D. Additional Information.

12. Have you paid an **attorney** any money for services in connection with this case, including the completion of this form, the bankruptcy petition, or schedules? Yes ___ No ___
If yes, how much have you paid? $ _____

13. Have you promised to pay or do you anticipate paying an **attorney** in connection with your bankruptcy case? Yes ___ No ___
If yes, how much have you promised to pay or do you anticipate paying? $ _____

14. Have you paid **anyone other than an attorney** (such as a bankruptcy petition preparer, paralegal, typing service, or another person) any money for services in connection with this case, including the completion of this form, the bankruptcy petition, or schedules? Yes ___ No ___
If yes, how much have you paid? $ _____

15. Have you promised to pay or do you anticipate paying **anyone other than an attorney** (such as a bankruptcy petition preparer, paralegal, typing service, or another person) any money for services in connection with this case, including the completion of this form, the bankruptcy petition, or schedules? Yes ___ No ___
If yes, how much have you promised to pay or do you anticipate paying? $ _____

16. Has anyone paid an attorney or other person or service in connection with this case, on your behalf? Yes ___ No ___

If yes, explain.

Form B3B Cont.
(04/09/06)

17. Have you previously filed for bankruptcy relief during the past eight years? Yes ____ No ____

Case Number (if known)	Year filed	Location of filing	Did you obtain a discharge? (if known)
_____	_____	_____	Yes ____ No ____ Don't know ____
_____	_____	_____	Yes ____ No ____ Don't know ____

18. Please provide any other information that helps to explain why you are unable to pay the filing fee in installments.

19. I (we) declare under penalty of perjury that I (we) cannot currently afford to pay the filing fee in full or in installments and that the foregoing information is true and correct.

Executed on: _____

      Date   Signature of Debtor

      Date   Signature of Co-debtor

DECLARATION AND SIGNATURE OF BANKRUPTCY PETITION PREPARER (See 11 U.S.C. § 110)

I declare under penalty of perjury that: (1) I am a bankruptcy petition preparer as defined in 11 U.S.C. § 110; (2) I prepared this document for compensation and have provided the debtor with a copy of this document and the notices and information required under 11 U.S.C. §§ 110(b), 110(h), and 342(b); and (3) if rules or guidelines have been promulgated pursuant to 11 U.S.C. § 110(h) setting a maximum fee for services chargeable by bankruptcy petition preparers, I have given the debtor notice of the maximum amount before preparing any document for filing for a debtor or accepting any fee from the debtor, as required under that section.

_____

Printed or Typed Name and Title, if any, of Bankruptcy Petition Preparer   Social Security No. (Required by 11 U.S.C. §110.)

If the bankruptcy petition preparer is not an individual, state the name, title (if any), address, and social security number of the officer, principal, responsible person, or partner who signs the document.

_____

_____

Address

x_____   _____
Signature of Bankruptcy Petition Preparer   Date

Names and Social Security numbers of all other individuals who prepared or assisted in preparing this document, unless the bankruptcy petition preparer is not an individual:

If more than one person prepared this document, attach additional signed sheets conforming to the appropriate Official Form for each person.
A bankruptcy petition preparer's failure to comply with the provisions of title 11 and the Federal Rules of Bankruptcy Procedure may result in fines or imprisonment or both. 11 U.S.C. § 110; 18 U.S.C. § 156.

Form B3B
(04/09/06)

United States Bankruptcy Court
_____ District of _____

In re: _____   Case No. _____
      Debtor(s)

ORDER ON DEBTOR'S APPLICATION FOR WAIVER OF THE CHAPTER 7 FILING FEE

Upon consideration of the debtor's "Application for Waiver of the Chapter 7 Filing Fee," the court orders that the application be:

[   ] GRANTED.

    This order is subject to being vacated at a later time if developments in the administration of the bankruptcy case demonstrate that the waiver was unwarranted.

[   ] DENIED.

    The debtor shall pay the chapter 7 filing fee according to the following terms:

    $ _____ on or before _____

    $ _____ on or before _____

    $ _____ on or before _____

    $ _____ on or before _____

    Until the filing fee is paid in full, the debtor shall not make any additional payment or transfer any additional property to an attorney or any other person for services in connection with this case.

    IF THE DEBTOR FAILS TO TIMELY PAY THE FILING FEE IN FULL OR TO TIMELY MAKE INSTALLMENT PAYMENTS, THE COURT MAY DISMISS THE DEBTOR'S CHAPTER 7 CASE.

[   ] SCHEDULED FOR HEARING.

    A hearing to consider the debtor's "Application for Waiver of the Chapter 7 Filing Fee" shall be held on _____ at _____ am/pm at _____.
                                            (address of courthouse)

    IF THE DEBTOR FAILS TO APPEAR AT THE SCHEDULED HEARING, THE COURT MAY DEEM SUCH FAILURE TO BE THE DEBTOR'S CONSENT TO THE ENTRY OF AN ORDER DENYING THE FEE WAIVER APPLICATION BY DEFAULT.

                                             BY THE COURT:

DATE: _____

                                           _____
                                           United States Bankruptcy Judge

UNITED STATES BANKRUPTCY COURT

_____ DISTRICT OF _____

In re: _____,   Case No. _____
          Debtor   (if known)

STATEMENT OF FINANCIAL AFFAIRS

This statement is to be completed by every debtor. Spouses filing a joint petition may file a single statement on which the information for both spouses is combined. If the case is filed under chapter 12 or chapter 13, a married debtor must furnish information for both spouses whether or not a joint petition is filed, unless the spouses are separated and a joint petition is not filed. An individual debtor engaged in business as a sole proprietor, partner, family farmer, or self-employed professional, should provide the information requested on this statement concerning all such activities as well as the individual's personal affairs. Do not include the name or address of a minor child in this statement. Indicate payments, transfers and the like to minor children by stating "a minor child." See 11 U.S.C. § 112; Fed. R. Bankr. P. 1007(m).

Questions 1 - 18 are to be completed by all debtors. Debtors that are or have been in business, as defined below, also must complete Questions 19 - 25. **If the answer to an applicable question is "None," mark the box labeled "None."** If additional space is needed for the answer to any question, use and attach a separate sheet properly identified with the case name, case number (if known), and the number of the question.

DEFINITIONS

"In business." A debtor is "in business" for the purpose of this form if the debtor is a corporation or partnership. An individual debtor is "in business" for the purpose of this form if the debtor is or has been, within six years immediately preceding the filing of this bankruptcy case, any of the following: an officer, director, managing executive, or owner of 5 percent or more of the voting or equity securities of a corporation; a partner, other than a limited partner, of a partnership; a sole proprietor or self-employed full-time or part-time. An individual debtor also may be "in business" for the purpose of this form if the debtor engages in a trade, business, or other activity, other than as an employee, to supplement income from the debtor's primary employment.

"Insider." The term "insider" includes but is not limited to: relatives of the debtor; general partners of the debtor and their relatives; corporations of which the debtor is an officer, director, or person in control; officers, directors, and any owner of 5 percent or more of the voting or equity securities of a corporate debtor and their relatives; affiliates of the debtor and insiders of such affiliates; any managing agent of the debtor. 11 U.S.C. § 101.

---

1. Income from employment or operation of business

None
☐

State the gross amount of income the debtor has received from employment, trade, or profession, or from operation of the debtor's business, including part-time activities either as an employee or in independent trade or business, from the beginning of this calendar year to the date this case was commenced. State also the gross amounts received during the **two years** immediately preceding this calendar year. (A debtor that maintains, or has maintained, financial records on the basis of a fiscal rather than a calendar year may report fiscal year income. Identify the beginning and ending dates of the debtor's fiscal year.) If a joint petition is filed, state income for each spouse separately. (Married debtors filing under chapter 12 or chapter 13 must state income of both spouses whether or not a joint petition is filed, unless the spouses are separated and a joint petition is not filed.)

         AMOUNT   SOURCE

2. Income other than from employment or operation of business

None ☐

State the amount of income received by the debtor other than from employment, trade, profession, operation of the debtor's business during the **two years** immediately preceding the commencement of this case. Give particulars. If a joint petition is filed, state income for each spouse separately. (Married debtors filing under chapter 12 or chapter 13 must state income for each spouse whether or not a joint petition is filed, unless the spouses are separated and a joint petition is not filed.)

AMOUNT   SOURCE

3. Payments to creditors

Complete a. or b., as appropriate, and c.

None ☐

a. *Individual or joint debtor(s) with primarily consumer debts:* List all payments on loans, installment purchases of goods or services, and other debts to any creditor made within **90 days** immediately preceding the commencement of this case if the aggregate value of all property that constitutes or is affected by such transfer is not less than $600. Indicate with an asterisk (*) any payments that were made to a creditor on account of a domestic support obligation or as part of an alternative repayment schedule under a plan by an approved nonprofit budgeting and creditor counseling agency. (Married debtors filing under chapter 12 or chapter 13 must include payments by either or both spouses whether or not a joint petition is filed, unless the spouses are separated and a joint petition is not filed.)

NAME AND ADDRESS OF CREDITOR	DATES OF PAYMENTS	AMOUNT PAID	AMOUNT STILL OWING

None ☐

b. *Debtor whose debts are not primarily consumer debts:* List each payment or other transfer to any creditor made within **90** days immediately preceding the commencement of the case if the aggregate value of all property that constitutes or is affected by such transfer is not less than $5,000. (Married debtors filing under chapter 12 or chapter 13 must include payments and other transfers by either or both spouses whether or not a joint petition is filed, unless the spouses are separated and a joint petition is not filed.)

NAME AND ADDRESS OF CREDITOR	DATES OF PAYMENTS/ TRANSFERS	AMOUNT PAID OR VALUE OF TRANSFERS	AMOUNT STILL OWING

None ☐

c. *All debtors:* List all payments made within **one year** immediately preceding the commencement of this case to or for the benefit of creditors who are or were insiders. (Married debtors filing under chapter 12 or chapter 13 must include payments by either or both spouses whether or not a joint petition is filed, unless the spouses are separated and a joint petition is not filed.)

NAME AND ADDRESS OF CREDITOR AND RELATIONSHIP TO DEBTOR	DATE OF PAYMENT	AMOUNT PAID	AMOUNT STILL OWING

4. Suits and administrative proceedings, executions, garnishments and attachments

---

None ☐ a. List all suits and administrative proceedings to which the debtor is or was a party within **one year** immediately preceding the filing of this bankruptcy case. (Married debtors filing under chapter 12 or chapter 13 must include information concerning either or both spouses whether or not a joint petition is filed, unless the spouses are separated and a joint petition is not filed.)

CAPTION OF SUIT AND CASE NUMBER	NATURE OF PROCEEDING	COURT OR AGENCY AND LOCATION	STATUS OR DISPOSITION

None ☐ b. Describe all property that has been attached, garnished or seized under any legal or equitable process within **one year** immediately preceding the commencement of this case. (Married debtors filing under chapter 12 or chapter 13 must include information concerning property of either or both spouses whether or not a joint petition is filed, unless the spouses are separated and a joint petition is not filed.)

NAME AND ADDRESS OF PERSON FOR WHOSE BENEFIT PROPERTY WAS SEIZED	DATE OF SEIZURE	DESCRIPTION AND VALUE OF PROPERTY

5. Repossessions, foreclosures and returns

None ☐ List all property that has been repossessed by a creditor, sold at a foreclosure sale, transferred through a deed in lieu of foreclosure or returned to the seller, within **one year** immediately preceding the commencement of this case. (Married debtors filing under chapter 12 or chapter 13 must include information concerning property of either or both spouses whether or not a joint petition is filed, unless the spouses are separated and a joint petition is not filed.)

NAME AND ADDRESS OF CREDITOR OR SELLER	DATE OF REPOSSESSION, FORECLOSURE SALE, TRANSFER OR RETURN	DESCRIPTION AND VALUE OF PROPERTY

6. Assignments and receiverships

None ☐ a. Describe any assignment of property for the benefit of creditors made within **120 days** immediately preceding the commencement of this case. (Married debtors filing under chapter 12 or chapter 13 must include any assignment by either or both spouses whether or not a joint petition is filed, unless the spouses are separated and a joint petition is not filed.)

NAME AND ADDRESS OF ASSIGNEE	DATE OF ASSIGNMENT	TERMS OF ASSIGNMENT OR SETTLEMENT

None ☐ b. List all property which has been in the hands of a custodian, receiver, or court-appointed official within **one year** immediately preceding the commencement of this case. (Married debtors filing under chapter 12 or chapter 13 must include information concerning property of either or both spouses whether or not a joint petition is filed, unless the spouses are separated and a joint petition is not filed.)

NAME AND ADDRESS OF CUSTODIAN	NAME AND LOCATION OF COURT CASE TITLE & NUMBER	DATE OF ORDER	DESCRIPTION AND VALUE Of PROPERTY

---

7. Gifts

None ☐ List all gifts or charitable contributions made within **one year** immediately preceding the commencement of this case except ordinary and usual gifts to family members aggregating less than $200 in value per individual family member and charitable contributions aggregating less than $100 per recipient. (Married debtors filing under chapter 12 or chapter 13 must include gifts or contributions by either or both spouses whether or not a joint petition is filed, unless the spouses are separated and a joint petition is not filed.)

NAME AND ADDRESS OF PERSON OR ORGANIZATION	RELATIONSHIP TO DEBTOR, IF ANY	DATE OF GIFT	DESCRIPTION AND VALUE OF GIFT

---

8. Losses

None ☐ List all losses from fire, theft, other casualty or gambling within **one year** immediately preceding the commencement of this case **or since the commencement of this case**. (Married debtors filing under chapter 12 or chapter 13 must include losses by either or both spouses whether or not a joint petition is filed, unless the spouses are separated and a joint petition is not filed.)

DESCRIPTION AND VALUE OF PROPERTY	DESCRIPTION OF CIRCUMSTANCES AND, IF LOSS WAS COVERED IN WHOLE OR IN PART BY INSURANCE, GIVE PARTICULARS	DATE OF LOSS

---

9. Payments related to debt counseling or bankruptcy

None ☐ List all payments made or property transferred by or on behalf of the debtor to any persons, including attorneys, for consultation concerning debt consolidation, relief under the bankruptcy law or preparation of a petition in bankruptcy within **one year** immediately preceding the commencement of this case.

NAME AND ADDRESS OF PAYEE	DATE OF PAYMENT, NAME OF PAYER IF OTHER THAN DEBTOR	AMOUNT OF MONEY OR DESCRIPTION AND VALUE OF PROPERTY

---

10. Other transfers

None ☐
a. List all other property, other than property transferred in the ordinary course of the business or financial affairs of the debtor, transferred either absolutely or as security within **two years** immediately preceding the commencement of this case. (Married debtors filing under chapter 12 or chapter 13 must include transfers by either or both spouses whether or not a joint petition is filed, unless the spouses are separated and a joint petition is not filed.)

NAME AND ADDRESS OF TRANSFEREE, RELATIONSHIP TO DEBTOR	DATE	DESCRIBE PROPERTY TRANSFERRED AND VALUE RECEIVED

None ☐
b. List all property transferred by the debtor within **ten years** immediately preceding the commencement of this case to a self-settled trust or similar device of which the debtor is a beneficiary.

NAME OF TRUST OR OTHER DEVICE	DATE(S) OF TRANSFER(S)	AMOUNT OF MONEY OR DESCRIPTION AND VALUE OF PROPERTY OR DEBTOR'S INTEREST IN PROPERTY

11. Closed financial accounts

None ☐
List all financial accounts and instruments held in the name of the debtor or for the benefit of the debtor which were closed, sold, or otherwise transferred within **one year** immediately preceding the commencement of this case. Include checking, savings, or other financial accounts, certificates of deposit, or other instruments; shares and share accounts held in banks, credit unions, pension funds, cooperatives, associations, brokerage houses and other financial institutions. (Married debtors filing under chapter 12 or chapter 13 must include information concerning accounts or instruments held by or for either or both spouses whether or not a joint petition is filed, unless the spouses are separated and a joint petition is not filed.)

NAME AND ADDRESS OF INSTITUTION	TYPE OF ACCOUNT, LAST FOUR DIGITS OF ACCOUNT NUMBER, AND AMOUNT OF FINAL BALANCE	AMOUNT AND DATE OF SALE OR CLOSING

12. Safe deposit boxes

None ☐
List each safe deposit or other box or depository in which the debtor has or had securities, cash, or other valuables within **one year** immediately preceding the commencement of this case. (Married debtors filing under chapter 12 or chapter 13 must include boxes or depositories of either or both spouses whether or not a joint petition is filed, unless the spouses are separated and a joint petition is not filed.)

NAME AND ADDRESS OF BANK OR OTHER DEPOSITORY	NAMES AND ADDRESSES OF THOSE WITH ACCESS TO BOX OR DEPOSITORY	DESCRIPTION OF CONTENTS	DATE OF TRANSFER OR SURRENDER, IF ANY

13. Setoffs

None ☐ List all setoffs made by any creditor, including a bank, against a debt or deposit of the debtor within **90 days** preceding the commencement of this case. (Married debtors filing under chapter 12 or chapter 13 must include information concerning either or both spouses whether or not a joint petition is filed, unless the spouses are separated and a joint petition is not filed.)

NAME AND ADDRESS OF CREDITOR | DATE OF SETOFF | AMOUNT OF SETOFF

14. Property held for another person

None ☐ List all property owned by another person that the debtor holds or controls.

NAME AND ADDRESS OF OWNER | DESCRIPTION AND VALUE OF PROPERTY | LOCATION OF PROPERTY

15. Prior address of debtor

None ☐ If debtor has moved within **three years** immediately preceding the commencement of this case, list all premises which the debtor occupied during that period and vacated prior to the commencement of this case. If a joint petition is filed, report also any separate address of either spouse.

ADDRESS | NAME USED | DATES OF OCCUPANCY

16. Spouses and Former Spouses

None ☐ If the debtor resides or resided in a community property state, commonwealth, or territory (including Alaska, Arizona, California, Idaho, Louisiana, Nevada, New Mexico, Puerto Rico, Texas, Washington, or Wisconsin) within **eight years** immediately preceding the commencement of the case, identify the name of the debtor's spouse and of any former spouse who resides or resided with the debtor in the community property state.

NAME

17. Environmental Information.

For the purpose of this question, the following definitions apply:

"Environmental Law" means any federal, state, or local statute or regulation regulating pollution, contamination, releases of hazardous or toxic substances, wastes or material into the air, land, soil, surface water, groundwater, or other medium, including, but not limited to, statutes or regulations regulating the cleanup of these substances, wastes, or material.

"Site" means any location, facility, or property as defined under any Environmental Law, whether or not presently or formerly owned or operated by the debtor, including, but not limited to, disposal sites.

"Hazardous Material" means anything defined as a hazardous waste, hazardous substance, toxic substance, hazardous material, pollutant, or contaminant or similar term under an Environmental Law.

None ☐ a. List the name and address of every site for which the debtor has received notice in writing by a governmental unit that it may be liable or potentially liable under or in violation of an Environmental Law. Indicate the governmental unit, the date of the notice, and, if known, the Environmental Law:

SITE NAME AND ADDRESS	NAME AND ADDRESS OF GOVERNMENTAL UNIT	DATE OF NOTICE	ENVIRONMENTAL LAW

None ☐ b. List the name and address of every site for which the debtor provided notice to a governmental unit of a release of Hazardous Material. Indicate the governmental unit to which the notice was sent and the date of the notice.

SITE NAME AND ADDRESS	NAME AND ADDRESS OF GOVERNMENTAL UNIT	DATE OF NOTICE	ENVIRONMENTAL LAW

None ☐ c. List all judicial or administrative proceedings, including settlements or orders, under any Environmental Law with respect to which the debtor is or was a party. Indicate the name and address of the governmental unit that is or was a party to the proceeding, and the docket number.

NAME AND ADDRESS OF GOVERNMENTAL UNIT	DOCKET NUMBER	STATUS OR DISPOSITION

18 . Nature, location and name of business

None ☐ a. *If the debtor is an individual*, list the names, addresses, taxpayer identification numbers, nature of the businesses, and beginning and ending dates of all businesses in which the debtor was an officer, director, partner, or managing executive of a corporation, partner in a partnership, sole proprietor, or was self-employed in a trade, profession, or other activity either full- or part-time within **six years** immediately preceding the commencement of this case, or in which the debtor owned 5 percent or more of the voting or equity securities within **six years** immediately preceding the commencement of this case.

If the debtor is a partnership, list the names, addresses, taxpayer identification numbers, nature of the businesses, and beginning and ending dates of all businesses in which the debtor was a partner or owned 5 percent or more of the voting or equity securities, within **six years** immediately preceding the commencement of this case.

If the debtor is a corporation, list the names, addresses, taxpayer identification numbers, nature of the businesses, and beginning and ending dates of all businesses in which the debtor was a partner or owned 5 percent or more of the voting or equity securities within **six years** immediately preceding the commencement of this case.

NAME	LAST FOUR DIGITS OF SOC. SEC. NO./ COMPLETE EIN OR OTHER TAXPAYER I.D. NO.	ADDRESS	NATURE OF BUSINESS	BEGINNING AND ENDING DATES

None ☐   b. Identify any business listed in response to subdivision a., above, that is "single asset real estate" as defined in 11 U.S.C. § 101.

     NAME   ADDRESS

     The following questions are to be completed by every debtor that is a corporation or partnership and by any individual debtor who is or has been, within **six years** immediately preceding the commencement of this case, any of the following: an officer, director, managing executive, or owner of more than 5 percent of the voting or equity securities of a corporation; a partner, other than a limited partner, of a partnership, a sole proprietor, or self-employed in a trade, profession, or other activity, either full- or part-time.

     *(An individual or joint debtor should complete this portion of the statement **only** if the debtor is or has been in business, as defined above, within six years immediately preceding the commencement of this case. A debtor who has not been in business within those six years should go directly to the signature page.)*

19. Books, records and financial statements

None ☐   a. List all bookkeepers and accountants who within **two years** immediately preceding the filing of this bankruptcy case kept or supervised the keeping of books of account and records of the debtor.

     NAME AND ADDRESS   DATES SERVICES RENDERED

None ☐   b. List all firms or individuals who within **two years** immediately preceding the filing of this bankruptcy case have audited the books of account and records, or prepared a financial statement of the debtor.

     NAME   ADDRESS   DATES SERVICES RENDERED

None ☐   c. List all firms or individuals who at the time of the commencement of this case were in possession of the books of account and records of the debtor. If any of the books of account and records are not available, explain.

     NAME   ADDRESS

None ☐ d. List all financial institutions, creditors and other parties, including mercantile and trade agencies, to whom a financial statement was issued by the debtor within **two years** immediately preceding the commencement of this case.

|NAME AND ADDRESS|DATE ISSUED|

20. Inventories

None ☐ a. List the dates of the last two inventories taken of your property, the name of the person who supervised the taking of each inventory, and the dollar amount and basis of each inventory.

| DATE OF INVENTORY | INVENTORY SUPERVISOR | DOLLAR AMOUNT OF INVENTORY (Specify cost, market or other basis) |

None ☐ b. List the name and address of the person having possession of the records of each of the inventories reported in a., above.

| DATE OF INVENTORY | NAME AND ADDRESSES OF CUSTODIAN OF INVENTORY RECORDS |

21 . Current Partners, Officers, Directors and Shareholders

None ☐ a. If the debtor is a partnership, list the nature and percentage of partnership interest of each member of the partnership.

| NAME AND ADDRESS | NATURE OF INTEREST | PERCENTAGE OF INTEREST |

None ☐ b. If the debtor is a corporation, list all officers and directors of the corporation, and each stockholder who directly or indirectly owns, controls, or holds 5 percent or more of the voting or equity securities of the corporation.

| NAME AND ADDRESS | TITLE | NATURE AND PERCENTAGE OF STOCK OWNERSHIP |

22 . Former partners, officers, directors and shareholders

None ☐ a. If the debtor is a partnership, list each member who withdrew from the partnership within **one year** immediately preceding the commencement of this case.

| NAME | ADDRESS | DATE OF WITHDRAWAL |

None ☐ b. If the debtor is a corporation, list all officers, or directors whose relationship with the corporation terminated within **one year** immediately preceding the commencement of this case.

NAME AND ADDRESS	TITLE	DATE OF TERMINATION

23 . Withdrawals from a partnership or distributions by a corporation

None ☐ If the debtor is a partnership or corporation, list all withdrawals or distributions credited or given to an insider, including compensation in any form, bonuses, loans, stock redemptions, options exercised and any other perquisite during **one year** immediately preceding the commencement of this case.

NAME & ADDRESS OF RECIPIENT, RELATIONSHIP TO DEBTOR	DATE AND PURPOSE OF WITHDRAWAL	AMOUNT OF MONEY OR DESCRIPTION AND VALUE OF PROPERTY

24. Tax Consolidation Group.

None ☐ If the debtor is a corporation, list the name and federal taxpayer identification number of the parent corporation of any consolidated group for tax purposes of which the debtor has been a member at any time within **six years** immediately preceding the commencement of the case.

NAME OF PARENT CORPORATION	TAXPAYER IDENTIFICATION NUMBER (EIN)

25. Pension Funds.

None ☐ If the debtor is not an individual, list the name and federal taxpayer identification number of any pension fund to which the debtor, as an employer, has been responsible for contributing at any time within **six years** immediately preceding the commencement of the case.

NAME OF PENSION FUND	TAXPAYER IDENTIFICATION NUMBER (EIN)

* * * * * *

[If completed by an individual or individual and spouse]

I declare under penalty of perjury that I have read the answers contained in the foregoing statement of financial affairs and any attachments thereto and that they are true and correct.

Date _____   Signature _____
                                          of Debtor

Date _____   Signature_____
                                          of Joint Debtor
                                          (if any)

_____

[If completed on behalf of a partnership or corporation]

I, declare under penalty of perjury that I have read the answers contained in the foregoing statement of financial affairs and any attachments thereto and that they are true and correct to the best of my knowledge, information and belief.

Date _____   Signature _____

                                          _____
                                          Print Name and Title

[An individual signing on behalf of a partnership or corporation must indicate position or relationship to debtor.]

_____ continuation sheets attached

Penalty for making a false statement: Fine of up to $500,000 or imprisonment for up to 5 years, or both. 18 U.S.C. §§ 152 and 3571

DECLARATION AND SIGNATURE OF NON-ATTORNEY BANKRUPTCY PETITION PREPARER (See 11 U.S.C. § 110)

I declare under penalty of perjury that: (1) I am a bankruptcy petition preparer as defined in 11 U.S.C. § 110; (2) I prepared this document for compensation and have provided the debtor with a copy of this document and the notices and information required under 11 U.S.C. §§ 110(b), 110(h), and 342(b); and, (3) if rules or guidelines have been promulgated pursuant to 11 U.S.C. § 110(h) setting a maximum fee for services chargeable by bankruptcy petition preparers, I have given the debtor notice of the maximum amount before preparing any document for filing for a debtor or accepting any fee from the debtor, as required by that section.

_____   _____
Printed or Typed Name and Title, if any, of Bankruptcy Petition Preparer   Social Security No.(Required by 11 U.S.C. § 110.)

If the bankruptcy petition preparer is not an individual, state the name, title (if any), address, and social security number of the officer, principal, responsible person, or partner who signs this document.
_____

_____
Address

X _____   _____
Signature of Bankruptcy Petition Preparer   Date

Names and Social Security numbers of all other individuals who prepared or assisted in preparing this document unless the bankruptcy petition preparer is not an individual:

If more than one person prepared this document, attach additional signed sheets conforming to the appropriate Official Form for each person.

A bankruptcy petition preparer's failure to comply with the provisions of title 11 and the Federal Rules of Bankruptcy Procedure may result in fines or imprisonment or both. 18 U.S.C. § 156.

United States Bankruptcy Court

_____ District Of _____

In re _____,
      Debtor

Case No. _____

Chapter 7

CHAPTER 7 INDIVIDUAL DEBTOR'S STATEMENT OF INTENTION

☐ I have filed a schedule of assets and liabilities which includes debts secured by property of the estate.
☐ I have filed a schedule of executory contracts and unexpired leases which includes personal property subject to an unexpired lease.
☐ I intend to do the following with respect to the property of the estate which secures those debts or is subject to a lease:

Description of Secured Property	Creditor's Name	Property will be Surrendered	Property is claimed as exempt	Property will be redeemed pursuant to 11 U.S.C. § 722	Debt will be reaffirmed pursuant to 11 U.S.C. § 524(c)

Description of Leased Property	Lessor's Name	Lease will be assumed pursuant to 11 U.S.C. § 362(h)(1)(A)

Date: _____

_____
Signature of Debtor

DECLARATION OF NON-ATTORNEY BANKRUPTCY PETITION PREPARER (See 11 U.S.C. § 110)

  I declare under penalty of perjury that: (1) I am a bankruptcy petition preparer as defined in 11 U.S.C. § 110; (2) I prepared this document for compensation and have provided the debtor with a copy of this document and the notices and information required under 11 U.S.C. §§ 110(b), 110(h), and 342(b); and, (3) if rules or guidelines have been promulgated pursuant to 11 U.S.C. § 110(h) setting a maximum fee for services chargeable by bankruptcy petition preparers, I have given the debtor notice of the maximum amount before preparing any document for filing for a debtor or accepting any fee from the debtor, as required in that section.

_____
Printed or Typed Name of Bankruptcy Petition Preparer

_____
Social Security No. (Required under 11 U.S.C. § 110.)

If the bankruptcy petition preparer is not an individual, state the name, title (if any), address, and social security number of the officer, principal, responsible person or partner who signs this document.

_____

_____
Address

X_____
Signature of Bankruptcy Petition Preparer

Date

_____

Names and Social Security Numbers of all other individuals who prepared or assisted in preparing this document unless the bankruptcy petition preparer is not an individual:

If more than one person prepared this document, attach additional signed sheets conforming to the appropriate Official Form for each person.

A bankruptcy petition preparer's failure to comply with the provisions of title 11 and the Federal Rules of Bankruptcy Procedure may result in fines or imprisonment or both. 11 U.S.C. § 110; 18 U.S.C. § 156.

Form 16A. CAPTION (FULL)

United States Bankruptcy Court

_____ District Of _____

In re _____,)
      [Set forth here all names including married,)
      maiden, and trade names used by debtor within)
      last 8 years.])
                    Debtor)   Case No. _____
)

Address _____)

            _____)   Chapter _____

Last four digits of Social Security No(s).: _____)
_____)
Employer's Tax Identification No(s). *[if any]:* _____)
_____)

[Designation of Character of Paper]

United States Bankruptcy Court

_____ District Of _____

In re _____,
     Set forth here all names including married,
     maiden, and trade names used by debtor within
     last 6 years.]
           Debtor

Address _____

_____

Employer's Tax Identification (EIN) No(s). _[if any]:_ _____

_____

Last four digits of Social Security No(s).: _____

)
)
)
)
) Case No. _____
)
)
)
) Chapter _____
)
)
)
)
)

NOTICE OF [MOTION TO   ] [OBJECTION TO   ]

_____has filed papers with the court to [relief sought in motion or objection].

Your rights may be affected. **You should read these papers carefully and discuss them with your attorney, if you have one in this bankruptcy case. (If you do not have an attorney, you may wish to consult one.)**

If you do not want the court to [relief sought in motion or objection], or if you want the court to consider your views on the [motion] [objection], then on or before _(date)_, you or your attorney must:

[File with the court a written request for a hearing {_or, if the court requires a written response_, an answer, explaining your position} at:

{address of the bankruptcy clerk's office}

If you mail your {request}{response} to the court for filing, you must mail it early enough so the court will **receive** it on or before the date stated above.

You must also mail a copy to:

{movant's attorney's name and address}

{names and addresses of others to be served}]

[Attend the hearing scheduled to be held on __(date)__, _(year)_, at ____a.m./p.m. in Courtroom ____, United States Bankruptcy Court, {address}.]

[Other steps required to oppose a motion or objection under local rule or court order.]

If you or your attorney do not take these steps, the court may decide that you do not oppose the relief sought in the motion or objection and may enter an order granting that relief.

Date: _____   Signature: _____
                                               Name:
                                               Address:

FORM 21. STATEMENT OF SOCIAL SECURITY NUMBER

[Caption as in Form 16A.]

STATEMENT OF SOCIAL SECURITY NUMBER(S)

1.Name of Debtor (enter Last, First, Middle):_____
(Check the appropriate box and, if applicable, provide the required information.)

      / /Debtor has a Social Security Number and it is: _ _ _-_ _-_ _ _ _
                (If more than one, state all.)
      / /Debtor does not have a Social Security Number.

2.Name of Joint Debtor (enter Last, First, Middle):_____
(Check the appropriate box and, if applicable, provide the required information.)

      / /Joint Debtor has a Social Security Number and it is: _ _ _-_ _-_ _ _ _
                (If more than one, state all.)
      / /Joint Debtor does not have a Social Security Number.

I declare under penalty of perjury that the foregoing is true and correct.

     X   _____
           Signature of Debtor   Date

     X   _____
           Signature of Joint Debtor   Date

_____

*Joint debtors must provide information for both spouses.
Penalty for making a false statement: Fine of up to $250,000 or up to 5 years imprisonment or both. 18 U.S.C. §§ 152 and 3571.

In re _____
Debtor(s)

Case Number: _____
(If known)

According to the calculations required by this statement:

☐ **The presumption arises.**

☐ **The presumption does not arise.**

(Check the box as directed in Parts I, III, and VI of this statement.)

STATEMENT OF CURRENT MONTHLY INCOME AND MEANS TEST CALCULATION
FOR USE IN CHAPTER 7 ONLY

In addition to Schedule I and J, this statement must be completed by every individual Chapter 7 debtor, whether or not filing jointly, whose debts are primarily consumer debts. Joint debtors may complete one statement only.

Part I. EXCLUSION FOR DISABLED VETERANS

1	If you are a disabled veteran described in the Veteran's Declaration in this Part I, (1) check the box at the beginning of the Veteran's Declaration, (2) check the box for "The presumption does not arise" at the top of this statement, and (3) complete the verification in Part VIII. Do not complete any of the remaining parts of this statement. ☐ **Veteran's Declaration.** By checking this box, I declare under penalty of perjury that I am a disabled veteran (as defined in 38 U.S.C. § 3741(1)) whose indebtedness occurred primarily during a period in which I was on active duty (as defined in 10 U.S.C. § 101(d)(1)) or while I was performing a homeland defense activity (as defined in 32 U.S.C. §901(1)).

Part II. CALCULATION OF MONTHLY INCOME FOR § 707(b)(7) EXCLUSION

2	**Marital/filing status.** Check the box that applies and complete the balance of this part of this statement as directed. a. ☐ Unmarried. **Complete only Column A ("Debtor's Income") for Lines 3-11.** b. ☐ Married, not filing jointly, with declaration of separate households. By checking this box, debtor declares under penalty of perjury: "My spouse and I are legally separated under applicable non-bankruptcy law or my spouse and I are living apart other than for the purpose of evading the requirements of § 707(b)(2)(A) of the Bankruptcy Code." **Complete only Column A ("Debtor's Income") for Lines 3-11.** c. ☐ Married, not filing jointly, without the declaration of separate households set out in Line 2.b above. **Complete both Column A ("Debtor's Income") and Column B (Spouse's Income) for Lines 3-11.** d. ☐ Married, filing jointly. **Complete both Column A ("Debtor's Income") and Column B ("Spouse's Income") for Lines 3-11.**

		Column A Debtor's Income	Column B Spouse's Income
	All figures must reflect average monthly income for the six calendar months prior to filing the bankruptcy case, ending on the last day of the month before the filing. If you received different amounts of income during these six months, you must total the amounts received during the six months, divide this total by six, and enter the result on the appropriate line.		
3	Gross wages, salary, tips, bonuses, overtime, commissions.	$	$
4	Income from the operation of a business, profession or farm. Subtract Line b from Line a and enter the difference on Line 4. Do not enter a number less than zero. **Do not include any part of the business expenses entered on Line b as a deduction in Part V.**	$	$

4	a.	Gross receipts	$
	b.	Ordinary and necessary business expenses	$
	c.	Business income	Subtract Line b from Line a

		Column A	Column B
		$	$

5	Rent and other real property income. Subtract Line b from Line a and enter the difference on Line 5. Do not enter a number less than zero. **Do not include any part of the operating expenses entered on Line b as a deduction in Part V.**		

5	a.	Gross receipts	$
	b.	Ordinary and necessary operating expenses	$
	c.	Rental income	Subtract Line b from Line a

		Column A	Column B
		$	$
6	Interest, dividends and royalties.	$	$
7	Pension and retirement income.	$	$
8	Regular contributions to the household expenses of the debtor or the debtor's dependents, including child or spousal support. Do not include contributions from the debtor's spouse if Column B is completed.	$	$

9	Unemployment compensation. Enter the amount in Column A and, if applicable, Column B. However, if you contend that unemployment compensation received by you or your spouse was a benefit under the Social Security Act, do not list the amount of such compensation in Column A or B, but instead state the amount in the space below: Unemployment compensation claimed to be a benefit under the Social Security Act Debtor $ _____ Spouse $ _____	$	$
10	Income from all other sources. If necessary, list additional sources on a separate page. **Do not include** any benefits received under the Social Security Act or payments received as a victim of a war crime, crime against humanity, or as a victim of international or domestic terrorism. Specify source and amount. a. _____ $ _____ b. _____ $ _____ Total and enter on Line 10	$	$
11	**Subtotal of Current Monthly Income for § 707(b)(7).** Add Lines 3 thru 10 in Column A, and, if Column B is completed, add Lines 3 through 10 in Column B. Enter the total(s).	$	$
12	**Total Current Monthly Income for § 707(b)(7).** If Column B has been completed, add Line 11, Column A to Line 11, Column B, and enter the total. If Column B has not been completed, enter the amount from Line 11, Column A.	$	

Part III. APPLICATION OF § 707(b)(7) EXCLUSION

13	**Annualized Current Monthly Income for § 707(b)(7).** Multiply the amount from Line 12 by the number 12 and enter the result.	$
14	**Applicable median family income.** Enter the median family income for the applicable state and household size. (This information is available by family size at www.usdoj.gov/ust/ or from the clerk of the bankruptcy court.) a. Enter debtor's state of residence: _____ b. Enter debtor's household size: _____	$
15	**Application of Section 707(b)(7).** Check the applicable box and proceed as directed. ☐ **The amount on Line 13 is less than or equal to the amount on Line 14.** Check the box for "The presumption does not arise" at the top of page 1 of this statement, and complete Part VIII; do not complete Parts IV, V, VI or VII. ☐ **The amount on Line 13 is more than the amount on Line 14.** Complete the remaining parts of this statement.	

Complete Parts IV, V, VI, and VII of this statement only if required. (See Line 15.)

Part IV. CALCULATION OF CURRENT MONTHLY INCOME FOR § 707(b)(2)

16	Enter the amount from Line 12.	$
17	**Marital adjustment.** If you checked the box at Line 2.c, enter the amount of the income listed in Line 11, Column B that was NOT regularly contributed to the household expenses of the debtor or the debtor's dependents. If you did not check box at Line 2.c, enter zero.	$
18	**Current monthly income for § 707(b)(2).** Subtract Line 17 from Line 16 and enter the result.	$

Part V. CALCULATION OF DEDUCTIONS ALLOWED UNDER § 707(b)(2)

Subpart A: Deductions under Standards of the Internal Revenue Service (IRS)

19	**National Standards: food, clothing, household supplies, personal care, and miscellaneous.** Enter "Total" amount from IRS National Standards for Allowable Living Expenses for the applicable family size and income level. (This information is available at www.usdoj.gov/ust/ or from the clerk of the bankruptcy court.)	$
20A	**Local Standards: housing and utilities; non-mortgage expenses.** Enter the amount of the IRS Housing and Utilities Standards; non-mortgage expenses for the applicable county and family size.	$

	(This information is available at www.usdoj.gov/ust/ or from the clerk of the bankruptcy court).

20B	**Local Standards: housing and utilities; mortgage/rent expense.** Enter, in Line a below, the amount of the IRS Housing and Utilities Standards; mortgage/rent expense for your county and family size (this information is available at www.usdoj.gov/ust/ or from the clerk of the bankruptcy court); enter on Line b the total of the Average Monthly Payments for any debts secured by your home, as stated in Line 42; subtract Line b from Line a and enter the result in Line 20B. **Do not enter an amount less than zero.** a. IRS Housing and Utilities Standards; mortgage/rental expense — $ b. Average Monthly Payment for any debts secured by your home, if any, as stated in Line 42 — $ c. Net mortgage/rental expense — Subtract Line b from Line a.	$
21	**Local Standards: housing and utilities; adjustment.** if you contend that the process set out in Lines 20A and 20B does not accurately compute the allowance to which you are entitled under the IRS Housing and Utilities Standards, enter any additional amount to which you contend you are entitled, and state the basis for your contention in the space below: _____ _____ _____	$
22	**Local Standards: transportation; vehicle operation/public transportation expense.** You are entitled to an expense allowance in this category regardless of whether you pay the expenses of operating a vehicle and regardless of whether you use public transportation. Check the number of vehicles for which you pay the operating expenses or for which the operating expenses are included as a contribution to your household expenses in Line 8. ☐ 0 ☐ 1 ☐ 2 or more. Enter the amount from IRS Transportation Standards, Operating Costs & Public Transportation Costs for the applicable number of vehicles in the applicable Metropolitan Statistical Area or Census Region. (This information is available at www.usdoj.gov/ust/ or from the clerk of the bankruptcy court.)	$
23	**Local Standards: transportation ownership/lease expense; Vehicle 1.** Check the number of vehicles for which you claim an ownership/lease expense. (You may not claim an ownership/lease expense for more than two vehicles.) ☐ 1 ☐ 2 or more. Enter, in Line a below, the amount of the IRS Transportation Standards, Ownership Costs, First Car (available at www.usdoj.gov/ust/ or from the clerk of the bankruptcy court); enter in Line b the total of the Average Monthly Payments for any debts secured by Vehicle 1, as stated in Line 42; subtract Line b from Line a and enter the result in Line 23. **Do not enter an amount less than zero.** a. IRS Transportation Standards, Ownership Costs, First Car — $ b. Average Monthly Payment for any debts secured by Vehicle 1, as stated in Line 42 — $ c. Net ownership/lease expense for Vehicle 1 — Subtract Line b from Line a.	$
24	**Local Standards: transportation ownership/lease expense; Vehicle 2.** Complete this Line only if you checked the "2 or more" Box in Line 23. Enter, in Line a below, the amount of the IRS Transportation Standards, Ownership Costs, Second Car (available at www.usdoj.gov/ust/ or from the clerk of the bankruptcy court); enter in Line b the total of the Average Monthly Payments for any debts secured by Vehicle 2, as stated in Line 42; subtract Line b from Line a and enter the result in Line 24. **Do not enter an amount less than zero.** a. IRS Transportation Standards, Ownership Costs, Second Car — $ b. Average Monthly Payment for any debts secured by Vehicle 2, as stated in Line 42 — $ c. Net ownership/lease expense for Vehicle 2 — Subtract Line b from Line a.	$
25	**Other Necessary Expenses: taxes.** Enter the total average monthly expense that you actually incur for all federal, state and local taxes, other than real estate and sales taxes, such as income taxes, self employment taxes, social security taxes, and Medicare taxes. **Do not include real estate or sales taxes.**	$
26	**Other Necessary Expenses: mandatory payroll deductions.** Enter the total average monthly payroll deductions that are required for your employment, such as mandatory retirement contributions, union dues, and uniform costs. **Do not include discretionary amounts, such as non-mandatory 401(k) contributions.**	$

27	**Other Necessary Expenses: life insurance.** Enter average monthly premiums that you actually pay for term life insurance for yourself. **Do not include premiums for insurance on your dependents, for whole life or for any other form of insurance.**	$
28	**Other Necessary Expenses: court-ordered payments.** Enter the total monthly amount that you are required to pay pursuant to court order, such as spousal or child support payments. **Do not include payments on past due support obligations included in Line 44.**	$
29	**Other Necessary Expenses: education for employment or for a physically or mentally challenged child.** Enter the total monthly amount that you actually expend for education that is a condition of employment and for education that is required for a physically or mentally challenged dependent child for whom no public education providing similar services is available.	$
30	**Other Necessary Expenses: childcare.** Enter the average monthly amount that you actually expend on childcare. **Do not include payments made for children's education.**	$
31	**Other Necessary Expenses: health care.** Enter the average monthly amount that you actually expend on health care expenses that are not reimbursed by insurance or paid by a health savings account. **Do not include payments for health insurance listed in Line 34.**	$
32	**Other Necessary Expenses: telecommunication services.** Enter the average monthly expenses that you actually pay for cell phones, pagers, call waiting, caller identification, special long distance or internet services necessary for the health and welfare of you or your dependents. **Do not include any amount previously deducted.**	$
33	**Total Expenses Allowed under IRS Standards.** Enter the total of Lines 19 through 32.	$

Subpart B: Additional Expense Deductions under § 707(b)
Note: Do not include any expenses that you have listed in Lines 19-32

34	**Health Insurance, Disability Insurance and Health Savings Account Expenses.** List the average monthly amounts that you actually expend in each of the following categories and enter the total.	
	a. Health Insurance — $	
	b. Disability Insurance — $	
	c. Health Savings Account — $	
	Total: Add Lines a, b and c	$
35	**Continued contributions to the care of household or family members.** Enter the actual monthly expenses that you will continue to pay for the reasonable and necessary care and support of an elderly, chronically ill, or disabled member of your household or member of your immediate family who is unable to pay for such expenses.	$
36	**Protection against family violence.** Enter any average monthly expenses that you actually incurred to maintain the safety of your family under the Family Violence Prevention and Services Act or other applicable federal law.	$
37	**Home energy costs in excess of the allowance specified by the IRS Local Standards.** Enter the average monthly amount by which your home energy costs exceed the allowance in the IRS Local Standards for Housing and Utilities. **You must provide your case trustee with documentation demonstrating that the additional amount claimed is reasonable and necessary.**	$
38	**Education expenses for dependent children less than 18.** Enter the average monthly expenses that you actually incur, not to exceed $125 per child, in providing elementary and secondary education for your dependent children less than 18 years of age. **You must provide your case trustee with documentation demonstrating that the amount claimed is reasonable and necessary and not already accounted for in the IRS Standards.**	$
39	**Additional food and clothing expense.** Enter the average monthly amount by which your food and clothing expenses exceed the combined allowances for food and apparel in the IRS National Standards, not to exceed five percent of those combined allowances. (This information is available at www.usdoj.gov/ust/ or from the clerk of the bankruptcy court.) **You must provide your case trustee with documentation demonstrating that the additional amount claimed is reasonable and necessary.**	$
40	**Continued charitable contributions.** Enter the amount that you will continue to contribute in the form of cash or financial instruments to a charitable organization as defined in 26 U.S.C. § 170(c)(1)-(2).	$
41	**Total Additional Expense Deductions under § 707(b).** Enter the total of Lines 34 through 40	$

	Subpart C: Deductions for Debt Payment			
42	**Future payments on secured claims.** For each of your debts that is secured by an interest in property that you own, list the name of the creditor, identify the property securing the debt, and state the Average Monthly Payment. The Average Monthly Payment is the total of all amounts contractually due to each Secured Creditor in the 60 months following the filing of the bankruptcy case, divided by 60. Mortgage debts should include payments of taxes and insurance required by the mortgage. If necessary, list additional entries on a separate page.			

	Name of Creditor	Property Securing the Debt	60-month Average Payment
a.			$
b.			$
c.			$
			Total: Add Lines a, b and c.

(Line 42 total) $

43	**Past due payments on secured claims.** If any of the debts listed in Line 42 are in default, and the property securing the debt is necessary for your support or the support of your dependents, you may include in your deductions 1/60th of the amount that you must pay the creditor as a result of the default (the "cure amount") in order to maintain possession of the property. List any such amounts in the following chart and enter the total. If necessary, list additional entries on a separate page.

	Name of Creditor	Property Securing the Debt in Default	1/60th of the Cure Amount
a.			$
b.			$
c.			$
			Total: Add Lines a, b and c

(Line 43 total) $

44	**Payments on priority claims.** Enter the total amount of all priority claims (including priority child support and alimony claims), divided by 60.	$

45	**Chapter 13 administrative expenses.** If you are eligible to file a case under Chapter 13, complete the following chart, multiply the amount in line a by the amount in line b, and enter the resulting administrative expense.	

	a.	Projected average monthly Chapter 13 plan payment.	$
	b.	Current multiplier for your district as determined under schedules issued by the Executive Office for United States Trustees. (This information is available at www.usdoj.gov/ust/ or from the clerk of the bankruptcy court.)	x
	c.	Average monthly administrative expense of Chapter 13 case	Total: Multiply Lines a and b

(Line 45 total) $

46	**Total Deductions for Debt Payment.** Enter the total of Lines 42 through 45.	$

	Subpart D: Total Deductions Allowed under § 707(b)(2)	
47	**Total of all deductions allowed under § 707(b)(2).** Enter the total of Lines 33, 41, and 46.	$

Part VI. DETERMINATION OF § 707(b)(2) PRESUMPTION

48	**Enter the amount from Line 18 (Current monthly income for § 707(b)(2))**	$
49	**Enter the amount from Line 47 (Total of all deductions allowed under § 707(b)(2))**	$
50	**Monthly disposable income under § 707(b)(2).** Subtract Line 49 from Line 48 and enter the result	$
51	**60-month disposable income under § 707(b)(2).** Multiply the amount in Line 50 by the number 60 and enter the result.	$

52	**Initial presumption determination.** Check the applicable box and proceed as directed. ☐ **The amount on Line 51 is less than $6,000** Check the box for "The presumption does not arise" at the top of page 1 of this statement, and complete the verification in Part VIII. Do not complete the remainder of Part VI. ☐ **The amount set forth on Line 51 is more than $10,000.** Check the box for "The presumption arises" at the top of page 1 of this statement, and complete the verification in Part VIII. You may also complete Part VII. Do not complete the remainder of Part VI. ☐ **The amount on Line 51 is at least $6,000, but not more than $10,000.** Complete the remainder of Part VI (Lines 53 through 55).

53	Enter the amount of your total non-priority unsecured debt	$
54	**Threshold debt payment amount.** Multiply the amount in Line 53 by the number 0.25 and enter the result.	$

55	**Secondary presumption determination.** Check the applicable box and proceed as directed. ☐ **The amount on Line 51 is less than the amount on Line 54.** Check the box for "The presumption does not arise" at the top of page 1 of this statement, and complete the verification in Part VIII. ☐ **The amount on Line 51 is equal to or greater than the amount on Line 54.** Check the box for "The presumption arises" at the top of page 1 of this statement, and complete the verification in Part VIII. You may also complete Part VII.

Part VII: ADDITIONAL EXPENSE CLAIMS

56	**Other Expenses.** List and describe any monthly expenses, not otherwise stated in this form, that are required for the health and welfare of you and your family and that you contend should be an additional deduction from your current monthly income under § 707(b)(2)(A)(ii)(I). If necessary, list additional sources on a separate page. All figures should reflect your average monthly expense for each item. Total the expenses.

	Expense Description	Monthly Amount
a.		$
b.		$
c.		$
	Total: Add Lines a, b and c	$

Part VIII: VERIFICATION

57	I declare under penalty of perjury that the information provided in this statement is true and correct. *(If this a joint case, both debtors must sign.)* Date: _____ Signature: _____ (Debtor) Date: _____ Signature: _____ (Joint Debtor, if any)

Form 23
(10/05)

United States Bankruptcy Court

_____ District Of _____

In re _____,   Case No. _____
                          Debtor

                                                   Chapter _____

DEBTOR'S CERTIFICATION OF COMPLETION OF INSTRUCTIONAL COURSE CONCERNING PERSONAL FINANCIAL MANAGEMENT

[Complete one of the following statements.]

☐ I/We, _____. the debtor(s) in the above-
          (Printed Name(s) of Debtor and Joint Debtor, if any)
styled case hereby certify that on _____ I/we completed an instructional
                                         (Date)
course in personal financial management provided by _____,
                                                          (Name of Provider)
an approved personal financial management instruction provider. If the provider furnished a
document attesting to the completion of the personal financial management instructional
course, a copy of that document is attached.

☐ I/We, _____, the debtor(s) in the above-
styled
          (Printed Names of Debtor and Joint Debtor, if any)
case, hereby certify that no personal financial management course is required because:
[Check the appropriate box.]
☐ I am/We are incapacitated or disabled, as defined in 11 U.S.C. § 109(h);
☐ I am/We are on active military duty in a military combat zone; or
☐ I/We reside in a district in which the United States trustee (or bankruptcy administrator) has
determined that the approved instructional courses are not adequate at this time to serve the
additional individuals who would otherwise be required to complete such courses.

Signature of Debtor: _____

Date: _____

Signature of Joint Debtor: _____

Date: _____

UNITED STATES BANKRUPTCY COURT

NOTICE TO INDIVIDUAL CONSUMER DEBTOR UNDER § 342(b) OF THE BANKRUPTCY CODE

In accordance with § 342(b) of the Bankruptcy Code, this notice: (1) Describes briefly the services available from credit counseling services; (2) Describes briefly the purposes, benefits and costs of the four types of bankruptcy proceedings you may commence; and (3) Informs you about bankruptcy crimes and notifies you that the Attorney General may examine all information you supply in connection with a bankruptcy case. You are cautioned that bankruptcy law is complicated and not easily described. Thus, you may wish to seek the advice of an attorney to learn of your rights and responsibilities should you decide to file a petition. Court employees cannot give you legal advice.

1. Services Available from Credit Counseling Agencies

With limited exceptions, § 109(h) of the Bankruptcy Code requires that all individual debtors who file for bankruptcy relief on or after October 17, 2005, receive a briefing that outlines the available opportunities for credit counseling and provides assistance in performing a budget analysis. The briefing must be given within 180 days **before** the bankruptcy filing. The briefing may be provided individually or in a group (including briefings conducted by telephone or on the Internet) and must be provided by a nonprofit budget and credit counseling agency approved by the United States trustee or bankruptcy administrator. The clerk of the bankruptcy court has a list that you may consult of the approved budget and credit counseling agencies.

In addition, after filing a bankruptcy case, an individual debtor generally must complete a financial management instructional course before he or she can receive a discharge. The clerk also has a list of approved financial management instructional courses.

2. The Four Chapters of the Bankruptcy Code Available to Individual Consumer Debtors

Chapter 7: Liquidation ($245 filing fee, $39 administrative fee, $15 trustee surcharge: Total fee $299)
1. Chapter 7 is designed for debtors in financial difficulty who do not have the ability to pay their existing debts. Debtors whose debts are primarily consumer debts are subject to a "means test" designed to determine whether the case should be permitted to proceed under chapter 7. If your income is greater than the median income for your state of residence and family size, in some cases, creditors have the right to file a motion requesting that the court dismiss your case under § 707(b) of the Code. It is up to the court to decide whether the case should be dismissed.
2. Under chapter 7, you may claim certain of your property as exempt under governing law. A trustee may have the right to take possession of and sell the remaining property that is not exempt and use the sale proceeds to pay your creditors.
3. The purpose of filing a chapter 7 case is to obtain a discharge of your existing debts. If, however, you are found to have committed certain kinds of improper conduct described in the Bankruptcy Code, the court may deny your discharge and, if it does, the purpose for which you filed the bankruptcy petition will be defeated.
4. Even if you receive a general discharge, some particular debts are not discharged under the law. Therefore, you may still be responsible for most taxes and student loans; debts incurred to pay nondischargeable taxes; domestic support and property settlement obligations; most fines, penalties, forfeitures, and criminal restitution obligations; certain debts which are not properly listed in your bankruptcy papers; and debts for death or personal injury caused by operating a motor vehicle, vessel, or aircraft while intoxicated from alcohol or drugs. Also, if a creditor can prove that a debt arose from fraud, breach of fiduciary duty, or theft, or from a willful and malicious injury, the bankruptcy court may determine that the debt is not discharged.

Chapter 13: Repayment of All or Part of the Debts of an Individual with Regular Income ($235 filing fee, $39 administrative fee: Total fee $274)
1. Chapter 13 is designed for individuals with regular income who would like to pay all or part of their debts in installments over a period of time. You are only eligible for chapter 13 if your debts do not exceed certain dollar amounts set forth in the Bankruptcy Code.

2. Under chapter 13, you must file with the court a plan to repay your creditors all or part of the money that you owe them, using your future earnings. The period allowed by the court to repay your debts may be three years or five years, depending upon your income and other factors. The court must approve your plan before it can take effect.

3. After completing the payments under your plan, your debts are generally discharged except for domestic support obligations; most student loans; certain taxes; most criminal fines and restitution obligations; certain debts which are not properly listed in your bankruptcy papers; certain debts for acts that caused death or personal injury; and certain long term secured obligations.

Chapter 11: Reorganization ($1000 filing fee, $39 administrative fee: Total fee $1039)

Chapter 11 is designed for the reorganization of a business but is also available to consumer debtors. Its provisions are quite complicated, and any decision by an individual to file a chapter 11 petition should be reviewed with an attorney.

Chapter 12: Family Farmer or Fisherman ($200 filing fee, $39 administrative fee: Total fee $239)

Chapter 12 is designed to permit family farmers and fishermen to repay their debts over a period of time from future earnings and is similar to chapter 13. The eligibility requirements are restrictive, limiting its use to those whose income arises primarily from a family-owned farm or commercial fishing operation.

3. Bankruptcy Crimes and Availability of Bankruptcy Papers to Law Enforcement Officials

A person who knowingly and fraudulently conceals assets or makes a false oath or statement under penalty of perjury, either orally or in writing, in connection with a bankruptcy case is subject to a fine, imprisonment, or both. All information supplied by a debtor in connection with a bankruptcy case is subject to examination by the Attorney General acting through the Office of the United States Trustee, the Office of the United States Attorney, and other components and employees of the Department of Justice.

WARNING: Section 521(a)(1) of the Bankruptcy Code requires that you promptly file detailed information regarding your creditors, assets, liabilities, income, expenses and general financial condition. Your bankruptcy case may be dismissed if this information is not filed with the court within the time deadlines set by the Bankruptcy Code, the Bankruptcy Rules, and the local rules of the court.

Certificate of [Non-Attorney] Bankruptcy Petition Preparer

I, the [non-attorney] bankruptcy petition preparer signing the debtor's petition, hereby certify that I delivered to the debtor this notice required by § 342(b) of the Bankruptcy Code.

_____

Printed name and title, if any, of Bankruptcy Petition Preparer

Address:

_____

X_____
Signature of Bankruptcy Petition Preparer or officer, principal, responsible person, or partner whose Social Security number is provided above.

Social Security number (If the bankruptcy petition preparer is not an individual, state the Social Security number of the officer, principal, responsible person, or partner of the bankruptcy petition preparer.) (Required by 11 U.S.C. § 110.)

Certificate of the Debtor

I (We), the debtor(s), affirm that I (we) have received and read this notice.

_____

Printed Name(s) of Debtor(s)

Case No. (if known) _____

X_____
Signature of Debtor   Date

X_____
Signature of Joint Debtor (if any)   Date

B 240 - Reaffirmation Agreement
(10/05))

United States Bankruptcy Court
_____District of _____

In re _____,   Case No._____
                        Debtor   Chapter _____

REAFFIRMATION AGREEMENT

[Indicate all documents included in this filing by checking each applicable box.]

☐ Part A: Disclosures, Instructions, and   ☐ Part D: Debtor's Statement in Support of
   Notice to Debtor (Pages 1 - 5)   Reaffirmation Agreement
☐ Part B: Reaffirmation Agreement   ☐ Part E: Motion for Court Approval
☐ Part C: Certification by Debtor's   ☐ Proposed Order Approving Reaffirmation
   Attorney   Agreement

☐ *[Check this box if]* Creditor is a Credit Union as defined in §19(b)(1)(a)(iv) of the
   Federal Reserve Act

PART A: DISCLOSURE STATEMENT, INSTRUCTIONS AND NOTICE TO DEBTOR

1.   DISCLOSURE STATEMENT

Before Agreeing to Reaffirm a Debt, Review These Important Disclosures:

SUMMARY OF REAFFIRMATION AGREEMENT
This Summary is made pursuant to the requirements of the Bankruptcy Code.

AMOUNT REAFFIRMED

a.   The amount of debt you have agreed to reaffirm: $_____

b.   All fees and costs accrued as of the date of this
      disclosure statement, related to the amount of debt
      shown in a., above: $_____

c.   The total amount you have agreed to reaffirm
      (Debt and fees and costs) (Add lines a. and b.): $_____

***Your credit agreement may obligate you to pay additional amounts which may come
due after the date of this disclosure. Consult your credit agreement.***

ANNUAL PERCENTAGE RATE

[The annual percentage rate can be disclosed in different ways, depending on the type of debt.]

a. If the debt is an extension of "credit" under an "open end credit plan," as those terms are defined in § 103 of the Truth in Lending Act, such as a credit card, the creditor may disclose the annual percentage rate shown in (I) below or, to the extent this rate is not readily available or not applicable, the simple interest rate shown in (ii) below, or both.

(I) The Annual Percentage Rate disclosed, or that would have been disclosed, to the debtor in the most recent periodic statement prior to entering into the reaffirmation agreement described in Part B below or, if no such periodic statement was given to the debtor during the prior six months, the annual percentage rate as it would have been so disclosed at the time of the disclosure statement: _____%.

— And/Or ---

(ii) The simple interest rate applicable to the amount reaffirmed as of the date this disclosure statement is given to the debtor: _____%. If different simple interest rates apply to different balances included in the amount reaffirmed, the amount of each balance and the rate applicable to it are:

$ _____ @ _____%;
$ _____ @ _____%;
$ _____ @ _____%.

b. If the debt is an extension of credit other than under than an open end credit plan, the creditor may disclose the annual percentage rate shown in (I) below, or, to the extent this rate is not readily available or not applicable, the simple interest rate shown in (ii) below, or both.

(I) The Annual Percentage Rate under §128(a)(4) of the Truth in Lending Act, as disclosed to the debtor in the most recent disclosure statement given to the debtor prior to entering into the reaffirmation agreement with respect to the debt or, if no such disclosure statement was given to the debtor, the annual percentage rate as it would have been so disclosed: _____%.

— And/Or ---

(ii) The simple interest rate applicable to the amount reaffirmed as of the date this disclosure statement is given to the debtor: _____%. If different simple interest rates apply to different balances included in the amount reaffirmed,

the amount of each balance and the rate applicable to it are:
$ _____ @ _____%;
$_____ @ _____%;
$_____ @ _____%.

c. If the underlying debt transaction was disclosed as a variable rate transaction on the most recent disclosure given under the Truth in Lending Act:

The interest rate on your loan may be a variable interest rate which changes from time to time, so that the annual percentage rate disclosed here may be higher or lower.

d. If the reaffirmed debt is secured by a security interest or lien, which has not been waived or determined to be void by a final order of the court, the following items or types of items of the debtor's goods or property remain subject to such security interest or lien in connection with the debt or debts being reaffirmed in the reaffirmation agreement described in Part B.

<u>Item or Type of Item</u>   <u>Original Purchase Price or Original Amount of Loan</u>

Optional---*At the election of the creditor, a repayment schedule using one or a combination of the following may be provided:*

Repayment Schedule:

Your first payment in the amount of $_____ is due on _____(date), but the future payment amount may be different. Consult your reaffirmation agreement or credit agreement, as applicable.

---Or---

Your payment schedule will be: _____(number) payments in the amount of $_____ each, payable (monthly, annually, weekly, etc.) on the _____ (day) of each _____ (week, month, etc.), unless altered later by mutual agreement in writing.

---Or---

A reasonably specific description of the debtor's repayment obligations to the extent known by the creditor or creditor's representative.

2. INSTRUCTIONS AND NOTICE TO DEBTOR

Reaffirming a debt is a serious financial decision. The law requires you to take certain steps to make sure the decision is in your best interest. If these steps are not completed, the reaffirmation agreement is not effective, even though you have signed it.

1. Read the disclosures in this Part A carefully. Consider the decision to reaffirm carefully. Then, if you want to reaffirm, sign the reaffirmation agreement in Part B (or you may use a separate agreement you and your creditor agree on).

2. Complete and sign Part D and be sure you can afford to make the payments you are agreeing to make and have received a copy of the disclosure statement and a completed and signed reaffirmation agreement.

3. If you were represented by an attorney during the negotiation of your reaffirmation agreement, the attorney must have signed the certification in Part C.

4. If you were not represented by an attorney during the negotiation of your reaffirmation agreement, you must have completed and signed Part E.

5. The original of this disclosure must be filed with the court by you or your creditor. If a separate reaffirmation agreement (other than the one in Part B) has been signed, it must be attached.

6. If the creditor is not a Credit Union and you were represented by an attorney during the negotiation of your reaffirmation agreement, your reaffirmation agreement becomes effective upon filing with the court unless the reaffirmation is presumed to be an undue hardship as explained in Part D. If the creditor is a Credit Union and you were represented by an attorney during the negotiation of your reaffirmation agreement, your reaffirmation agreement becomes effective upon filing with the court.

7. If you were not represented by an attorney during the negotiation of your reaffirmation agreement, it will not be effective unless the court approves it. The court will notify you and the creditor of the hearing on your reaffirmation agreement. You must attend this hearing in bankruptcy court where the judge will review your reaffirmation agreement. The bankruptcy court must approve your reaffirmation agreement as consistent with your best interests, except that no court approval is required if your reaffirmation agreement is for a consumer debt secured by a mortgage, deed of trust, security deed, or other lien on your real property, like your home.

YOUR RIGHT TO RESCIND (CANCEL) YOUR REAFFIRMATION AGREEMENT

You may rescind (cancel) your reaffirmation agreement at any time before the bankruptcy court enters a discharge order, or before the expiration of the 60-day period that begins on the date your reaffirmation agreement is filed with the court, whichever occurs later. To rescind (cancel) your reaffirmation agreement, you must notify the creditor that your reaffirmation agreement is rescinded (or canceled).

Frequently Asked Questions:

<u>What are your obligations if you reaffirm the debt?</u> A reaffirmed debt remains your personal legal obligation. It is not discharged in your bankruptcy case. That means that if you default on your reaffirmed debt after your bankruptcy case is over, your creditor may be able to take your property or your wages. Otherwise, your obligations will be determined by the reaffirmation agreement which may have changed the terms of the original agreement. For example, if you are reaffirming an open end credit agreement, the creditor may be permitted by that agreement or applicable law to change the terms of that agreement in the future under certain conditions.

<u>Are you required to enter into a reaffirmation agreement by any law?</u> No, you are not required to reaffirm a debt by any law. Only agree to reaffirm a debt if it is in your best interest. Be sure you can afford the payments you agree to make.

<u>What if your creditor has a security interest or lien?</u> Your bankruptcy discharge does not eliminate any lien on your property. A ''lien'' is often referred to as a security interest, deed of trust, mortgage or security deed. Even if you do not reaffirm and your personal liability on the debt is discharged, because of the lien your creditor may still have the right to take the security property if you do not pay the debt or default on it. If the lien is on an item of personal property that is exempt under your State's law or that the trustee has abandoned, you may be able to redeem the item rather than reaffirm the debt. To redeem, you make a single payment to the creditor equal to the current value of the security property, as agreed by the parties or determined by the court.

> **NOTE:** When this disclosure refers to what a creditor ''may'' do, it does not use the word ''may'' to give the creditor specific permission. The word ''may'' is used to tell you what might occur if the law permits the creditor to take the action. If you have questions about your reaffirming a debt or what the law requires, consult with the attorney who helped you negotiate this agreement reaffirming a debt. If you don't have an attorney helping you, the judge will explain the effect of your reaffirming a debt when the hearing on the reaffirmation agreement is held.

PART B: REAFFIRMATION AGREEMENT.

I (we) agree to reaffirm the debts arising under the credit agreement described below.

1. Brief description of credit agreement:

2. Description of any changes to the credit agreement made as part of this reaffirmation agreement:

SIGNATURE(S):

Borrower: Co-borrower, if also reaffirming these debts:

_____   _____
(Print Name)   (Print Name)
_____   _____
(Signature)   (Signature)
Date: _____   Date: _____

Accepted by creditor:

_____
(Print Name)
_____
(Signature)
Date of creditor acceptance: _____

PART C: CERTIFICATION BY DEBTOR'S ATTORNEY (IF ANY).

[Check each applicable box.]

☐ I hereby certify that (1) this agreement represents a fully informed and voluntary agreement by the debtor; (2) this agreement does not impose an undue hardship on the debtor or any dependent of the debtor; and (3) I have fully advised the debtor of the legal effect and consequences of this agreement and any default under this agreement.

☐ *[If applicable and the creditor is not a Credit Union.]* A presumption of undue hardship has been established with respect to this agreement. In my opinion, however, the debtor is able to make the required payment.

Printed Name of Debtor's Attorney: _____

Signature of Debtor's Attorney: _____

Date: _____

PART D: DEBTOR'S STATEMENT IN SUPPORT OF REAFFIRMATION AGREEMENT

[Read and complete numbered paragraphs 1 and 2, <u>OR</u>, if the creditor is a Credit Union and the debtor is represented by an attorney, read the un- numbered paragraph below. Sign the appropriate signature line(s) and date your signature.]

1. I believe this reaffirmation agreement will not impose an undue hardship on my dependents or me. I can afford to make the payments on the reaffirmed debt because my monthly income (take home pay plus any other income received) is $_____, and my actual current monthly expenses including monthly payments on post-bankruptcy debt and other reaffirmation agreements total $_____, leaving $_____ to make the required payments on this reaffirmed debt. I understand that if my income less my monthly expenses does not leave enough to make the payments, this reaffirmation agreement is presumed to be an undue hardship on me and must be reviewed by the court. However, this presumption may be overcome if I explain to the satisfaction of the court how I can afford to make the payments here: _____.

2. I received a copy of the Reaffirmation Disclosure Statement in Part A and a completed and signed reaffirmation agreement.

Signed: _____
　　　　 (Debtor)

　　　　 _____
　　　　 (Joint Debtor, if any)
Date: _____

— *Or*
[If the creditor is a Credit Union and the debtor is represented by an attorney]

I believe this reaffirmation agreement is in my financial interest. I can afford to make the payments on the reaffirmed debt. I received a copy of the Reaffirmation Disclosure Statement in Part A and a completed and signed reaffirmation agreement.

Signed: _____
　　　　 (Debtor)

　　　　 _____
　　　　 (Joint Debtor, if any)
Date: _____

PART E: MOTION FOR COURT APPROVAL
(To be completed only if the debtor is not represented by an attorney.)

MOTION FOR COURT APPROVAL OF REAFFIRMATION AGREEMENT

I (we), the debtor(s), affirm the following to be true and correct:

I am not represented by an attorney in connection with this reaffirmation agreement.

I believe this reaffirmation agreement is in my best interest based on the income and expenses I have disclosed in my Statement in Support of this reaffirmation agreement, and because (provide any additional relevant reasons the court should consider):

Therefore, I ask the court for an order approving this reaffirmation agreement.

Signed:_____
      (Debtor)

_____
      (Joint Debtor, if any)

Date: _____

United States Bankruptcy Court
_____ District of _____

In re _____,   Case No._____
                    Debtor   Chapter _____

ORDER APPROVING REAFFIRMATION AGREEMENT

    The debtor(s) _____ have filed a motion for approval of the
                     (Name(s) of debtor(s))

reaffirmation agreement dated _____ made between the debtor(s) and
                      (Date of agreement)
_____. The court held the hearing required by 11 U.S.C. § 524(d)
     (Name of creditor)
on notice to the debtor(s) and the creditor on _____.
                             (Date)

COURT ORDER: The court grants the debtor's motion and approves the reaffirmation
                    agreement described above.

                             BY THE COURT

Date: _____   _____
                             United States Bankruptcy Judge

UNITED STATES BANKRUPTCY COURT

_____ DISTRICT OF _____

In re _____)
      [Set forth here all names including)
      married, maiden, and trade names used)
      by debtor within last 8 years])
                                Debtor(s))   Case No. _____

Address _____)

      _____)   Chapter _____

Employer's Tax Identification (EIN) No(s). *[if any]:*)

_____)

Last four digits of Social Security no(s): _____)

AMENDMENT COVER SHEET

Presented herewith are the original and one copy of the following:

☐ Voluntary Petition (Note: Spouse may not be added or deleted subsequent to initial filing.)

☐ Schedule A—Real Property

☐ Schedule B—Personal Property

☐ Schedule C—Property Claimed as Exempt

☐ Schedule D—Creditors Holding Secured Claims

☐ Schedule E—Creditors Holding Unsecured Priority Claims

☐ Schedule F—Creditors Holding Unsecured Nonpriority Claims

☐ Schedule G—Executory Contracts and Unexpired Leases

☐ Schedule H—Codebtors

☐ Schedule I—Current Income of Individual Debtor(s)

☐ Schedule J—Current Expenditures of Individual Debtor(s)

☐ Summary of Schedules

☐ Statement of Financial Affairs

☐ I have enclosed a $26 fee because I am adding new creditors or changing addresses after the original Meeting of Creditors Notice has been sent.

_____   _____
Signature of Debtor   Signature of Debtor's Spouse

I (we) _____ and

_____, the debtor(s)

in this case, declare under penalty of perjury that the information set forth in the amendment attached hereto

consisting of _____ pages is true and correct to the best of my (our) information and belief.

Dated: _____, 20_____

_____   _____
Signature of Debtor   Signature of Debtor's Spouse

UNITED STATES BANKRUPTCY COURT

_____ DISTRICT OF _____

In re _____)
　　　[Set forth here all names including)
　　　married, maiden, and trade names used)
　　　by debtor within last 8 years])
　　　　　　　　　　　　　　Debtor(s))　Case No. _____
Address _____)
　　　　　　　　　　　　　　　　　　)
　　　_____)　Chapter _____
　　　　　　　　　　　　　　　　　　)
Employer's Tax Identification (EIN) No(s). [if any]:)
_____)
Last four digits of Social Security no(s): _____)

NOTICE OF CHANGE OF ADDRESS

MY (OUR) FORMER MAILING ADDRESS AND PHONE NUMBER WAS:

Name: _____

Street: _____

City: _____

State/Zip: _____

Phone: (_____) _____

PLEASE BE ADVISED THAT AS OF_____, 20_____, MY (OUR) NEW
MAILING ADDRESS AND PHONE NUMBER IS:

Name: _____

Street: _____

City: _____

State/Zip: _____

Phone: (_____) _____

_____
Signature of Debtor

_____
Signature of Debtor's Spouse

UNITED STATES BANKRUPTCY COURT

_____ DISTRICT OF _____

In re) Case No. _____

    [Set forth here all names including) Chapter _____

    married, maiden, and trade names used)

    by debtor within last 8 years]) SUPPLEMENTAL SCHEDULE FOR

) PROPERTY ACQUIRED AFTER

    Debtor(s)) BANKRUPTCY DISCHARGE

TO:_____, Trustee

This is to inform you that I (we) have received the following item of property since my (our) discharge but within the 180-day period after filing my (our) Bankruptcy Petition under Bankruptcy Rule 1007(h):

This property was obtained through an inheritance, marital settlement agreement or divorce decree, death benefits or life insurance proceeds, or other (specify):

☐ I (we) claim this property exempt under the following law:

I (we) _____ and

_____, the debtor(s)

in this case, declare under penalty of perjury that the foregoing is true and correct.

Dated: _____, 20_____   _____

                                        Signature of Debtor

                                  _____

                                        Signature of Debtor's Spouse

UNITED STATES BANKRUPTCY COURT

_____ DISTRICT OF _____

In re _____   )
    [Set forth here all names including   )
    married, maiden, and trade names used   )
    by debtor within last 8 years]   )
                    Debtor(s)   ) Case No. _____
Address _____   )
)
    _____   ) Chapter 7
)
Employer's Tax Identification (EIN) No(s). _[if any]_:)
_____   )
Last four digits of Social Security no(s): _____   )

PROOF OF SERVICE BY MAIL

I, _____, declare that: I am a resident or

employed in the County of _____, State of _____ .

My residence/business address is _____

_____ .

I am over the age of eighteen years and not a party to this case.

On _____, 20___, I served the:

on _____,

by placing true and correct copies thereof enclosed in a sealed envelope with postage thereon fully prepaid

in the United States Mail at _____, addressed as follows:

I declare under penalty of perjury that the foregoing is true and correct, and that this declaration was

executed on

Date: _____ , 20___ at _____
                                        City and State

_____
Signature

1

2

3

4

5

6

7

8

9

10

11

12

13

14

15

16

17

18

19

20

21

22

23

24

25

26

27

28

Index

	PRICE	CODE

BUSINESS

Becoming a Mediator: Your Guide to Career Opportunites	$29.99	BECM
Business Buyout Agreements (Book w/CD-ROM)	$49.99	BSAG
The CA Nonprofit Corporation Kit (Binder w/CD-ROM)	$69.99	CNP
California Workers' Comp: How to Take Charge When You're Injured on the Job	$34.99	WORK
The Complete Guide to Buying a Business (Book w/CD-ROM)	$24.99	BUYBU
The Complete Guide to Selling Your Business (Book w/CD-ROM)	$24.99	SELBU
Consultant & Independent Contractor Agreements (Book w/CD-ROM)	$29.99	CICA
The Corporate Records Handbook (Book w/CD-ROM)	$69.99	CORMI
Create Your Own Employee Handbook (Book w/CD-ROM)	$49.99	EMHA
Dealing With Problem Employees	$44.99	PROBM
Deduct It! Lower Your Small Business Taxes	$34.99	DEDU
Effective Fundraising for Nonprofits	$24.99	EFFN
The Employer's Legal Handbook	$39.99	EMPL
Federal Employment Laws	$49.99	FELW
Form Your Own Limited Liability Company (Book w/CD-ROM)	$44.99	LIAB
Home Business Tax Deductions: Keep What You Earn	$34.99	DEHB
How to Create a Noncompete Agreement (Book w/CD-ROM)	$44.95	NOCMP
How to Form a California Professional Corporation (Book w/CD-ROM)	$59.99	PROF
How to Form a Nonprofit Corporation (Book w/CD-ROM)—National Edition	$49.99	NNP
How to Form a Nonprofit Corporation in California (Book w/CD-ROM)	$49.99	NON
How to Form Your Own California Corporation (Binder w/CD-ROM)	$59.99	CACI
How to Form Your Own California Corporation (Book w/CD-ROM)	$34.99	CCOR
How to Get Your Business on the Web	$29.99	WEBS
How to Run a Thriving Business: Strategies for Sucess & Satisfaction	$19.99	THRV
How to Write a Business Plan	$34.99	SBS
Incorporate Your Business	$49.95	NIBS
The Independent Paralegal's Handbook	$34.99	PARA
Legal Forms for Starting & Running a Small Business (Book w/CD-ROM)	$29.99	RUNSF
Legal Guide for Starting & Running a Small Business	$34.99	RUNS
LLC or Corporation?	$24.99	CHENT
The Manager's Legal Handbook	$39.99	ELBA
Marketing Without Advertising	$20.00	MWAD
Mediate, Don't Litigate	$24.99	MEDL

Prices subject to change.

	PRICE	CODE
Music Law (Book w/CD-ROM)	$39.99	ML
Negotitate the Best Lease for Your Business	$24.99	LESP
Nolo's Guide to Social Security Disability	$29.99	QSS
Nolo's Quick LLC	$29.99	LLCQ
Nondisclosure Agreements (Book w/CD-ROM)	$39.95	NAG
The Partnership Book: How to Write a Partnership Agreement (Book w/CD-ROM)	$39.99	PART
The Performance Appraisal Handbook	$29.99	PERF
The Small Business Start-up Kit (Book w/CD-ROM)	$24.99	SMBU
The Small Business Start-up Kit for California (Book w/CD-ROM)	$24.99	OPEN
Starting & Running a Successful Newsletter or Magazine	$29.99	MAG
Tax Savvy for Small Business	$36.99	SAVVY
Workplace Investigations: A Step by Step Guide	$39.99	CMPLN
Working for Yourself: Law & Taxes for Independent Contractors, Freelancers & Consultants	$39.99	WAGE
Working With Independent Contractors (Book w/CD-ROM)	$29.99	HICI
Your Crafts Business: A Legal Guide (Book w/CD-ROM)	$26.99	VART
Your Limited Liability Company: An Operating Manual (Book w/CD-ROM)	$49.99	LOP
Your Rights in the Workplace	$29.99	YRW

CONSUMER

	PRICE	CODE
How to Win Your Personal Injury Claim	$29.99	PICL
Nolo's Encyclopedia of Everyday Law	$29.99	EVL
Nolo's Guide to California Law	$24.99	CLAW

ESTATE PLANNING & PROBATE

	PRICE	CODE
8 Ways to Avoid Probate	$19.99	PRAV
Estate Planning Basics	$21.99	ESPN
The Executor's Guide: Settling a Loved One's Estate or Trust	$34.99	EXEC
How to Probate an Estate in California	$49.99	PAE
Make Your Own Living Trust (Book w/CD-ROM)	$39.99	LITR
Nolo's Simple Will Book (Book w/CD-ROM)	$36.99	SWIL
Plan Your Estate	$44.99	NEST
Quick & Legal Will Book	$16.99	QUIC
Quicken Willmaker: Estate Planning Essentials (Book with Interactive CD-ROM)	$49.99	QWMB
Special Needs Trust: Protect Your Child's Fianancial Future	$34.99	SPNT

FAMILY MATTERS

	PRICE	CODE
Building a Parenting Agreement That Works	$24.99	CUST
The Complete IEP Guide	$34.99	IEP
Divorce & Money: How to Make the Best Financial Decisions During Divorce	$34.99	DIMO
Do Your Own California Adoption: Nolo's Guide for Stepparents and Domestic Partners (Book w/CD-ROM)	$34.99	ADOP
Every Dog's Legal Guide: A Must-Have Book for Your Owner		

ORDER 24 HOURS A DAY @ www.nolo.com
Call 800-728-3555 • Mail or fax the order form in this book

	PRICE	CODE
Get a Life: You Don't Need a Million to Retire Well	$24.99	LIFE
The Guardianship Book for California	$39.99	GB
A Legal Guide for Lesbian and Gay Couples	$34.99	LG
Living Together: A Legal Guide (Book w/CD-ROM)	$34.99	LTK
Living Wills and Powers of Attorney in California (Book w/CD-ROM)	$21.99	CPOA
Nolo's IEP Guide: Learning Disablities	$29.99	IELD
Prenuptial Agreements: How to Write a Fair & Lasting Contract (Book w/CD-ROM)	$34.99	PNUP
Using Divorce Mediation: Save Your Money & Your Sanity	$29.99	UDMD

GOING TO COURT

	PRICE	CODE
Beat Your Ticket: Go To Court & Win! (National Edition)	$21.99	BEYT
The Criminal Law Handbook: Know Your Rights, Survive the System	$34.99	KYR
Everybody's Guide to Small Claims Court (National Edition)	$26.99	NSCC
Everybody's Guide to Small Claims Court in California	$29.99	CSCC
Fight Your Ticket & Win in California	$29.99	FYT
How to Change Your Name in California	$34.99	NAME
How to Collect When You Win a Lawsuit (California Edition)	$29.99	JUDG
The Lawsuit Survival Guide	$29.99	UNCL
Nolo's Deposition Handbook	$29.99	DEP
Represent Yourself in Court: How to Prepare & Try a Winning Case	$34.99	RYC
Win Your Lawsuit: A Judge's Guide to Representing Yourself in CA Superior Court	$29.99	SLWY

HOMEOWNERS, LANDLORDS & TENANTS

	PRICE	CODE
California Tenants' Rights	$27.99	CTEN
Deeds for California Real Estate	$24.99	DEED
Every Landlord's Legal Guide (National Edition, Book w/CD-ROM)	$44.99	ELLI
Every Landlord's Tax Deduction Guide	$34.99	DELL
Every Tenant's Legal Guide	$29.99	EVTEN
For Sale by Owner in California	$29.99	FSBO
How to Buy a House in California	$34.99	BHCA
The California Landlord's Law Book: Rights & Responsibilities (Book w/CD-ROM)	$44.99	LBRT
The California Landlord's Law Book: Evictions (Book w/CD-ROM)	$44.99	LBEV
Leases & Rental Agreements	$29.99	LEAR
Neighbor Law: Fences, Trees, Boundaries & Noise	$26.99	NEI
The New York Landlord's Law Book (Book w/CD-ROM)	$39.99	NYLL
New York Tenants' Rights	$27.99	NYTEN
Renters' Rights (National Edition)	$24.99	RENT

IMMIGRATION

	PRICE	CODE
Becoming A U.S. Citizen: A Guide to the Law, Exam and Interview	$24.99	USCIT
Fiancé & Marriage Visas (Book w/CD-ROM)	$44.99	IMAR
How to Get a Green Card	$29.99	GRN

	PRICE	CODE
Student & Tourist Visas	$29.99	ISTU
U.S. Immigration Made Easy	$44.99	IMEZ

MONEY MATTERS

	PRICE	CODE
101 Law Forms for Personal Use (Book w/CD-ROM)	$29.99	SPOT
Bankruptcy: Is It the Right Solution to Your Debt Problems?	$21.99	BRS
Chapter 13 Bankruptcy: Repay Your Debts	$36.99	CHB
Credit Repair (Book w/CD-ROM)	$24.99	CREP
Getting Paid: How to Collect form Bankrupt Debtors	$29.99	CRBNK
How to File for Chapter 7 Bankruptcy	$29.99	HFB
IRAs, 401(k)s & Other Retirement Plans: Taking Your Money Out	$34.99	RET
Solve Your Money Troubles	$29.99	MT
Stand Up to the IRS	$29.99	SIRS
Surviving an IRS Tax Audit	$24.95	SAUD
Take Control of Your Student Loan Debt	$26.95	SLOAN

PATENTS AND COPYRIGHTS

	PRICE	CODE
All I Need is Money: How to Finance Your Invention	$19.99	FINA
The Copyright Handbook: How to Protect and Use Written Works (Book w/CD-ROM)	$39.99	COHA
Copyright Your Software (Book w/CD-ROM)	$34.95	CYS
Getting Permission: How to License and Clear Copyrighted Materials Online and Off (Book w/CD-ROM)	$34.99	RIPER
How to Make Patent Drawings	$29.99	DRAW
What Every Inventor Needs to Know About Business and Taxes (Book w/CD-ROM)	$21.99	ILAX
The Inventor's Notebook	$24.99	INOT
License Your Invention (Book w/CD-ROM)	$39.99	LICE
Nolo's Patents for Beginners	$29.99	QPAT
Patent, Copyright & Trademark	$39.99	PCTM
Patent It Yourself	$49.99	PAT
Patent Pending in 24 Hours	$29.99	PEND
Patenting Art & Entertainment: New Stategies for Protecting Creative Ideas	$39.99	PATAE
The Public Domain	$34.99	PUBL
Trademark: Legal Care for Your Business and Product Name	$39.99	TRD
Web and Software Development: A Legal Guide (Book w/ CD-ROM)	$44.99	SFT

RESEARCH & REFERENCE

	PRICE	CODE
Legal Research: How to Find & Understand the Law	$39.99	LRES

SENIORS

	PRICE	CODE
Long-Term Care: How to Plan & Pay For It	$21.99	ELD
Social Security, Medicare & Goverment Pensions	$29.99	SOA